Modern Canadian Plays

revised edition

MODERN CANADIAN PLAYS

revised edition

edited by Jerry Wasserman

TALONBOOKS   •   VANCOUVER   •   1986

published with assistance from the Canada Council

Talonbooks
201 / 1019 East Cordova
Vancouver
British Columbia V6A 1M8
Canada

This book was typeset by Mary Schendlinger and Baseline Type & Graphics Cooperative, and printed in Canada by Hignell Printing Ltd.

First Printing: January 1985
First Printing (Revised Edition): August 1986
Second printing (revised edition): February 1989

Canadian Cataloguing in Publication Data

Main entry under title:

Modern Canadian plays

    Bibliography: p.
    ISBN 0-88922-243-6

    1. Canadian drama (English)-20th century.*
I. Wasserman, Jerry, 1945-
PS8315.M63 1986   C812'.54'08   C86-091458-5
PR9196.6.M63 1986

CONTENTS

PREFACE

This book grew out of the need to solve what I perceived to be two related problems. The first was finding a reasonably priced textbook for my Canadian Drama classes. Studying ten or twelve plays in a term, students were each having to spend upwards of $50 on individual playtexts, and the costs were rising every year. None of the available anthologies was suitable for a general purpose university or college textbook; in fact none of them included even one of the plays I teach. Looking over those anthologies, I also found myself wondering what sort of general impression of Canadian drama they might give a reader with only casual knowledge of the field. After all, an anthology is a sampler, and one might expect to be able to sample the best or most successful or historically most important work of whatever the subject—in this case, the Canadian theatre. Unfortunately, no single publication provided that perspective.

Probably because indigenous Canadian drama is such a recent phenomenon, Canadians on the whole seem puzzled about it. This has been as true within the academic community as in the public at large, and to some extent it applies to Canadian theatre professionals as well. When I first put together the Canadian Drama course at UBC in 1979, students and colleagues would ask me only half-jokingly how I could possibly fill up a whole term. Some of these people taught or studied drama themselves—British or World—and some were involved with Canadian literature, but Canadian drama seemed to fall between the cracks. Almost everyone I talked to had seen some Canadian plays and knew a few names and titles. They also knew that something was going on out there, but they didn't have a clear sense of what, or whether it was really any good. And who could blame them, since there existed no book-length critical introduction nor collection of plays that in any way defined the field. I first came to Canadian drama myself as an actor. But even in the professional theatre, outside of some artistic directors there is only the haziest sense of the *body* of Canadian plays that comprises our national repertoire. This is due to a number of factors including geography and economics. But it is also due to the lack of any easily identifiable list of our major plays and playwrights, accessible from a single source.

Modern Canadian Plays is intended to fill both these needs. As a textbook it should be useful for surveys as well as specialized courses in drama. Outside the classroom I hope it will be the book that anyone interested in an overview of Canadian drama in English will turn to for a sense of its highlights since 1967. I have tried to avoid all extrinsic criteria (regional representation, generic variety, etc.), and have included only those plays and playwrights that have had a major impact on the Canadian theatre so far, and that promise to remain significant for a long time to come. (My only regret is the absence of Michel Tremblay, whose reluctance to allow any of his plays to be anthologized leaves an unfortunate gap.) The General Introduction provides historical and critical contexts for the twelve plays. Each play is also preceded by a brief biographical and critical commentary. The book concludes with a three-part Selective Bibliography of Source Material—general surveys and studies of modern Canadian drama, critical and biographical material specific to each playwright, and selected reviews of each play. The reviews should be of particular value, since for many of these plays there is little else available in the way of formal critical analysis. I have tried to choose the most informative and astute reviews regardless of their opinions of the play, and to include reviews of various productions in different cities.

Many people had a hand in this book, directly or indirectly, besides all those responsible for writing the plays, putting them on stage, getting them into print, and laying the bibliographical and critical groundwork: the students of English 313, 423 and 504 whose enthusiasm for Canadian plays helped feed my own, and who generated so many good ideas for me to steal; Michael Cook, Errol Durbach, Sherrill Grace, John Gray, Pam Hawthorn, Eva-Marie Kröller, Beverlee Larsen, Bill New, Erika Ritter, George Ryga, the Vancouver East Cultural Centre staff, and Glenn

Wasserman among others for their encouragement, cooperation and generosity; my wife Susan for her editorial assistance, good judgment and love; David Robinson, formerly of Talonbooks, and Karl Siegler for keeping the faith; and especially Mary Schendlinger who played as many parts in this project as Eric Peterson in *Billy Bishop Goes to War*, and deserves as many plaudits. I am also grateful to the University of British Columbia for a research grant at an early stage of the project. *Modern Canadian Plays* is dedicated to the memory of Susan Wood.

A Note on the Revised Edition:

Revisions to this edition of *Modern Canadian Plays* have been made in three major areas. Biographical introductions to each playwright have been brought up to date. The critical bibliography has also been updated. And a substantially revised version of *Jitters* takes the place of the original, incorporating all of David French's most recent changes to the play. The script that appears here is *Jitters* as it is currently being performed. My thanks to all those—teachers, students, critics, friends, actors, colleagues, directors and reviewers—who have provided helpful feedback and suggestions for improving the text.

Jerry Wasserman
August 1986

INTRODUCTION

Theatrical activity in Canada has a long and fascinating history. Canadian plays go back as far as 1606 when Marc Lescarbot wrote *Le Théâtre de Neptune en la Nouvelle-France* and staged it in Indian war canoes to honour the arrival of French dignitaries at Port Royal. Playwriting in Canada in English dates back to the eighteenth century, and in the nineteenth century Canadian playhouses sprang up in substantial numbers, though mainly to accommodate American and British touring companies. The first half of the twentieth century saw the development of a thriving amateur theatre movement and the best radio drama on the continent, as well as the emergence of a handful of playwrights of distinction. But as late as 1945 there were no Canadian professional theatre companies. As late as 1959 the foremost theatre critic in the country could write, "there is not in Canada a single person who earns a living as a playwright, or who has any practical hope of doing so."[1] Even as late as 1965 a report on "Trends in Canadian Theatre" could omit any mention of the role of Canadian plays or playwrights.[2]

The remarkable fact is that Canadian theatre as an indigenous professional institution dates only as far back as the end of World War II. And English-Canadian *drama*, in the sense of a body of dramatic work by Canadian playwrights written for performance in professional theatres, is a more recent development still. Modern drama in Quebec had its inception with Gratien Gélinas' *Tit-Coq* in 1948. For English Canada the key date was 1967: Centennial Year, the year of Expo and of the first (and last) all-Canadian Dominion Drama Festival. With due respect to Robertson Davies and James Reaney whose plays highlighted theatre in English Canada from the late 1940s through the mid-sixties, 1967 was also the year that English-Canadian drama began to achieve legitimacy.

Over the course of that year amateur companies presented sixty-two Canadian plays in French and English in the Dominion Drama Festival competitions, twenty-nine of which were performed for the first time. (Not surprisingly, a play from the already more mature Quebec theatre, Robert Gurik's *Le Pendu*, took home all the major awards.)[3] More important was the success of the new plays given professional productions literally from coast to coast as part of the Centennial celebrations: Gélinas' *Yesterday the Children Were Dancing* in English translation at the Charlottetown Festival, Reaney's *Colours in the Dark* at Stratford, Ann Henry's *Lulu Street* in Winnipeg, John Coulter's *The Trial of Louis Riel* in Regina, George Ryga's *The Ecstasy of Rita Joe* in Vancouver. Right across the country audiences and critics, buoyed by a new national self-consciousness and pride, were taking note of this latest cultural phenomenon—plays written by Canadian playwrights, performed by Canadian actors in Canadian theatres. And they were good! And in New York, meanwhile, Toronto's John Herbert had a major hit with *Fortune and Men's Eyes*.

These events and the subsequent explosion of Canadian drama over the next decade seem in retrospect products of a particular historical moment, like the new European theatre that appeared in the 1870s, the new American theatre of the 1920s and the British theatrical renaissance of the mid-1950s. Yet all these movements were culminations of social and cultural forces that had been gathering momentum for many years. In the case of Canadian theatre the revolution of 1967 was rooted in an evolutionary process that began to take shape clearly around the time of the First World War.

I.

Inspired by the vogue of European art theatres at the turn of the century—especially the Irish Abbey Theatre which would be cited time and again as a positive model for Canadians—amateur groups such as Toronto's Arts and Letters Club Players devoted themselves to performing contemporary works from the world repertoire as an alternative to the predictable fare, commercialism and imported talent offered by the circuit theatres. (Three of the same complaints would help give rise to a second wave of Canadian alternative theatres in the early 1970s.) One thing that became clear in the midst of these first stirrings was that a genuine Canadian theatre would need its own dramatists. "There are no signs as yet upon our literary horizon of the arrival of our dramatist," a writer for *The Canadian Magazine* concluded poignantly in 1914, "but we are waiting expectantly, for we feel that he should soon come now."[4] At about the same time theatre pioneer Vincent Massey realized that "if we are to have a Canadian drama we must have a Canadian theatre in which to produce it."[5]

Under Massey's auspices both these ideals began to take form with the founding of Hart House Theatre in 1919. This was a well-equipped building as well as a company of the most talented actors, designers and directors in Toronto, dedicated to doing plays which would otherwise have gone unproduced in that city, including plays written by Canadians. Encouraged by this policy dramatists did arrive, enough to fill two modest volumes of *Canadian Plays from Hart House Theatre* by 1927. The most interesting was Merrill Denison. His Hart House successes, especially the satirical comedy "Brothers in Arms," and his 1923 published collection, *The Unheroic North*, established him as Canada's first playwright of note. Unable to make a living writing for the stage in Canada, Denison eventually moved to the United States in 1931 to write for American radio. But Hart House remained a focal point of the developing Canadian theatre for many more years.

Throughout the 1920s and into the thirties amateur theatre flourished under the umbrella of the Little Theatre movement, a burgeoning of homegrown playmaking in large and small communities on both sides of the Canada-U.S. border. Some Canadian commentators, ever on the lookout for the theatrical messiah, saw these companies as the route to deliverance "because they build the foundation for more mature creative theatres and develop an audience for the Ultimate National Canadian theatre."[6] That hazy ideal of a National Theatre (always capitalized) seemed to move a large step closer to realization with the establishment in 1932 of the Dominion Drama Festival, a nationwide competition organized by the new Governor General, Lord Bessborough, and chaired by Vincent Massey. The Festival was to consist of an annual series of regional playoffs climaxing in a final (held in a different city each year) at which various awards would be given for production and performance. Community theatres, school and university drama groups and such established amateur companies as Hart House would all be eligible, and adjudicators would provide helpful comments as well as determining the winners. The aim of the Festival was to showcase theatre in Canada and at the same time upgrade the quality of Canada's theatrical arts and crafts through competition and cross-fertilization.

During the years of its existence (1933-70, with a hiatus from 1940-46 due to the war), the DDF helped institutionalize amateur theatre in Canada. Whether it accomplished much more than that has been a matter of some debate. It certainly provided a proving ground for Canadian talent which often went on to New York, London, Hollywood, or by the 1950s to Stratford or other areas of the nascent Canadian professional theatre. Through special trophies and cash prizes the DDF also encouraged the writing and production of Canadian plays, an encouragement which proved at least statistically impressive. In 1934 the Festival organizers could come up with just nine Canadian titles for inclusion on its list of suggested plays sent out to participating groups; by 1966 the list contained 240 Canadian titles in English alone. But the quality and adventurousness of the work the Festival inspired were often questionable.

One damning indictment of the limitations of the DDF was its inability to contend with the multi-media expressionism of Herman Voaden's plays, which consistently failed to advance beyond regional competitions because the adjudicators did not know what to make of them.[7] Voaden was an ardent nationalist and theatrical innovator who desired a Canadian dramatic art as distinctive as the paintings of the Group of Seven. To that end he sponsored a playwriting competition in Toronto in 1929 which required that each play be set in the Canadian North and suggested that the play's subject or mood be based on the writer's favourite Canadian painting.

Voaden himself combined an obsession with the Canadian landscape and such disparate theatrical influences as modern dance, Wagnerian opera and symbolist drama to create a synaesthetic form he called "symphonic expressionism" in plays with titles like *Rocks*, *Earth Song* and *Hill-Land*. The Play Workshop he ran from 1934 to 1936 with the aim of encouraging Canadian playwriting and an indigenous theatrical style resulted in the production of twenty-five new works as well as continued experiments in total theatre. For all his eccentric and sometimes brilliant work as playwright, producer, director and educator, Voaden probably made his greatest impact on the development of Canadian drama as a persistent lobbyist for increased government support for the theatre, leading to his election as the first president of the new Canadian Arts Council in 1945.

The Play Workshop and Hart House were not the only centres of Canadian playwriting activity. A group of women journalists organized the Playwrights' Studio Group in Toronto in 1932 and by the end of the decade they had produced more than fifty new plays, mainly society comedies. At the other end of the spectrum were the Progressive Arts Clubs in Toronto, Montreal, Winnipeg and Vancouver, leftist workers' theatre groups that created and performed agitprop and social protest plays throughout the Depression years. Meanwhile in Alberta the Banff School of the Theatre was founded in 1933, later evolving into the Banff School of Fine Arts which is still an important centre for theatre training and workshop production. Associated with Banff from the beginning was Gwen Pharis Ringwood, whose stark prairie tragedies "Still Stands the House" and *Dark Harvest* were among the strongest Canadian plays of the thirties and forties. (Later she would teach playwriting at Banff to George Ryga among others.) Ringwood remained a prolific and popular dramatist (in amateur circles) until her death in 1984, but her residence in northern B.C. left her out of the mainstream of the new Canadian professional theatre that grew up during the last thirty years of her life.

Probably the most significant development of the 1930s and '40s in terms of the creation of a genuine Canadian drama was the rise of radio. The CBC had been established in 1932, and in 1936 it began broadcasting radio plays for which it actually paid writers, producers, directors, actors, musicians and technicians. What came to be known as "The Golden Age" of Canadian radio began when Andrew Allan became Supervisor of Drama for CBC and producer of its weekly *Stage* series. Under Allan from 1944 to 1955 *Stage* and *Wednesday Night* created consistently bold and imaginative drama that maintained high standards of excellence while proving broadly popular— only *Hockey Night in Canada* drew more listeners than *Stage* in the 1940s. The stable of writers and actors that Allan assembled was "far and away the most exciting repertory group that can be heard," *The New York Times* proclaimed in 1946,[8] and it became Canada's equivalent of a national professional theatre. Hundreds of original scripts by Allan's house writers such as Lister Sinclair and Len Peterson were produced for broadcast. Even though radio's golden age faded with the coming of television in the fifties, CBC radio drama still pays the bills for a lot of Canadian playwrights who wouldn't otherwise be able to afford the luxury of writing for the chronically impecunious live stage.

In spite of the varied successes of the DDF and the CBC, neither amateur theatricals nor radio drama amounted to a real Canadian theatre. John Coulter, who quickly became an award-winning DDF playwright and one of the most frequently produced CBC dramatists after emigrating to Canada from Ireland in 1936, was a vocal critic of the Canadian theatre scene. In "Canadian Theatre and the Irish Exemplar," an article published in 1938, he passionately held up Dublin's Abbey Theatre as a model for Canadians, a theatre "showing the Irish to themselves . . . Irish mugs in Irish mirrors." Canadians too, he argued, could find dramatic subject matter in indigenous situations: "in prairie droughts and crop failures, in mining disasters, in the poverty of slum dwellers of city streets or country shacks" (a catalogue of the kinds of naturalistic subjects that have in fact occupied a good many Canadian plays ever since). "But if there were a great Canadian play," he concluded, "would Canadians bother to stage it? Till someday Americans or British do it and tell them not to be ashamed."[9] After a series of plays set in Ireland, Coulter took his own advice and turned to Canadian history (about which he had already written for radio), achieving his greatest success with a trilogy of stage plays about Louis Riel. First produced in 1950, *Riel* would serve as a paradigm for the history plays of James Reaney and the Theatre Passe Muraille dramatists of the 1970s: revisionist Canadian history with the rebel or underdog as hero, presented as a synthesis of documentary and myth.

Coulter was fortunate that by the time *Riel* was ready for production there was a professional company to do it: the New Play Society, founded by Dora Mavor Moore in 1946. From 1950 it also included a drama school, one of whose students would be John Herbert (who later went on to act, design and stage manage for the company). Though the New Play Society remained active until 1971, its glory years were 1946-50 when its full seasons of plays in the Royal Ontario Museum Theatre proved to many skeptics the viability of a professional Canadian stage. Its most substantial success was *Spring Thaw*, a musical revue satirizing all things topical in the Great White North, first staged in 1948 and remounted with increased popularity annually for the next twenty years. The ice was broken; Canada finally had a homegrown professional theatre.

In 1954 Toronto found itself with a second, the Crest, which soon superceded the New Play Society in importance, presenting quality theatre in continuous repertory for thirteen seasons until its demise in 1966. The major Canadian playwright associated with the Crest was Robertson Davies, whose *A Jig for the Gypsy* and *Hunting Stuart* premiered there in 1954-55. Davies had already become English Canada's foremost playwright on the amateur circuit with "Eros at Breakfast," "Overlaid" and *Fortune, My Foe* in 1948-49, satires of Canadian philistinism and the national disease, "emotional understimulation." Like the Crest itself, Davies remained a significant force in Canadian theatre until the mid-sixties when his playwriting career gave way to his work as a novelist.

Aside from his playwriting, Davies' journalism made a strong contribution to the developing Canadian theatre in the 1940s and '50s. Both in his own name and under the pseudonym of Samuel Marchbanks, he raised his voice in continual protest like Voaden and Coulter against the conditions under which would-be Canadian theatre professionals had to labour—what he called in 1952 "the seedy amateurism which has afflicted the arts here for so long."[10] No wonder then that he reacted with enthusiasm to the idea of a world-class Shakespeare festival theatre in Stratford, Ontario. Davies, along with Dora Mavor Moore, was instrumental in arranging for the innovative British producer-director Tyrone Guthrie to head the venture, which held its first season of two plays under a tent in the summer of 1953. Guthrie imported Alec Guinness and Irene Worth to play the leads and fleshed out the rest of the company with Canadian actors, a policy that by and large became standard for Stratford. Reviewing that first season, Davies concluded that it had given Canadians "a new vision of the theatre":

> This cannot help but have its effect on work everywhere in the country. For one thing, many of our best Canadian actors are working at Stratford.... Are these actors, who have tasted the wine of true theatre, ever again to be satisfied with the sour slops of under-rehearsed, under-dressed, under-mounted, underpaid, and frequently ill-considered and ill-financed theatre projects?... The Stratford Festival is an artistic bombshell, exploded just at the time when Canadian theatre is most ready for a break with the dead past and a leap into the future.[11]

There is no doubt that the Stratford Festival did have an enormous impact on theatre and the *idea* of theatre in Canada. It became an event of international importance and influence (its new non-proscenium thrust stage designed by Guthrie and Tanya Moisiewitsch made waves in theatres world-wide). Thus it raised the profile of theatre in Canada as nothing else had been able to do and served as a focus of national cultural pride. Stratford also became a training ground for many of the best actors who emerged in Canada over the next three decades, making stars of Christopher Plummer, Frances Hyland and others. Moreover, it was argued,

Stratford created a model for indigenous Canadian theatre: a non-profit organization, unconcerned with the values of New York, unashamedly using imported personnel where Canadian expertise was lacking, equally unashamedly welcoming subsidy support in return for placing its destiny—at a policy-making level—in the hands of a volunteer citizen Board of Governors, and representative of the community in which it found itself.[12]

But Stratford did little to effect or support the development of Canadian playwriting. Writers like Herbert and Reaney would receive workshop and small-scale public performances of their plays there in the late sixties, and in 1971 a Third Stage was added, in part to produce Canadian work. But by that time Stratford was no longer an adequate model. With its huge financial operation it became in many eyes a cultural dinosaur, devouring large subsidies at the expense of the smaller theatres whose productions of Canadian plays, often on shoestring budgets, were perceived as being more central to an emerging national drama than a theatre devoted to Shakespeare. Ironically, while Stratford feasted, Canadian drama came of age in the early seventies as a kind of poor theatre nourished on just those "sour slops" that Davies had complained of in 1953.

In any case by 1956 there was good reason for the feeling that "the Canadian theatre . . . like the stock market, is bullish these days. . . ."[13] The success of Stratford and the other new professional theatres was being augmented by CBC television, which from its inception in 1952 gave starts to a number of important dramatists who would later go on to write for the stage, including George Ryga, David French and Michel Tremblay. On the horizon as well was the Canada Council, whose founding in 1957 would change the nature of theatre in Canada more than any other single development, providing a sudden massive influx of government funding for buildings, companies and individuals engaged in the arts.

The Canada Council was the most concrete manifestation of the Royal Commission on National Development in the Arts, Letters and Sciences appointed by Prime Minister St. Laurent in 1949 with Vincent Massey as chairman. Its mandate was to examine how government could contribute to the development of those areas of endeavour "which express national feeling, promote common understanding and add to the variety and richness of Canadian life."[14] The Massey Commission's Report in 1951 proved a tremendous national consciousness-raiser. It found that Canadian culture was being stifled by the omnipresence of American influences and the lack of support and facilities for artists in Canada. Its major recommendation was the formation of the Canada Council for the Encouragement of the Arts, Letters, Humanities and Social Sciences to support Canadian culture at home and abroad. From an initial outlay of $2.6 million in arts grants in 1957, the Council's investment in individuals and groups totalled more than $60 million by 1970, a quantum leap in the funds available to fuel the engine of Canadian cultural nationalism.

Money wasn't the only catalyst for change, though. In 1958 in Winnipeg, with virtually no capital but their missionary commitment to convert a whole province to the ideal of a regional professional theatre, Tom Hendry and John Hirsch merged their amateur Theatre 77 with the Winnipeg Little Theatre to create the Manitoba Theatre Centre, with Hirsch as its first artistic director. From the start the MTC "was meant to be more than a theatre, something that could in fact become a focus for all theatrical energy and resources in one community."[15] Combining mainstage productions in Winnipeg with a touring company, children's theatre and a school, the MTC succeeded so well in galvanizing the support and resources of its constituency that it became the basis for a new concept: a Canadian national theatre that would be decentralized and regional, like the nation itself—a professional theatre version of the Canadian mosaic. With support and encouragement from the Canada Council a network of regional theatres spread across the country: Vancouver's Playhouse and Halifax's Neptune in 1963, Edmonton's Citadel in 1965 and Regina's Globe in 1966. By 1970 Montreal, Calgary, Fredericton and Toronto also had theatres catering in principle to regional communities.

Canada, it seemed, had indeed become bullish on theatre. The building boom didn't stop with the regionals, either. To train and supply actors for the new national theatre network, the National Theatre School was opened in Montreal in 1960. At Niagara-on-the-Lake the Shaw Festival began operation in 1962, and P.E.I.'s Charlottetown Festival was inaugurated in 1964 specializing in Canadian musical theatre. St. John's got its Arts and Culture Centre in 1967. Finally, in 1969-70 the completion of three major Centennial construction projects—Ottawa's National Arts Centre, Toronto's St. Lawrence Centre, and a new building for the MTC—rounded out a decade of extraordinary growth for the Canadian theatre.

II.

With the superstructure finally intact the question now was, where were the plays? In particular where was *the play* that might crystallize the new drama in English Canada the way Gélinas' *Tit-Coq* and John Osborne's *Look Back in Anger* had done in Quebec and Britain, implanting it at the heart of the nation's cultural life. Those plays had had in common vernacular speech, anti-establishment anger, and characters, settings and situations that were definitively of their own time and place. So too had the play that finally touched the nerve of English Canada. *The Ecstasy of Rita Joe* premiered at the Vancouver Playhouse on November 23, 1967, in a landmark production that was remounted for the opening of the National Arts Centre in 1969. That year the play was also broadcast on CBC-TV and produced in a French translation by Gratien Gélinas in Montreal, as *Rita Joe* reverberated through the nation's collective consciousness. In a review of a later production, Jamie Portman recalled that "*Rita Joe* happened during Centennial year when Canadians were anxious to look at themselves. But the look that this play provided was an unsettling one. It punctured the euphoria and the smug complacency of Canada's birthday celebrations and declared unequivocally that all was not well with this country and its institutions." Its implications for Canadian playwriting were equally dramatic:

> This was an indigenous Canadian drama that surfaced and succeeded at a time when indigenous Canadian drama was generally considered to be an aberration. It was a play of merit, worthy of production in any Canadian theatre. It prompted an awareness of the existence of other plays potentially worthy of production. It provided resounding evidence that it was not necessary for any Canadian theatre to rely solely on imported fare. With the arrival of *The Ecstasy of Rita Joe*, Canadian plays ceased to be a rarity in English-speaking Canada. Companies dedicated to the production of new Canadian drama sprang up, and in so doing nurtured the further growth of playwriting activity. Canada's regional theatres—some of them grudgingly—found themselves forced to take the Canadian playwright seriously for the first time.[16]

Yet the battle for credibility was not quite so easily won. Just how grudgingly the theatre establishment came to accept the Canadian playwright was vividly registered by a 1971 study that found that in the previous year, the seven major regional theatres had produced the work of a total of two Canadian dramatists, and paid them less than $5000 out of combined budgets of more than $2 million.[17] Consider the case of the once pioneering Manitoba Theatre Centre. Despite its success with Winnipeg writer Ann Henry's *Lulu Street*, more than a decade would pass before the MTC presented another new play by a local playwright. The flurry of Canadian play production in 1967 had obviously been in some respects no more than Centennial Year tokenism.

The stage history of John Herbert's *Fortune and Men's Eyes* is especially revealing of the difficulties faced by Canadian playwrights. *Fortune* had been workshopped at Stratford in 1965. But denied a full production there or anywhere else in Canada, the play opened in New York in 1967 and ran for a year off-Broadway. By the end of 1968 it had had a long run in London and become a full-scale international hit. By 1969 it was already being revived in New York. The play's impact on other Canadian dramatists was immediate and inspirational: "the ice-breaker in the channel," George Ryga called it.[18] But for all that, professional productions of *Fortune and Men's Eyes* in Canada to 1970 consisted of a week at the Vancouver Playhouse's "experimental" Stage 2 and a brief run in the MTC's Studio Theatre. There was not a mainstage production to be seen.

What had gone wrong? The expectations and struggles of a half-century had resulted in a Canadian theatre that by the late 1960s had already become entrenched and conservative. Rather than living up to the original promise of the regionals to create new models adapted to the distinctive needs of their communities, which surely should have meant presenting plays written about those communities from within them, the large subsidized theatres mostly tried to emulate Broadway and the West End. When artistic directors were asked about Canadian plays and playwrights, their responses were often remarkably similar:

> I don't see how a play can be Canadian.
> I don't think there are any plays that you could call strictly Canadian.
> But if you start to define what is a Canadian and what is a Canadian playwright, what do you end up with?
> What does the phrase mean?[19]

With few exceptions the regionals served up homogenized theatre: safe, commercial seasons of British and American hits plus a smattering of world classics. Moreover, it was theatre as Cultural Event, like the opera or the symphony, the kind of thing you got dressed up for.

But in the late sixties, the Age of Aquarius and the Generation Gap, many theatre artists and much of the potential audience were evolving in a different direction. The Canadian Centennial just happened to coincide with the most radical cultural upheaval of the century in the Western world. There was a sexual revolution, a musical revolution, a drug revolution; long hair, peace marches and a Summer of Love. By 1968 in Chicago, Paris and Prague the revolution would spill over into the streets. Canada wasn't immune to these forces nor could its theatre be, no matter how stubbornly it tried to remain middle-aged and middle-class.

That the most significant Canadian plays of the decade should both have appeared in 1967 was not coincidental. *The Ecstasy of Rita Joe* and *Fortune and Men's Eyes* are plays very much of their age, marked by strong social consciousness and critical, anti-establishment perspectives. The playwrights too, by virtue of their alienation from the cultural mainstream, were in sync with the temper of the times. Both Ryga and Herbert were outspoken and uncompromising in their social, artistic, sexual and political views. It was characteristic of their outsider status that neither was initially allowed entry into the United States to see his own play in production; characteristic that Herbert refused the DDF's Massey Award (and its $1000 cash prize) for Best Play for *Fortune* in 1968; characteristic that the politics of Ryga's 1970 play *Captives of the Faceless Drummer* would so enrage the Board of the Vancouver Playhouse, which had commissioned it, that they would refuse it production. It was ironic but perhaps also inevitable that the two writers whose plays brought modern Canadian drama into existence would eventually find themselves virtually unproduced by the major Canadian theatres.

Modern Canadian drama was born out of an amalgam of the new consciousness of the age—social, political and aesthetic—with the new Canadian self-consciousness. Since the larger theatres were generally unsympathetic and unaccommodating to both these forces, an even newer Canadian theatre had to be invented, an alternate theatre. One of its prime movers in Toronto was Martin Kinch, who describes those first heady days as having little to do with nationalism:

> The real influences were Fritz Perls and Timothy Leary, Peter Brook and Jerzy Grotowski, Tom O'Horgan, Cafe La Mama, Julian Beck, Judith Malina, and the ensemble of the Living Theatre; in short, a host of European and American artists, most of them primarily dedicated to the ethic and the aesthetic of "doing your own thing." . . . It was

an exciting time, a time of experiment and exploration . . . expressionism, hallucination, confrontation, and audience participation flourished. Perhaps most important, however, there existed a definite bond between the theatres and their audience; an audience that was characterized by long hair, beards, bells, and babies in the front rows of the most outrageous plays. Its concerns were the concerns of "the sixties": the breaking of sexual taboo, the problems of individual freedom, and the yearning for community.[20]

In 1969 Kinch became a co-director of Toronto's Theatre Passe Muraille, founded the previous year by Jim Garrard. As its name suggests, Passe Muraille was to be a theatre without walls: neither the traditional fourth wall between actors and audience nor necessarily even the walls of a theatre building. Garrard envisioned "a guerilla theatre": "Theatre in the subways, get a truck and do theatre in small towns, real circuses, grab people in the streets. . . . I'd like to make theatre as popular as bowling."[21] A milestone for the new alternate theatre movement was Passe Muraille's production of Rochelle Owens' *Futz* in February 1969. An American play about a man in love with a pig (!), in both style and content it established the parameters of the alternate theatre's self-conscious anti-conventionality. The sex, obscenity and nudity it featured would become almost obligatory. When the show was closed by the morality squad, and the company charged and subsequently acquitted, the new movement had its red badge of courage.

By the summer of 1970 alternate theatre in Toronto had developed to the point where it could celebrate itself with a Festival of Underground Theatre. When the smoke from the festival cleared, the emphasis of the alternates could be seen to have undergone something of a shift from sensationalism to nationalism. Central to the new emphasis were Ken Gass and his Factory Theatre Lab, and the new artistic director of Theatre Passe Muraille, Paul Thompson.

Gass, who had been helping run John Herbert's tiny Garret Theatre, set out to prove that there was no lack of Canadian playwrights; they were just waiting to be discovered and encouraged. His theatre would be both a factory and a laboratory, presenting polished new works as well as works-in-progress, fragments, staged ideas. Most importantly it would be "The Home of the Canadian Playwright." His concept paid off almost immediately with a string of notable new plays: David Freeman's *Creeps*, Herschel Hardin's *Esker Mike and His Wife, Agiluk* and George Walker's *Prince of Naples* all in 1971; most of Walker's other plays over the next dozen years; and exciting (though not necessarily enduring) work by Hrant Alianak, Larry Fineberg, Bryan Wade and Gass himself.

Paul Thompson came to Passe Muraille after working in France with Roger Planchon, whose process-oriented, political brand of theatre was in direct contrast with Thompson's experiences during a brief apprenticeship at Stratford. Rejecting the Stratford model, Thompson steered his company towards a focus on local subject matter and collective creation, involving his actors in first-hand research, improvisation and continual revision, and utilizing their particular skills as key elements in the play wherever possible. When Thompson took over Passe Muraille there was already a precedent for this kind of theatre in Toronto. George Luscombe had been involved with Joan Littlewood's Theatre Workshops in England in the mid-fifties and had put together Toronto Workshop Productions in 1959 based on Littlewood's political and stylistic principles: left-wing politics and an eclectic style that integrated improvs, documentary, *commedia* and often collective scripting. In the late sixties and early seventies TWP was creating potent socio-political theatre with agitprop pieces like *Mister Bones* and *Chicago '70* on race and politics in America, and its bittersweet evocation of the Canadian Depression, *Ten Lost Years*. In 1984, the partnership of Luscombe and Toronto Workshop Productions celebrated its twenty-fifth year, still very much a going concern.

Nevertheless it was Passe Muraille under Paul Thompson's stewardship that became the most important theatre in Canada in the early seventies. Creations like *Doukhobors, The Farm Show* (first performed in a Clinton, Ontario barn), *Under the Greywacke* and *The Adventures of an Immigrant* (performed in Toronto streetcars among other venues) made often stirring theatrical poetry out of material that was sometimes mundane and always local. Docudrama with a high degree of theatricality became the Passe Muraille trademark: a small company of actors using little but their own bodies and voices to create ingenious stage metaphors. They inspired countless imitators across the country, though in less talented hands the deceptively rigorous demands of collective scripting and Passe Muraille's presentational style sometimes had unfortunate results. Among the best of their offshoots was Twenty-Fifth Street House Theatre in Saskatoon, whose *Paper Wheat* was in the finest Passe Muraille tradition, and Newfoundland's CODCO. In addition the company specialized in resurrecting, popularizing, dramatizing and often mythicizing Canadian history in collective scripts or in conjunction with a writer. *Buffalo Jump* with Carol Bolt, *1837: The Farmers' Revolt* with Rick Salutin, *Them Donnellys* with Frank MacEnany and *Far as the Eye Can See* with Rudy Wiebe were some of the best of the collaborations. Later in the decade two Passe Muraille alumni would create *Billy Bishop Goes to War*, and Linda Griffiths (with Paul Thompson) would let loose *Maggie & Pierre* upon the country. Perhaps the most exciting Canadian playwright to emerge in the 1980s, Judith Thompson, also came out of Passe Muraille with her extraordinary first play, *The Crackwalker*.

Not everything was happening in Toronto. In Vancouver, where John Juliani's experimental Savage God project had been operating since 1966, John Gray, Larry Lillo and a group of other UBC theatre graduates formed Tamahnous Theatre in 1971, a collective that would remain Vancouver's most original and progressive company for the next ten years. Its most enduring legacy may prove to be the special brand of small-cast musical best represented by Gray's *Billy Bishop* and Morris Panych's "post-nuclear cabaret," *Last Call!* Meanwhile the New Play Centre had come into being in 1970 dedicated to developing new scripts by local writers with production as only a secondary priority. Under the direction of Pamela Hawthorn since 1972, the New Play Centre has had a hand in most of the drama to come out of B.C., including the work of Margaret Hollingsworth, Tom Walmsley, Ted Galay, John Lazarus, Sheldon Rosen, Betty Lambert, Eric Nicol and Sherman Snukal.

Seeded by government grants from Local Initiatives Programs (LIP) and Opportunities for Youth (OFY), new companies doing indigenous theatre sprouted everywhere in 1971-72: Edmonton's Theatre 3, Calgary's Alberta Theatre Projects, Pier One in Halifax, the Mummers Troupe in St. John's. Lennoxville, Quebec even provided a kind of "alternate" festival theatre. Festival Lennoxville presented all-Canadian summer seasons of plays by the likes of Michael Cook, Herschel Hardin and Sharon Pollock from 1972 until its demise in 1982, a victim of poor demographics and Parti Québécois cultural policy.

Toronto, though, was where most of the action was, and nothing did more to cement its position at the centre of the new movement than Tarragon Theatre. Founded in 1971 by Bill Glassco, who had directed *Creeps* at the Factory Lab earlier in the year, Tarragon opened with a revised version of *Creeps* that proved even more successful than the original. The first Tarragon season ended with a new work which was to become probably the single most influential Canadian play of the 1970s, David French's *Leaving Home*. Its story of generational conflict and a singularly Canadian form of immigrant alienation (ex-Newfoundlanders spiritually adrift in Toronto) elicited strong audience identification, and its straightforward, accessible style had broad appeal. *Leaving Home* created a vogue for domestic realism that some have argued was a debilitating counterforce to the more adventurous directions that Canadian drama seemed to be taking at the time. Tarragon soon became identified with that particular style, especially in light of Glassco's productions of subsequent plays by Freeman and French that were stylistically tame. But it wasn't really a fair reputation. Tarragon also introduced English Canada to the plays of Michel Tremblay with Glassco as director and co-translator—plays that are domestic in setting but hardly realistic in style. Moreover, from 1973-75 Tarragon produced James Reaney's Donnelly trilogy, which is about as far removed from stylistic realism or naturalism as plays can get. Unlike the great majority of companies devoted to Canadian works, Tarragon managed both to combine artistic and commercial success and to sustain it over a number of years. More than any other theatre it succeeded in bringing Canadian drama into the mainstream.

The great wave of new alternate theatres in Toronto crested in 1972 with the founding of Toronto Free Theatre by Tom Hendry, Martin Kinch and John Palmer. Subsidized by LIP grants, performances were literally free until 1974 when the impossible economics of that policy led to gradually increasing admissions. But Toronto Free's cultivation of an excellent ensemble of actors and a distinctive taste for the psychologically bizarre in plays and production has remained constant. Many of its early successes were plays by its in-house triumvirate—especially Hendry and Palmer—along with Carol Bolt. George Walker and Erika Ritter were among the most noteworthy later additions to Toronto Free's playwriting corps.

Notwithstanding the dynamism of the alternate theatres, drama in Canada in the early seventies was in danger of falling victim to an insidious form of ghettoization. Canadian plays were relegated to small, low-budget theatres that lacked the financial and technical resources available to the heavily subsidized festivals and regionals. While non-Canadian works had access to lush productions, large casts and relatively highly paid actors, Canadian plays were doomed to what George Ryga called "beggars theatre."[22] Concurrently, of course, Canadian playwrights were denied the financial opportunities that might allow them to actually make a living by practicing their craft. In an attempt to remedy this situation a group of playwrights met in the summer of 1971 to consider "The Dilemma of the Playwright in Canada." What ensued was a series of strongly worded recommendations, the most contentious of which called for a 50% Canadian content quota for all theatres receiving government funding. Most artistic directors and editorialists were predictably outraged. ("If it ever happened, then critics should also get Canada Council grants for sitting through the plays," was one wit's response.[23]) Though no formal quota system was ever adopted, the controversy led to a full public airing of the situation and, more importantly, to an informal policy decision by the Canada Council to "appeal" to its client theatres to do more Canadian plays. The results were startling. By the 1972-73 season nearly 50% of the plays produced by subsidized theatres were in fact Canadian.

Among the most tangible consequences of this new policy was a return to one of the original precepts of the "regional" ideal, the commissioning of new plays by regional theatres from playwrights with local roots and interests. These arrangements have proven mutually fruitful for playwrights and theatres alike, especially Sharon Pollock's work for the Vancouver Playhouse and Theatre Calgary, John Murrell and W.O. Mitchell also at Theatre Calgary, Ken Mitchell and especially Rex Deverell with Regina's Globe, and David Fennario with the Centaur in Montreal. The Blyth and Kawartha Summer Festivals, in their cultivation of Anne Chislett, have proven the value of a homegrown product even in the traditionally more commercial milieu of summer theatre. In each of these cases plays written with very specific associations for local audiences have made their way into theatres across the country with no lack of success. Maybe Canada has achieved its long-elusive "national theatre" after all.

Following the tremendous expansion of the Canadian theatre in the first half of the 1970s, a certain amount of retrenchment was inevitable. Tougher economic times and a general trend towards conservatism have put additional strains on an endeavour that is economically marginal even under the best conditions. Theatres as widely divergent as Stratford and Twenty-Fifth Street House have had to weather financial and artistic crises that threatened their survival. Some have gone under: Vancouver's Westcoast Actors, Edmonton's Theatre 3, Montreal's Saidye Bronfman. Robin Phillips' ambitious Grand Theatre Company in London, Ontario, couldn't survive its first season. Facing new audience expectations and a changing ideological climate, the major "alternate" theatres (the term is no longer really accurate) in Toronto and Vancouver have all undergone structural reorganization and found new artistic directors.

But Passe Muraille, Tarragon, Factory Lab, Toronto Free and Tamahnous are still very much in operation, still providing a springboard for Canadian plays along with the resurgent regionals and theatres like Vancouver's Arts Club that have successfully occupied the middle ground. And a new generation of neo-alternates has arisen to take the place of those that have fallen by the wayside or entered into the mainstream, companies like Theatre Network in Edmonton, Touchstone in Vancouver, Prairie Theatre Exchange in Winnipeg, and Toronto's Actor's Lab, Necessary Angel and Buddies in Bad Times. The Toronto International Theatre Festival in 1981 showcased Canadian plays and productions alongside some of the best theatre companies in the world, and no one had to apologize for the quality of the domestic product. The eighties have seen, too, the establishment of a series of new awards. Joining the prestigious Chalmers Award (given by the Toronto Drama Bench since 1972 for best Canadian play produced each year in Toronto) are the Governor-General's Award in Drama for the best new Canadian play in publication, and Vancouver and Toronto's equivalents to New York's Tony Awards, the Doras in Toronto (after Dora Mavor Moore) and the Jessies in Vancouver (after Jessie Richardson). More than just self-congratulations, these plaudits signify that Canadian drama and theatre are a *fait accompli*, occupying at last a prominent place in the nation's cultural profile. And the prognosis for the future is very good, the Canadian play even threatening to become an exportable commodity. "The next ten years," the dramaturge of New York's Public Theater predicted in 1979, "are going to be the decade of the Canadian playwright."[24]

III.

Hyperbole aside, Canadian theatre since 1967 has brought forth a substantial body of plays worthy of continued attention both as scripts to be performed and texts to be read and studied. The intention of *Modern Canadian Plays* is to present as definitively as possible the highlights of modern Canadian drama in English. *Rita Joe* and *Fortune and Men's Eyes* set it all in motion in 1967 and became its first true classics. *Creeps* helped launch both the Factory Lab and Tarragon theatres and defined the brutal naturalism that characterized a good deal of Canadian theatre through the first half of the seventies, just as *1837: The Farmers' Revolt* epitomized Passe Muraille's influential collective, quasi-documentary style. The history play took new directions in the prairies with *Walsh* and in Ontario with the brilliant theatricality of the Donnelly trilogy, perhaps the masterwork of Canadian drama. *Jacob's Wake* was a family play with a powerful Newfoundland accent while *Balconville* was the most eloquent of David Fennario's chronicles of the Montreal working class. *Zastrozzi* spoke with the distinctive voice of genre parody leavened with pop metaphysics that George Walker has made his own. *Jitters* and *Automatic Pilot* blazed bright comic paths in the urbane style that reflected a new national sophistication. And *Billy Bishop* flew higher and further than anything else to date.

These plays are also, in a variety of ways, representative of the primary patterns into which modern Canadian drama has shaped itself. Probably the strongest impression made by Canadian plays through the mid-1970s was of a theatre of the underdog and the outsider. This is not entirely surprising in the context of Canadian literature generally, which shows many of the same impulses. Although Margaret Atwood pays virtually no attention to drama in her thematic study of Canadian literature, *Survival*, her arguments concerning the characteristic "victim-positions" of Canadian protagonists are applicable to a formidable number of plays. In *Rita Joe*, *Fortune* and *Creeps*, and nearly everything written for the stage by Fennario and Tremblay, the victimization is played out in the mode of social protest within a contemporary landscape. But even when the perspective is historical, as in *1837*, *Walsh* and the Donnelly plays, the dramatic focus is on the losers rather than the winners, the victims (or the process of victimization) rather than the victors. From *Riel* onwards there have been few exceptions to this rule.

The alienated Outsider is the central figure not just in modern Canadian plays, of course, but in modern literature as a whole, and particularly in the post-war drama. Gélinas' bastard hero Tit-Coq, the British "angry young men" and the American rebels without a cause of the 1950s are the true spiritual ancestors of Rita Joe, Fennario's workers, Tom Walmsley's outlaws and even some of the playwrights themselves. (David French tells a good story in *Stage Voices* about going to his first acting class dressed like James Dean.) New dramatic movements seem in fact to thrive on the outsider status of their plays' characters: witness Ibsen's artists and social rebels and O'Neill's early protagonists. Perhaps the dramatist's own position in the vanguard of a new movement, himself alienated from the establishment and challenging its order, demands his sympathy for the outsider.

In that regard it is useful to consider the autobiographical nature of much of the new Canadian drama. Writing about *Fortune and Men's Eyes* in 1968, Nathan Cohen attributed the play's success to its origins in Herbert's own experience, and he noted critically "how seldom the [Canadian playwright] bases himself on his own involvements and observations, or how rarely he takes for his point of artistic departure the social tensions of life in his own backyard."[25] But all that changed very quickly. Many of the best plays of the era were autobiographically based (*Creeps, Lulu Street, Leaving Home*) or at least drawn from immediate personal observation (*Rita Joe, Les Belles Soeurs*). A favourite theme was the experience of coming of age (French's *Of the Fields, Lately* and *Leaving Home*, Tom Hendry's *Fifteen Miles of Broken Glass*) with its attendant disillusionment and revisionism. Considering that even the history plays shared those attitudes, and that the Centennial experience was something like a national coming of age, it is possible to see the Canadian drama of this period as embodying a kind of collective national autobiography. (In James Reaney's *Colours in the Dark* the autobiographical impulse surges beyond the personal and national into the archetypal.) In the best dramatic tradition the playwrights insisted on holding up a mirror before their audiences so that Canadians might see themselves, no matter how flawed or unflattering the reflection.

But what were the images being reflected? Frequently they were Indians or Newfoundlanders, criminals, the handicapped or homosexuals; the socially marginal and disenfranchised took centre stage. Outsiders became insiders as the revolutionary impulses of the late sixties and early seventies counterculture inverted the traditional aesthetic order. Cultural militancy in the Third World and among Black Americans also helped to awaken a new awareness of and among Canadian minorities. All this worked to accelerate a process noted by Northrop Frye in his analysis of the "garrison mentality" in Canadian literature:

> As the centre of Canadian life moves from the fortress to the metropolis, the garrison mentality changes correspondingly. It begins as an expression of the moral values generally accepted in the group as a whole, and then, as society gets more complicated and more in control of its environment, it becomes more of a revolutionary garrison within a metropolitan society.... It changes from a defence of to an attack on what society accepts as conventional standards.... [26]

The courtroom (and even the city itself) from which Rita Joe can't escape, the prison in *Fortune and Men's Eyes*, the sheltered workshop in *Creeps*, the shipping room in Fennario's *On the Job*—these are all more than just physical settings. They are metaphors of a repressive System which paradoxically keeps its outsiders shut up inside, creating garrisons with revolutionary potential. As Canadian history and history plays tell us, however, from 1837 to Riel to the FLQ, Canadian revolutions don't succeed. At best all these plays celebrate moral victories, preservations of integrity, possibilities of escape.

Perhaps because the Canadian mosaic and our domestic geopolitics make nearly *everyone* here feel like something of an outsider, the family looms large in Canadian drama. Those who don't have one (Tit-Coq, *Lulu Street*'s Elly) idealize it as the locus of security and identity. At its best, as in the Donnelly plays, it really is that and more—the source of all strength. The family provides the ultimate garrison for the Donnellys and others who feel themselves surrounded by hostility or stranded in an alien environment, like the elder Mercers in David French's plays. But for young Ben Mercer who has set his sights wider, the family is a trap, stifling and devouring where it purports to nourish and protect. Modern drama from Strindberg through O'Neill to Miller and Pinter has more often than not portrayed the family as a battleground on which primal wars are fought, and so it is too in Canadian plays as different as *Leaving Home*, *Jacob's Wake*, Pollock's *Blood Relations*, Margaret Hollingsworth's *War Baby*, Timothy Findley's *Can You See Me Yet?* and Tremblay's *Forever Yours Marie-Lou*. In the latter play Carmen, like Ben Mercer, fights to become a creative outsider, to escape the terrible grip of what her mother calls with bitter irony "the family cell": the garrison become prison. Ironically, such plays present the family as a microcosm of the larger society of which it is a part. The convicts in *Fortune and Men's Eyes* construct a surrogate family every bit as corrupt and self-destructive as those they grew up in on the outside.

Surrogate families don't have to be destructive. The "family" of theatre people in *Jitters* manages, in spite of its tensions, to achieve a delicate equilibrium that gets them through the toughest times. The same is true of the tenement-dwellers in *Balconville*. A different kind of surrogate family is constituted in plays like Sheldon Rosen's *Ned and Jack* and Tremblay's *Hosanna* which investigate the way relationships between people of the same sex can grow into a mutuality like the family at its best (or degenerate into a parody of family role-playing at its very worst). With the decline of the nuclear family and the advent of gay liberation and women's liberation has come a testing of new sexual attitudes and domestic arrangements. This has found its most popular expression in contemporary comedies of manners like *Automatic Pilot*, Anne Chislett's *The Tomorrow Box* and Sherman Snukal's *Talking Dirty* that may prove to be the "family plays" of the 1980s.

Because the rise of Canadian drama coincided with a surge of nationalism and national self-awareness, the history play has had a prominent place in the developing repertoire. Canadian plays about non-Canadian history have been relatively rare, but perhaps not surprisingly they have tended to concern themselves almost exclusively with revolutionaries. (Carol Bolt's *Red Emma*, Ryga's *Paracelsus*, Michael Cook's *The Gayden Chronicles* and Ken Mitchell's *The Great Cultural Revolution* are typical examples.) Plays about Canadian history have a slightly more complex range of concerns. For a time their primary purpose seemed to be to make Canadians aware that they *had* a history and that it was actually interesting (both assumptions about which many Canadians remain skeptical). Beyond that, there were a number of different messages: that Canadian history hadn't always happened the way it was taught in school, if it had been taught at all; that it had sometimes been shameful; and that it was full of genuine Canadian heroes, some of them relatively unknown and most extremely unlikely.

The harshest dramatic treatments have been reserved for various acts of genocide committed against native Indians in Canada—*Walsh*, Cook's *On the Rim of the Curve*, Herschel Hardin's *The Great Wave of Civilization*—and similar expressions of racism (Pollock's *The Komagata Maru Incident*). In a lighter vein politicians have made ripe pickings for critical portraits, Mackenzie King in particular (in Reaney's *The Dismissal* and Alan Stratton's *Rexy!*). But on the whole, Canadian playwrights have been more interested in accentuating the historically positive. Coulter and Reaney resurrect Louis Riel and the Black Donnellys, polish up their badly tarnished reputations and turn them from villains into heroes. William Lyon Mackenzie in *1837*, Dr. Norman Bethune in Rod Langley's *Bethune* and Billy Bishop are all reintroduced as legitimate Canadian heroes, even if contentious men. *1837* also celebrates a *collective* hero—it is after all *The Farmers' Revolt*—using agitprop techniques borrowed from the political theatre of the 1930s. The collective struggles of Saskatchewan farmers (*Paper Wheat*), unemployed workers (Bolt's *Buffalo Jump*) and coal miners (Rex Deverell's *Black Powder*) have been chronicled and lionized in similar ways.

"Chronicled" is not really the right word. The history play is a problematical genre by definition. History is supposed to be true whereas a play is of course fictional. Canadian history plays often take the form of "docudrama," combining the truthfulness of documentary with the imaginative freedom of drama. But what proportions of fact and fiction are necessary to ensure that Canadian history turns out, in the eyes of the playwright, satisfactorily? How does one mitigate the fact that the good guys have rarely won? In a comment on his own pseudo-history play, *The Boy Bishop*, Ken Gass proposes that "the only important thing about history is that it needs to be transcended.

We should lie about our history or make one up if we don't like the one we have."[27] Other playwrights prefer less radical terminology. In his preface to *The Crime of Louis Riel*, John Coulter refers to his Riel as a "legendary hero." Both Rick Salutin (referring to his *Les Canadiens*) and Carol Bolt use the term "myth" to describe their plays. "Myth is more appealing than fact," says Bolt. "It postulates that heroism is possible, that people can be noble and effective and change things."[28]

Myth as the expression of a fundamental human desire for some kind of heroism or nobility or efficacy animates every play in this collection. But is there also an identifiable *Canadian* myth that runs through these plays, a "distinctive mythology which reflects . . . who we are and how we got that way"?[29] If there is, maybe it is the awareness implicit in all of them that, though winning might be nice, the quality of experience is more important than the final score. This is true even of *Zastrozzi* and *Billy Bishop Goes to War*. Both plays deliver a special kind of satisfaction by celebrating unabashed winners in theatrically exciting ways, but a peculiar sense of melancholy hangs over them as well. Victory is somehow tainted, even a little distasteful. "You're a typical Canadian, / You're modesty itself," Lady St. Helier sings to Billy Bishop. That too is part of the Canadian myth. But is it true? Maybe. What is undoubtedly true, as these plays confirm, is that theatre at its best always brings us closer to ourselves.

NOTES

[1] Nathan Cohen, "Theatre Today: English Canada," *Tamarack Review*, 13 (Autumn 1959), 28.

[2] Thomas B. Hendry, "Trends in Canadian Theatre," *Tulane Drama Review*, 10 (Fall 1965), 62-70. That same year Michael Tait concluded his survey of "the grey wastes of Canadian drama" from 1920-60 by noting "perhaps the most depressing feature of theatre in Canada: the lack of any vital and continuing relation between theatrical activity and the work of the Canadian playwright." See "Drama and Theatre," *Literary History of Canada*, ed. Carl F. Klinck, 2nd ed. (Toronto: Univ. of Toronto Press, 1976), II, 159, 167.

[3] Betty Lee, *Love and Whiskey: The Story of the Dominion Drama Festival* (Toronto: McClelland and Stewart, 1973), 296.

[4] Fred Jacobs, "Waiting for a Dramatist," *The Canadian Magazine*, 43 (June 1914), 146.

[5] Vincent Massey, "The Prospects of a Canadian Drama," *Queen's Quarterly*, 30 (October 1922), 200.

[6] Rupert Caplan, "The Ultimate National Theatre," *Canadian Forum*, 9 (January 1929), 143-44.

[7] See Anton Wagner, "The Developing Mosaic: English Canadian Drama to Mid-Century," in *Canada's Lost Plays, Volume Three*, ed. Anton Wagner (Toronto: CTR Publications, 1980), 19-21.

[8] Jack Gould, "Canada Shows Us How," *New York Times*, 1 Sept. 1946, Sec. II, 7.

[9] John Coulter in *Stage Voices*, ed. Geraldine Anthony (Toronto: Doubleday, 1978), 19-20.

[10] Robertson Davies, *The Well-Tempered Critic: One Man's View of Theatre and Letters in Canada*, ed. Judith Skelton Grant (Toronto: McClelland and Stewart, 1981), 66.

[11] Davies, 74.

[12] Hendry, "Trends in Canadian Theatre," 64-65.

[13] Mavor Moore, "A Theatre for Canada," *University of Toronto Quarterly*, 26 (October 1956), 2.

[14] Quoted in Don Rubin, "Creeping Toward a Culture: The Theatre in English Canada Since 1945," *Canadian Theatre Review*, 1 (Winter 1974), 8.

[15] Tom Hendry, "MTC: A View from the Beginning," *Canadian Theatre Review*, 4 (Fall 1974), 16.

[16] Jamie Portman, "*Ecstasy of Rita Joe* Still Manages to Shock and Scourge," *Vancouver Province*, 12 April 1976, p. 10. Cf. Neil Carson, "Towards a Popular Theatre in English Canada," *Canadian Literature*, 85 (Summer 1980), 64-65.

[17] David Gustafson, "Let's Really Hear It for Canadian Theatre," *Maclean's*, 84 (October 1971), 84.

[18] George Ryga, "Contemporary Theatre and Its Language," *Canadian Theatre Review*, 14 (Spring 1977), p. 8.

[19] Quoted verbatim from a series of interviews with artistic directors of regional theatres in *The Stage in Canada*: Edward Gilbert (MTC), 3 (May 1967), p. 14; Robert Glenn (Citadel), 3 (June 1967), p. 7; Joy Coghill (Playhouse), 3 (Sept. 1967), p. 10; Kurt Reis (MTC), 5 (Nov. 1969), p. 13.

[20] Martin Kinch, "Canadian Theatre: In for the Long Haul," *This Magazine*, 10 (Nov.-Dec. 1976), 4-5.

[21] Quoted in Robert Wallace, "Growing Pains: Toronto Theatre in the 1970s," *Canadian Literature*, 85 (Summer 1980), 77.

[22] George Ryga, "Theatre in Canada: A Viewpoint on Its Development and Future," *Canadian Theatre Review*, 1 (Winter 1974), 30.

[23] Bill Thomas in the *Victoria Colonist*, quoted in "Playwrights," *The Stage in Canada*, 6 (January 1972), p. 17.

[24] John Bentley Mays, "Taking It on the Road," *Maclean's*, 92 (4 June 1979), 60.

[25] Nathan Cohen, "John Herbert," in *Canadian Writing Today*, ed. Mordecai Richler (Harmondsworth: Penguin, 1970), 212.

[26] Northrop Frye, "Conclusion," *Literary History of Canada*, II, 346.

[27] "Postscript: Interview with Ken Gass," *Canadian Theatre Review*, 12 (Fall 1976), 123.

[28] *Playwrights in Profile: Carol Bolt* (Toronto: Playwrights Co-op, 1976), 8.

[29] George Ryga, "The Need for a Mythology," *Canadian Theatre Review*, 16 (Fall 1977), 5.

GEORGE RYGA (b. 1932)

"Playwright George Ryga Thursday night peeled a cicatrice off Canadian society and showed the bleeding flesh beneath." Jack Richards, reviewing the first performance of *The Ecstasy of Rita Joe* for the *Vancouver Sun* in 1967, identified an essential quality of Ryga's work that has proven to be one of his major strengths and most serious difficulties. With stubborn integrity and singlemindedness Ryga has made a career of tearing at sensitive wounds, stirring up controversy and sometimes making himself unpopular in the process. Outspoken, abrasive and always fiercely committed to social justice and the defense of human dignity, he has created a body of dramatic work that is among the most impressive and least well known in Canada.

Ryga gave warning of his uncompromising political views soon after leaving the Ukrainian community in northern Alberta where he had grown up. At the Banff School of Arts in 1950 he lost a scholarship for writing a poem critical of the Korean War. Four years later he was forced to resign his job as a radio producer in Edmonton because of his public protests against the Rosenberg trial. When in 1962 after a decade of writing poetry and fiction Ryga turned his hand to drama, the imprint of his convictions was immediately clear.

His first play, *Indian*, written for television, is an austere, powerful work that announced a remarkable dramatic talent. The nameless Indian of the title is initially seen as a stereotype but gradually reveals a desperate humanity in whose light his white employer and the complacent government agent (a recurrent character type in Ryga's work) seem bloodless ciphers. The abrupt plunges into memory that punctuate the naturalism of *Indian* look forward to the more sophisticated stylization of Ryga's stage plays, just as the play's tone of anger combined with deep sadness would mark the best of Ryga's work to come.

In 1963 Ryga settled in Summerland, B.C., where he still lives, and after publishing two novels about the harshness of prairie life, *Hungry Hills* (1963) and *Ballad of a Stonepicker* (1966), he was commissioned to write a Centennial play for the Vancouver Playhouse. *The Ecstasy of Rita Joe* was the result, and he followed it with an even bigger box-office hit, *Grass and Wild Strawberries* (1969), a multi-media exploration of the conflict between sixties youth culture and the adult establishment. When his third commission from the Playhouse coincided with the October Crisis in 1970, Ryga reshaped his work-in-progress into a confrontation between a government mandarin and the terrorist holding him hostage. Upset by the politics of the script, the theatre's board refused to produce it and months of bitter public controversy ensued. For a short time *Captives of the Faceless Drummer* became a *cause célèbre*; but long after the play was forgotten the bitterness lingered and Ryga became increasingly alienated from the mainstream of Canadian theatre.

Since 1971 Ryga's new plays have been produced in the relative obscurity of Banff (*Sunrise on Sarah* and *Portrait of Angelica*), Edmonton's Theatre Network (*Seven Hours to Sundown*), Western Canada Theatre Company in Kamloops (*Ploughmen of the Glacier*) and Kam Theatre Lab of North Bay, Ontario (the excellent *Letter to My Son*, perhaps Ryga's best play since *Rita Joe*). Few of the larger theatres have ever done any of his work except *Rita Joe*. One of his most interesting and ambitious plays, *Paracelsus*, first published in 1974, didn't receive a professional production until 1986. Ryga has written two more novels, *Night Desk* (1976) and *In the Shadow of the Vulture* (1985), and a book about his trip to China, *Beyond the Crimson Morning* (1979). Currently he spends much of his time adapting his plays for European radio. His work is extremely popular in both Eastern and Western Europe where it is regularly produced on radio and stage, winning awards and setting attendance records.

Ryga's popularity on the other side of the Atlantic may be partly attributable to the European sensibility in his writing, especially *The Ecstasy of Rita Joe*. Though the play's major social concern—the plight of the Indian in the white man's city—is distinctively Canadian, the quality of Rita's suffering, her passivity and sense of spiritual homelessness are evocative of Dostoevsky (whom Ryga claims to have read in full). The nightmarishness of Rita's experience, her feelings of entrapment and unaccountable guilt have roots that go back through Kafka to early expressionist drama—to Büchner's *Woyzeck*, for example (or a later American instance, O'Neill's *The Hairy Ape*). Rita takes her place in that tradition: the outsider perceived as a sort of freak, struggling to preserve her integrity in the face of a system socially and politically designed to frustrate her every attempt to make sense of her life; struggling to avoid internalizing the guilt imposed by a world that grows increasingly monstrous until it completes its inevitable process of destruction.

Central to Rita's torment is the cultural and epistemological schism between whites and Indians, represented in its extreme form by the contrast between the mechanical, life-denying pseudo-rationalism of the Magistrate and the humane, intuitive impressionism of David Joe. These ways of seeing and understanding the world are so fundamentally different that the results of their clashes are sometimes comical. When Rita claims to have seen God in the sky she's told to call the Air Force. When Jaimie Paul sees a TV commercial that shows a knife "cutting up good shoes like they were potatoes," he reacts with comic bewilderment (edged with the bitter irony that he and Rita have nothing to eat). But Rita's inability to assimilate is also the real crime of which the white Witnesses along with the Teacher and Priest, the Magistrate and Mr. Homer take turns accusing her. In court, while the Magistrate rambles on about "the process of legal argument," Rita asks him if she can bum a cigarette; in the stage direction the Policeman "smiles and exits"—he rests his case. Later the Magistrate tells Rita, "the obstacles to your life are here . . . in your thoughts . . . possibly even in your culture," and he suggests that she fix her hair, tame her accent, "perhaps even change your name."

But Rita won't be helped and can't be saved. She certainly gets no help from the hollow paternalism of the Priest, the Magistrate or the ironically named Mr. Homer. Nor can Rita be aided by her own father. For all the sympathy Ryga invests in him, David Joe is impotent to save his people, just as Jaimie Paul says. And when he comes to take Rita home to the reserve from the city, she refuses to go. Rita is trapped. The rural past, though pastoral in her memory, she knows is a dead-end. The urban present holds only degradation and the promise of an early death. And what about the future? The circular ramp that comprises the set traces Rita's futile journey through the play; the shadowy Murderers who appear and reappear symbolize her doom, immanent from the start; the Brechtian Singer who sings of the fate of Rita and Jaimie forecloses any hope of salvation. The one rich fantasy she and Jaimie indulge turns quickly sour: their dream of having children in the city collides with the ugly fact that Clara Hill has had to give hers away. The scene that begins with the implied promise of lovemaking in Jaimie's room ends in frustration, disgust and despair.

Is Rita Joe tragic? Does she retain her selfhood with a stubborn persistence that transforms her death from a sordid ritual of rape and murder into the "ecstasy" of a martyr? Or is she merely a passive victim doomed by birth, culture and her own feeble resignation? George Ryga's probing of this terrible wound near the heart of Canadian society provides no clear answer. But no one seeing or reading this play can ever look upon the "Indian problem" in the same way again.

•

The Ecstasy of Rita Joe first opened at the Vancouver Playhouse on November 23, 1967, featuring Frances Hyland as Rita Joe, August Schellenberg as Jaimie Paul, Chief Dan George as David Joe, Henry Ramer as the Magistrate, Robert Clothier as the Priest, Patricia George as Eileen Joe, and Walter Marsh as Mr. Homer. Ann Mortifee played the Singer and wrote the music with Willy Dunn. The production was designed by Charles Evans and directed by George Bloomfield.

THE ECSTASY OF RITA JOE

CHARACTERS

RITA JOE
JAIMIE PAUL
DAVID JOE, *Rita's father*
MAGISTRATE
MR. HOMER
FATHER ANDREW, *a priest*
EILEEN JOE, *Rita's sister*
OLD INDIAN WOMAN
MISS DONAHUE, *a teacher*
POLICEMAN
WITNESSES
MURDERERS
YOUNG INDIAN MEN
SINGER

SET

A circular ramp beginning at floor level stage left and continuing downward below floor level at stage front, then rising and sweeping along stage back at two-foot elevation to disappear in the wings of stage left. This ramp dominates the stage by wrapping the central and forward playing area. A short approach ramp, meeting with the main ramp at stage right, expedites entrances from the wings of stage right. The MAGISTRATE's chair and representation of court desk are situated at stage right, enclosed within the sweep of the ramp. At the foot of the desk is a lip on stage right side.

The SINGER sits here, turned away from the focus of the play. Her songs and accompaniment appear almost accidental. She has all the reactions of a white liberal folklorist with a limited concern and understanding of an ethnic dilemma which she touches in the course of her research and work in compiling and writing folk songs. She serves too as an alter ego to RITA JOE.

No curtain is used during the play. At the opening, intermission and conclusion of the play, the curtain remains up. The onus for isolating scenes from the past and present in RITA JOE's life falls on highlight lighting.

Backstage, there is a mountain cyclorama. In front of the cyclorama there is a darker maze curtain to suggest gloom and confusion, and a cityscape.

ACT ONE

The house lights and stage work lights remain on. Backstage, cyclorama, and maze curtains are up, revealing wall back of stage, exit doors, etc.

CAST and SINGER enter offstage singly and in pairs from the wings, the exit doors at the back of the theatre, and from the auditorium side doors. The entrances are workmanlike and untheatrical. When all the CAST is on stage, they turn to face the audience momentarily. The house lights dim.

The cyclorama is lowered into place. The maze curtain follows. This creates a sense of compression of stage into the auditorium. Recorded voices are heard in a jumble of mutterings and throat clearings. The MAGISTRATE enters as the CLERK begins.

CLERK *recorded* This court is in session. All present will rise....

The shuffling and scraping of furniture is heard. The CAST repeat "Rita Joe, Rita Joe." A POLICEMAN brings on RITA JOE.

MAGISTRATE Who is she? Can she speak English?

POLICEMAN Yes.

MAGISTRATE Then let her speak for herself!

He speaks to the audience firmly and with reason.

To understand life in a given society, one must understand laws of that society. All relationships...

CLERK *recorded* Man to man...man to woman ...man to property...man to the state...

MAGISTRATE ...are determined and enriched by laws that have grown out of social realities. The quality of the law under which you live and function determines the real quality of the freedom that was yours today.

The rest of the CAST slowly move out.

Your home and your well-being were protected. The roads of the city are open to us. So are the galleries, libraries, the administrative and public buildings. There are buses, trains...going in and coming out. Nobody is a prisoner here.

RITA *with humour, almost a sad sigh* The first time I tried to go home I was picked up by some men who gave me five dollars. An' then they arrested me.

The POLICEMAN retreats into the shadows. The SINGER crosses down.

MAGISTRATE   Thousands leave and enter the city every day . . .

RITA   It wasn't true what they said, but nobody'd believe me . . .

SINGER   *singing a recitivo searching for a melody*
Will the winds not blow
My words to her
Like the seeds
Of the dandelion?

MAGISTRATE   *smiling, as at a private joke*
Once . . . I saw a little girl in the Cariboo country. It was summer then and she wore only a blouse and skirt. I wondered what she wore in winter?

The MURDERERS hover in the background on the upper ramp. One whistles and one lights a cigarette—an action which will be repeated at the end of the play.

RITA   *moving to him, but hesitating*   You look like a good man. Tell them to let me go, please!

The MAGISTRATE goes to his podium.

MAGISTRATE   Our nation is on an economic par with the state of Arkansas. . . . We are a developing country, but a buoyant one. Still . . . the summer report of the Economic Council of Canada predicts a reduction in the gross national product unless we utilize our manpower for greater efficiency. Employed, happy people make for a prosperous, happy nation. . . .

RITA   *exultantly*   I worked at some jobs, mister!

The MAGISTRATE turns to face RITA JOE. The MURDERERS have gone.

MAGISTRATE   Gainful employment. Obedience to the law . . .

RITA   *to the MAGISTRATE*   Once I had a job . . .

He does not relate to her. She is troubled. She talks to the audience.

Once I had a job in a tire store . . . an' I'd worry about what time my boss would come. . . . He was always late . . . and so was everybody. Sometimes I got to thinkin' what would happen if he'd not come. And nobody else would come. And I'd be all day in this big room with no lights on an' the telephone ringing an' people asking for other people that weren't there. . . . What would happen?

As she relates her concern, she laughs. Towards the end of her monologue she is so amused by the absurdity of it all that she can hardly contain herself.

Lights fade on the MAGISTRATE who broods in his chair as he examines his court papers.

Lights up on JAIMIE PAUL approaching on the backstage ramp from stage left. He is jubilant, his laughter blending with her laughter. At the sound of his voice, RITA JOE runs to him, to the memory of him.

JAIMIE   I seen the city today and I seen things today I never knew was there, Rita Joe!

RITA   *happily*   I seen them too, Jaimie Paul!

He pauses above her, his mood light and childlike.

JAIMIE   I see a guy on top of a bridge, talkin' to himself . . . an' lots of people on the beach watchin' harbour seals. . . . Kids feed popcorn to seagulls . . . an' I think to myself . . . boy! Pigeons eat pretty good here!

RITA   In the morning, Jaimie Paul . . . very early in the morning . . . the air is cold like at home. . . .

JAIMIE   Pretty soon I seen a little woman walkin' a big black dog on a rope. . . . Dog is mad. . . . Dog wants a man!

JAIMIE PAUL moves to RITA JOE. They embrace.

RITA   Clouds are red over the city in the morning. Clara Hill says to me if you're real happy . . . the clouds make you forget you're not home. . . .

They laugh together. JAIMIE PAUL breaks from her. He punctuates his story with wide, sweeping gestures.

JAIMIE   I start singin' and some hotel windows open. I wave to them, but nobody waves back! They're watchin' me, like I was a harbour seal!   *He laughs.*   So I stopped singin'!

RITA   I remember colours, but I've forgot faces already. . . .

JAIMIE PAUL looks at her as her mood changes. Faint light on the MAGISTRATE brightens.

RITA   A train whistle is white, with black lines. . . . A sick man talkin' is brown like an overcoat with pockets torn an' string showin'. . . . A sad woman is a room with the curtains shut. . . .

MAGISTRATE   Rita Joe?

She becomes sobered, but JAIMIE PAUL continues laughing. She nods to the MAGISTRATE, then turns to JAIMIE PAUL.

RITA   Them bastards put me in jail. They're gonna do it again, they said. . . . Them bastards!

JAIMIE   Guys who sell newspapers don't see nothin' . . .

RITA   They drive by me, lookin' . . .

JAIMIE   I'm gonna be a carpenter!

RITA   I walk like a stick, tryin' to keep my ass from showin' because I know what they're thinkin'. . . . Them bastards!

JAIMIE   I got myself boots an' a new shirt. . . . See!

RITA   *worried now*   I thought their jail was on fire. . . . I thought it was burning.

JAIMIE   Room I got costs me seven bucks a week. . . .

RITA   I can't leave town. Every time I try, they put me in jail.

A POLICEMAN enters with a file folder.

JAIMIE   They say it's a pretty good room for seven bucks a week. . . .

JAIMIE PAUL begins to retreat backwards from her, along the ramp to the wings of stage left. She is isolated in a pool of light away from the MAGISTRATE. The light isolation between her and JAIMIE PAUL deepens, as the scene turns into the courtroom again.

MAGISTRATE   Vagrancy. . . . You are charged with vagrancy. —

JAIMIE   *with enthusiasm, boyishly*   First hundred bucks I make, Rita Joe . . . I'm gonna buy a car so I can take you every place!

RITA   *moving after him*   Jaimie!

He retreats, dreamlike, into the wings. The spell of memory between them is broken. Pools of light between her and the MAGISTRATE spread and fuse into a single light area. She turns to the MAGISTRATE, worried and confused.

MAGISTRATE   *reading the documents in his hand* The charge against you this morning is vagrancy. . . .

The MAGISTRATE continues studying the papers he holds. She looks up at him and shakes her head helplessly, then blurts out to him.

RITA   I had to spend last night in jail. . . . Did you know?

MAGISTRATE   Yes. You were arrested.

RITA   I didn't know when morning came . . . there was no windows. . . . The jail stinks! People in jail stink!

MAGISTRATE   *indulgently*   Are you surprised?

RITA   I didn't know anybody there. . . . People in jail stink like paper that's been in the rain too long. But a jail stinks worse. It stinks of rust . . . an' old hair. . . .

The MAGISTRATE looks down at her for the first time.

MAGISTRATE   You . . . are Rita Joe?

She nods quickly. A faint concern shows in his face. He watches her for a long moment.

I know your face . . . yet . . . it wasn't in this court-room. Or was it?

RITA   I don't know . . .

MAGISTRATE   *pondering*   Have you appeared before me in the past year?

RITA   *turning away from him, shrugging*   I don't know. I can't remember. . . .

The MAGISTRATE throws his head back and laughs. The POLICEMAN joins in.

MAGISTRATE   You can't remember? Come now. . . .

RITA   *laughing with him and looking to the POLICEMAN*   I can't remember. . . .

MAGISTRATE   Then I take it you haven't appeared before me. Certainly you and I would remember if you had.

RITA   *smiling*   I don't remember. . . .

The MAGISTRATE makes some hurried notes, but he is watching RITA JOE, formulating his next thought.

RITA   *naively*   My sister hitchhiked home an' she had no trouble like I . . .

MAGISTRATE   You'll need witnesses, Rita Joe. I'm only giving you eight hours to find witnesses for yourself. . . .

RITA   Jaimie knows . . .

She turns to where JAIMIE PAUL had been, but the back of the stage is in darkness. The POLICEMAN exits suddenly.

Jaimie knew . . .

Her voice trails off pathetically. The MAGISTRATE shrugs and returns to studying his notes. RITA JOE chafes during the silence which follows. She craves communion with people, with the MAGISTRATE.

My sister was a dressmaker, mister! But she only worked two weeks in the city. . . . An' then she got sick and went back to the reserve to help my father catch fish an' cut pulpwood.   *smiling*   She's not coming back . . . that's for sure!

MAGISTRATE   *with interest*   Should I know your sister? What was her name?

RITA   Eileen Joe.

EILEEN JOE appears spotlit behind, a memory crowding in.

MAGISTRATE   Eileen . . . that's a soft, undulating name.

RITA   Two weeks, and not one white woman came to her to leave an order or old clothes for her to fix. No work at all for two weeks, an' her money ran out. . . . Isn't that funny?

The MAGISTRATE again studies RITA JOE, his mind elsewhere.

MAGISTRATE   Hmmmmm. . . .

EILEEN JOE disappears.

RITA   So she went back to the reserve to catch fish an' cut pulpwood!

MAGISTRATE   I do know your face. . .yes! And yet. . . .

RITA   Can I sit someplace?

MAGISTRATE   *excited*   I remember now. . . .Yes! I was on holidays three summers back in the Cariboo country. . .driving over this road with not a house or field in sight. . .just barren land, wild and wind-blown. And then I saw this child beside the road, dressed in a blouse and skirt, barefooted. . .

RITA   *looking around*   I don't feel so good, mister.

MAGISTRATE   My God, she wasn't more than three or four years old. . .walking towards me beside the road. When I'd passed her, I stopped my car and then turned around and drove back to where I'd seen her, for I wondered what she could possibly be doing in such a lonely country at that age without her father or mother walking with her. . . .Yet when I got back to where I'd seen her, she had disappeared. She was nowhere to be seen. Yet the land was flat for over a mile in every direction. . . .I had to see her. But I couldn't. . . .

He stares down at RITA JOE for a long moment.

You see, what I was going to say was that this child had your face! Isn't that strange?

RITA   *with disinterest*   Sure, if you think so, mister. . .

MAGISTRATE   Could she have been. . .your daughter?

RITA   What difference does it make?

MAGISTRATE   Children cannot be left like that. . . .It takes money to raise children in the woods as in the cities. . . .There are institutions and people with more money than you who could. . .

RITA   Nobody would get my child, mister!

She is distracted by EILEEN JOE's voice in her memory. EILEEN's voice begins in darkness, but as she speaks, a spotlight isolates her in front of the ramp, stage left. EILEEN is on her hands and knees, two buckets beside her. She is picking berries in mime.

EILEEN   First was the strawberries an' then the blueberries. After the frost. . .we picked the cranberries. . .

She laughs with delight.

RITA   *pleading with the MAGISTRATE, but her attention on EILEEN*   Let me go, mister. . .

MAGISTRATE   I can't let you go. I don't think that would be of any use in the circumstances. Would you like a lawyer?

Even as he speaks, RITA JOE has entered the scene with EILEEN picking berries. The MAGISTRATE's light fades on his podium.

RITA   You ate the strawberries an' blueberries because you were always a hungry kid!

EILEEN   But not cranberries! They made my stomach hurt.

RITA JOE goes down on her knees with EILEEN.

RITA   Let me pick. . . .You rest.   *holding out the bucket to EILEEN*   Mine's full already. . . .Let's change. You rest. . . .

During the exchange of buckets, EILEEN notices her hands are larger than RITA JOE's. She is both delighted and surprised by this.

EILEEN   My hands are bigger than yours, Rita. . . .Look!   *taking RITA JOE's hands in hers*   When did my hands grow so big?

RITA   *wisely and sadly*   You've worked so hard. . . .I'm older than you, Leenie. . . .I will always be older.

The two sisters are thoughtful for a moment, each watching the other in silence. Then RITA JOE becomes animated and resumes her mime of picking berries in the woods.

We picked lots of wild berries when we were kids, Leenie!

They turn away from their work and lie down alongside each other, facing the front of the stage. The light on them becomes summery, warm.

In the summer, it was hot an' flies hummed so loud you'd go to sleep if you sat down an' just listened.

EILEEN   The leaves on the poplars used to turn black an' curl together with the heat. . .

RITA   One day you and I were pickin' blueberries and a big storm came. . . .

A sudden crash of thunder and a lightning flash. The lights turn cold and blue. The three MURDERERS stand in silhouette on a riser behind them. EILEEN cringes in fear, afraid of the storm, aware of the presence of the MURDERERS behind them. RITA JOE springs to her feet, her being attached to the wildness of the atmosphere. Lightning continues to flash and flicker.

EILEEN   Oh, no!

RITA   *shouting*   It got cold and the rain an' hail came. . .the sky falling!

EILEEN   *crying in fear*   Rita!

RITA   *laughing, shouting*   Stay there!

A high flash of lightning, silhouetting the MURDERERS harshly. They take a step forward on the lightning flash. EILEEN dashes into the arms of RITA JOE. She screams and drags RITA JOE down with her. RITA JOE struggles against EILEEN.

Let me go! What in hell's wrong with you? Let me go!

MAGISTRATE   I can't let you go.

The lightning dies, but the thunder rumbles off into the distance. EILEEN subsides, and pressing herself into the arms of RITA JOE as a small child to her mother, she sobs quietly.

RITA   There, there. . . .   *With infinite tenderness* You said to me, "What would happen if the storm hurt us an' we can't find our way home, but are lost together so far away in the bush?"

EILEEN looks up, brushing away her tears and smiling at RITA JOE.

RITA and EILEEN   *in unison*   Would you be my mother then?

RITA   Would I be your mother?

RITA JOE releases EILEEN who looks back fearfully to where the MURDERERS had stood. They are gone. She rises and, collecting the buckets, moves hesitantly to where they had been. Confident now, she laughs softly and nervously to herself and leaves the stage. RITA JOE rises and talks to EILEEN as she departs.

We walked home through the mud an' icy puddles among the trees. At first you cried, Leenie. . .and then you wanted to sleep. But I held you up an' when we got home you said you were sure you would've died in the bush if it hadn't been for us being together like that.

EILEEN disappears from the stage. The MAGISTRATE's light comes up. RITA JOE shakes her head sadly at the memory, then comes forward to the apron of the stage. She is proud of her sister and her next speech reveals this pride.

She made a blouse for me that I wore every day for one year, an' it never ripped at the armpits like the blouse I buy in the store does the first time I stretch.   *She stretches languidly.*   I like to stretch when I'm happy! It makes all the happiness go through me like warm water. . . .

The PRIEST, the TEACHER, and a YOUNG INDIAN MAN cross the stage directly behind her. The PRIEST wears a Roman collar and a checked bush-jacket of a worker-priest. He pauses before passing RITA JOE and goes to meet her.

PRIEST   Rita Joe? When did you get back? How's life?

RITA JOE shrugs noncommittally.

RITA   You know me, Father Andrew. . .could be better, could be worse. . . .

PRIEST   Are you still working?

RITA JOE is still noncommittal. She smiles at him. Her gestures are not definite.

RITA   I live.

PRIEST   *serious and concerned*   It's not easy, is it?

RITA   Not always.

The TEACHER and the YOUNG INDIAN MAN exit.

PRIEST   A lot of things are different in the city. It's easier here on the reserve. . .life is simpler. You can be yourself. That's important to remember.

RITA   Yes, Father. . . .

The PRIEST wants to ask and say more, but he cannot. An awkward moment between them and he reaches out to touch her shoulder gently.

PRIEST   Well. . .be a good girl, Rita Joe. . . .

RITA   *without turning after him*   Goodbye, Father.

MAGISTRATE   *more insistently*   Do you want a lawyer?

The PRIEST leaves stage right. As he leaves, cross light to where a happy JAIMIE PAUL enters from stage left. JAIMIE PAUL comes down to join RITA JOE.

JAIMIE   This guy asked me how much education I got, an' I says to him, "Grade six. How much education a man need for such a job?". . .An' the bum, he says it's not good enough! I should take night school. But I got the job, an' I start next Friday. . .like this. . . .

JAIMIE PAUL does a mock sweeping routine as if he was cleaning a vast office building. He and RITA JOE are both laughing.

Pretty good, eh?

RITA   Pretty good.

JAIMIE   Cleaning the floors an' desks in the building. . . .But it's a government job, and that's good for life. Work hard, then the government give me a raise. . . .I never had a job like that before. . . .

RITA   When I sleep happy, I dream of blueberries an' sun an' all the nice things when I was a little kid, Jaimie Paul.

The sound of an airplane is heard. JAIMIE PAUL looks up. RITA JOE also stares into the sky of her memory. JAIMIE PAUL's face is touched with pain and recollection. The TEACHER, RITA JOE's FATHER, an OLD WOMAN, four YOUNG INDIAN MEN and EILEEN JOE come into the background quietly, as if at a wharf watching the airplane leave the village. They stand looking up until the noise of the aircraft begins to diminish.

JAIMIE   That airplane. . .a Cessna. . . .

He continues watching the aircraft and turns, following its flight path.

She said to me, maybe I never see you again, Jaimie Paul.

There is a faint light on the MAGISTRATE in his chair. He is thoughtful, looking down at his hands.

MAGISTRATE   Do you want a lawyer?

RITA   *to JAIMIE PAUL*   Who?

JAIMIE   Your mother.... I said to her, they'll fix you up good in the hospital. Better than before.... It was a Cessna that landed on the river an' took her away.... Maybe I never see you again, Jaimie, she says to me. She knew she was gonna die, but I was a kid and so were you.... What the hell did we know? I'll never forget....

JAIMIE PAUL joins the village group on the upper level.

SINGER   *singing an indefinite melody developing into a square-dance tune*
There was a man in a beat-up hat
Who runs a house in the middle of town,
An' round his stove-pipe chimney house
The magpies sat, just a-lookin' round.

The Indian village people remain in the back of the stage, still watching the airplane which has vanished. JAIMIE PAUL, on his way, passes MR. HOMER, a white citizen who has the hurried but fulfilled appearance of the socially responsible man. MR. HOMER comes to the front of the stage beside RITA JOE. He talks directly to the audience.

MR. HOMER   Sure, we do a lot of things for our Indians here in the city at the Centre.... Bring 'em in from the cold an' give them food.... The rest ... well, the rest kinda take care of itself.

RITA JOE lowers her head and looks away from him. MR. HOMER moves to her and places his hand on her shoulders possessively.

When your mother got sick we flew her out.... You remember that, Rita Joe?

RITA   *nodding, looking down*   Yes, Mr. Homer. ... Thank you.

MR. HOMER   And we sent her body back for the funeral.... Right, Rita Joe?

The people of the village leave except for the YOUNG INDIAN MEN who remain and mime drinking.

MR. HOMER   And then sometimes a man drinks it up an' leaves his wife an' kids and the poor dears come here for help. We give them food an' a place to sleep. ... Right, Rita?

RITA   Yes.

MR. HOMER   Clothes too.... White people leave clothes here for the Indians to take if they need 'em. Used to have them all up on racks over there ... just like in a store.... *pointing*   But now we got them all on a heap on a table in the basement.

He laughs and RITA JOE nods with him.

MR. HOMER   Indian people... 'specially the women ...get more of a kick diggin' through stuff that's piled up like that....

MR. HOMER chuckles and shakes his head. There is a pale light on the MAGISTRATE, who is still looking down at his hands.

MAGISTRATE   There are institutions to help you....

MR. HOMER again speaks to the audience, but now he is angry over some personal beef.

MR. HOMER   So you see, the Centre serves a need that's real for Indians who come to the city. *wagging his finger at the audience angrily*   It's the do-gooders burn my ass, you know! They come in from television or the newspaper...hang around just long enough to see a drunken Indian...an' bingo!

JAIMIE   Bingo!

MR. HOMER   That's their story! Next thing, they're seeing some kind of Red Power...

The YOUNG INDIAN MEN laugh and RITA JOE gets up to join them.

...or beatin' the government over the head! Let them live an' work among the Indians for a few months...then they'd know what it's really like....

The music comes up sharply.

SINGER
Round and round the cenotaph,
The clumsy seagulls play.
Fed by funny men with hats
Who watch them night and day.

The four YOUNG INDIAN MEN join with RITA JOE and dance. Leading the group is JAIMIE PAUL. He is drunk, dishevelled. Light spreads before them as they advance onstage. They are laughing rowdily. RITA JOE moves to them.

RITA   Jaimie Paul?

MR. HOMER leaves. JAIMIE PAUL is overtaken by two of his companions who take him by the arms, but he pushes them roughly away.

JAIMIE   Get the hell outa my way!...I'm as good a man as him any time....

JAIMIE PAUL crosses downstage to confront a member of the audience.

You know me?...You think I'm a dirty Indian, eh? Get outa my way!

He puts his hands over his head and continues staggering away.

Goddamnit, I wanna sleep....

The YOUNG INDIAN MEN and JAIMIE PAUL exit. RITA JOE follows after JAIMIE PAUL, reaching out to touch him, but the SINGER stands in her way and drives her back, singing. . . .Music up tempo and volume.

SINGER
Oh, can't you see that train roll on,
Its hot black wheels keep comin' on?
A Kamloops Indian died today.
Train didn't hit him, he just fell.
Busy train with wheels on fire!

The music dies. A POLICEMAN enters.

POLICEMAN   Rita Joe!

He repeats her name many times. The TEACHER enters ringing the school handbell and crosses through.

TEACHER   calling   Rita Joe! Rita Joe! Didn't you hear the bell ring? The class is waiting. . . .The class is always waiting for you.

The TEACHER exits.

MAGISTRATE and POLICEMAN   sharply, in unison Rita Joe!

The POLICEMAN grabs and shakes RITA JOE to snap her out of her reverie.

Light up on the MAGISTRATE who sits erect, with authority.

MAGISTRATE   I ask you for the last time, Rita Joe. . . .Do you want a lawyer?

RITA   defiantly   What for?. . .I can take care of myself.

MAGISTRATE   The charge against you this morning is prostitution. Why did you not return to your people as you said you would?

The light on the backstage dies. RITA JOE stands before the MAGISTRATE and the POLICEMAN. She is contained in a pool of light before them.

RITA   nervous, with despair   I tried. . . .I tried. . . .

The MAGISTRATE settles back into his chair and takes a folder from his desk, which he opens and studies.

MAGISTRATE   Special Constable Eric Wilson has submitted a statement to the effect that on June 18th he and Special Constable Schneider approached you on Fourth Avenue at nine-forty in the evening. . .

POLICEMAN   We were impersonating two deck-hands newly arrived in the city. . .

MAGISTRATE   You were arrested an hour later on charges of prostitution.

The MAGISTRATE holds the folder threateningly and looks down at her. RITA JOE is defiant.

RITA   That's a goddamned lie!

MAGISTRATE   sternly, gesturing to the POLICE-MAN   This is a police statement. Surely you don't think a mistake was made?

RITA   peering into the light above her, shuddering Everything in this room is like ice. . . .How can you stay alive working here?. . .I'm so hungry I want to throw up. . .

MAGISTRATE   You have heard the statement, Rita Joe. . . .Do you deny it?

RITA   I was going home, trying to find the highway. . . .I knew those two were cops, the moment I saw them. . .I told them to go f. . .fly a kite! They got sore then an' started pushing me around. . . .

MAGISTRATE   patiently now, waving down the objections of the POLICEMAN   Go on.

RITA   They followed me around until a third cop drove up. An' then they arrested me.

MAGISTRATE   Arrested you. . . .Nothing else?

RITA   They stuffed five dollar bills in my pockets when they had me in the car. . . .I ask you, mister, when are they gonna charge cops like that with contributing to. . .

POLICEMAN   Your worship. . .

MAGISTRATE   irritably, indicating the folder on the table before him   Now it's your word against this! You need references. . .people who know you. . . who will come to court to substantiate what you say. . .today! That is the process of legal argument!

RITA   Can I bum a cigarette someplace?

MAGISTRATE   No. You can't smoke in court.

The POLICEMAN smiles and exits.

RITA   Then give me a bed to sleep on, or is the sun gonna rise an' rise until it burns a hole in my head?

Guitar music cues softly in the background.

MAGISTRATE   Tell me about the child.

RITA   What child?

MAGISTRATE   The little girl I once saw beside the road!

RITA   I don't know any girl, mister! When do I eat? Why does an Indian wait even when he's there first thing in the morning?

The pool of light tightens around the MAGISTRATE and RITA JOE.

MAGISTRATE   I have children. . .two sons. . .

RITA   nodding   Sure. That's good.

The MAGISTRATE gropes for words to express a message that is very precious to him.

MAGISTRATE My sons can go in any direction they wish....into trades or university....But if I had a daughter, I would be more concerned....

RITA What's so special about a girl?

MAGISTRATE I would wish...well, I'd be concerned about her choices...her choices of living, school...friends....These things don't come as lightly for a girl. For boys it's different....But I would worry if I had a daughter.... Don't hide your child! Someone else can be found to raise her if you can't!

RITA JOE shakes her head, a strange smile on her face.

Why not? There are people who would love to take care of it.

RITA Nobody would get my child....I would sooner kill it an' bury it first! I am not a kind woman, mister judge!

MAGISTRATE *at a loss* I see....

RITA *a cry* I want to go home....

Quick up tempo music is heard. Suddenly, the lights change.

JAIMIE PAUL and the YOUNG INDIAN MEN sweep over the backstage ramp, the light widening for them. RITA JOE moves into this railway station crowd. She turns from one man to another until she sees JAIMIE PAUL.

EILEEN JOE and an OLD WOMAN enter.

RITA Jaimie!

EILEEN *happily, running to him* Jaimie Paul! God's sakes....When did you get back from the north?...I thought you said you wasn't coming until breakup....

JAIMIE *turning to EILEEN* I was comin' home on the train...had a bit to drink and was feeling pretty good....Lots of women sleeping in their seats on the train....I'd lift their hats an' say, "Excuse me, lady...I'm lookin' for a wife!" *turning to the OLD WOMAN* One fat lady got mad, an' I says to her, "That's alright, lady....You got no worries....You keep sleepin'!"

Laughter.

JAIMIE PAUL and the OLD WOMAN move away. EILEEN sees RITA JOE who is standing watching.

EILEEN Rita!...Tom an' I broke up...did I tell you?

RITA No, Leenie...you didn't tell me!

EILEEN He was no good....He stopped comin' to see me when he said he would. I kept waiting, but he didn't come....

RITA I sent you a pillow for your wedding!

EILEEN I gave it away....I gave it to Clara Hill.

RITA *laughing bawdily and miming pregnancy* Clara Hill don't need no pillow now!

JAIMIE *smiling, crossing to her and exiting* I always came to see you, Rita Joe....

RITA JOE looks bewildered.

OLD WOMAN *exiting* I made two Saskatoon pies, Rita....You said next time you came home you wanted Saskatoon pie with lots of sugar....

EILEEN and the OLD WOMAN drift away. JAIMIE PAUL moves on to the shadows. The THREE MURDERERS enter in silhouette; one whistles. RITA JOE rushes to the YOUNG INDIAN MEN in stagefront.

RITA This is me, Rita Joe, God's sakes....We went to the same school together....Don't you know me now, Johnny? You remember how tough you was when you was a boy?...We tied you up in the Rainbow Creek and forgot you was there after recess....An' after school was out, somebody remembered. *laughing* And you was blue when we got to you. Your clothes was wet to the chin, an' you said, "That's a pretty good knot....I almost gave up trying to untie it!"

The music continues. RITA JOE steps among the YOUNG INDIAN MEN and they mime being piled in a car at a drive-in.

Steve Laporte?...You remember us goin' to the drive-in and the cold rain comin' down the car windows so we couldn't see the picture show anyhow?

She sits beside STEVE LAPORTE. They mime the windshield wipers.

A cold white light comes up on the playing area directly in front of the MAGISTRATE's chair. A MALE WITNESS of dishevelled, dirty appearance steps into the light and delivers testimony in a whining, defensive voice. He is one of the MURDERERS, but apart from the other three, he is nervous.

FIRST WITNESS I gave her three bucks...an' once I got her goin' she started yellin' like hell! Called me a dog, pig...some filthy kind of animal....So I slapped her around a bit....Guys said she was a funny kind of bim...would do it for them standing up, but not for me she wouldn't....So I slapped her around....

The MAGISTRATE nods and makes a notation. The light on the FIRST WITNESS dies. RITA JOE speaks with urgency and growing fear to STEVE LAPORTE.

RITA Then you shut the wipers off an' we were just sitting there, not knowing what to do....I wish...we could go back again there an' start livin' from that day on....Jaimie!

RITA JOE looks at STEVE LAPORTE as at a stranger. She stands and draws away from him. JAIMIE PAUL enters behind RITA JOE.

There is a cold light before the MAGISTRATE again and another MALE WITNESS moves into the light, replacing the FIRST WITNESS. He too is one of the MURDERERS. This SECOND WITNESS testifies with full gusto.

SECOND WITNESS Gave her a job in my tire store . . . took her over to my place after work once. . . . She was scared when I tried a trick, but I'm easy on broads that get scared, providin' they keep their voices down. . . . After that, I slipped her a fiver. . . . Well, sir, she took the money, then she stood in front of the window, her head high an' her naked shoulders shakin' like she was cold. Well, sir, she cried a little an' then she says, "Goddamnit, but I wish I was a school teacher. . . ."

He laughs and everyone onstage joins in the laughter. The light dies out on the SECOND WITNESS. JAIMIE PAUL enters and crosses to RITA JOE. They lie down and embrace.

RITA You always came to see me, Jaimie Paul. . . . The night we were in the cemetery . . . you remember, Jaimie Paul? I turned my face from yours until I saw the ground . . . an' I knew that below us . . . they were like us once, and now they lie below the ground, their eyes gone, the bones showin'. . . . They must've spoke and touched each other here . . . like you're touching me, Jaimie Paul . . . an' now there was nothing over them, except us . . . an' wind in the grass an' a barbwire fence creaking. An' behind that, a hundred acres of barley.

JAIMIE PAUL stands.

RITA That's something to remember, when you're lovin', eh?

The sound of a train whistle is heard. JAIMIE PAUL goes and the lights onstage fade. The music comes up and the SINGER sings. As JAIMIE PAUL passes her, the SINGER pursues him up the ramp, and RITA JOE runs after them.

SINGER
Oh, can't you see that train roll on,
Gonna kill a man, before it's gone?
Jaimie Paul fell and died.
He had it comin', so it's alright.
Silver train with wheels on fire!

The music dies instantly. RITA JOE's words come on the heels of the music as a bitter extension of the song. She stands before the MAGISTRATE, again in the court, but looks back to where JAIMIE PAUL had been in the gloom. The POLICEMAN enters where JAIMIE PAUL has exited, replacing him, for the fourth trial scene.

RITA Jaimie, why am I here? . . . Is it . . . because people are talkin' about me and all them men. . . . Is

that why? I never wanted to cut cordwood for a living. . . . *with great bitterness* Never once I thought . . . it'd be like this. . . .

MAGISTRATE What are we going to do about you, Rita Joe? This is the seventh charge against you in one year. . . . Laws are not made to be violated in this way. . . . Why did you steal?

RITA I was hungry. I had no money.

MAGISTRATE Yet you must have known you would be caught?

RITA Yes.

MAGISTRATE Are you not afraid of what is happening to you?

RITA I am afraid of a lot of things. Put me in jail. I don't care. . . .

MAGISTRATE *with forced authority* Law is a procedure. The procedure must be respected. It took hundreds of years to develop this process of law.

RITA I stole a sweater. . . . They caught me in five minutes!

She smiles whimsically at this. The MAGISTRATE is leafing through the documents before him. The POLICEMAN stands to one side of him.

MAGISTRATE The prosecutor's office has submitted some of the past history of Rita Joe. . . .

POLICEMAN She was born and raised on a reservation. Then came a brief period in a public school off the reservation . . . at which time Rita Joe established herself as something of a disruptive influence . . .

RITA What's that mean?

MAGISTRATE *turning to her, smiling* A trouble maker!

RITA JOE becomes animated, aware of the trap around her closing even at moments such as this.

RITA Maybe it was about the horse, huh? . . .

She looks up at the MAGISTRATE who is still smiling, offering her no help.

There was this accident with a horse. . . . It happened like this . . . I was riding a horse to school an' some of the boys shot a rifle an' my horse bucked an' I fell off. I fell in the bush an' got scratched. . . . The boys caught the horse by the school and tried to ride him, but the horse bucked an' pinned a boy against a tree, breaking his leg in two places. . . .

She indicates the place the leg got broken.

They said . . . an' he said I'd rode the horse over him on purpose!

MAGISTRATE Well . . . did you?

RITA It wasn't that way at all, I tell you! They lied!

The POLICEMAN and the SINGER laugh.

MAGISTRATE   Why should they lie, and Rita Joe alone tell the truth?...Or are you a child enough to believe the civilization of which we are a part...

He indicates the audience as inclusive of civilization from his point of view.

...does not understand Rita Joe?

RITA   I don't know what you're saying.

MAGISTRATE   *with a touch of compassion*   Look at you, woman! Each time you come before me you are older. The lines in your face are those of...

RITA   I'm tired an' I want to eat, mister! I haven't had grub since day before yesterday.... This room is like a boat on water.... I'm so dizzy.... What the hell kind of place is this won't let me go lie down on grass?

She doubles over to choke back her nausea.

MAGISTRATE   This is not the reservation, Rita Joe. This is another place, another time....

RITA   *straining to remember, to herself*   I was once in Whitecourt, Alberta. The cops are fatter there than here. I had to get out of Whitecourt, Alberta...

MAGISTRATE   Don't blame the police, Rita Joe! The obstacles to your life are here...   *He touches his forefinger to his temples.*   ...in your thoughts ...possibly even in your culture....

RITA JOE turns away from him, searching the darkness behind her.

What's the matter?

RITA   I want to go home!

MAGISTRATE   But you can't go now. You've broken a law for which you will have to pay a fine or go to prison....

RITA   I have no money.

MAGISTRATE   *with exasperation*   Rita Joe.... It is against the law to solicit men on the street. You have to wash....

RITA JOE begins to move away from him, crossing the front of the stage along the apron, her walk cocky. The light spreads and follows her.

You can't walk around in old clothes and running shoes made of canvas.... You have to have some money in your pockets and an address where you live. You should fix your hair...perhaps even change your name. And try to tame that accent that sounds like you have a mouthful of sawdust. ...There is no peace in being extraordinary!

The light dies on the MAGISTRATE and the POLICEMAN.

RITA JOE is transported into another memory. JAIMIE PAUL enters and slides along the floor, left

of centre stage. He is drunk, counting the fingers on his outstretched hands. MR. HOMER has entered with a wagon carrying hot soup and mugs. Four YOUNG INDIAN MEN come in out of the cold. MR. HOMER speaks to the audience in a matter-of-fact informative way.

MR. HOMER   *dispensing soup to the YOUNG INDIAN MEN*   The do-gooders make something special of the Indian....There's nothing special here.... At the centre here the quick cure is a bowl of stew under the belt and a good night's sleep.

JAIMIE   Hey, Mister Homer! How come I got so many fingers? Heh?

He laughs. MR. HOMER ignores JAIMIE PAUL and continues talking to the audience.

MR. HOMER   I wouldn't say they were brothers or sisters to me...no sir! But if you're...

JAIMIE PAUL gets up and embraces RITA JOE.

JAIMIE   I got two hands an' one neck.... I can kill more than I can eat.... If I had more fingers I would need mittens big as pie plates.... Yeh?

MR. HOMER   *to JAIMIE PAUL*   Lie down, Jaimie Paul, an' have some more sleep. When you feel better, I'll get you some soup.

RITA JOE laughs. JAIMIE PAUL weaves his way uncertainly to where MR. HOMER stands.

JAIMIE   *laughing*   I spit in your soup! You know what I say?...I say I spit in your soup, Mister Homer....

He comes to MR. HOMER and seems about to do just what he threatens.

MR. HOMER   *pushing him away with good humour*   I'll spit in your eyeball if you don't shut up!

JAIMIE   *breaking away from MR. HOMER, taunting*   You...are not Mister Homer!

MR. HOMER   I'm not what?

JAIMIE   You're not Mister Homer....You're somebody wearing his pants an' shirt...   *stumbling away*   But you're not Mister Homer....Mister Homer never gets mad....No sir, not Mister Homer!

MR. HOMER   I'm not mad....What're you talkin' about?

JAIMIE PAUL turns and approaches the YOUNG INDIAN MEN. He threatens to fall off the apron of the stage.

JAIMIE   No...not Mister Homer! An' I got ten fingers.... How's that?

MR. HOMER   For Chris' sake, Jaimie...go to sleep.

JAIMIE PAUL stops and scowls, then grins knowingly. He begins to mime a clumsy paddler paddling a boat.

JAIMIE *laughing again* I know you.... Hey? I know you!... I seen you up Rainbow Creek one time.... I seen you paddling!

He breaks up with laughter.

MR. HOMER *amused, tolerant* Oh, come on ... I've never been to Rainbow Creek.

JAIMIE *controlling his laughter* Sure you been to Rainbow Creek.... *He begins to mime paddling again.* Next time you need a good paddler, you see me. I have a governmen' job, but screw that. I'm gonna paddle! I seen you paddle....

Again he breaks up in laughter as he once more demonstrates the quality of paddling he once saw. RITA JOE is fully enjoying the spectacle. So are the YOUNG INDIAN MEN. MR. HOMER is also amused by the absurdity of the situation. JAIMIE PAUL turns, but chokes up with laughter after saying...

I have seen some paddlers...but you!

JAIMIE PAUL turns and waves his hand derisively, laughing.

MR. HOMER It must've been somebody else. ...I've never been to Rainbow Creek.

JAIMIE Like hell, you say!

JAIMIE PAUL paddles the soup wagon out. Guitar music comes in with an upbeat tempo. RITA JOE and the YOUNG INDIAN MEN dance to the beat. The YOUNG INDIAN MEN then drift after MR. HOMER.

The light fades slowly on centre stage and the music changes.

RITA JOE, happy in her memory, does a circling butch walk in the fading light to the song of the SINGER. At the conclusion of the song, she is on the apron, stage right, in a wash of light that includes the MAGISTRATE and the SINGER.

SINGER
I woke up at six o'clock
Stumbled out of bed,
Crash of cans an' diesel trucks
Damned near killed me dead.

Sleepless hours, heavy nights,
Dream your dreams so pretty.
God was gonna have a laugh
An' gave me a job in the city!

RITA JOE is still elated at her memory of JAIMIE PAUL and his story. With unusual candour, she turns girlishly before the MAGISTRATE, and in mild imitation of her own moment of drunkenness, begins telling him a story. Faint guitar music in the background continues.

RITA One night I drank a little bit of wine, an' I was outside lookin' at the stars...thinking...when I was a little girl how much bigger the trees were

...no clouds, but suddenly there was a light that made the whole sky look like day...

Guitar out.

...just for a moment...an' before I got used to the night...I saw animals, moving across the sky ...two white horses.... A man was takin' them by the halters, and I knew the man was my grandfather....

She stares at the MAGISTRATE, unsure of herself now.

MAGISTRATE Yes! Is that all?

RITA No.... But I never seen my grandfather alive, and I got so sad thinkin' about it I wanted to cry. I wasn't sure it was him, even.... *She begins to laugh.* I went an' telephoned the police and asked for the chief, but the chief was home and a guy asks what I want.

MAGISTRATE *mildly amused* You...called the police?

RITA I told the guy I'd seen God, and he says, "Yeh? What would you like us to do about it?" An' I said, "Pray! Laugh! Shout!"

MAGISTRATE Go on....

RITA He...asked where I'd seen God, an' I told him in the sky. He says you better call this number. ...It's the Air Force. They'll take care of it!

She laughs and the MAGISTRATE smiles.

I called the number the guy gave me, but it was nighttime and there was no answer! If God was to come at night, after office hours, then....

A terrible awkwardness sets in. There is a harsh light on her. She turns away, aware that she is in captivity. The MAGISTRATE stirs with discomfort.

RITA *with great fear* How long will this be? Will I never be able to...

MAGISTRATE *annoyed at himself, at her* There is nothing here but a record of your convictions ...nothing to speak for you and provide me with any reason to moderate your sentence! What the hell am I supposed to do? Violate the law myself because I feel that somehow...I've known and felt....No! *turning from her* You give me no alternative...no alternative at all!

The MAGISTRATE packs up his books.

RITA I'll go home...jus' let me go home. I can't get out of jail to find the highway...or some kind of job!

MAGISTRATE *standing* Prison and fines are not the only thing.... Have you, for instance, considered that you might be an incurable carrier? There are people like that.... They cannot come into contact with others without infecting them.

They cannot eat from dishes others may use. . . . They cannot prepare or touch food others will eat. . . . The same with clothes, cars, hospital beds!

The MAGISTRATE exits. RITA JOE shakes her head with disbelief. The idea of perpetual condemnation is beyond her comprehension. She falls to the floor. Guitar music is heard in the background.

She turns away from the MAGISTRATE and the light comes up over the ramp at the back of the stage. Another light comes up on centre stage left. Here, EILEEN JOE and the OLD WOMAN are miming clothes washing using a scrubbing board and placing the wash into woven baskets. The woman and the girl are on their knees, facing each other.

On the ramp above them, JAIMIE PAUL is struggling with a POLICEMAN who is scolding him softly for being drunk, abusive and noisy. JAIMIE PAUL is jocular; the POLICEMAN, harassed and worried. They slowly cross the ramp from stage left.

SINGER
Four o'clock in the morning,
The sailor rides the ship
An' I ride the wind!

Eight o'clock in the morning,
My honey's scoldin' the sleepyheads
An' I'm scoldin' him.

JAIMIE *to the POLICEMAN* On the Smoky River . . . four o'clock in the morning . . . hey? There was nobody . . . just me. . . . You know that?

POLICEMAN No, I don't. Come on. Let's get you home.

JAIMIE PAUL moves forward and embraces the POLICEMAN.

JAIMIE . You wanna see something?

JAIMIE PAUL takes out a coin to do a trick.

OLD WOMAN *to EILEEN* Your father's been very sick.

EILEEN He won't eat nothing. . . .

OLD WOMAN Jus' sits and worries. . . . That's no good.

JAIMIE PAUL *finishing his coin trick* You like that one? Hey, we both work for the government, eh?

They exit laughing.

Watch the rough stuff. . . . Just don't make me mad.

OLD WOMAN If Rita Joe was to come and see him . . . maybe say goodbye to him. . . .

RITA *calling from her world to the world of her strongest fears* But he's not dying! I saw him not so long ago. . . .

The women in her memory do not hear her. They continue discussing her father.

OLD WOMAN He loved her an' always worried. . . .

RITA I didn't know he was sick!

OLD WOMAN You were smart to come back, Eileen Joe.

RITA *again calling over the distance of her soul* Nobody told me!

SINGER
Nine o'clock in the evening,
Moon is high in the blueberry sky
An' I'm lovin' you.

JAIMIE *now passing along the apron beside RITA JOE, talking to the POLICEMAN* You seen where I live? Big house with a mongolia in front. . . . Fancy place! You wanna see the room I got?

POLICEMAN *gruffly, aware that JAIMIE PAUL can become angry quickly* When I get holidays, we'll take a tour of everything you've got . . . but I don't get holidays until September!

From the apron they cross to the stage rear diagonally, between the OLD WOMAN with EILEEN, and RITA JOE.

JAIMIE You're a good man . . . good for a laugh. I'm a good man . . . you know me!

POLICEMAN Sure, you're first class when you're sober!

JAIMIE I got a cousin in the city. He got his wife a stove an' washing machine! He's a good man. . . . You know my cousin maybe?

Fading off. They leave the stage.

The OLD WOMAN has risen from her knees and wearily collected one basket of clothes. She climbs the ramp and moves to the wings, stage right. EILEEN is thoughtful and slower, but she also prepares her clothes wash and follows.

OLD WOMAN Nothing in the city I can see . . . only if you're lucky. A good man who don't drink or play cards . . . that's all.

EILEEN And if he's bad?

OLD WOMAN Then leave him. I'm older than you, Eileen. . . . I know what's best.

The OLD WOMAN exits. The guitar music dies out. JAIMIE PAUL's laughter and voice is heard offstage.

JAIMIE *offstage, loud, boisterous* We both work for the gov'ment! We're buddies, no? . . . You think we're both the same?

Laughter. The lights on the ramp and centre stage die.

RITA *following JAIMIE PAUL's laughter* Good or bad, what difference? So long as he's a livin' man!

RITA JOE and EILEEN giggle. The light spreads around her into pale infinity.

The TEACHER enters on the ramp. She rings a handbell and stops a short distance from the wings to peer around. She is a shy, inadequate woman who moves and behaves jerkily, the product of incomplete education and poor job placement.

TEACHER   *in a scolding voice*   Rita! Rita Joe!

The bell rings.

The class is waiting for you. The class is always waiting.

RITA JOE is startled to hear the bell and see the woman. She comes to her feet, now a child before the TEACHER, and runs to join EILEEN. JAIMIE PAUL and the YOUNG INDIAN MEN have entered with the bell and sit cross-legged on the floor as school children.

RITA   The sun is in my skin, Miss Donohue. The leaves is red and orange, and the wind stopped blowin' an hour ago.

The TEACHER has stopped to listen to this. RITA JOE and EILEEN, late again, slip into class and sit on the floor with the others.

TEACHER   Rita! What is a noun?

No answer. The kids poke RITA JOE to stand up.

Did you hear what I asked?

RITA   *uncertain*   No . . . yes?

TEACHER   There's a lot you don't know. . . . That kind of behaviour is exhibitionism! We are a melting pot!

RITA   A melting pot?

TEACHER   A melting pot! Do you know what a melting pot is?

RITA   It's . . .   *She shrugs.*   . . . a melting pot!

The class laughs.

TEACHER   Precisely! You put copper and tin into a melting pot and out comes bronze. . . . It's the same with people!

RITA   Yes, Miss Donohue . . . out comes bronze. . . .

Laughter again. The TEACHER calls RITA JOE over to her. The light fades on the other children.

TEACHER   Rita, what was it I said to you this morning?

RITA   You said . . . wash my neck, clean my finger-nails. . . .

TEACHER   *cagey*   No, it wasn't, Rita!

RITA   I can't remember. It was long ago.

TEACHER   Try to remember, Rita.

RITA   I don't remember, Miss Donohue! I was thinkin' about you last night, thinkin' if you knew some . . .

TEACHER   You are straying off the topic! Never stray off the topic!

RITA   It was a dream, but now I'm scared, Miss Donohue. I've been a long time moving about . . . trying to find something! . . . I must've lost . . .

TEACHER   No, Rita. That is not important.

RITA   Not important?

TEACHER   No, Rita. . . . Now you repeat after me like I said or I'm going to have to pass you by again. Say after me . . .

RITA   Sure. Say after you . . .

TEACHER   Say after me . . . "A book of verse underneath the spreading bough . . ."

RITA   "A book of verse underneath the spreading bough . . ."

TEACHER   "A jug of wine, a loaf of bread and thou beside me . . . singing in the wilderness."

RITA   *the child spell broken, she laughs bawdily*   Jaimie said, "To heck with the wine an' loaf. . . . Let's have some more of this here thou!"

Her laughter dies. She wipes her lips, as if trying to erase some stain there.

TEACHER   *peevish*   Alright, Rita. . . . Alright, let's have none of that!

RITA   *plaintively*   I'm sorry, Miss Donohue. . . . I'm sure sorry!

TEACHER   That's alright.

RITA   I'm sorry!

TEACHER   Alright. . . .

RITA   Sorry . . .

TEACHER   You will never make bronze! Coming from nowhere and going no place! Who am I to change that?

RITA JOE grips the edge of the desk with both hands, holding on tightly.

RITA   No! They said for me to stay here, to learn something!

TEACHER   *with exasperation*   I tried to teach you, but your head was in the clouds, and as for your body. . . . Well! I wouldn't even think what I know you do!

The TEACHER crosses amongst the other children.

RITA   I'm sorry . . . please! Let me say it after you again . . .   *blurting it out*   "A book of verse underneath the spreading . . ."

TEACHER   Arguing . . . always trying to upset me . . . and in grade four . . . I saw it then . . . pawing the ground for men like a bitch in heat!

RITA   *dismayed*   It . . . isn't so!

TEACHER   You think I don't know? I'm not blind...I can see out of the windows.

The TEACHER marches off into the wings and the class runs after her leaving RITA JOE alone onstage.

RITA   That's a lie! For God's sake, tell the judge I have a good character....I am clean an' honest. ...Everything you said is right, I'm never gonna argue again....I believe in God...an' I'm from the country and lost like hell! Tell him!

She shakes her head sadly, knowing the extent of her betrayal.

They only give me eight hours to find somebody who knows me....An' seven and a half hours is gone already!

The light on the scene dies.

SINGER   *recitivo*
Things that were...
Life that might have been...

A pale backlight on the back of the ramp comes up. Recorded sounds of crickets and the distant sound of a train whistle are heard.

RITA JOE's FATHER and JAIMIE PAUL enter on the ramp from stage left. The FATHER leads the way. JAIMIE PAUL is behind, rolling a cigarette. They walk slowly, thoughtfully, following the ramp across and downstage. RITA JOE stands separate, watching.

SINGER
The blue evening of the first
Warm day
Is the last evening.
There'll not be another
Like it.

JAIMIE   No more handouts, David Joe....We can pick an' can the berries ourselves.

FATHER   We need money to start a cooperative like that.

JAIMIE   Then some other way!

The old man listens, standing still, to the sounds of the train and the night.

FATHER   You're a young man, Jaimie Paul...young an' angry. It's not good to be that angry.

JAIMIE   We're gonna work an' live like people ...not be afraid all the time...stop listening to an old priest an' Indian Department guys who're working for a pension!

FATHER   You're a young man, Jaimie Paul....

JAIMIE   I say stop listening, David Joe!...In the city they never learned my name. It was "Hey, fella"...or "You, boy"...that kind of stuff.

Pause. The sound of the train whistle is heard.

FATHER   A beautiful night, Jaimie Paul.

JAIMIE   We can make some money. The berries are good this year!

JAIMIE PAUL is restless, edgy, particularly on the train whistle sound.

FATHER   Sometimes...children...you remember every day with them....Never forget you are alive with children.

JAIMIE PAUL turns away and begins to retrace his steps.

JAIMIE   You want us all to leave an' go to the city? Is that what you want?

The FATHER shakes his head. He does not wish for this, but the generation spread between them is great now. JAIMIE PAUL walks away with a gesture of contempt.

The sounds die. The light dies and isolates the FATHER and RITA JOE.

RITA   You were sick, an' now you're well.

FATHER   *in measured speech, turning away from RITA JOE, as if carefully recalling something of great importance* You left your father, Rita Joe ...never wrote Eileen a letter that time....Your father was pretty sick man that time...pretty sick man....June ninth he got the cold, an' on June twenty he...

RITA   But you're alive! I had such crazy dreams I'd wake up laughing at myself!

FATHER   I have dreams too....

RITA JOE moves forward to him. She stops talking to him, as if communicating thoughts rather than words. He remains standing where he is, facing away from her.

RITA   I was in a big city...so many streets I'd get lost like nothin'....When you got sick I was on a job...

FATHER   June ninth I got the cold...

RITA   Good job in a tire store...Jaimie Paul's got a job with the government, you know?

FATHER   Pretty sick man, that time...

RITA   A good job in a tire store. They was gonna teach me how to file statements after I learned the telephone. Bus ticket home was twenty dollars. ...But I got drunk all the same when I heard an' I went in and tried to work that day.... *smiling and shaking her head* Boy, I tried to work! Some day that was!

FATHER   I have dreams....Sometimes I'm scared....

They finally look at each other.

RITA   *shuddering* I'm so cold....

FATHER   Long dreams....I dream about Rita Joe. ... *sadly* Have to get better. I've lived longer, but I know nothing . . . nothing at all. Only the old stories.

RITA JOE moves sideways to him. She is smiling happily.

RITA   When I was little, a man came out of the bush to see you. Tell me why again!

The FATHER hesitates, shaking his head, but he is also smiling. The light of their separate yearnings fades out and the front of the stage is lit with the two of them together. The FATHER turns and comes forward to meet her.

FATHER   You don't want to hear that story again.

He sits on the slight elevation of the stage apron. RITA JOE sits down in front of him and snuggles between his knees. He leans forward over her.

RITA   It's the best story I ever heard!

FATHER   You were a little girl . . . four years old already . . . an' Eileen was getting big inside your mother. One day it was hot . . . sure was hot. Too hot to try an' fish in the lake, because the fish was down deep where the water was cold.

RITA   The dog started to bark . . .

FATHER   The dog started to bark. . . . How!

FATHER and RITA   *in unison*   How! How! How!

FATHER   Barking to beat hell an' I says to myself why . . . on such a hot day? Then I see the bushes moving . . . somebody was coming to see us. Your mother said from inside the house, "What's the matter with that dog?" An' I says to her, "Somebody coming to see me." It was big Sandy Collins, who ran the sawmill back of the reserve. Business was bad for big Sandy then . . . but he comes out of that bush like he was being chased . . . his clothes all wet an' stickin' to him . . . his cap in his hands, an' his face black with the heat and dirt from hard work. . . . He says to me, "My little Millie got a cough last night an' today she's dead.". . . ."She's dead," big Sandy says to me. I says to him, "I'm sorry to hear that, Sandy. Millie is the same age as my Rita." And he says to me, "David Joe . . . look, you got another kid coming . . . won't make much difference to you. . . . Sell me Rita Joe like she is for a thousand dollars!"

RITA JOE giggles. The FATHER raises his hand to silence her.

"A thousand dollars is a lot of money, Sandy," I says to him . . . "lots of money. You got to cut a lot of timber for a thousand dollars." Then he says to me, "Not a thousand cash at once, David Joe. First I give you two hundred fifty dollars. . . . When Rita Joe comes ten years old and she's still alright, I give you the next two hundred fifty. . . . An' if she don't die by fifteen, I guarantee you five hundred dollars cash at once!"

RITA JOE and the FATHER break into laughter. He reaches around her throat and draws her close.

FATHER   So you see, Rita Joe, you lose me one thousand dollars from big Sandy Collins!

They continue laughing. A harsh light on the MAGISTRATE, who enters and stands on his podium.

MAGISTRATE   Rita Joe, when was the last time you had dental treatment?

RITA JOE covers her ears, refusing to surrender this moment of security in the arms of her FATHER.

RITA   I can't hear you!

MAGISTRATE   *loudly*   You had your teeth fixed ever?

RITA   *coming to her feet and turning on him*   Leave me alone!

MAGISTRATE   Have you had your lungs X-rayed recently?

RITA   I was hungry, that's all!

MAGISTRATE   *becoming staccato, machine-like in his questions*   When was your last Wasserman taken?

RITA   What's that?

RITA JOE hears the TEACHER's voice. She turns to see the approaching TEACHER give the MAGISTRATE testimony. The stage is lit in a cold blue light now.

TEACHER   *crisply to the MAGISTRATE as she approaches, her monologue a reading*   Dear Sir. . . . In reply to your letter of the twelfth, I cannot in all sincerity provide a reference of good character for one Rita Joe. . . .

The WITNESSES do not see her and the testimony takes on the air of a nightmare for RITA JOE. She is baffled and afraid. The TEACHER continues to quietly repeat her testimony. RITA JOE appeals to the MAGISTRATE.

RITA   Why am I here? What've I done?

MAGISTRATE   You are charged with prostitution.

Her FATHER stands and crosses upstage to the ramp to observe. He is joined by EILEEN JOE, the OLD WOMAN and the PRIEST. MR. HOMER approaches briskly from stage left.

MR. HOMER   She'd been drinking when she comes into the centre. . . . Nothing wrong in that I could see, 'specially on a Friday night. So I give her some soup an' a sandwich. Then all of a sudden in the middle of a silly argument, she goes haywire . . . an' I see her comin' at me. . . . I'll tell you, I was scared! I don't know Indian women that well!

MAGISTRATE   Assault!

RITA JOE retreats from him. The TEACHER and MR. HOMER now stand before the MAGISTRATE as if they were frozen. MR. HOMER repeats his testimony under the main dialogue. JAIMIE PAUL staggers in from stage right, over the ramp, heading to the wings of lower stage left.

JAIMIE *to himself* What the hell are they doing?

RITA *running to him* Say a good word for me, Jaimie!

JAIMIE They fired me yesterday.... What the hell's the use of living?

JAIMIE PAUL leaves the stage as the SCHOOL BOARD CLERK enters to offer further testimony to the MAGISTRATE.

SCHOOL BOARD CLERK I recommended in a letter that she take school after grade five through correspondence courses from the Department of Education ... but she never replied to the form letter the school division sent her....

RITA *defending herself to the MAGISTRATE* That drunken bastard Mahoney used it to light fire in his store.... He'd never tell Indians when mail came for us!

SCHOOL BOARD CLERK I repeat... I wish our position understood most clearly.... No reply was ever received in this office to the letter we sent Rita Joe!

RITA One letter... one letter for a lifetime?

TEACHER Say after me! "I wandered lonely as a cloud, that floats on high o'er vales and hills. ... When all at once I saw a crowd... a melting pot..."

A POLICEMAN and a MALE WITNESS enter. The PRIEST crosses downstage. The testimonies are becoming a nightmare babble. RITA JOE is stung, stumbling backward from all of them as they face the MAGISTRATE with their condemnations.

POLICEMAN We were impersonating two deckhands....

The PRIEST is passing by RITA JOE. He makes the sign of the cross and offers comfort in a thin voice, lost in the noise.

PRIEST Be patient, Rita.... The young are always stormy, but in time, your understanding will deepen. ... There is an end to all things.

WITNESS I gave her a job, but she was kind of slow.... I can't wait around, there's lots of white people goin' lookin' for work... so I figure, to hell with this noise...

MAGISTRATE *loudly over the other voices* Have your ears ached?

RITA No!

MAGISTRATE Have you any boils on your back? Any discharge? When did you bathe last?

The MURDERERS appear and circle RITA JOE.

MAGISTRATE Answer me! Drunkenness! Shoplifting! Assault! Prostitution, prostitution, prostitution, prostitution!

RITA *her voice shrill, cutting over the babble* I don't know what happened... but you got to listen to me and believe me, mister!

The babble ceases abruptly. RITA JOE pleads with them as best she knows.

You got rules here that was made before I was born.... I was hungry when I stole something... an' I was hollerin' I was so lonely when I started whoring....

The MURDERERS come closer.

MAGISTRATE Rita Joe... has a doctor examined you?... I mean, really examined you? Rita Joe... you might be carrying and transmitting some disease and not aware of it!

RITA *breaking away from the MURDERERS* Bastards! *to the MAGISTRATE* Put me in jail... I don't care.... I'll sign anything. I'm so goddamn hungry I'm sick.... Whatever it is, I'm guilty!

She clutches her head and goes down in a squat of defeat.

MAGISTRATE Are you free of venereal disease?

RITA I don't know. I'm not sick that way.

MAGISTRATE How can you tell?

RITA *lifting her face to him* I know.... A woman knows them things....

Pause.

MAGISTRATE Thirty days!

The POLICEMAN leads RITA JOE off and the house lights come up. The ACTORS and the SINGER walk off the stage, leaving emptiness as at the opening of the act.

ACT TWO

The house lights dim. A POLICEMAN brings RITA JOE in downstage centre. She curls up in her jail cell and sleeps. RITA JOE's FATHER enters on the ramp and crosses down to the audience. The stage work lights die down. Lights isolate RITA JOE's FATHER. Another light with prison bar shadows isolates RITA JOE in her area of the stage.

FATHER *looking down on RITA JOE* I see no way... no way.... It's not clear like trees against snow... not clear at all....

To the audience.

But when I was fifteen years old, I leave the reserve to work on a threshing crew. They pay a dollar a day for a good man... an' I was a good strong man. The first time I got work there was a girl about as old as I. . . . She'd come out in the yard an' watch the men working at the threshing machine. She had eyes that were the biggest I ever seen. . . like fifty-cent pieces. . . an' there was always a flock of geese around her. Whenever I see her I feel good. She used to stand an' watch me, an' the geese made a helluva lot of noise. One time I got off my rick an' went to get a drink of water. . . but I walked close to where she was watching me. She backed away, and then ran from me with the geese chasin' after her, their wings out an' their feet no longer touching the ground. . . . They were white geese. . . . The last time Rita Joe come home to see us. . . the last time she ever come home. . . I watched her leave. . . and I seen geese running after Rita Joe the same way . . .white geese. . .with their wings out an' their feet no longer touching the ground. And I remembered it all, an' my heart got so heavy I wanted to cry. . . .

The light fades to darkness on the FATHER, as he exits up the ramp and off. RITA JOE wakes from her dream, cold, shaking, desperate.

SINGER
The blue evening of the
First warm day
Is the last evening.
There'll not be another
Like it.

The PRIEST enters from darkness with the POLICEMAN. He is dressed in a dark suit which needs pressing. He stops in half shadow outside RITA JOE's prison light. The scene between them is played out in the manner of two country people meeting in a time of crisis. Their thoughts come slowly, incompletely. There is both fear and helplessness in both characters.

PRIEST   I came twice before they'd let me see you. . . .

RITA JOE jumps to her feet. She smiles at him.

RITA   Oh, Father Andrew!

PRIEST   Even so, I had to wait an hour.

A long pause. He clumsily takes out a package of cigarettes and matches from his pocket and hands them to her, aware that he is possibly breaking a prison regulation.

I'm sorry about this, Rita.

RITA JOE tears the package open greedily and lights a cigarette. She draws on it with animal satisfaction.

RITA   I don't know what's happening, Father Andrew.

PRIEST   They're not. . .hurting you here?

RITA   No.

PRIEST   I could make an appointment with the warden if there was something . . .

RITA   What's it like outside?. . .Is it a nice day outside? I heard it raining last night. . . . Was it raining?

PRIEST   It rains a lot here. . .

RITA   When I was a kid, there was leaves an' a river. . . . Jaimie Paul told me once that maybe we never see those things again.

A long pause. The PRIEST struggles with himself.

PRIEST   I've never been inside a jail before. . . . They told me there was a chapel. . . .

He points indefinitely back.

RITA   What's gonna happen to me?. . .That judge sure got sore. . . .

She laughs.

PRIEST   *with disgust, yet unsure of himself*   Prostitution this time?

RITA   I guess so. . . .

PRIEST   You know how I feel. . . . City is no place for you. . .nor for me. . . . I've spent my life in the same surroundings as your father!

RITA   Sure. . .but you had God on your side!

She smiles mischievously. The PRIEST angers.

PRIEST   Rita, try to understand. . . . Our Lord Jesus once met a woman such as you beside the well. . . . He forgave her!

RITA   I don't think God hears me here. . . . Nobody hears me now, nobody except cops an' pimps an' bootleggers!

PRIEST   I'm here. I was there when you were born.

RITA   You've told me lots of times. . . . I was thinkin' about my mother last night. . . . She died young. . . . I'm older than she was. . . .

PRIEST   Your mother was a good, hard-working woman. She was happy. . . .

A pause between them.

RITA   There was frost on the street at five o'clock Tuesday morning when they arrested me. . . . Last night I remembered things flyin' and kids runnin' past me trying to catch a chocolate wrapper that's blowin' in the wind. . . . *She presses her hands against her bosom.*   It hurts me here to think about them things!

PRIEST   I worry about you. . . . Your father worries too. . . . I baptized you. . . .I watched you and Leenie grow into women!

RITA   Yes. . .I seen God in what you said. . .in your clothes! In your hair!

PRIEST   But you're not the woman I expected you to be. . . . Your pride, Rita. . .your pride. . .may bar you from heaven.

RITA *mocking him* They got rules there too...in heaven?

PRIEST *angry* Rita!...I'm not blind...I can see! I'm not deaf...I know all about you! So does God!

RITA My uncle was Dan Joe....He was dyin' and he said to me, "Long ago the white man come with Bibles to talk to my people, who had the land. They talk for hundred years...then we had all the Bibles, an' the white man had our land...."

PRIEST Don't blame the Church! We are trying to help...

RITA *with passion* How? I'm looking for the door....

PRIEST *tortured now* I...will hear your confession...

RITA But I want to be free!

PRIEST *stiffly* We learn through suffering, Rita Joe....We will only be free if we become humble again. *Pause.* Will you confess, Rita Joe? *A long pause.* I'm going back on the four o'clock bus. *He begins walking away into the gloom.* I'll tell your father I saw you, and you looked well.

He is suddenly relieved.

RITA *after him as he leaves* You go to hell!

The PRIEST turns sharply.

Go tell your God...when you see him...tell him about Rita Joe an' what they done to her! Tell him about yourself too!...That you were not good enough for me, but that didn't stop you tryin'! Tell him that!

The PRIEST hurries away. Guitar in. RITA JOE sits down, brooding.

SINGER
I will give you the wind and a sense of wonder
As the child by the river, the reedy river.
I will give you the sky wounded by thunder
And a leaf on the river, the silver river.

A light comes up on the ramp where JAIMIE PAUL appears, smiling and waving to her.

JAIMIE *shouting* Rita Joe! I'm gonna take you dancing after work Friday....That job's gonna be alright!

RITA JOE springs to her feet, elated.

RITA Put me back in jail so I can be free on Friday!

A sudden burst of dance music. The stage lights up and JAIMIE PAUL approaches her. They dance together, remaining close in the front centre stage.

SINGER
Round an' round the cenotaph;
The clumsy seagulls play.

Fed by funny men with hats
Who watch them night and day.

Sleepless hours, heavy nights,
Dream your dreams so pretty.
God was gonna have a laugh
An' gave me a job in the city!

The music continues for the interlude.

Some YOUNG INDIAN MEN run onto the stage along the ramp and join JAIMIE PAUL and RITA JOE in their dance. The MURDERERS enter and elbow into the group, their attention specifically menacing towards JAIMIE PAUL and RITA JOE. A street brawl begins as a POLICEMAN passes through on his beat. The MURDERERS leave hastily.

I woke up at six o'clock,
Stumbled out of bed.
Crash of steel and diesel trucks
Damned near killed me dead.

Sleepless hours, heavy nights,
Dream your dreams so pretty.
God was gonna have a laugh
An' gave me a job in the city!

Musical interlude. RITA JOE and JAIMIE PAUL continue dancing languidly. The YOUNG INDIAN MEN exit.

I've polished floors an' cut the trees,
Fished and stooked the wheat.
Now "Hallelujah, Praise the Lord,"
I sing before I eat!

Sleepless hours, heavy nights,
Dream your dreams so pretty.
God was gonna have a laugh
An' gave me a job in the city!

Musical interlude.

The music dies as the YOUNG INDIAN MEN wheel in a brass bed, circle it around and exit. The stage darkens except for a pool of light where RITA JOE and JAIMIE PAUL stand, embracing. JAIMIE PAUL takes her hand and leads her away.

JAIMIE Come on, Rita Joe...you're slow.

RITA *happy in her memories, not wishing to forget too soon, hesitating* How much rent...for a place where you can keep babies?

JAIMIE I don't know...maybe eighty dollars a month.

RITA That's a lot of money.

JAIMIE It costs a buck to go dancin' even....

They walk slowly along the apron to stage left, as if following a street to JAIMIE PAUL's rooming house.

It's a good place....I got a sink in the room. Costs seven bucks a week, that's all!

RITA That's good....I only got a bed in my place....

JAIMIE   I seen Mickey an' Steve Laporte last night.

RITA   How are they?

JAIMIE   Good.... We're goin' to a beer parlour Monday night when I get paid...the same beer parlour they threw Steve out of! Only now there's three of us goin' in!

They arrive at and enter his room. A spot illuminates the bed near the wings of stage left. It is old, dilapidated. JAIMIE PAUL and RITA JOE enter the area of light around the bed. He is aware that the room is more drab than he would wish it.

How do you like it...I like it!

RITA   *examining room critically*   It's...smaller than my place.

JAIMIE   Sit down.

She sits on the edge of the bed and falls backward into a springless hollow. He laughs nervously. He is awkward and confused. The ease they shared walking to his place is now constricted.

I was gonna get some grub today, but I was busy. ...Here....

He takes a chocolate bar out of his shirt pocket and offers it to her. She opens it, breaks off a small piece, and gives the remainder to him. He closes the wrapper and replaces the bar in his pocket. She eats ravenously. He walks around the bed nervously.

No fat d.p.'s gonna throw me or the boys out of that beer parlour or he's gonna get this!

He holds up a fist in a gesture that is both poignant and futile. She laughs and he glowers at her.

I'm tellin' you!

RITA   If they want to throw you out, they'll throw you out.

JAIMIE   Well, this is one Indian guy they're not pushing around no more!

RITA   God helps them who help themselves.

JAIMIE   That's right! *laughing* I was lookin' at the white shirts in Eaton's and this bugger comes an' says to me, you gonna buy or you gonna look all day?

RITA   *looking around her*   It's a nice room for a guy, I guess...

JAIMIE   It's a lousy room!

RITA JOE lies back lengthwise in the bed. JAIMIE PAUL sits on the bed beside her.

RITA   You need a good job to have babies in the city....Clara Hill gave both her kids away they say....

JAIMIE   Where do kids like that go?

RITA   Foster homes, I guess.

JAIMIE   If somebody don't like the kid, back they go to another foster home?

RITA   I guess so....Clara Hill don't know where her kids are now.

JAIMIE   *twisting sharply in his anger*   Goddamn it!

RITA   My father says...

JAIMIE PAUL rises, crosses round the bed to the other side.

JAIMIE   *harshly*   I don't want to hear what your father got to say! He's like...like the kind of Indian a white man likes! He's gonna look wise and wait forever...for what? For the kids they take away to come back?

RITA   He's scared...I'm scared....We're all scared, Jaimie Paul.

JAIMIE PAUL lies face down and mimes a gun through the bars.

JAIMIE   Sometimes I feel like takin' a gun and just....

He waves his hand as if to liquidate his environment and all that bedevils him. He turns over on his back and lies beside RITA JOE.

I don't know....Goddamnit, I don't know what to do. I get mad an' then I don't know what I'm doing or thinkin'....I get scared sometimes, Rita Joe.

RITA   *tenderly*   We're scared...everybody....

JAIMIE   I'm scared of dyin'...in the city. They don't care for one another here....You got to be smart or have a good job to live like that.

RITA   Clara Hill's gonna have another baby...

JAIMIE   I can't live like that....A man don't count for much here....Women can do as much as a man....There's no difference between men and women. I can't live like that.

RITA   You got to stop worrying, Jaimie Paul. You're gonna get sick worryin'.

JAIMIE   You can't live like that, can you?

RITA   No.

JAIMIE   I can't figure out what the hell they want from us!

RITA   *laughing*   Last time I was in trouble, the judge was asking me what I wanted from him! I could've told him, but I didn't!

They both laugh. JAIMIE PAUL becomes playful and happy.

JAIMIE   Last night I seen television in a store window. I seen a guy on television showing this knife that cuts everything it's so sharp....He was cutting up good shoes like they were potatoes. ...That was sure funny to see!

Again they laugh in merriment at the idea of such a demonstration. JAIMIE PAUL continues with his story, gesturing with his hands.

Chop...chop...chop....A potful of shoes in no time! What's a guy gonna do with a potful of shoes? Cook them?

They continue laughing and lie together again. Then JAIMIE PAUL sobers. He rises from the bed and walks around it. He offers his hand to RITA JOE, who also rises.

JAIMIE *drily* Come on. This is a lousy room!

SINGER *reprise*
God was gonna have a laugh,
And gave me a job in the city!

The light goes down on RITA JOE and JAIMIE PAUL. The YOUNG INDIAN MEN clear the bed. Cross fade to the rear ramp of the stage. RITA JOE's FATHER and the PRIEST enter and cross the stage.

PRIEST She got out yesterday, but she wouldn't let me see her. I stayed an extra day, but she wouldn't see me.

FATHER *sadly* I must go once more to the city. ...I must go to see them.

PRIEST You're an old man....I wish I could persuade you not to go.

FATHER You wouldn't say that if you had children, Andrew....

The lights go down on them. The lights come up on centre stage front. Three YOUNG INDIAN MEN precede MR. HOMER, carrying a table between them. MR. HOMER follows with a hamper of clothes under his arm.

MR. HOMER Yeh...right about there is fine, boys. Got to get the clutter out of the basement....There's mice coming in to beat hell.

MR. HOMER empties the clothes hamper on the table. The YOUNG INDIAN MEN step aside and converse in an undertone. On the ramp, a YOUNG INDIAN MAN weaves his way from stage left and down to centre stage where the others have brought the table. He is followed by JAIMIE PAUL and RITA JOE, who mime his intoxicated progress.

MR. HOMER *speaking to the audience* The Society for Aid to the Indians sent a guy over to see if I could recommend someone who'd been...well, through the mill, like they say...an' then smartened up an' taken rehabilitation. The guy said they just wanted a rehabilitated Indian to show up at their annual dinner. No speeches or fancy stuff...just be there.

The YOUNG INDIAN MAN lies down carefully to one side of MR. HOMER.

MR. HOMER Hi, Louie. Not that I would cross the street for the Society....They're nothing but a pack of do-gooders out to get their name in the papers....

The YOUNG INDIAN MAN begins to sing a tuneless song, trailing off into silence.

Keep it down, eh, Louie? I couldn't think of anybody to suggest to this guy...so he went away pretty sore....

RITA JOE begins to rummage through the clothes on the table. She looks at sweaters and holds a red one thoughtfully in her hands. JAIMIE PAUL is in conversation with the YOUNG INDIAN MEN to one side of the table. MR. HOMER turns from the audience to see RITA JOE holding the sweater.

Try it on, Rita Joe....That's what the stuff's here for.

JAIMIE PAUL turns. He is in a provocative mood, seething with rebellion that makes the humour he triggers both biting and deceptively innocent. The YOUNG INDIAN MEN respond to him with strong laughter. JAIMIE PAUL takes a play punch at one of them.

JAIMIE Whoops! Scared you, eh?

He glances back at MR. HOMER, as if talking to him.

Can't take it, eh? The priest can't take it. Indian Department guys can't take it....Why listen to them? Listen to the radio if you want to hear something.

The YOUNG INDIAN MEN laugh.

Or listen to me! You think I'm smart?

YOUNG INDIAN MAN You're a smart man, Jaimie Paul.

JAIMIE Naw...I'm not smart... *pointing to another YOUNG INDIAN MAN* This guy here ...calls himself squaw-humper...he's smart! ...Him...he buys extra big shirts...more cloth for the same money....That's smart! *Laughter.* I'm not smart. *seriously* You figure we can start a business an' be our own boss?

YOUNG INDIAN MAN I don't know about that....

JAIMIE PAUL leaves them and goes to lean over the YOUNG INDIAN MAN who is now asleep on the floor.

JAIMIE Buy a taxi...be our own boss....

He shakes the sleeping YOUNG INDIAN MAN, who immediately begins his tuneless song.

Aw, he's drunk....

JAIMIE PAUL goes over to the table and stares at the YOUNG INDIAN MAN beyond the table.

JAIMIE *soberly* Buy everything we need.... Don't be bums! Bums need grub an' clothes.... Bums is bad for the country, right Mr. Homer?

MR. HOMER *nodding* I guess so.... *to RITA JOE who is now wearing the old sweater* Red looks good on you, Rita Joe.... Take it!

JAIMIE PAUL goes over and embraces RITA JOE, then pushes her gently away.

JAIMIE She looks better in yellow. I never seen a red dandelion before.

He and the YOUNG INDIAN MEN laugh, but the laughter is hollow.

MR. HOMER Come on, Jaimie! Leave the girl alone. That's what it's here for.... Are you working?

JAIMIE *evasive, needling* Yeh!...No!..."Can you drive?" the guy says to me. "Sure, I can drive," I says to him. "Okay," he says, "then drive this broom until the warehouse is clean."

They all laugh.

MR. HOMER That's a good one.... Jaimie, you're a card.... Well, time to get some food for you lot....

MR. HOMER leaves. RITA JOE feels better about the sweater. She looks to one of the YOUNG INDIAN MEN for approval. JAIMIE PAUL becomes grim-faced.

RITA Do you like it?

YOUNG INDIAN MAN Sure. It's a nice sweater. ...Take it.

JAIMIE Take it where? Take it to hell.... Be men! *pointing after MR. HOMER* He's got no kids. ...Guys like that get mean when they got no kids.... We're his kids an' he means to keep it that way! Well, I'm a big boy now! *to RITA JOE* I go to the employment office. I want work an' I want it now. "I'm not a goddamned cripple," I says to him. An' he says he can only take my name! If work comes he'll call me! "What the hell is this," I says to him. "I'll never get work like that.... There's no telephone in the house where I got a room!"

MR. HOMER returns pushing a wheeled tray on which he has some food for sandwiches, a loaf of bread and a large cutting knife. He begins to make some sandwiches.

RITA *scolding JAIMIE PAUL* You won't get work talking that way, Jaimie Paul!

JAIMIE Why not? I'm not scared. He gets mad at me an' I say to him...."You think I'm some stupid Indian you're talkin' to? Heh? You think that?"

JAIMIE PAUL struts and swaggers to demonstrate how he faced his opponent at the employment office.

MR. HOMER *cutting bread* You're a tough man to cross, Jaimie Paul.

JAIMIE *ignoring MR. HOMER, to the YOUNG INDIAN MEN* Boy, I showed that bastard who he was talkin' to!

RITA Did you get the job?

JAIMIE *turning to her, laughing boyishly* No! He called the cops an' they threw me out!

They all laugh. The YOUNG INDIAN MEN go to the table now and rummage through the clothes.

MR. HOMER Take whatever you want, boys ...there's more clothes comin' tomorrow.

JAIMIE PAUL impulsively moves to the table where the YOUNG INDIAN MEN are fingering the clothes. He pushes them aside and shoves the clothes in a heap leaving a small corner of the table clean. He takes out two coins from his pockets and spits in his hands.

JAIMIE I got a new trick....Come on, Mister Homer...I'll show you! See this!

He shows the coins, then slams his hands palms down on the table.

Which hand got the coins?

MR. HOMER Why...one under each hand....

JAIMIE Right! *turning up his hands* Again? *He collects the coins and slaps his hands down again.* Where are the coins now? Come on, guess!

MR. HOMER is confident now, and points to the right hand with his cutting knife. JAIMIE PAUL laughs and lifts his hands. The coins are under his left hand.

MR. HOMER Son of a gun.

JAIMIE You're a smart man.

He puts the coins in his pockets and, laughing, turns to RITA JOE who stands uncertainly, dressed in the red sweater. She likes the garment, but she is aware JAIMIE PAUL might resent her taking it. The YOUNG INDIAN MEN again move to the table, and MR. HOMER returns to making sandwiches.

MR. HOMER There's a good pair of socks might come in handy for one of you guys!

A YOUNG INDIAN MAN pokes his thumbs through the holes in the socks, and laughs.

JAIMIE Sure...take the socks! Take the table!

He slaps the table with his hands and laughs.

Take Mister Homer cutting bread! Take everything!

MR. HOMER Hey, Jaimie!

JAIMIE Why not? There's more comin' tomorrow, you said!

RITA Jaimie!

MR. HOMER You're sure in a smart-assed mood today, aren't you?

JAIMIE   *pointing to the YOUNG INDIAN MAN with the socks, but talking to MR. HOMER*   Mister, friend Steve over there laughs lots.... He figures...the way to get along an' live is to grab his guts an' laugh at anything anybody says. You see him laughing all the time. A dog barks at him an' he laughs.... *Laughter from the YOUNG INDIAN MAN.*   Laughs at a fence post fallin'.... *Laughter.*   Kids with funny eyes make him go haywire.... *Laughter.* Can of meat an' no can opener....

MR. HOMER watches the YOUNG INDIAN MEN and grins at JAIMIE PAUL.

MR. HOMER   Yeh...he laughs quite a bit....

JAIMIE   He laughs at a rusty nail.... Nice guy ...laughs all the time.

MR. HOMER   *to JAIMIE PAUL, holding the knife* You wanted mustard on your bread or just plain?

JAIMIE   I seen him cut his hand and start laughin'. ...Isn't that funny?

The YOUNG INDIAN MEN laugh, but with less humour now.

MR. HOMER   *to JAIMIE PAUL*   You want mustard? ...I'm talkin' to you!

JAIMIE   I'm not hungry.

The YOUNG INDIAN MEN stop laughing altogether. They become tense and suspicious of JAIMIE PAUL, who is watching them severely.

MR. HOMER   Suit yourself. Rita?

She shakes her head slowly, her gaze on JAIMIE PAUL's face.

RITA   I'm not hungry.

MR. HOMER looks from RITA JOE to JAIMIE PAUL, then to the YOUNG INDIAN MEN. His manner stiffens.

MR. HOMER   I see....

JAIMIE PAUL and RITA JOE touch hands and come forward to sit on the apron of the stage, front. A pale light is on the two of them. The stage lights behind them fade. A low light that is diffused and shadowy remains on the table where MR. HOMER has prepared the food. The YOUNG INDIAN MEN move slowly to the table and begin eating the sandwiches MR. HOMER offers to them. The light on the table fades very low. JAIMIE PAUL hands a cigarette to RITA JOE and they smoke.

Light comes up over the rear ramp. RITA JOE's FATHER enters onto the ramp from the wings of stage right. His step is resolute. The PRIEST follows behind him a few paces. They have been arguing. Both are dressed in work clothes: heavy trousers and windbreakers.

JAIMIE   When I'm laughing, I got friends.

RITA   I know, Jaimie Paul....

PRIEST   That was the way I found her, that was the way I left her.

JAIMIE   *bitterly*   When I'm laughing, I'm a joker ...a funny boy!

FATHER   If I was young...I wouldn't sleep. I would talk to people...let them all know!

JAIMIE   I'm not dangerous when I'm laughing....

PRIEST   You could lose the reserve and have no-where to go!

FATHER   I have lost more than that! Young people die...young people don't believe me....

JAIMIE   That's alright...that's alright....

The light dies out on JAIMIE PAUL and RITA JOE. The light also dies out on MR. HOMER and the YOUNG INDIAN MEN.

PRIEST   You think they believe that hot-headed ...that troublemaker?

FATHER   *turning to face the PRIEST*   Jaimie Paul is a good boy!

PRIEST   David Joe...you and I have lived through a lot. We need peace now, and time to consider what to do next.

FATHER   Eileen said to me last night...she wants to go to the city. I worry all night....What can I do?

PRIEST   I'll talk to her, if you wish.

FATHER   *angry*   And tell her what?...Of the animals there...   *gesturing to the audience*   who sleep with sore stomachs because...they eat too much?

PRIEST   We mustn't lose the reserve and the old life, David Joe.... Would you...give up being chief on the reserve?

FATHER   Yes!

PRIEST   To Jaimie Paul?

FATHER   No...to someone who's been to school ...maybe university...who knows more.

PRIEST   *relieved by this, but not reassured*   The people here need your wisdom and stability, David Joe. There is no man here who knows as much about hunting and fishing and guiding. You can survive.... What does a youngster who's been away to school know of this?

FATHER   *sadly*   If we only fish an' hunt an' cut pulpwood...pick strawberries in the bush...for a hundred years more, we are dead. I know this, here....   *He touches his breast.*

The light dies on the ramp. A light rises on stage front, on JAIMIE PAUL and RITA JOE sitting at the apron of the stage. MR. HOMER is still cutting bread for sandwiches. The three YOUNG INDIAN MEN have eaten and appear restless to leave. The fourth YOUNG INDIAN MAN is still asleep on the floor. RITA JOE has taken off the red sweater, but continues to hold it in her hand.

JAIMIE to MR. HOMER One time I was on a trapline five days without grub. I ate snow an' I walked until I got back. You think you can take it like me?

MR. HOMER approaches JAIMIE PAUL and holds out a sandwich to him.

MR. HOMER Here . . . have a sandwich now.

JAIMIE PAUL ignores his hand.

RITA Mister Homer don't know what happened, Jaimie Paul.

MR. HOMER shrugs and walks away to his sandwich table.

JAIMIE Then he's got to learn. . . . Sure he knows! to MR. HOMER Sure he knows! He's feedin' sandwiches to Indian bums. . . . He knows. He's the worst kind!

The YOUNG INDIAN MEN freeze and MR. HOMER stops.

MR. HOMER coldly I've never yet asked a man to leave this building.

RITA JOE and JAIMIE PAUL rise to their feet. RITA JOE goes to the clothes table and throws the red sweater back on the pile of clothes. JAIMIE PAUL laughs sardonically.

MR. HOMER to RITA JOE Hey, not you, girl. . . . You take it!

She shakes her head and moves to leave.

RITA I think we better go, boys.

The sleeping YOUNG INDIAN MAN slowly raises his head, senses there is something wrong, and is about to be helped up when . . .

JAIMIE After five days without grub, the first meal I threw up . . . stomach couldn't take it. . . . But after that it was alright. . . . to MR. HOMER, with intensity I don't believe nobody . . . no priest nor government. . . . They don't know what it's like to . . . to want an' not have . . . to stand in line an' nobody sees you!

MR. HOMER If you want food, eat! You need clothes, take them. That's all. . . . But I'm runnin' this centre my way, and I mean it!

JAIMIE I come to say no to you. . . . That's all . . . that's all!

He throws out his arms in a gesture that is both defiant and childlike. The gesture disarms some of MR. HOMER's growing hostility.

MR. HOMER You've got that right . . . no problems. There's others come through here day an' night. . . . No problems.

JAIMIE I don't want no others to come. I don't want them to eat here! indicating his friends If we got to take it from behind a store window, then we break the window an' wait for the cops. It's better than . . . than this!

He gestures with contempt at the food and the clothes on the table.

MR. HOMER Rita Joe . . . where'd you pick up this . . . this loudmouth anyway?

RITA slowly, firmly I think . . . Jaimie Paul's . . . right.

MR. HOMER looks from face to face. The three YOUNG INDIAN MEN are passive, staring into the distance. The fourth is trying hard to clear his head. JAIMIE PAUL is cold, hostile. RITA JOE is determined.

MR. HOMER decisively Alright! You've eaten . . . looked over the clothes. . . . Now clear out so others get a chance to come in! Move!

He tries to herd everyone out and the four YOUNG INDIAN MEN begin to move away. JAIMIE PAUL mimics the gestures of MR. HOMER and steps in front of the YOUNG INDIAN MEN herding them back in.

JAIMIE Run, boys, run! Or Mister Homer gonna beat us up!

RITA JOE takes JAIMIE PAUL's hand and tries to pull him away to leave.

RITA Jaimie Paul . . . you said to me no trouble!

JAIMIE PAUL pulls his hand free and jumps back of the clothes table. MR. HOMER comes for him, unknowingly still carrying the slicing knife in his hand. An absurd chase begins around the table. One of the YOUNG INDIAN MEN laughs, and stepping forward, catches hold of MR. HOMER's hand with the knife in it.

YOUNG INDIAN MAN Hey! Don't play with a knife, Mister Homer!

He gently takes the knife away from MR. HOMER and drops it on the food table behind. MR. HOMER looks at his hand, an expression of shock on his face. JAIMIE PAUL gives him no time to think about the knife and what it must have appeared like to the YOUNG INDIAN MEN. He pulls a large brassiere from the clothes table and mockingly holds it over his breasts, which he sticks out enticingly at MR. HOMER. The YOUNG INDIAN MEN laugh. MR. HOMER is exasperated and furious. RITA JOE is frightened.

RITA It's not funny, Jaimie!

JAIMIE It's funny as hell, Rita Joe. Even funnier this way!

JAIMIE PAUL puts the brassiere over his head, with the cups down over his ears and the straps under his chin. The YOUNG INDIAN MEN are all laughing now and moving close to the table. MR. HOMER makes a futile attempt at driving them off.

Suddenly JAIMIE PAUL's expression turns to one of hatred. He throws the brassiere on the table and gripping its edge, throws the table and clothes over, scattering the clothes. He kicks at them. The YOUNG INDIAN MEN all jump in and, picking up the clothes, hurl them over the ramp.

RITA JOE runs in to try and stop them. She grips the table and tries lifting it up again.

MR. HOMER *to JAIMIE PAUL* Cut that out, you sonofabitch!

JAIMIE PAUL stands watching him. MR. HOMER is in a fury. He sees RITA JOE struggling to right the table. He moves to her and pushes her hard.

MR. HOMER You slut!. . . You breed whore!

RITA JOE recoils. With a shriek of frustration, she attacks MR. HOMER, tearing at him. He backs away, then turns and runs. JAIMIE PAUL overturns the table again. The others join in the melee with the clothes. A POLICEMAN enters and grabs JAIMIE PAUL. RITA JOE and the four YOUNG INDIAN MEN exit, clearing away the tables and remaining clothes.

A sharp, tiny spotlight comes up on the face and upper torso of JAIMIE PAUL. He is wild with rebellion as the POLICEMAN forces him, in an arm lock, down towards the audience.

JAIMIE *screaming defiance at the audience* Not jus' a box of cornflakes! When I go in I want the whole store! That's right. . . the whole goddamned store!

Another sharp light on the MAGISTRATE standing on his podium looking down at JAIMIE PAUL.

MAGISTRATE Thirty days!

JAIMIE *held by POLICEMAN* Sure, sure. . . . Anything else you know?

MAGISTRATE Thirty days!

JAIMIE Gimme back my truth!

MAGISTRATE We'll get larger prisons and more police in every town and city across the country!

JAIMIE Teach me who I really am! You've taken that away! Give me back the real me so I can live like a man!

MAGISTRATE There is room for dialogue. There is room for disagreement and there is room for social change. . . but within the framework of institutions and traditions in existence for that purpose!

JAIMIE *spitting* Go to hell!. . . I can die an' you got nothing to tell me!

MAGISTRATE *in a cold fury* Thirty days! And after that, it will be six months! And after that. . . God help you!

The MAGISTRATE marches off his platform and offstage. JAIMIE PAUL is led off briskly in the other direction offstage.

The lights change. RITA JOE enters, crossing the stage, exchanging a look with the SINGER.

SINGER
Sleepless hours, heavy nights,
Dream your dreams so pretty.
God was gonna have a laugh
An' gave me a job in the city!

RITA JOE walks the street. She is smoking a cigarette. She is dispirited.

The light broadens across the stage. RITA JOE's FATHER and JAIMIE PAUL enter the stage from the wings of centre stage left. They walk slowly towards where RITA JOE stands. At the sight of her FATHER, RITA JOE moans softly and hurriedly stamps out her cigarette. She visibly straightens and waits for the approaching men, her expression one of fear and joy.

FATHER I got a ride on Miller's truck. . . took me two days. . . .

JAIMIE It's a long way, David Joe.

The FATHER stops a pace short of RITA JOE and looks at her with great tenderness and concern.

FATHER *softly* I come. . . to get Rita Joe.

RITA Oh. . . I don't know. . . .

She looks to JAIMIE PAUL for help in deciding what to do, but he is sullen and uncommunicative.

FATHER I come to take Rita Joe home. . . . We got a house an' some work sometime. . . .

JAIMIE She's with me now, David Joe.

RITA *very torn* I don't know. . . .

JAIMIE You don't have to go back, Rita Joe.

RITA JOE looks away from her FATHER with humility. The FATHER turns to JAIMIE PAUL. He stands ancient and heroic.

FATHER I live. . . an' I am afraid. Because. . . I have not done everything. When I have done everything. . . know that my children are safe . . . then. . . it will be alright. Not before.

JAIMIE *to RITA JOE* You don't have to go. This is an old man now. . . . He has nothing to give . . . nothin' to say!

RITA JOE reacts to both men, her conflict deepening.

FATHER *turning away from JAIMIE PAUL to RITA JOE* For a long time. . . a very long time. . . she was in my hands. . . like that! *He cups his hands into the shape of a bowl.* Sweet. . . tiny. . . lovin' all the time and wanting love.... *He shakes his head sadly.*

JAIMIE *angrily* Go tell it to the white men! They're lookin' for Indians that stay proud even when they hurt . . . just so long's they don't ask for their rights!

The FATHER turns slowly, with great dignity, to JAIMIE PAUL. His gestures show JAIMIE PAUL to be wrong; the old man's spirit was never broken. JAIMIE PAUL understands and looks away.

FATHER You're a good boy, Jaimie Paul . . . a good boy.... *to RITA JOE, talking slowly, painfully* I once seen a dragonfly breakin' its shell to get its wings.... It floated on water an' crawled up on a log where I was sitting.... It dug its feet into the log an' then it pulled until the shell bust over its neck. Then it pulled some more . . . an' slowly its wings slipped out of the shell . . . like that!

He shows with his hands how the dragonfly got his freedom.

JAIMIE *angered and deeply moved by the FATHER* Where you gonna be when they start bustin' our heads open an' throwing us into jails right across the goddamned country?

FATHER Such wings I never seen before . . . folded like an accordion so fine, like thin glass an' white in the morning sun....

JAIMIE We're gonna have to fight to win . . . there's no other way! They're not listenin' to you, old man! Or to me.

FATHER It spread its wings . . . so slowly . . . an' then the wings opened an' began to flutter . . . just like that . . . see! Hesitant at first . . . then stronger . . . an' then the wings beatin' like that made the dragonfly's body quiver until the shell on its back falls off . . .

JAIMIE Stop kiddin' yourself! We're gonna say no pretty soon to all the crap that makes us soft an' easy to push this way . . . that way!

FATHER . . . An' the dragonfly . . . flew up . . . up . . . up . . . into the white sun . . . to the green sky . . . to the sun . . . faster an' faster.... Higher . . . higher!

The FATHER reaches up with his hands, releasing the imaginary dragonfly into the sun, his final words torn out of his heart. RITA JOE springs to her feet and rushes against JAIMIE PAUL, striking at him with her fists.

RITA *savagely* For Chris' sakes, I'm not goin' back! . . . Leave him alone.... He's everything we got left now!

JAIMIE PAUL stands, frozen by his emotion which he can barely control. The FATHER turns. RITA JOE goes to him. The FATHER speaks privately to RITA JOE in Indian dialect. They embrace. He pauses for

a long moment to embrace and forgive her everything. Then he goes slowly offstage into the wings of stage left without looking back.

FATHER Goodbye, Rita Joe.... Goodbye, Jaimie Paul....

RITA Goodbye, Father.

JAIMIE PAUL watches RITA JOE who moves away from him to the front of the stage.

JAIMIE *to her* You comin'?

She shakes her head to indicate no, she is staying. Suddenly JAIMIE PAUL runs away from her diagonally across to the wings of rear stage left. As he nears the wings, the four YOUNG INDIAN MEN emerge, happily on their way to a party. They stop him at his approach. He runs into them, directing them back, his voice breaking with feelings of love and hatred intermingling.

JAMIE *shouting at them* Next time . . . in a beer parlour or any place like that . . . I'll go myself or you guys take me home.... No more white buggers pushin' us out the door or he gets this!

He raises his fist. The group of YOUNG INDIAN MEN, elated by their newly-found determination, surround JAIMIE PAUL and exit into the wings of the stage. The light dies in back and at stage left.

The MAGISTRATE enters. There is a light on RITA JOE where she stands. There is also a light around the MAGISTRATE. The MAGISTRATE's voice and purpose are leaden. He has given up on RITA JOE. He is merely performing the formality of condemning her and dismissing her from his conscience.

MAGISTRATE I sentence you to thirty days in prison.

RITA *angry, defiant* Sure, sure.... Anything else you know?

MAGISTRATE I sentence you to thirty days in prison, with a recommendation you be examined medically and given all necessary treatment at the prison clinic. There is nothing . . . there is nothing I can do now.

RITA *stoically* Thank you. Is that right? To thank you?

MAGISTRATE You'll be back . . . always be back . . . growing older, tougher . . . filthier . . . looking more like stone and prison bars . . . the lines in your face will tell everyone who sees you about prison windows and prison food.

RITA No child on the road would remember you, mister!

The MAGISTRATE comes down to stand before her. He has the rambling confidence of detached authority.

MAGISTRATE   What do you expect? We provide schools for you and you won't attend them because they're out of the way and that little extra effort is too much for you! We came up as a civilization having to . . . yes, claw upwards at times. . . . There's nothing wrong with that. . . . We give you X-ray chest clinics. . . .

He turns away from her and goes to the apron of the stage and speaks directly to the audience.

We give them X-ray chest clinics and three-quarters of them won't show up. . . . Those that do frequently get medical attention at one of the hospitals. . .

RITA   *interjecting*   My mother died!

MAGISTRATE   *not hearing her*   But as soon as they're released they forget they're chronically ill and end up on a drinking party and a long walk home through the snow. . . . Next thing . . . they're dead!

RITA   *quietly*   Oh, put me in jail an' then let me go.

MAGISTRATE   *turning to her*   Some of you get jobs. . . . There are jobs, good jobs, if you'd only look around a bit . . . and stick with them when you get them. But no . . . you get a job and promise to stay with it and learn, and two weeks later you're gone for three, four days without explanation. . . . Your reliability record is ruined and an employer has to regard you as lazy, undependable. . . . What do you expect?

RITA   I'm not scared of you now, bastard!

MAGISTRATE   You have a mind . . . you have a heart. The cities are open to you to come and go as you wish, yet you gravitate to the slums and skid rows and the shanty-town fringes. You become a whore, drunkard, user of narcotics. . . . At best, dying of illness or malnutrition. . . . At worst, kicked or beaten to death by some angry white scum who finds in you something lower than himself to pound his frustrations out on! What's to be done? You Indians seem to be incapable of taking action to help yourselves. Someone must care for you. . . . Who? For how long?

RITA   You don't know nothin'!

MAGISTRATE   I know . . . I know. . . . It's a struggle just to stay alive. I know . . . I understand. That struggle is mine, as well as yours, Rita Joe! The jungle of the executive has as many savage teeth ready to go for the throat as the rundown hotel on the waterfront. . . . Your days and hours are numbered, Rita Joe. . . . I worry for the child I once saw. . . . I have already forgotten the woman!

He turns away from her and exits into the wings of stage right.

The lights on RITA JOE fade. Lights of cold, eerie blue wash the backdrop of the stage faintly. RITA JOE stands in silhouette for a long moment.

Slowly, ominously, the three MURDERERS appear on the ramp backstage, one coming from the wings of stage right; one from the wings of stage left; and one rising from the back of the ramp, climbing it. One of the MURDERERS is whistling, a soft nervous noise throughout their scene onstage.

RITA JOE whimpers in fear, and as the MURDERERS loom above her, she runs along the apron to stage left. Here she bumps into JAIMIE PAUL who enters. She screams in fear.

JAIMIE   Rita Joe!

RITA   *terrorized*   Jaimie! They're comin'. I seen them comin'!

JAIMIE   Who's coming? What's the matter, Rita Joe?

RITA   Men I once dreamed about. . . . I seen it all happen once before . . . an' it was like this. . . .

JAIMIE PAUL laughs and pats her shoulders reassuringly. He takes her hand and tries to lead her forward to the apron of the stage, but RITA JOE is dead, her steps wooden.

JAIMIE   Don't worry . . . I can take care of myself!

A faint light on the two of them.

RITA   You been in jail now too, Jaimie Paul. . . .

JAIMIE   So what? Guys in jail was saying that they got to put a man behind bars or the judge don't get paid for being in court to make the trial. . . . Funny world, eh, Rita Joe?

RITA   *nodding*   Funny world.

The light dies on them. They come forward slowly.

JAIMIE   I got a room with a hot plate. . . . We can have a couple of eggs and some tea before we go to the movie.

RITA   What was it like for you in jail?

JAIMIE   So so. . . .

JAIMIE PAUL motions for RITA JOE to follow him and moves forward from her. The distant sound of a train approaching is heard. She is wooden, coming slowly after him.

RITA   It was different where the women were. . . . It's different to be a woman. . . . Some women was wild . . . and they shouted they were riding black horses into a fire I couldn't see. . . . There was no fire there, Jaimie!

JAIMIE   *turning to her, taking her arm*   Don't worry . . . we're goin' to eat and then see a movie. . . . Come on, Rita Joe!

She looks back and sees the MURDERERS rise and slowly approach from the gloom. Her speech becomes thick and unsteady as she follows JAIMIE PAUL to the front of the ramp.

RITA   One time I couldn't find the street where I had a room to sleep in . . . forgot my handbag . . . had no money. . . . An old man with a dog said hello, but I couldn't say hello back because I was worried an' my mouth was so sticky I couldn't speak to him. . . .

JAIMIE   Are you comin'?

RITA   When you're tired an' sick, Jaimie, the city starts to dance. . . .

JAIMIE   *taking her hand, pulling her gently along* Come on, Rita Joe.

RITA   The street lights start rollin' like wheels an' cement walls feel like they was made of blanket cloth. . . .

The sound of the train is closer now. The lights of its lamps flicker in back of the stage. RITA JOE turns to face the MURDERERS, one of whom is whistling ominously. She whimpers in fear and presses herself against JAIMIE PAUL. JAIMIE PAUL turns and sees the MURDERERS hovering near them.

JAIMIE   Don't be scared. . . . Nothing to be scared of, Rita Joe. . . .   *to the MURDERERS*   What the hell do you want?

One of the MURDERERS laughs. JAIMIE PAUL pushes RITA JOE back behind himself. He moves towards the MURDERERS, taunting them.

You think I can't take care of myself?

With deceptive casualness, the MURDERERS approach him. One of them makes a sudden lurch at JAIMIE PAUL as if to draw him into their circle. JAIMIE PAUL anticipates the trap and takes a flying kick at the MURDERER, knocking him down.

They close around JAIMIE PAUL with precision, then attack. JAIMIE PAUL leaps, but is caught mid-air by the other two. They bring him down and put the boots to him. RITA JOE screams and runs to him. The train sound is loud and immediate now.

One of the MURDERERS has grabbed RITA JOE. The remaining two raise JAIMIE PAUL to his feet and one knees him viciously in the groin. JAIMIE PAUL screams and doubles over. The lights of the train are upon them. The MURDERERS leap off the ramp leaving JAIMIE PAUL in the path of the approaching train. JAIMIE PAUL's death cry becomes the sound of the train horn. As the train sound roars by, the MURDERERS return to close in around RITA JOE. One MURDERER springs forward and grabs RITA JOE. The other two help to hold her, with nervous fear and lust. RITA JOE breaks free of them and runs to the front of the stage. The three MURDERERS come after her, panting hard. They close in on her leisurely now, playing with her, knowing that they have her trapped.

Recorded and overlapping voices.

CLERK   The court calls Rita Joe . . .

MAGISTRATE   Who is she? . . . Let her speak for herself . . .

RITA   In the summer it was hot, an' flies hummed . . .

TEACHER   A book of verse, a melting pot . . .

MAGISTRATE   Thirty days!

FATHER   Barkin' to beat hell. . . . How! How!

JAIMIE   *laughing, defiant, taunting*   You go to hell!

PRIEST   A confession, Rita Joe . . .

Over the voices she hears, the MURDERERS attack. Dragging her down backwards, they pull her legs open and one MURDERER lowers himself on her.

RITA   Jaimie! Jaimie! Jaimie!

RITA JOE's head lolls over sideways. The MURDERERS stare at her and pull back slightly.

MURDERER   *thickly, rising off her twisted, broken body*   Shit . . . she's dead. . . . We hardly touched her.

He hesitates for a moment, then runs, joined by the SECOND MURDERER.

SECOND MURDERER   Let's get out of here!

They run up onto the ramp and watch as the THIRD MURDERER piteously climbs onto the dead RITA JOE.

Sounds of a funeral chant. MOURNERS appear on riser backstage. RITA JOE's FATHER enters from the wings of stage left, chanting an ancient Indian funeral chant, carrying the body of JAIMIE PAUL. The MURDERER hesitates in his necrophilic rape and then runs away.

The YOUNG INDIAN MEN bring the body of JAIMIE PAUL over the ramp and approach. The body is placed down on the podium, beside RITA JOE's. All the Indians, young and old, kneel around the two bodies. The FATHER continues his death chant. The PRIEST enters from the wings of stage right reciting a prayer. The TEACHER, SINGER, POLICEMAN and MURDERERS come with him forming the outside perimeter around the Indian funeral.

PRIEST   Hail Mary, Mother of God . . . pray for us sinners now and at the hour of our death.

Repeated until finally EILEEN JOE slowly rises to her feet and, turning to the PRIEST and WHITE MOURNERS, says softly . . .

EILEEN   *over the sounds of chanting and praying* No! . . . No! . . . No more!

The YOUNG INDIAN MEN rise one after another facing the outer circle defiantly and the CAST freezes on stage, except for the SINGER.

SINGER
Oh, the singing bird
Has found its wings
And it's soaring!

My God, what a sight!
On the cold fresh wind of morning!...

During the song, EILEEN JOE steps forward to the audience and as the song ends, says...

EILEEN   When Rita Joe first come to the city, she told me...the cement made her feet hurt.

JOHN HERBERT (b. 1926)

Although John Herbert Brundage was a prime mover in the creation of Toronto's alternate theatre in the 1960s—"the single most important figure of the decade," according to Bill Glassco— his success as a playwright, to a much greater extent even than George Ryga's, has happened outside of Canada. And more so than Ryga's it rests on a single play. At last count *Fortune and Men's Eyes* had been performed in over a hundred countries in at least forty different translations. It has sold, in an American edition, more copies than any other published Canadian play. It even led to the founding of the Fortune Society, an organization devoted to prison reform in the United States. Yet *Fortune* was an established international success for nearly eight years before Herbert got to see a professional production in his home and native city, "cold, bitter, suspicious Toronto," as he entitled a 1971 *Saturday Night* article.

Herbert's bitterness about Toronto stems in part from an incident in 1946 when, as he tells it, he was beaten and robbed by a street gang. Instead of laying charges against his assailants, the police charged Herbert with having sexually propositioned them and he was convicted of gross indecency. The six months he spent in Guelph reformatory would later become the basis for *Fortune and Men's Eyes*. The vivid third-person description of his time in prison that Herbert contributed to Geraldine Anthony's *Stage Voices* makes clear that the characters of both Mona and Queenie in *Fortune* are projections of his own experience behind bars.

Herbert's theatrical career began in 1955 when he enrolled in the New Play Society School of Drama, studying acting, directing and production for three years followed by two years of dance training at the National Ballet school. In 1960 he founded Adventure Theatre in Toronto and from 1962-65 was artistic director of the New Venture Players with whom he produced and directed his own early plays "Private Club," "A Household God" and an adaptation from Dumas, "A Lady of Camelias." In 1965 he opened a fifty-seat theatre over a pizzeria on Yonge Street. The Garret Theatre ran off and on until 1970, subsidized by Herbert's labours as a waiter. Among its productions were his plays "Closer to Cleveland" and "World of Woyzeck," adapted from Büchner.

Meanwhile Herbert had written *Fortune and Men's Eyes* in 1964, and while serving drinks at the University Club he had mentioned it to Robertson Davies who suggested submitting the play to a summer workshop at Stratford. *Toronto Star* critic Nathan Cohen got wind of the 1965 workshop production, read the script and sent it to New York producer David Rothenberg. *Fortune and Men's Eyes* opened off-Broadway in 1967, and within a few years it was making its way around the world.

The international success of *Fortune* did little, however, for Herbert's fortunes in Canada. Unable to get a major Canadian production of the play and with the Garret devouring his foreign royalties, Herbert closed the theatre permanently in 1970 (deeding its equipment to Ken Gass who promptly set up the Factory Lab) and left in frustration to live in England. But two years later he was back in Toronto to stay, trying again to establish his presence in the Canadian theatre. Between 1972 and 1974 he staged two ambitious new plays, *Born of Medusa's Blood* and *Omphale and the Hero*, and four one-acts under the title *Some Angry Summer Songs*, but no one seemed to be listening. By 1975, when *Fortune* won the Chalmers Award for its first professional production in Toronto, Herbert had pretty well retired from the theatre. He has since written a novel (*The House That Jack Built*), taught drama and creative writing, worked as an art and theatre critic, and served as Associate Editor of *Onion*, a Toronto arts newsletter.

All Herbert's full-length plays and many of his one-acts concern relationships characterized by selfishness and betrayal usually resulting in destruction. At the centre of both *Born of Medusa's Blood* and *Omphale and the Hero* are female figures of redemption (who both happen to be whores) destroyed by perverse machismo and a corrupt social order. *Fortune and Men's Eyes* uses the same formula but in a much more dramatically compelling way. The prison environment enforces a distinctive kind of garrison mentality among its inhabitants whose struggle for survival involves not just their physical well-being but their ethical and sexual identities as well.

Fortune and Men's Eyes (originally titled *The Christmas Concert*) has the structure of a morality play. Smitty, as his name suggests, is the Everyman character. He enters the prison world an innocent and is immediately confronted by a distorted value system which demands from him a series of unpalatable choices. As represented by his three cellmates, his choices are to accept, reject or accommodate himself to the prison's values. Rocky has clearly adopted those values as his own. His authoritarianism and racism, his blackmail of the guard and manipulation of Catso show him to be completely at home in the prison system, the jungle in which he calls himself king. At the other extreme is Mona who transcends "her" surroundings by separating body and spirit, preserving—only at a terrible price—an essentially feminine gentleness and sensitivity inimical to the perverted masculinity of the prison that expresses itself through homosexual gang rapes and brutal beatings. In between these two is Queenie. He knows the prison game even better than Rocky and can be just as vicious; yet like Mona he has not entirely lost himself to the system. His outrageous drag routines are a personal signature marking his distance from the prison's drab conformity (and making him the play's most entertaining character). But behind the personae of the clown and the helpful "mother" that Queenie plays in the prison's travesty of domestic order is just one more sad, damaged boy.

"I feel like I'm in another country," Smitty says when he first enters the cellblock. But it's not long before he's forced to adopt native customs, and by Scene Two he's already speaking the language. He comes under the influence first of Rocky, then of Queenie, learning the rules of the game so well that by the end he is almost too far gone to embrace the possibility of salvation held out by Mona and amplified in the Shakespeare sonnet from which the play's title comes. After their moment of communion is shattered by the brutality of the others and the prison's injustice, Smitty shows that he has become another Rocky: cruel, desensitized, irrevocably lost.

Although *Fortune and Men's Eyes* is certainly an exposé of the brutalizing effects of prison life, environment is not the only operative factor in the play. Herbert's naturalism also encompasses the other traditional element, heredity. In his study *Modern Tragedy*, Raymond Williams describes how "in Ibsen, the hero defines an opposing world, full of lies and compromises and dead positions, only to find, as he struggles against it, that as a man he belongs to this world and has its destructive inheritance in himself." Smitty too carries within him a destructive inheritance. Like his father, the practical businessman who turns out to be a "hardhearted bastard," Smitty reveals a coldblooded pragmatism that leaves him emotionally crippled. He no sooner complains that his father treats his mother like a prostitute than he offers Mona the same treatment. Just as Rocky is an inevitable product and victim of his criminal family, Queenie of his mother's abandonment, and Mona of an effeminate physical appearance, Smitty is doomed by a condition more devastating than anything symbolized by the final clang of the jail door.

•

Fortune and Men's Eyes opened at the Actors Playhouse in New York on February 23, 1967, directed by Mitchell Nestor, with set design by C. Murawski. It featured Terry Kiser as Smitty, Victor Arnold as Rocky, Bill Moor as Queenie, Robert Christian as Mona and Clifford Pellow as the Guard.

FORTUNE AND MEN'S EYES

CHARACTERS

SMITTY, a good-looking, clean-cut youth of clear intelligence, aged seventeen years. He has the look of a collegiate athlete. The face is strong and masculine with enough sensitivity in feature and expression to soften the sharp outline. He is of a type that everyone seems to like, almost on sight.

ROCKY, a youth of nineteen years who seems older and harder than his age should allow, though there is an emotional immaturity that reveals itself constantly. He has a nature, driven by fear, that uses hatred aggressively to protect itself, taking pride in harbouring no soft or gentle feelings. He lives like a cornered rat, vicious, dangerous and unpredictable. He is handsome in a lean, cold, dark, razor-featured way.

QUEENIE, a large, heavy-bodied youth of nineteen or twenty with the strength of a wrestler but the soft white skin of a very blond person. Physical appearance is a strange combination of softness and hulking strength. For a large person he moves with definite grace and fine precision, almost feminine in exactness, but in no way frivolous or fluttery. Movements, when exaggerated purposely, are big, showy and extravagant. The face is dainty in features as a "cupie-doll's"—plump-cheeked and small-nosed. The mouth has a pouting, self-indulgent look, but the eyes are hard, cold, and pale blue like ice. The hair is fair, fine, and curly, like a baby's. One looks at him and thinks of a madam in a brothel . . . coarse, cruel, tough and voluptuously pretty.

MONA, a youth of eighteen or nineteen years, of a physical appearance that arouses resentment at once in many people, men and women. He seems to hang suspended between the sexes, neither boy nor woman. He is slender, narrow-shouldered, long-necked, long-legged, but never gauche or ungainly. He moves gracefully, but not self-consciously. His nature seems almost more feminine than effeminate because it is not mannerism that calls attention to an absence of masculinity so much as the sum of his appearance, lightness of movement, and gentleness of action. His effeminacy is not aggressive . . . just exists. The face is responsible for his nickname of "Mona Lisa." Features are madonna-like, straight-nosed, patrician-mouthed and sad-eyed. Facial contour is oval and the expression enigmatic. If he had been a woman, some would have described him as having a certain ethereal beauty.

GUARD, a rugged-faced man of about forty-five to fifty, who looks like an ex-army officer. He has a rigid military bearing, a look of order and long acquaintance with discipline. He presents an impressive exterior of uniformed law enforcement, but one senses behind the unsmiling features some nagging doubt or worry, as if something of his past returned occasionally to haunt him, when he would prefer it forgotten. At these moments, his actions are uneasy and he does not seem so impressive, in spite of his uniform. He has a stomach ulcer that causes him much physical discomfort, manifesting itself in loud belching.

SCENE

A Canadian reformatory, prep school for the penitentiary. The inmates are usually young, but there are often older prisoners, as indicated by the dialogue in places. We are primarily concerned here with four who are young, though they tell us others exist. The overwhelming majority of prisoners in a reformatory are in the late teens and early twenties. Those who are older have been convicted of offenses that do not carry a sentence large enough to warrant sending them to a penitentiary.

SET

The setting is a dormitory with four beds and two doorways. One door leads to the corridor, but we do not see it. There is a stone alcove, angled so that we get the impression of a short hall. We hear the guard's key open this unseen door whenever he or the four inmates enter or exit. The whole upstage wall is barred so that we look into the corridor where the guard and inmates pass in entrance and exit. Another doorway leads to the toilet and shower room.

ACT ONE

Scene One

Mid-October, evening.

Overture: 3 songs—"Alouette" (sung by Group of Boys' Voices); "Down in the Valley" (One Male Voice); "Jesus Loves Me" (sung by Group of Boys' Voices).

ROCKY is stretched on his bed like a prince at rest; QUEENIE sits on his own bed upstage; MONA leans against the wall of bars, upstage of QUEENIE. In the distance we hear the clang of metal doors, and a gruff voice issuing orders. MONA turns at the sounds, and looks along the hall.

Just before lights come up, after curtain has opened, a BOY'S VOICE is heard singing, at a distance—as if farther along a corridor.

BOY'S VOICE   *singing*
Oh, if I had the wings of an angel
Over these prison walls would I fly—

Sound of metal doors clanging open and shut. And sound of heavy boots marching along corridor.

VOICE   *English accent*   Halt! Attention! Straighten that line! Guard! Take this one down and put him in Observation!

GUARD   Yes sir! Smith! Step out—and smartly!

Lights come up.

BOY'S VOICE   *singing*   Oh, if I had the wings of—

QUEENIE   *on stage*
Oh, if I had the wings of an angel
And the ass of a big buffalo,
I would fly to the heavens above me,
And crap on the people below.

VOICE   *English accent; raised now, the voice is not only gruff as before but high and shrill in overtone, like Hitler's recorded speech*   And you, Canary-Bird—shut that bloody row, or I shall cut off your seed supply.

Repeated sound of metal doors, and of boots marching away.

QUEENIE   Oh, oh! That's Bad Bess. The Royal Sergeant don't come this close to the common folk, except when they're bringin' in a batch o' fish.

ROCKY   What's the action out there, Queenie?

MONA   *standing nearest the bars*   It's the new arrivals.

ROCKY   Anybody ask you to open your mouth, fruity?

QUEENIE   Oh, lay off the Mona Lisa, for Christ sake, Rocky.

ROCKY   Always getting her jollies looking out that hole.

QUEENIE   Does Macy's bother Gimbel's?

ROCKY   They got their own corners.

QUEENIE   Well she ain't in yours, so dummy up!

ROCKY   Don't mess with the bull, Queenie!

QUEENIE   Your horn ain't long enough to reach me, Ferdinand.

ROCKY   You might feel it yet.

QUEENIE   Worst offer I've had today, but it's early.

ROCKY   Screw off!   *turning toward MONA*   Look at the queer watchin' the fish! See anything you can catch, Rosie?

QUEENIE   How's the new stock, Mona? Anything worth shakin' it for?

MONA   They're all so young.

QUEENIE   That'll suit Rocky. If he could coop a new chicken in his yard, he might not be so salty.

ROCKY   Where'd you get all that mouth . . . from your mother?

QUEENIE   The better to gobble you up with, Little Red Riding Wolf!

ROCKY   Tell it to your old man.

QUEENIE   Which one? Remember me? I'm my own P.I.

ROCKY   You got a choice?

QUEENIE   I don't mean pimp, like you, I mean political influence, like me!

ROCKY   So you got a coupla wheels in the office! Big deal!

QUEENIE   I like it that way . . . makes it so I don't have to take no crap from a would-be hippy like you.

MONA   They're coming this way.

QUEENIE   Hell! And I didn't set my hair in toilet-paper curls last night. Oh well! I'll try to look seductive.

ROCKY   You better turn around then.

QUEENIE   Well, my backside looks better than your face, if that's what you wanta say.

ROCKY   *with disdain*   Queers!

Enter GUARD with a youth who is about seventeen.

ROCKY   Hi, screw! What's that . . . your new baby?

GUARD   You planning a return trip to the tower, smart boy?

ROCKY   Just bein' friendly, Captain! I like to make the kids feel at home.

GUARD   So I've noticed.   *to the new boy*   Okay, Smith, this is your dormitory for now. Try to get along with the others and keep your nose clean. Do as you're told, keep your bunk tidy, and no talking after lights out. You'll be assigned your work to-morrow. Meanwhile, follow the others to washup and meals. Pick up the routine and don't spend too much time in the craphouse, or you'll end up in an isolation cell.

ROCKY   He means Gunsel's Alley. Too bad all the queers don't make it there.

QUEENIE   *to the GUARD*   Now he wants a private room. Take him away, Nurse!

GUARD   Okay you two! Turn off the vaudeville. You'll get your chance to do your number at the Christmas concert.

He exits.

QUEENIE   The Dolly Sisters! After you got your royal uniform, in the delousing room, did Bad Bess challenge you to a duel?

SMITTY   Who?

QUEENIE   Little Sergeant Gritt—that chalk-faced, pea-eyed squirt in the rimless goggles! He's always goin' on about the "Days of Empire" and "God and Country" and all suchlike Bronco Bullcrap.

SMITTY   Oh, yes! He did most of the talking.

QUEENIE   That's our Cockney cunt—never closes her hole. Didn't he want you to square off for fisticuffs, old chap? Sporting chance an' all that stale roast beef an' Yorkshire pudding?

SMITTY   Well, he did say he'd been boxing champion at some school in England, and that, if any of us thought we were tough, this was our chance to prove it—man to man, with no interference.

QUEENIE   Yeah—that's his usual pitch. Corny, ain't it? It makes him feel harder than those stone lions out front o' Buckingham Palace. Yellow-bellied little rat! When he's outa that uniform, he's scared to death o' any eleven-year-old kid he meets on the street. Did his Lordship get any challengers?

SMITTY   Well, no! I wasn't surprised at that. I felt sure it was just a way of letting the prisoners know who's boss.

QUEENIE   I must say—you ain't exactly a idiot.

ROCKY   One o' these farty Fridays, he's gonna get it good, from some guy faster'n that goddam Indian.

QUEENIE   How stupid kin a Iroquois be? Imagine this jerky Indian from Timmins, takin' that fish-faced little potato chip at his word. The only one ever took the chance—far as I know.

SMITTY   He'd have to have a lot of guts.

QUEENIE   Oh yeah—and they showed them to him fast. He was a brave brave all right—an' stupid as a dead buffalo. The second he an' Bad Bess squared off at each other, two guards jumped Big Chief Running Blood, an' the three British bully boys beat the roaring piss outa him. Heroes all!

ROCKY   What a mess they made o' that squaw-banger!

QUEENIE   You couldn't exactly put that profile on a coin no more—not even a cheap little copper. Oh, well—let's look on the bright side o' the penny; he's in pretty good shape for the shape he's in. After all, he got a free nose-bob an' can pass for a pale nigger now. A darkie can get a better job 'n a redskin any day.

ROCKY   Whoever heard of a Indian what worked? They git government relief.

QUEENIE   Howdya think he got here, Moronia? He was one o' them featherheads from Matachewan Reservation, tryin' t' get a job in the mines. There was this great big ol' riot, an' the cowboys won again. Pocahontas' husband is up here because he tried t' scalp some Timmins cop. An', believe you me, that's the wrong way to get yourself a wig in that tin town.

ROCKY   An' you believe that crap, like he tells you his stories about how some stinkin' bird got its name? Jeez! Maybe you should git yerself a blanket an' become a squaw—you dig these tepee tales so much.

QUEENIE   I dig all kinds o' tail, pale-ass—except yours.

ROCKY   All Indians is screwin' finks an' stoolies, an' I woulden trust 'em with a bottle o' cheap shavin' lotion; and that Blackfeet bum probably slugged some ol' fairy in a public crapper, t' git a bottle o' wine.

QUEENIE   Always judgin' everybody by yourself! Tch! Tch! That's the sign of a slow con man, Sweetie.

MONA   *to new boy* What's your name? I'm Jan.

SMITTY   Smith.

QUEENIE   But you can call her Mona, and I'm Queenie.

ROCKY   Look at the girls givin' the new boy a fast cruise. Give him time to take his pants off, Queenie.

QUEENIE   So you can get into them, Daddy-O? Don't let him bug you, Smitty. He thinks he's the big rooster here.

ROCKY   You know it too. Welcome home, punk!

SMITTY   This is my first time.

ROCKY   Braggin' or complainin'?

SMITTY   Neither. It's just a fact.

ROCKY   Well, that's nice. You shouldn't be here at all I guess. Got a bum beef?

SMITTY   A . . . a what?

ROCKY   Crap! A beef! A rap! Whose cookies did you boost . . . your mother's?

QUEENIE   What the judge wants to know, honey, is what special talent brought you this vacation . . . are you a store-counter booster or like myself do you make all your house calls when nobody's home?

SMITTY   Neither!

QUEENIE   Rolled a drunk . . . autographed somebody's cheques . . . raped the girl next door?

SMITTY   No, and I . . . I don't want to talk about it.

QUEENIE   You might as well spill it, kid. I can't stand suspense. Ask Mona . . . she screwed all around the mulberry bush until I finally had to go find out in the office.

ROCKY   I coulda saved you the trouble and told you she reached for the wrong joy stick. Did you ever get one you didn't like, Mona?

MONA   *to SMITTY*   I've learned it doesn't matter what you've done. If you don't say, everyone assumes it's something far worse, so you might as well get it over with.

SMITTY   I just can't.

QUEENIE   OKAY Smitty . . . skip it! I'll find out on the Q.T., but I won't spill it.

ROCKY   Ottawa's First Lady! How did you do it, Ladybird?

QUEENIE   Well . . . I lifted my left leg and then my right, and between the two of them, I rose right to the top.

ROCKY   Of a pile of bull!

MONA   How long is your sentence?

SMITTY   Six months.

MONA   Same as mine. I have a few to go.

SMITTY   Does . . . does it seem as long as . . . as . . . .

MONA   Not after a while. You get used to the routine, and there are diversions.

ROCKY   That's an invitation to the crapper.

MONA   Do you like to read?

SMITTY   I never did . . . much.

MONA   Well, this is a good place to acquire the habit.

ROCKY   Yeah! Let Mona the fruit teach you her habits, then you can go and make yourself an extra pack of weed a week.

QUEENIE   She don't go as cheap as you, Rocky. We're tailor-made cigarette girls or nothin'.

ROCKY   I get what I want without bending over.

QUEENIE   Sure! You can always con some stupid chicken into doing it for you. How many left in your harem now, Valentino?

ROCKY   My kids wouldn't spit on the best part of you.

QUEENIE   Who's interested in a lot of little worn-out punks? I've seen them all hustling their skinny asses in the Corner Cafeteria, and if it wasn't for the old aunties who feel them up in the show and take them for a meal, they'd starve to death. Did you tell them before they left that you'd provide them with a whole bus terminal to sleep in when you get out?

ROCKY   After I smarten them up, they don't have to flop in your hunting grounds. They go where the action is and cruise around in Cadillacs.

QUEENIE   Yours, of course?

ROCKY   What I *take*, you can call *mine*.

QUEENIE   What a pity you couldn't get a judge to see it the same way.

ROCKY   You're cruisin' for a bruisin', bitch!

QUEENIE   Thanks awfully, but I'm no maso-sissy, sad-ass. I always kick for the balls when attacked.

He sings to the tune of "Habanera" from Carmen:

My name is Carmen,
I am a whore,
And I go knocking
From door to door.

ROCKY   I'll meet you in front of the city hall next Christmas.

QUEENIE   Lovely, but don't ask me for a quarter, like last time.

ROCKY   Since when did you walk on the street with more than a dime?

QUEENIE   After I stopped letting bums like you roost at my place overnight.

ROCKY   Cripes! You'll never forget you played Sally Ann to me once. When you sobered up and felt like a little fun, did you miss me?

QUEENIE   . . . Yeah—also my marble clock, my garnet ring, and eleven dollars.

ROCKY   *laughing*   Oh jeez, I wish I coulda seen your face. Was your mascara running?

QUEENIE   He's having such a good time, I hate to tell him I like Bob Hope better. So where did you come from Smitty . . . the big corner?

MONA   That means the city . . . it's a slang term. You'll get used to them.

SMITTY   I feel like I'm in another country.

ROCKY   What's your ambition, kid? You wanna be a Square John . . . a brown nose?

QUEENIE   Ignore the ignoramus. He loves to play the wise guy.

SMITTY   I'm willing to catch on.

QUEENIE   You will, but you gotta watch yourself . . . play it cool and listen to the politicians.

SMITTY   Politicians?

QUEENIE   The hep guys . . . hippos, who are smart enough to make it into the office. They get the best of it . . . good grub, new shirts and jeans, lightweight booties and special privileges . . . extra gym, movie shows, and sometimes even tailor-made cigarettes. Like to get in on that?

SMITTY   I don't smoke.

QUEENIE   Well for cripes' sake don't tell them. Take your deck of weed and give it to your mother.

SMITTY   My...

QUEENIE   Me, honey! Who else!

SMITTY   Oh! Okay!

MONA   Tailor-made cigarettes are contraband, but your package of tobacco is handed out with a folder of cigarette papers and a razor blade when you go for clothing change once a week...it's sort of a payday!

ROCKY   Listen to our little working girl. She works in the gash-house sewing pants together for the guys to wear. Her only complaint is there's nothing in 'em when they're finished.

SMITTY   Is that what I'll be doing...?

QUEENIE   No baby, you won't. The tailor shop and the laundry are especially for us girls. They can make sure, that way, we don't stray behind a bush. But I like the laundry since they made me forelady. It's a sweet act of fate because it's the only place in the joint where I can get Javex—to keep myself a natural blonde.

ROCKY   And it's easier to show your ass bending over a tub than under a sewing machine or a wheelbarrow.

QUEENIE   You've got a one-track mind, and it's all dirt.

ROCKY   My shovel's clean.

QUEENIE   I don't know how. Every time you get in a shower, you've got it in somebody's ditch.

ROCKY   Don't be jealous. I'll get around to shoveling in yours.

QUEENIE   Be sure you can fill it with diamonds when you come callin'.

ROCKY   You'd be happy with a fistful of chocolates.

QUEENIE   Feed the Lauras to your chickens at jug-up, eh Smitty?

SMITTY   Jug-up?

QUEENIE   Meals! Didn't they yell jug-up at you before you ate today?

SMITTY   I wasn't hungry. I thought the food would be the same as at the city jail, and it always made me sick after.

QUEENIE   Don't remind me of that sewage dump on the River. I think they bought that bloody old baloney and those withered wieners once a year ...and you could put up wallpaper forever with

that goddam porridge. Don't worry...the pigs they keep here are fed better than that.

MONA   Yes, the meals are good, Smitty. This place has its own farm, so the animals and vegetables are all raised by the prisoners.

SMITTY   I once worked on a farm, between school terms. I wouldn't mind if they put me on that...the time would go fast.

QUEENIE   That's the idea, honey! I'll try to wangle you a good go so you don't hafta do hard time. I got some pull in the office.

ROCKY   You'll have to serve a little keester to the politicians who wanna put you in the barn.

SMITTY   What?

ROCKY   But I guess you been in the hay before. Queenie's all for fixin' you up with an old man. You're ripe for tomato season.

QUEENIE   One thing about it, Rockhead. It'll be a hippy who's got it made, and no crap disturber like you that picks him off my vine.

SMITTY   I don't want to hurt anybody's feelings, but I'm not...queer. I've got a girl friend: she even came to court.

ROCKY   You shoulda brought her with you. I'da shared my bunk with her.

SMITTY   You don't understand, she's not that kind of...

MONA   It's all right, Smitty; he's just teasing you. Life inside is different, but you still don't have to do anything you don't want to, not if you—

QUEENIE   I'm tryin' to smarten him up, Mona, and you try to queer the play. Has sittin' outside the fence got you anything? At jug-up some punk's always grabbin' the meat off your plate and you're scared to say boo.

MONA   I get enough to eat. If anybody's that hungry, I don't begrudge it.

QUEENIE   And look at your goddam rags. They give you that junk on purpose, to make a bloody clown outa you. You ain't had a garment that fits since you come in.

MONA   I can fix them to look better at the shop when the guard's not looking.

QUEENIE   Well I like everything new. I can't feel sexy in rags.

MONA   I don't really care what I look like here.

QUEENIE   *sigh of despair* See, Smitty! I try to sharpen the girls I like and she don't listen to a screwin' word I say. I coulda got her a real good old man, but she told him she liked her "independence" if you can picture it.

SMITTY   I can understand that.

QUEENIE   Yeah? So what happens? One day in the gym a bunch of hippos con her into the storeroom to get something for the game, and teach her another one instead. They make up the team, but she's the only basket. They all took a whack, now she's public property. You can't say no around here unless you got somebody behind you. Take it from your mother . . . I know the score.

SMITTY   I'll have to think about it.

QUEENIE   Well don't wait until they give you a gang splash in the storeroom. Mona had to hold on to the wall to walk, for a week.

MONA   They won't do it to him. He doesn't look gay, and he's probably not here on a sex charge. They felt I had no rights.

SMITTY   That doesn't seem fair.

MONA   I didn't think so either. It takes a while to get used to the rules of the game, and I've made a few concessions since . . . just to make life bearable. One thing, Smitty; don't depend on protection from the guards, and don't ever go to them. You have to solve your own problems.

ROCKY   And Mona'll show you her scars to prove it . . . fink! Squealed to a goddam screw! Cut you up pretty good after that, didn't we, bitch?

SMITTY   But how could they get away with it?

QUEENIE   The usual way . . . it was an "accident."

SMITTY   Jan?

MONA   Everyone agreed it was an accident . . . including me. Be careful, Smitty!

QUEENIE   Now Mona's givin' you some smart news. There's only two kinds of guards: the ones you can use like Holy Face who brought you in—and the fink screws that go straight to the General. When you see one comin' give six so we can play it safe.

SMITTY   Six?

QUEENIE   Say "six" instead of "nix". . . a warning!

SMITTY   Oh, I get it.

QUEENIE   It's no game, Honey! They got a nice cold tower here with no blankets or mattresses on the iron bunks and a diet of bread and water to tame you. If that don't work, there's a little machine that fastens your hips and ankles, while some sad-ass screw that's got a rod on for you bangs you across the ass with a leather belt fulla holes, and some other son of a bitch holds your arms over your head, twisted in your shirt. They can make you scream for God and your mother before they let you go.

SMITTY   *aghast*   It sounds like the late late show.

QUEENIE   It's no Hollywood horror-vision. Ask Mona; she was in a fog for a month after.

SMITTY   Mona? . . . Jan?

MONA   I don't want to talk about that, Smitty.

ROCKY   No. She'd rather dream about it.

QUEENIE   She wakes the whole place in the middle of the night with those bloody awful screams— "Mother! Mother!" Crap!

SMITTY   *petrified*   You're only trying to scare me . . . all of you.

MONA   *gently*   No, we're not, Smitty . . . someone's always waiting for you to make a misstep. Please be careful.

SMITTY   I've heard of lashes, but I thought it was only in very special cases.

MONA   *bitterly*   They don't keep those little goodies because they have to but because they want to. Learn to look into their eyes before you stick out a hand.

SMITTY   Thanks, Mona. I'll remember.

QUEENIE   Well, now we're gettin' someplace. You see what a wise girl Mona's gettin' to be? She'll know the ropes better than me next time around.

SMITTY   Same thing happen to you?

QUEENIE   Well not exactly, but then I handle myself a little different. Mona's a girl who's gotta learn the hard way. I always see the trap before it springs. But then I have the advantage of early training. I was a Children's Aid ward, and shuffled around from foster homes to farms, to God knows what. I been locked in closets so my foster mother could drink and play cards unseen; I had farmers treat me worse'n their dogs, and I learned before I was twelve that nobody gives a crap about you in this cruddy world. So I decided to do something about it. Queenie looks after Queenie, and pretty good too let me tellya.

SMITTY   Sounds like you've had a rough time.

QUEENIE   Skip it! I wouldn't trade places with any soft son of a bitch who needs a goddam mother to tell it what to do and a lousy house in some phony suburb with home-baked pies, and a lot of chitchat around a kitchen table. I've seen what that does to people, and I hate them gutless bastards who go to work eight hours a day, to parties and shows the rest of the time, and walk around with their noses in the air like their own crap don't stink.

MONA   Queenie's never been able to find her mother. The Children's Aid wouldn't give the address because of her criminal record.

QUEENIE   Who wants it anyway? She's probably a pukin' prostitute somewhere, walkin' around the street with a gutful of gin. What dirty bitch would leave a kid before its eyes was open to be pushed around by a buncha bastards who only want some sucker to do the housework for them? I bailed myself outa that crap when I was lucky thirteen and found out somebody liked my body. I been renting it out ever since.

ROCKY But the offers are gettin' fewer and the rates are gettin' lower. Next year you'll be dishwasher at the corner lunch.

QUEENIE Listen, asshole, as long as there's houses fulla jewelry an' furs, this girl's hands will help to keep the insurance companies in business, and don't you forget it. It's you stinkin' pimps who better move fast an' get it made before your hair an' teeth rot out on the sidewalk. I'll wave at your bench as I ride past the park in my limousine.

MONA *seeing the GUARD approach* Six!

Enter the GUARD called "Holy Face."

GUARD Book-up! Okay Curlylocks, it's your turn to wheel the library around, I'm advised from the office, so try not to spend too much time visiting your friends en route . . . everybody's entitled to a book, too. Your pram's in the corridor.

QUEENIE Thanks Daddy-O, I'll save you a Baby Bunting book.

QUEENIE combs his hair in preparation for the excursion.

GUARD We have another nice little detail in the V.D. ward. A new patient just puked all over his cell, but he's too weak to mop it up.

MONA The poor kid!

GUARD Okay, beautiful. I figure even you might be trusted up there.

QUEENIE Always the little mother, but don't go giving any kisses till he's had his shots, Nurse.

QUEENIE exits into the corridor wheeling the library cart.

Cigars, cigarettes, vaseline! Everything for the home!

ROCKY Thanks, Captain! I was just about to bash their heads together when you made the scene. You saved me a trip to the tower.

GUARD It's temporary, believe me. You've been getting closer to it every day. Don't start brooding, Smith . . . that doesn't help in here. Get yourself a book or something before lights out.

SMITTY Yes sir.

ROCKY My, my! What a polite little chap. Isn't he sweet, Officer?

GUARD Lay off him Tibber, or I'll have you moved to a stricter dormitory. Can't you get along anywhere?

ROCKY Sure, outside!

GUARD Is that why we're honoured by your presence so often?

ROCKY Well the law don't like to see a smart guy get ahead. They want suckers who'll take a few cents a week, a row of brass buttons, and call it a living.

GUARD But we can walk home when the work's done without an armed escort. Think about that, big shot!

ROCKY I'm thinkin'.

He gives the GUARD a look that seems to make the GUARD uneasy.

You wanta stay nice an' honest—and keep it that way. Like, I mean next year ya kin take off wit' yer pension, ain't it? That is—if nothing don't go wrong.

GUARD Lights out at eight o'clock, Smith! Be ready for bed by then.

SMITTY Eight?

GUARD That's right. You're up at six. It won't seem so early when you get used to the idea that, in the evening, there's no place to go.

SMITTY I guess so.

GUARD Okay, Florence Nightingale—on the double!

He exits with MONA.

ROCKY Oh boy! That sucker's ulcer's gonna kill'im afore he gits the chance t' sit at home in a rockin' chair.

SMITTY He sure did look sick when he went out.

ROCKY He's sick an' he makes me sick. You ain't smart, ya know, Smitty!

SMITTY How come?

ROCKY Fruits always get ya in the deep crap.

SMITTY I don't know; I never knew any before.

ROCKY You ain't been around.

SMITTY No, I guess not.

ROCKY They'll screw you up every time.

SMITTY How?

ROCKY 'Cause they're all phonies . . . gutless; they're all finks.

SMITTY You sound like you've had experience with them.

ROCKY An overdose! But no more! I gotta get me one when I get outa the joint. I'm gonna break both her legs . . . then I'm gonna put a coupla sharp chicks out on the hustle for me. That's the real dough.

SMITTY You mean . . . women?

ROCKY Let me tell ya! They were fallin' all over Rocky for me to be their boy, but I latched on to this one homo first to make a fast buck. Took him for everything he had . . . almost!

SMITTY   The homo?

ROCKY   Fag!

SMITTY   Oh—queer.

ROCKY   More money than bloody brains! Crazy about me! Old man's a big shot millionaire—stock exchange, race horses—the whole bit, but his one son was real fruit. It took some connin', but I got in solid...weekly allowance, swell apartment, lotsa booze and company and a Cadillac convertible.

SMITTY   All yours?

ROCKY   Except the heap! That's how she got me. I was browned off with the freak and split. Sold the works...television set, cut-glass decanters and whisky glasses, paintin's and statoos...all that crap! I split in the Caddy with a roll would choke an elephant an' had me a ball...hotel rooms an' motels from Montreal to Windsor....Forty-two Street, Frisco...dames, cards, booze! Man, was I livin' high!

SMITTY   Money run out?

ROCKY   Hell no! When ya got it, ya can always make it, but that fruit had the brass to call the bulls and get me picked up for takin' the Caddy.

SMITTY   Because it wasn't yours?

ROCKY   What I take is mine—that's my motto. But these queers always like one string to keep ya in line. This bastard kept the car in her name so she could screw me up when the time came.

SMITTY   So he...she laid a charge?

ROCKY   Hell, no! She wanted me back, that's all! We agreed on a story to cover all the crap stirred up, but her old man and the bulls stepped in anyways and fixed me good. They tried to throw the book at me. Now, I'm gonna fix her, an' when I'm finished she won't be able to cruise no more little boys for about a year, except out a window or on a stretcher!

SMITTY   If you do that, maybe they'll send you back again.

ROCKY   You sure are dumb. After you do a job, like I'm gonna, on somebody, they're scared crapless ...glad to give ya both sides o' the street. Never let a fruit scare ya...the cops don't like them either, so underneath they're yellow as a broken egg. Don't ever forget that.

SMITTY   I'll remember.

ROCKY   Ya know, I could make a real sharp guy outa you. Ya got a head an' ya don't shoot your mouth too much.

SMITTY   I don't know too much.

ROCKY   You'll learn, kid! You'll learn. Listen to old Rocky an' you'll get to sit on the sunny side of the yard. See...I'm in this dormitory because I raise

hell a bit. That's why they put me with these two fruits—to watch me. But there's bigger an' better dorms with more guys, an' that's where I'll be goin' back to...an' so could you, if you play along with Rocky.

SMITTY   How do you mean?

ROCKY   Well ya gotta have a buddy, see? Ya can't get chummy with the whole joint, an' specially no fruits. If ya get that name, your ass is cooked when you get to a good dorm. Why d'ya think I give 'em a hard time here? If you're smart, you'll do the same thing. There's real guys in some corridors, so ya wanna keep your nose clean.

SMITTY   I sure don't want anybody to think I'm queer.

ROCKY   Good! That's what I like t' hear.

SMITTY   Why would they put me in this particular dormitory, I wonder? To watch me, too?

ROCKY   Ya musta done somethin' goofy before your bit here...took a poke at a copper or somethin' like that. They won't leave ya here if Rocky can swing somethin' for us. The other blocks are probably filled up, but we'll be movin' soon. Would you go for that, kid?

SMITTY   Maybe it would be better.

ROCKY   Stick with the Rock an' you'll be looked up at. That ain't easy in the joint. Every jerk's lookin' for your jelly-spot. I didn't get the name I got by takin' it off these goons. Even the screws step easy on me. See how I talk to Holy Face? His blood turns to crap around Rocky.

SMITTY   He doesn't seem to stop you too much.

ROCKY   Nobody stops this boy. Besides I got somethin' on Holy Face. I'll tell you if you make up your mind who your buddy's gonna be. Remember what happened to Mona. You're sittin' duck for a gang splash if ya ain't got a old man. I'm offerin' to be your old man, kid, an' if you're wise you'll think fast. Whadda ya say?

SMITTY   Would it keep me from...what happened to Mona...in the storeroom?

ROCKY   Ya wouldn't want all those goons to pile on ya, would ya now?

SMITTY   No...for God's sake, no!

ROCKY   Am I your old man then?

SMITTY   Like...a buddy, you mean?

ROCKY   Sure, that's the score. I'll kill any son of a bitch lays a hand on ya.

SMITTY   Okay...and...thanks!

ROCKY   *tossing* SMITTY *his cigarette lighter*   Here's a firebox for ya, kid. Keep it! We're gonna get along good, Smitty. Ya wanna know what I got on Holy Face?

SMITTY   Well, sure!

ROCKY   He took a pigeon outa the joint for a pal o' mine, so I know all about it, an' he knows I got the goods on him. I throw him a hint every once in a while when he thinks he's gonna push me around.

SMITTY   A pigeon?

ROCKY   A letter...a message! Jailbird lingo for stuff that ain't allowed— *with a confiding wink* like a punk kid is a chicken an' if he gives ya a kiss, that's a bluebird. Everythin' you write's gotta go through a censor in the office, but if ya got somethin' goin' for ya, ya can allays buy some screw. One o' my buddies gave Holy Face fifty bucks t' get a pigeon out for him. That's about as much dough as a lousy screw makes in a week, an' Holy Face ain't so holy as he acts when it comes to makin' hisself a buck.

SMITTY   But there's no money in here. They kept mine at the office.

ROCKY   You're green, kid. There's all kinds of lines goin' around the joint.

SMITTY   But how?

ROCKY   Easy! Some relative calls in for a Sunday visit, slips Holy Face the dough, an' next chance he's got, he divvies up, takes out his half-C note and posts your pigeon.

SMITTY   Why not get the relatives to take a message for nothing?

ROCKY   There's things some relatives won't do. This was a junk deal...dope...big-time stuff!

SMITTY   What kind of excuse could you give to ask fifty dollars from a relative...here?

ROCKY   Plenty! Tell 'em the meals are crap an' cash could get ya candy, magazines, or nice face soap...some story like that. Say ya can only get stuff through a good-hearted screw who's takin' a chance for ya. Play it hearts and flowers...works good on most relatives.

SMITTY   I guess so.

ROCKY   So come on, baby, let's me and you take a shower before bedtime.

SMITTY   A shower?

ROCKY   Sure! I like one every night before lights out!

SMITTY   Go ahead! I had one this afternoon when they brought me in and gave me a uniform.

ROCKY   It ain't gonna kill ya t' take another. I like company.

SMITTY   Tomorrow, Rocky.

ROCKY   Right now!

SMITTY   No...thanks!

ROCKY   I like my kids clean.

SMITTY   I'm clean.

ROCKY   Get up!

SMITTY   What...

ROCKY   Get movin'...into that shower room.

SMITTY   Rocky, you're not...

ROCKY   I said *move*, boy!

SMITTY   No! I changed my mind. I don't want an old man.

ROCKY   You got a old man, an' that's better than the storeroom, buddy boy!

SMITTY   I'll take a chance.

ROCKY   I'll make sure it's no chance. It's me or a gang splash. Now move your ass fast. I'm not used to punks tellin' me what they want.

He grabs SMITTY's arm, twisting it behind the boy's back. SMITTY gives a small cry of pain, but ROCKY throws a hand over his mouth, pushing him toward the shower room. SMITTY pulls his face free.

SMITTY   Rocky...please...if you like me...

ROCKY   I like you...an' you're gonna like me!

Blackout.

Scene Two

Three weeks later, evening.

As the scene opens, SMITTY and MONA are lying or sitting on their own cots, each reading his own book. ROCKY can be heard offstage, singing in the shower room. QUEENIE and the GUARD are both absent.

ROCKY   *singing*   Oh, they call me The Jungle King, The Jungle King...   *shouting*   Hey-y—Smitty!

SMITTY   Yeah?

He continues reading.

ROCKY   *offstage*   Hey, Smitty!

SMITTY   Yeah, Rocky?

ROCKY   *offstage*   Roll me some smokes!

SMITTY   Okay, okay.

He moves, still reading, to ROCKY's cot, where he finds packages of tobacco, but no papers.

ROCKY   *still offstage and singing*   Oh, the Lion and the Monkey...

SMITTY   What you got there, Jan? You must have had thirty takeouts in three weeks.

MONA   It's a book of poems.

SMITTY   Any good?

MONA   Yes, but it's not exactly what I wanted.

SMITTY   I've got something better; well, more useful, anyway. Come here; have a look.

MONA   *after crossing to join SMITTY on ROCKY's bed* "Advanced Automobile Mechanics." Very practical!

SMITTY   I'm a practical guy. You see, I figure I might not be able to get a job in an office, because—well—bonding, and all that. You know what I mean. Anyway, I worked evenings after school and all day Saturday in my fath—in a garage. I learned a lot about car motors, so I might as well put it to use. Mechanics are paid pretty good, you know.

MONA   That's wonderful, Smitty. This way, your time won't be wasted. You can make your six months really tell, and then after . . .

ROCKY   *entering singing and combing his hair*   The Jungle King, the Jungle King. . . . Say-y! Whadya call this here scene—squatters' rights? Let me tellya somethin'—quick! In good ol' Cabbage-town, there's a li'l joint where me gang hangs out; it's called the Kay Won Cafe. Guess who runs it?

SMITTY   A Chinaman?

ROCKY   Wrong! Charlie owns it, but Rocky runs it. A pretty-boy comes in there 'n' I don't like his face much—me boys wait fer 'im outside, an' grab aholt his arms 'n' legs, an' Rock, who's welterweight champ 'round there, changes the smart guy's kisser a li'l.

SMITTY   You don't like your punching bag to swing too free. Your toughs have to hold him, eh?

ROCKY   I do things *my* way. There's another spot, on the roughest corner in town, called Eddie's Poolroom. Now—guess who runs it?

SMITTY   Eddie?

ROCKY   Oh boy, do you learn slow! Same story. Eddie owns the shack, but ya kin bet yer sweet billiard cue The Rock says who's behin' the eight ball 'round there.

MONA   *rising from ROCKY's bed*   All right, Rocky—I get the point.

ROCKY   Ya better see it, Pinhead—or I'll give ya a fat eye t' wear. Now beat it!

SMITTY   Leave him alone.

ROCKY   Oh, you ain't talkin' t' me.

SMITTY   Just don't touch him.

ROCKY   Whadya think he is—precious or somethin'?

SMITTY   Lay off, that's all.

ROCKY   How come ya talk t' me like that? Ain't I good t'ya kid? Don't I getya cookies outa the kitchen? An' rubber t' chew, off Holy Face?

SMITTY   You're so good to me—and I'm so sick of it all.

ROCKY   Now, now! That ain't a nice way t' talk, when I just bin fixin' it up wit Baldy t' git us in "D" Dorm. Ain't that whatya wanted all along?

SMITTY   Let's not overdo this "togetherness."

ROCKY   Sad—sad—sad! We-ell—I guess I'll just hafta 'range us a li'l extra gym, so's ya don't feel too neglected. The boys'll wanna meet ya before we move inta their Big Dorm. Tomorrow afternoon, Smitty? Get together wit de gang—just like at Eddie's or the Kay Won?

SMITTY   No, Rocky—no!

ROCKY   No what? No ketchup or no applesauce?

SMITTY   No—no extra gym.

MONA   Please, Rocky—we were only . . .

ROCKY   Shut up, ya wall-eyed whore!

MONA   I only . . .

QUEENIE is heard singing, approaching in corridor.

SMITTY   Six! Six! Forget it!

QUEENIE   *offstage, singing*
I'm a big girl now,
I wanna be handled like a big girl now;
I'm tired a stayin' home each evenin' after dark,
Tired a bein' dynamite without a spark . . .

Let me in.   *stamping his feet*   Let me in this cell!

QUEENIE and the GUARD called Holy Face enter, QUEENIE carrying a small, white, cone-shaped Dixie cup. He continues singing.

I wanna learn what homos do in Old Queen's Park. . . .

GUARD   I wanna learn what you do up in that hospital so often.

QUEENIE   I show the surgeon my stretch marks.

GUARD   I know it can't be only for that coneful of cold cream. I'll bet if I gave you a frisk, I'd find scissors or a scalpel tucked in the seam of your shirt. I oughta search you every time out.

QUEENIE   *throwing open his arms*   Oh do, Daddy-O! I just can't wait t' feel your big callous hands on m' satin-smooth bod-ee!

GUARD   I'd as soon have syphilis.

QUEENIE   Who's she? Any relation to Gonorita?

GUARD   Cut it! Let's have a little common decency.

QUEENIE   What's that—somethin' ya eat? Ya know, you're not well at all; the way you been belchin' and turnin' green around here lately. Maybe that ulcer of yours has soured into cancer, an' you'll never make that first pension cheque.

GUARD   I'll live to collect it all, and my stomach will sweeten considerably next winter, when I'm down in Florida—away from you bunch of bums.

GUARD belches loudly.

QUEENIE   Pardon *you*! Will the rest be up in a minute? Maybe if the Doc finds out you ain't fit to work, they'll fire ya. Part-pension won't pay the shot for Palm Beach.

GUARD   One thing—I'm going to find out what you do with all those gobs of goo from the dispensary. I suspect it's got somethin' to do with the backside of decency.

GUARD exits to shower room.

QUEENIE   How gross of you, Gertrude. No secret at all! I mix the cold cream with coal dust off the window sills, an' sell it to the screws for mascara. Helen Roobenbitch ain't got nothin' on me.

He exits to shower room. Sound of a slap.

offstage   Brutality! Brutality!

GUARD   *entering*   Next stop for that one is the bug wing. It might as well wear its jacket the same way it does everything else—backwards!

ROCKY   Take it an' tie it up an' don't never ever bring it back no more.

GUARD   Okay. Book-up time. Anybody want a trip to the library?

ROCKY   Yeah! I'll take a book o' matches—t' the works.

GUARD   Pyromania would become you, Tibber; you got all the other bugs.

ROCKY   It bugs me sometimes watchin' noses stuck into sheets o' paper day 'n' night. Ain't that right, Smitty?

GUARD   Keep right on reading, Smith! There's no safer pastime around here. Tibber never got past Super-Rat. Well—if that's it, I'll head for a smoke in the lock—

MONA   I'd like to go to the library.

GUARD   Again? You're there every time the doors open. Can't you wait for the cart to come around?

MONA   It won't have what I'm looking for.

GUARD   Cripes! If there wasn't bars on that book room, you'd be breakin' in.

MONA   Mr. Benson said that I could find something to do for the Christmas concert.

He shows GUARD a library pass-card.

GUARD   I thought Benson ran the orchestra. Why don't he get you to play the skin flute?

ROCKY   Yah! Yah! The Minnie-Lousy could give him lessons.

MONA   Mr. Benson's in charge of drama for the concert, too. I'm going to do something like that.

GUARD   Why don't you do "I'm a Big Girl Now"? Sassy-face in there could teach you the words.

MONA   I don't sing.

GUARD   Oh, hell! Come on, Hortense; your carriage awaits without.

MONA   Thank you.

SMITTY   See you after, Jan.

MONA   See you, Smitty.

GUARD and MONA exit.

ROCKY   *singing introduction to "I'm a Big Girl Now"*
Me 'n' my chilehood sweetheart
Ha' come t' de partin' o' de ways . . .

SMITTY   Oh, you're really funny.

QUEENIE   *entering from shower room singing*
He still treats me like he did
In our bab-ee days,
But I'm a little bit older
And a little bit bolder
Since both of us were three . . .

ROCKY   Put down that bloody book, kid!

SMITTY does so, and sits looking at ROCKY.

QUEENIE   *still singing*
I'm a little more padded
Somethin' new has been added . . .

ROCKY   I got best bunk in this joint; can see everything comin' at us down the hall. I wantya t' know I'm real particular who uses it. That thing don't sit on my bunk no more.

SMITTY   *rising*   That'll make two of us . . .

ROCKY   *pushing him back*   What's mine is yours, kid.

QUEENIE   An' what's urine is my-un.

SMITTY   Keep it! I only want what's mine.

He gets up again and goes to lie face down on his own cot.

ROCKY   Come again on them mashed potatoes.

SMITTY   You heard me.

ROCKY   Watchit! I warned ya 'bout the tomato sauce. Be a good kid now, an' roll me a smoke.

SMITTY casually rolls a cigarette, as though it is second nature to do so for ROCKY.

QUEENIE   And when you've done that, Cinderella—mop the floor, wash the windows, shake the rugs and . . .

SMITTY   Aw, cut it, Queenie!

ROCKY   Smitty likes to keep the old man happy, don't you, kid?

SMITTY   Sure!

QUEENIE   *singing to the tune of "Old Man River"*
Far far be it from me to free the slaves;
I'm not honest, and my name ain't Abe.
He just keeps rollin'—rollin' those ciggie-boos.

ROCKY   Yer name'll be mud if you keep that up.

QUEENIE   Queen Mud to you, peasant!

ROCKY   I think she's jealous, Smitty.

QUEENIE   Of what, for crap's sake?

ROCKY   'Cause me an' Smitty is such good buddies. Bugs you, don't it?

QUEENIE   I don't give a damn if you legalize it in church-up next Sunday, and have fourteen babies. It ain't green you see in my eye, it's red, 'cause I hate to see a guy who could be a hippo playin' bumboy to a haywire loony who'll get him an ass-beat or a trip to the tower before his time's up.

ROCKY   You're really askin' for it, ain't ya?

QUEENIE   I'd like nothin' better than for you to take a swing at me, rockhead. Then we'll see who's gonna be called mud!

ROCKY   I'll find a better way, and you can believe it.

QUEENIE   It'll have to be while I'm asleep, 'cause I can see your next move like you drew me a map.

ROCKY   How come you're so smart . . . for a queer?

QUEENIE   'Cause I get to bed bright an' early, and I'm up with the jailbirds—fresh as a pansy! We can't all be as dumb as you, Dora; it makes for bad publicity.

ROCKY   When you find me underneath, class me with you. For right now you call me Mister!

QUEENIE   How'd you like to say hello to your dear old friend Baldy in the office? He tells me he knows you from your first semester here, when you were chicken, like Smitty. I believe he gave your coming-out party, and made you debutante of the year.

ROCKY   I ain't interested in no old fairy's tales.

QUEENIE   May I quote you, or don't you want Baldy to pick you out a nice private room, where you can count your bellybutton and say your prayers, to pass the time?

ROCKY   Shoot off your mouth any way you want. Baldy an' me get along just fine.

QUEENIE   Yeah, he's got a soft spot in his head for you . . . except when he sees Smitty. Your sonny outshines you, it seems.

ROCKY   If he likes me, he's gotta like my buddy too.

QUEENIE   He does. Oh yes indeedy, *how* he does!

SMITTY   Why don't you two turn it off? What am I anyways, a piece of goods on the bargain counter?

QUEENIE   That's up to you, honey. If you smartened up, you could be as high-priced as you want.

SMITTY   I just don't want to be bugged, that's all. Let me do my time the easy way.

QUEENIE   Like the Mona Lisa?

SMITTY   What's Mona got to do with it?

QUEENIE   Well, she don't believe in wheelin' and dealin' either, and you see what she gets. You gotta hustle inside too, you know, or you end up like a chippy-ass, wipin' up somebody's puke.

SMITTY   I thought you were Mona's friend.

QUEENIE   I am, and I guess I like her 'cause she's different from me. But that don't mean a comer like you has got to settle for the crappy end of the stick. You could have it all your own way . . . by just reachin' for it. You can't park your keester in a corner 'round here.

SMITTY   I'm satisfied to sit it out.

QUEENIE   Okay. Play it safe, but don't be sorry later. Nobody'll bother you while you got a old man, but you'll be anybody's baby when he drops you for a new chicken.

ROCKY sings first two lines of "Jalousie."

QUEENIE   It's Catso-Ratso, your old gearbox buddy who's got the greenies. That Wop's gonna get you good.

ROCKY   No Macaroni scares me, sister!

Sound of metal door opening and closing at a distance.

VOICE   *at distance, along corridor*   Tower up!

SECOND VOICE   Tower screw!

THIRD VOICE   *closer*   Hack from Tower!

FOURTH VOICE   Holy Face with hack!

FIFTH VOICE   *nearby*   Who they after?

SIXTH VOICE   *next cell*   They're still comin'. Must be after Rocky!   *same*   Hey Rocky! What'd ya do now?

GUARD   *offstage*   Shut those goddam traps!

VOICE   *at distance*   Holy Face is a stinkin' lush.

On-stage cell inmates pick it up.

ROCKY   Beats his wife an' bangs his daughter.

QUEENIE   Not our Holy Face! He does it on his dear ol' granny.

GUARD   *offstage*   Who in hell said that?

A short silence.

VOICE *at distance* It was me, Sir—Gawd! Ain't you ashamed o' yerself?

General laughter from all voices along corridor and on stage.

GUARD *to unseen tower guard* Jenkins! Go get those bastards!

Sound of a heavy stick banging on metal doors, fading into distance—then silence. GUARD appears.

ROCKY *singing old hymn*
Rock of ages, cleft for me-ee
Let me hide meself in thee-hee—

GUARD *entering cell* That's just lovely—Tibber! I can hardly wait to hear the rest at the Christmas concert.

ROCKY Thanks, Cap! Bring the wife and kids. They deserve a treat for living with you all year.

GUARD I'd as soon see them into a monkey cage at the zoo.

ROCKY Fine sense of loyalty to your students, professor! Tch-tch. . . . You hurt my feelin's.

QUEENIE How do you think the monkeys must feel? Speakin' of monkeys, where in hell's the Mona Lisa?

GUARD I took it over to the library. It's tryin' to find some book it needs for a number in the Christmas concert.

QUEENIE I don't need no book for my act! What's she gonna do. . . read "Alice in Wonderland"?

GUARD I believe it's hunting on the Shakespeare shelf.

QUEENIE Oh no, who does she think she is. . . Bette Davis?

GUARD As long as it doesn't ask me to play Romeo, I couldn't care less.

QUEENIE "But soft, what balcony from yonder Juliet breaks. . ."

SMITTY Mona shouldn't try to do Shakespeare here. They'd probably laugh, and. . .

QUEENIE And what? Don't you think we could use a good laugh around this dump? Let her do it if she's fool enough. She'd be worse tryin' to do my act.

SMITTY But they might hurt her feelings. . .

QUEENIE Yeah? Maybe *you* should play Romeo. What do you think, Captain?

GUARD I suppose a little Shakespeare's all right. We've never had the classics before. Maybe it'll start a whole new trend in Christmas concerts.

QUEENIE Well, I'll stick to song and dance and a few bumps and grinds.

SMITTY *thinking aloud* But why?

QUEENIE Why bumps and grinds?

SMITTY Huh? No. . .no, I was thinking of something else.

GUARD Come on, Tibber. . .on your feet! They want you in the big office.

ROCKY What in hell for?

GUARD Well, I'm reasonably sure it's not to give you the Nobel Peace Prize.

ROCKY I ain't done nothin'.

GUARD I wouldn't know. I got a few dozen other characters to watch besides you. Make it fast. I've got to bring the Shakespearean actress back before lights out.

ROCKY Crap! Roll me some smokes for later, Smitty!

SMITTY Yeah! I'll try to keep busy so I don't miss you.

ROCKY and GUARD exit.

QUEENIE *singing first three lines of "I'll See You Again" after them* You don't smoke, an' you spend half your time rollin' smokes for that haywire goon. What's the matter with you?

SMITTY *dryly* We're "buddies."

QUEENIE I'd like to know how he got you to make a mistake like that! I had an idea when I first saw you that you're the kind of guy who'd like to be on top.

SMITTY Of what?

QUEENIE Of everything. You're no lolliflier—you don't have to play it the way I do. Whatever you're gonna be here. . .you gotta be it in a big way. My way, I'm happy. The hippos know I'm a mean bitch, so I got no questions to answer. But I'm nobody's punk, and you shouldn't be either.

SMITTY So what am I supposed to do. . .let you pick me an old man? How the hell would that make any difference?

QUEENIE You don't need a old man, you could be a hippo, if you play your cards right.

SMITTY So deal me a hand, and see if it comes up a winner.

QUEENIE Okay. Here's a straight. Rocky's nowhere near top dog in this joint. . .just a hard crap disturber who gets a wide berth from everybody. He ain't in at all, and as long as you're with him, you ain't either. If you get out from under Rocky, and I spread the news you're boss in this block, they'll listen.

SMITTY So how do I do it? Give him to some sucker for Christmas?

QUEENIE   Who'd take him as a gift? You could wrap him up, just the same.

SMITTY   I'm tempted. What would I use, crap paper?

QUEENIE   You ain't scared of Rocky?

SMITTY   Hell, no! I just figured he helped to keep me out of the storeroom. He said if I was asked to that party, I wouldn't be a guest, and I didn't like the idea of providing entertainment for anybody's wolf pack.

QUEENIE   So that's how he caught you . . . the cagey bastard.

SMITTY   You going to sound off about that?

QUEENIE   Not on your life! It wouldn't do me any good to broadcast how Rocky conned you into his nest. When I tipped you off to the storeroom gang splash, it was a cue to get next to the politicians who can do you some good. You shouldn't have give in so soon, or so easy.

SMITTY   Were you here?

QUEENIE   No, damn it!

SMITTY   Well, let me tell you, it wasn't so easy.

QUEENIE   Yeah? Can you go?

SMITTY   You think I didn't fight?

QUEENIE   So how come Rocky won?

SMITTY   With his mouth! Every time he said storeroom, I remembered about Mona, and my fists melted like candy floss.

QUEENIE   *excited*   You takin' a shower tonight?

SMITTY   I don't know. I try to make them few and far between. If I had a choice, I'd be dirty as a craphouse rat before taking a shower with Rocky.

QUEENIE   Take one tonight, and I'll give six. One thing about Rocky, he don't squeal.

SMITTY   What did you say?

QUEENIE   I'll . . . give . . . *six!*

SMITTY   Well! How do you think I should play it?

QUEENIE   You wanta be on top, don't ya? I ain't interested in no stars can't live up to their billing. If I put it out that you're tellin' me an' Rocky what to do, I gotta believe half of it.

SMITTY   I begin to read you. You want me to punch his head in. Right?

QUEENIE   Have you got what it takes?

SMITTY   All stored up!

QUEENIE   Then let it go.

SMITTY   In the crapper?

QUEENIE   I'll give you six in case Holy Face is hangin' around, but try and make it fast. Turn on a coupla showers to cover the slammin'.

SMITTY   You're on! Oh! Oh! Hold it a minute! What about after?

QUEENIE   What about it?

SMITTY   What will I owe you? You're not doing this out of sweet charity.

QUEENIE   Am I so hard to be nice to?

SMITTY   That depends . . .

QUEENIE   I mean . . . when you want and how you want—I'm nobody's old man, if you know what I mean.

SMITTY   It'd be a change, anyway.

QUEENIE   Whatever you want. You'll be top dog in this corner.

SMITTY   Six!

Sound of key in corridor door . . . enter GUARD and ROCKY.

GUARD   Slipped out of that one like a snake, didn't you, Tibber?

ROCKY   Sure! I don't let no finks hang me on the hook.

GUARD   You'll get caught one day, and when you do, I want to be there.

ROCKY   And here I thought you was my true friend.

GUARD   You make no friends, Tibber!

ROCKY   I got Smitty. I tell him everything . . . but everything, screw.

GUARD   That's his business.

ROCKY   Now, don't ya wish ya hadn't slapped me across the mouth three years ago, Mr. Screw?

GUARD   If I had to worry about every mouth I slapped around here, I'd be better off working as a wet nurse.

ROCKY   Well, maybe ya slug so many, ya forgot, but I ain't. It was my first day in the joint, an' I didn't call you "sir."

GUARD   You always were a nervy little brat.

ROCKY   So ya said, an' ya smashed me across the jaw wit' both sides o' yer big mitt, an' when I says, "Ain't y'afraid I'll tell the Warden?" ya says, why should ya be; twenty years ago ya smacked me father in the mouth, an' he was a thief an' a pimp just like me. Ain't that so, Hack?

GUARD   Yeah, that's it all right.

ROCKY   So-o, how's it feel t' have yer own arse roastin' over the pit—an' fer a little fifty-buck boo-boo?

GUARD   You bastard!

He exits.

ROCKY   Oh, how sweet it is. *laughing* See how I shake 'em up, Smitty old kid? *stretching out on his bed* Say, where's my weeds, pal?

SMITTY   Roll your own—pal.

ROCKY rolls a cigarette without taking his eyes from SMITTY's face.

ROCKY   Gimme a light, kid!

SMITTY   *tossing a lighter to ROCKY* Light on your ass!

ROCKY   *carefully* You two take a shower while The Rock was out on business?

QUEENIE   *coyly* I should be so lucky.

ROCKY   Smitty, come here. I'm gonna tell you what happens to jokers what try to give Rocky the dirty end.

SMITTY   I can hear you.

ROCKY   That phony Wop, Catsolini, finked to a shop screw on me, an' now he's all wrapped up in the General's office...wishin' he'd kept his hole closed.

QUEENIE   I thought good old Catso was your machine-shop buddy.

ROCKY   Think again. He mouthed off to the machine-shop screw I lifted his lousy firebox, so they hauled me up to the General, give me a quick frisk, an' when they couldn't find nothin', put the pressure on me. I took it good for you, Smitty.

SMITTY   For me?

ROCKY   Sure! Where d'ya think you got your screwin' firebox—from Ronson's?

SMITTY   But I didn't want the bloody lighter. All I used it for was to light your crappin' smokes when you ask me to come on like your butler.

ROCKY   Alla same, I took it good so's they wouldn't put you on the spot, kid.

QUEENIE   My hero! They make medals for people like you and Saint Joan.

ROCKY   Can it! One thing about it, old Catso's headed for the tower as sure as Christ made little apples an' his mother's ass. His Wop temper got riled up when the screws started shovin' him, and he gave old Sad-Ass Shriker a punch in the mouth. He sure picked the wrong target. Shriker's had a rod-on for that Wop a mile long. Shriker don't like no sissies, Micks, Wops, or Kikes, an' when he gets ahold of one, he's just gotta get 'em into the butcher shop so he can have his jollies.

QUEENIE   That's Mona's dearest boy friend...the one who slapped her little keester for her. I think she still dreams about him.

SMITTY   That's not funny, Queenie.

QUEENIE   Who says so? It gives me a laugh.

ROCKY   Six!

Sound of key in the door. Enter GUARD and MONA.

GUARD   Make way for the great Sarah Bernhardt ...or is it Heartburn?

He exits.

QUEENIE   Don't stand up; she's just passing through. No autographs, no interviews, no pictures, and please desist from climbing up on her balcony. Cripes! Look at the expression. She's takin' this tragic stuff serious. Pardon me, madam...do we perchance breathe the same air?

SMITTY   Leave her alone, Queenie. You look upset, Mona, what's eating you?

MONA   *trembling* I...I saw something awful as I passed the hospital door.

QUEENIE   Don't tell me one of the boys was havin' a baby?

MONA   Tony...

QUEENIE   *quickly interested* Catsolino?

MONA   Yes, he...

ROCKY   Cripes! Those screws musta really marked him up. That circus troupe he calls his family'll be cut off from Sunday visits while old Catso's walkin' around lookin' like a road map.

MONA   It wasn't just that.

SMITTY   What then, for God's sake?

MONA   The doctor was holding a stethoscope to his heart.

ROCKY   Maybe they wanted t' see if Wops has got one.

QUEENIE   I know what she means, an' so do you, rat. Some buddy you are to let him get it. See where Rocky takes his pals, Smitty?

SMITTY   What? Let me in on it.

QUEENIE   You wouldn't know of course. The butcher always tests your heart before he lets 'em cut you up in the kitchen.

SMITTY   What are you blowing about?

QUEENIE   There's a little room off the kitchen where they keep a machine an' a coupla long pieces of cowhide...only that torture chamber ain't for the dumb animals.

SMITTY   They're not going to...

QUEENIE   You're goddam right they are. You don't slug a screw in the chops an' get off light. Catso's going to get the cat-o'-nine- tails.

SMITTY   God help him.

QUEENIE   Shall we pray?

ROCKY   The only time you get on your knees, bitch, it ain't to pray.

SMITTY   Over a lousy little firebox . . .

QUEENIE   Ease off Smitty. It ain't your beef.

SMITTY   The lighter was lifted for me.

ROCKY   That ain't what he's gettin' a ass-beat for. I got no sympathy for a bloody fink. All squealers oughta be shot.

SMITTY   Because of me . . .

ROCKY   You're buggy . . .

SMITTY   *to MONA*   What are you doing that for?

MONA is standing close to the upstage bars at the extreme end of the wall, near the exit hall, poised in a position of straining to hear some sound from a great distance away. He seems completely occupied with the effort, unaware of the others in the room.

QUEENIE   She's listening for the screams. Sometimes the screws leave the kitchen door open, an' you can just hear from that corner. Once I even heard the bloody slaps of the belt. Musta been old Shriker swingin'.

MONA   Oh-h-h . . .

He does not seem to hear or see SMITTY.

QUEENIE   Oh, let her get 'er kicks. I think she's a goddam masochist.

SMITTY crosses to pull MONA from the bars almost brutally, but the boy does not seem to care; he only covers his ears with both hands, as though to shut out some sound.

SMITTY   *voice shaking*   What do you want to do that for? You trying to bug me? Make me feel guilty?

MONA   *dazed*   I'm sorry . . . I'm sorry.

He sits in a trance on his bed.

ROCKY   I'm sick of this crap. Come on, Smitty, let's take a shower. For some reason I feel real good tonight.

SMITTY   Glad to hear it!

ROCKY   Jesus! Don't tell me you're actual gettin' co-operative?

SMITTY   I am . . . tonight.

ROCKY   We-ll, it's about time! Give us six, Mona, if you can come outa that stupor.

QUEENIE   Don't bug her! I'll give ya six tonight.

ROCKY   When did you get so friendly? I had the impression you didn't exactly like us leavin' you alone, Mother dear.

QUEENIE   *sweetly*   Tonight I like it. I'll baby-sit.

ROCKY   I smell a sardine, or two.

QUEENIE   What are ya worried about, Rocky? You must have a guilty conscience!

ROCKY   I got no conscience an' no fat fruit worries me either. Come on, buddy boy.

SMITTY   You can call me Smith.

ROCKY   I don't care what I call ya as long as y' do like you're told. Now move your ass.

SMITTY walks into the shower room. ROCKY turns a questioning look on QUEENIE who smiles in reply like the Cheshire cat. ROCKY goes out to shower room and QUEENIE crosses to stand near door to corridor, without looking toward shower-room door.

MONA   *starting*   Something's wrong in there. What's that?

QUEENIE   Mind your screwin' business.

MONA   But Smitty . . .

QUEENIE   Can take care of himself. He's my boy now, and don't you forget it.

MONA   But Rocky . . .

QUEENIE   Is getting a lesson he's needed for a long time.

MONA   How do you . . . ?

QUEENIE   Because I can pick 'em real good, honey. I know a born hippo when I see one. I ain't spent time around these joints since I was fourteen for nothing. Smitty's got everythin' it takes to run his own show, but he needs me t' help him. I'm big-hearted that way.

MONA   There's no sound now . . .

QUEENIE   I said to make it fast. You give me six. I'm gonna check the damage.

QUEENIE goes to shower room, returning almost at once.

You still got that alcohol an' bandages I give you t' hide under your mattress?

MONA   You planned this—to get Smitty.

QUEENIE   Right where I can see him—like I got all the other suckers on this street.

MONA   He could have been caught—or killed. You're not even on his side.

QUEENIE   If he's got a side! Shut your nellie jaw, before I blind you, bitch—an' get me that goddam medicine bag.

MONA   Yes—I'll get it.   *He does so.*

QUEENIE   An' get ready to bow low, Miss Shakespeare. This block had a good queen; all it needed was a king.

He exits triumphantly, leaving MONA looking lost and alone.

Curtain.

ACT TWO

Christmas Eve.

At one end of the dormitory, ROCKY lies smoking on his bed; at the other end, SMITTY is propped up on his with a book, reading; the GUARD, Holy Face, sits on a high stool upstage, and a portable record player is going, the music filling the dormitory with something of a night-club atmosphere.

ROCKY Crap, Captain! The Christmas stunt is lousy enough, without havin' t' watch stinkin' rehearsals.

GUARD We could always arrange to reserve you a private room, Mr. Tibber. There's a vacancy right now in Gunsel's Alley...

ROCKY Screw off!

GUARD If you think this is any treat for me, guess again. I got a television when I want to be entertained. The tumblers and acrobats and what-have-you are using up the stage and gym floor, so the leading ladies will just have to practise here at home, with the family. You are what might be described as a captive audience. *walking toward shower-room door* Move it, girls...you're on! These critics of yours will be asleep before you get into those costumes.

QUEENIE *calling from shower room* Thank you, Mr. Sullivan. A little cruisin' music, please, while I remove my jock. I'll take it from the top...as we used to say at the Casino.

The GUARD crosses to reset the record, and QUEENIE enters, looking like a combination of Gorgeous George, Sophie Tucker and Mae West. He wears a platinum-blond wig, spangled sequin dress, long black gloves, large rhinestone jewelry on ears, neck and wrists, heavy make-up, and is carrying a large feather fan. There is no self-consciousness or lack of confidence: movements are large, controlled, voluptuous and sure. He throws open the fan, as ROCKY, SMITTY and the GUARD watch, bending his knees in a slow dip, so the tight gown pulls across his heavy, rounded body, giving the look of an overweight strip teaser beginning the act; slowly he undulates the hips forward and upward in a series of professionally controlled bumps and grinds, the meat and muscle of burlesque dancing. As the record plays the opening to a song, an old night-club favourite, QUEENIE prepares the way with these bold, sex-conscious movements.

SMITTY Holy mother of...you look sexy as hell. Look what we had here, and didn't know it.

QUEENIE It's all yours, honey—every precious pound.

He picks up the melody from the recording, a parody of "A Good Man Is Hard to Find."

Here is a story, without morals
An' all you fags better pay some mind
'Cause if ya find a man worth keepin'
Be satisfied—an' treat him kind.

A hard man is good to find
I always get the other kind
Just when I think that he's my pal
I turn around an' find him actin' like somebody's gal
And then I rave; I even crave
To see him lyin' dead in his grave.
So if your hippo's nice
Take my advice
Hug him in the shower, kiss him every night
Give him plenty oompah, treat him right
'Cause a hard man nowadays is good to find.

There is spontaneous applause, from even ROCKY and the GUARD, for there is an all-embracing extrovert quality to QUEENIE's performance that is somehow contagious, partly because of a warmth generated by a feeling that QUEENIE seems completely happy with himself and his surroundings.

ROCKY Come on, Queenie...give us another one...real lowdown and dirty.

SMITTY Yeah, Queenie...sing it for Daddy, and don't forget I like the wiggle accompaniment.

QUEENIE *like a famous star* Sorry, boys...that's gotta wait for the show. Get your tickets early, before the front seats are sold out. I wouldn't wantya t' miss anything headed your way.

SMITTY Throw it here, kid; I don't need a catcher's mitt.

ROCKY Turn that stuff on again, Queenie; I might get in the mood.

QUEENIE Put your gloves on, boys. We ain't got that much time before the show starts, an' this is more or less a costume an' make-up rehearsal. We got our numbers down already, but they didn't get these Christmas decorations in till today. Ain't this gown a flip?

SMITTY Fits like a second skin. What did you do...grow into it?

QUEENIE I hadda get Mona to shove me with a shoehorn.

SMITTY What you hiding under there?

QUEENIE Nothing, baby—but your Christmas box.

ROCKY I'll look after the diamonds for ya.

QUEENIE They musta took a chandelier apart to get all this glass. Feels good, but you couldn't hock it for a plate o' beans.

ROCKY   Looks like they shot a ostrich for ya, too.

QUEENIE   *waving the fan*   I hope it ain't moulting season in Africa.

SMITTY   You sprung those curls awful fast.

QUEENIE   My teeth an' my ass are my own, Honey!

GUARD   *caught in the mood*   If my wife could see me now, she'd start divorce proceedings.

QUEENIE   Never mind, baby; think of the beautiful music you an' me could make while she's in Mexico.

ROCKY   As long as you're spreadin' it around, Queenie . . . my pad's over here. Holy Face ain't got anythin' I can't better.

QUEENIE   *enjoying every moment*   What am I bid? Line up the Cadillacs on stage left an' the mink coats on the right. What's your offer, Smitty?

SMITTY   All I got is this book on auto mechanics.

QUEENIE   *with a wink*   Oh, that ain't all you got, Honey.

SMITTY   *laughing*   You've been peeking again.

ROCKY   Turn on the walkin' music, Queenie, an' give us the strip you did at the last Christmas concert.

QUEENIE   Are you kidding? I did a week in the tower for that surprise performance. I could hear the boys still whistlin', when they turned the key on your mother. Oh well, the bread an' water was good for my figure. I started the New Year lookin' like a cover off *Vogue!*

GUARD   No more surprises like that one, Queenie, or your concert days will be over. The conveners of this one had a hell of a time getting the General to trust you again.

QUEENIE   Oh, I told them how to fix that up.

GUARD   That's news to me. What did you do?

QUEENIE   I promised the General a little bit.

ROCKY, SMITTY and the GUARD laugh uproariously. At this moment, MONA enters, wearing a makeshift costume for Portia's court scene in The Merchant of Venice. It is a converted red velvet curtain and becomes him somewhat, but contrast between the graceful, almost classic costume and Queenie's glittering ensemble seems incongruous.

ROCKY   Flyin' crap! What's that supposed to be? Your bathrobe an' nightcap? What're you gonna do . . . "The Night Before Christmas"?

QUEENIE   *in impresario fashion*   Ladies and gentlemen, I want you all to meet Tillie—The Birdwoman, God's gift to the Tree People.

ROCKY, SMITTY and GUARD howl at the announcement, but MONA remains as enigmatic in expression as the painting he is named for.

QUEENIE   What kinda music do you want, Tillie . . . a slow waltz or a minuet? You'll never get those window drapes off the ground.

MONA   I won't need music.

QUEENIE   Well, you need something.   *proffering the fan*   How about these feathers? If you wave 'em hard enough, they might lift you up on your toes; you could call it "The Dying Duck" ballet.

ROCKY   Maybe she oughta have a window to hang herself in.

QUEENIE   You better not do a strip, 'cause you'd hafta have red flannel underwear to go with that smock.

MONA   It's from *The Merchant of Venice.*

QUEENIE   Well, I'd take it back to him, dearie; you got gypped, whatever you paid.

MONA   This costume is for the courtroom scene . . .

QUEENIE   Oh, I get it. You're gonna play a judge. That should go over big in this joint.

MONA   It's Portia . . .

QUEENIE   It's poor something.

SMITTY   *sober and fierce suddenly*   Cut it, Queenie!

QUEENIE   What's biting your backside, big boy? She oughta be able to take a little fun.

SMITTY   You go past the point where it's funny.

QUEENIE   When I want you to tell me what to laugh at, I'll write you a certificate of authority.

GUARD   *standing*   Okay, children . . . cool it! Or we cut the run-through right here.

QUEENIE   Let's have Miss Shakespeare's number. I'm sure Rocky and the other boys will just love it, especially the ones who write poems on the wall of the crapper.

SMITTY   I know the scene, Mona; we took it in high-school English. It's where Portia goes to court for her boyfriend. Isn't that the part?

MONA   *attention on SMITTY only*   Yes . . . it is the plea she makes in the name of human charity and . . .

SMITTY   *gently*   Mercy?

MONA   Yes.

SMITTY   I'd like to hear it again. Will you say it for me?

QUEENIE   Oh mercy my me!

The others move into the background, sitting on beds; the GUARD returns to his stool. They watch, as though at some amusing spectacle where one should not laugh but cannot resist. QUEENIE pokes ROCKY in the ribs with his elbow, then opens the fan over his face, holding it as a shield. ROCKY casually lights a cigarette and the GUARD yawns with indifference. Only SMITTY moves to hear MONA, looking into the serious, sad face.

MONA begins very hesitantly, stuttering (with comic pathos and badly spoken)—as the others giggle and roll eyes, etc.

QUEENIE and ROCKY interrupt MONA's speech throughout.

MONA   The quality of mercy is not strained,
It droppeth, as the gentle rain from heaven
Upon the place beneath: it is twice blessed;
It blesseth him that gives, and him that takes:
'Tis mightiest in the mightiest; it becomes
The throned monarch better than his crown;
His sceptre shows the force of temporal power
The attribute to awe and majesty,
Wherein doth sit the dread and fear of kings;
But mercy is above this sceptred sway,
It is enthroned in the hearts of kings,
It is an attribute of God himself;
And earthly power doth then show likest God's,
When mercy seasons justice.

QUEENIE   *to SMITTY, standing*   Down in front.

SMITTY sits and MONA strives to continue.

QUEENIE   *with finality*   Thank you!

MONA continues

ROCKY   Take it off.

QUEENIE   Put it on.

ROCKY   Ya dropped yer lunch.

QUEENIE   Encore!

ROCKY   Turn off the lights.

QUEENIE   Gee, you're pretty, lady!

ROCKY   Pretty ugly.

QUEENIE   Would you mind terribly—coming out of a cake?

MONA falters and seems unable to continue.

Oh, she doesn't know it by heart.

SMITTY   *turning to the GUARD*   Will you make them shut up?

GUARD   Okay. Good enough! The guys are waitin' and they won't know them words any better 'n you do. Let's go, Christmas dolls! Come on, Shirley, Dimples—and you too, Raggedy Ann!

QUEENIE   *grabbing MONA away from SMITTY*   Laws has muhcy, Miss Melanie—de Yankees is hyeah. Ain' you skeered dey gonna find yoah sissy brudder in dat closet?   *propelling MONA toward corridor and concert*   Run foh yoah life; all Atlanta am on fiyah!

They exit.

GUARD   *to ROCKY and SMITTY*   You bums get busy with a boot brush, and button up those shirt fronts. The General's wife and the Salvation Army are out there tonight.

He exits.

ROCKY   *shouting after him*   Yeah! I'll wear me best tie—de one wit' de stripes. Queenie's browned off with you, Smitty.

SMITTY   Who gives a screw?

ROCKY   Mona...maybe?

SMITTY   How come Mona bothers you so much? You got a rod-on for her?

ROCKY   I got something I'd like t' give all fruits, but it ain't what they're lookin' for.

SMITTY   Seems to me that Mona doesn't know you're alive.

ROCKY   Oh, the Mona knows I'm here all right, only it's too lily-livered to look.

SMITTY   For a joker who claims he doesn't go in that direction, it looks to me like you ride the train awful hard.

ROCKY   You tryin' t' prove somethin', wise guy?

SMITTY   I don't have to. You prove the point every time you open your trap...it snaps shut on what you are.

ROCKY   Don't ever get the idea I'm a pansy, punker!

SMITTY   Watch your words there, Rocky. I'm no-body's punker these days, or have you forgotten what the floor of the crapper smells like...up close?

ROCKY   I ain't forgot.

SMITTY   Don't make me remind you too often.

ROCKY   Y'use yer meat hooks pretty good, but that don't make you big time, Mister. Queenie tells me you're doin' a lousy little joy-ride rap. That's kid stuff.

SMITTY   It's big enough for me.

ROCKY   Ya didn't know yer ass from a hole in the ground before ya hit this joint here. It took me and Queenie t' smarten y' up.

SMITTY   I'm not interested in getting smart like you or Queenie. Did you get a chance to keep any of the stuff you got knocked off for? I guess not. And it must have taken a lot of Queenie's guts to smash a little old lady over the head for a closetful of diamonds and furs.

ROCKY   I'da got away clean if the lousy heap didn't run outa stinkin' gas, but Queenie screwed herself ...she hadda play the actress before sluggin' some old bitch, by standin' in the hall singin' Happy Birthday to cover up the screams. Too bad the next-door neighbour knew it wasn't the old dame's birthday, and called the cops. Crap! I'da gave my right eye to 'a seen Queenie's face when they put the arm on her with that load of mink coats and diamonds. I'll bet she was plannin' to wear 'em, like Queen Elizabeth, on Halloween.

SMITTY   So today she's wearing a neckload of cheap glass and singing her songs to a gymnasium full of pickpockets and petty boosters.

ROCKY   Well, I ain't in that class. When my bit's up here, my real old man'll be outa Kingston, and me and him's gonna hit the big time together. I guess a pun . . . *thinking better of using the term* . . . a joy-rider like you don't know who Tiger Tibber is.

SMITTY   Sure . . . I've read about your father . . . the high priest of pipe dreams.

ROCKY   But you wouldn't know what kinda cash a guy gets, dealin' out the junk.

SMITTY   Look Rocky. I don't give a crap what you and your old man do to get back here or someplace else. Queenie's always telling me what a big thing it is to pry open somebody's door or window, and you want to impress me by telling me your father peddles dope and your mother sells bingo to wine-hounds. Well, it cuts no ice with me. If I was to choose a racket it wouldn't be lousy drugs and cheap booze.

ROCKY   Well, ya better find somethin', buddy boy, 'cause y'ain't gonna be able t' git a decent job no more—maybe not even a half-assed one. Lookit Queenie! She wuz workin' the counter o' a Chinatown restaurant, after her first bit here. She wuzn't there two weeks when Seven-Foot Tiny o' the Morality Squad steps inta the kitchen t' scoff a free cuppa coffee. He catches sight o' sweet Queenie playin' tea maid t' all them tourists 'n' square Chinks, so sends down t' the cash register for the manager. He asks him does he know he's got a queer an' a thief workin' fer 'im. Dear Queenie, who planned on gittin' fat that winter, wuz out in the alley wit' the rest o' the cats—before Big Tiny finishes his bummy cuppa coffee.

SMITTY   So? Queenie made a try, anyway. It was probably better than selling bingo to wine-hounds. You pick your form of animal life; I'll find mine.

ROCKY   You keep my old lady outa it. When she was a big-time bootlegger she use'ta eat little boys like you for breakfast.

SMITTY   I can believe it!

ROCKY   And she still rakes in more dough in a day than you seen in a year.

SMITTY   I hope she saves it to pay her fines. They must love her at City Hall.

ROCKY   Can it.

SMITTY   You started this bomb rolling, big mouth.

ROCKY   That's what I get for tryin' to level withya about Queenie! She's bugged by you playin' nurse-maid to Mona.

SMITTY   I don't like to see somebody shoved around by a couple of yellow-bellied crapheads.

ROCKY   You tangled with Queenie yet?

SMITTY   I'm ready when it comes!

ROCKY   I got news for you. Queenie's in solid with the politicians. She keeps old Baldy fixed up with punkers, and he pays by takin' the jokers she fingers, and lockin' em up in Gunsel's Alley.

SMITTY   I'm worried sick; notice how my nails are chewed to the elbow.

ROCKY   You ain't done hard time till they make you sit it out in Gunsel's Alley. Y'eat, crap, wash, jerk an' flop . . . all in a lonely little six-by-six. It's real cozy if ya don't go haywire the first month. A couple goons smashed their own heads on the brick wall . . . wide open like eggs. They figgered they was better off in the hospital than locked alone in a cage, like a screwin' canary.

SMITTY   I'd sing all day long, if I thought I wouldn't have to look at your ugly map for the rest of my time.

ROCKY   Yeah? Well they don't let little Mona drop in for visits, y'know.

SMITTY   Let's take a shower, Rocky!

ROCKY   I'm nice and clean right now, thanks.

SMITTY   Well don't rub any more of your dirt on me, 'cause I'll get the urge to clean it off . . . on you. Dig me, punk?

GUARD   *entering with MONA*   Okay Hans and Fritz! Patch it up and come on to the Christmas concert. They've got a bag of candies and an orange waiting for you at the door.

SMITTY   Why aren't you backstage, Mona? It's about time to start.

MONA   They decided I shouldn't do any Shakespeare.

SMITTY   Who decided?

MONA   Mr. Benson said they would only laugh at me and make life more unpleasant afterwards.

SMITTY   Well come on and watch with me, then.

GUARD   No, leave it here! Whenever that one gets into an assembly, there's trouble. Last time it was at church-up . . . somebody split its pants down the back with a razor blade.

SMITTY   You wouldn't call that his fault.

GUARD   Look, Junior! If you had a bunch of hunters waving rifles around, you wouldn't throw a bird in the air, and expect nobody to shoot, would ya? It stays here.

SMITTY   This is Christmas!

GUARD   I don't care if it's the day of the Second Coming, the target stays here. Anyhow, it's got the whole corridor to roam around in tonight. The cell doors are all open, an' silly-bitch can go sniffin' around the empty beds for entertainment.

SMITTY   Isn't there a rule that says everybody attends the Christmas concert?

GUARD   You ask too many questions, Smith.

SMITTY   I thought you went by *all* the rules.

GUARD   *uneasy, as sometimes with ROCKY's words* Yeah! Come on, let's go.

SMITTY   I'll celebrate right here.

GUARD   Pick the kind of company you want, Smitty, but take my advice . . . don't get caught. Come on, Tibber.

ROCKY   Let's move! The concert can't be as corny as this act. So long, sweethearts.

GUARD and ROCKY exit.

In the distance, BOYS' voices can be heard singing a round of:

Row, row, row your boat,
Gently down the stream
Merrily, merrily, merrily, merrily,
Life is but a dream . . .

Sounds are from gathering in the auditorium.

SMITTY   I hate that son of a bitch, and I'm soon going to show him how much. Then, he'll know the shower of knuckles I gave him was only a baptism.

MONA   Rocky can destroy himself soon enough.

SMITTY   He ought to be squashed—like a bedbug.

MONA   What would you expect of him? Do you know that his father . . .

SMITTY   Hell, yes! He takes great pride in his parents—the famous dope-peddler and the fabulous bootlegger. He sure rounds out that family circle.

MONA   Before he came here, this time, his mother was sent to jail. She's been convicted so many times, the court wouldn't accept another fine.

SMITTY   My heart bleeds for the dear, lost lady and her deprived offspring. Who'll make the pancakes now and run the still?

MONA   Rocky's sixteen-year-old brother took over the bootlegging and began, besides, to sell his teen-age girlfriends to anybody who has five dollars.

SMITTY   Say! Outside, did you live near that slum?

MONA   No, I probably wouldn't have lived this long, or, at least, my nose would be a different shape.

SMITTY   How come you know so much about the rockhead?

MONA   I listen to him and read between the lines.

SMITTY   What a waste of time! That's their mess—not ours. I'm interested in you and me. You make excuses for them, but you keep your secrets, like Greta Garbo—under a hat.

MONA   You haven't said much about your life outside.

SMITTY   I'm forgetting, that's why—I'm going to spend the rest of my life forgetting my father. He put me here. To hell with him! Who put you in?

MONA   No one—really! It just—happened.

SMITTY   Happened? How can a thing like getting here just happen?

MONA   My life—like that from the start; I expect what comes.

SMITTY   That tells me a lot.

MONA   It's just that I can't . . .

SMITTY   So shove it, then!

MONA   A gang—of guys—in the neighbourhood—that night—pushed me around. My payday—had it on me—they knew. Next thing—I'm on the ground—kicking me—kicking. I look up—all those legs, but there's a big cop. Thank God! Thank God! Bleeding—numb—on my feet at last! Then—he looked at me, and I saw his sympathy shift—to the gang. Forgot my money—excited, asked were they mixed up with me—sexually. Smitty?

SMITTY   Don't get off the damn pot! Crap it out!

MONA   A—a huddle—like a football game—formation; all came out, laid charges—said I made passes. Four gave witness in court. Only voice for me—my poor, shocked mother, and sitting out there, trying to smile at me—eyes dark, afraid—God help her—my young sister!

SMITTY   But you should have had a lawyer.

MONA   Oh, I had one—or did I? Yeah—too late, after he got his money—we saw he didn't care—to tarnish his reputation. No real defense. A deal. Magistrate's court is like trial in a police station—all pals, lawyers and cops together! Threw me on the mercy of the court. Oh, Christ—that judge, with his hurry-up face, heard the neat police evidence and my lawyer's silly, sugar-sweet plea. So half-hearted—I wanted to shout, "Let me speak; leave me some damn dignity!" The fat, white-haired frown looked down on me— "Go to jail for six months!"

—like I'd dirtied his hands, and that would wipe them clean. Six months! Six thousand would have sounded the same.

SMITTY   Well, things are going to be a lot different by next month. There's a brand new year on the way.

MONA   How—"different"?

SMITTY   I mean, you're not going to be pushed around by anybody—goons, like Rocky and Queenie. They taught me more than was good for them. I'm on my way to being a politician, and I don't plan to do anymore hard time because of anybody. We've had it rough lately, but I'm about to even the score.

MONA   I don't know how that can be done.

SMITTY   Hell, kid! What I'm saying is we're going to wear the best of everything—new shirts, fresh from the tailor shop, and lightweight boots. We'll get extra grub—candy and fresh fruit— everything good that's going around. What do you say to that?

MONA   What do you expect me to say—about those things?

SMITTY   Well, for cripe's sake you might say "thanks." I'll have to. Or, "I like you, Smitty," or even—you might—

MONA   What's happened to you, Smitty?

SMITTY   I discovered I'm human. You're not blind. Who's been acting like your old man lately?

MONA   I don't have any old man. I thought you understood that.

SMITTY   You only think you don't. Look, Jan, when I came to this joint, I didn't know up from down. I've made a few mistakes since the one that got me here, and that's the only one I'm not sorry for. I stole a car—to get my mother out of town, away from my drunken slob of a father. I had to—he had the keys. I was helping her to run away with Ben— Ben's a nice guy. They tried to get me out of this jackpot, together, but I slugged a cop when they were arresting me. My dear father got back at us all. He didn't have a good word for me in court. After all, he was the respectable married man, a substantial citizen with his own business—the hardhearted bastard! Hard is a good word for him. He likes hard women, hard liquor, and hard words. For all he wanted from my mother, he might as well have hired a housekeeper and visited a prostitute regularly. Screw him! What I'm saying is you've got to work at it to make things go your way.

MONA   I can see you're not going to park your keester in a corner. Your father and Queenie have taught you well.

SMITTY   And I'm sick of that fat whore treating me like a piece of her property. I'll pick my own bedmate from here in. I shouldn't have to give you

all this jazz, you know what I need. Haven't you any feelings after all?

MONA   Yes—some, but not the kind you're getting at—at least, not with you.

SMITTY   What did you say?

MONA   I said—not with you, Smitty.

SMITTY   Saving yourself for those dirty bastards in the gym? Is that what you enjoy—being forced into a corner?

MONA   It's better that way.

SMITTY   Better? Are you playing hard to get or something? Because I know different; anybody who grabs you, gets you.

MONA   Slicings—patterns—blind and empty release; sure, I'll go on being a party to it.

SMITTY   Do you like that? I thought you liked me.

MONA   I do, Smitty—a great deal.

SMITTY   I knew you put up with what you got because you had no choice; that you really went for me. You showed it in a hundred ways, so now, while we're alone—a chance—

MONA   Just a minute! How do you feel with Queenie—afterward?

SMITTY   I could spit on her.

MONA   It would be the same with me; it's not in your nature.

SMITTY   I came to you.

MONA   No! Just circumstance! You're looking for a girl—not for me.

SMITTY   Do I smell or something? What's wrong with *my* body?

MONA   Nothing—it's very—Smitty, don't ask me to.

SMITTY   Should I ask you to do it with somebody else? Keep on being public property? I guess you like change—a different one every day, for variety. What do you do? Make comparisons?

MONA   I—separate! Yes, that's right. I separate things in order to live with others and myself. What my body does and feels is one thing, and what I think and feel apart from that is something else.

SMITTY   You're crazy.

MONA   It's to the world I dream in you belong. It endures better. I won't let you move over, into the other, where I would become worthless to you— and myself. I have a right to save something.

SMITTY   I was afraid of everyone—everything— except you—until now. You're trying to shake me.

MONA   You're trying to kill me. You think I can be used just any old way—even by you.

SMITTY   To hell with me then!

MONA   No—listen! It's the sight of myself I can't stand—the way you throw it back.

SMITTY   Where do you get the goddam gall to tell me how I see you?

MONA   The right to say or be anything or everything or nothing to myself—and not a tame little fruit. Wasn't that it—soft, worshipping, harmless? Now you've flexed your muscles and found power, I'm an easy convenience. Not a Queenie! Oh no; I'd never turn on you. If I mattered, you'd be afraid of my feelings—not sure of them. You're offering me—indifference. Well, I don't want it.

SMITTY   Did you think I wanted your body? You make me sick. I wanted some kind of reaction to me, and only because I'm caught in this hellhole, you filthy fairy! You cocksucker!

MONA   You see? You see?

SMITTY   *running to the bars*   Let me out of here! I'll go to the bloody concert—anywhere—where there's life—

He bangs wildly on the bars with his fists. MONA follows to stand behind SMITTY, puts out a hand gently, but not touching him, then with difficulty punches him on the shoulder. SMITTY reacts violently, turning on MONA.

MONA   No! Wait a minute!

He goes to SMITTY's bunk, picks up a book and holds it out.

Look—listen—you read it.

SMITTY goes slowly to sit beside MONA and begins to read, clumsily, haltingly. They laugh, embarrassed, and continue to read until they are in a slight hysteria of laughter that causes them to break up and fall against each other.

When in disgrace with fortune and men's eyes
I, all alone, beweep my outcast state,
And trouble deaf heaven with my bootless cries,
And look upon myself, and curse my fate,
Wishing me like to one more rich in hope,
Featur'd like him, like him with friends possess'd,
Desiring this man's art, and that man's scope,
With what I most enjoy, contented least;
Yet in these thoughts myself almost despising,
Haply I think on thee, and then my soul
(Like to the lark at break of day arising,
From sullen earth) sings hymns at heaven's gate;
For thy sweet love remembered such wealth brings,
That then I scorn to share my state with kings.

SMITTY and MONA are laughing, heads close together, when QUEENIE and ROCKY enter.

QUEENIE   I'll give the bitch a bluebird!

He smashes his fist into MONA's cheek.

ROCKY   Give it to the dirty little fruit.

SMITTY has leaped up, fists ready to swing. He punches QUEENIE on the jaw.

SMITTY   Screw off, bastard!

QUEENIE   *backing away, but preparing to fight*   I'll take the punk, Rocky. Put your boots to the bitch.

SMITTY turns to take ROCKY, and QUEENIE uses the advantage to put a wrestling hold on SMITTY, pinning his arms behind his back.

QUEENIE   I got him. Go, Rocky! Go!

ROCKY   *shaking MONA as though he were a rag doll*   I'm gonna smash your face, fairy.

He throws MONA to the floor, raising his foot to kick, but SMITTY breaks from QUEENIE, hurling the heavy blond to the floor, and kicks ROCKY in the groin. ROCKY screams, doubling over with pain. SMITTY then goes after QUEENIE just as the GUARD comes in, gun drawn.

GUARD   To the wall fast, or I cut your feet off.

All except MONA, who lies on the floor, move toward the wall.

Raise those mitts, children!

The three raise their hands.

Okay, crap-disturbers, what's the score here?

QUEENIE, ROCKY and SMITTY   *together*   That dirty little bitch. . . . The goddam fruit. . . . These filthy bastards. . . .

GUARD   Cut it! One at a time!   *to QUEENIE*   You, Goldilocks, what's your story?

QUEENIE   When me an' Rocky come in from the concert, that lolliflier on the floor was tryin' to make the kid here.   *wide-eyed*   We done it for his own good, Cap!

GUARD   Yeah! I can just imagine your motives.   *to ROCKY*   Okay, you now, Terrible Tibber! Let's hear your phony. Who were you saving?

ROCKY   Queenie give it to you straight, Cap; an' I'm stickin' with that story. The fruit was gropin' pretty good when we made the scene. We don't want that kinda stuff in here. You know how it is. Just turn your back an' that little queer's reachin'. . .

GUARD   Okay, turn it off, Tibber! Next thing you'll be telling me you want to go to church next Sunday to pray.   *to SMITTY*   All right, Romeo! Let's have your version of the balcony scene.

SMITTY   My name is Smith.

GUARD   Well, well! May I call you Mister Smith? Names don't mean a damned thing in here, sonny.

Actions mean everything. Did that thing on the floor make a pass at you?

SMITTY   Nobody made a pass.

GUARD   Oh, now, this isn't your mother or a judge you're talking to, Smarty Smith. We know by now a pass was made. I'm not asking you if you liked it. I want to know who made the pass.

SMITTY   Nobody made a pass at anybody.

GUARD   Real stubborn, aren't you?

SMITTY   You asked me. I can't help it that you don't believe me. We were talking when these haywire goons hit the block. They started the hey rube and I took over, since they seemed to want to play.

GUARD   You're not only getting too smart, Smith, you're becoming arrogant as well. Where do you think this attitude's going to lead you?

SMITTY   Into the office, where I can put an end to this crap.

GUARD   You're right . . . the General's office, where you'll need some much smarter answers.

SMITTY   I've got them.

GUARD   Your answers aren't worth much when you get hauled up on the big guy's carpet, kid.

SMITTY   Says you! Don't you think they might be worth about . . . fifty bucks?

The GUARD is stunned into silence. He steals a quick accusing look at ROCKY, who averts his eyes carefully.

GUARD   *shakily*   I don't think you know what you're talking about. What is this . . . some kind of bluff?

SMITTY   I don't say anything I can't back up with facts . . . like names, dates and letters. Dig me, screw?

GUARD   *enraged but cornered*   You crapping fink! Learned it all, haven't you? Found a way to save your precious little hide?   *to ROCKY*   I ought to shoot you a second mouth, Tibber.

ROCKY just grins in reply, now enjoying the GUARD's discomfiture.

GUARD   There's one hide's not gonna get off so easy.   *pushing MONA with his foot*   Up off your ass, you little pansy! You know what you got the last time this happened, don't you?

He pushes MONA ahead of him, toward the corridor door.

You can bend over all you want, in the kitchen.

MONA   *realizing*   No! Oh, no, no, no, no . . .

His protests mount to screams offstage.

SMITTY   *running to the bars*   Stop it! Stop it! I did it! I made the pass.   *shouting after them*   Do you hear? I made the pass . . . I made the . . .

QUEENIE and ROCKY begin to laugh in derision.

SMITTY   *turning vicious*   Shut up you yellow bastards! I'll wipe the floor with your rotten guts. One more laugh out of your ugly kissers and I'll spray teeth from here to hell.

QUEENIE   We didn't mean anything, Smitty. What are you so hot about? That little . . .

SMITTY   Shut your filthy hole, you fat whore!

ROCKY   Jeez, Smitty; that thing ain't worth . . .

SMITTY   Listen to me, Rock-ass! Before I leave this stinking joint I'm going to demolish your mug so bad that no fruit will ever look at you again . . . let alone a woman. When will depend on you. Ask for it once and you've got it. This is my show from now on. I got that lousy screw over a barrel, and I'm going to keep him there. Also, Baldy's making me a politician . . . a wheel in the office. You see, Queenie, I wasn't hustling my little ass in the park at thirteen for peanuts. I went to school; I got typing and bookkeeping, so Baldy's put me where I can make things move my way. If you'd learned to write, maybe you'd be better off . . . but you'll swallow chicken crap when I make up the menu. And you, monkey; would you like to be my punchin' bag around here or should I ship you into Gunsel's Alley for safekeeping? Choose fast!

ROCKY   I . . . I'll take it off you.

SMITTY   Okay. You'll volunteer to be my sparring partner in the gym every time I want to box somebody, and sweetie, I'm gonna knock you senseless. Now get into that goddam crapper and stick your heads into a coupla bowls till I yell for you to come out. That'll be after lights out, 'cause I don't want to see your ugly maps again today.

ROCKY and QUEENIE look at each other, dazed.

You know who Baldy is? You know what he can do? Well, I'm his boy now.

QUEENIE   Ain't it the bitter truth?   *pulling ROCKY away*   Come on, Snake-Eyes; we rolled too low in the game—this time around.

SMITTY   So move, goddam it!

He takes a step toward them. In their haste to get out, the two bump into each other, ridiculous and clumsy in their new roles. SMITTY laughs loudly, revealing a cruelty that fills the room with its sound. Suddenly his head turns in another direction as though just recalling something. He steals a quick look toward the shower room, then stealthily and lithely as a cat, he moves to the corner of the dorm where MONA had listened to the sound of Catsolino's beating. From an attitude of strained listening, SMITTY suddenly contorts in pain as MONA had done before, but there is no sound from his distorted mouth. He seems to be whipped by unseen strokes of a lash, until he is spread-eagled across the upstage bars. When it seems he can bear no more he covers his ears with both hands, stumbling blindly downstage. Standing thus, head and shoulders down, he rises slowly out of the hunched position to full height, hands lowering. His face now seems to be carved of stone, the mouth narrow, cruel and grim, the eyes corresponding slits of hatred. He speaks in a hoarse, ugly whisper.

I'm going to pay them back.

He then walks, almost casually, down to ROCKY's bunk where cigarettes, which we have not seen him use before, and a lighter lie on the side table. He picks up a cigarette, lights it, then stretches out on ROCKY's bed, torso upright against the back of it. Looking coolly out to the audience with a slight, twisted smile that is somehow cold, sadistic and menacing, he speaks his last line.

I'll pay you all back.

Light fades to black, and there is heard a final slam of the jail door.

Curtain.

DAVID FREEMAN (b. 1945)

At the age of seventeen David Freeman found himself at a dead end, sanding wooden blocks in Toronto's Adult Interfraternity Workshop, a job for which he was paid seventy-five cents every two weeks. Freeman had been born with cerebral palsy. As a spastic CP who drooled and slurred his speech and lacked coordination in his limbs, he seemed doomed to the circumscribed world of the severely handicapped. But his whole life had been a series of battles against heavy odds. By his own account, "When I was born, the doctor predicted I wouldn't last the night. When I lasted the night he predicted I wouldn't last the week. When the week was over, I wouldn't last the month. After a year, the doctor realized a CP could be damn stubborn." Before he was thirty Freeman would parlay that stubbornness into a career as one of the most dynamic young playwrights in the Canadian theatre.

Born in Toronto, Freeman spent his childhood in the Sunny View School for handicapped children where he was encouraged by a speech teacher to try writing stories. By sixteen, with the help of a special typewriter, he was able to type up to two pages a day with one finger. But when he left Sunny View in 1962 he was shocked to find that no one took his education or aspirations seriously. Instead he was expected to live off charity, filling his time with such therapeutic exercises as sanding blocks or sorting nuts and bolts all day in a sheltered workshop. Feeling patronized and belittled—"they tend to build a wall of tinsel between us and reality"—Freeman left the workshop after six months to look for work as a journalist. In 1964 Maclean's published his first article, "The World of Can't," telling of his frustrations as a CP victim trying to live a normal life in the face of misunderstanding and condescension. In further pursuit of that life, he enrolled at McMaster University in 1966, graduating in 1971 with a B.A. in political science.

Creeps had its genesis in 1964 when a CBC-TV producer asked Freeman to write a dramatic script based on "The World of Can't." But when it was finished the producer rejected it on the grounds that the characters were too unattractive for television. The script didn't re-emerge until 1970 when Freeman's old friend Bill Glassco, looking for Canadian plays to direct at the newly opened Factory Theatre Lab, suggested he rewrite it for the stage. As Freeman recalls in Stage Voices, "I found the rewriting of Creeps painful primarily because I lived it. I knew every inch of that washroom and every dream and fantasy, depraved or wholesome, that every one of those four characters had. This was because I happened to be every one of those four characters. . . ." Creeps became a major success for the Factory early in 1971 and an even bigger hit later that year when Glassco remounted it as the first production of his new Tarragon Theatre. It won the Chalmers Award for best Canadian play in 1972, and when a Washington, D.C. production moved to off-Broadway in 1973 it won Freeman the New York Drama Desk Award for Outstanding New Playwright. Since then the play has been frequently produced, recently completing a tour of Great Britain and a run of almost two years in Los Angeles.

Freeman retained a high profile with his subsequent plays Battering Ram (1973) and You're Gonna Be Alright, Jamie Boy (1974), both first successfully presented by Bill Glassco at the Tarragon, followed by productions across Canada. Neither, however, lived up to the expectations raised by Creeps. In 1976 Freeman's weakest play to date, Flytrap, was staged in Montreal where he has since made his home. With each successive work Freeman moved further away from the radical physical disabilities of the characters in Creeps to explore the emotionally crippled of the "normal" world, a realm of sexual frustration, alcohol and addiction to T.V. In his newest play, Scar, as yet unstaged, he imagines a post-holocaust future. But he has yet to recapture the power or three-dimensional humanity that made Creeps such a major dramatic achievement.

Freeman can hardly be blamed for his difficulty in writing another Creeps, for it is a very special play. Even the usually jaded New York critics found it an unforgettable experience—"like a punch in the mouth," wrote Douglas Watt in the Daily News—and their reactions have been typical. For Kevin Sanders on WABC-TV it was "the most harrowing evening I've ever spent in the theater." Edith Oliver of *The New Yorker* was left shaking her head: "There are people on that stage. Watching them is all but unbearable. I wish I could forget them, but I doubt I ever will."

The primary impact of *Creeps* derives from its two-fold naturalism. The play's dramatic conflict unfolds in the sordid washroom setting as the spastics fight among themselves and against the do-gooders whose "pityshit" degrades them and impedes their attempts at self-sufficiency. At the same time, and ultimately even more central to the play's potency, there is the conflict inherent in the characters' own bodies. Every movement involves an enormous physical struggle; every speech is an effort. In his prefatory notes Freeman suggests that *Creeps* not even be attempted unless the actors have access to first-hand observation of CPs' various physical problems. The realism of the presentation must be absolute, and the characters must seem grotesque, embarrassing, and even horrifying. Only in the full light of their disabilities, the ways in which they are not like us, do we in the audience get to experience the ways in which they are.

In contrast to its documentary naturalism are the play's fantasy sequences—the Shriners' visits and the carnival barker's "brain speech"—which not everyone has found effective. Walter Kerr for one, in his *New York Times* review, objected that their superimposed theatricality interfered with the "gut accuracy" of the play and impeded audience involvement. But in fact the black comedy of these scenes reinforces rather than undermines the horror of the characters' situation (in ways similar to the vaudeville routines played out by the parents of the brain-damaged child in Peter Nichols' *A Day in the Death of Joe Egg*). They are a further manifestation of the grim humour and self-mockery of the spastics themselves, the angry laughter that keeps them sane and alive.

Like *The Ecstasy of Rita Joe* and *Fortune and Men's Eyes*, *Creeps* depicts a repressive system whose agents (flat characters in all three plays) thwart the protagonists' desire for freedom and fulfillment. But the real thematic focus of all three plays is the *self*-imprisonment, the self-condemnation and self-destruction of those who internalize the system's view of them and thus become incapable of freeing themselves from it. The other two plays allow no exit for their protagonists; in *Creeps* at least Tom walks out the door at the end, perhaps echoing the liberating exit of Nora at the end of Ibsen's *A Doll's House*. Alternatively, we might be reminded of the ominous final slam of the jail door in *Fortune and Men's Eyes* as the lights fade on an unliberated Jim sitting dejectedly, while the triumphant Mr. Carson stands over him and the offstage voice of Thelma cries for a priest. That impotent cry, the refrain that runs through the play, is for help from outside the self, and on that score David Freeman is unequivocal. "The play was about freedom and having the guts to reach for it," he has written. "No one can give another person freedom."

•

Creeps first opened at Toronto's Factory Theatre Lab on February 5, 1971, and reopened in this revised version at the Tarragon Theatre on October 5, 1971. Both productions were directed by Bill Glassco and designed by Peter Kolisnyk, and featured Victor Sutton as Pete, Robert Coltri as Jim, Steven Whistance-Smith as Sam, Frank Moore as Tom, and Len Sedun as Michael.

CREEPS

CHARACTERS

PETE
JIM
SAM
TOM
MICHAEL
MISS SAUNDERS
MR. CARSON
GIRL, *"Miss Cerebral Palsy"*
2 SHRINERS
THELMA, *an offstage voice*

The actor playing the role of Michael also plays the Chef, Puffo the Clown, and the Carnival Barker in the three Shriner sequences.

SOME NOTES ON THE CHARACTERS' MOVEMENTS

Each actor taking a role of one of the characters with cerebral palsy is faced, as the character, with major physical problems, the practical solution of which is paramount to a successful rendering of the play. It is to be noted that there are many kinds of spasticity, and each actor should base his movements on one of these. There can be no substitute for the first-hand observation of these physical problems, and one might even suggest that the play not be attempted if opportunities for such first-hand observation are not available. These notes indicate the approach taken by the actors in the original production.

PETE: The actor in the original production developed a way of speaking that is common to many spastics. The effort required to speak causes a distortion of the facial muscles. The actor was able to achieve this by thrusting the jaw forward, and letting the lower jaw hang. Whatever speech problem is adopted for this role, no actor should attempt it unless he has an opportunity for first-hand observation.

    The deformed hand was not held rigid in one position. The actor used the hand for many things, keeping the fist clenched and employing the fingers in a claw-like manner.

JIM: The actor walked with his knees almost touching, feet apart, back bent much of the time, using his arms more than any other part of his body for balance.

SAM: Sam is a diaplegic, his body dead from the waist down (except for his genitals). He is in a wheelchair. The problem for this actor was to find how to make the wheelchair an extension of his body.

TOM: The actor walked with one hip thrust out to the side. Forward motion always began with the foot of the other leg, rising up on the toe, and then thrusting downward with the heel. His arms were held in front of him, his fingers splayed, upper arms and shoulders constantly being employed for balance.

MICHAEL: The actor always staggered, his head lolling, his body very loose, constantly on the edge of falling. He fell, or collapsed, rather than sat, and grinned most of the time. He too had a speech problem, very slurred, not employing the facial muscles like Pete.

SCENE

The play is set in the washroom of a sheltered workshop for cerebral palsy victims. A "sheltered workshop" is a place where disabled people can go and work at their own pace without the pressure of the competitive outside world. Its aim is not to provide a living wage for the C.P., but rather to occupy his idle hours.

SET

A men's washroom in a sheltered workshop. The hall leading to the washroom is visible. In the washroom are two urinals and two stalls. A chair is set against one of the stalls and there is a bench.

When the lights go up one of the stalls is occupied. MICHAEL, a mentally retarded C.P. of about eighteen, comes along the hall, enters the door of the washroom, and starts flushing the toilets, beginning with the urinals. He comes to the occupied stall and knocks on the door.

PETE   Who is it?

THELMA   *(An offstage voice. It is important that this voice be spastic, but that what she is saying always be clear)*   I need a priest!

MICHAEL chuckles to himself, does not answer. Meanwhile TOM has entered, walking in a sway and stagger motion. Having observed the game MICHAEL is playing on PETE, he ushers MICHAEL out, then sits in the chair up against the stall occupied by PETE. PETE drops his pack of cigarettes.

TOM   *disguising his voice*   Hey, Pete, you dropped your cigarettes.

Pause. A comic book falls.

Hey, Pete, you dropped your comic book.

PETE's pants drop to the floor.

TOM   *his own voice*   Hey, Pete, you dropped your pants.

PETE   That you, Tom?

TOM   Course it's me. Who were you expecting, Woody the Pecker?

PETE   Why didn't you answer?

TOM   When?

PETE   Didn't you knock on the door just now?

TOM   No.

PETE   Must have been Michael flushing toilets.

TOM   Doing his thing.

PETE   He wants to be toilet flushing champion of the world.

TOM   Well at least he's not like some lazy bastards who sit on their ass all day reading comic books.

PETE   I'm on strike. They only pay me seventy-five cents a week. I'm worth eighty.

TOM   You're always on strike.

PETE   How many boxes did you fold today, smart ass?

TOM   Oh, about two hundred. How's the rug?

PETE   Fucking rug. I wish to hell she'd put me on something else. At least for a day or two. It's getting to be a real drag.

TOM   Yeah, that's the way I feel about those boxes.

THELMA   I need a priest! Get me a priest!

TOM   *wearily*   Oh, God.

PETE   Old Thelma kind of gets on your nerves, doesn't she?

TOM   Yeah.

THELMA   Someone get me a priest!

TOM   Pete, I gotta talk to you about something.

PETE   Okay, shoot.

TOM   No, I'll wait till you're out of the can.

Knock at the door.

SAM   Open up!   *Pause.*   Who's in there?

TOM moves to open the door.

SAM   Come on, for Chrissake.

TOM   All right, hang on.

With difficulty TOM gets the door open. SAM wheels by him into the washroom.

TOM   Wanna take a leak, Sam?

SAM   No, I wanna join the circle jerk. Where's Pete?

PETE   In here.

SAM   Well, well, Pete is actually using the shithouse to take a shit.

PETE   Okay, Sam, knock it off.

Pause.

TOM   *to SAM*   How are you making out with the blocks?

SAM   Screw the blocks. You know how many of those fuckin' things I done today? Two. Do you know why? Because that half-ass physical therapist . . .

TOM   Physio.

SAM   Physio, physical, what the fuck's the difference? They're all after my body. She keeps making me do the same damn blocks over again. "That's not good enough," she says. "Get the edges smoother," she says.   *pointing to his crotch*   Take a bite of this.

PETE   *flushing the toilet*   She can be a pretty miserable old cunt at times.

SAM   All the time. How's the rug, Pete?

PETE   That thing.

TOM   I told him, he's never gonna finish it sitting in the john all day.

PETE   *emerging from the stall*   I've been weaving that stupid rug beside that hot radiator every day now for three months. And what has it got me? A big fat zero.

SAM   That's because you're a lazy bugger. You know what that stupid idiot who runs this dump says about you.

PETE   Yeah, I know. "Pete, if you worked in my factory, you wouldn't last a day . . ."

TOM   "But since you're a helpless cripple, I'll let you work in my workshop . . ."

SAM   "For free!"

PETE   And the government will give me a pension, just for breathing.

TOM   And the Rotary and the Shriners will provide hot dogs and ice cream.

SAM   And remember, boys, "If they won't do it . . ."

ALL   "Nobody else will!"

Blackout. Circus music and bright lights. Enter two SHRINERS, a GIRL (Miss Cerebral Palsy) in a white bathing suit, and a CHEF. They dance around the boys, posing for pictures, blowing noisemakers, and generally molesting them in the name of charity. The CHEF stuffs hot dogs into their hands. They exit, the music fades, the light returns to normal. The boys throw their hot dogs over the back of the set.

PETE   Sometimes I wonder how I ever got myself into this.

TOM   Good question, Pete. How did you?

PETE   Another time, Tom, another time.

THELMA   I need a priest!

PETE   What's this big piece of news you have to tell me?

TOM   It doesn't matter.

PETE   Come on, Tom, crap it out.

TOM   It's okay, forget it.

PETE   I postponed my shit for this.

TOM   That's your problem.

SAM   Hey, I bet he's gonna get laid and he doesn't know what to do.

PETE   Well the first thing he better learn is how to get undressed faster.

TOM   Very funny.

PETE   What's the matter? This place still getting you down?

TOM   Yeah, I can't hack it much longer.

SAM   Can't hack what?

TOM   Everything. Folding boxes, the Spastic Club, Thelma, the whole bit.

PETE   How's the art coming?

TOM   Didn't you hear me?

PETE   Sure I heard you. You said you couldn't hack folding boxes. Well I can't hack weaving that goddamn rug. So how's the art?

TOM   Screw the art. I don't want to talk about art.

PETE   Okay.

SAM   Chickentracks.

TOM   What's that?

SAM   Chickentracks. That's what you paint, Tom. Chickentracks.

TOM   I paint abstract. I know to some ignorant assholes it looks like chickentracks . . .

SAM   Listen, Rembrandt, anything you ever tried to paint always looked like shit warmed over, so you try to cover it up by calling it an abstract. But it's chickenshit and you know it.

TOM   You wouldn't know the difference between a tree and a telephone pole, Sam.

SAM   There isn't any difference. A dog'll piss on both of them.

TOM   And you'll piss on anything, won't you?

PETE   Okay, Tom, cool it.

TOM   Why the fuck should I cool it? This prick's attacking my art.

PETE   You shouldn't take yourself so seriously.

TOM   Oh, do forgive me, gentlemen. I took myself seriously.   *getting up*   I shall go to Miss Saunders and insist she castrate me.

He starts for the door.

SAM   Castrate what?

PETE   Where are you going?

TOM   Where does it look like?

PETE   Dammit, Tom, come on back and stop acting like an idiot.

TOM   Why should I? Whenever anyone tries to talk serious around here, you guys turn it into a joke.

PETE   Nobody's making a joke.

SAM   Look, Tom, even if you do have talent, which I seriously doubt, what good is it to you? You know bloody well they're not going to let you use it.

TOM   Who's they, Sam?

SAM   The Rotary, the Shriners, the Kiwanis, the creeps who run this dump. In fact, the whole goddamn world. Look, if we start making it, they won't have anyone to be embarrassed about.

PETE   Come on, Sam, there's always the blacks.

TOM   And the Indians.

SAM   Yeah, but we're more of a challenge. You can always throw real shit at a black man or an Indian, but at us you're only allowed to throw pityshit. And pityshit ain't visible.

TOM   I think you're stretching it just a bit.

SAM   The only way you're going to get to use that talent of yours, Tom, is to give someone's ass an extra big juicy kiss. And you ought to know by now how brilliantly that works for some people round here.

TOM   You mean Harris?

SAM   If the shoe fits.

TOM   You lay off Jim, 'cause if you'd had the same opportunity you'd have done the same thing.

SAM   So now he licks stamps in the office on a weekly salary, and he's president of the Spastic Club. Whoopee!

TOM *to PETE* Are you going to talk to me or not?

JIM enters and goes to the urinal. He is surprised to see TOM. His walk is slow and shaky, almost a drunken stagger.

SAM Here's Mommy's boy now.

Pause.

PETE Things slack in the office, Jim?

JIM Naw, I just thought I might be missing something.

SAM Oh you're sweet. Isn't he sweet? I love him.

PETE Cigarette?

JIM *flushing the urinal* No thanks, I'm trying to give them up.

SAM Shouldn't be difficult. Giving up is what you do best.

JIM Aren't you guys worried about getting caught? *to PETE* You know you've been in here for over an hour.

SAM Shit time. Push me into the crapper, will ya, Pete.

PETE Saunders won't come in here.

JIM She might, Pete. Remember Rick and Stanley.

PETE I do, but I'm not Rick and Stanley.

TOM Jim, that story's horseshit. Those guys weren't queer.

SAM *from the stall* Sure they were queer. Why do you think they always sat together at lunch, for Chrissake?

PETE I'll never forget the day she caught them in here necking. Screamed her bloody head off. *to TOM* Of course the reason she gave for separating them was that they were talking too much and not getting their work done. Right, Jim?

JIM says nothing.

No, Saunders won't come in here now. Not after a shock like that.

SAM Maybe not, but she might send Cinderella to check up on us. How 'bout it, Princess?

JIM Why would I do a thing like that?

PETE Then why did you come in?

JIM Is this washroom exclusive or something?

TOM It's not that, Jim. It's just that you haven't been to one of our bull sessions for a long time. Not since your promotion.

JIM I already told you. I just wanted to see if I was missing something.

SAM You are. Your balls.

Knock at the door.

SAUNDERS Jim! What's happening in there? I haven't got all day.

Silence. PETE and TOM look at JIM.

JIM Okay, so she asked me. But I didn't come in here to spy.

SAM Well move your ass, Romeo. You heard what the lady said, she can't wait all day.

SAUNDERS Jim?

SAM Bye-bye.

SAUNDERS Jim, are you there?

JIM moves towards the door.

TOM Wait, Jim, you don't have to go.

SAM Dammit, let the fucker go. His mommy wants him.

PETE Shut up, Sam.

SAM I wasn't talking to you.

TOM Why don't you stay for a while?

PETE Yeah, tell old tight-cunt you're on the can or something.

He grabs JIM and pulls him away from the door.

SAUNDERS Jim Harris! Do you hear me!?

PETE signals to JIM to answer.

JIM Yes, Miss Saunders, I hear you. But I'm on the toilet at the moment.

SAUNDERS What are you doing on the toilet?

PETE *at the door* He's taking a shit. What do you do on the toilet?

SAUNDERS If you boys aren't back to work in five minutes I'm reporting you to Mr. Carson.

She walks back down the hall.

SAM Once upon a time, boys, there was a boudingy bird, and the cry of the boudingy went like this . . .

TOM and PETE *in falsetto, forestalling SAM* Suck my boudingy!

Silence while PETE listens at the door.

JIM I could use that cigarette now.

PETE *bringing him one* Thought you were trying to quit.

JIM I am.

Pause.

TOM Jim, why did you lie?

JIM I did not lie. Saunders saw me coming in, and she thought I might remind you that you'd been in here a long time. That's all.

TOM Then why didn't you say so when Sam asked you?

SAM Because he's so used to telling lies, if anyone said he was spastic, he'd deny it.

TOM Will ya shut up, Sam.

JIM That's okay. Sam didn't care for me when I was sanding blocks with him.

SAM Pete, push that chair in here, will you?

JIM Now that he thinks I've gone over to the other side, he's got even less reason to like me.

SAM Listen, Princess, nobody likes a white nigger.

TOM What's that mean, Sam?

PETE *as he holds the chair for SAM* Why don't you use a bedpan?

SAM Why do you think, dummy? Because my ass begins to look like the other side of the moon. *By now he is off the toilet and back in the chair.* All right, all right.

He wheels backwards out of the stall.

JIM Well, Sam?

SAM Well what, stooge?

JIM What do you mean, white nigger?

SAM Well since you're so all fired fuckin' dyin' to know, I'll tell you. You finished high school, didn't you?

JIM Yes.

SAM And you got a degree?

JIM So?

SAM Well, you went to university. You wrote all that crap for the paper about how shitty it was to be handicapped in this country. Then what do you do? You come running down here and kiss the first ass you see. That's what I mean by being a white nigger, and that's what fuckin' well pisses me off.

JIM All right, Sam, now you listen to me. I still believe everything I wrote, and I intend to act on it. But you can't change things until you're in a position to call the shots. And you don't get there without being nice to people. By the way, what are you doing about it? All I ever get from you is bitch, bitch, bitch!

SAM I got every fuckin' right to bitch. You expect me to sand blocks and put up with the pityshit routine for ninety-nine years waiting for you to get your ass into a position of power? Fuck you, buddy! You give me a choice and I'll stop bitching.

TOM Now look who's taking himself seriously.

SAM *to TOM and PETE* What do you guys know about the bullshit I put up with? My old lady, now get this, my old lady has devoted her entire goddamn life to martyrdom. And my old man, you ever met my old man? Ever seen him give me one of his "Where have I failed?" looks? Wait'll ya hear what happened last night. He invited his boss over for dinner, and you know where the old bugger wanted me to eat? In the kitchen. First I told him to go screw the dog—that's about his style—and then, at the height of the festivities, just when everything was going real nice for Daddy, I puked all over the table.

TOM Charming.

SAM It was beautiful. Stuck my finger down my throat and out it all came: roast beef, mashed potatoes, peas, olives. There was a *real* abstract painting, Tom. You should have seen the look on his boss's face. Be a long time before he gives at the office again.

MICHAEL enters. During the ensuing dialogue he attempts to flush the urinals, but is stopped by signals from PETE.

JIM You know, Sam, you amaze me. You say you don't want to wait ninety-nine years, but you're happy if you can set us back a few. A stunt like that doesn't make Carson's job any easier.

PETE Okay, Timmy, you're not addressing the Spastic Club.

SAM Piss on Carson! He doesn't give a shit about us and you know it.

JIM I don't know it. I don't know what his motives are. But I do know he's trying to help us.

PETE His motives are to keep the niggers in their place.

SAM Yeah, by getting Uncle Timmy here to watch over them.

TOM *to SAM and PETE* What are you guys, the resident hypocrites? Look, no one twists your arm to go to those Spastic Club meetings. No one forces those hot dogs down your throat.

PETE Sure, we take them. Why not? They're free. Why look a gift horse in the mouth? But at least we don't kiss ass.

JIM No, you let me do it for you. *Slight pause.* But that's beside the point. The point is that Carson does care about what happens to us.

SAM He does?

JIM You're darn right he does.

SAM You ever been over to his house for dinner?

JIM Yes.

SAM Ever been back?

JIM No.

SAM   In other words, you got your token dinner, and now you only see him at Spastic Club meetings and here at the workshop?

JIM   That's not true. He comes to my place sometimes, doesn't he, Tom?

TOM   Yeah, but what about all those times your mother invited him for dinner and he cancelled out at the last minute?

JIM   So? That doesn't prove anything.

SAM   It proves a helluva lot to me.

MICHAEL pokes PETE on the shoulder.

PETE   What is it, Michael?

MICHAEL   Cigarette, please.

PETE   Okay, Michael, but smoke it this time, don't eat it. Last time everyone accused me of trying to poison you.

Banging at the door.

SAUNDERS   Boys! What's going on in there? If you don't come out this minute I'm coming in.

SAM   We dare you!

TOM   Shut up, Sam.

SAUNDERS   What was that?

PETE   Nothing, Miss Saunders. Sam just said, "We hear you."

SAUNDERS   Oh no he didn't. I know what he said. He said, "We dare you."

PETE   Well Christ, if you already knew, what the fuck did you ask for?   *to himself*   Stupid bitch!

SAUNDERS   Jim. What's happening in there? Are they doing something they shouldn't?

SAM   Yeah, we're pissing through our noses!

JIM   Cut it out, Sam. No, Tom and Pete are on the toilets and I'm holding the bottle for Sam.

SAM   Hey, that hurts! Don't pull so hard, you idiot!

SAUNDERS   *nonplussed*   Well hurry up, and stop fooling around. I can't wait on you all day.

She starts down the hallway, stops when she hears . . .

SAM   *to the door*   That's it, Pete, no more blowjobs for cigarettes! Jim, take your hands off me, I've only got one! Michael, don't use your teeth! Christ, I've never seen so many queers in one place. I could open a fruit stand!

SAUNDERS listens, horrified, then runs off down the hall. MICHAEL sits on the floor and begins to eat the cigarette. The laughter subsides.

PETE   I think she left.

Pause.

TOM   Do I finally get to say something?

PETE   Oh yeah, where were we? You couldn't hack folding boxes.

TOM   Or the Spastic Club.

PETE   Or the Spastic Club.

TOM   Or Thelma.

PETE   Or Thelma.

TOM   Pete.

PETE   What's the matter now?

TOM   Cochran, for once in your life, will you be serious?

PETE   I'm fucking serious.

SAM   It's the only way to fuck.

PETE   If I was any more serious, I'd be dead. I wish to hell you'd get on with it, Tom.

Pause.

TOM   You guys ever read a story called "Premature Burial"?

SAM and JIM shake their heads.

PETE   What comic was it in?

TOM   Edgar Allan Poe.

PETE   Oh.

TOM   Anyway, it's about this guy who has this sickness that puts him into a coma every so often. And he's scared as hell someone's going to mistake him and bury him alive. Well, that's the way I feel about this workshop. It's like I'm at the bottom of a grave yelling "I'm alive! I am alive!" But they don't hear me. They just keep shovelling in the dirt.

THELMA   I need a priest!

JIM   Tom, if you really feel that way, you ought to talk to Carson.

TOM   Oh, fuck off.

JIM   He's not an idiot, you know.

PETE   Tom, you want to know what I think? I think you should stop reading junk like Edgar Allen Poe. You take that stuff too seriously.

SAM   Pete's right. You should stick to your regular diet.

TOM   What's that crack supposed to mean?

SAM   It's sticking out of your back pocket, sexy.

TOM   *reaching round, removing a book from his pocket, and tossing it to SAM*   Here, Sam, why don't you take it for a while? Maybe it'll shut you up.

SAM   *as he flicks through the book*   Hey, he's got the dirty parts underlined in red.

PETE   Read some.

SAM   *reading*   "Nothing like a nice yellow banana," she said aloud. It touched every sensitive area of her pussy. Tears came to her eyes in shots of violent lust. Then her movements began to increase and she spliced herself repeatedly...

TOM   That's enough, Sam.

SAM   The thick banana swirled in her cunt like a battering ram. She grasped it hard and shoved it faster and faster. Then she sat up, still gorged with the banana...

TOM   I said, that's enough!

He gets up and moves to take the book away from SAM.

SAM   *who has not stopped reading*   It hit high up against the walls of her wet cunt. She could move whichever way she liked. "Oh, shit, this is juicy," she said aloud. The reflection she saw in the mirror was ludicrous and made her even more hot. "Oh you big banana, fuck me!..."

TOM grabs the book.

PETE   Wait. I want to find out about the banana split.

TOM   If you're so hot about the banana, you can have the goddamn book.

He gives it to him.

SAM   It'll only cost you a nickel, Pete, it's underlined.

TOM   Okay. So I get a charge out of dirty books. What does that make me, a creep?

SAM   Well, at least I don't pretend to be something I'm not. I don't work myself up during office hours.

TOM   No, you just do it at picnics.

SAM   What about a goddamn picnic?

JIM   Come on, Sam, you remember the Rotarian's daughter.

SAM   So I remember a Rotarian's daughter. What now?

PETE   She was sitting beside you and you were feeling her up like crazy, that's what now.

SAM   If the silly little fart is stupid enough to let me, why not?

JIM   You were making a bloody spectacle of yourself.

SAM   Love is where you find it.

PETE   Yeah, but with you working her over like that, I could hardly keep my mind on the three-legged race. Didn't she even say anything?

SAM   Nope, she just sat there. Smiled a lot.

THELMA   I need a priest!

Pause.

JIM   There's a girl who isn't smiling, is she, Sam?

SAM   Shut up, Harris.

THELMA   Get me a priest!

TOM   Ever since I've been here, Thelma's always calling for a priest. How come?

PETE   Sam knows.

SAM   Yeah, well mind your own business.

THELMA   Someone get me a priest!

SAM   *screams, overlapping THELMA*   Dry up, you stupid fuckin' broad!

PETE   Why don't you go comfort her, Sam? You used to be pretty good at comforting old Thelma.

JIM   Yeah, you couldn't keep your hands off her.

SAM   What's the matter, were ya jealous, princess?

TOM   Hey, I'd like to know what the hell's going on.

PETE   This was before your time, Tom. Thelma was all right then. Cute kid, as a matter of fact. Until old horny here got his hands on her and drove her off her rocker.

SAM   That's a fuckin' lie. The doctors said it wasn't my fault.

JIM   They only told you that to make it easy for you.

SAM   Look, it wasn't my fault.

JIM   What you did sure didn't help any.

SAM   Well why bring it up now?

PETE   Because we're sick and tired of having you put everybody down. It's time someone put you down for a change.

TOM   Well, what did he do? Will you please tell me?

PETE   From the day Thelma got here, Sam was after her like a hot stud. Being so nice to her, and then coming in here and bragging how she was letting him feel her up, and bragging how he was gonna fuck the ass off her soon.

THELMA   I want a priest!

PETE   Maybe you've heard, Tom, that Thelma's parents are religious. I don't just mean they're devout, they're real dingalings about it. Like they believe Thelma's the way she is because of some great sin they've committed. Like that. Anyway, she was home in bed one weekend with a cold, and Sam went over to visit her, and her parents weren't out of the room two seconds when Sam was into her pants.

SAM   That's another goddamn lie. It didn't happen that way.

PETE   Okay, so it took a full minute. Don't quibble over details.

SAM   Look, I didn't mean for anything to happen that day. What do you think I am, stupid? In the first place, she had a cold, and in the second place, her parents were out on the goddamn porch. I just wanted to talk. She started fooling around, trying to grab my cannon and everything. Naturally I get a hard-on. What am I supposed to do? Silly little bitch! We were just going real good when she changed her mind. That's one helluva time to exercise her woman's prerogative, isn't it? Anyway, we . . . she fell out of bed. In a few seconds in come Mommy and Daddy. They thought I'd fallen out of my chair or something. Well, there I am in bed with my joint waving merrily in the breeze and Thelma's on the floor minus her PJs, and all hell broke loose. You'd have thought they'd never seen a cock before. The old man, he bounced me out of bed along the floor and into the hallway. The old lady, she dragged Thelma up behind. Then they held us up in front of a little Jesus statue and asked it to forgive us 'cause we didn't know what we were doing.   *Pause.*   The doctors said it wasn't my fault.

JIM   They were only feeling sorry for a horny cripple in a wheelchair.

PETE   Yeah, but we all know the truth, don't we Sam?

SAM   *overlapping*   Why don't you shut the fuck up, Cochran!

JIM   Hey Pete, remember how Thelma used to dress before Sam put his rod to her? So pretty.

TOM   Okay, guys, knock it off.

PETE   Yeah, but that's all over now. Now she only wears black and brown, and everything's covered, right up to the neck.

JIM   She used to laugh a lot too.

TOM   That's enough!

THELMA   I need a priest!

MICHAEL   *sing-song*   Thelma needs a priest. Thelma needs a priest.

SAM   Fuck off! Piece of shit!

SAM goes for MICHAEL, who is sitting on the floor, and hits out at him. MICHAEL is surprised, but hits back. To stop the fight, PETE grabs SAM's chair from behind. SAM then lashes out at PETE. At the same time, JIM and TOM go to rescue MICHAEL. JIM falls while TOM tries to get MICHAEL's attention away from SAM. Throughout the commotion MICHAEL continues to yell, "Thelma needs a priest." Finally, SAM wheels angrily away and PETE helps JIM up.

TOM   *at one of the urinals*   Hey, Michael, look, a cockroach. Big fat one.

MICHAEL sees the cockroach and gets very excited. PETE, TOM and JIM gather round him at the urinal.

PETE   Hey, Sam, there's livestock in the pisser.

TOM   *to MICHAEL*   Why don't you use your ray gun and disintegrate it?

MICHAEL   What ray gun? I got no ray gun.

SAM   Yes, you have. That thing between your legs. It's a ray gun.

MICHAEL looks down and makes the connection.

MICHAEL   *delighted*   I disintegrate it. I disintegrate it all up.

He turns into the urinal.

SAM   You do that.

SAUNDERS returns and knocks at the door.

SAUNDERS   For the last time, are you boys coming out or not?

SAM   Go away, we're busy.

SAUNDERS   Very well, then, I'm coming in.

She enters the washroom.

PETE   Have you no sense of decency?

SAUNDERS   All right, I don't know what you boys have been doing in here, but I want you back to work immediately. Pete, you've still that rug. Tom, there's boxes to be folded. Sam, you'd better get busy and sand down the edges of those blocks if you expect to earn anything this week. As for you, Jim, well, I'm beginning to have second thoughts.

JIM   Yes, ma'am.

Pause. No one makes a move to go.

SAUNDERS   Well, get moving!

PETE   I have to take a crap.

He heads into one of the stalls.

TOM   Me too.

He goes into the other one.

SAM   I have to use the bottle.

SAUNDERS   And how about you, Jim? Don't you have something to do?

SAM   He has to hold the bottle for me.

SAUNDERS   He has to what, Sam?

SAM   Well, it's like this. I don't have a very good aim, so Princess here is gonna get down on her hands and knees . . .

SAUNDERS *cutting him off* All right, that's quite enough. When you're through here, I want you back to work. And fast. Michael, you come with me.

MICHAEL turns around from the urinal. His pants are open, his penis exposed.

MICHAEL *to SAUNDERS* I'm gonna disintegrate you.

SAUNDERS *screams* Michael! Oh, you boys, you put him up to this! Didn't you?

PETE We did not.

SAUNDERS Right! Mr. Carson will be here any minute. We'll see what he has to say.

She opens the door to leave.

SAM *calling after her* Hey, be careful. He's got one too.

More screams. She exits, and is seen running down the hall. PETE and TOM emerge from the stalls laughing. JIM tidies MICHAEL and sends him out the door.

PETE Sam, you have a warped sense of humour.

SAM Yeah, just like the rest of me.

JIM Proud of that, aren't you Sam? Professional cripple.

SAM Eat shit, princess.

JIM And such a sterling vocabulary.

Pause. JIM begins to pick up cigarette butts and matches, which by now litter the floor.

TOM Hadn't you better go before Carson gets back?

JIM The office can wait.

TOM What'll you do when he gets here?

JIM I'll cross that bridge when I come to it.

TOM Well, we'll all have to cross that bridge soon. We've been in here for over half an hour.

SAM Yeah, we do tend to take long craps.

PETE I don't care how long it takes me to crap.

Pause.

TOM Did you get your typewriter fixed yet, Jim?

JIM No, I haven't had time.

TOM Well, my dad's offer still stands . . . if you'd like him to take a look at it.

JIM Thanks, I would. How is your father?

TOM He's okay. Why don't you bring it over Sunday?

JIM I'll have to see. I'm kind of busy at the club. Christmas is coming.

TOM It will only take an hour.

JIM You wouldn't like to give us a hand this year, would you?

TOM What did you have in mind?

JIM I thought you might like to do our Christmas mural.

TOM No, I don't think so.

JIM Spastic Club's not good enough for chicken-tracks, eh? Seriously, Tom, I could use some help. Not just for the mural, but to paint posters, stuff like that.

TOM How much is the Spastic Club willing to pay for all this?

JIM Come on, you know there's no payment. All the work for the club is done on a voluntary basis. Carson's never paid anyone before.

SAM So why should the old fart break his record of stinginess just for you?

JIM It may interest you to know, Sam, that Carson doesn't get paid for his services either.

SAM Bwess his wittle heart.

TOM In that case, the answer's no. If I get paid for folding boxes, why the hell should I paint a lousy mural for free?

JIM I just thought it might keep you busy.

TOM I'm busy enough.

JIM gets up, staggers over to the waste basket and deposits his litter. SAM applauds.

PETE Jim, what's the Spastic Club planning for us boys and girls this year?

JIM Oh, we've got a few things up our sleeve. Actually, we'd appreciate it if some of the members were a bit more co-operative. So far the response has been practically nil.

TOM That's horseshit.

PETE What about my idea of having that psychologist down from the university?

JIM Well, since you're so interested, Pete, I'll tell you. Carson didn't think too much of it. He was afraid the members would be bored. I don't happen to agree with him, but that's the way he feels.

SAM What about my idea for installing ramps in the subway?

JIM It's a good idea, Sam, but that sort of thing doesn't come under our jurisdiction.

SAM Who says so?

JIM It's up to the city. We're not in a position . . .

TOM Okay, Jim, what does the Spastic Club have up its sleeve for this year?

JIM There's a trip to the Science Centre. One to the African Lion Safari. We're organizing a finger painting contest, that sorority is throwing a Valentine's Day party for us . . .

PETE Wheee! A party!

Circus music is heard low in the distance.

TOM What's the entertainment, Jim?

JIM Puffo the Clown, Merlin the Magician . . .

PETE And Cinderella, and Snow White and the Seven Fucking Dwarfs. Jesus Christ, Jim, Puffo the Clown! What do you and Carson think you're dealing with, a bunch of fucking babies?

Blackout, circus music at full and bright lights. PUFFO, in clown suit, has arrived, carrying balloons. Enter also the GIRL and two SHRINERS, the GIRL dressed in circus attire. She is marching and twirling a baton. One of the SHRINERS is wearing a Mickey Mouse mask and white gloves. He follows the GIRL, weaving in and around the boys, dancing in time to the music. The other SHRINER appears on a tricycle (or on roller skates, if preferred) waving to the audience. PUFFO presents SAM, TOM and PETE each with a balloon, and exits following the GIRL and SHRINERS. The music fades.

PETE Who was that masked man, anyway?

On a signal from PETE, the boys burst their balloons with their lighted cigarettes.

JIM Wait a minute, Pete, let me finish. We've got other things planned.

PETE Like what?

JIM Well, for one, we're planning a trip to a glue factory.

TOM You're kidding.

JIM No, I'm not. Carson thinks it might be very educational.

TOM What do you think, Jim? Do you think it will be very educational?

JIM I don't know. I've never seen them make glue before.

PETE Well, you take one old horse, and you stir well . . .

JIM We're planning other things too, you know.

TOM What other things?

JIM Well you know, theatre trips, museum trips. These things take time, Tom. We've written letters and . . .

TOM What letters? To whom?

JIM Letters. Lots of letters. They're at home in my briefcase. I'll show them to you tomorrow.

TOM Any replies?

JIM What?

TOM How many replies did you get to the letters?

JIM Look, am I on trial or something?

TOM I don't know, Jim. Are you?

JIM Okay, maybe some of the things we do aren't as exciting as you and I'd like them to be, but I'm doing the job as well as I can, and I can't do it all on my own. You guys bitch about the program, but you won't get off your asses and fight for something better. That idea of Pete's about the psychologist, I really pushed that idea. Pushed it to the hilt . . .

PETE But Carson didn't like it.

JIM Carson didn't like it, and the more I pushed the firmer he got.

SAM Why didn't you push it right up his ass?

JIM *ignoring this* So I told Pete he should go down and talk to Carson himself. I even made him an appointment. But he never showed up, did you, Pete?

PETE I was busy.

TOM Why the hell should you or Pete or anyone else have to beg that prick for anything?

JIM Tom, that's not fair. So he's a little stuffy, at least he's interested. He does give us more than the passing time of day.

PETE Sure, he was in for a whole hour this morning.

JIM Pete, you may not like Carson, but just remember. If he, or the Kiwanis, or any of the other service clubs decide to throw in the towel, we're in big trouble.

SAM "If they won't do it . . ."

JIM If they won't do it, who will? You?

A long pause.

PETE I've got nothing against the Rotary or the Kiwanis. If they want to give me a free meal just to look good, that's okay with me.

TOM You're sure of that?

PETE Tom, the Bible says the Lord provides. Right now He's providing pretty good. Should I get upset if He sends the Kiwanis instead of coming Himself?

JIM If you feel like getting something, why don't you give something?

PETE No, sir. I don't jump through hoops for nobody, and certainly not for a bastard like Carson. I might have nothing to say against the groups, but I don't have anything to say for them either.

TOM You can't stay neutral all the time.

PETE Tell that to Switzerland. Tom, you're young. You don't realize how tough it is for people like us. Baby, it's cold outside.

SAM *under his breath* Christ!

PETE When I came to this dump eleven years ago, I wanted to be a carpenter. That's all I could think about ever since I can remember. But face it, whoever heard of a carpenter with a flipper like that? *holding up his deformed hand* But I had a nice chat with this doc, and he told me I'd find what I'm looking for down here. So I came down here, and one of Saunders' flunkies shoves a bag of blocks in my hand. "What gives?" I said. And then it slowly dawned on me that as far as the doc is concerned, that's the closest I'll ever get to carpentry.

And I was pissed off, sure. But then I think, good old doc, he just doesn't understand me. 'Cause I still have my ideals. So in a few days I bust out of this place and go looking for a job—preferably carpentry. What happens? I get nothing but aching feet and a flat nose from having fucking doors slammed in my face all the fucking time.

And I'm at my wits' end when I get a letter from the Spastic Club. And I said fuck that. I'm about to throw it in the furnace, but I get curious. I've heard of the Spastic Club and I always figured it was a load of shit. But I think one meeting isn't going to kill me.

So I go, and I find out I'm right. It's a load of shit. It's a bunch of fuckheads sitting around saying, "Aren't we just too ducky for these poor unfortunate cripples?" But I got a free turkey dinner.

When I got home I took a good look at myself. I ask myself what am I supposed to be fighting? What do these jokers want me to do? The answer is they want to make life easier for me. Is that so bad? I mean, they don't expect me to keep you guys in your place or nothing. They just want me to enjoy life. And the government even pays me just for doing that. If I got a job, I'd lose the pension. So why have I been breaking my ass all this time looking for a job? And I got no answers to that. So I take the pension, and come back to the workshop. The only price I gotta pay is listening to old lady Saunders giving me hell for not weaving her goddamn rug.

Blackout. Fanfare. Lights up on far side of the stage. The actor playing MICHAEL enters dressed as a freak show barker. With him is the GIRL, his assistant, dressed in similar carnival attire. The following sequence takes place in a stage area independent of the washroom.

BARKER *to the audience* Are you bored with your job? Would you like to break out of the rat race? Does early retirement appeal to you? Well, my friends, you're in luck. The Shriners, the Rotary, and the Kiwanis are just begging to wait on you hand and foot.

Charleston music. The BARKER and the GIRL dance. The music continues through the next several speeches until he is handed the brain.

To throw you parties, picnics. To take you on field trips. To the flower show, the dog show, and to the Santa Claus Parade.

More dancing.

Would you like to learn new skills? Like sanding blocks, folding boxes, separating nuts and bolts? My friends, physiotherapists are standing by eager to teach you.

The GIRL hands the BARKER a wooden block and another block covered with sandpaper. More dancing as he sands the block.

Whoopee, is this ever fun.

He hands the block back to the GIRL.

Now, I suppose you good people would like to know, how do I get this one-way ticket to paradise? My props, please.

The GIRL hands him a life-size model of a human brain which has the various sections marked off, and a hammer. The music stops. He walks downstage into a pool of light directly in front of the audience.

Now all you do is take a hammer and adjust the motor area of the brain. Like this. Not too hard, now, we wouldn't want to lose you.

He taps the brain gently.

Having done that, you will have impaired your muscle co-ordination, and will suddenly find that you now *speaking with the speech defect of the character MICHAEL* "talk with an accent." You will then be brought to our attention either by relatives who have no room for you in the attic, or by neighbours who are distressed to see you out in the street, clashing with the landscape.

Now, assuming you are successful in locating the proper point of demolition, we guarantee that this very special euphoria will be yours not for a day, not for a week, but for a lifetime. There's no chance of relapse, regression, or rehabilitation because, my friends, it's as permanent as a hair transplant. It's for keeps. Should you, however, become disenchanted with this state, there is one recourse available to you, which while we ourselves do not recommend it, is popular with many, and does provide a final solution to a very complex problem. All you do is take the hammer and simply tap a little harder.

He smashes the brain. At the moment of impact, he becomes spastic, and slowly crumbles to the floor. Blackout.

The lights come up on the four boys.

SAM Guys like you really bug me. You got two good legs and one good hand. So the other's deformed. Big Fuckin' Deal. By the way, who the hell said you couldn't be a carpenter? You had your loom fixed up in five minutes last week while that old fart of a handyman was running around town looking for something to fix it with.

PETE   That was just lucky.

TOM   You know what I think, Cochran? I think you're lazy. I think eleven years ago you were looking for a grave to fall into, and you found it in the Spastic Club.

PETE   Don't be self-righteous about things you don't understand.

TOM   I understand laziness.

PETE   You don't understand. I tried.

TOM •   Aw, c'mon, Pete, you didn't try very hard.

PETE   There's no place in the outside world for a guy who talks funny.

SAM   Aw, you poor wittle boy. Did the big bad mans hurt your wittle feelings?

PETE goes for SAM, is about to hit him, but is restrained by TOM.

TOM   That's not funny, Sam.   *to PETE*   But it is a bit ridiculous. Here you are, you're thirty-seven years old, and you're still worried about something as small as that.

PETE   It may be a small thing to you, Tom. It's not to me.

JIM   Howdya like to have kids following you down the street calling you drunk? I get that all the time, but you learn to live with it.

SAM   Sure you learn to live with it. You learn to rub their noses in it too. Last week I was at this show and I had to be bounced about twenty steps in the chair just to get to the lobby. Well, you know what that does to my bladder, eh? So naturally I make for the washroom. The stalls are two inches too narrow, of course. As for the urinals, I never claimed to be Annie Oakley. They don't have urinal bottles 'cause they'd fuck up the interior decoration. But then I did spy this little Dixie cup dispenser. . .

JIM   Sam, you didn't!

SAM   Yeah, sweetie, I did. I was just doing up my fly when the usher walked in, saw the cup sitting on the edge of the sink. He thought it was lemonade. Told me patrons weren't allowed to bring refreshments into the washroom. Then he moved closer and got a whiff.

PETE   What happened?

SAM   Another United Appeal supporter had his dreams all crushed to ratshit.

JIM   And Sam set us back another twenty years.

SAM   What do you expect me to do, Harris? Piss my pants waiting for everything to come under your jurisdiction?

PETE   Sam's right. It's like you said, Jim. You do the best with what you got.

TOM   Come on, Pete, that's a cop-out and you know it. Sam should have got rid of that cup as soon as he took his leak. Putting it on the sink in plain view of everyone, for Chrissake!

PETE   Don't be so smug. A guy survives the best way he knows how. You wait, you'll find out. They don't want us creeps messing up their world. They just don't want us.

TOM   Tough! They're going to get me whether they want me or not. I'm a man, and I've got a right to live like other men.

PETE   You're the only man I know who can make a sermon out of saying hello.

He goes into one of the stalls, slamming the door behind him.

TOM   Yeah and pretty soon I'm gonna say goodbye. You expect me to spend the rest of my life folding boxes?

PETE   *over the top of the stall*   Look, Rembrandt, we know you're a great artist and all that shit. But if you paint like you fold, forget it.

JIM   Wait a minute, Pete. I've seen some of Tom's paintings. I'm no expert on abstract, but I think they're pretty good. They're colourful and. . .

SAM   Colourful chickentracks?

TOM   Fuck off!

JIM   Still, I'm not other people. I might like them, but folks on the outside might not. People get pretty funny when they find out something's been done by a handicapped person. Besides, we both know you can't draw.

TOM   That doesn't make any difference. I paint abstract.

SAM   So you'll win the finger painting contest.

JIM   Tom, we've been over this I don't know how many times. Name me one good abstract painter who isn't a good draftsman.

SAM   Name me one good writer who'd be caught dead in a glue factory.

JIM   Seriously, can you think of one famous artist who was spastic?

TOM   Jim, if you're sure I can't make it, what about the letter?

PETE   What letter?

JIM   *shrugs*   Oh, a letter he got from an art critic.

PETE   *emerging from the stall*   What did it say?

TOM   Here, you can read it yourself.

He hands the letter to PETE who begins to read it to himself.

SAM   Out loud.

PETE starts to read it, gives up, hands the letter to JIM.

JIM   *reading*   Dear Mr. March, I was fascinated by the portfolio you submitted. I cannot recall an artist in whose work such a strong sense of struggle was manifest. You positively stab the canvas with bold colour, and your sure grasp of the palette lends a native primitivism to your work. I am at once drawn to the crude simplicity of your figures and repulsed by the naive grotesqueries which grope for recognition in your tortured world. While I cannot hail you as a mature artist, I would be interested in seeing your work in progress this time next year.

SAM   Which one of your father's friends wrote it?

TOM   None of them.

SAM   One of your mother's friends?

TOM   The letter's authentic. I'll bring the guy's magazine column if you don't believe me.

PETE   Oh, we believe you, Tom. Critics are so compassionate.

TOM   You shit all over everything, don't you?

PETE   *handing TOM the letter*   It's a good letter, I guess.

TOM   You guess?

PETE   Well, what the hell am I supposed to say? You're the artist. I don't even like the Mona Lisa. To me she's just a fat ugly broad. But I can't help wondering, Tom . . .

TOM   What?

PETE   If he wouldn't have said the same thing if you'd sent him one of your boxes.   *TOM starts to protest but PETE goes on.*   Like when I'm weaving that goddamn rug and we have visitors. Now I'm no master weaver. Matter of fact, I've woven some pretty shitty rugs in my time. But whenever we have visitors, there are always one or two clowns who come over and practically have an orgasm over my rug, no matter how shitty we both know it is.

SAM   It's the same with the blocks. They pick one up, tell me how great it is, and then walk away with a handful of splinters.

TOM   It's not the same. This guy happens to be one of the toughest art critics around.

JIM   Even tough art critics give to the United Appeal.

TOM   Yes, and sometimes writers write for it.

JIM   Well, it keeps me off the streets.

SAM   Yeah, Jim peddles his ass indoors where it's warm.

PETE   And Carson has an exclusive contract on it. Right Jim?

JIM   I work because I want to work. It's a challenge, I enjoy it, and I can see the results.

PETE   Sure. So can we. Hot dogs, ice cream, balloons, confetti . . .

JIM   Well at least I don't have illusions of grandeur.

TOM   What illusions have you got, Jim?

JIM   Tom, you've got to come down to earth sooner or later. For someone in my situation the workshop makes sense. I can be more useful in a place like this.

TOM   Useful to Carson?

JIM   No, to people like Michael and Thelma.

TOM   What about Carson? Are you going to go on kissing his ass?

JIM   Call it what you like. In dealing with people, I have to be diplomatic. .

TOM   Fine, Jim.   *getting up*   You be diplomatic for both of us.

PETE   Where are you going?

TOM   I'm bored. I'm leaving.

PETE   What's the matter?

TOM   Nothing, Cochran, go back and finish your shit.

JIM   Tom, what is it?

TOM   I'm quitting.

JIM   You're not serious?

TOM   Getting more serious by the minute.

JIM   You're building a lot on a few kind words, aren't you?

TOM   The man doesn't know I'm spastic.

JIM   He's going to find out. And you know what'll happen when he does. You'll be his golden boy for a few weeks, but as soon as the novelty wears off, he'll go out of his way to avoid you.

TOM   What if the novelty doesn't wear off?

JIM   Tom, I don't think you should rush into this.

TOM   How long do I have to stay, Jim?

JIM   Stay until Christmas. Stay and do the mural.

TOM   No.

JIM   But you like painting. It won't hurt you.

TOM   I said no!

JIM   Why not?

TOM moves toward the door.

JIM   Won't you at least talk about it?

TOM   *turning and looking at JIM*   That's all you know how to do now, isn't it? No writing, no thinking, just talking., Well get this straight. I don't want any part of the Spastic Club or the Workshop. It's finished, okay?

JIM   Look, I know this place isn't perfect. I agree. It's even pretty rotten at times. But, Tom, out there, you'll be lost. You're not wanted out there, you're not welcome. None of us are. If you stay here we can work together. We can build something.

SAM   Yeah, a monument to Carson. For the pigeons to shit on.

TOM   How long are *you* going to stay here?

JIM   How long?

TOM   Are you going to spend the rest of your life being Carson's private secretary?

JIM   Well, nothing's permanent. Even I know that.

TOM   Stop bullshitting and give me a straight answer.

JIM   Okay, I'll move on. Sure.

TOM   And do what?

JIM   Maybe I'll go back to my writing.

TOM   When?   *No reply.*   When was the last time you wrote anything?

JIM   Last month I wrote an article for "The Sunshine Friend."

PETE   *joined by SAM*   "You are my sunshine, my only sunshine . . ."

TOM   Shut up! I mean when was the last time you wrote something you wanted to write?

JIM   Well, you know, my typewriter's bust . . .

TOM   Don't give me that crap about your typewriter. You don't want to get it fixed.

JIM   That's not true . . .

TOM   Do you know what you're doing here? You're throwing away your talent for a lousy bit of security.

JIM   Tom, you don't understand . . .

TOM   You're wasting your time doing a patch up job at something you don't really believe in.

JIM does not reply. TOM moves towards him.

Jim, there are stacks of guys in this world who haven't the intelligence to know where they're at. But you have. You *know*. And if you don't *do* something with that knowledge, you'll end up hating yourself.

JIM   What the hell could I do?

TOM   You could go into journalism, write a book. Listen, in this job, who can you tell it to? Spastics. Now think. Think of all the millions of jerks on the outside who have no idea of what it's really like in here. Hell, you could write a best-seller.

JIM   I've thought about it.

TOM   Well, *do* something about it.

JIM   Don't you think I want to?

TOM   Jim, I know you're scared. I'm scared. But if I don't take this chance, I won't have a hope in hell of making it. And if you keep on doing something you don't want to do, soon you won't even have a mind. Do you think if Michael had a mind like yours he'd be content to hang around here all day flushing toilets?

PETE   He's right, Jim. You don't belong here. Why don't you and Tom go together?

TOM   Look, I'll help you. We can go, we can get a place, we can do it together. Come on, what do you say?

SAUNDERS and CARSON enter the hallway.

SAUNDERS   They've been in here all afternoon. I tried to reason with them, but they refused to come out. I know you're busy, and I hate to bring you down here, but I'm really afraid this Rick and Stanley business is repeating itself . . .

CARSON   Miss Saunders.

SAUNDERS   Yes?

CARSON   Thanks, I can take it from here.

SAUNDERS exits. CARSON opens the door and stands in the doorway.

CARSON   Okay, guys, out.

Brief pause, then JIM moves to go.

TOM   Jim, how about it?

JIM   Later, Tom.

CARSON   Much later. It's time to get back to work.

TOM   I'm quitting, Carson.

CARSON   First things first. We can discuss that in the morning.   *He waits.*   Let's go.

JIM   I'm quitting too, sir.

CARSON   Right now I've got a good mind to fire you. Go to my office and wait for me.

SAM   He's making it real easy for you Jim. He just fired you.

CARSON   You too, Sam. Out.

SAM   I need the bottle. Hand me the bottle, Carson.

CARSON   You've had all afternoon to use the bottle. Now, out!

SAM   I need the fucking bottle!

TOM goes to get the bottle, is stopped by CARSON.

CARSON   You leave that bottle alone. I want you all out of here.

PETE gets the bottle, gives it to SAM.

CARSON   Pete! Goddamn it, what's wrong with you guys?

SAM now has the bottle in his lap.

CARSON   Give me that bottle!   *He takes it away from SAM.*   Now get out of here, all of you.

Nothing happens, so he starts to wheel SAM's chair.

SAM   Take your fuckin' hands off my chair!

JIM   Listen! You never listen to me!

CARSON   For God's sake, Jim, I'll listen, but in my office.

JIM   No, here. Now!

CARSON   What's eating you?

SAM   Give me the goddamn bottle.

He tries to get it, but CARSON holds it out of his reach.

CARSON   Get out of here, Sam!

He pushes the chair away.

SAM   Fucking prick!

CARSON   *shaken*   All right, what is it?

TOM   Jim, he's listening.

JIM   I don't want to spend the rest of my life here.

CARSON   Fine. You probably won't. Now can we all get back to work?

SAM   I need the fucking bottle!

TOM   Didn't you hear what he said? He said he doesn't want to spend his whole life in this dump.

CARSON   Look, March, you've been in here all the afternoon. You've got Miss Saunders all upset because of Michael, and . . .

SAM   *I need the bottle!*

CARSON   Shut up, Sam!

TOM   Do you know why we've been here all afternoon? Did you ever think of that?

SAM   Son of a bitch! Do you want me to piss my pants?

CARSON shoves the bottle at him. SAM wheels into the doorway of one of the stalls.

TOM   Did it ever enter your head that we might think of something besides the workshop, the club, and making you look good?

CARSON   Look, I don't know what you think, and right now I really don't care. All I'm concerned with is that you get out of this washroom. If you've got a complaint, you can come and talk to me.

TOM   I won't be there. Neither will Jim.

CARSON   I said, we can discuss that in the morning. *He turns to SAM and PETE.*   Come on Sam, Pete, let's go.

PETE   He can't find it, Carson.

JIM   I want to be a writer.

CARSON   *to SAM and PETE*   Quit fooling around, and hurry up.

JIM   I want to be a writer!

CARSON   You are a writer.

JIM   You don't understand. I want to make my living from it.

CARSON   Maybe you will, some day. But it's not going to happen overnight, is it?

TOM   If you stay here, Jim, it won't happen at all.

CARSON   It sure as hell won't if he runs off on some half-assed adventure with you.

TOM   Come on, Jim, the man's deaf.

CARSON   And what is it this time, Rembrandt? Poverty in a garret somewhere?

TOM   Better than poverty at the workshop.

CARSON   What are you going to paint, nude women?

TOM   You son of a bitch!

CARSON   Okay, Tom. Let's go.

He moves to usher TOM out.

TOM   You fucking son of a bitch!

In pushing him off, TOM loses his balance and falls. CARSON tries to help him up.

Get the fuck off me, Carson!

Slowly JIM and PETE help him to his feet.

Jim, you can stay and fart around as much as you like, but I'm going. Now are you with me or not?

CARSON   No, he's not. Now beat it.

TOM   Is that your answer, Jim?

JIM   Tom, wait . . .

TOM   I'm tired of waiting.

JIM   Maybe if I had just a little more time.

TOM   There's no time left.

JIM   Couldn't we wait till the end of the week?

CARSON   No, Jim. If you're serious about going, go now.

JIM   What about the Christmas program?

CARSON   I can find someone else.

JIM   But Christmas is the busiest time.

PETE   Go, Jim! Go with Tom!

SAM   *overlapping*   Don't let him do it to you, baby. Go!

JIM   But Tom, it's Christmas!

TOM   Jim, please!

JIM   I can't let him down now. Maybe after Christmas. . .

SAM   Fuck Christmas! What about Tom?

JIM   I've written all these letters, made all the arrangements. . .

TOM turns and moves towards the door.

SAM   Piss on the arrangements! Are you going to let him walk out that door alone?

PETE   If you don't go now, Tom will be alone, but you'll be more alone. Believe me, I know.

JIM   I can't go! I can't go, Tom, because, if you fall, I'll be the only one there to pick you up. And I can hardly stand up myself.

TOM has gone.

SAM   How did you get around on campus, princess? Crawl on your belly?   *He wheels angrily to the door.*   Fuckin' door! Hey, Carson, how about one cripple helping another?

CARSON   Get him out, Pete.

SAM and PETE exit. They wait outside the door, listening. JIM staggers over to the bench and sits.

CARSON   Why don't we talk about this over dinner? At my place, if you like.

THELMA   I need a priest! Get me a priest! Someone get me a priest!

Slow fade to the sound of THELMA's sobbing. PETE wheels SAM down the hallway. SAM is laughing.

RICK SALUTIN and
THEATRE PASSE MURAILLE

(b. 1942)

In his production diary of *1837*, the original version of *1837: The Farmers' Revolt*, Rick Salutin remarks how the opening night audience in Toronto laughed at the mention of Bay and Adelaide, a downtown intersection. That reaction brought into sharp focus for Salutin the reasons for having created the play in the first place, the bizarre attitudes typically held by Canadians towards their own history. "We are so imbued with self-denial," he concluded, "so colonized, that the very thought of something historic happening *here*, at Bay and Adelaide, draws laughs." His ongoing project and that of Theatre Passe Muraille under Paul Thompson has been to get Canadian audiences to laugh at themselves in the *right* places, presenting the everyday life and history of Canadians in theatrically playful and often brilliantly comical ways while at the same time insisting that they are subjects worthy of serious dramatic treatment.

Ironically, the man *Maclean's* has called "the country's foremost nationalist playwright" was educated almost entirely in the United States. Between 1960 and 1970 Salutin earned a B.A. in Near Eastern and Judaic Studies at Brandeis University, an M.A. in religion from Columbia, and was doing a Ph.D. in philosophy at New York's New School when he decided to return home to Toronto in 1970 after reading Harold Innis' *The Fur Trade in Canada*, an economic history that Salutin says "made sense of the present by making sense of the past." While working as a journalist and trade union organizer, he wrote his first play, *Fanshen*, produced in 1972 by Toronto Workshop Productions. An adaptation of William Hinton's classic study of the effects of the Chinese Revolution on the life of a small village, the play epitomizes Salutin's concern with the way history and politics are enacted in the daily lives of ordinary people. That concern would be at the heart of his next project, *1837*.

While Salutin was studying in the United States, Paul Thompson was getting an eclectic education in Canada and abroad: a B.A. in English and French from the University of Western Ontario in 1963 followed by a year at the Sorbonne; an M.A. in history at the University of Toronto in 1965 followed by two years' theatrical apprenticeship with Roger Planchon in Lyons. Thompson returned to Canada in 1967 and finally planted himself in Toronto with Theatre Passe Muraille just about the time Salutin came home. By the fall of 1972 when Thompson, Salutin and six Passe Muraille actors set to work creating *1837*, Thompson had been artistic director for a year and had already put his strong personal stamp on the company with innovative productions of Carol Bolt's *Buffalo Jump* and the collectively created *Doukhobors* and *The Farm Show*. The essence of Thompson's dramaturgy, as Brian Arnott has pointed out, "was a conscientious effort to give theatrical validity to sounds, rhythms and myths that were distinctively Canadian." The political and theatrical interests of Salutin and Thompson meshed perfectly with the skills of the Passe Muraille company on *1837* and a year later on *1837: The Farmers' Revolt*, which has become one of the most popular plays in the Canadian repertoire.

Since *1837* both Rick Salutin and Theatre Passe Muraille have thrived, the company under the direction of Paul Thompson until 1982 and subsequently under Clarke Rogers. Salutin worked with Passe Muraille again on the collective *Adventures of an Immigrant* (1974) and on his own plays *The False Messiah* (1975) and *Nathan Cohen: A Review* (1981). He has also pursued the collective form with two Newfoundland companies in theatrical examinations of that province's history, *I.W.A.* with the Mummers Troupe (1976) and *Joey* with Rising Tide (1982). His play about hockey and nationalism in Quebec, *Les Canadiens*, first produced at the Centaur in 1977, won the Chalmers Award and has been widely performed across Canada. Most recently he has collaborated with Ian Adams on the stage version of *S: Portrait of a Spy* (1984) and written *Grierson and*

Gouzenko (1986), a TV drama for CBC. Salutin's book *Marginal Notes* (1984) provides a lively selection of his journalism, some of it originally written for *This Magazine* of which he has been a long-time editor.

The politics of *1837: The Farmers' Revolt* are very much Salutin's own. The play presents a Canada lacking independence and subservient to British imperialism, finding its revolutionary impulse in the ordinary people of the time. Created during the heyday of Canadian nationalism, it was meant to speak to the contemporary sense of American imperial domination and economic, political and cultural colonialism many Canadians still feel. Salutin also intended the play as a corrective to what he called "The Great Canadian History Robbery" in a 1973 *Maclean's* article: the textbook view of Canadian history in which "we learned that all our problems were resolved 'peaceably' long ago; that there is nothing in our history to get excited over; that Canadians don't *get* excited; that they never fight back against things as they've always been."

Ideology, however, was probably less crucial to the play's success than its theatricality, a product of the unique collective chemistry brought to bear in its creation. Salutin's diary reveals how he would bring in Mackenzie's newspaper article on the Family Compact or Robert Davis' book *The Canadian Farmer's Travels in the U.S.A.*, and Thompson would lead the actors on improvisational forays through it. The wittiest scenes in Act One, including "The Head" and "The Lady in the Coach," grew out of improvisations based on documentary material. The actors were also asked to improvise 1837 objects and do 1837 "anger exercises," the latter shaped by Salutin into the final scene of Act One. When necessary Salutin would script a scene (like "Doel's Brewery" opening Act Two), but as much as possible the emphasis was on the actors' imaginative reconstructions of the 1837 world, coaxed out of them by Thompson's sympathetic direction.

Salutin's final role was to shape the resulting material into a coherent, dramatically effective whole, and his success in that regard can be seen most clearly in Act One. Its non-linear arrangement of scenes masks a clever and deceptively rigorous dialectical structure. The farmers' struggle with the stump in "Clearing" and Mackenzie's with the mud in "Hat" are both amplified and clarified in "The Tavern" where the people learn that the system itself is the obstacle: the swamp that can only be cleared through collective action. The ensuing scene, "The Family Compact," further illuminates the system by individualizing the forces of oppression. Then the lovely "Mary Macdonald" introduces a wholly different kind of family compact, what Mackenzie will later call "the real nobility of Upper Canada." As Edward exits with Mary he warns, "there's ruts," and "The Lady in the Coach" bogs down in them. That scene provides a wonderful comic illustration of the imperialist approach to problem-solving—let the colonials pull us out of the mud while we give the orders—a view reaffirmed by Sir Francis' speech in "The Head" promising "paternal care" of his subjects. The self-fulfilling nature of such colonialist attitudes is vividly shown in "The Election of '36." Obviously the farmers *haven't* learned how to take care of themselves politically. Their only solution will be to develop a revolutionary consciousness.

The play's imaginative energy flags a little in the second act. Both Salutin and Thompson have acknowledged feeling "handcuffed by history" into presenting a more or less chronological narrative of the events of the rebellion ending with its defeat. Still, the historical narrative is leavened and humanized by the reintroduction of the non-historical characters we've met in Act One. The farmers, the collective hero, become almost as individualized as their catalyst, Mackenzie himself. And while history dictates that they must fail in the end, Salutin has taken mild dramatic license to ensure that defeat doesn't mean despair; we haven't really lost, we just haven't won. . .yet. Salutin's preface, which follows, illuminates this distinction along with many of the other agonies and ecstasies involved in the making of the play.

•

1837: The Farmers' Revolt opened June 7, 1974, on tour in southwestern Ontario, designed by Paul Williams and directed by Paul Thompson. The actors were Doris Cowan, David Fox, Eric Peterson, Miles Potter and Terry Tweed.

1837: THE FARMERS' REVOLT

PREFACE

1837 was first produced at Theatre Passe Muraille in Toronto in January, 1973. Here is a "diary" of that production.

Fall, 1972

Last year, while I was in rehearsal with a play called *Fanshen*, about the Chinese Revolution, the director said, "Now what we ought to do *next* year is—Quebec!"

Oh no, I thought. No more getting off on these exotic foreign revolutions. Next year if we do a revolution it will be right here in Ontario.

Sunday, Dec. 3

Drove out to the Niagara Peninsula with Paul (director) and Williams (designer). On a winding narrow road that once was the thoroughfare between Hamilton and the frontier we found a neglected monument, high as my waist and shaped like a gravestone. Divided into crescents, it read:

Up the hill 50 feet stood the home of Samuel Chandler Patriot
He guided Mackenzie to Buffalo
And here they had supper
Dec. 10, 1837

It is encouraging. With all the denigration spattered on the rebellion during our schooldays and since, I was beginning to ponder whether we were the first who had ever thought to treat it as a serious national event.

Wednesday, Dec. 6

Rehearsals begin tomorrow, the 7th, the anniversary of the Battle of Montgomery's Tavern. The 7th was also a Thursday in 1837. Odd how those things fuel you. We have no script yet, only general ideas of why and how we want to do it. I've tried too. In September, I sketched out scenes, then showed it to L. "Looks just the way we learned it in school," she said. Back to the drawing board. Paul is delighted. He's said all along we're better off without a script, that it makes the actors lazy. Even if we had one, he'd be for hiding it. Fine—but what do they need me for?

Thursday Dec. 7

We have six actors. Three men and three women. Two I know from *Fanshen*. The rest are strangers. I brought in a few goodies: maps and pictures of Old Toronto. Great stir at finding the *history* of places we've all lived around. We're starting very far back: other countries may have to relive or reinterpret their past, but they know they *have* a past. In Quebec they may hate it, but it's sure as hell there. English Canadians, at least around here, must be convinced there *is* a past that is their own.

We paraded to Mackenzie House on Bond St. in midafternoon where little Wasp women in period dress served us tea and apple butter. I nearly choked on it, and the rest of what they've wreaked on our only militant independantiste. Our work is cut out.

Before splitting up, we asked each of the actors to present an 1837 object. The best was Clare. She set herself before us and said:

I'm William Lyon Mackenzie's house. My feet are spread wide apart and are firmly planted. My hands are on my hips and I look straight ahead. I have *lots* of windows and any question you ask me, I'm not afraid to answer.

It's already apparent that Paul is right. The absence of a script is drawing material out of the actors. After all, they have more theatre experience than anyone, and they're almost never asked to draw on it.

Friday Dec. 8

We gave the actors anger exercises today. Each had to simulate anger around 1837. For some it was agony—or constipation. Neil was superb. "Nobody," he roared, "is going to make me speak with an English accent." That is a true Canadian actor's anti-imperialism. Theatre is one of the few areas left in Canada where the main imperial oppressor remains England and not the U.S. They run every regional theatre in the country; Englishmen waft over and drown in role offers. Stratford—our *national* theatre—gobbling public money to become an acknowledged *second* best in *another* country's national playwright. Neil was one of Stratford's golden boys—an apprentice—in its early years. Then he rebelled by going to act for twelve years in New York, instead of London. He's been back about two years now.

Last spring, when Paul and I first talked about this play, I said it was to be an anti-imperialist piece. He leaped joyfully and cried, "Right—we'll really smash the Brits"—making me wince, but in theatre he was right.

Monday Dec. 11

First resistance. From Clare. She looked to me and said, "*There's* all the research—bottled up in your head—and we can't get at it."

Actors have been so infantilized. Writers tell them what to say and directors tell them where to stand and no one asks them to think for themselves. They come to work with Paul because they want to break that pattern, but then they freeze up. I remember my first horrified encounter with actors, during *Fanshen*. They were treating this play exactly as they would any other; it might have been *Barefoot in the Park*. Like the mailman, they'd deliver anything. It shocked me that they were like any other group in the country, politically, that is. But the actors are also the real proletariat of the theatre; that too was clear from the first rehearsal. They are the bottom rung. They take shit from everyone else, and *their* labour holds it all up: reproduces it all, night after night.

This matter of research: the material on 1837 is endless, to my surprise. The collective method takes the pressure off me for digesting all of it. Everyone reads like crazy. Mornings, before we start, the rehearsal room looks like a library.

Tuesday Dec. 12

We're still concentrating on texture, and haven't begun to build scenes.

The woman problem remains completely unsolved, although we are ignoring it at this point. Paul originally wanted only one woman. I insisted on at least two and claimed we could show the class conflict through two women. He went along, and since Suzette became available, we now have three, in addition to the three men. But what will we do with them, given the paucity of the sources on women? I've ransacked the records, talked with historians, writers, feminists. All we find are interminable journals by the *gentle*women of the time, who complain of their hard life in the Bush, and how tough it is to get servants. Women didn't fight, and they didn't legislate. Clearly they worked. But what they did, and how they felt, in specifics . . . ? Every time I go back over it, I end up nowhere. In *Fanshen*, the woman issue was so *clear*.

Wednesday Dec. 13

Williams brought in the set—that is, a mockup in a shoebox. What a triumph. A series of four platforms ranging from 2 to 8 feet off the floor connected by ramps which will be corduroyed. Plus five enormous trees set throughout the theatre that will tower up through the roof.

The effect of the platforms will be to give us the possibility of isolation and concentration— *plus* the possibility of movement (between the platforms); it is the best of all possible worlds, in terms of design. Instantly all our thinking about the play is transformed. I keep wandering by it and conjuring miniature people on the ramps.

Thursday Dec. 14

We tried Mackenzie's newspaper piece on the Family Compact today. It's a fine hatchet job. He numbers them from one to thirty, and cross references them by number. We did it with five people taking all the roles—switching—and Neil reading. It will, I hope, become the definitive version of the Family Compact. I suppose I like it because I have been writing political satire for radio three years now and see Mackenzie's piece as the start of a Canadian tradition.

I gave Miles *The Canadian Farmer's Travels in the U.S.A.* to read. Written by an Upper Canadian farmer named Davis in 1836. I discovered it in the rare book room of the public library. Heartsick at the election of '36, he went travelling in the U.S., was thrilled by the abundance he saw everywhere and the efficacy of the democratic system, and resolved to return home and struggle for improvement here. He published the book, and died in the fighting in 1838. It's a very naive book—he's so overwhelmed by what he saw, that he loves *everything*—slavery, Indians— all of it. It's a trip scene and should work well, especially with the kind of energy Miles can give it.

More texturing: we've given everyone a minor character to do from the time. Someone who's barely mentioned in the records. Sally Jordan, who worked for Anne Langton, who wrote a journal. Ira Anderson, innkeeper, who's on the arrest record. A name mentioned in Mackenzie's paper as seconding a motion at a meeting. They must build their character according to what they know of the time. We'll quiz the actors in coming days on what may come out of it, but more important is the *thickness*—to pour into and onto whatever and whoever we end up using. We have to build the reality of the ordinary people of the time. They are the core of our past we have to get through to; they must be the centre of the play—not any of the "great" individuals who hog most of the records.

Friday Dec. 15

Blizzard. After the break Janet said, "Can I go home?" and Paul said, "If you walk all the way up Yonge St. and do it in character." Upshot was we bundled up and trekked through Old Toronto. Down to the site of the hangings on King St., along King to Berkeley, up Parliament and over to the cemetery where Mackenzie, Lount and Matthews are buried. It was locked when we arrived. One thing we concluded: December was a hell of a time to make a revolution here.

Monday Dec. 18

A row at the end of the day. "I'm sick of our Canadian politeness," Paul complained. We'd been doing break-ins by loyalists at the homes of rebels after the battle. The traditional Canadian knock at the door. Our intruders had tied themselves in knots trying not to be too, too nasty.

It is a crux: the ability to *really* identify with the main struggles and passions of the people at the time; else it will be just play-acting, better or worse. Clare dealt it back the strongest. "One of the nicest things about Canadians is that they *don't* get angry," she yelled.

I argued—academically I fear—that this "typical" Canadian reserve is not genetically rooted; that Canadians did fight and shout in 1837; and that our esteemed diffidence is the result of the failure and repression of such moments of resistance and assertion. If it is that historically based, we're not going to shake it loose by doing a passionate play; still, we may gain an inch or two.

Wednesday Dec. 20

Pictures: we give the actors five minutes to rummage through books, choose an image, and give it back.

David plunged: "Now sir, when we moved onto that plot, there was nothing there. All I'm asking is . . ." Suzette hauled a table and chair in front of him, and leaned back like a contemptuous land agent. As he stammered on, about how he and his family had worked, the others filled in behind, chopping and clearing. Hewers of wood and drawers of water. Very strong. David is our staunchest, in a way. Our oak—(and we have Miles chop him down in a scene). He grew up in Kirkland Lake, taught high school ten years in Brantford, and did his first professional acting this past summer.

Janet did a brilliant picture. Back to us, passed her palm above her head, saying, "A smooth broad forehead." Then she stood Suzette and Neil side by side facing us as, "Two piercing eyes." Drew their inner arms forward together as, "A classic nose." Got Clare in to make a mouth; and announced it was John Beverley Robinson, one of the leading members of the Compact. Now to find a way of integrating it into the production so that it becomes more than a *tour de force* of theatricality.

(The "Head" developed this way: Paul felt we had to make it the head of Lieutenant Governor Francis Bond Head, not Robinson, since Mackenzie had been so fond of punning on Head's name. Neil found a speech by Bond Head that was the quintessence of the Imperial attitude; as one of the eyes he also delivered it. It fit perfectly as the prelude to the Canadian Farmer's Travels to the U.S. The whole didn't come together until weeks after Janet had given us the original image.)

Friday Dec. 22

There was no point trying to rehearse today. Everyone is gripped with job insecurity, because Actors' Equity is about to shut down Factory Theatre Lab, and is preparing an offensive against the other small Canadian theatres like ourselves. Ostensibly the issue is kickbacks. Equity actors who work at the small theatres must sign contracts at Equity rates, but since these are unrealistic for the small theatres, they often return a part of what they are paid. We have four Equity actors and they've all received threatening letters from *their* union. (They can't seem to get the incongruity of this through their heads.) They fear they'll be expelled. We talked all day, mostly about American unions and how typical this is of the way they operate in Canada—and about other forms of imperialism, especially American. I am the only one with a thoroughly paranoid interpretation: that Equity's real purpose is to shut down the small Canadian theatres because they provide increasing competition and audience drain from the downtown mausoleums that house touring Broadway shows, American-mounted productions, to which Equity gives its main allegiance. I was alone in deeming it a conspiracy, but various forms of fear and indignation reign among the rest. They're tired of yearly questionnaires from Equity asking how many hours they've worked on-Broadway, off-Broadway, etc. There is certainly no way of avoiding this discussion in the context of the play we are making.

Boxing Day

Finally tried Ventriloquism. Inspired by a handbill for an 1830's travelling show (". . . and featuring—VENTRILOQUISM"). It's a perfect metaphor for colonialism—maybe too perfect? Divided our actors into teams of dummy and master; David and Clare were far the best technically. Now to work on the problem of what they're to say.

Thursday Dec. 28

We had our good day today, as Janet said.

For his anger homework, David came in with a team stuck in the mud. Got off his wagon, stuffed his shoulder against a wheel, shoved and cursed. Others moved in as horses etc., and Janet sang God Save the Queen. *Finally* we got behind the academicism of the "roads" issue. Each time someone uses it, it sounds plucked from the section of the textbook called Causes of the Rebellion. We've taken to barking "Cause Three" when they mention roads, and "Cause Four" to the Clergy Reserves. But this was real and *felt*.

Neil began musing about the secret meeting at Doel's Brewery in Toronto before the rebellion — the night when the city was unguarded and Mackenzie urged his fellow reformers to seize it and the four thousand arms that were there. I've yearned to do it from the start. It was the time to act, but they stalled till they could bring down the farmers to take the risks for them. Had they acted there is no doubt our history would have been different. The British would have been forced to return half their forces from Quebec, where fighting had already begun; the French just might then have succeeded; in Ontario there'd have been arms and impetus.... Still, dreams aside, the point of the scene is not to show what might have been, but the unreliability and timidity of bourgeois leadership in a struggle for Canadian independence. Then as now, Paul felt it was too programmatic to get out of the actors, but Neil was so keen on it that we both gulped, "Let's try it." It went not badly, broad lines emerged, and in this one case, I am going to write it up as a scene, based on the improvised work. My first chance to be a playwright. Now they get a chance to judge my work.

We finally got the Davis scene, the Canadian farmer travelling in the U.S. Miles had had an anxiety attack each time he moved into it. Today we literally sat on him, holding him down, and by the time he finally escaped he'd gathered so much energy it carried him right through the trip. The key is to satirize the farmer's enthusiasm for all things American. To put through our eyes what we saw through his. On one side lethargic Windsor (yawns) and then — Industrious Detroit — everyone pumping and rushing and HAPPY. He adores it all; Neil ran up and said, "Excuse me sir, I'm a runaway slave, which way is Canada?" and he said — "No, don't go, it'll get better here." Got quite wild, snatches of Aquarius, etc. Very exciting. I'm still excited about it.

Friday Dec. 29

I've got a last line. Talking with Suzette about Canadian plays and what downers they are — always about losers. Yet what to do? Our past is negative. The country has remained a colony; the struggle in 1837 did not succeed. I've thought of changing the ending, having the rebels win (Stop that Hanging!); or cutting off before the battle and the defeat, at, say, the high point in October '37. But finally we have to wrestle with what actually happened and wring something positive out of that. Losing, I argued, does not have to make you a "Loser"; there are winners who lose. It is the difference between saying, "We lost," and saying, "No, we just haven't won yet." There it is.

Saturday Dec. 30

The Family Compact is turning into a hell, more demoralizing each time we run it. The novelty of the numbering has worn off, they are reaching for ever more corn to cover their changes. We're down to staging numbers 21-25 as a bloody cricket match. Paul can't get it. Damn. Paul's strength — his genius — is working with people and eliciting their creativity. I try to help — but I'm no director. Christ what a loss it would be — it's right there!

Sunday Dec. 31

They showed me a scene Suzette had improvised yesterday while I was out. An English gentlewoman doing the tour of the colonies gets stuck in her coach on the road from Toronto to

Niagara, blusters at the driver, fidgets about her manservant, yammers endlessly, but together they push free and suddenly she is ecstatic about the "adventure" they've just had. ("My cousin Stephanie was one experience up on me, you know.") I loathed her—extolling "Nature's cathedral" which only she and not the gruff coachman could appreciate, bidding "Goodbye Brave Bush," before she'd climb back in the coach. I grabbed for one of our stage rifles and would gladly have plugged her through her "jaded, civilized eyes." But she is so right and brilliant and hilarious—I suppose there will be no way of keeping it out of the play.

We are starting to think about how to shape these things. About time. It is New Year's Eve. We open on the 17th.

Tuesday Jan. 2

Working with Mackenzie's newspaper again. Divided them, as usual, into an upper class and a dirt poor family, each reacting to the same articles differently. Today though, they fell into interrupting each other's readings and emerged in fullblown battle. All the good arguments were with the reactionaries. And all the articulateness. "My dear man, you can't expect illiterate farmers to actually *govern*?" "What do *you* know about economics?" "Are you admitting then that you are *disloyal*?" On and on, Neil and his gathering steam; David and his, being ground down. Miles (for the rich) made some patronizing analogy, to which David tried pathetically to respond. Janet got closer to the class reality, barging in with, "That's a stupid argument!" Suzette cooed, "Why can't we all get *along*?" in a perfect Rosedale tone. Janet tore through the paper looking for counterarguments, looking to us—what she really felt was—If only Mac was here, *he'd* tell them. We suddenly saw Mackenzie's real importance for these people. The oppressed never control the ideological apparatus; it is always used by the ruling classes to confuse and demoralize them. Mackenzie took the ideological skills he possessed and put them at the disposal of the oppressed instead of the oppressors, doing for them what they had not been given the resources to do for themselves. He really served the people. What nonsense the way we learned it—as if it was Mackenzie against the Family Compact in personal combat. It was the working people against the Empire. They were the centre, but they needed him.

Wednesday Jan. 3

I distributed the script for the brewery scene today; reaction was astounding. They blinked and wouldn't believe—a real script—went berserk with gratitude and joy. Much feigned, of course, but it came from somewhere. The pressure and demands on them in this method of work are vast. That we knew; but not quite how *much*.

Most striking was how the presence of a script shot everyone into an instant role. They became actors, underlining their speeches and saying bitchy things like, "Let me feel my way into this, will you?" Paul became a director urging interpretations and line readings on them ("Let me coach you"). And I became a writer, skulking in back, gritting my teeth at what they were doing to "my" lines, nodding when they "got it," and not intervening except to occasionally whisper to Paul. Till now, roles have been loose; everyone was writing, directing and acting, though of course not all to the same extent. With the script, compartmentalization sets in like terminal cancer. I'm glad we did it—just this one scene—to watch it happen.

Toward the end of the day, with everyone tired and loath to take on a bummer like the Compact, Paul spied a length of rope in the corner, looped it six times, put it over their heads and told them they were prisoners being returned to Toronto after the rebellion. They trudged and told us what they felt and saw. Too much self-pity at the moment, but a strong image and one that will work on our set. Where did that come from? I asked Paul. Desperation, he said.

Friday Jan. 5

Last night I read through seven or eight accounts of the Seige of Toronto between Dec. 4 and 7, culminating with the Battle, and typed a composite account, very long and detailed. Then I cut it up with scissors into thirty different pieces, numbered, and this morning gave five pieces to each actor. Each has to say his section as they come up in sequence, though everyone acts out the events. It will take lots of choreography and coordination, and we will be at it once a day till we open—like taking vitamins, says Paul. I think our audiences will be captivated—all those warlike events up and down Yonge St.

I feel less guilt about my contribution, now that I've done some scripting. And I think I can see the shape of Act II. From Doel's, through the Battle, the march of the prisoners, the hangings. We'll be leaping right into the maw of the defeat, and see what kind of victory we can bring from it. But as for Act I, God only knows. . . .

Monday Jan. 8

Awful. Just awful. I can't say how bad. There is nothing there. And they will not work, will not give. The Family Compact is a horror; we haven't dared touch it in five days. Miles is stumped on his Farmer's Travels. We all see what a good scene it is; we've seen him do it brilliantly; but he's clogged up, he makes excuses and accuses Paul of not directing him. Paul fires back that Miles won't commit himself. I stalk around the theatre—we moved in today out of the rehearsal room—wanting to rip Miles into bits for his stingy withholding. I know that's false, but it's what I feel. Paul and I confer hostilely, and they pick it up and sulk or fling back angry glares—Janet is doing that more and more. We are at a dead halt—no, we are careening backwards. There is no giving, no expansiveness—and no script to fall back on!

Christ, I said to Paul, is it this way every time?

I don't know, he sighed. I can't remember. I guess so.

How do you stand it?

I must forget. If I remembered, I would never do it again.

Tuesday Jan. 9

Today it was Clare. She has no lines in the Doel's scene, but is a brewery hand who sets it up and works away in the background while the leaders of the rebellion are conspiring below. She is the lurking presence of the ordinary working people who will have to take all the chances while most of their "leaders" sit tight. But she's been a lump. I challenged her on it and she maintained that since she knows nothing about brewing beer, she can't act it. I said she should figure out something that seemed to her like brewing and do that. She pouted that she'd take off the rest of the day and go research brewing in the library. More tight-assed withholding—I stormed off. Paul? I don't know where he gets the patience. Like a shrink fighting through layers of resistance, he patiently counters argument after argument of hers till she admits she just doesn't want to take a chance. Then she went ahead and did it—beautifully. I don't know what the hell *she* thought she was doing, but at the least it didn't look like *not* brewing beer.

Wednesday Jan. 10

The Ventriloquism is in trouble. We haven't figured out how to use it—is it metaphor, is it to the audience, is it within the play itself? David and Clare are balking, say it's no fun, no point. I'll try and script it as a two minute skit—as if I were writing for radio.

We did get the Family Compact. We'd written it off regretfully but I was looking at the set today—ramps running down from platform to platform—and said, Why don't we try it on the ramps, unwinding the Compact from top to bottom? So we did, and we have a scene.

Thursday Jan. 11

Came up with an Act I closing. Our anger exercises. Spread our people over the set, doing bursts of anger one after another. They made them up on the spot; some were extraordinary.

> MILES *climbing off the floor onto the set* I don't care who you are and what your name is. From now on you can clean the muck out from under your own damned English footbridge.
>
> NEIL See this cabinet. Took me six months. Know why I can't sell it? Because it was made in *an awful angry whine* Torrrrooonnnttoooo—
>
> JANET So I sez to her—Milk your *own* cow!

And finally a chance to use Suzette's Quebec half: Moé-la, j'aimais plus je'n chant'ra pour les Anglais!

It is the boiling point of 1837, where grievances and resentments are irrepressible and have to burst into the action of the rebellion itself—in Act II.

Friday Jan. 12

Just what we'd considered our strongest suit—the pictures—just won't work down here in the theatre. They were grand in the little rehearsal room with the low ceiling but—ah well, they served their purpose: got us into the texture of the time.

Saturday Jan. 13

Worked with David on his (Lount's) gallows speech. He's been to the provincial archives mornings this week, reading accounts of the trial of Lount and Matthews.

Finally found a use for those lists I like so much—the names of those arrested or charged in the aftermath of the rebellion. 885 men, their homes, and occupations. Fine names—Caleb Kipp, Josiah Dent, Joshua Doan: yeoman, labourer, tanner, etc. When I have been stymied by this work both before and then during rehearsals, I've taken to reading through those names. I've wanted to employ them as a sort of litany. They work well into the rope scene, the march of the prisoners. Each gives his name and when they've gone round once, they go round again, and then again, creating with the six an endless line of captured revolutionaries. I gave a page of names to each actor; they can choose the ones they'll use each night.

The final form is now clear. Act I will be fairly diffuse, a view of the life of the times—our blessed texture—though building to the inevitability of the outbreak. It should end high, with the feeling, This Can't Miss. After intermission we change pace completely.

Act II drives right through with the line of the rebellion, defeat and aftermath. It will have the guts of our politics, what we make of this event and why we are returning to it now.

Monday Jan. 15

We hit the crunch today with the Farmer's Travels. Miles capsized again midway. He tried to get Paul to call it off, cut the scene, give it to someone else—do *something*. I could see Paul struggling with the offer; then he leapt up on the set and refused. Said he would not become the paternalistic director at this point. If Miles really wanted to do the scene, Paul would stand by him no matter how much it seemed to lack—and he was sure the audience would accept it. Or—if Miles really didn't want to do it, *he* would have to say so. It was a trap for Paul and he was magnificent in avoiding it. Suzette, bless her, said, "I vote to have it in," not pressing but making the point that, if not Miles, then someone else should do it. Miles wrestled with it, started the trip again, stalled, slumped down, and said, "I don't want to do it like this." "O.K.," said Paul, "Janet—will you try it?"

Janet looked to Miles, he nodded generously, she launched it, and was fine. When we tried it again later, Miles came in as the wife, urging the farmer not to leave for the States. It works, and I think it also means we've solved the women problem as far as we can. Clare argued with me the other day that one of the men on the scaffold should be played by a woman, and I argued back that it would be so obtrusive that we would end up with a scene about the equality of women, not about 1837. It might be right politically, but if it doesn't work as theatre there is no point in doing it in a play. Janet plays a man because it has become dramatically necessary in the travel scene. We have women playing men in the battle and the brewery scene for the same reason and it is unobtrusive there. We've failed to find a centrality for women in 1837 terms. But we are *doing* the play in *our* terms—with an equal cast, fair distribution of parts, etc. It is an attempt to portray an oppressive reality in a liberated way.

Tuesday Jan. 16

We've put the Ventriloquism unit as the introduction to the meeting Mackenzie addresses before the rebellion. As a skit presented by two farmers for their friends at the rally. Agitprop of '37. Allows the other actors to react to it as *its* audience, drains off the heavy symbolism, and clarifies that Clare is playing a real person who is *playing* a dummy.

Great consternation about the newspaper scene with which we'd wanted to open. It is important for me 1) to open a play about Canadian history with a scene of class conflict, and 2) to show the centrality of Mackenzie's paper—its propaganda and education—for the movement. Paul's retort was—it's not doing either of those things as it is now. I had to agree. We put it to them and—wonder of wonders—they say they want to do it as we have it and are sure they can pull it off tomorrow night, though they'd like me to settle on four or five articles and choose an order for them. Instead of suggesting another cut, they propose an inclusion—a good, good sign.

The programs came today, and I like them. They are a piece with the rest of this work: single sheets with a map of Old Toronto and an alphabetical list of the people who made the play.

I think I see now Paul's vision of theatre and the value he places on improvisation. Without a script, there is real tension and the possibility of creative breakthrough on stage at any moment. It is not *set*. People come to plays thinking of them as movies or TV gone live, perfect realizations of a script or theme, and frozen at that point of perfect realization. But a play is made live each night, and its possibility is not frozen perfection but ongoing re-creation. The edge for an audience should not be awe at a perfect performance, but anxiety about something new and possibly better at any moment.

Opening Night

Two instructive things happened. When Clare started Act II with "Bay and Adelaide, the northwest corner," the audience laughed. If an actor said, "Montmartre, 4 a.m.," or "Piccadilly Circus, twelve noon," no audience anywhere would laugh. But we are so imbued with self-denial, so colonized, that the very thought of something historic happening *here*, at Bay and Adelaide, draws laughs.

Again, during the Battle, in the nighttime skirmish when both inexperienced sides broke ranks and fled, Miles lost his line for a moment, and the audience laughed. Miles—American Miles— said that moment made clear to him for the first time what I'd been saying about the problem of Canadian history for a Canadian audience. There was nothing funny about the moment. It was terrifying or should have been.

Three Weeks Later

The actors have come to take it as a challenge to deliver those lines so that the audience cannot laugh at them. At the same time, Janet says the response to *1837* is different from any play she's ever appeared in. It's not just appreciation. It's something warmer.

It is, I think, identification. Beyond the identification you get in any good theatre. It is a meeting with ourselves.

Over a year later, the play was reworked. The result—amounting to a new play—was called *1837: The Farmers' Revolt*. It was produced in the spring, summer and fall of 1974—first in the auction barns of southwestern Ontario, then in the Victoria Playhouse in Petrolia, Ontario, and then in Toronto. It has since had many productions throughout the country. It is the script of this latter production which is included below.

1837: The Farmers' Revolt was developed in exactly the same way as the first version of the play. But it was meant for a tour of farming communities instead of an urban theatre audience and it differed from the earlier play in the following ways.

It was not Toronto-centred. In the first *1837* we had made hay of the events and locales of early Toronto. We de-emphasized these in the country, and looked for elements that reflected what had happened out there, where we were planning to tour the show.

So, for instance, we cleared a larger space for Anthony van Egmond, the old colonel who led the revolutionary force at Montgomery's Tavern. Van Egmond had lived just outside Seaforth—in the village now called Egmondville. The family home is still standing, and local people are restoring it.

Instead of showing the entire four days of fighting around Toronto, we showed only the final battle there. For the first three days, we went out to the country, and followed Van Egmond, as he marched from his home down to Toronto, to take command of the forces there.

Numerous such changes in the script occurred. Another change which took place was, in a way, political.

The earlier play—beamed into the Toronto milieu—could assume a somewhat left-of-liberal politics on the part of its audience; more or less of a sympathy, or at least tolerance, for the revolutionary sentiments of the play. But the farming community is, at least in its explicit attitudes, far more conservative. So some of the rhetoric—what Miles called the "bombast"—came out. And more justification of the movement for change went in. For instance, we had *two* scenes, instead of one, depicting the bitterness of the farmers over the land policies of the 1830s.

The play also changed dramatically, or artistically.

It became much tighter than the earlier version. In the first version, for example, we served the battle up whole. In the second, by concentrating on the experience of Van Egmond, we gave the scene a dramatic focus it had lacked. In the end, I would say version two (the one included here) is a far better play.

This is largely so because on the first time round we were intent on getting clear *what* we were going to say about 1837. By round two, that most crucial of matters was basically settled; we could concentrate on *how* to say it most effectively, refining scenes, characters, etc. The resulting script proves, I think, that the collective process can produce a play as dramatically tight as the more typical scripting approach.

In some ways though, I preferred the earlier version. It would not make as good reading, and it did not play as well. Yet it had a rawness and a timeliness. It felt to me, when we first put this show up in January of 1973, that we were expressing something of what was happening in the country at the time: a determination to throw off colonial submissiveness in all areas. *1837* was a theatrical expression of that feeling, making it more of a political event, and not just, or even primarily, a theatrical one.

By the second time round, a mere year and a half later, things seemed to have changed, have slowed. The movement for Canadianization of trade unions had *not* yet taken off; the universities were more dominated than ever by Americans; the Waffle had been expelled from the NDP, largely for its nationalism; the cries for economic control had muted. The nationalist, anti-imperialist impetus was still present, and *more* necessary than ever; but it was less fresh, was in a bit of a withdrawal.

And so the play became more of a theatrical, and less of a political, event. That is why I preferred version one, though version two is no doubt superior "theatre."

1837: The Farmers' Revolt had an original cast of five: three men and two women. Men played women, and women men, or animals or objects or parts of the body—depending on the needs of the scene. There were very few props. I mention this because anyone reading the script will be tempted to imagine a well-equipped cast of thousands.

The actors who worked on the various productions were Janet Amos, Clare Coulter, Suzette Couture, Doris Cowan, David Fox, Eric Peterson, Miles Potter, Terry Tweed, and Neil Vipond. I had a notion of including a list with this script indicating which actors were primarily responsible for which scenes—but when it comes to the doing it is terrifically difficult to assign such credit. So I will just reiterate that the play is *entirely* a creation of the company in rehearsals and performance. The present script is an after-the-fact, somewhat composite, effort, assembled *following* the close of the fall 1974 run.

The director of *1837* was Paul Thompson. The designer was Paul Williams. I was the writer on—but not of—*1837*.

Rick Salutin

1837: THE FARMERS' REVOLT

ACT ONE
Walking

A man is walking on the set. He carries an axe and a sack. He walks and walks, seeing the forests and the occasional cleared farm of Upper Canada pass by him as he goes. The audience are still entering. They are asking each other, Who is he? Where's he going? What's he got with him? *He keeps walking. This is a play about a time when people in Canada walked to get anywhere and do anything. Eventually two* FARMERS *enter, one stage left and one stage right. They are taking a rest. They watch him go by their field.*

FIRST FARMER   Who is that fellow?

SECOND   Name's Thomas Campbell.

FIRST   Where's he from?

SECOND   Glasgow.

He walks. Enter two more FARMERS.

THIRD FARMER   Where's he going?

FOURTH   He's bought a plot of land near Coldwater.

They watch him awhile. They are all tired from hard work.

SECOND   How much did it cost him?

FIRST   Twenty dollars down—he'll work the rest out.

FOURTH   How long has he been walking?

THIRD   Four and a half days.

FIRST   *feeling his own feet*   Ouch.

SECOND   Does he have any family?

FOURTH   Wife. Son. Three daughters. Younger brother. All back in Scotland. They'll be over later.

THIRD   What's he got with him?

FIRST   Everything he owns.

SECOND   Think he knows how to use that axe?

THIRD   If he doesn't, he'll learn.

FIRST   What does he see?

THIRD   Trees.

SECOND   Trees.

FOURTH   Trees.

FIRST   Trees and trees and trees and trees—

They all fill in the word "trees" as he speaks. They are planting a forest of trees with their voices. It mounts, then recedes and dies.

THIRD   What's he going to do when he gets there?

He gets there. He puts down his load, very weary. Looks around at the trees, up at the trees, tries to see through to the sky. He decides not to rest, raises his axe, and begins clearing his land.

Blackout.

Clearing

Grunts and sounds of straining in the dark. Lights up slowly. Four people working around a great (imaginary) stump, hacking it and hauling it. With one mighty heave it comes loose and they fall away from it, spent.

VOICE   *offstage*   Halloooo—

STEADMAN   *panting*   Hallooo—

VOICE   *offstage*   Is there a Peter Steadman there?

They lie there, too exhausted to respond. Enter MAGISTRATE THOMPSON, obviously an official. He approaches one of them.

MAGISTRATE   Peter Steadman?

He is motioned toward STEADMAN.

Magistrate Thompson, from Richmond Hill.

STEADMAN   Magistrate, how do you do?   *With distaste, the MAGISTRATE shakes STEADMAN's sweaty hand.*   It's a long ride from Richmond Hill. Will you take something to drink? Sit down?

MAGISTRATE   Thank you, no.

STEADMAN'S WIFE   Can I get you anything?

MAGISTRATE   No. I was told I would find you here.

STEADMAN   We've been here a long time.

MAGISTRATE   How long, exactly?

STEADMAN   Close to two years.

MAGISTRATE   This is fine land. How much have you cleared?

STEADMAN   Eighteen acres.

STEADMAN'S BROTHER   Eighteen acres in two years!

STEADMAN'S WIFE   We've been working hard.

MAGISTRATE   Yes. Congratulations. That's a fine home.

STEADMAN'S WIFE   First one I've ever had that was my own.

STEADMAN   We were going to come up to Toronto to see you people pretty soon.

MAGISTRATE   Good, black, fertile soil.

STEADMAN   Yes, it's a good farm.

MAGISTRATE   Could I see your deed please, Mr. Steadman?

STEADMAN   I don't have a deed.

MAGISTRATE   Then your letter of license.

STEADMAN   Now I wouldn't have one of those without a deed, would I?

MAGISTRATE   Mr. Steadman, don't presume to tell me my business.   *He unrolls a survey map, which looks to us like a Union Jack.*   Your lot is number seventeen. On this government survey map, lot seventeen, here in this corner—I see no record whatever of the name Steadman. But it *is* part of a parcel of one thousand acres which was granted three weeks ago to Colonel Sparling of the Forty-Eighth Highlanders.

STEADMAN   Granted!

MAGISTRATE   By the Lieutenant-Governor.

STEADMAN'S SISTER-IN-LAW   This farm is not for sale!

STEADMAN'S BROTHER   You listen—we home-steaded this land.

MAGISTRATE   I choose to call it squatting.

STEADMAN'S BROTHER   Call it what you want. It's what everybody does when they don't have any money to start.

MAGISTRATE   And everybody who does it accepts the risk that something of this sort will happen.

STEADMAN   *trying to be reasonable*   I'll be glad to go down to Toronto and talk to this Colonel and buy the land from him.

MAGISTRATE   Mr. Steadman, I know with certainty that he simply does not want you on his land. He is not however an ungenerous man, and if you approach him on the right footing, he might be willing to recompense you for your labour on his land.

STEADMAN'S BROTHER   How's he going to pay us for two years of clearing?

MAGISTRATE   He wants you off the land. You have one week, Steadman.

STEADMAN   *burning*   You have one minute, Magistrate—to get off my farm.

STEADMAN'S BROTHER picks up his axe. The MAGISTRATE beats a retreat.

MAGISTRATE   *as he goes*   One week, Steadman—

STEADMAN   *calling after him*   We'll be here a week from now, Magistrate. We'll be here long after you're dead—

Now that they are left alone again, the anger quickly drops away and doubt sets in.

STEADMAN'S WIFE   What do we do now?

STEADMAN   *ponders, then—*   Go back to work. Come on—

They set in around the stump again, straining and grunting. Lights down slowly to black.

Hat

Lights up on MACKENZIE.

MACKENZIE   My name is William Lyon Mackenzie. I run a small newspaper here in Toronto—it's called *The Advocate.* Used to be *The Colonial Advocate,* but I decided it was high time to get rid of the "Colonial" part. It's a good paper, pick one up if you get a chance. Now I was on my way down King Street to the office the other day—and it had rained just the night before. Well any time it rains here the roads turn into quagmires, and the only way you can use them is to pick your way from one high, dry spot to another. So I was picking my way along King—just outside here—when I noticed this hat lying in the mud in the middle of the road. Well it looked like a good hat and I decided it was worth muddying my boots to get it, so I picked my way over...   *He is doing it.*   ...best I could, and I picked up the hat.

As he lifts the hat he uncovers a MAN's head. The MAN spits out a mouthful of mud.

MACKENZIE   There was a man under it!   *to MAN* It looks like you're in trouble.

MAN   Yes, I certainly am.

MACKENZIE   *bending down to hoist him*   Here, let me give you a hand.

MAN   You're quite a little fellow. I think you'd better go for some help.

MACKENZIE   Oh I'm pretty tough. I think I can pull you out myself.

MAN   But it's not just me I'm worrying about. It's the wagon and the two oxen!

Blackout.

The Tavern

Onstage right: ISAAC CASSELMAN, Tavernkeeper; EMMA, his wife; RUTH, a friend and customer; and JAMEY, local drunk and part-time help at the tavern.

ISAAC   *singing*
When I got up in the morning,
My heart did give a wrench,
For lying on the table
Was the captain and a wench—

Freeze. Enter FRED BENCH, stage left. Addresses audience.

FRED   That's why you cut your roots and come thousands of miles across the ocean—to buy your own land, be your own boss. I just got back from Toronto about that very thing—

Tavern action resumes.

ISAAC   *singing*
And then one fine spring morning,
I did a dancing jig—

Freeze.

FRED   This is Isaac Casselman's Inn. When I'm not working in the bush I spend most of my time right here.

Tavern resumes.

ISAAC   For lying on the table was the captain and—

Enter FRED.

Fred Bench! You're back—

EMMA   Fred—welcome home.

FRED   Hello Emma. Jamey! Hasn't Isaac fired you yet?

JAMEY   He can't fire me Fred.

FRED   Why not?

JAMEY   *tottering into cellar*   I'm the only one who knows the inventory—

FRED   Ruth—

They embrace. RUTH is so excited she can't talk. Enter JAMEY, carrying a keg.

JAMEY   In your honour Fred. The best keg of rum in Isaac's cellar.

FRED   How do you know that Jamey?

JAMEY   Because I tested four others before I found it. It's the best.

EMMA   Fred—come on and tell us some good stories about Toronto.

RUTH   And show us what you've got!

ISAAC   Now first things first. In honour of the traveller's return—a toast!

ALL   Hear hear; a toast; *etc.*

They all take mugs.

ISAAC   To Fred Bench—and his new land.

ALL BUT FRED   To Fred Bench and—

FRED   Hold it. That's not quite right. To Fred Bench—and his *almost* land.

ISAAC   Wha—?

EMMA   Have you been drinking Fred?

JAMEY   *undaunted*   To Fred Bench and the almost land.   *Down the hatch.*

RUTH   What do you mean?

FRED   Haven't touched a drop Emma. At least not yet. But now I'll tell you that story. Do you want to hear it?

ALL   Yes; *etc.*

FRED   It's a story about Toronto. What a city! For three days I walked through the bush. It was dark. Trees blocking out almost all the light. But when you get to the top of Yonge St., that bush just sweeps away. And there's Toronto. Morning fog coming in off the lake. Spires poking through here and there. It was like a dream. And I knew that day the city belonged to Fred Bench! Down into it I went—why, do you know they've got it built up all the way to Queen St.?   *disbelief*   I walked right in alongside the gentlemen and ladies. Isaac—you should see the taverns they've got now. And the traffic. Right along the flagstone sidewalks of King Street to the Courthouse—that's where the Land Office is. Up the steps—just a whiff of fish coming in from the wharf—inside are pillars that lay the fear of God in you. And *there's* the Land Office. And behind its thick oak door sits the Commissioner of Crown Lands.   *He is seized with an idea.*   Jamey—c'mere. You want to help me show these fine people some of the facts of life?

JAMEY   *stumbling to FRED's side*   Facts of life? You've come to the right man for the facts of life.

FRED   Stand over here Jamey. Peter Robinson, Commissioner of Crown Lands.   *JAMEY looks around.*   No. That's you. Straight and tall. Fine satin shirt. Stiff collar.   *JAMEY begins to assume the role.*   Velvet trousers. And boots that you can see your face in.

JAMEY   *He has become the Lands Commissioner.* Shine my boots Fred!

FRED   Oh yes sir! Because you see, you control all the government land in the province.

JAMEY   All the land in the province? Mine?

FRED   Lord Jamey!

JAMEY   That's me—Lord Jamey!

FRED moves away from JAMEY.

FRED   Now on the other side of this oak door is the waiting room, three times the size of your tavern Isaac. And it's packed with people like me—all wanting land.

RUTH   Come on, let's help him out.

They all join FRED in the waiting room.

FRED   And we're packed in so tight—fifty or sixty of us—that we can't even sit down. Hey, Jamey, we got no land, you got it all. What do you think of us?

JAMEY   *swaggering*   I think you're all—pieces of dirt!

FRED   We just couldn't get past the door. We waited one, two, three, four days, and never saw the Commissioner. Then, on the fifth day, in walks a private land agent—a Mr. Bronlyn.   *ISAAC assumes the role as FRED talks.*   A rich man, in a grey suit, with a bit of paunch and cold grey eyes that look right through anything and anyone they—

BRONLYN barges right through the waiting room, slapping people out of his way. The COMMISSIONER opens the door to him.

ISAAC   *as BRONLYN*   Ah, Mr. Commissioner—

JAMEY   Mr. Bronlyn, come in.   *to the others*   Slam!

EMMA   Fred—you mean he just walked in there—nice as you please!

FRED   Just like that.

EMMA   What'd you do?

FRED   What would you do?

EMMA stalks up to the door and knocks.

EMMA   Mr. Commissioner! I want to talk to you. We were promised land. We've been waiting here for five days. Some of us are hungry. You've got to—

JAMEY   *without opening door*   My dear woman—who do you think you're talking to? The Commissioner of Crown Lands—that's who you're talking to. Now can't you see I'm busy? Go away. I've got important business to discuss with my friend, Mr. Bronlyn. If you want, you can leave your names with my clerk.

FRED   So we left our names with the clerk, walked out of the waiting room, and stood around Toronto for another two days. And then, in comes Mr. Bronlyn.

ISAAC   Is there a Mr. Bench here? A Mr. Fred Bench?

FRED   Yeah?

ISAAC   Mr. Bench, I understand that you wish to purchase some land.

FRED   Oh yes, yes sir—you bet I do.

ISAAC Well I have just the land for you. One hundred acres of good, fertile—

FRED And I have the twenty dollars here to buy it.

ISAAC You don't understand Mr. Bench. This land sells for two dollars an acre.

RUTH What?

EMMA But that's two hundred dollars—

ISAAC That's correct, Madam. Well Mr. Bench—

FRED Now hold on. I got the newspaper that says I can get one hundred acres of government land for twenty dollars.

ISAAC That might be, Mr. Bench—though I rather doubt it. But I do not represent the government. I am a private land agent. I sell land for a profit.

FRED *to EMMA and RUTH* Now where did he get my name?

JAMEY *still in his "office"* I gave it to him, Fred. I gave him all your names—for a little . . . consideration.

FRED A little consideration. You see, they're in it together. Two crooks working hand in glove.

ISAAC Well Mr. Bench? Do you or do you not want to buy the land? *reverting to himself* What'd you do, Fred?

FRED I laughed in his face, grabbed him by his fancy shirt, and threw him out—because nobody makes a fool of Fred Bench!

EMMA Good for you, Fred!

JAMEY You really did, did you Fred?

RUTH You mean . . . you didn't get the land . . . there's nothing. . . .

FRED *keeping up the bravado* Well—no. But I've still got twenty dollars, and if it's not going for land, it's going for the biggest party we've ever had around here! Jamey—come on—

JAMEY I'm with you Fred—

FRED Isaac, more drinks—

All but RUTH cheer and raise their glasses. Freeze. Lights down on them. RUTH, alone on the other side of the stage, wails her disappointment.

Blackout.

The Family Compact

MACKENZIE Ladies and gentlemen, this evening for your entertainment, and with the help of my charming assistant . . . *enter charming ASSISTANT* . . . I would like to demonstrate for you a magical trick. Now the thing that interests me about magic is not so much the phenomenon of the trick itself, as how it is actually accomplished, and I shall try to perform this trick in such a way that you can share its secret with me. *to ASSISTANT* We need the volunteers onstage. *to audience* I would have got volunteers from the audience, but you're all far too respectable for that.

Enter the three VOLUNTEERS. They are a sullen, brutish lot.

Now this trick will go down in the annals of conjuring history as one of the most remarkable ever performed anywhere in the world, for you are about to see this gang of thieves, rogues, villains and fools transformed before your very eyes into the ruling class of this province. Yes indeed—this band of criminals, by magical transformation, will become the government of Upper Canada. Now I've said I was going to do this trick slowly, so that you'll be able to see the positions they hold in the government, as well as the bonds that tie them together: bonds of blood, marriage, or greed—and in most cases it's all three. Anyway, on with the trick. Number one—

The ASSISTANT covers up the first VOLUNTEER with her cape.

Presto—Darcy Boulton Sr.

The cape is whisked away, revealing VOLUNTEER transformed into member of the Family Compact.

Retired pensioner, at a pension of five hundred pounds a year, paid by the people of Upper Canada. Number two—Presto—Henry Boulton, son to number one. *So on with the cape. After three she begins again with one.* Now Henry is the Attorney General for Upper Canada as well as being bank solicitor. Number three—Presto!—Darcy Boulton Jr., Auditor-General for Upper Canada as well as being Master in Chancery and a commissioner in the police. Numbers four and five—William and George Boulton—Presto!—also sons to number one, brothers to two and three, and holding various positions in the government. Number six—Presto!——John Beverley Robinson. Now Robinson is a brother-in-law to the Boultons there. He is the Chief Justice for Upper Canada. He's a member of the Legislative Council and the Speaker of the Legislative Council. Number seven—Peter Robinson, brother to number six. He's a member of the Executive Council, he's a member of the Legislative Council, he's the Commissioner of Crown Lands and Commissioner of the Clergy Reserves, as well as being the Surveyor-General of Woods. Number eight—William Robinson, brother to numbers six and seven. He's the Postmaster for Newmarket, he's a member of the Assembly for Simcoe, he's a government contractor, a colonel in the militia, and a Justice of the Peace.

MACKENZIE claps his hands twice. This brings the VOLUNTEERS out of their trance. They are dumbfounded.

We'll skip over nine, ten, eleven, twelve, thirteen, fourteen, and fifteen. They're just more of the same: they're all related to each other and they all hold various positions in the government. Which brings us to sixteen.

He claps again, thrusting VOLUNTEERS back into character. The ASSISTANT can barely keep the blistering pace.

—James B. Macaulay. Macaulay is a justice of the court of King's Bench. Number seventeen—Christopher Alexander Hagerman—presto!—Now Hagerman is a brother-in-law to Macaulay—

The cape is still in place, and a struggle is evidently taking place behind it. MACKENZIE rushes across, and snatches it away to reveal HAGERMAN in an unseemly clinch with the ASSISTANT.

This man is the Solicitor-General of Upper Canada! Now we won't do eighteen to twenty-two for the same reason we skipped the earlier batch, which brings us to twenty-three, twenty-four and twenty-five—the Jarvis family: Samuel Peter Jarvis, Grant Jarvis—his son—and William Jarvis, his brother. They hold such varied positions between them as clerk of the Crown in Chancery, Secretary of the Province, bank solicitor, clerk of the Legislative Council, police justice, judge, Commissioner of Customs, and two high sheriffs. And that brings us to twenty-six, the biggest fish in this small pond of Upper Canada—Archdeacon John Strachan, family tutor and political schoolmaster to this mob. This man is the archdeacon and rector of York. He's a member of the Executive Council, he's a member of the Legislative Council, he's President of the University, President of the Board of Education, and twenty other situations. *MACKENZIE and STRACHAN glare at each other.* Oh I almost forgot—twenty-seven—Thomas Mercer Jones. He's the son-in-law to Strachan and he's the agent and director for the Canada Company land monopoly here in Upper Canada. And there you have it—the government of this fair colony. *They take a bow.*

Now this family connection rules Upper Canada according to its own good pleasure. It has no effective check from the country to guard the people against its acts of tyranny and oppression. It includes the whole of the judges of the supreme civil and criminal tribunals; it includes the agents and directors for the Canada Company land monopoly; it includes the president and solicitor and members of the board of the Bank of Upper Canada; it includes half of the Executive Council and all of the Legislative Council. *They are chortling with self-satisfaction.* Now this is pretty impressive, I'd say—criminals into government. But there's one piece of magic even more mind-boggling than that you've already seen—and that is how this Family Compact of villainy stays in power in Upper Canada!

They laugh him off the stage.

Mary MacDonald

EDWARD PETERS, a farmer, is stage left. He is waiting for someone to arrive. Enter MARY MAC-DONALD, stage right. She is expecting to be met. She does not notice him. He approaches her nervously.

EDWARD   Excuse me, are you Miss Mary Macdonald?

MARY   I am.   *She is very Scottish.*

EDWARD   Oh. I'm Edward Peters.

They are both horribly awkward.

MARY   I'm very pleased to make your acquaintance Mr. Peters.

EDWARD   I'm very pleased to meet you.   *A painful silence.*   You must be tired after such a long trip.

MARY   Yes, I am—a bit.

EDWARD   They have benches here for people if you'd care to—um—

MARY   Oh, thank you.

They cross and sit down.

EDWARD   *plunging*   I wrote you a letter, Miss Macdonald. I don't know if you received it, proposing a date for the—um—for our wedding.

MARY   *nearly choking with nervousness*   Yes. I got it.

EDWARD   Ah. Well. Would two weeks be satisfactory then?

MARY   Yes. That would be just fine. I wouldn't want to put you to any trouble.

EDWARD   No. It's no trouble.

They sit in awful silence. He leans over and away from her, to spit. He notices her watching him and swallows it instead.

MARY   Oh feel free.

EDWARD   Ah, no. I didn't really feel like it.

MARY   It's quite hot, is it not?

EDWARD   Yes. It's usually quite hot here in August. It's going to get a lot colder though.

MARY   What kind of farm do you have Mr. Peters?

EDWARD   It's a *good* farm. I raise wheat, built most of a barn, got a good frame house. I think you'll be very comfortable there. Nice furniture. Rough, but it's usable. I built it myself. I'm good with my hands.

MARY   *trying hopelessly to relax him and herself* Yes—

EDWARD   And I don't drink.

MARY   *not really happy about it*   Oh.

EDWARD   I bought a cow.

MARY   You did—

EDWARD   Yes. I thought you'd be used to fresh milk so I went and bought a cow.

MARY   *pleased*   And what's her name?

EDWARD   *embarrassed again*   Cow.

MARY   Cow?

EDWARD   Well when you only have one, you just . . . call it . . . cow. . . .

MARY   *feeling their lack of success in communicating*   Oh—

EDWARD   But you could go ahead and give her a nice name.

MARY   I could?

EDWARD   Sure. You'll be milking her and looking after her. You could go ahead and name her.

MARY   Thank you.

EDWARD   You're welcome.

With great relief he spots someone coming up the street.

That's George. See that big fellow on the wagon there? That's my brother George. He's come down to take us back to the farm.

MARY   Now?

EDWARD   Yes.

They start across the stage. MARY is in front of EDWARD. MARY stumbles and almost falls. EDWARD catches her by the arm. It is the first time they've touched. They smile.

EDWARD   You've got to watch where you're walking, Mary. There's ruts.

MARY   Yes.

They go off together.

The Lady in the Coach

Enter LADY BACKWASH, an English gentlewoman of the memoir-writing ilk. (Note: This role has been played by both male and female actors.)

LADY B.   Ladies, I should like to talk to you this evening about my adventures in Upper Canada. I call this lecture—Roughing It In The Bush. The Bush is a term which these quaint Canadians use when describing the vast trackless forests which cover nine-tenths of the colony; dark impenetrable woods much like a jungle, complete with insects, but not the heat. I was on my way to visit a very old and dear friend, Colonel Stockton, in Niagara-on-the-Lake.

As she speaks, the COACH DRIVER appears, brings in and harnesses his horse to the coach and settles in for the ride.

LADY B.   We were to have a sumptuous meal and then witness the spectacular beauty of Niagara Falls by moonlight, which I shall describe later in this evening's talk. Our transportation from Toronto to Niagara was to be accomplished by coach. Now I use this word in the broadest sense of the term, for the vehicle which was produced for our conveyance, if 'twere in England, would not be called a coach. It would be called a great many things, but certainly not a coach. However, despite this hardship, it was with the greatest of anticipation that I set out, with my man Johnson . . . *Enter JOHNSON, with a discreet bow toward the audience. JOHNSON is a young lad, notably Cockney.* . . . to travel from Toronto to Niagara.

They enter and are seated in the coach. The DRIVER lets out a "hyaaah" to his horse and they are off with much bumping.

DRIVER   Giddup Winnifred—whoa—hyaah—giddup. . . .

LADY B.   Johnson, have they never heard of springs in this country?

JOHNSON   I don't believe so madam—

They hit an enormous bump, then bounce, stop, and the coach rocks from side to side. The LADY and her man are discomfitted. The DRIVER has leapt from his seat down to the side of the coach and is straining to push it out of the hole in which it is stuck.

LADY B.   Johnson—the driver has jumped off!

JOHNSON   I don't blame him. I'd get off too if I could.

LADY B.   Driver.   *The DRIVER does not respond.* Driver! We've stopped.

DRIVER   *hoping she'll go away*   That's right, ma'am.

LADY B.   Why have we stopped?

DRIVER   Well ma'am—it's the mud.

LADY B.   Mud? You hear that Johnson—mud! My dear man, I have a very important dinner engagement in Niagara-on-the-Lake this evening, and with some candor I might tell you that if I am forced to go without my dinner tonight, you shall be obliged to do without your job tomorrow. Mud or no mud!

DRIVER   Ma'am—if you think this is bad, why we've got bogs up the way ahead of us that'll make this look like a puddle. Now we'll be able to get on our way in a minute if you'll just step out of the coach.

LADY B.   Out? Get out? My dear man, your impertinence is only matched by your incompetence as a driver. It is my duty to ride in this coach from Toronto to Niagara. It is yours to get me there. Now I am doing my duty. Kindly do yours.

DRIVER   *patience, patience*   Ma'am—if you won't get out of the coach, to lighten the load, so that I can push her out of this hole, we'll never get to Niagara.

JOHNSON   *aping his mistress' tone*   Absolutely not. We paid good money to ride in this coach and we're not getting out of it.   *turning to LADY B., pleased with himself*   Got to be firm with his type.

LADY B.   *interrupting*   Johnson, you and I shall get out of the coach.

JOHNSON   *stung*   Wot—

LADY B.   *firmly*   —thereby lightening the load, thereby facilitating this nincompoop in getting us out of here.

DRIVER   Thank you ma'am. There's a dry spot here—

JOHNSON   I don't see no dry spot—

The DRIVER tries to help JOHNSON down. JOHNSON tries to avoid being dropped in the mud. The upshot is, the DRIVER is holding JOHNSON aloft. LADY B. stands up grandly and strides out of the other door of the coach onto the side of the road. She notices the confusion with JOHNSON and upbraids him.

LADY B.   Johnson, come over here. Don't worry about a little mud. Where would the glorious Empire be today if it weren't above mud?

JOHNSON crosses to her and stands beside her. The DRIVER puts his shoulder to the wheel.

DRIVER   Now pull Winnifred. Pull girl—

LADY B.   *to DRIVER*   Oh you'll not do it that way. You're not strong enough.

DRIVER   *straining*   Hyaah, hyaah—

JOHNSON   He's not smart enough either.

LADY B.   He's not smart enough to know he's not strong enough.

DRIVER   *giving up*   Whoa Winnifred—

LADY B.   Told you so. No, Johnson shall have to help you push from behind.

JOHNSON   *stung*   Wot?

LADY B.   Yes, Johnson shall have to get in the mud and help you push from behind.

JOHNSON   Wot—me get in the mud and push that thing. Not likely—

LADY B.   *cutting him off with great master-servant authority*   Johnson!

JOHNSON breaks off his tirade and assumes instant humility. He has remembered his place.

This colony is having a most disturbing effect on your personality. Now into the mud and push! *JOHNSON jumps obediently into the mud.*   That's British pluck.

DRIVER   Alright Mr. Johnson. You just put your back into it, right about there, and give it what you've got—

JOHNSON wrinkles his nose at the DRIVER.

LADY B.   Johnson, push with a will—the eyes of England are upon you.

DRIVER   Alright, Winnifred, pull girl, hyaah—

They strain away. Enter, rear of LADY BACKWASH, an INDIAN carrying an axe. He is amused by the sight and wanders up. LADY B. hears his laughs, turns to see him and emits a shriek.

LADY B.   Eeek. Johnson, I'm being attacked by a savage!

JOHNSON   *springing to the rescue*   Savage is it? That's my job.   *running up to confront the savage*   Alright Savage—put 'em up. I studied with the Marquess of Queensbury, I did—Omygawd, he's got an axe!

He flees to the other side of the stage and climbs a tree.

DRIVER   *to INDIAN*   Hello Bart. How are you today?

INDIAN   *moving over to LADY B.*   Fine. Hello Ma'am, Wells is the name.

He offers his hand which she shakes, her mind already grinding away about how she can use this new arrival.

INDIAN   *moving on to DRIVER*   Where did you find that one?

LADY B.   Johnson, come down from that tree. You're not a monkey.   *JOHNSON obeys.*   Johnson, it *referring to the INDIAN*   speaks English. And if it speaks English, it can take orders. Johnson, you shall take the savage in hand and push from behind. Driver—Johnson and the savage shall push from behind. While they push, you shall lift from the middle, and I myself shall take Winnifred by the head, and encourage her to greater effort. Right Winnifred?

WINNIFRED whinnies. They assume their appointed positions.

LADY B.   Altogether now—push, pull, come on Winnifred, it's coming—

They are straining, pushing, lifting. Suddenly, with a lurch, the coach comes free. They are all—except for LADY B.—panting from the effort. She is babbling more than ever.

LADY B.   *elated*   There! We did it! What did I tell you? Just needed a little leadership. Johnson—you were superb. Driver—you were tremendous. Savage—you were alright. And Winnifred—you pulled with a will.

INDIAN   *to DRIVER*   You sure it's safe for me to leave you alone with her?

LADY B.   Johnson, I haven't felt so good since I arrived in this wretched colony.   *a sudden inspiration*   Johnson—quickly, my diary.

JOHNSON fetches it and takes down her dictation. She addresses posterity.

We had fought the good fight and won. We had been faced with insurmountable obstacles and we had overcome them. And now we took the rest of the victorious, and what better place than here, in Nature's Cathedral.

JOHNSON   *copying*   Oh, I like that.

LADY B.   I looked up at the tall trees, like giant columns supporting the vast infinite blue of the sky above. The birds sang, the bees—um, the bees— *She searches.*

JOHNSON   Might I suggest "buzzed"?

LADY B.   *accepting with alacrity*   Buzzed. Of course—buzzed. Very good, Johnson. And everywhere was peace, tranquillity and beauty.

WINNIFRED whinnies impatiently.

DRIVER   Ma'am can I suggest you get back into the coach. Once Winnifred gets us out of one bog, she just can't wait to get us into the next one.

JOHNSON   Huh?

LADY B.   An example of Canadian humour, I believe, Johnson.   *They chuckle.*   That's enough, Johnson.

They get back into the coach. The DRIVER is about to crack the whip. LADY BACKWASH takes one final look at the site of this enchanted event.

LADY B.   Farewell, brave bush!

DRIVER   Hyaah!

The coach bounces into motion. They are bouncing with it.

Blackout.

The Head

Note: Sir Francis Bond Head was Lieutenant-Governor of Upper Canada in 1837. Mackenzie could rarely resist punning on his name. In this scene four actors comprise themselves as Head's head. Two of their heads are his eyes, two arms his arching eyebrows, two other arms his nose. So on for his mouth, dimple, etc. The scene begins with the narrated, piece by piece construction of the head, after which the "head" talks.

VOICE   Two piercing blue eyes . . .   *Enter the eyes.*   . . . arching eyebrows, a long aristocratic nose, a firm mouth—and a dimple on the chin. Sir Francis Bond Head, Lieutenant-Governor of Upper Canada, addresses an assembly of voters before the election of 1836.

HEAD   *sniffing, scowling, smiling etc., as the speech proceeds*   Gentlemen, as your district now has the important duty to perform of electing representatives for the new Parliament, I think it might practically assist if I clearly lay before you the conduct I intend inflexibly to pursue. If you choose to dispute with me and live on bad terms with the Mother Country, you will—to use a homely phrase—only quarrel with your own bread and butter. If you choose to try this experiment by again electing members who will oppose me, do so. On the other hand, if you choose to embark your interests with my character, I will take paternal care of them both. Men—women and money are what you want. And if you send to Parliament members who will assist me, you can depend upon it, you will gain far more than you possibly can by trying to insult me. But—let your conduct be what it may—I am quite determined, so long as I occupy this station, neither to give offense, nor to take it. Gentlemen, you may now cast your ballots.

Blackout.

Further note: The above is a quotation from an actual speech by Sir Francis at the time.

The Election of '36

A TORY and a REFORMER.

TORY   Hey!

REFORMER   Yeah?

TORY   How're you voting?

REFORMER   Me? Reform.

TORY   Oh Yeah?   *Ploughs him one.*

ANOTHER REFORMER   Well—you're obviously voting Tory.

TORY   That's right.

REFORMER   Uh-huh.   *Ploughs the TORY. Then loudly proclaims:*   Reform!

ANOTHER TORY   Didn't hear that. All votes have to be heard to be recorded.

REFORMER   I said—Reform!

TORY   That's what I thought you said.   *Wham.*

ROBERT DAVIS   *(This character has, for some reason, been played by a woman in all productions of 1837 so far.)*   Hey, don't hit him like that. This is no way to carry on an election—

All then turn on this poor peacemaker and attack him, screaming their political slogans as they flail away at each other and particularly at ROBERT DAVIS. The cry of "Tory" rings above the others. The Tories are obviously most proficient at this political bullying. The mayhem concludes with the brutal cry, "God—Save—The—Queen!" Freeze.

The Canadian Farmer's Travels in the U.S.A.

ROBERT DAVIS, Upper Canadian farmer, drags himself out from the bottom of the brawl during the election of 1836.

DAVIS   Would you believe that was an election? I would! Lost two teeth in it—and that proves it's an election around here. My name's Robert Davis. I have a small farm here in Nissouri Township. Lived here all my life. Got two fine kids. Taught myself to read and write. But this election was just about the end for me. Why we've been working for reform for fifteen years—and now things in Upper Canada are worse than ever. I'd about lost hope. And I needed to get my hope back somehow. So I decided I'd take a trip to the United States. I'd heard things were different down there, and I thought—if I can see that someone else has succeeded, maybe I can keep on trying myself. So I started out.

He walks.

Now the first place I came to on my way to the border was the little town of Chatham. Beautiful little place for a town, but very sleepy. . . .

The Town Council of Chatham comes to order.

MAYOR   My friends, as members of the Town Council of Chatham I think we should establish what is going to be happening here for the next twenty years.

DAVIS   Good. I'd like to see that. What have you got in mind?

The members of the Council yawn, fall flat on their backs, and snore.

DAVIS   See that! That's despair—I'm not going to stay around here.   *Walks.*   So I kept on, till I came to the town of Sandwich, that's right across the river from Detroit. Look around. There's nothing happening here.

BOATMAN   All aboard for Detroit.

DAVIS   Can you take me to Detroit?

BOATMAN   Yup. Get aboard fast. Miss this boat and there isn't another one for a week.

DAVIS   That's ridiculous—one boat a week!

They start across the river.

And as we left Sandwich snoozing in the sunshine, I could see a kind of stir on the other side of the river. And sounds—sounds like I'd never heard before—

The bustling sounds of Detroit begin to come up.

DAVIS   And suddenly we were surrounded by boats, big and little, carrying grain, and goods, and *people*—

BOATMAN   *yelling*   Detroit! Gateway to the American Dream—

The sounds of industry and trade explode around poor DAVIS. People rush back and forth past him, happy, productive—

AMERICAN   Howdy stranger, I'd like to stay and shoot the breeze, but I'm too busy getting rich.

DAVIS   Look at all these people—and this *industry*, and—and—two thousand immigrants a day—most of them from Upper Canada!

IMMIGRANT   *kissing the ground*   America! America!

RUNAWAY SLAVE   *to DAVIS*   Excuse me sir, I'm a runaway slave. Which way is Canada?

DAVIS   No, no. Don't go there. It's terrible. Stay here. I'm sure things will get better for you.   *turning*   Oh—look. A four-storey brick building!   *Someone plays it.*   Isn't it wonderful?

WRECKER   'Scuse me fella. Gotta tear down this four-storey building.

DAVIS *horrified* Why?

WRECKER *knocking it down* 'Cause we're gonna put up a *six*-storey one in its place! There—Whoosht—up it goes.

DAVIS Oh—and look at what it says on it—Museum!

MUSEUM Sure. Come on in—

DAVIS enters, sees statues of American heroes—"We got more than we know what to do with"—Whistler's Mother, or some such nonsense. (By the way, this scene has never been "set." DAVIS has seen different things nearly every time he has taken his trip.)

DAVIS This is all fine, but you know I'm a farmer, and I'll really know what to make of your country when I see what's happening outside the cities. So can you tell me how I can get to the country?

AMERICAN Sure. How'd you like to go?

DAVIS How? I thought I'd walk—

AMERICAN Pshaw—nobody walks down here. Now you can go by coach, or canal—

DAVIS Don't talk to me about canals! Did you ever hear of the Welland Canal? They've been building it for twelve years! It's only twelve miles long. It's cost us millions of dollars and you *still* have to dig your way through!

AMERICAN No kidding. Well we've got the Erie Canal. Five hundred miles and clear straight through—

DAVIS *stunned* Five hundred miles. . . .

AMERICAN But if you don't like that, you can always take the train.

DAVIS Train? What was that word you just said?

Zip. He is suddenly in the country.

DAVIS So I went to the country. Acre after acre of cleared, fertile land—

FARMER Excuse me friend, would you mind moving your foot?

DAVIS My foot? Why?

FARMER Well, do you feel something moving under it?

DAVIS Moving? Why yes—I do!

FARMER Just move it aside—there.

They both watch as a crop of wheat grows from the floor to the ceiling.

Crop of wheat I planted this morning. A little small this year. Well, watch yourself while I harvest it. *with his axe* Timber!

DAVIS Wheat—and apple orchards—and thousands of head of cattle—and sixty pound cheeses!

These appear—or fail to do so—at the whim of the other actors onstage. The most fun occurs when someone introduces into the scene something DAVIS and the others have not expected.

And then I went to one of the hundreds of thriving country towns—

SCHOOLHOUSE Bong! Bong! Come on kiddies—everybody into school for your free universal education.

DAVIS Free? Universal? You mean your schools aren't just for your aristocracy?

SCHOOLHOUSE You watch your language down here. We don't use words like that!

DAVIS Everyone can go to school! Does it work?

SCHOOLHOUSE Hah! Where's that dumb kid. C'mere kid, get inside.

The DUMB KID walks through one door of the schoolhouse and emerges from the other.

FORMERLY DUMB KID $E=mc^2$.

CHURCH Ding Dong—Methodist.

ANOTHER Ding Dong—Lutheran.

ANOTHER Ding Dong—Quaker.

Somebody has not declared himself.

DAVIS What are you?

TOWNSMAN I'm an atheist.

DAVIS You allow atheists down here too?

CHURCH We don't like them but we allow them.

DAVIS But which one is your established church, you know, the official church?

They all laugh.

TOWNSMAN Say—you must be a Canadian.

DAVIS *delighted* I am. How'd you know?

TOWNSMAN Say house.

DAVIS House.

TOWNSMAN Say about.

DAVIS About.

TOWNSMAN I knew it. Now excuse us, we're going to have an election.

DAVIS *panicking* An election? Let me out of here—I'm going to hide—I've lost enough teeth.

He watches from a distance.

FIRST VOTER Having searched my conscience, I have decided to cast my vote as a Democrat.

The next VOTER steps up. DAVIS winces in expectation of the clash.

SECOND VOTER Well, in that case, I'm going to vote Republican.

THIRD VOTER   Then I vote Democrat.

FOURTH VOTER   Let's see—the Republicans won last time, so I'll vote Democrat too.

ALL   Hurray!

They all commiserate with the lone Republican.

DAVIS   Hey—wait a minute. When does the fight start?

VOTER   Fight? What do you mean? This is an election. Now come here, uh, what's your name?

DAVIS   Davis.

VOTER   No, I mean your first name. We all use first names here.

DAVIS   Bob.

VOTER   Well, Bob, I'd like you to meet the new governor of our state. This is Ole. Ole, this is Bob, from Canada—

OLE   *a very slow speaking farmer*   Well, how do you do. You wouldn't like to buy a pig would you?

DAVIS   Pig? You mean you're the governor of this state and you still work as a farmer.

OLE   Well, gotta make some money somehow—

DAVIS   You know, you've all given me new hope. You've proven to me it can be done. This is what we've been working for for years, and I can go home now and—

VOTER   Home? Wait a minute Bob. Why don't you stay right here with us and make this your new home?

DAVIS   Here? But why should I?

ANOTHER VOTER   Because it's the best darned country in the world. That's why.

DAVIS   But—but I've got my family back there.

ANOTHER   Bring 'em down here. Bring your whole country.

DAVIS   But—but there's my farm.

ANOTHER   Tell you what we'll do Bob. We'll give you a four hundred acre cleared farm right here. Just for you.

DAVIS   *getting excited*   Cleared?   *suspicious* How much?

ANOTHER   Nothing. Just take good care of it.

DAVIS   I can have that farm?

ANOTHER   Sure. We'll just sweep those Indians off it and—

DAVIS   Why that's wonderful! You're all so generous! This must be the finest—

ANOTHER   See. He's starting to act like an American already. Being happy and talking loud—

DAVIS   No. No, I can't do it.

ANOTHER   Those words don't exist in America.

DAVIS   I can't stay. You see—it's not my home. I can't just leave Canada. It's up to us to do there what you've done here. But you've given me hope. Now I know it can be done—   *He is leaving.*   So I went home.

Lethargic, snoring, apathetic Canadians surround him.

DAVIS   And I said—Don't lie around. Get up. Help each other. You can do it.

He drags them to their feet. They are rubbery-legged. They cling to each other and anything they can find.

I've seen it now. I know it can be done. We can do it too, if we stay together. Now is not the time for Reformers to fawn and crouch. Now is the time to unite and fight!

Blackout.

The Dummy

A political rally in rural Upper Canada attended by angry Reform farmers.

FARMER   He's here, he's here alright. The great man is here. I saw him just out back.

They cheer.

He's come down here to talk to all of us—now you put that jug away, this is a dry meeting—but before the great man talks to us, a couple of the folks have worked up one of their little skits to do for us. So come on up here and get it over with, so we can all get on with hearing the great man's speech.   *Two farmers come up front.*   And don't forget your lines this time.

The two stand in front of the rally. One assumes the role of the VENTRILOQUIST. The other plays his DUMMY.

VENTRILOQUIST   Ladies and gentlemen. Presenting for your enjoyment, straight from England, John Bull—your Imperial ventriloquist—and his companion, Peter Stump—the Canadian axeman. Say hello to the people, Peter.

PETER   *The VENTRILOQUIST is throwing his voice.* Hello.

JOHN   Aren't you forgetting to add something, Peter?

PETER   God Save The Queen.

JOHN   Good, Peter. Very loyal. I say—what is that in your hand?

PETER   My axe.

JOHN   What do you do with your axe, Peter?

PETER   Chop down trees.   *He chops.*   Timber!

JOHN   And what do you do with the wood you cut?

PETER   Send it to you in England, John.

JOHN   Very fine Peter. Say, what else do you have there?

PETER   My rifle.

JOHN   Aha—and who are you going to shoot?

PETER   Yankees.

JOHN   Good. And quickly too—   *He hides behind PETER.*

PETER   Bang, bang, bang, bang—

JOHN   *emerging*   Whew! Well done, lad. Now could you loan me twenty of your dollars?

PETER   *protesting*   John, I'm short myself—

JOHN   *picking his pocket*   There. I knew you wouldn't mind. Now is there anything else I can do for you?

PETER   Yes.

JOHN   What's that?

PETER   Please take your hand away from my neck.

JOHN   *surprised*   I beg your pardon?

PETER   Take your hand away from me.

JOHN   If I do that, you will be helpless. Do you understand?

PETER   I want to try.

CROWD   Let him go. Give him a chance.

JOHN   Very well, Peter—

He yanks his hand out. PETER stands stock still. JOHN moves away from him.

Now Peter, now let's hear you speak. Ha! Chop down trees Peter! Shoot Yankees! Can't do a thing can you?

CROWD   Come on, Peter. You can do it.

JOHN   Without me, John Bull, you are nothing. Pathetic isn't he, ladies and gentlemen? A pitiable, colonial—

PETER   *with his own voice, for the first time*   Mm—

JOHN   *stunned*   What? What was that?

PETER   *louder*   Mm—mm—I—I—

JOHN   Peter, Peter—what are you up to?

PETER   *slowly finding his voice*   I want to say: *more confidently*   Thank God for the man who is giving me a voice—   *shouting, no longer a dummy at all*   William Lyon Mackenzie!

The CROWD cheers. Enter MACKENZIE and bounds onto the rostrum.

The Speech

MACKENZIE   Thank you, ladies and gentlemen, thank you. Now let's start off this meeting by giving three cheers for the men who made it possible, or rather I should say necessary. Let's have three cheers for Archdeacon John Strachan. Hip hip hurray! Hip hip hurray!—

CROWD   Booo—

MACKENZIE   Come now my friends, you won't cheer John Strachan? I didn't realize feelings ran that high. Now I was talking to someone the other day who said about Strachan—if that man's godliness were gunpowder, he couldn't blow his own nose. Alright then, if you won't cheer Strachan, let's have three cheers for Christopher Alexander Hagerman. Hip hip hurray—

CROWD   Booo—

MACKENZIE   My friends, these people tell us over and over that they are the nobility of this colony so we should cheer them. Come on now—

CROWD   No!

MACKENZIE   Alright then, let's give three cheers for the real nobility of Upper Canada. Three cheers for the farmers!

CROWD   Hip hip hurray! Hip hip hurray! Hip hip hurray!

MACKENZIE   Alright now, I'm going to tell you a story. It's an old story, but there's no stories like the old stories. It concerns a little Reformer who goes to the Assembly to see what he can do to rectify the wrongs in this colony. So he puts forward all those bills he feels are for the general good and he opposes all those bills he feels are against the general good, please or offend whom it might. And it seemed to offend some people. For Bolton called him a reptile and Hagerman called him a spaniel dog. Now that shows you one thing about Hagerman, and that is—that his knowledge of dogs is only equalled by his knowledge of decent government. For anybody who knew anything about dogs could tell you that this Reformer was not a spaniel dog—but a Scots terrier hot on the tail of a rat!

The CROWD cheers.

MACKENZIE   But these men didn't stop at calling him names. They thought that more forceful action was necessary. So they grabbed him by the seat of the pants and the collar of the coat, and they threw him out of the Assembly!   *MACKENZIE leaps into the CROWD.*   But what did the people do?

CROWD   We put you back.   *They hoist him back onto the platform.*

MACKENZIE   And they threw him out again!   *He leaps out.*

CROWD   And we put you back—

MACKENZIE   And out again—

CROWD   And back again—

MACKENZIE   And a fourth time—

CROWD   And back a fourth time—

MACKENZIE   Yes, four times they threw him out, and four times the people sent him back. And that's round one for the people. For try as they might, these men cannot oppose the will of the people to send to the Assembly who they want. So the little Reformer finds himself securely in the Assembly. But what can he do? His hands are tied. So he says to himself, I've got to go above the heads of these people, above Strachan and Bolton, and Hagerman. I've got to go to the top—to the King of England! So the little Reformer goes to England, and he's armed with a petition of grievances that's half a mile long. And the signatures on that petition aren't one, two, three, or four names. Oh no no no—there's twenty-five thousand names on that petition. And the King of England looks at it, and he goes—Oh my my my my! And he calls for the Colonial Secretary, and the Colonial Secretary gets the Colonial Office moving, and the Colonial Office gets our government over here moving, so everybody's moving hither-thither, helter-skelter, but out of all this government activity what real good comes? What happens here in this colony?

CROWD   Nothing!

MACKENZIE   Nothing? Not quite. For the Pharaoh of England in his wisdom sends us a saviour—a new Lieutenant-Governor, Sir Francis *Bone* Head. Now what are Sir Francis' credentials for holding this very important office?

CROWD   None! He hasn't got any!

MACKENZIE   Oh yes he does. It's a long and impressive list and I'm going to tell you what they are. Number one. He's a damn fool. Number two. He's English. Number three. He's arrogant. And number four. He's very good with a lasso.

CROWD   What?

MACKENZIE   The lasso. Sir Francis' specialty is the lasso—a skill he picked up in Argentina, used there for herding cattle. So the first thing Sir Francis does when he gets to our colony is he gets out his lasso, and he circles it above his head once, twice, three times—and he lets it go! And who does he catch? You! He catches the people of Upper Canada, and there we all are in Sir Francis' lasso. And he pulls it a little tighter and he says—alright, now it's time for an election; all those in favour of Reform, stand up! And he pulls very hard and he pulls all of us off our feet. Now how did one man pull all of us off our feet? I'll tell you how he did it. We're all in that lasso and we're pushing this way and pulling that way in our frustration and despair. But I tell you that, if as one man we took hold of that rope and turned to Sir Francis, then with one mighty tug, we could pull him off his high horse and send him back to England on his ass!

The CROWD cheers.

MACKENZIE   And that's what I want to talk to you about today. Pulling as one man—Union! For the power of the people is as nothing without union and union is nothing without confidence and discipline. Now the Tories have been following me around to these various meetings, taking what I say back to Toronto, and I'm flattered by the attention. But I don't want to get in trouble with the authorities—treason or anything of that sort, so I'm going to talk to you now in a roundabout manner. Now first of all I think we have to form ourselves into small groups—say fourteen to forty people—just to talk. There's no law against talking. And each of those groups is in contact with other such groups around the province, so we know who our friends are in case of an emergency. But I think the time for talking is past. It's gone by. And I think now it's time for us to work on our muscle power, develop our strength—and I think the best way to do that is through turkey shoots.

CROWD   Turkey shoots?

MACKENZIE   Yes—

CROWD   We know how to shoot turkeys!

MACKENZIE   But don't you think a turkey shoot would be more fun if there was a little drilling beforehand? And don't you think you could shoot turkeys a bit better if everyone shot at once—bang bang bang bang. Because you see, the thing about a Tory—I mean a turkey—the thing about a turkey is you can shoot it with a rifle, you can cut its head off with an axe, a pike is an excellent tool for getting turkeys out of high places—and if worse comes to worst, you can always grab a turkey in your own bare hands and wring its bloody neck!

The CROWD cheers.

MACKENZIE   Now once we get very good at killing turkeys, we go down to that turkey parliament, and we say—this is what we want! And this is what we intend to get! And if they refuse—

CROWD   Yes! What then?

MACKENZIE   We declare open season on turkeys and you'll all have one on your plate this year for Christmas!

The CROWD cheers.

MACKENZIE   Now who's going to be the first to come up here and sign the paper and pledge themselves to shooting turkeys?

CROWD   Me! I will!

MACKENZIE   That's the spirit!

Freeze. Blackout.

Lount's Forge

SAMUEL LOUNT's blacksmith shop at Holland Landing. LOUNT is at stage centre, hammer in hand, standing over his anvil. Around him are various voices of discontent. All lines are spoken to the audience.

LOUNT   Oh yes! I'm back—doing what I know how to do. I've been a farmer, a surveyor, mostly a blacksmith—but the most useless job I ever tried was politics!

MAN   It took me twelve years to drain the swamp off my land. Then, last summer, the Canada Company dams up the river and floods all the low lands. You look now—you've never seen such bog!

LOUNT   Samuel Lount for the Assembly! Sam— you've got to run. Sam—we need you.

WOMAN   I can work in her kitchen, but she doesn't want me in the rest of her house. Well I know all about it anyway—because my husband built it!

LOUNT   So off I go to the Assembly. Every man's vote behind me. And went to sleep for two years.

WOMAN   Sure it's a nice farm. And the town's over there, two miles. But there's no road between our farm and the town—because all the land in between belongs to John Strachan and his accursed Church of England!

LOUNT   I'd no sooner stand up to propose a bill, than some Tory would call for a recess.

MAN   Here's a road. Fine road too. Except for the river that runs across it. Now they won't build the bridge. Now what the hell good is a road without a bridge?

LOUNT   Tories got you scared Sam? That why you're not going back? Yes I'm scared. Scared if we waste two more years with this government, there won't be anything left in this country worth saving!

MAN   Now I don't know anything about politics. But there must be *something* wrong in this province. Because there ain't no women!

LOUNT   So Mackenzie comes to me. "Sam, it's time. We need you." I've heard that one before.

MAN   See this cabinet? Took me four months to make. Know why I can't sell it? Because it was made in Toronto!

WOMAN   Yes, I took in travellers for the night. And maybe I did a few favours for men in return for money. But what else can a woman alone with six children do? So they put me in jail and took away my children. Well watch out Mister—because your turn is coming and it's coming soon!

LOUNT   Mac—I said—I'm a blacksmith, not a politician. "Fine, Sam—that's just what we need. A blacksmith."

MAN   I voted Reform in the last election so the Colonel foreclosed on my mortgage. Now that's four years work all gone. But that's all right. Because now I've got nothing to lose!

LOUNT   So I'm back. But I'm not making horseshoes. And I'm not making laws. I'm making pikes—

He raises the redhot pike he has had on the anvil and lowers it into a bucket of water.

ALL   Sssssssssss—

Blackout.

ACT TWO
Doel's Brewery

MACKENZIE sets the scene. Onstage with him are three of his Reform associates, and a BREWERY WORKER.

MACKENZIE   November 11, 1837. Doel's Brewery, at the corner of Bay and Adelaide Streets, in Toronto. I've called an emergency meeting of the leading Reformers of this city: John Doel—he owns this brewery; lawyer Parsons; Dr. Rolph. These gentlemen are all leading and respected citizens. And this man over here—he's one of Doel's workers—and a good man he is too. We don't seem to have any influence with the government of this country. We have none at all with the King of England. But to my surprise and delight, I find we have some influence with someone up there *skyward* for the opportunity which has been presented to us can only be described as heaven-sent. The brave French patriots under Papineau in Lower Canada have struck for their own freedom. Now that means two things to us. First—it indicates to us in Upper Canada the route we too must take to achieve our ends. Second— and even more important—it means there isn't one English soldier left here in Toronto tonight. They've all marched off to Lower Canada. But our blessings don't stop there. No no no no—for in City Hall are four thousand muskets, still in their crates, not even unpacked yet. Guarded by only two men! Now anyone who would leave four thousand muskets guarded by only two men cannot be averse to them being used. At Government House, Sir Francis Bond Head has just come in from his ride; he sits before his fire, feet up on the fender, sipping a glass of expensive French brandy, and imagines he presides over the most contented colony in the entire Empire. He is guarded by only one sentry. At Kingston, Fort Henry lies open and deserted. A steamer only has to sail up to the wharf and it's ours. *turning to his colleagues* Now here's the plan—we seize Sir Francis, we take him to City Hall and seize the arms, which we distribute to our friends here and in the country. We then declare a Provisional Government and demand of Sir Francis a Legislative Council responsible to a new and fairly elected Assembly. If he refuses—

DOEL   Yes? If he refuses?

MACKENZIE   We go at once for Independence and take whatever steps are necessary to secure it! *He grabs DOEL and pilots him across the stage.* Doel, it's so easy, all you have to do is come along here, pick up those muskets, and we've won!

DOEL   *pulling away* Shhhh. Now we all want the same things Mac—but we *don't* want to cause trouble.

MACKENZIE   Right! And if we do it this way it'll be no trouble at all—

PARSONS   *trying to settle him down* Now Mackenzie—you're our leader, we all agree to that. But why don't you just sit down for a moment and—

MACKENZIE   *springing back up* This is no time to sit down! It's time to rise up and act!

ROLPH   *authoritatively* Mackenzie! What if we fail?

MACKENZIE   Rolph, with this much nerve—this much courage—we cannot fail.

DOEL   Now Mac—don't rush like this. We've put four months of careful organization and preparation into this.

MACKENZIE   Doel, what in God's name have we been organizing *for*?

PARSONS   Mac, I want to go with you, but I just don't know how to make the jump—   *He mimes it.*

MACKENZIE   If you want to jump—you jump.   *He leaps across the stage.*

ROLPH   We don't have the men.

MACKENZIE   We do! We've got Doel's own workers. We've got Armstrong's axemakers, Dutcher's foundrymen—they're strong, dependable, and they're ready to *act*—

The WORKER starts moving determinedly toward the stand of muskets (indicated by one or two guns). The three REFORMERS scurry to interpose themselves before the weapons actually are seized. They head off the WORKER by a whisker.

ROLPH   Mackenzie—we have pledged ourselves to Reform—not Revolution.

MACKENZIE   It doesn't matter what you call it Rolph. The question is, what are you going to do about it?

DOEL   Well, if it's force we want, I move we bring down our friends from the country.

MACKENZIE   That's the way is it, Doel? Bring down the farmers to do your dirty work? Besides—it will take four weeks to get the farmers down here.

PARSONS   Well alright then—four weeks. That makes it what?—December seventh.

DOEL   Yes. Agreed. December seventh.

ROLPH   December seventh.

DOEL   Mackenzie?

MACKENZIE   *with a helpless look at the WORKER, and a gesture of disgust toward his colleagues* Alright—December seventh!

Blackout.

Drilling

A FARMER is alone onstage, with a pitchfork, drilling with it as one would with a rifle.

FARMER   Present. . . . Attack! Present. . . . Attack! Present. . . . Attack!

Enter another FARMER, who sees the drill and starts to chuckle about it. FIRST continues drilling, but is irked by the derision.

SECOND   Come on. Come on now.

FIRST   Present. . . . Attack!. . .

SECOND   You're not going to march to Toronto with that?

FIRST   Present. . .

SECOND   What are you going to do with it? Feed hay to the British?

FIRST wheels on SECOND and presses the very menacing point of the pitchfork against his throat. (In fact, this scene has always been played by two women.)

SECOND   Wait—what're you doing?

FIRST   Go on. Laugh some more.

SECOND   Alright. Stop.

FIRST continues pressing. It is quite ominous. That is a real pitchfork up there onstage.

FIRST   Say it—

SECOND   Alright, alright—

FIRST   *Say* it!

SECOND   Say what?

FIRST   Present—

SECOND   *practically a whimper*   Present—

FIRST   *whirling and stabbing the fork directly out toward the audience*   Attack!

Tiger Dunlop

DUNLOP   The date is November 19. The place—Gairbraid, near Goderich, home of William "Tiger" Dunlop—raconteur, wit, doctor of medicine, and arch-Tory.

Enter MACKENZIE and COLONEL ANTHONY VAN EGMOND, an older man. They join DUNLOP and all three participate in a hearty after-dinner laugh.

DUNLOP   Yes—I believe that was the same evening we were dining at your home, Van Egmond, and your housekeeper said to me—   *imitating the housekeeper*   Doctor, why is it sir, we never see you in church? And I said, Because, Madam, I have an abiding distrust of any place where one man does all the talking, you're liable to meet your wife, and people sing without drinking!

They all laugh.

VAN EGMOND   An amazing likeness, Tiger, and I must tell you that she still anxiously awaits your return. Tiger here is one of the most eligible bachelors in the tract.

DUNLOP   And intending to remain so. But—that was a long time ago. Strange, isn't it, what time does—to men like Van Egmond and myself, who spent so much time in the same camp in the bush—yet now find ourselves in such separate camps.

VAN EGMOND   Perhaps.

DUNLOP   But, times being what they are, I'm sure you gentlemen haven't come here to hear my old stories. Not with having brought this screaming Reformer with you. I imagine you've come for something—so tell me—What can Tiger Dunlop do for you?

MACKENZIE   Tiger Dunlop can let us help him.

DUNLOP   I beg your pardon.

MACKENZIE   Let us help you.

DUNLOP   What could you possibly do to help me?

MACKENZIE   What do you think of John Strachan?

DUNLOP   I hate the bastard.

MACKENZIE   And Thomas Mercer Jones?

DUNLOP   Jones. Well, anyone who would marry Strachan's daughter can't be all good.

MACKENZIE   Dunlop, you and I seem to concur in our opinions of these people.

DUNLOP   Yes. I believe we do.

MACKENZIE   Every time we turn around in this colony, we see its wealth being carted off someplace else. And what about the honest, hardworking people—the farmers and the labourers? The fruits of their effort are being scooped up to support the idle dandies in Toronto or London—

DUNLOP   Just a moment, Mr. Mackenzie. When you start in about the honest, hardworking people, it's obvious you're about to launch one of your famous political speeches. Now don't let my reputation fool you. I'm still a man who likes plain speaking. I beg you—speak to me plainly.

MACKENZIE   Alright, I'll speak to you plainly. There's going to be some changes in this colony, Dunlop. Big changes. It's going to be out with the old and in with the new. Now the question is, Tiger—are you going to be part of the new or are you going out with the old?

DUNLOP   You talk about changes. Now I have always stood for change in this colony. Isn't that true, Colonel?

VAN EGMOND   Yes. Yes, Tiger—that's the man I remember. Long ago, before this part of the country was even opened up, Tiger here, John Galt—remember him, Tiger?—and myself, we used to go up on a rise by the lake, look about us and talk of the tremendous potential of the country. And Tiger had the most vivid dreams of all. Eighty thousand families, I believe you said, could be supported by the Huron Tract alone. And we set about to make that a reality. We built roads—remember, Tiger?—pushing the roads through the bush to bring in the settlers—built mills, provided for schools, and churches, shipped in supplies—anything that would bring in the settlers. And the towns. That you founded.

But look about you, Tiger. Where are the eighty thousand? For every one settler there should be a hundred more. The roads that were built to bring people in are leading them out. By the thousands. Land value is where it was five, ten years ago. Why? What has happened? I think you have let go of your dream, Tiger. Given it up to men like Jones, Strachan, Hagerman. Fops and dandies. Mushroom aristocrats. Bladders of pride and arrogance—who care not a damn for the country—but only for their own fiefdoms—filling their pockets. I don't think you are the kind of man to let this abuse continue. John Galt could not tolerate such leadership and he resigned his post with the Canada Company. I rather think you are cast in the same mould as Galt.

DUNLOP   Time brings changes, Colonel, and might I say—compromise?

MACKENZIE   Compromise! Dunlop, I've been from one end of this colony to the other. Now there is discontent, vengeance, rage—in men's minds. But not compromise! I've seen it at over two hundred public meetings. Thousands of signatures, names of men pledging themselves to use force of arms if necessary to alleviate their suffering. This colony wants cheap, efficient responsible government and it's going to have it, and there's nothing that the Lieutenant-Governor, or the King of England, or the whole British army can do to stop it.

VAN EGMOND   Tiger, you know what the people want, what they think. You talk to them, high and low alike. They admire you. You are a brilliant man — I don't flatter — you have ideas, and you have the energy to put those ideas into effect.

MACKENZIE   An independent country. A new nation. Think of it, Tiger. Think what this country could be with its natural bounty, under the leadership which men like yourself could provide — it could be one of the greatest in the world. It's a tremendous responsibility staring you right in the face. Now are you man enough to meet that responsibility, Dunlop?

DUNLOP   *He deliberates a long while then chuckles.* Excuse me, gentlemen, but you remind me of a couple of Yankee schoolboys who just read the Declaration of Independence. Now I'm a political realist. Change is one thing, but I call what you're talking about rebellion.

MACKENZIE   Call it revolution if you want, Tiger.

DUNLOP   Well, I don't think you're the man to lead it. My God, man, you can't even buy a cow without offending the herdsman. Colonel, you're a dear and old friend, but it is the truth sir — you are old. Waterloo was long ago. Now if you gentlemen will permit me, I believe I have a responsibility to history. Dr. William Dunlop does not join in insurrection against the rightful government of—

MACKENZIE   I take it all this pomposity is leading up to a "no."

DUNLOP   Yes — I mean, no.

MACKENZIE   Well, it's a long ride back to Toronto, Dunlop. Goodbye.

He exits.

VAN EGMOND   Tiger, do you know that you are twice as old as I am?

VAN EGMOND starts out. DUNLOP calls to him as he is almost out the door.

DUNLOP   Van Egmond—

VAN EGMOND   Goodnight.

He exits. Light on TIGER alone. Fade to black.

Leaving

The following six scenes concern people leaving for the battle. Each is introduced by a verse from the song "Across Toronto Bay."

ALL
Up now and shoulder arms, and join this free men's march boys,
It's time to show the Tories that this country's no man's toy.
So it's march, march, march to Toronto town today,
And we'll use that fork to pitch Bond Head — across Toronto Bay.

A MERCHANT and the man who does his chores. The EMPLOYEE is carrying an armful of wood. He drops it with a crash.

MERCHANT   Rather sloppy of you Thomas.

THOMAS   That's just my way of saying goodbye sir.

MERCHANT   Goodbye?

THOMAS   Yes sir. I'm going to be leaving your employ.

MERCHANT   You've never mentioned anything of this before.

THOMAS   Well, you see the way I figure it sir, I think there's going to be a fight and I have just the merest suspicion that you and me are going to be on different sides.

MERCHANT   Thomas, I would not become embroiled in this if I were you.

THOMAS   I just don't think it would be fair, sir, for me to keep taking your wages, in case we met on the battlefield — and I had to shoot you dead. *chortling* So I'll just be off now sir. Goodbye — and good luck.   *A hearty laugh as he goes out.*

ALL
It's time to do a different job and take a different stand,
They said we're good for chopping wood and clearing off the land.
So it's march, march, march to Toronto town today,
And we'll use that fork to pitch Bond Head — across Toronto Bay.

HAROLD, a farmer, holding a pistol.

HAROLD   I just can't do it. I never thought I'd have to really shoot somebody when we were drilling. I — I'll tell them I can't go. No that's no good. I know — I'll say I can't go tonight. I'll meet them tomorrow.

Enter his friend TOM.

TOM   Ready, Harold?

HAROLD   Tom — uh, yeah, I'm ready.

TOM   Good!

HAROLD   Uh, look—I even stole a pistol.

TOM   A pistol! Well then—you're in charge!

They exit together.

ALL
So let those Tories have their fun and slop up all
    that tea.
I'd just as soon I killed myself a Tory as a tree.
So it's march, march, march to Toronto town today,
And we'll use that fork to pitch Bond Head—across
    Toronto Bay.

*FRED BENCH and his new wife RUTH, both of
whom we met in the tavern scene in Act One. They
are in bed.*

RUTH   Fred—I heard awful stories in town today.
People were talking about the Rebels. They say that
they're going to burn Toronto.

FRED   Some people have just cause Ruth.

RUTH   Fred Bench, don't you talk that way. Oh
Fred! You wouldn't yourself—don't tell me that
you'd—

FRED   Now Ruth—I'll do what I think is best for
you.

RUTH   Well that's better. Don't let me even think
that you'd . . . oh well, I'm sure the Governor will
soon put a stop to all this.

FRED   Uh-huh.

RUTH   Goodnight.

FRED   Goodnight Ruth.

*She falls asleep. He feigns sleep, then rolls out of
bed, grabs his boots and rifle, and steals toward the
door.*

ALL
A war will bring some death, boys, it's sure to bring
    you sorrow,
But if we stand back to back today, we'll own this
    land tomorrow.
So it's march, march, march to Toronto town today,
And we'll use that fork to pitch Bond Head—across
    Toronto Bay.

*A BOY sneaking through the woods. His younger
BROTHER and SISTER intercept him.*

BOY   How'd you two get in front of me?

SISTER   We followed you.

BOY   Well, you're not supposed to. Go home.

BROTHER   You're supposed to be looking after us.

BOY   I can't for now. So get on home.

SISTER   We know where you're going.

BOY   I don't care if you know. You're not coming
with me.

BROTHER   We'll tell.

BOY   Don't you dare tell! Just take your sister and
get on home.

They whine.

BOY   Get going. I'll be back.

*He exits. His BROTHER darts after him. The SISTER
looks around, lost, and cries.*

ALL
Now Old Mac says we've got a cause to load our
    rifles for,
So leave that stove and woman home and march
    right out the door.
For it's march, march, march to Toronto town today,
And we'll use that fork to pitch Bond Head—across
    Toronto Bay.

*ISAAC CASSELMAN's Tavern, as in Act One. EMMA
and JAMEY are cleaning around. Enter ISAAC,
carrying his rifle and pistol.*

ISAAC   Emma, put out the fire. Jamey, you lock
the tavern. This tavern is closed.

EMMA   What's going on?

ISAAC   There's a war on, by God, and Isaac Casselman is going off to fight.

JAMEY   Isaac—gimme your pistol.

He grabs it and points it into his mouth.

ISAAC   Jamey—what're you doing?

JAMEY   I'm going to kill myself.

ISAAC   *grabbing the pistol back*   Why?

JAMEY   Well if you're closing the tavern, I've got
no reason to go on living.

ISAAC   Jamey—why don't you come along?

JAMEY   *scornful*   Naaa—

ISAAC   Maybe there'll be a rum ration.

JAMEY   Rum?   *He grabs the pistol and leads the
way.*   Forward—

ALL
Now all across this country, you can hear the Rebel
    yell,
We'll follow you Mackenzie, to Toronto or to hell.
So it's march, march, march to Toronto town today,
And we'll use that fork to pitch Bond Head—across
    Toronto Bay.

*MARY MACDONALD, whom we met in Act One,
fresh from Scotland, is sitting in her farmhouse
doing some chore. She is singing to herself.*

MARY   Speed, bonnie boat, like a bird on the wing.
Onward the sailors cry—

Enter her husband EDWARD.

MARY   Edward, you're home early.

EDWARD *kissing her* Mary—

MARY Is anything wrong? *EDWARD sits down uncomfortably.* What is it, Edward?

EDWARD You remember when we first met—and we didn't know each other at all—and we were afraid things wouldn't work out—

MARY Yes, I remember—

EDWARD I know I've never said very much. That's just my way. But I want you to know that it's been. . . . Hell—I've got to go fight.

MARY *accepting it with difficulty* Yes. Of course.

EDWARD *relieved* Of course? Do you think it's wrong—us being married such a short time?

MARY No. I don't. Of course you must go.

EDWARD is immensely grateful that she accepts it.

MARY When do you have to go?

EDWARD They said they'd come by about day-break.

MARY Oh. We have some time then.

EDWARD Yes. *getting her drift* Oh. You mean. . .

He takes her hand and leads her upstairs. There is a knock at the door.

Who's there?

FLETCHER *outside* It's Fletcher, Edward. There's been a change in plans. We have to go meet Lount at the crossroads right now.

EDWARD But they said tomorrow—

FLETCHER I don't care what they said. We have to leave right away.

EDWARD I'll be right out.

FLETCHER Right now!

EDWARD *angrily* I *said* I was coming!

MARY I'll get your things.

She hands him his coat and his rifle. They embrace. He starts toward the door, stops, returns to her.

EDWARD I love you. By God I do. I love you.

He rushes out.

MARY *sobbing* Oh no. No. He never said that to me before. No. No—

Fade to black.

Van Egmond's March

During this scene, the focus is on COLONEL ANTHONY VAN EGMOND as he travels toward Toronto. But around him many things take place: the daily work of the people he passes; events occurring in Toronto; encounters with people on the road. A small table serves as VAN EGMOND's horse.

VAN EGMOND Colonel Anthony Van Egmond— age sixty-seven, veteran of the Napoleonic Wars, owner of a parcel of fourteen thousand acres in the Huron Tract near Goderich—is appointed commander-in-chief of the Patriot forces. December 3, 1837, he sets out from his farm on horseback, to meet with his troops at Montgomery's Tavern, north of Toronto, on December 7—the date set for the advance on the city.

He mounts his horse and begins his march.

Day one. There is a light snow falling, muffling the sound. I shall travel alone to avoid suspicion. If we are to get the advantage of the enemy, we must take them by surprise. *Notes as he goes:* St. Columban—

MESSENGER *rushing from the opposite direction* Colonel! Colonel—I'm glad I caught you sir. There's been a change—

VAN EGMOND Change?

MESSENGER Yes sir—they've changed the date. From the seventh to the fourth.

VAN EGMOND Who issued this change?

MESSENGER It's a message sir—from that Dr. Rolph.

VAN EGMOND Dr. Rolph does not have the power to make such changes. Only Mackenzie does.

MESSENGER Yes he does. He said—

VAN EGMOND There has been no change! December 7 is the date for the advance on the city!

MESSENGER Yes sir. No change.

He exits.

VAN EGMOND *continuing his march* We could not possibly muster enough men before December 7. *Noting his progress:* Mitchell. Ah—another homesteader. He shall see such changes made!

A TORY PICKET IN TORONTO Anderson!

He fires a shot. ANTHONY ANDERSON, a rebel, is hit, lurches across the stage, and falls dead at the feet of VAN EGMOND.

A FARMER *to VAN EGMOND* You—you hear the news?

VAN EGMOND News?

FARMER Yup. Seems a man named Anderson— Anthony Anderson—and another fellow named Moodie—both shot outside of Toronto. Don't know any more about it.

VAN EGMOND *dismounting for the night* Seebach's Inn. Sebringville. *to the INNKEEPER* What do you know of events in Toronto?

INNKEEPER I heard that a government man named Moodie'd been shot. And a Rebel name of Anderson.

VAN EGMOND Confirmed.

INNKEEPER No, no—that's just talk as far as I know.

VAN EGMOND Anthony Anderson was the only other Rebel leader with military experience.

Freeze.

VAN EGMOND Day two. *He remounts his horse.* Stratford. There's much more activity on the roads today.

A TRAVELLER Where are you going, sir?

VAN EGMOND Toronto.

TRAVELLER You can't go there. The Americans have attacked. They're going to burn the city—

VAN EGMOND The Americans have not attacked.

TRAVELLER Yes they have. I heard it from somebody who heard it from someone who was there—

VAN EGMOND Nonsense.

TRAVELLER I'm warning you. I wouldn't go on—

He exits, blathering.

VAN EGMOND Mackenzie, you must hold fast for more forces!

A MOUNTED HORSEMAN enters, dismounts and posts a handbill advertising a reward for MACKENZIE. (This was done using the actor who played MACKENZIE and, as it were, nailing him to the wall as though he were the poster.)

HORSEMAN By authority of the Lieutenant-Governor, a reward of one thousand pounds is hereby offered to anyone who will apprehend and deliver up to justice William Lyon Mackenzie. God Save the Queen.

VAN EGMOND *dismounting* Helmer's Inn. Waterloo.

He approaches the "handbill" and addresses it, with MACKENZIE's own call to arms.

Canadians, do you love freedom?

MACKENZIE *i.e., the MACKENZIE in the handbill* I know you do. Do you hate oppression? Who would deny it. Then buckle on your armour and drive out these villains who enslave and oppress our country.

VAN EGMOND *responding* Long after we are dead, free men shall salute us.

They embrace. Freeze. VAN EGMOND remounts.

Day three. Breslau.

OLD MAN Sir—have you heard the news from Toronto?

As he tells this news to VAN EGMOND, someone else recounts it directly to the audience.

A REBEL Well I can tell you exactly how it happened because I was there. It was a hell of a battle and it was right there at the corner of Yonge and College. You see, Sheriff Jarvis stationed his men behind a fence, just waiting for the Rebels to come marching down. Well, we came alright—in the dead of night. We moved out of the tavern, formed up at the tollgate at Bloor Street and then marched down Yonge, proud as peacocks, five abreast. They waited till we got really close, and then they let loose. Well they cut some of us down, but we fired back. And then we dropped down to let the men behind us fire. But the men behind—they were green—they thought we'd dropped because we were all dead. So they turned around and ran back to the tavern. Sheriff Jarvis' men—they were even greener than that—they threw away their guns and ran back to Toronto.

Great confusion onstage. People milling and fleeing. VAN EGMOND tries to stem the tide.

VAN EGMOND Wait! If you want something you stay and fight for it!

But they push past him, leaving him alone and dejected. He dismounts and sits down despairingly.

What is happening in Toronto? Why didn't they wait? Fools—so much at stake—if only I *knew!* I am an old man; there is still honour in retreat. I shall return home—

Enter a REBEL, overhears VAN EGMOND.

REBEL Yah, you go home, go back to your farm. Whatever you do, don't go to Toronto.

VAN EGMOND Have you come from Toronto?

REBEL I *ran* from Toronto. I'm going home.

VAN EGMOND What is happening there?

REBEL Macnab's in the city. He's brought four hundred armed militiamen. They're barricading the city. They're going to shoot us like rats—

VAN EGMOND Macnab? I'd like to fight Macnab.

REBEL You're welcome to him.

VAN EGMOND What is the condition of the patriot forces?

REBEL Bad.

VAN EGMOND   Are they still coming in?

REBEL   Yah, they're coming in—

VAN EGMOND   They are—

REBEL   But they're leaving just as fast as they come in.

VAN EGMOND   Why?

REBEL   Because there's no leadership there. Nobody knows what they're doing. Someone orders this. Another one orders that—

VAN EGMOND   If there had been a leader there—whom you trusted—would you have fled?

REBEL   I'm no coward. I'd have stayed.

VAN EGMOND   *extending his hand*   Colonel Anthony Van Egmond, son—

REBEL   Colonel—

VAN EGMOND   Will you march back to Toronto with me?

REBEL   Yes sir.

A chorus of "yes sir" begins to build in the background.

VAN EGMOND   You see Macnab is no soldier. He is a bully but he has no strategy. Help me up.   *He mounts.*   Have you ever been in a real battle, boy?

REBEL   Only on Yonge Street, sir.

VAN EGMOND   That was no battle. It was a skirmish. Do you know—I was fifteen years in the Napoleonic Wars. Wounded fourteen times and never once in the back.

The chorus of "yes sir" builds and transforms into the Marseillaise.

A REBEL   Remember Moscow!

VAN EGMOND   Macnab, you'll rue the day—

REBEL   Remember Waterloo!

VAN EGMOND   Mackenzie, hold fast now—

REBEL   Think of Montgomery's Tavern!

VAN EGMOND   Lancers ho—

A SENTRY   Halt!

Silence.

Who goes there?

VAN EGMOND   Colonel Van Egmond.

SENTRY   Hot damn general—are we glad to see you!

VAN EGMOND   Where is Mackenzie?

SENTRY   He's inside, sir. I'll show you. We didn't know if you were coming at all. Some said you weren't.

VAN EGMOND   Well I'm here aren't I?

SENTRY   Yes sir. You are. He's right in there. Don't tell him I forgot to salute—

VAN EGMOND   Mackenzie—

He storms in.

The Battle

This scene continues directly from the previous scene.

VAN EGMOND   Mackenzie, what in hell is going on here?

MACKENZIE   Colonel, thank God you're here. Rolph changed the date. Everything's in a mess. Macnab's in the city with four hundred men.

VAN EGMOND   How many do we have?

MACKENZIE   Two hundred and fifty.

VAN EGMOND   Not enough. When do we expect more?

MACKENZIE   Tonight. December 7. They'll be down tonight.

VAN EGMOND   Then we wait till they arrive.

MACKENZIE   Colonel, we can't wait to be attacked.

VAN EGMOND   You cannot go against Macnab with a handful of men.

MACKENZIE   We've got to do something—

REBEL SOLDIER   *to audience*   It is finally decided to send a diversionary force under Peter Matthews to the east to burn the Don Valley Bridge and draw off the main Loyalist force. The rest wait at Montgomery's for reinforcements. Meanwhile, back in Toronto, the Loyalist army is drawn up in front of Archdeacon Strachan's residence—known as The Palace—on Front Street.

The Loyalist army forms up.

BOND HEAD   I am Sir Francis Bond Head. I have a double-barrelled pistol in my bandolier, a rifle leaning against my thigh, and a brace of pistols in my belt. So good to see so many respected citizens standing in the ranks today.

THE RANKS   Pip pip—Hear hear—

BOND HEAD   We march at noon. Forward—march!

They set out.

REBEL SOLDIER   Meanwhile to the east, Matthews and his men have crossed the bridge and moved west on King Street. They meet a contingent of militia and retreat back across the bridge, attempting to burn it as they go. In the exchange of fire, one man is fatally shot through the throat. *This all is acted out.* The bridge itself is saved.

A LOYALIST But the main Loyalist force is already moving north toward Montgomery's. *Shouts.* Bugler—strike up a tune!

The Loyalist army marches to "Yankee Doodle"—an old British parody of Americans and Americanizers.

LOYALIST Six hundred men remain in the centre with Bond Head. One hundred fifty off to the right flank. Two hundred on the left.

A REBEL SENTRY Hey wake up—

HIS FRIEND What? *looking out at the approaching army* Good God!

SENTRY There must be thousands of them—

FRIEND I'll stay and watch them. You go tell Mackenzie—

SENTRY *riding off* Mackenzie! They're coming this way—you'd better go see—

MACKENZIE Form up the men! *The Rebels form up.* There is the enemy! They outnumber us. They are better armed. And they have artillery—but they are the men we came to fight. Will you fight them?

A hearty Rebel cheer.

MACKENZIE Forward—

A REBEL A force of two hundred and fifty under Van Egmond and Samuel Lount advance into the woods to the south of the tavern. Another sixty position themselves behind rail fences on the other side of the road. Two hundred yet unarmed men remain in the tavern.

The battle is staged. The Rebel soldiers talk frantically among themselves as they watch the overwhelming force of the Loyalists moving toward them. The battle itself is bitter and very brief. The two nine-pound cannons of the Loyalists decimate the Rebel formations. The Rebels are crushed. In the end the Loyalists are totally triumphant. The bodies and weapons of the Rebels litter the field. The Loyalists clean up. All of this with much screaming, swearing and writhing.

MACKENZIE *as he escapes* Mackenzie is the last man to leave the field. Together with Van Egmond he goes to a nearby farmhouse. The farmer's wife diverts soldiers while Mackenzie escapes, but Van Egmond, exhausted, is captured. Mackenzie heads west toward the Niagara border. Rewards are offered for him everywhere, but not a soul who sees him reports him. Within days he has established the provisional government of the State of Upper Canada on Navy Island in the Niagara River. He arrives with twenty-six men but soon has hundreds more. Macnab encamps on the opposite shore with a government force of five thousand. Mackenzie gathers the arms and provisions which will enable him to return and join Dr. Charles Duncombe, who has raised a Rebel army near London. He waits for his chance to move. *stepping into character* And while I wait, I fire my four cannons here at Macnab across the river—just to let him know I'm still here!

Boom. Boom. Boom. Boom.

Blackout.

Knocks on the Door

An old Canadian tradition. The following three scenes depict break-ins by government forces at the homes of suspected Rebels. Knock, knock, knock in the dark. Lights up as a SOLDIER breaks through the door and in on a WOMAN alone.

SOLDIER Get the hell out of here. We're burning this house down!

She screams. He shoves her out. Blackout.

Knock, knock, knock in the dark.

SOLDIER Open up in the name of the Queen!

Lights up. A WOMAN opens. He barges in.

Where's your husband, Mrs. Polk?

WOMAN I have no husband.

SOLDIER No? Then who's that ugly man you've been living with for the last seven years.

WOMAN Go away—

SOLDIER *searching* Where is he?

WOMAN He's dead. There's nothing here for you, so please leave my house—

SOLDIER He's been seen Mrs. Polk. He's gone too far this time—

He is bashing away at her belongings with his rifle butt. She leaps on him furiously from behind. He wrestles her to the ground, pins her there. She struggles futilely.

SOLDIER We're going to get him, and we're going to hang him, but before we do, I'm going to punch his face off. And then, Mrs. Polk, what're you going to do for a man—

She spits in his face. He raises his fist.

ANOTHER SOLDIER *from outside* Come on George. There's no one here.

SOLDIER I'll be back.

He exits.

Blackout.

Knock, knock, knock in the dark.

Lights up. Enter HAROLD, the fellow from the earlier scene who was afraid to go off to fight. He rushes in and hides under a stair, floorboard or the like. Enter TOM, the friend with whom he'd left to fight the rebellion. TOM is carrying a rifle and clearly searching for Rebels. (Because of all the doubling in this play, it is not immediately evident to the audience that these are HAROLD and TOM from an earlier scene. This works to the advantage of this brief scene as it develops.)

TOM   *nervously*   Now I seen you come in here. So come on out.

HAROLD coughs.

TOM   If you don't come out by the time I count three, I'll shoot—   *He aims at the place HAROLD is hiding.*   One, two, three—   *He shoots, but his gun misfires.*   Goldarn gun—

HAROLD leaps out of his hiding place and jumps on TOM; the two struggle for several seconds before they recognize each other.

TOM   Harold!

HAROLD   Tom!

TOM   What're you doing here?

HAROLD   I'm hiding! What're you doing? You were with me at Montgomery's Tavern!

TOM   I doubled back through the woods and joined up. Otherwise they'd have arrested me. They're making everyone search. Harold, they know who you are—

HAROLD   I know. They nearly got me twice today. Tom, you gotta help me. I haven't even got a—gimme your gun.

TOM   I can't do that. They'll ask me where it went.

HAROLD   *grabbing it*   Tell them—tell them you were searching down a well and it fell in. Thanks Tom—

He rushes off.

TOM   *calling after*   You hide good next time, Harold—   *looking down at his hands, realizing he's stuck without a gun*   What in hell am I—

Blackout.

The Rope

Captured Rebels being led to jail in Toronto. A rope is looped over each of their necks. Their hands are tied behind their backs. They march single file. They state their names in turn. When they have gone round once, they go round again.

REBELS   Jacob Beemer, farmer. Taken January 3, 1838, near Stratford.
Richard Thorpe, labourer. Taken December 7, at Montgomery's Tavern.

Caleb Kipp, yeoman. Taken on the road to Buffalo.
John Bradley, teacher. I'm no Rebel. I voted Reform but I'm no Rebel.
Absalom Slade, farmer.
Elijah Rowe, tinker. Taken December 7, at Montgomery's. But it took six of them.
They're burning. Look at that smoke—
I can't feel my toes.
William Stockdale, farmer.
Jonathan Grimes, ropemaker.
Damn the Tories! What're you looking at, lady?

They reach their destination.

Hey, lookit who's here!
There's thousands of us!
Hey, anybody here from Newmarket?
Hell, the whole country's in here—
Newmarket?—

A rising babble of greetings etc.

Blackout.

Emigrating

A REBEL WOMAN. She is packing, and talking to a neighbour.

REBEL WOMAN   Now the coach is coming at four, got to be ready. And my brother is picking that up, and this is for you. You always admired it and I want you to have it now. We won't need no winter coats where we're going. Yes, I finally convinced my Dan, I just sat down the other day, had the kids all around—they've been getting an awful time from the other kids—and I said, Now Dan, we've tried. We voted Reform, we did what we thought was best, we lost, it's time to face facts. And I just got this letter from my sister. She's got a farm and a fine husband and she said we could go down and stay with them as long as we want, and oh the kids were yelling and screaming and—well what can he say? So we're going.
   You know, this place, it's my home, the kids were both born here, but times have changed and we're going to change with them. I wouldn't stay in Stouffville one more day, I'll tell you. But I want you to know you're welcome to come down and visit us any time you want. Oh, it's going to be so fine down there, we'll have a big house, and the kids will go to school—   *calling out the window*   Hey, Mrs. Phipps, you know those two plates you borrowed from me two years ago? You can keep them. She never did like me. What are you people staring at? Anything else in here you can come and take when we're gone. We're leaving it behind. We're going to have five times better. You know why? Because we're going to the Yew-Nited States!

Blackout.

The Hangings

Toronto City Jail.

VAN EGMOND April 12, 1838. Government forces have scattered Dr. Duncombe's army in the west. Mackenzie himself has fled Navy Island for the United States. Toronto City Jail. Near King and Church Streets. The cells are cold, dark, wet, filled for the most part with patriots awaiting trial and sentencing on charges of high treason. Today they press against the bars of their cells to witness the executions of two of the patriot leaders, Peter Matthews and Samuel Lount. It is the laws, and not their crimes, that condemn them. Anthony Van Egmond might also have been witness to this spectacle but he died, untried, in his cell, December 30, 1837.

MATTHEWS and LOUNT advance to the gallows.

LOUNT My friends, I address as friends all those in the jail behind me, in all the jails across this province, in the ships bound for Van Diemen's Land, in exile in the United States—there are over eight hundred of us. I am proud to be one of you. John Beverley Robinson—Chief Justice Robinson—you seem to fear we will become martyrs to our countrymen. Well still your fears. This country will not have time to mourn a farmer and a blacksmith. It will be free, I am certain, long before our deaths have time to become symbols. It cannot remain long under the hell of such merciless wretches that they murder its inhabitants for their love of liberty.

As for us, I do not know exactly how we came to this. Except by a series of steps, each of which seemed to require the next. But if I were to leave my home in Holland Landing again, and march down Yonge Street, I would go by the same route, only hoping that the journey's end would differ. And there will be others coming down that road you know, and others after them, until it does end differently. But for us, the only way on now is by the rope.

MATTHEWS laughs bitterly.

LOUNT What Peter? What?

MATTHEWS Sam, we lost—

LOUNT No! We haven't won yet.

The trap falls. They dangle by the ropes.

Blackout.

SHARON POLLOCK (b. 1936)

In the preface to her play *The Komagata Maru Incident*, Sharon Pollock writes, "As a Canadian, I feel that much of our history has been misrepresented and even hidden from us. Until we recognize our past, we cannot change our future." The sentiments are similar to those of Rick Salutin, and like him, Pollock delivered to the stage in 1973 a dramatization of nineteenth-century Canadian history meant to change irrevocably the way we view ourselves. *Walsh* was the prototype of a playwriting career that has persisted in bringing to light injustices done in the name of a higher good, past and present, in both formal "history plays" and family histories, utilizing multiple levels of chronology and perspective, and usually featuring a man or woman caught in the squeeze between personal inclination and political or familial pressures. With *Walsh* Sharon Pollock first revealed herself to a national audience as one of the major dramatists of the modern Canadian theatre.

Pollock was born Sharon Chalmers in Fredericton, N.B., where she first became involved in the theatre at university. Later, with the Prairie Players she toured B.C. and Alberta in 1966, and was voted Best Actress at the Dominion Drama Festival. Pollock settled in Calgary the next year, and while pregnant with her sixth child she began writing her first play. The absurdist farce *A Compulsory Option* won the 1971 Alberta Playwriting Competition and was produced in 1972 by the New Play Centre in Vancouver, where Pollock and family were now living. *Walsh* was her next project, followed by a productive association with the Vancouver Playhouse between 1973 and 1976 that resulted in six plays for children as well as *And Out Goes You?* (1975), a political comedy about eviction, expropriation and urban redevelopment, and *The Komagata Maru Incident* (1976), which powerfully dissects the politics of racism behind the refusal to admit Sikh immigrants into Vancouver in 1914. Pollock herself played the title role of Lizzie Borden in a local college production of her next play, *My Name Is Lisbeth* (1976), which would go on to become her most popular success, *Blood Relations*, first staged professionally in 1980 by Edmonton's Theatre Three.

Pollock moved to Edmonton in 1976 to teach playwriting at the University of Alberta, but since 1977 she has made her home in Calgary. From 1977-79 she ran the summer Playwrights' Colony at Banff and was playwright-in-residence for Alberta Theatre Projects which produced her fine study of a family of prairie farmers, *Generations*, in 1980. In the same year the Citadel mounted *One Tiger to a Hill*, her dramatization of a notorious hostage-taking at the B.C. Pen. She spent 1981-82 as artist-in-residence at the National Arts Centre, then returned to Theatre Calgary to present *Whiskey Six* (1983) and *Doc* (1984). The former is a tale of rum-running and coal mining in 1920s Alberta, the latter an autobiographical treatment of a ravaged New Brunswick family. *Doc* has had a number of major productions including one directed by Pollock herself. To round out her accomplishments, Pollock has served as Chairman of the Canada Council's Advisory Arts Panel and, for a brief period in 1984, artistic director of Theatre Calgary. One of her many radio plays, *Sweet Land of Liberty*, received ACTRA's Best Radio Drama award in 1980, and her volume *Blood Relations and Other Plays* won the Governor-General's Literary Award for 1981.

Walsh had its genesis in Vancouver in 1972-73. While Pollock was researching and writing the play, the artistic director of Theatre Calgary, Harold Baldridge, was reading Dee Brown's *Bury My Heart at Wounded Knee* and becoming interested in the story of Sitting Bull's stay in Canada. He contacted Pollock when he heard about *Walsh*, and after substantial revisions in a New Play Centre workshop the play opened at Theatre Calgary in November 1973. Further revised, *Walsh* was done again the next summer at Stratford's Third Stage with the addition of the Prologue and the characters Mary and Pretty Plume, but minus the recorded readings from documents of the day that preceded each scene in the original production. A new scene involving the American General Terry was added for the play's 1983 revival at the National Arts Centre (the version reprinted here).

Walsh is grounded very firmly in historical fact. Major James Walsh did command the North West Mounted Police detachment that was charged with keeping order in the area that is now the southern Alberta-Saskatchewan border during the period (1877-81) that Sitting Bull and his Sioux spent there in exile. Two histories published the same year as *Walsh*, Grant MacEwan's *Sitting Bull* and C. Frank Turner's *Across the Medicine Line*, also confirm the basic accuracy of Pollock's presentation: the exemplary behaviour of the Sioux while in Canada, the great respect they developed for Walsh, and the political machinations that eventually drove the survivors back across the line. Only at the end does Pollock take liberty with historical fact, telescoping the time between Sitting Bull's return to the U.S. in 1881 and his assassination in 1890 so it appears one followed hard upon the other.

But like British playwright Peter Shaffer, whose *Royal Hunt of the Sun* shares numerous similarities with *Walsh*, Pollock is less interested in documentary on an epic scale than in history as personal drama. Assuming the real sources of political power to be distant, faceless and bureaucratic, Pollock focuses instead on an intermediary, a well-intentioned local functionary who acts as the instrument of authority and oppression—the prison warden and social worker of *One Tiger to a Hill*, the immigration officer in *The Komagata Maru Incident*, and the good soldier Walsh. Walsh's drama is particularly compelling because he is so fundamentally humane and so ambivalent. As his admiration for Sitting Bull and the Sioux grows, Walsh's loyalty to the Force is stretched to its breaking point until, like Shaffer's Pizarro, he is forced to make the choice that destroys himself as surely as it does the Indians.

Walsh's dilemma is that he cannot ultimately be both a private person and an officer at the service of his political masters. At first he is confident he can juggle the two roles, telling Sitting Bull, "I am a soldier, and I must follow orders, but I am a friend also." "White Forehead" is the friend, "Major Walsh" the soldier. But such a split is both unnatural and unsustainable. Eventually he *must* choose. And when he can no longer avoid committing himself, he chooses duty over friendship, Major Walsh over White Forehead. In the climactic scene where Sitting Bull makes his last appeal to Walsh's sense of charity and justice, Walsh literally buttons himself up in the red tunic that symbolizes his official self. Once having denied his humanity he becomes a broken man, a travesty of the brave soldier he once was and, eventually, the wreck we meet in the Yukon at the beginning of the play, years after his betrayal of Sitting Bull.

Walsh isn't the only character torn between two loyalties. Sitting Bull himself must make the painful choice to protect his own people's status in Canada rather than help the Nez Percés. Louis, the Métis scout, has a foot in both the white and Indian worlds and sees the contradictions with terrible clarity. And Clarence, the naive recruit who grows in sympathy and understanding through the play, idolizes Walsh yet comes to love Sitting Bull and Crowfoot like his own family. His enduring faith in the fundamental goodness and rationality of the Canadian government whose policies effectively condemn the Sioux to extinction prompts Walsh to remark, "That young man should never make the Force his life"—a sad self-commentary on the bitter fate of a professional soldier who would also be a good man.

•

Walsh premiered at Theatre Calgary on November 7, 1973, directed by Harold Baldridge and designed by Richard Roberts. It featured Michael Fletcher as Walsh, August Schellenberg as Sitting Bull, Hardee T. Lineham as Clarence, Jean Archambault as Louis, Frank J. Adamson as Harry, Ron Chudley as McCutcheon and Hutchinson Shandro as Colonel MacLeod.

WALSH

CHARACTERS

HARRY, *a wagon master*
CLARENCE, *a new recruit to the NWMP*
LOUIS, *a Métis scout*
WALSH, *a superintendent of the NWMP in charge of Fort Walsh*
MRS. ANDERSON, *a settler*
CROW EAGLE, *a Cree*
McCUTCHEON, *a sergeant in the NWMP*
MARY, *wife of Major Walsh*
SITTING BULL, *a chief of the Hunkpapa Sioux*
PRETTY PLUME, *wife of Sitting Bull*
CROWFOOT, *son of Sitting Bull*
GALL, *a chief of the Hunkpapa Sioux*
WHITE DOG, *an Assiniboine*
TERRY, *a general in the U.S. Army*
COLONEL MacLEOD, *commissioner of the NWMP*

PROLOGUE

The characters in the prologue become the characters in the play proper. McCUTCHEON plays IAN, the bartender. SITTING BULL is the PROSPECTOR; CROW EAGLE is BILLY, the harmonica player in the saloon. LOUIS and MacLEOD are a couple of poker players. CROWFOOT is JOEIE, the newspaper boy. JENNIE is MRS. ANDERSON. WALSH and HARRY play themselves. WALSH is in civvies, impeccably dressed, in contrast to the other characters who look dirty and disreputable. The atmosphere in the prologue is smoky, as if the scene were lit by a coal-oil lamp with a dirty chimney.

The scene is from WALSH's point of view, and the freezes are momentary arrests in the action and are broken by the character's speech or action following. The impression given is similar to that experienced when one is drunk or under great mental stress. CLARENCE stands outside of the prologue scene, never taking his eyes off WALSH. He has on his red tunic and he exists only in WALSH's mind. He is not part of the prologue scene and his scream is heard only by WALSH.

There is no break in staging between the prologue and Act One.

The sound of wind is heard—a mournful sound. In a very dim light, the characters suddenly appear on the periphery of the playing area. WALSH is not among them. They freeze there for a moment, and then, quickly and silently, like ghosts, take their positions onstage, with the exception of HARRY, JOEIE and CLARENCE, who remain in the shadows.

The characters freeze on stage, all facing WALSH's entrance. There is an increase in the howling of the wind and WALSH appears in a spotlight somewhat brighter than the general dim lighting. The wind fades as WALSH enters. He is walking very slowly and carefully, as if he were the tiniest bit drunk. As he enters, JENNIE pulls out a chair at a table and IAN pours a drink into a glass on the table. The PROSPECTOR is blocking WALSH's way and WALSH stops. The PROSPECTOR steps aside and WALSH continues toward the table. All the characters watch him. WALSH stops at the chair, looks out at CLARENCE and turns the chair so that he no longer faces CLARENCE. He sits. There is a momentary freeze, then WALSH reaches for his drink, breaking the freeze. BILLY begins playing the harmonica; JENNIE begins to sing and move among the characters, tipping a hat here and rubbing an arm there as she passes. The characters come alive and the light brightens a bit so that WALSH's spotlight is gone—although the light is still not full.

JENNIE *singing*
George Carmack on Bonanza Creek
Went out to look for gold,
I wonder why, I wonder why.
Oldtimers said it was no use,
The water was too cold.
I wonder why, I wonder why.

PROSPECTOR   Another verse, Jennie!

JENNIE   Is there somethin' else you'd have me do, Mr. Walsh?

WALSH   Do you know..."Break the News to Mother"?

JENNIE   There's not much I don't know. How the hell did you think I ended up in Dawson?

Laughs and guffaws are heard from the boys.

WALSH   I always liked "Break the News to Mother."

JENNIE   *singing*   I wonder why, I wonder why.

HARRY   *entering from the shadows*   Jeeeesus Chriiiist! It's colder than a witch's diddy.

All the characters turn and look at him, with the exception of WALSH.

How about some eats here?

JENNIE   Girls, upstairs to the left: a drink, we can give you here.

BILLY   But you can't buy what there ain't none of....

PROSPECTOR   Which is grub.

There is a momentary freeze, which affects everyone but WALSH, who looks at HARRY.

JENNIE   *singing as BILLY plays the harmonica*
They said that he might search the creek
Until the world did end,
But not enough of gold he'd find
A postage stamp to send—

JENNIE stops singing abruptly as HARRY pulls out his poke. There is a momentary freeze. It affects everyone but WALSH. The freeze is broken by hoarse whispers.

BILLY   Better put away that poke, mister.

PROSPECTOR   We got a grafter in the room.   *He indicates WALSH.*   Ain't you noticed?

JENNIE   He'd as soon take ten percent off the top of that as look at you.

WALSH   *raising his glass to them*   Gentlemen—and sweet Jennie.

BILLY   *in a low voice*   To hell with Mr. Walsh.

There is a momentary freeze as they all watch WALSH drink. The freeze is broken by WALSH when he puts down his glass. IAN moves to fill it. BILLY begins playing "Garryowen" on his harmonica.

HARRY   Where'd you learn that song? You a Yankee fella? You a cavalry man?

BILLY   Don't have to be a cavalry man to know a song, mister.

He resumes playing his harmonica.

JENNIE   Here's a lady done a lot of ridin' and she don't know that song.

PROSPECTOR   "Garryowen."

WALSH knocks over his drink. There is a momentary freeze as they all look at WALSH and he stares at his spilled drink.

JENNIE   Ah, Mr. Walsh, you've spilled your drink. A drink for Mr. Walsh.

IAN rights his glass and pours him another drink.

BILLY   To hell with Mr. Walsh.

He resumes playing his harmonica and "Garryowen" builds with the sound of a military band creeping in and growing in volume.

HARRY   "Garryowen." Marching song of the 7th Cavalry. Custer's outfit.

JENNIE   Who's that?

HARRY   A long hair killed with long knives at the Greasy Grass.

JENNIE   We speak English here, mister.

"Garryowen" stops abruptly. WALSH bangs down his glass. There is another freeze as he looks around slowly and speaks clearly, carefully, announcing it, giving the impression once again of perhaps being drunk, but really being completely under control.

WALSH   General George Armstrong Custer . . . killed with 261 men of the 7th Cavalry of the United States Army . . . at the Little Big Horn, Montana, June 25th, 1876.

There is a pause. The freeze is broken as he picks up his drink. BILLY begins playing a ragtime tune on his harmonica. The lights brighten. The characters resume their talk.

HARRY   Who's your grafter?

IAN   That's Major Walsh—but he's not with the force. He's Commissioner of the Yukon now.

JENNIE   Did you see me front? Not a bit of snow to the street. Walsh may not be with the force, but he gets a good day's work out of 'em.   *She laughs.*   I must be the only whorehouse in the north whose front is shovelled clear by the North West Mounted on the orders of the Commissioner of the Yukon. *They all look at WALSH.*   He knows what those boys are good for.

JOEIE   *moving out of the shadows*   Anyone want to buy a paper?

JENNIE   Hey, Joeie's here with the *Nugget.* . . . Pass the hat round for Joeie! Isn't he a dear?

The PROSPECTOR starts around with the hat. JENNIE puts her arm around JOEIE.

His Da froze and his Mum takes in washin'. He's sweet Jennie's dear, aren't you, Joeie? You're sweet Jennie's sweetheart, aren't you?

The PROSPECTOR approaches WALSH after collecting some money from the others.

PROSPECTOR   *holding out the hat*   For Joeie.

WALSH looks at him. There is a look of incomprehension in his gaze.

I'm askin' for somethin' for the little boy.

WALSH   I can give you nothing.

PROSPECTOR   You and your kind have taken enough off us. You kin spare somethin' for the little boy.

WALSH   I can give you nothing!

PROSPECTOR   It ain't enough you're a son-of-a-bitch, you gotta be a cheap son-of-a-bitch!

WALSH hits him in the face, knocking him down. As he goes to get up, WALSH plants a foot in his back, sending him sprawling.

CLARENCE   *screaming from the shadows*   Nooooooooo!

There is a freeze with WALSH with his hand upraised to hit the PROSPECTOR; IAN with the bottle raised as a club; JENNIE drawing JOEIE to her. All of the characters in the saloon are in positions of action, except for HARRY who is a spectator. There is a pause, then HARRY sets forward, moving among the frozen characters.

HARRY *addressing the audience* The Klondike! 1898! And the end for Major James A. Walsh, formerly of the North West Mounted Police, an original member of the first contingent of that force, formed in 1873 by Sir John A. MacDonald to police the Canadian West!

He smashes his fist on the table. The freeze ends. HARRY continues as the actors leave.

Major Walsh never met General Custer, which was kinda a pity, 'cause the day Custer met Sittin' Bull was the beginning of the end for Major Walsh. . . . Old Glory Hound Custer—now he had a fail-proof plan for killin' off Injuns. First off, you found yourself some friendlies. You was forced to kill friendlies 'cause it was too difficult findin' hostiles, but friendlies camped near the forts, to show their goodwill kinda like, and it weren't too hard to come across a bunch of 'em set up in some cozy little hollow, flyin' the 'merican flag for good measure.

He laughs a dry chuckle.

Well now, once you picked yourself some Injuns, you gotta pick yourself a time. Custer thought winter was the best, for the Injun had always figured fightin' in winter wasn't sportin' like, and avoided it if he could. . . . Custer was an early riser—and if you team up a winter date with a 4 a.m. charge, when the Injuns was all asleep, you pretty well had it made. . . . Course, tactics comes into it. Custer did all right there too. 'Member that cozy little hollow I mentioned? Sorta a tube-like hollow was best, 'cause what you did was send a bunch of men in one end of the tube and, of course, all hell broke loose there, what with kids screamin', women runnin' and men lookin' for somethin' to hit back with, and the whole works naked as the day they was born, it bein' the middle of the night as far as they was concerned. Anyway, as their attention was somewhat di-verted by this here attack at one end of the tube, Custer, with a bunch of the boys, would sneak round t'other end and ride through, hell-bent for whoop-up, killin' off the strays, and generally gettin' a lot of 'em in the back while they was lookin' t'other way. . . . It were a pretty efficient way to fight a war. . . . The flag did its bit too, for the Injuns was prone to rally under it, thinkin' maybe the fact they was friendly had been missed; occasionally one of 'em even had time to run up a white flag.

He reminisces.

There was almost a kinda festive at-mos-phere to a Custer attack, what with his marchin' band playing "Garryowen." Custer liked to charge to music, and "Garryowen" was his favourite, although he was fond of "The Girl I Left Behind" too. . . . Still, generally, it was "Garryowen."

He whistles a few bars of "Garryowen." The tune begins brightly, but becomes slower and slower, then stops. There is silence for a second. He continues speaking—not as lightly as in the first part of his monologue.

The Little Big Horn. . . June 25th. . . 1876. . . . First off, wrong time! June ain't December—and that's a fact. Just shows how success kin go to your head. And the Injuns at the Little Big Horn weren't friendly. They was hostile. They was hostile as hell. Sittin' Bull and the Sioux had listened to the 'merican government say, "The utmost good faith shall always be observed towards the Indians, and their land and property shall never be taken from them without their consent." They had taken the government at its word—bein' savages, they weren't too familiar with governments and all, so it was an understandable mistake. . . . So, we got wrong month, and wrong bunch of Injuns. These Sioux weren't sittin' under no flag waitin' to be popped off like passenger pigeons. . . . On June 25th, Custer was up at 4 a.m. all right. Trouble was he never found no Injuns till noon time. His fail-proof plan for killin' off Injuns was goin' to hell in a hand basket. On top of everythin' else, the marchin' band had a prior engagement with General Terry.

So here's Custer. . . at noon time. . . in late June . . . with no marchin' band. . . comin' upon a camp of hostiles. Well now, it weren't hardly a camp either. It was a gathering together, under Sittin' Bull, of the last of those Injuns who weren't willin' to swap their huntin' grounds and freedom for a small corner of a reservation, 'bout 4,000 warriors, plus women and children. And what they was camped in wasn't, by no stretch of the imagination, a tube-like hollow. It was a gentle rollin' sweep of Montana prairie.

Custer, seein' it was gettin' later in the day by the minute, and probably wantin' to avoid that early afternoon slump most early risers suffer from, decided to attack without sendin' out a scout to see how far this here camp of Injuns extended. He had 'bout 500 men, and he figured that would be enough with some left over. . . . "Take no prisoners" was the order. . . . Major Reno, who, incidentally, had never fought Injuns before, only other 'mericans in the Civil War. . . this here Reno was given the honour of ridin' with 'bout half the men into one end of the non-tube. Which he did. And got the bejesus beat out of him. He made a hasty retreat to a bluff where he sat with his men for two days, cursin' Custer for runnin' off and leavin' them to the mercy of the Injuns and the sun. Forgot to mention that Custer did have this unfortunate habit of cuttin' his losses and ridin' off.

This time, Custer hadn't ridden off. He wasn't goin' nowhere. He had taken his half of the 7th, ridden a couple of miles, and cut down to what he figured was the outskirts of the camp. Two miles. His figurin' was 'bout eight miles out. He found Injuns aplenty—and none of them was facin' the other way.

On June 28th, General Terry came on a yellow-brown slope dotted with dead horses and pale white bodies—the dead—stripped of arms, ammunition, equipment . . . and clothin'. . . . At the summit of the slope stood a horse. The sole survivor of Custer's Last Stand was a clay-coloured horse—Comanche —still on his feet with ten bullet holes in him. The bullet holes eventually healed and on April 10th, 1878, the horse was commissioned "second commandin' officer" of the 7th Cavalry . . . and, on all occasions of ceremony, saddled, bridled, draped in mournin' and led by a mounted trooper, Comanche paraded with the regiment. . . . I hear tell, that when Terry looked on Custer's dead body, he wept, and said, "The flower of the American Army is gone."

Well now, the rest of the 'merican Army was out to avenge the "Custer Massacre." Sittin' Bull and the Sioux were hard to lay hands on, but there was always the friendlies.

ACT ONE

The action continues without a break.

HARRY *beginning to move treaty goods* Across the line, in the country of the Great White Mother, Major James A. Walsh of the North West Mounted was enforcin' law and order as decreed by Her Majesty's Government.

CLARENCE *offstage* Hey, Harry!

HARRY I had . . . what you might call, vacated the U-nited States and had myself a job as wagon master. . . .

CLARENCE *offstage* Harry! What're you doin'? Come on!

HARRY I'm comin'! I was running treaty goods for Canadian Injuns into Fort Walsh.

CLARENCE *offstage* Jesus Christ, Harry! Would you give me a hand!

HARRY *without moving to go* I said, I'm comin'!

CLARENCE Never mind, you lazy bastard! *Grunts and groans of effort are heard.* I'll do it myself!

HARRY Be right with you.

CLARENCE enters, bent double under a packing case. HARRY sits and watches him.

Hey, you better watch out for . . .

CLARENCE trips over a ploughshare. He falls flat on his face, spilling the packing case which is full of shovels.

. . . the ploughshare.

CLARENCE sits up, looking around at the shovels, the packing case.

CLARENCE *speaking plaintively* What the hell are they goin' to do with these?

HARRY *matter-of-factly* Nothin'.

CLARENCE What do you mean, nothin'?

HARRY *explaining a fact of life* They're gonna do nothin' with these. We're gonna haul 'em over here, your Major's gonna pass 'em all out and they're gonna haul 'em all away. And they ain't gonna do nothin' with 'em. The seed's gonna rot, the 'shares gonna rust and them goddamn shovels is just gonna lie where they flung 'em.

CLARENCE If they aren't gonna use 'em, why're we luggin' them around?

HARRY I'll tell you somethin', your Major's gonna be madder than a wet hen when he sees this lot. Second lot I brung in this month. First lot, the Major, he threw a real fit, said he was gonna write the Prime Minister, tell 'im to stuff his farm u-tensils.

CLARENCE Hey, did you hear the talk over at the fort?

HARRY *biting off a chaw of tobacco and looking at CLARENCE disdainfully* That talk's everywhere, Clarence.

CLARENCE Do you believe it?

HARRY Don't see why it couldn't be true.

CLARENCE Aren't you scared?

HARRY Now, why'd I be scared, Clarence?

CLARENCE We're gonna have ourselves an Injun War, just like the States, that's why!

HARRY gives him a dry look.

CLARENCE The Sioux are headed north. . . . An Injun War! . . . I could get to kill the man who killed Custer!

HARRY And who might that be?

CLARENCE Why, Sittin' Bull, of course.

HARRY How'd you know it was him personally killed Custer?

CLARENCE *defensively* Well . . . everybody says so! It was Sittin' Bull himself killed Custer at the Little Big Horn—with his huntin' knife! *He thinks about it and backs down a bit.* I guess the only ones know for sure are the men who died with Custer, eh?

HARRY *politely* Ain't you forgettin' somethin'?

CLARENCE What?

HARRY I seem to recollect there was some other people present at the event.

CLARENCE Who?

HARRY   Jesus Christ, Clarence! The Indians, that's who! You think a white man's the only person kin know anythin' for sure! Whyn't you try askin' an Injun who killed Custer? You bleedin' redcoats don't know nothin'!

CLARENCE   *insulted*   You wanna fight?

HARRY looks at CLARENCE and directs a spittle of tobacco juice at CLARENCE's feet. CLARENCE hauls back his fist.

LOUIS   *from the shadows, speaking to CLARENCE*   'Ey!

WALSH enters, his attention fixed on the crates.

WALSH   What the hell's this?

HARRY   *clearing his throat*   Well, sir, I 'spect you'd say. . .it was more. . . .

WALSH   And this. . .and this. . .and this!

He slaps each item with his riding crop.

LOUIS   *attempting to be helpful*   'Dat's plough-share. We got 'em last time.

WALSH   I know we got them last time. Why're we getting them this time?

LOUIS shrugs. WALSH's glance falls on CLARENCE. He notices him for the first time. CLARENCE feels obliged to say something.

CLARENCE   I. . .I don't know, sir.

WALSH's irritation seems to go and his manner changes.

WALSH   A new recruit, aren't you?

CLARENCE   Yes, sir.

WALSH   Name?

CLARENCE   Constable Clarence Underhill, sir!

WALSH   Welcome to the fort, Constable. Keep your eyes, ears and mind open. . . .

CLARENCE   Yes, s. . . .

WALSH   . . .and your mouth shut.   *He turns to HARRY and speaks real friendly.*   All right, Harry. *He leans on a crate beside HARRY and indicates the implements with his riding crop.*   What is all this?

HARRY   Well, sir. . . .

WALSH   *exceedingly friendly*   Some immigrant family ordered it, I suppose. . . .

HARRY   Ah. . .I can't rightly say that, sir.

WALSH   Aha. . . .Then you're taking it up to Calgary, are you, for some poor witless farmer there?

HARRY   No, sir. . . .Not that either.

WALSH   Mmmm. . . .Planning on homesteading yourself, are you?

HARRY smiles. The idea amuses him.

HARRY   Not very likely, sir.

WALSH stares at HARRY for a second. He lowers his voice and his speech builds.

WALSH   Are you telling me, man, that once again the government has seen fit to burden me and the natives of these parts with another load of seed and equipment to rot and rust when they know goddamn well, because I've told them time and again, that these Indians are not, and will never be, farmers!

There is a pause as WALSH stares at HARRY.

HARRY   *answering weakly*   That's it, sir.

WALSH   Right!   *His anger seems to subside.*   Well. . .can't be helped, can it?

He walks around one of the crates, tapping it with his riding crop, then, extending his hand, he barks.

Bill of lading!

CLARENCE   *startled*   Ah! Yes, sir!

He feels in his pocket as WALSH watches him expressionlessly. He finds the bill, presents it to WALSH—but not quite in his hand. The bill begins to float to the ground. He retrieves it and places it in WALSH's hand.

WALSH   *dryly*   Thank you, Constable.

CLARENCE   Yes, sir!

WALSH looks at CLARENCE, then moves away with HARRY.

WALSH   What have you got there, Harry?

He and HARRY begin to check the number of crates. LOUIS looks over to CLARENCE.

LOUIS   'Ey. . .'ey dere. . . .

He beckons him with his finger. CLARENCE moves over to him, although he's still more or less at attention and focused on WALSH in case he should suddenly want something.

Dis. . .a. . .first time you meet da. . . *nodding towards WALSH*   . . .commandin' officer up close, eh?

CLARENCE nods and looks at LOUIS warily. LOUIS looks somewhat disreputable in his scout outfit.

What you think of 'im?

CLARENCE   He seems a little. . . .

He casts a nervous glance at WALSH.

WALSH   *to HARRY*   Read it yourself!   *thrusting the bill at HARRY*   What does that look like to you?

CLARENCE smiles weakly at LOUIS, who smiles back.

HARRY   It. . .ah. . .looks like we're missin' one crate, Major.

WALSH I trust you'll find it.

HARRY I'll do that . . . yes, I will, Major. First thing I hit Fort MacLeod.

WALSH Right.

He takes the bill and begins to check it against the goods listed on the outside of the crates.

So . . . contents . . . .

HARRY assists him.

LOUIS *indicating himself* Louis Leveille. *shaking hands with CLARENCE.* Fort Walsh scout. . . . Mother red, father white . . . but not so white as da Major dere. . . . Louis' father, French.

He laughs. CLARENCE realizes it's a joke and smiles back.

WALSH Mark it off! Mark it off!

HARRY does so. CLARENCE glances at them nervously.

LOUIS Ah . . . don't worry . . . mean nothin'. . . . Just 'is way. He care a lot and so he yell a lot, eh?

CLARENCE Yeah. I guess you gotta know a lot to be an officer.

LOUIS Louis tell yuh somethin'. . . . Take all da books, da news dat da white man prints, take all dat Bible book, take all dose things you learn from . . . lay dem on da prairie . . . and da sun . . . da rain . . . da snow . . . pouf! You wanna learn, you study inside here . . . *He taps his head.* . . . and here . . . *He taps his chest.* . . . and how it is wit' you and me . . . *He indicates the two of them.* . . . and how it is wit' you and all. . . . *He indicates the surroundings.* Travel 'round da Medicine Wheel. Den you know somethin'.

WALSH *approaching LOUIS and CLARENCE* Well, Louis, there's another lot, courtesy of those fools in Ottawa.

LOUIS Dose fools dat're sittin' dere ain't such fools as da people dat sent dem dere, eh, Major?

WALSH chuckles. HARRY begins to clear away the treaty goods.

MRS. ANDERSON *offstage* Major Walsh! Oh, Major!

WALSH sighs. MRS. ANDERSON enters almost hysterical.

Major Walsh!

WALSH *smiling at MRS. ANDERSON* Yes, Mrs. Anderson.

MRS. ANDERSON *almost in tears* Major Walsh, the most terrible thing has happened.

CROW EAGLE enters with great dignity. He walks a bit ahead of Sergeant McCUTCHEON. He is in custody, although there is no hand on him.

WALSH Now, it's all right, Mrs. Anderson. Just tell us what this is all about.

MRS. ANDERSON Ah, Major . . . this savage . . . this heathen . . . this . . . Indian has stolen my washtub!

A pained expression passes over WALSH's face. He shakes his head and makes an almost inaudible tut-tut sound.

Yes! It was right outside the door and these heathens snuck up and stole it! I'm counting on you, Major, to return that tub! I mean, what am I to rinse in otherwise?

WALSH Well, Crow Eagle, did you take this white lady's tub?

CROW EAGLE That is so.

MRS. ANDERSON What did I tell you? *circling CROW EAGLE in a rage.* Mark my words, they'll be killing us in our sleep next!

WALSH *placating her* Mrs. Anderson. . . . *turning to CROW EAGLE* Why'd you take the tub?

CROW EAGLE We needed a drum.

WALSH The Great White Mother'd be very angry if she discovered you'd taken this white lady's washtub.

CROW EAGLE I am sure if the Great White Mother knew how much we needed that drum, she would be glad to let us keep it.

MRS. ANDERSON As if the Queen cared about them!

CROW EAGLE We have cut the bottom out of that tub and covered it with buffalo skin. It makes a very good drum.

LOUIS Da white lady has 'nother tub . . . why does she not use dat?

MRS. ANDERSON *going to seize CROW EAGLE's arm* What's mine's my own! You'll not take. . . .

WALSH *taking her arm and drawing her aside* Mrs. Anderson!

MRS. ANDERSON Whose side are you on, Jim?

WALSH I was unaware we were choosing sides. My job is to keep the peace and see that justice is done.

MRS. ANDERSON Then get me my tub!

WALSH *a trifle tired* Louis, explain it to him.

LOUIS *explaining to CROW EAGLE in Cree* Na-mo-ya ta-ki otin-a-man ki-kwhy a-ka a-tipaý-hitaman (It is not lawful to take what is not your own). . . .

CROW EAGLE *dismissing LOUIS and speaking directly to WALSH* White Forehead Chief! Why we should not keep it?

WALSH *after a pause* You must not take articles from the whites again. They need even what they appear not to need.... And you must bring skins in payment for the...drum....Make sure he understands, Louis.

LOUIS draws CROW EAGLE aside and speaks to him in muffled conversation while WALSH continues with MRS. ANDERSON.

LOUIS   Wapi-ka-tik-oki-maw it-o-wew-may-scootch ata-yuk ta-pa-so-wa-chik to tippo-what misti-kwa-shihk-asa kotin-nut (The White Forehead Chief says you must bring skins in payment for the drum you have taken).

CROW EAGLE   Ni-ka-to-tayn namaya-ni-nistotayn ma-ka ni-ka-to- tayn keespin wapi-ka-tik ekosi it-o-wen-ni-ka-to-tayn (I will do it. I do not understand it, but I will do it. If the White Forehead Chief says it...I will do it).

LOUIS   Pi-ko ta-na-hi-ta-wat Okimaskoew Kwa-yask ta-pa-mi-hayew ki-ta-yes-si-ni-ma apo tchi ke-yom ta-wan-kiski-sew kiya (You must obey the Great White Mother's law. She will look after your people if you do. Otherwise, she will forget you).

CROW EAGLE   Wapi-ka-tik chee pa-taw aso-ta-ma-to-aina paski-si- gana, mosiniya nin-ta wahitaynan paskowaw mastosak aya-wak sa-ka- staynok (Has she sent the White Forehead Chief the goods that I asked for my people? We need ammunition, we have seen buffalo to the south).

WALSH   *steering MRS. ANDERSON away*   Now, look, Emma....

MRS. ANDERSON   What about my tub?

WALSH   Emma...the Indians, they see two tubs in your yard....You have to remember they've a different background from us....

MRS. ANDERSON   Background? They don't have any background.

WALSH   Well, as I was saying....

MRS. ANDERSON   Are you telling me I'm not getting my tub back?

WALSH   That's right, Emma.

MRS. ANDERSON   What will you do when they murder us in our beds? You're nothing but a...

WALSH   Would you have me throw him in chains? To hell with your damned old tub! We're not going to start an Indian War over it!

MRS. ANDERSON   No! You'll sit by and let the Sioux do that!

She whirls around and exits. WALSH stands stiff and tense as she exits, then he relaxes and turns to McCUTCHEON. He smiles, sighs and shakes his head.

WALSH   The Sioux?...Well, McCutcheon...hell hath no fury like a woman deprived of her washtub.

He walks around the equipment, looking at it casually. You'd think it was her very existence.

McCUTCHEON   Aye, sir. You're right there. I tell ye, I'd rather face a hostile in a fit of pique than Mrs. Anderson with her dander up....

LOUIS   Crow Eagle asks for ammunition to hunt da buffalo. His scouts have seen a small herd to da south.

WALSH   Every year there're fewer buffalo and soon there will be no more. His people must think of next year and the year after.

LOUIS   *almost gently*   Ever since he was born, he has eaten wild meat. His father and his grandfather ate wild meat. He cannot give up quickly the customs of his fathers.

WALSH speaks directly to CROW EAGLE.

WALSH   *speaking formally*   When the white man comes, the buffalo goes....And with the buffalo goes the life you have known. You cannot stop this happening any more than you can stop the sun or the moon. You must find a new life....That is why the Great White Mother sends you these...   *He indicates the implements.*   ...so you can start a new life.

CROW EAGLE   I do not wish to be servant to a cow.

HARRY   *laughing*   He's got somethin' there....

WALSH   Yes, well...McCutcheon, take him over to the post and see he gets ammunition for the hunt.

McCUTCHEON   Aye, sir.

He and CROW EAGLE go to leave.

WALSH   Crow Eagle, you must think of the time when there are no more buffalo.

CROW EAGLE   When there are no more buffalo ...there are no more Indians.

He and McCUTCHEON exit. WALSH watches them leave.

WALSH   *to himself*   I ask you, can you see that man bent double over a hoe?

HARRY   Don't appear likely they'll ever be farmers, that's a fact.

WALSH   Farmers? Not farmers! If they're to grow anything in this dust bowl, the government'll have to turn them into magicians!

CLARENCE   *standing at attention*   Excuse me, sir ...permission to speak, sir.

WALSH appears lost in his thoughts as he stares after CROW EAGLE.

WALSH   Yes...what is it?

CLARENCE   There's been some talk, sir, among the men at the post...about the hostiles from the States.

WALSH   *still not particularly attentive*   Go on....

CLARENCE   *encouraged*   About them comin' up into Canada....Sittin' Bull and the whole Sioux nation comin' up into Canada to get away from the U.S. Army....

Sometime during CLARENCE's speech, WALSH becomes alert and is listening.

WALSH   Yes?

CLARENCE   Well...I was just wonderin', sir, if that was true...I mean, the whole Sioux nation, sir? And we only got 'bout 60 men here...

WALSH   Yes.

CLARENCE   ...and you know...I'm not askin' for myself, sir, it's just that I'd like to write a last letter home to me Mum if we...if we were on the verge of war, sir, or anything like that...sir.

WALSH   *speaking quietly*   What have the Sioux done?

CLARENCE   *blurting it out*   They killed Custer!

WALSH   And Custer killed them.

CLARENCE   Yes, sir.

WALSH   What have the Sioux done to us?

CLARENCE   *looking nervously at HARRY, then back to WALSH*   Nothin', sir?

WALSH   In which case, I don't believe we're on the verge of war with them.   *to LOUIS, lightly*   What do you say, Louis?

LOUIS   *smiling*   I think our redcoats too damn busy chasin' 'merican whiskey traders. Dey much worse trouble dan any Sioux I run across.

WALSH   *smiling*   My sentiments exactly.

He and LOUIS start off. The sound of the arrival of the Sioux creeps in very softly—muted voices, horses, faint drums and singing. It can barely be heard.

CLARENCE   Sir!

WALSH   *turning back to him*   Yes, Constable?

CLARENCE   *speaking quickly*   Request permission to accompany the Major when he rides out to meet Sittin' Bull and the Sioux, sir!

WALSH   What about that letter to your mother?

CLARENCE   I'll write it tonight, sir.

WALSH has a hard time keeping a smile off his face.

WALSH   Permission granted.

WALSH exits as CLARENCE and HARRY watch him. CLARENCE is tense and HARRY is casual, then

CLARENCE looks at HARRY, relaxes, grins and leaps into the air, throwing his hat off. There is a certain similarity to an Indian youth after his first coup.

CLARENCE   Yip yip yip yip yipeeeeeeeeeeeeeeeee! Whahooo!

CLARENCE and HARRY exit. The lights dim as LOUIS crouches, listening to the sound of the Sioux arriving. As it builds, LOUIS moves about as if he were watching the arrival of the Sioux. The sound is well established before he speaks.

LOUIS   Tabernacle!   *casting a glance over his shoulder*   Major! Dis way!

WALSH and McCUTCHEON enter. They stand on a slight rise.

See...da village is dere.   *pointing*   Dat dust, dat is more joinin' dose already camped.

WALSH hands his binoculars to McCUTCHEON. He gazes at the village, using only his naked eye, as the scout does.

WALSH   Must be...what...two miles away? What would you say, Louis?

LOUIS   *smiling*   Louis say you damn good pupil.

WALSH   *smiling*   Louis damn good teacher.

McCUTCHEON   *looking through the binoculars, then lowering them*   Must be 2,000 people there.

LOUIS   Maybe so...5,000.

CLARENCE enters.

CLARENCE   The horses're picketed, sir.

WALSH turns to CLARENCE and speaks to him with an intensity that indicates he is taut as a bow string and ready for anything.

WALSH   You wanted to see the Sioux, Constable ...all right, here they come. I want you to remember something....You do not draw your gun unless you see me draw mine. You will follow orders exactly, precisely and immediately. If you do one thing that precipitates trouble between us and the Sioux, you need not worry about a redskin taking your scalp. I myself will place a bullet between your eyes faster than you can say write-a-letter-home.

It is a threat he means.

Do you understand?

For the first time, CLARENCE is aware of the potential explosiveness of the situation.

CLARENCE   I do, sir.

The sound is building.

WALSH   Louis, beside me....McCutcheon and Underhill, behind....

They take up their positions. WALSH gives a quick look to CLARENCE.

I rely on you to uphold the honour of the force.

The sound is at its crescendo—all around the audience—for several seconds. The sound stops. There is a pause.

GALL enters. He is followed by SITTING BULL, who looks austere. He has one feather in his hair. They stop a short distance from WALSH. WALSH raises his hand, palm outward. GALL returns the gesture. There is silence for a second.

WALSH   Louis, tell them....

GALL   We speak as men—to each other.

He means that they do not need an interpreter.

I am Gall of the Hunkpapa Lakota.

WALSH   You've crossed the line into the country of the Great White Mother.

GALL stares at WALSH impassively. SITTING BULL follows their conversation. His movements, if any, are slow and deliberate. He is a man of great presence and personal magnetism. It is not necessary for him to speak or to draw attention to himself in any way for one to be aware of his strength of character. It is his custom to carefully size up a situation before committing himself to a course of action.

WALSH   I am a soldier of the Great White Mother. You may know me, and others like me, by my red coat.   *He indicates his tunic.*

GALL   *offering WALSH a George III medal*   My grandfather was a soldier for the grandfather of Queen Victoria. At that time, your people told him that the Sioux nation belonged to that grandfather of the Queen. My people fought against the Long-knives for your people then. We were told that you would always look after your red children. Now the Longknives have stolen our land. We have no place to go. We come home to you asking for that protection you promised.

WALSH takes the medal from GALL and examines it. He looks at GALL. He is not actually prepared for this specific argument about Canada's obligation to the Sioux.

McCUTCHEON   *speaking quietly*   What is it, sir?

WALSH   *passing the medal to McCUTCHEON*   It's a George III medal. The Sioux fought for the British in 1776 against the Americans.

He looks at GALL and speaks carefully. His orders from Ottawa have not covered this exigency.

We are your friends, that is true....

GALL   The Lakota has need of friends. I want you to know this trouble was not begun by us. The Long-knives have come out of the night and for camp-fires they have lit our lodges. Our women weep and the nostrils of our babies must be pinched lest they cry out and give us away. At the Greasy Grass, the Long Hair attacked our camp and we

rose up like the buffalo bull when the cows are attacked and we rubbed him out. Now we are hunted as we hunt animals . . . and we have crossed the line.

LOUIS   *nudging WALSH*   'Ey . . . on the ridge . . . is dat not da horse of Père de Corbay?

WALSH   *looking, frowning towards the hills*   Whose horses graze there?

GALL   *looking at the hills*   White Dog's, our Assini-boine brother.

WALSH   I wish to speak to him.

The sound of rattles and drums is heard. GALL exits. CLARENCE shifts from side to side nervously. McCUTCHEON gives him a look.

McCUTCHEON   *in a low voice*   Easy, laddie.

CLARENCE   *taking a slow look over his shoulder*   We're bloody well surrounded, Sergeant.

McCUTCHEON   Never ye mind, laddie. Just keep your eye on the Major.

WALSH takes a slow walk. He whistles, then he stops, looking directly at SITTING BULL.

WALSH   Gall!   *GALL turns toward him.*   I ask the name of the man who stands with us.

GALL   A wise man....

WHITE DOG enters. He carries a rifle in one hand.

WALSH   *speaking quickly*   McCutcheon!

WHITE DOG   *belligerently*   White Dog.

WALSH   The horses on the ridge, are they yours?

WHITE DOG   *antagonistically*   You say!

WALSH   *snapping*   McCutcheon!

McCUTCHEON moves quickly and seizes WHITE DOG's arms. WHITE DOG resists, but McCUTCHEON holds him immobile. WALSH's hand rests easily, almost casually, on his holstered gun. As McCUT-CHEON seizes WHITE DOG, he cries out. There is a swelling of sound from the surrounding Sioux. WALSH raises his voice and announces as the sound continues in the background.

Those are the horses of Père de Corbay! His brand can be seen from here! White Dog is under arrest for stealing!

WHITE DOG   I find loose! It is custom, horses taken! No law!

WALSH   *after a pause*   Release him!

McCUTCHEON releases him.

Next time, you find horses not belonging to you, they must be left alone!

WHITE DOG   *as he turns to leave, calling back threateningly*   Meet again, Wichitas!

WALSH   White Dog!

He walks up to WHITE DOG, oblivious of his rifle.

Repeat your words.

WHITE DOG   *a coward*   Meet again sometime.

WALSH   *speaking quietly but now without menace*
Take back those words.

WHITE DOG hesitates a minute, then looks to SIT-TING BULL and back at WALSH.

WHITE DOG   White Dog not threaten.

WALSH   *inclining his head slightly*   Then go. I have no grudge against White Dog.

WHITE DOG hurries off. The background sound swells. WALSH walks over to SITTING BULL, who raises his hand. The noise stops.

SITTING BULL   These people are my people. I am Sitting Bull.

WALSH   Major James Walsh of the North West Mounted Police.

He extends his hand and after a second's hesitation, SITTING BULL takes it.

SITTING BULL   My people need ammunition.

WALSH   *beginning his "government" statement*
The Queen will not tolerate raiding from her soil, nor does she . . .

SITTING BULL   Hard times have come to us. My warriors use the lasso to bring down meat.

WALSH stares at him for a split second and decides to trust him.

WALSH   Ammunition will be issued sufficient for hunting purposes. McCutcheon, take the Constable and see to it.

McCUTCHEON   Aye, sir!

McCUTCHEON and CLARENCE exit. The lights begin to dim.

SITTING BULL   We shall meet again.

WALSH   *smiling*   I look forward to it.

GALL, WALSH and SITTING BULL exit. PRETTY PLUME enters, unrolls a buffalo skin for the floor of the tent, as LOUIS, singing softly, removes his pack and sits a distance from the tent.

LOUIS   En roulant ma boule roulant, enroulant ma boule.
En roulant ma boule roulant, enroulant ma boule.
Derrier' chez nous, 'y a-t'un e-tang, enroulant ma boule,
Trois beaux canards s'en vont baignant, roulant ma boule, roulant. .

The lights brighten as McCUTCHEON and CLARENCE enter, carrying bowls of food. McCUTCHEON passes a bowl of food to LOUIS.

McCUTCHEON   Here y'are, Louis.

McCUTCHEON and CLARENCE sit. All three of them begin to eat. LOUIS eats with relish; McCUTCHEON eats simply; CLARENCE sloshes his bowl around, peering into it with apprehension. He is reassured by LOUIS' appreciation of the contents. He dips his fingers into the bowl and comes up with something unpleasant. He quickly drops it back into the bowl and grimaces. He looks at McCUTCHEON, who tilts his bowl a bit and drains it. CLARENCE swallows and looks down at his bowl. LOUIS glances over at him.

LOUIS   *teasing CLARENCE*   Dat some good, eh?

CLARENCE smiles weakly and nods half-heartedly. LOUIS gets up.

'Nother one?

McCUTCHEON   *putting his empty bowl down*   Not for me, Louis.

LOUIS looks at CLARENCE.

CLARENCE   I still got some. Thanks anyway.

LOUIS exits to get some more.

McCUTCHEON   *calling after him*   My compliments to the chef, Louis!

CLARENCE stares at McCUTCHEON, then down at his own bowl. McCUTCHEON suppresses a smile.

Laddie, ye better be eatin' that up, if ye want to keep your forelock.

CLARENCE   What do you mean?

McCUTCHEON   *whispering to him*   It's a great insult not to eat what's put before ye when y're visitin' the Sioux. . . . Men have been known to lose their scalps over such an insult.

CLARENCE   *sickly*   That so?

He dips his fingers into his bowl again, comes in contact with something unpleasant, drops it back into the bowl, sits for a second, then makes up his mind.

Well, I don't give a damn! I'd sooner be scalped than eat any more of this stuff! Here, you take it!

McCUTCHEON   *laughing and pushing the bowl away*   I've done my duty, laddie. Now it's up to you.

LOUIS returns, dejected.

LOUIS   Merde, McCutch. Dey eat it all up. Dere's none left.

CLARENCE   *looking up, brightening*   Say, Louis, I think . . .   *He feels his forehead.*   . . . I think I overdid it a bit today . . . don't really feel too much like eatin' tonight. . . . If you want mine, well, no sense seein' it wasted.

He offers his bowl hopefully to LOUIS. LOUIS smiles, recognizing his ploy.

LOUIS   Dat so? Weeeellllllll....

He takes his bowl, squats and eats. CLARENCE smiles at McCUTCHEON.

McCUTCHEON   Now I wonder how the Major's makin' out.

LOUIS   *looking up*   Da Major and Sittin' Bull over in da big tipi dere. Dey send Louis away, but he keep an eye out all da same.

He goes back to his food. McCUTCHEON gets out his pipe and stretches his legs, but remains sitting.

McCUTCHEON   The Sioux have behaved themselves, there's no denyin' that. Six months it's been, and they're as good as gold.

LOUIS   *putting down his bowl and looking at McCUTCHEON*   Dese Sioux, dey not stupid, you know. Make trouble and dey know what happens. 'Mericans send Longknives up here. Dey kill every Indian dey see—little ones, big ones, mama with bébé—dey don't give a good goddamn, friendly or hostile.... You got red skin...   *He points his finger.*   ...bang-bang!...Louis' skin got reddish tinge.

There is an awkward silence. The lights dim a bit. McCUTCHEON and CLARENCE look down. LOUIS shrugs and gets out his pipe.

McCUTCHEON   *passing LOUIS his pouch of tobacco*   Try mine.

LOUIS   *taking the pouch and fingering it*   You buy new one, eh?

McCUTCHEON   I got it at the post before we left. Feel that leather...soft, isn't it?

LOUIS   Dat's nice....   *He gazes off into space.*   But not so nice as 'nother pouch I see once...many year ago, before the redcoats come...I see white man at Fort Whoop-Up, a Longknife....He show everybody mighty nice tobacco pouch he have ...made from breast of Indian woman he killed at Sand Creek.

He looks in the direction of SITTING BULL's tipi. McCUTCHEON and CLARENCE follow suit. As the lights dim on them, they begin to come up on the tipi. There is a soft background sound of Indian rattles and bells, which continues until the scene with SITTING BULL is established. WALSH and SITTING BULL are eating. WALSH looks up from his bowl after a moment.

WALSH   Louis tells me you've been visiting the Blackfoot and the Cree.

SITTING BULL   They tell me that Major Walsh is the White Forehead Chief...and the White Forehead Chief is the Indian's friend. If trouble strikes your camp, they say, send for the White Forehead Chief.

WALSH   The Blackfoot...

SITTING BULL   Do you ride out to speak only of the Blackfoot and the Cree....Have you no news for the Sioux?

WALSH   Yes, I have news...and it's not good news....My chief says the Queen is not responsible for you.   *He holds up the George III medal.*   This happened a long time ago. The Great White Mother has made peace with the Americans.

SITTING BULL   *with a hint of sarcasm*   Whose red children are we then?

WALSH   It was decided the Sioux belonged to the President in Washington.

SITTING BULL   It was decided....You are few and we are many. Will you try to drive us back across the line?

WALSH   You're welcome to stay here so long as your young men don't cross the line to raid and so long as the Sioux are self-sufficient....The Queen won't feed or clothe you as she does her own Indians.

SITTING BULL   *leaning towards WALSH*   My people have never accepted the annuities....We have never touched the pen....We have never sold our land! It has been stolen from us! You need not feed or clothe us. The Hunkpapa Lakota feed and clothe themselves!

WALSH   *speaking gently*   Soon you won't be able to do that. The buffalo will be gone. You must return to your home before that happens.

SITTING BULL   The Black Hills is our home! And the white man has stolen them! I cannot sign away the Black Hills. They are not mine alone. Before me, they were my father's. After me, they shall be my children's. Do you sign away the birthright of your children?

WALSH   I tell you this because I am a soldier and I must follow orders, but I am a friend also. White Forehead...   *indicating himself*   ...does not say this, Major Walsh says this.   *He speaks officially.*   The President in Washington has requested the Sioux to return...and promises fair treatment to all.

SITTING BULL stares at WALSH for a moment, then begins to speak conversationally, casually.

SITTING BULL   Let me tell you what I have heard today....Today, I have news of my good friend Crazy Horse of the Oglala. He was a dreamer, wishing only to serve his people...and they loved him well....Brave in battle. Wise in council. He loved the little children and could not bear to see them suffer. The Oglala and the Hunkpapa fought together at the Greasy Grass where Custer died. I brought my people across the line, but Crazy Horse and the Oglala remained behind. Since that time, they've known no peace. General Terry pursued them like a wolf who tears at the soft underbelly of a fleeing doe.... There are two reservation chiefs across the line named Red Cloud and Spotted Tail. Some say they are paper chiefs created by the white man to betray their red brothers. . . . Red Cloud and Spotted Tail met Crazy Horse in council and begged him to bring his people in, to touch the pen, to lead a reservation life. They told him, "You will be a great chief!". . . The Sioux are proud; we love position. . . . My good friend Crazy Horse is dead. He brought his people in and when he stepped into the meeting place, he saw the windows all were barred and 'round about stood soldiers pointing longknives at him . . . and when he turned to run, his arms were pinioned by his red brothers and a white soldier pushed his bayonet into Crazy Horse's stomach! It took one night for him to die. He sang his death song and his mother and father stood outside and sang back, for the white soldiers would not let them enter where he lay dying. And where he stood when he was struck, there is a great gouge gone from the wall, for the soldier's longknife passed through Crazy Horse and lodged there till he withdrew it. . . . I am told that men with skin like yours gaze at that gouge and laugh and joke and say: "There stood a good Indian . . . a dead Indian." . . . My good friend Crazy Horse of the Oglala.

WALSH   Aren't things sometimes done in your name? Things you do not wish? It can be that way with white men too. . . . I am your friend.

SITTING BULL   I have no white friends.

WALSH   For Christ's sake, forget the colour of our skin! If you've got no more to say than that, let's all line up and have it out! To hell with it! Is that what you want?

SITTING BULL   Red men choke and die on white men's words!

WALSH   When have my actions betrayed my words? I came here to speak to you as a man and I expect the same from you! What's past is past! Crazy Horse is dead, but others live and you and I are here to talk of them! . . . People are coming from the White Father in Washington. I ask you to see them. If you don't want to return with them, I will tell them so. I promise you, I'll stand by you.

SITTING BULL   Who do they send?

WALSH   General Terry.

SITTING BULL   You ask me to see this man? The man who burnt my mother earth and killed my friends! You tell me, see this man!

WALSH   If you wish to negotiate a reservation here in Canada, you must make your peace with the Americans first.

There is silence as WALSH and SITTING BULL sit staring at one another.

There's something more I have to say. . . . Last night, two men rode into your camp.

SITTING BULL   With news of Crazy Horse.

WALSH   And news of something more than that, I think.

SITTING BULL   They had a request to make of me.

WALSH   Nez Percés, weren't they?

SITTING BULL   Nez Percés . . . from the valley of the Winding Waters.

WALSH   The Wallowa Valley no longer belongs to them.

SITTING BULL   A thief treaty . . . Chief Joseph did not sign!

WALSH   Nevertheless, the President has put aside a reservation and the Indians must go onto it.

SITTING BULL   What right has he to tell the Indian where he must go in his own land?

WALSH   Is Chief Joseph trying to bring his people into Canada?

SITTING BULL   I tell you what you already know . . . the Nez Percés are on the run. They have come to me. They request the Sioux to help them fight their way across the line.

WALSH   What I do not know is your decision.

SITTING BULL   I have not made it.

WALSH   Then listen to me. If it can be proven that you've carried out an act of war against the Americans while camping here in Canada, your refuge will be in jeopardy.

SITTING BULL   What could you do?

WALSH   We could open the border and allow the American Army in to drive you out.

SITTING BULL   Even though you know you send us to our death?

WALSH   We don't know that.

SITTING BULL   As we speak, Nez Percés are rotting, their bodies full of bullet holes, their heads smashed in with gunstocks and boot heels. Would you term this a natural death?

WALSH   You see my red coat . . . it represents the Queen and the Canadian government. My duty is to inform you of my government's position . . . and it is this: "Armed excursions across the line . . . for whatever reason . . . will not be tolerated!" *speaking gently to SITTING BULL* I'd advise you to deny the Nez Percés.

SITTING BULL   Men, women, children? . . . They have travelled 1,300 miles.

WALSH   Another 60 and they're across the line. My government won't try to stop them, but you must not try to aid them either. They must make it on their own.

SITTING BULL   You ask me to deny them.

WALSH   It's for the good of your people. You can see that.

SITTING BULL   Yes. . . I can see it. . . . Today is a sad day for me. . . . In the past, I have risen, toma-hawk in hand. I have done all the hurt to the whites that I could. . . . Now you are here. My arms hang to the ground as if dead. . . . I believe the Blackfoot and the Cree have judged you wisely. I will call you White Sioux and I will trust you. I will speak to General Terry. . . and I will deny the Nez Percés.

As the lights dim on WALSH and SITTING BULL, they come up blue and cold along with a back-ground sound of howling wind. The lights pick out McCUTCHEON and CLARENCE, who are bundled in greatcoats. A winter blizzard is blowing.

McCUTCHEON   *to CLARENCE who has stopped in front of him*   What is it?

CLARENCE   We've lost the Major.

McCUTCHEON   Keep goin', laddie.

CLARENCE   We've lost the Major.

McCUTCHEON   Here, let me. . . .

He moves ahead of CLARENCE and begins walking, holding his hand up to shield himself from the wind. CLARENCE follows him.

And we've no lost the Major. . . . Come on, laddie, we'll wait for Louis here.

He and CLARENCE huddle together.

CLARENCE   My God, I'm cold!

A blue light picks out WALSH, SITTING BULL and GALL as they enter in single file, leaning against the storm.

McCUTCHEON   *cupping his hands and calling*   Over here, sir!

WALSH   *as they approach*   Any sign of Louis?

McCUTCHEON   *shaking his head*   Are ye sure Sittin' Bull's information is correct?

WALSH looks at SITTING BULL.

SITTING BULL   The Longknives have surrounded the Nez Percés, but some have broken through.

WALSH   Well, if they're out there, Louis'll find them.

CLARENCE   Aren't you worried 'bout him?

McCUTCHEON   Ah, we've got naught to worry about Louis. . . . He can look after himself.

CLARENCE   My God, I'm cold!

They hear a noise. They all turn around and look. A blue light picks out LOUIS. He makes his way toward them. He comes to SITTING BULL and stands before him without speaking. There is a pause for a moment.

WALSH   Well. . . speak up, Louis, have the Nez Percés crossed the border?

LOUIS   *speaking to SITTING BULL*   I have found da tracks of a small number of people. Dey have few ponies and move slowly. Most are on foot. . . . Dere trail is easy to follow. . . it is marked with frozen blood. . . . Come with me.

SITTING BULL and GALL prepare to follow him. He speaks to WALSH.

Wait here. We speak to dem first. Dey will be frightened. We will bring dem back.

They exit. There is silence. McCUTCHEON moves toward WALSH, who stands at the edge of the light looking out. A wolf howls. There is silence again, then the whinnying of a pony. WALSH points.

McCUTCHEON   Is it them, sir?

SITTING BULL returns without his outer robes. He wears leggings and breeches. He stands outside the circle of light, a silhouette.

WALSH   Sergeant. . . Constable. . . . Help them!

He nods his head briskly in the direction from which SITTING BULL came. He gives them his greatcoat. They exit quickly.

SITTING BULL   *an honest question*   How does the white man sustain himself beneath the weight of the blood that he has shed?

WALSH looks at SITTING BULL, then off at the muffled sounds of people approaching. The light begins to flicker, as if people were passing in front of it. WALSH turns slowly, looking outside of the light. The sound of people moaning is heard. A blue light picks out CLARENCE as he makes his way toward WALSH.

CLARENCE   Is. . . is it all right, sir? My coat. . . I've. . . I've given it to. . .   *He indicates vaguely outside of the light.*   . . . to. . . to a little girl and her brother. Their feet are frozen, sir. . . . Will the government mind about the coat?

WALSH   *holding himself erect, military*   I'll speak on your behalf, Constable.

CLARENCE   It's just women and children. . . and a few men. . . . Most of them are. . . got wounds of one kind or another. Chief Joseph, he's not with them. He. . . didn't make it. . . . It's only just people, people that's been hurt! I don't see what they could have done to deserve this. . . . Do you know what they've done?

WALSH   There. . . see there. . . .

He hurriedly removes his tunic. He has on a long underwear top.

Take this. . . take this to the woman on the pony . . . there. . . with the papoose on her back. Take it to her.

CLARENCE   Yes, sir.

He moves toward the figure and freezes a ways from her. The wind howls. LOUIS stands on the rim of the light, watching. CLARENCE returns, moving slowly. He has the tunic with him.

She doesn't need it...she's been hit in the chest. The baby's dead. It's got a bit of blood on it....

He gives the tunic an ineffectual wipe, more a touch of the blood, then looks at WALSH.

I didn't notice till I put it 'round her that...she didn't need it.

WALSH slowly takes the tunic from him. CLARENCE moves away as WALSH stands there holding the tunic. He extends one arm slowly, deliberately. He drops the tunic and looks out. LOUIS steps forward, picks up the tunic and hands it to WALSH.

LOUIS   You can't just throw it away, sir. Dat's too easy.

WALSH looks at him, takes the tunic and slowly exits with it. LOUIS goes down on one knee. SITTING BULL steps forward slightly. The many voices of the Nez Percés are heard in the background saying "Ay Ay" as LOUIS speaks.

LOUIS   My father has given me this nation.
In protecting it,
A hard time I have.

Friends, hardships pursue me,
Fearless of them,
I live.
My chiefs of old are gone.
Myself, I shall take courage.

The voices grow in volume. They stop simultaneously. There is a second of blackout, then the light comes up on PRETTY PLUME and CROWFOOT who are with SITTING BULL, who is in his former position.

PRETTY PLUME   Tatanka Yotanka!

CROWFOOT runs toward SITTING BULL and SITTING BULL picks him up, laughing. As he swings him in the air, PRETTY PLUME approaches him and holds out a rawhide bag which contains sacred stones.

SITTING BULL   Aha, Little One! Get to work, your mother says. Clear a spot.

CROWFOOT   Now?

SITTING BULL   Now.

He sits. CROWFOOT kneels, smoothing a spot to lay out the sacred stones, then he sits beside SITTING BULL. PRETTY PLUME sits watching from a distance.

So.... *He arranges the stones in the shape of a Medicine Wheel.* To the Great Spirit belongs all things. The four-legged and the two-legged...but to the two-legged he gives the power to make live and to destroy....To you, he gives the cup of living water....Now...see? *He indicates the circle of stones.* It makes the sacred hoop. Here is the cross within the circle dividing it in four.

CLARENCE appears and stops before intruding. He draws near during the following speeches as he becomes interested.

The Great Spirit caused everything to be in fours and four is a sacred number. Four directions—north, east, south, west; four divisions of time—the day, the night, the month, the year; four parts of everything that grows—the root, the stem, the leaves, the fruit....What else?

CROWFOOT   Ahhhhh....

SITTING BULL holds out his hands, palms downward, his thumbs concealed. CROWFOOT thrusts out his hands likewise.

Four fingers on each hand...and...two arms, two legs....

He thrusts his limbs out, laughing.

Four in all!

CLARENCE casts a furtive look at his own hands.

SITTING BULL   *urging CROWFOOT on* Four things above the earth—the sun...the moon...

CROWFOOT   The sky, the stars!

SITTING BULL   *smiling and nodding at CROWFOOT* Good....All of the universe is enclosed and revealed in the sacred circle. *He traces the circle.* Do you see how the sundance is a sacred hoop...and the sundance pole, the sacred centre? What else?

CLARENCE   *caught up in it all, breaking in* The tipi!

SITTING BULL looks at him.

Like, it's a circle too and...the fire...that's the centre.

He shifts nervously, bumping one of the stones. He picks it up, then isn't sure where it goes. He hands it to SITTING BULL.

SITTING BULL   *holding up the stone* This is a sacred stone. See how round it is. Everything the Great Spirit does is done in a circle. The sun and moon are round; they come and go forth in a circle. The white man says the earth is round...and so are all the stars. What else?

CROWFOOT   Birds make their nests round!

WALSH enters quietly.

SITTING BULL   The winds whirl; the seasons form a great circle...and when we, the Sioux, meet as a nation, we set our tipis so.... *He describes an arc with the hand holding the stone.* The nation's hoop!

He puts the stone back in position, then looks at WALSH.

WALSH   It's time.

CLARENCE   *scrambling to his feet*   I'm sorry, sir. *to SITTING BULL*   The Major has asked me to inform you that they're ready. Everything's ready.

SITTING BULL inclines his head acknowledging CLARENCE.

A light comes up on GENERAL TERRY in uniform.

SITTING BULL places a hand on his son's shoulder. They make their way to the meeting place with GENERAL TERRY. GALL appears and joins them as well. PRETTY PLUME goes to leave.

SITTING BULL   Come...come.

PRETTY PLUME joins them. Eventually, GALL, SIT-TING BULL, CROWFOOT and PRETTY PLUME will range themselves for the meeting.

WALSH, LOUIS, CLARENCE and McCUTCHEON attend the meeting as well, CLARENCE almost sneaking in to observe. LOUIS, McCUTCHEON and WALSH are there in a more formal sense. McCUTCHEON joins GENERAL TERRY, acting as a temporary aide de camp for him.

CLARENCE   *to WALSH, as they make their way to the meeting place*   I got detained, sir. I got caught up.

WALSH places a hand on his shoulder and gives it a reassuring clasp.

When they enter, GENERAL TERRY ignores SITTING BULL's entrance. It is as if the Indians are not present.

WALSH   General Terry.

TERRY   Ah, Walsh. Wonderful man you got here. Been looking after me like I was one of his own.

WALSH   And so he does for me.

TERRY   Great country you have here. *WALSH nods.*   I'm impressed. Empty as yet, but a course that'll change. My God, man, the wagon trains never cease across the line, and it's settlers that'll open it up...economic base, possibilities endless. You follow me? *WALSH nods.*   Heavy responsibility on you and me, of course. And what's imperative ...safety, progress...is the elimination of the savage.

WALSH   Sir?

TERRY   Control of the savage, elimination of the savage aspects of the Indian's character.... Do you follow me? Though what you'd have left, be god-damned if I know. *He chuckles.*   However,

governments decree and we, poor bastards that we are, must deliver....

He looks toward the Sioux and sighs, then looks back at WALSH.

You ever meet George?

WALSH   General Custer?

TERRY   Great tragedy that...and there are the very devils themselves. Savage they may be, but I'll tell you this, Major, they are kittens compared to the Eastern press. I'll take a Sioux sittin' on my chest anyday to a scribe peerin' over my shoulder. You follow me? You know where you are with a Sioux. Headlines coast to coast lauding George...and between you and me, he was a man had his faults. ...Same goddamn papers up for court-martialing him over that Wichitas business, and now up on a pedestal, and bring the villains to justice, wipe them out...and of course the government's got to act.... Do you follow me? And it's yours and my head on the block.... That's the way of it. That's what we live with. So....

He looks at the Sioux and sniffs. He whispers to WALSH confidentially.

And I'll tell you this...whatever we do, by the time we're finished, they'll have flip-flopped to the other side of the fence. You follow me?

WALSH does not follow him.

The papers, man, the Eastern press.

WALSH   Yes, sir.

TERRY   Not a man among them I'd have at my back in a fight. *He whispers.*   Nor a position I'd give to George, if the truth be known. *He chuckles, stops, clears his throat.*   Still, a wonderful soldier, one of the best.

He gets out a pair of wire-rimmed glasses, studies a document and looks up.

I am empowered to speak to you on behalf of the American government.

PRETTY PLUME   We are listening.

TERRY   *looking at her, then continuing*   The Great White Father in Washington is a generous father.

PRETTY PLUME   We are listening.

TERRY   Who the hell is she?... Your deeds against the whites have been grievous. The mighty arm and righteous anger of the Great White Father has been raised against you. It is within his power to wipe you out. He has stayed that anger and that might. He has forgiven you.

PRETTY PLUME   We are listening.

TERRY   They got a goddamn woman speaking for them.... Who speaks for the Sioux?

SITTING BULL   The bearer of our children.

TERRY   I'm here to speak to you!

PRETTY PLUME   We are listening.

TERRY   The Great White Father holds your lives in his hands. The Indian is his . . . to do with as he pleases. You will return across the line. A reservation has been provided for you and you will go on it. Goods will be provided sufficient for your needs. Should you heed my words, you will be safe in the hand of the Great White Father. Should you not. . . .

He closes his hand tightly and makes a gesture of throwing away.

PRETTY PLUME   We have heard you.

TERRY   Get her out of here.   *McCUTCHEON looks at WALSH.*   Get her out! I'm here to talk to you! *The Sioux start to leave.*   Who the hell do they think they are? Stop them!

The Sioux exit, except for SITTING BULL.

WALSH   Do you realize what he's promised? A reservation, food and supplies for your people, an amnesty. No one will be punished or go to jail for acts of war committed against the government. All that will be forgiven and forgotten!

SITTING BULL   Forgotten? . . . When I was a boy, the Sioux owned the world. The sun rose and set on our land. We sent 10,000 men to battle. Where are those warriors now? Where are our lands? Who owns them? Tell me . . . what law have I broken? Is it because my skin is red? Because I am Sioux, because I was born where my fathers lived, because I would die for my people and my country? . . . This white man would forgive me . . . and while he speaks to me of forgiveness, what do his people say in secret? "Seize their guns and horses! Drive them back across the line! The more we kill this year, the less we have to kill next year." Is it not true?

TERRY   Goddamn waste of time.

He thrusts his fist towards SITTING BULL, then makes a throwing away gesture, and leaves. McCUTCHEON follows. LOUIS remains as SITTING BULL and WALSH speak. There is a pause. Eventually, SITTING BULL turns to WALSH and begins intimately.

SITTING BULL   You are a white man. The God whose son you killed must love you and your people well, for he has rewarded you with many gifts . . . and tools . . . and . . .   *indicating their uniforms, their guns, etc.*   . . . all this. . . . I am told wisdom is yours as well. Advise me now, White Sioux. Tell me what is best for my people. I will follow your advice . . . and the burden of it will be on your shoulders. . . .

WALSH does not answer him.

SITTING BULL   Shall I lead my people into the arms of the Longknives? Will they protect us as "feathers do a bird"? Look inside your heart! . . . You have a heart. I saw it the night the Nez Percés crossed the line. What does your heart say?

WALSH   *agitated*   You know, if you refuse this offer, there'll be nothing for you here. My government says they won't feed you or give you reservations.

SITTING BULL   Is your advice then to return with the Americans?

WALSH   My advice . . . is . . . to consider . . . to consider the consequences of your actions. That is my advice.

SITTING BULL   What does that mean?

WALSH   It means . . . if you stay . . . you're dependent on the buffalo . . . and when they go, as they are surely going, we won't care for you as we do our own Indians. . . . Now, if you go with General Terry, he has given his word that you won't be mistreated or. . . .

He stops himself from saying the word "killed."

You will be fed and clothed.

SITTING BULL   Would you choose to live as you advise me to do?

WALSH   I don't advise you to do this. I . . . merely state your choices.

SITTING BULL   I know many who took the white man's promise . . . Bear Ribs, White Antelope, Iron Shield, Black Kettle, Stirring Bear . . . Crazy Horse. I would ask their guidance, but all of them are dead.

WALSH   You . . . make your point.

SITTING BULL   *dropping all pretence of asking for advice*   Let us speak clearly to each other. . . . If the President in Washington can say: "Come, you are safe here" and then change his mind and let the Longknives kill us . . . can it not work the other way too?   *looking intently at WALSH*   Cannot the Great White Mother say: "No food or reservations," but then reconsider? Our brothers, the Santee Sioux, from across the line . . .

WALSH   . . . have been given a reservation in Manitoba. Quite right!

SITTING BULL   *opening up to WALSH, stating his secret fear*   I believe the Americans are only waiting to get us all together . . . and then they will slaughter us. That is what I believe.

WALSH   *thinking, then deciding*   Right! . . . Well now, I've delivered my government's message, to which your reply is. . . .

SITTING BULL   The Sioux are self-sufficient!

WALSH   Mmmm . . . and I shall give your final decision to General Terry, that is. . . .

SITTING BULL   *joking*   Tell him he can take it easy on the way back. The Sioux only fight with men.

WALSH *smiling* I was thinking of something a bit more formal.

SITTING BULL *begins by playing the role a bit* He came here to tell us lies, but we don't want to hear them. . . . I intend to stay here . . . and to raise my people in this country.

SITTING BULL leaves. The lights begin to fade. WALSH looks after him for a moment, then begins to leave.

LOUIS *speaking from the shadows* Major!

WALSH stops and looks at LOUIS.

Does da Major know what month dis is?

WALSH The month when the green grass comes up.

LOUIS *without humour* Major damn good pupil.

WALSH *almost abruptly* Louis damn good teacher.

He turns to go.

LOUIS *moving toward WALSH* Louis "request" permission to speak to da Major.

WALSH *with a trace of irritation* Here and now?

LOUIS Last fall, crossin' da Milk River, da Major's horse step in dat sink hole . . . and Louis, he grab da Major and pull 'im out . . . *WALSH nods.* Da other year, when Louis hear all kind of story 'bout da 'ssiniboine makin' trouble . . . Louis tell da Major . . . even t'ough dat 'ssiniboine is son of good friend of Louis' mother. . . .

WALSH The Major is in your debt.

LOUIS And some of Louis' mother's people don't speak to him no more, but dis don't matter, for Louis trust da Major to do da right thing. . . . Dis is da month when da green grass come up, da moon of makin' fat: dis is spring. . . . Can da Major make da spring come for da Sioux? What can you do for Sittin' Bull?

WALSH Everything within my power.

LOUIS How much is dat?

WALSH Say what you mean, Louis.

LOUIS Louis choose to trust, but da Indian can do nothin' else but trust. . . . Trust . . . or die. . . . Sometime, trust *and* die. . . . Can da Major make da spring come for da Sioux?

WALSH You trust in me . . . and I trust in those above me. . . . Quite simple, eh? . . . Now, let's get on. . . .

He goes to leave.

LOUIS Da Indian say he would trust da Great White Mother more if she did not have so many bald-headed thieves workin' for her!

WALSH *stopping and turning, angrily* The Sioux have a case . . . a strong case . . . and I shall present it!

LOUIS *softly* Who stands behind you dere?

WALSH Honourable men!

LOUIS spits.

Blackout.

ACT TWO

The lights come up on HARRY, CLARENCE, LOUIS and McCUTCHEON. The lights are punctuated by LOUIS throwing his knife into the floor of the stage. A dull thud is heard. LOUIS sits with his rifle unslung; McCUTCHEON sits cleaning his saddle. CLARENCE is attempting to thread a needle. As HARRY watches the three of them, McCUTCHEON leans over, picks up the needle from CLARENCE, threads it efficiently and passes it back. CLARENCE looks up at McCUTCHEON.

CLARENCE Thanks. . . .

He begins to mend a sock. HARRY and McCUTCHEON exchange a look of amusement.

HARRY Sewin' detail, eh?

He begins to roll a cigarette as he watches CLARENCE.

CLARENCE *intent on his sewing* Yeah . . . I wish me Mum were here. . . .

McCUTCHEON tosses HARRY a match for his cigarette.

CLARENCE This ain't my idea of police work.

McCUTCHEON Ah, laddie, your poor wee face would have been wet with tears for your Mum if ye'd been with the force on our march west in '73. I don't know what ye'd have called that.

HARRY *settling down to watch everyone work* It weren't the Mounted Police then, Clarence, it were the Dismounted Police. . . . Lost practically every horse they had. *He laughs.*

McCUTCHEON Aye, a man with the best will in the world couldn't call it the force's finest hour.

LOUIS Dey didn't have Louis with dem. Dey need a good scout.

McCUTCHEON I never saw so many bugs . . . black-flies so thick they clogged your nose so ye couldn't draw breath . . . and every man from the Colonel down infected with fleas. It's a lovely time y're havin', laddie. Ye don't appreciate it.

CLARENCE Yeah . . . well . . . me Mum always mended my things at home.

HARRY   Jesus Christ, Clarence, you had a good thing there, boy, your Mum waitin' on you hand an' foot. What'd you want to go and join up for? You could have had it easy in the East.

CLARENCE   My dad was a soldier.

HARRY   You don't say?

CLARENCE   Yup. Half-pay officer, served in the Crimean, he did. . . . And, after that, he and me Mum, they come out to Upper Canada in '60. First winter out, my Dad, he died. . . . I can't hardly remember him. . . . But, me Mum, she used to tell me 'bout him bein' a soldier and all. . . . It was hard goin' for us. . . . I think me Mum was the real soldier. . . .

McCUTCHEON   No brothers or sisters, laddie?

CLARENCE   Nope. . . . Mum's all alone back East.

HARRY   You ain't told us why you joined?

CLARENCE   Well . . . me Mum, she said I was a man like my Dad . . . and I had to find my own place. . . . Couldn't sit in Glengarry growin' potatoes and tendin' to her. And she was right. . . . I got to thinking . . .

HARRY   Yeah?

CLARENCE   You all'd laugh.

HARRY   No, we wouldn't.

CLARENCE   Well, I got to thinkin', out here in the territories, that was where everything was happenin' . . . the Indian Wars . . . and openin' the West . . . and Wild Bill Hickock sittin on the biggest, blackest horse you ever saw!

He looks at HARRY, McCUTCHEON and LOUIS, who regard him seriously.

I wanted to do what was right . . . and excitin' and . . . and make me Mum proud of me.

McCUTCHEON looks out at the horizon and sniffs.

HARRY   How do you figure it's turned out?

CLARENCE   I guess she's proud of me. . . . Not so excitin' as I thought it'd be . . . and as far as what's right goes . . . that don't seem to come into it. . . .

McCUTCHEON   What's that in the air, Louis? Smoke?

LOUIS   Lotta smoke. . . . Dere goin' be more.

CLARENCE   I don't smell nothin'.

HARRY   Hell, Clarence, you won't smell it till tomorrow or next day. . . . The Sergeant here, he smells it today . . . and Louis . . . *smiling at LOUIS* When'd you smell it, Louis?

LOUIS   *holding up two fingers*   Two days ago.

CLARENCE   What's it from?

LOUIS   Da 'mericans fire da border.

CLARENCE   *curious*   What?

LOUIS   'Merican soldiers, da Longknives, dey set fires all 'long da border, two or three hundred mile long, every ten mile or so.

CLARENCE   *to McCUTCHEON*   What's he sayin'? That don't make sense, Louis.

LOUIS   Make a lotta sense.

HARRY   It's this way, Clarence. . . . The buffalo across the line start movin' north, so the soldiers burn all along the border. The buffalo turn back and then the American government don't have to feed the reservation Indians.

CLARENCE looks at him blankly.

They're supposed to hunt and feed themselves!

CLARENCE   Well, what about *our* Indians?

LOUIS   *surprised*   You got some Indians?

CLARENCE   You know what I mean.

LOUIS ignores him and looks at his gun.

Okay. . . . What about *the* Indians livin' on the Canadian side of the line?

LOUIS   What about dem?

CLARENCE   What're they supposed to do?

HARRY   Eat grass.

CLARENCE   *angrily*   I don't believe you! Besides, I don't smell nothin'. It's all a lie. There's no smoke in the air! Do you smell smoke, Sergeant?

McCUTCHEON   Look at that haze over the hills, laddie.

CLARENCE   That's a heat haze . . . from the sun.

HARRY   You think so, eh?

CLARENCE   Well, I don't believe it! It ain't fair! And even if it was true . . . and there weren't no buffalo . . . and nothin' for them to eat, well then, the Canadian government, it'd send out food for them. It's got a responsibility!

LOUIS   *shrugging*   Maybe so.

HARRY   So the Canadian government feeds its own Indians. . . . Who's gonna feed the Sioux?

CLARENCE   They're people, aren't they?

McCUTCHEON, HARRY and LOUIS look at him.

You don't let people starve to death, do you? Just 'cause you wish they'd move someplace else, you don't let people starve! You can't do things like that. You can't do things like that!

He stares at HARRY, McCUTCHEON and LOUIS. They all freeze. HARRY pulls a document out and reads from it. The lights slowly dim.

HARRY MacDonald reports that though the Sioux have behaved themselves remarkably well since crossing into Canada, their presence in the North West Territories has been attended by serious consequences. The buffalo are rapidly diminishing and the advent of so large a body of foreign Indians has precipitated their diminution. The Sioux are already feeling the hardship and are hard pressed to avert danger and suffering from famine.

The lights black out. About four bars of calliope music are heard. The lights come back up. MARY is sitting there embroidering. WALSH is a distance away from her. The music fades as WALSH speaks.

WALSH My. . .dearest. . .Mary. . . .My dearest Mary.

MARY Jim.

WALSH Two letters came in today. . .along with a load of winter supplies. I don't know which I was happier to see.

MARY The girls are fine. . . . It's been a long time since they've seen you.

WALSH You'll think I've got a touch of prairie fever, but the solitude here, the emptiness of these Great Plains, fills me with a sense of timelessness.

MARY Both send their love.

WALSH Remember the day we picnicked on the river? Cora, plump and placid on the blanket; little Mary showing me her hands stained with the juice of flowers. . .and you bent over the basket, your hair hanging loose and laughing. . . .You looked eighteen.

MARY I hope you're looking after yourself. *laughing* How often do I say that?

WALSH You're not to worry about my health. McCutcheon's like a mother hen.

MARY Here in the East, we're always hearing grand tales of Major Walsh. . .how he's subdued the Sioux and Sitting Bull.

WALSH The Sioux. . . .Common sense, honesty and humanity.

MARY The treachery.

WALSH Ah, Mary, we call our actions strategy or tactics; we call theirs treachery. . . .My God, if I could only show you what I see every day. . . .The buffalo are gone, vanished. . .like frost at dawn . . .one minute here, the next. . .nowhere. In the fall, the Sioux were hungry. Now, it's winter. . .and they starve.

MARY After church supper, the choir sang.

WALSH Sickness, plain suffering kills them like flies. Most of their ponies are dead. . .and their rotting carcasses are cut up for food. . . .Yes, they're starving and destitute, yet they endure.

They share what little they have. . .and they observe the law. Goddamnit, they'd be a credit to any community. . . .Ottawa has not acknowledged my recommendations. . . .

MARY *smiling* You always say don't worry.

WALSH I wonder if Dewdney has even forwarded them.

MARY But, of course, I worry. It's natural to worry. *laughing* Yesterday I found another grey hair. You won't know me when you return.

WALSH I try to understand the government's viewpoint. . . . Jesus Christ, I'm no raw recruit! One thing I know, across the line there's been gross and continual mismanagement of the Sioux. An able and brilliant people have been crushed, held down, moved from place to place, cheated and lied to. . . .And now, they hold on here in Canada, the remnants of a proud race, and they ask for some sort of justice. . .which is what I thought I swore an oath to serve!

The lights begin to fade.

MARY *distant* Your "little" Mary's soon to be thirteen. . . . Don't forget her birthday, will you?

WALSH We carried great bouquets of flowers home that day. . . . *looking down at his hands* She's not thirteen. . . .

MARY Cora's getting thin.

WALSH Cora, red and bawling; and you with your hair spread on the pillow, smiling and offering me your hand. . . .

The lights go out on MARY. There is a spotlight on the figure of WALSH.

The girls, still babies; you, eighteen, in the East . . .suspended in amber. . .while I grow old in the West. . . .

McCUTCHEON Colonel MacLeod to see you, sir.

WALSH MacLeod? Send him on in.

MacLEOD enters. WALSH springs up to greet him sincerely. Both are original members of the force and are friends.

Welcome to the fort, Colonel. Pleasant journey, I trust?

MacLEOD Not bad, Major, not bad. . . .You're looking well.

McCUTCHEON Is there anything else, sir?

WALSH No, McCutcheon. Stand down.

McCUTCHEON leaves.

MacLEOD To tell the truth, Jim, you look like death. What the hell have you been up to?

WALSH If you think I look bad, you should see the horses.

MacLEOD   That so?

WALSH   It's been a hard winter.

MacLEOD   *clipping the end of a cigar*   Seems to be the case right across the West.

WALSH gets out a flask and looks at MacLEOD who nods "yes" to a drink.

WALSH   Are you doing the tour early? The boys at Fort Walsh are always on their toes. It'll be a . . .

MacLEOD   Nothing like that.

WALSH   *stiffening somewhat*   Do you bring news for the Sioux?

MacLEOD   Sit down, Jim. I'd like a wee informal talk with you.

WALSH   Well now, you've caught my interest. *sitting down*   What is it?

There is a pause as MacLEOD examines the end of his cigar. He looks up at WALSH and pauses again.

MacLEOD   Soooo . . . horses had a bad winter, eh?

WALSH   What the hell are you here for?

MacLEOD   *putting a letter on the desk*   Recognize that?

WALSH   *looking at the letter and dropping it back on the desk*   I usually recognize my own correspondence. It's a letter I sent Frank Mills at Fort Benton across the line. Why're you dropping it on my desk like a hot potato?

MacLEOD   I'd be most surprised to hear that you're unaware of the proper channels one must go through when making a suggestion of the nature contained in this letter.

WALSH   My note to Frank Mills suggests an exchange of stolen horses. American horses stolen by Canadian Indians to be exchanged for Canadian horses stolen by American Indians. . . . Hardly an international incident.

MacLEOD   And what is the proper channel through which we should negotiate an arrangement like this?

WALSH   The proper channel? Yes, sir. I should send a recommendation to my commanding officer, Colonel MacLeod. If he decides to act on it, he will send a recommendation to Ottawa. If it ever reaches the Prime Minister's office and he decides to act on it, he will send a recommendation to London. It is possible that London will send it to Washington, and Washington to Mills' commanding officer, and, God willing and the mails providing, Mills will receive a recommendation concerning the exchange of stolen horses. Jesus Christ, man! That's 6,000 miles and the Lord knows how many bureaucratic bunglers. Frank Mills is 60 miles south of me. Are you trying to tell me that you object to my simplifying matters?

MacLEOD   It's not my objecting to it. . . . Mills, apparently, objects to it.

WALSH   What the hell do you mean by that?

MacLEOD   He forwarded your "note" to Fort Robson. To make a long story short, the President has sent a formal protest to the Queen regarding the high-handed methods of a certain officer of the force serving the Canadian West. . . .

WALSH   Son-of-a-bitch! *to himself*   The next goddamn American horse the boys bring in, I'll have it shot.

MacLEOD   You realize as well as I do that this is only the tip of the iceberg.

WALSH   *back to MacLEOD*   Where are you now, Colonel . . . back on the cold winter again?

MacLEOD   I'm talking about the real reason for the American protest against your behaviour. I'm talking about Sitting Bull and the Sioux.

WALSH   *stiffening and becoming more formal*   I'm afraid I don't follow you, sir.

MacLEOD   Jim, the Americans believe . . . and they have convinced the Prime Minister . . . that you are privately urging Sitting Bull to remain in Canada while publically stating that he must leave.

WALSH   Which indicates how little they know of Sitting Bull. When his mind's made up, no man can sway him.

MacLEOD   Not even his friends?

WALSH   He has no white friends.

MacLEOD   He calls you White Sioux. What is that supposed to mean?

WALSH   We have an understanding.

MacLEOD   Oh? . . . Which means?

WALSH   We understand each other.

MacLEOD   *tapping the letter on the desk*   The protest over this is an attempt to discredit you and it all leads back to the Sioux. You're close to that old war horse. Persuade him to return across the line. Goddamn it, he's a thorn in our flesh. We can't discuss a bloody thing with the Americans without they bring it up!

WALSH   What up?

MacLEOD   Our giving sanctuary to those responsible for the Custer Massacre. They talk of nothing else.

WALSH   Custer was responsible for the death of himself and his men! For Christ's sake, speak the truth!

MacLEOD   I'm not here to argue with you. I'm here as a friend.

WALSH   I've had my orders and I've followed them.

MacLEOD   I'm asking you to do more than that. . . . He trusts you.

WALSH   Because he knows I won't deceive him.

MacLEOD   He'll listen to you.

WALSH   Because he trusts me and he knows I won't deceive him.

MacLEOD   *softly*   How am I asking you to deceive him? *Pause.* The Sioux have no future here in Canada.

WALSH   Tell me something. . . . It was you, as Commissioner of the North West Mounted Police, who impressed upon me that a part of my duty, no less important than the policing of this area, was the accurate observation and recording of events, no matter how minute. . . . Such a report, to be sent monthly, along with my recommendations for government policy.

MacLEOD   Quite correct.

WALSH   Then, why the hell is nothing acted upon?

MacLEOD   Did you not receive two stallions, come in with Harry, to sire your mares? Are you not now in the act of digging a new well?

WALSH   I'm not talking about domestic trivia! I don't need a statement from the goddamn Prime Minister to undertake a new well!

MacLEOD   Ah, but you do, Jim.

WALSH   My men are not in the act of digging a new well. . . . My men *dug* a new well two months before permission was granted! The entire fort would have been down with typhoid or dead of thirst had I waited for word from Ottawa.

MacLEOD sighs and shakes his head.

What about my recommendations concerning the Indians?

MacLEOD   What about them?

WALSH   The Sioux have as much legal right to a reservation here as the Santee Sioux had in Manitoba.

MacLEOD   The Santee Sioux did not kill Custer.

WALSH   They killed over 600 white settlers in Minnesota who were not engaged in an act of war against them. Why are my recommendations not acted upon?

MacLEOD   Out here, you don't see the whole picture. There're other considerations.

WALSH   My recommendations are ignored! I may as well post them in the privy!

MacLEOD   You play chess. . . . Sometimes a pawn is sacrificed on one side of the board to gain an advantage on the other.

WALSH   *in disbelief*   I am a pawn?

MacLEOD   No, no, Jim. . . . not you. . . . It might be possible to consider Sitting Bull and the Sioux as pawns.

WALSH   What are the advantages to be gained from this . . . this sacrifice?

MacLEOD   We can't know that, can we? That's the kind of weighty decision the Prime Minister and London must contend with.

WALSH   I demand to know what advantage is to be gained.

MacLEOD   The Prime Minister is not responsible to you, Jim!

WALSH   Goddamn it, he is! If I carry out his orders, he is responsible to me.

MacLEOD   You're talking nonsense. An army that operated like that couldn't navigate its way across a playing field! And you know it!

WALSH   What do you think happens when I take off this tunic? At night, in my quarters, what do you think happens to me?

MacLEOD   Jim . . .

WALSH   Do you think McCutcheon hangs me up from some goddamn wooden peg with all my strings dangling? Is that what you think happens? Do you think I'm a puppet? Manipulate me right and anything is possible. . . . I'm a person. I exist. I think and feel! And I will not allow you to do this to me!

MacLEOD   *softly*   To do what to you? I merely ask you to use your position with Sitting Bull to convince him to leave the country in the best interests of his people.

WALSH   I've had my orders and I've followed them. . . .

MacLEOD   You're tired, Jim.

WALSH   Ask my men if I'm tired. No one at this post rises earlier or is to bed later. Fatigue is unknown to me.

MacLEOD   You work yourself too hard.

WALSH   I have a job and I do it.

MacLEOD   It's a long time since you've been home.

WALSH   Home? I don't request a leave of absence, Colonel. . . . Shall we get on with the business at hand?

MacLEOD   I have two dispatches from the Prime Minister. The first concerns the Sioux.

WALSH   What is it?

MacLEOD   You are to see that no food stuffs, clothing, ammunition or supplies are given them . . . if they do not possess the money to pay for them.

WALSH   They have no money.

MacLEOD It has been brought to the attention of the Prime Minister that certain settlers as well as members of the force itself have been supplying the Sioux with various odds and ends of food and clothing. This must stop at once.

WALSH Yes, sir.

MacLEOD The Prime Minister feels that, whereas common sense has not prevailed upon the Sioux, hunger will.

He looks at WALSH for a moment, then back at his dispatch.

My second dispatch concerns your ill-advised note to Major Mills.

WALSH Yes, sir.

MacLEOD An apology is to be written, couched in the appropriate words, stating that you humbly beg the American government's pardon for over-stepping the limits of your authority. *Pause.* Is that understood?

WALSH I . . .

MacLEOD If you find yourself unable to do this, it is my sad duty to ask you for your resignation.

WALSH How well you know your men.

MacLEOD I pride myself on that.

WALSH They say one's strongest instinct is self-preservation . . . and I've made the force my life. . . . To whom do I send this letter?

MacLEOD To your commanding officer, myself, naturally.

WALSH Ah, yes.

MacLEOD I'll see that it's forwarded to Ottawa. . . . Well, Jim, how about a walk around the post before bed? . . . Bit of pleasure after a surfeit of business.

WALSH McCutcheon! . . . Sorry, Colonel, I've a few things to attend to. McCutcheon will see you to your quarters. *McCUTCHEON enters.* Goodnight, sir.

MacLEOD Goodnight, Jim.

WALSH stands rigid until McCUTCHEON and McLEOD exit. When they have gone, he pours himself another drink. He walks outside of his office and stands looking at the prairies, flask in hand. We hear someone whistling "Garryowen." He listens to the whistling, then speaks.

WALSH That you, Harry?

HARRY You give me a start there, Major. I didn't expect to see nobody up at this time of night.

WALSH takes a drink and extends the flask to HARRY.

HARRY Don't mind if I do. *He takes a drink and keeps the flask.* I been up visitin' with Sittin' Bull. . . . Always a dry night when you visit with the old man. . . . Lots of tobacco, but no booze.

WALSH Fraternizing, eh?

HARRY Oh, no, nothin' like that. . . . Just chewin' the fat. *Pause.* Hear MacLeod come in today. . . . Bit early, ain't he? *Pause.* Is he here for the tour?

WALSH *bringing his attention back to HARRY* No, no . . . he isn't.

HARRY O-fficial business, eh? O-fficial business.

WALSH Do you know Brockville, Harry?

HARRY Can't say as I do.

WALSH Pretty town. . . . Trees. Shade in the summertime . . . cool and green.

HARRY Hell of a change from this place, I reckon.

WALSH My wife lives in Brockville . . . and my two girls.

HARRY Ain't got a son?

WALSH No. . . . No son . . . just as well . . . no son. Pretty place, though.

HARRY What the hell! *passing the flask to him* Have another drink, Major!

WALSH *taking a drink and passing the flask back to HARRY* I've always thought of myself as a man of principle. . . . Honour, truth, the lot. . . . They're just words, Harry. They don't exist. I gave my life to them and they don't exist.

HARRY *staring at WALSH, uneasy* You should get to bed, Major. It ain't night, it's mornin'.

WALSH *smiling* Fatigue is unknown to me.

HARRY *smiling back, feeling he's back on more familiar ground* That's a fact, sir. That's a fact. Ain't never knowed you to be tired.

WALSH *reaching for the flask, taking a drink and handing it back to HARRY* You were up visiting the Sioux, were you?

HARRY Yessireee. Course, they knowed MacLeod's come in. Naturally, they's wonderin' if it means anythin' for them.

WALSH Oh yes, I should say it does.

HARRY Good news?

WALSH The Sioux have no future here in Canada.

HARRY They sure as hell don't have none south of the line.

WALSH The government's concern stops at the border.

HARRY   Major, you get yourself too het up.

WALSH   I see. . .larger issues at stake.

HARRY   Don't see what's a larger issue than a man's life. . . .No Injun agent's gonna put up with Sittin' Bull.

WALSH   You think not?

HARRY   They'll kill him off. . . .Only smart thing to do, ain't it?

WALSH   And how do you feel about that?

HARRY   Ain't nothin' I can do. . . .Goodnight, Major.

WALSH stares at HARRY as he exits, then WALSH exits. PRETTY PLUME enters, carrying a pipe. She is followed by CROWFOOT.

PRETTY PLUME   *singing*
Little One, Little One,
Loved by everyone.
Little One speaks sweet words to everyone.
That is why, that is why,
Little One is loved by everyone.

CROWFOOT puts his head in her lap in the semi-darkness outside of the scene. CLARENCE sneaks furtively into the light, carrying a small knapsack.

CLARENCE   *whispering* Pssssstttt!. . .Little One!
. . .Little One!

SITTING BULL   *from the shadows* Is it my son you seek?

CLARENCE   *frightened* Oh!. . .Ah. . .yes, sir. I was just. . .a. . .

He tries to conceal the knapsack behind him.

. . .I was just. . .lookin' for your little boy.

SITTING BULL comes into the light. He looks older, his face is drawn.

SITTING BULL   You are the young man who rides out with White Sioux. . . .Is he with you?

CLARENCE   Ah, well, no sir. . . .I. . .come by myself. . . .I brought. . . *He quickly thrusts the knapsack at SITTING BULL.* Ah. . . *nodding at the knapsack* . . .some things from the mess, sir. I'd like the little boy to have them.

SITTING BULL   *taking the knapsack and nodding his thanks* You have a good heart. . . .I have little to offer you in return. . . .

He sees the pipe that PRETTY PLUME has brought on. He checks his tobacco pouch and smiles.

Come! Have a pipe with me!

He sits and motions CLARENCE to sit.

CLARENCE   Well, I. . .don't know if I should.

SITTING BULL   Sit!

CLARENCE sits in silence as SITTING BULL prepares the pipe and passes it to him. There is silence as they smoke for a bit.

SITTING BULL   Times are bad. . . .They say there are still buffalo south of the line, but if we go to hunt them, the bluecoats will kill us. *laughing dryly* It hardly matters, as our ponies are too weak to carry us there in the first place. But my heart grows weak and trembles when I hear the little children cry for food. . . .It is a hard thing. *smiling at CLARENCE* And you feel that way too. See? We are not so different.

CLARENCE   Don't you think, maybe, you could think about goin' back? Everybody hungry and everythin'. Is it worth it?

SITTING BULL   Across the line, on the reservations, they are starving too. We hear these things and so must your people. *CLARENCE nods.* The white man is afraid to kill us outright, but he knows if he kills the buffalo, we must soon follow. . . .I myself do not understand why you should wish this on us.

CLARENCE   I don't wish nothin' like that.

SITTING BULL   And I think. . .if you give me nothing and you will not let me go where I can get something for myself, what is there? I would rather die fighting than die of starvation.

CLARENCE   *uneasy* You'd just all get killed that way.

SITTING BULL   Yes. That is the warrior's way out . . .but I am not only a warrior. I must think of *all* my people. I must think of the ones here now and the ones that come after. . .what is best for them. . . .I know we must change.

CLARENCE   Yeah. I guess that's it.

SITTING BULL   Sometimes one has something of value. Dogs come and spoil it for you, yet you do not wish to see it destroyed. . . .I am of the Hunk-papa Sioux of the prairie and the prairie will provide for me. When the buffalo are gone, my children will hunt mice. When my horse falls, I shall chase gopher. And when there is nothing else, we shall dig and eat roots. . . .And I pray to the Great Spirit that the White Mother gives the thought to her children that I give to mine.

We hear WALSH laughing harshly. The lights dim on SITTING BULL and CLARENCE and come up on WALSH, who is seated, looking at a letter. He rips the letter in half. McCUTCHEON is going through some papers. He concentrates on his business. He knows what's coming and he is preparing himself for it.

WALSH   Why is nothing simple in this life? It all seems perfectly simple to me. Why do people make it complex? The simplest thing. . .complex. . . .McCutcheon! Are you listening to me?

McCUTCHEON   Aye, sir.

WALSH   Well then, why is everything so goddamn complex?

McCUTCHEON   I don't know, sir.

WALSH   *leaping up and beginning to pace*   I write a report...a perfectly simple report...in which I state that our Indians as well as the Sioux are suffering severe deprivation because of the extinction of the buffalo. Is that simple or is it not?

McCUTCHEON   Perfectly simple, sir.

WALSH   Right! And if we do not make a sincere and whole-hearted effort to aid these Indians, we can expect trouble, necessitating a build-up in troops, horses and supplies, plus the possibility of loss of life as well as property.....And what is the government's reply to this?

McCUTCHEON   I don't know, sir.

WALSH   *exploding*   The son-of-a-bitch's going to send me more men! And, to top it all off, I'll probably get a recommendation for my foresight!

CLARENCE enters with some papers. WALSH takes the papers.

Were you in court yesterday?

CLARENCE   No, sir.

WALSH   I sat in judgement yesterday. I sat in judgement of a Sioux. His wife and child were starving. He slaughtered a cow belonging to a settler and then....

He laughs. CLARENCE looks nervously, quickly, to McCUTCHEON, then back to WALSH.

Do you know what the damn fool did?

CLARENCE   No sir, I...

WALSH   He took his horse...his only horse...told the settler what had happened and offered the horse in payment. The settler refused and pressed charges. And yesterday, I sentenced that Sioux to six months imprisonment and fined him twenty dollars, for that is the law! But where's the justice in it?

LOUIS enters. WALSH turns on him and barks.

What is it?

There is a quick look between LOUIS and McCUTCHEON.

For God's sake, man, did you come in here to gape? Speak up!

LOUIS   Sittin' Bull's outside.

WALSH stares at LOUIS for a moment, then he becomes very calm. He sits in a chair, picks up a pencil and begins to examine it.

WALSH   And why is Sitting Bull's geographical location supposed to be of interest to me?

LOUIS   He wants to see you.

WALSH   I'm busy.

LOUIS   *staring hard at WALSH*   I sent him on in!

He turns to go.

WALSH   Louis!

LOUIS stops.

Just...give me a minute.

LOUIS exits. WALSH puts his pencil down, looks at McCUTCHEON and CLARENCE, then turns around and does up the top button of his tunic. His shoulders stiffen. SITTING BULL enters. WALSH has his back to him. LOUIS follows SITTING BULL in. SITTING BULL has a ragged blanket wrapped around him. He looks gaunt; not well, although his personal magnetism is still evident. He stops and looks at WALSH's back.

SITTING BULL   White Sioux....

WALSH   *without turning*   Yes.

SITTING BULL   I wish to speak with you.

WALSH   *turning and looking at him*   I'm listening.

SITTING BULL   Have you had news from the Great White Mother?

WALSH   My news is always the same....No reservations, no food, no clothing, no supplies.

SITTING BULL   I wish you to send the Great White Mother a special message from Sitting Bull.

WALSH   What is it?

SITTING BULL   Tell her...once I was strong and brave. My people had hearts of iron....But now, my women are sick, my children are freezing and I have thrown my war paint to the wind. The suffering of my people has made my heart weak and I have placed nothing in the way of those who wish to return across the line. Many have done so. We who remain desire a home. For three years, we have been in the White Mother's land. We have obeyed her laws and we have kept her peace....I beg the White Mother to...to...

WALSH   Go on.

SITTING BULL   ...to have...pity...on us.

WALSH   Right!...Well then...I'll see that this goes off....

SITTING BULL makes no move to leave.

Is there anything else?

SITTING BULL   *gazing at WALSH*   White Sioux...

WALSH   Yes?

SITTING BULL   *speaking slowly and with effort* ...I find it necessary...to make a request...

WALSH *stares at him.*

. . . a request . . . for . . . provisions for my people. We have nothing.

WALSH *brusquely* Your provisions wait for you across the line. If you want provisions, go there for them.

SITTING BULL We hear you have a quantity of flour and I have come to ask you for it.

WALSH If you wish to do business, you do it at the trading post.

SITTING BULL takes off his ragged blanket. He holds out the blanket to WALSH. WALSH begins to breathe heavily as he struggles to retain control of himself.

I have appealed to the Great White Mother and the Great White Mother says no.

SITTING BULL I ask for only a little.

WALSH *exploding* And I can give you nothing! God knows, I've done my damnedest and nothing's changed. Do you hear that? Nothing's changed! Cross the line if you're so hungry, but don't, for Christ's sake, come begging food from me!

SITTING BULL *straightening up* You are speaking to the head of the Sioux nation!

WALSH I don't give a goddamn who you are! Get the hell out!

SITTING BULL goes for the knife in his belt. WALSH grabs him by the arm, twists it up and throws him to the floor. As SITTING BULL goes to get up, WALSH puts his foot in the middle of his back and shoves him, sending him sprawling. He plants his foot in the middle of his back. CLARENCE and McCUTCHEON enter.

CLARENCE *screaming* Noooooooo!

McCUTCHEON grabs CLARENCE. Everyone freezes for a moment.

WALSH *in a strained voice* McCutcheon, Underhill, go out and alert the boys in case of trouble. Throw a couple of poles across the road.

McCUTCHEON Yes, sir. *He starts off.* Laddie!

CLARENCE looks at him. McCUTCHEON speaks more gently to him.

Come on, laddie. *He takes CLARENCE off.* The Major's given an order.

LOUIS steps forward and pushes WALSH aside. He still has his foot in the middle of SITTING BULL's back. LOUIS starts to help SITTING BULL up, but SITTING BULL gets up by himself. LOUIS gets him his blanket. SITTING BULL picks up his knife. He stands there staring at WALSH. There is a pause. SITTING BULL replaces his knife in its sheath. WALSH's hand slowly reaches out to SITTING BULL as SITTING BULL slowly turns, takes his blanket and exits. LOUIS stares at WALSH.

LOUIS Is dat all for me, too?

WALSH looks up at him for a moment, then slowly nods his head. LOUIS exits. The sound of "Garryowen" is heard faintly in the background. It builds as WALSH straightens up and walks off. McCUTCHEON and CLARENCE march on, carrying a trunk. They drop it—bang—as the music ends. On the trunk is written: Major James Walsh, NWMP, No. 7 Garden Lane, Brockville, Ontario.

CLARENCE I've never seen a trunk so roped up. What's he got in it?

McCUTCHEON When the major says securely fastened, he means securely fastened.

CLARENCE I'd say that were excessive. You don't need that much rope. It's a waste.

McCUTCHEON If you want to get on in the force, laddie, know your place. The Major decrees the tying. I oversee the tying. . . and you tie.

CLARENCE Yes, Sergeant.

McCUTCHEON Now get on over to the post and saddle up.

CLARENCE When's the Major leaving?

McCUTCHEON Later.

CLARENCE I'd like to speak to him before he goes.

McCUTCHEON Sorry, Constable.

CLARENCE I've got to see him!

WALSH approaches the two of them. They do not see him.

McCUTCHEON Move your ass on over to that post!

CLARENCE I can't go till I see him!

WALSH coughs.

McCUTCHEON Constable!

CLARENCE straightens to attention. WALSH glares at McCUTCHEON for not getting rid of CLARENCE, then he looks to the trunk.

WALSH Ah, good.

CLARENCE Thank you, sir.

WALSH Bit too much rope, perhaps.

CLARENCE *with a brief look to McCUTCHEON* Yes, sir.

WALSH *tapping one of the lashings of rope with his riding crop* This, I think, can go.

CLARENCE *getting down on his hands and knees* Yes, sir.

WALSH You may go, Sergeant. . . .

McCUTCHEON exits.

A thing worth doing is worth doing well. . . . May take more time, but that's not the point, is it?

CLARENCE   No, sir.

WALSH   You wanted to speak to me?

CLARENCE   Yes, sir, I did. . . . Me and the men . . . a lot of us is upset, sir, about your leaving. . . .

WALSH   A simple leave of absence, Constable. I have a wife and children. It's been several years since I've seen them. Colonel MacLeod, upon my request, has kindly arranged several months off for me.

CLARENCE   It all seemed kinda sudden.

WALSH   I need the rest, Constable.

He regrets his statement. He moves around the trunk.

The lettering's not quite right. . . . Had to have it redone. . . . Been a long time since it's been in transit.

CLARENCE   There's something else.

WALSH   Yes?

CLARENCE   It's about Sitting Bull.

WALSH   You see a lot of him. . . . The little boy, rather.

CLARENCE   Yes, sir, I do. He's a very smart little boy and I have a lot of hope for the Sioux when I talk to him, sir.

WALSH   Do you?

CLARENCE   Sitting Bull still considers you his friend.

WALSH   I would have to deny that. I have my men and my wife and children . . . but I have no friends. Friends are a danger. You may not comprehend that statement, Constable, but Sitting Bull would.

CLARENCE   Maybe what I should have said was I still considered you his friend. I know you've seen me out with food and stuff, sir . . . and you haven't hauled me up. . . . I'm not much good at sneaking.

WALSH   That's true. *laughing* I would never send you out on reconnaissance.

CLARENCE   No, sir.

WALSH   What do you want to see me about, Constable?

CLARENCE   You're goin' East to Brockville, sir. That's not too far from Ottawa. I know you've been doin' all you can from this end, but I just wondered if maybe you couldn't go up to Ottawa and tell the Prime Minister how things are. It'd make a difference. You'd make him do something.

WALSH   Oh yes.

CLARENCE   Will you try and help Sittin' Bull?

WALSH   I shall give your proposition every consideration.

McCUTCHEON   Sorry to interrupt sir, but. . . .

WALSH   Quite right. I must get on, Constable.

CLARENCE   Can I tell Sittin' Bull that?

WALSH   Our chat has been most informative, Constable. No doubt I'll see you on my return.

CLARENCE exits.

Your timing is impeccable, McCutcheon.

McCUTCHEON   I know, sir.

WALSH   The trunk looks solid, don't you think?

McCUTCHEON   Aye, sir.

WALSH   *looking after CLARENCE* That young man should never make the force his life.

He looks at McCUTCHEON and exits. The lights dim. SITTING BULL enters. He rolls up his buffalo robe and looks at PRETTY PLUME and CROWFOOT. The lights come up on HARRY, who has a bottle and is singing.

HARRY   Oh, life in a prairie shack, when the rain begins to pour.
Drip, drip, it comes through the roof and I want to go home to my Ma—Maw.
Maw, Maw, I want to go home to my Maw.
This bloomin' country's a fraud and I want to go home to my Maw.

CLARENCE enters from one direction, carrying a cup; LOUIS and McCUTCHEON enter from the other direction.

LOUIS   Alors, je lui dirais, mange la merde!

McCUTCHEON   It's the pay, mostly . . . very poor pay, ye could say. . . .

LOUIS   Mange la merde!

McCUTCHEON   And nobody gives a damn!

CLARENCE   Shut up! This bloody bastard's talkin' French and you're talkin' at the same goddamn time. You make me dizzy!

They fall silent—and drink. There is a pause, then CLARENCE speaks quietly.

Where's the Major?

LOUIS   Eh?

McCUTCHEON   Never mind him, Louis.

CLARENCE   *louder* Where the hell's the goddamn Major?

McCUTCHEON   He's not here.

CLARENCE   I know he's not here. What kind of a fool do you take me for? I know he's not here.

McCUTCHEON   Give me another, Louis.

CLARENCE   What kind of a leave of absence is eighteen months? That's what I want to know.

LOUIS pours McCUTCHEON another drink. He looks at CLARENCE.

McCUTCHEON   He's had enough.   *leaning toward CLARENCE*   You've had enough, Clarence!

HARRY   *singing*   This bloomin' country's a fraud and I want to go home to my Maw.

McCUTCHEON   Come on, y'old buzzard. Sit down and shut up!

HARRY   *coming over*   I want to go home to my Maw. . . . You boys been celebratin'?

CLARENCE   What?

McCUTCHEON   When did ye get in?

HARRY   *filling CLARENCE's cup*   Done and over with. . . . Signed, sealed and delivered. I seen the last of Sittin' Bull.

CLARENCE   How'd it go?

HARRY   Me and five or six of the boys from C Troop, we escorted him down to the border with nary an incident. . . . The boys signed him over and then they came back up.

CLARENCE   Where was you?

HARRY   Sittin' Bull, he asked me to go on down to Fort Robson with him. That's where they was gonna be picked up and taken over to the reservation.

CLARENCE   Yeah?

HARRY   So I did!

CLARENCE   Everythin' go all right?

HARRY   You know that old horse he was ridin'? Bluecoats took that and everythin' else. . . . Said they wouldn't be needing guns or horses where they was goin'.

CLARENCE   I never seen a Sioux without some kind of horse standin' by.

He is insinuating that HARRY is a liar.

HARRY   Yeah. . . well, they sure looked a sight. Real ragtag bunch, I'm tellin' you.

There is a pause as they drink.

CLARENCE   How was they takin' them to the reservation with no horses?

HARRY   Walkin' them . . . 'cept Sittin' Bull.

CLARENCE   What about Sittin' Bull?

HARRY   They put him on some boat. Gonna take him down to Fort Randall.

CLARENCE   Fort Randall.

LOUIS   Dat's da military prison.

CLARENCE   Why's he goin' there?

HARRY   Why'd you think?

CLARENCE   The agreement was nobody'd be punished.   *Pause.*   Ain't that right?

HARRY   I don't know nothin' 'bout what's right. . . . All's I know is that Sittin Bull's in Fort Randall for killin' Custer.

CLARENCE   What . . . what'd he do when they told him?

HARRY   He said somethin' 'bout not goin' . . . not havin' to. . . . One of them bluecoats just give him a good clip on the side of the head with his rifle butt and they carried him aboard. . . . Weren't nothin' to it. Yessiree, I seen a historical sight. . . . I seen the end of the Sioux nation.

CLARENCE   That's not true!

HARRY   Was you there? . . . That boat moved off down the river and all them Injuns lined up along the bank makin' this terrible moanin' sound. I'm telling you, it was somethin' to see.   *Pause.*   What's the matter with you bastards? Me, Harry, is gonna propose a toast!

He holds up the bottle. LOUIS and McCUTCHEON hold up their glasses.

Here's to the Sioux! They won the battle, but they lost the war!

CLARENCE throws his drink in HARRY's face. HARRY stands up and throws one punch at CLARENCE which knocks him cold. McCUTCHEON and LOUIS carry CLARENCE off.

HARRY   *looking at the audience and proposing a toast*   Bottoms up!

He drinks.

Sir John A.'s policy for dealin' with the Sioux was an all round winner . . . beats Custer all to hell! Not half so messy as ridin' into tube-like hollows at ungodly hours of the mornin'. . . . and no need for a marchin' band. . . . Quiet, simple and effective. . . . Do not delay in returning to the United States, for that course is the only alternative to death by starvation. . . . So Sittin' Bull left the Canadian West . . .

WALSH enters and stands behind his desk.

. . . and Major Walsh returned to it. Yessireee, beats Custer all to hell!

McCUTCHEON formally carries on a large board with a map on it; toy soldiers, a train engine, trees. HARRY looks at the board as McCUTCHEON puts it on WALSH's desk. HARRY laughs.

HARRY   Je-sus!

He exits, shaking his head.

WALSH   The railway track is here.... There is a slight curve here around a grove of trees.... Do you see that, McCutcheon?

McCUTCHEON   Aye, sir.

WALSH   I think possibly twenty men could be concealed amongst those trees...twenty men.... Do we have twenty men we can rely on? Top notch fellows?

McCUTCHEON   Aye, sir.

WALSH   Good. In an operation like this, there is no room for error.... Image of the force and all that.... So...the men are concealed here. *tapping the map*   At 2:10 precisely the train should round this curve.... You follow me?

McCUTCHEON   Aye, sir.

WALSH   All right.... Now, as the train reaches this point, Harry pulls out with a full load across the tracks....

McCUTCHEON   Isn't that a bit dangerous, sir?

WALSH looks at him sharply.

I mean, sir...will the train have ample time to stop, sir?

WALSH   All that is calculated. *speaking coldly* Would you care to check my figures?

McCUTCHEON   No, sir...just wondering.

WALSH   *staring at him*   Good. *turning his attention back to the map*   Now, as the train pulls up, the men, myself at the head.... There'll be a dress parade before... I told you that, didn't I?

McCUTCHEON   Aye, sir.

WALSH   Right!... I will ride out from the woods, my men behind me, and all of us in full dress.... Tell the men to practice war whoops. I want good full-blooded Indian yells, you hear?

McCUTCHEON   Aye, sir.

WALSH   So, out we come...yelling bloody murder.... I'll swing aboard the train and ride it into Calgary. Well, what do you think? Is that a stirring sight or not?

McCUTCHEON   Very stirring, sir.

WALSH   When you open a railroad, you do it in style, I say! Bloody train will be full of Easterners and we'll scare the pants off every one of them! I want a good show!

CLARENCE enters, followed by LOUIS.

CLARENCE   Major.

WALSH   *stopping him*   Underhill! You have interrupted an important conference!

CLARENCE   Beggin' your pardon, sir.... Request permission to speak, sir.

WALSH   *long suffering*   What is it?

CLARENCE   A rider's come in from Standin' Rock. ... Been in the saddle all night.

WALSH   And?

LOUIS   He's dead.... Da white man have da Indian Police kill 'im.... Sittin' Bull is dead!... Da rider say he see his face bleed empty and death come starin' in its place.

CLARENCE   They shot him twice and put the boots to him... and Little Crow says the soldiers dropped him in a pit of lime, so's his people couldn't bury him proper.

WALSH stands there frozen, staring at CLARENCE.

And Crowfoot?... Do you remember Crowfoot, sir? He used to come up to the fort, sir, and us men, we used to play with him 'cause he was just a kid, and ain't none of us got kids here... and he was a real good boy... and I liked him, sir.... And they drug him out from under the bed where he was hidin' and they threw him down and they shot him and he's dead too!

His anger is spent.

I come in to tell you, sir...'cause...'cause...I didn't know what else to do.

WALSH stands so still he seems to be a statue. There is a long pause. At last, he speaks.

WALSH   Dis-missed....

McCUTCHEON, LOUIS and CLARENCE make no move to leave.

DIS-MISSED!

They exit. WALSH watches them leave. He moves to his desk and looks at it. He undoes his leather holster and takes out his gun. As he does this, we hear the sound of the Nez Percés from the end of Act One. That sound continues as he lays the gun on the desk and slowly, carefully, takes off his tunic, putting it on the desk as well. We hear SITTING BULL's voice as WALSH slowly lifts both hands over his head. SITTING BULL speaks softly, reminiscent of his speech to CROWFOOT early in Act Two.

SITTING BULL   In the beginning...was given...to everyone a cup.... A cup of clay. And from this cup, we drink our life. We all dip in the water...but the cups are different.... My cup is broken. It has passed away.

WALSH slams his hands down on his desk.

Blackout.

JAMES REANEY (b. 1926)

Observing how "life reflected art" in Stratford, Ontario, near where he was born and grew up, James Reaney wrote in a 1962 poem, "Let us make a form out of this: documentary on one side and myth on the other." Perhaps no other Canadian dramatist or poet has so successfully transmuted the local into the universal, the stuff of documentary into the stuff of myth. Avoiding for the most part the political edge that Salutin and Pollock give to their work, Reaney makes of the life and history of Souwesto—the small towns and farms of southwestern Ontario—a rich poetic brew steeped in Blake and the Brontës, Walt Disney and the Bible, and leavened with a childlike propensity to treat everything as creative play. In his hands the story of the Donnellys, local history and legend, emerges as an experience of extraordinary theatrical scope and complexity, a trilogy of plays that many consider the finest achievement of the Canadian theatre to date.

Reaney was well established as a poet and academic before attempting to write for the stage. He enrolled at the University of Toronto in 1944, and in 1949 earned an M.A. in English and a Governor-General's Award for his first book of poetry, *The Red Heart*. After teaching at the University of Manitoba for seven years, he returned to Toronto to pick up his Ph.D. in 1958 along with another Governor-General's Award for his second book of verse, *A Suit of Nettles*. In 1960 Reaney began teaching English at the University of Western Ontario, a position he still holds today, and founded the innovative journal *Alphabet* which he published and edited until 1971. He also made his remarkable debut in the theatre that year with *The Killdeer*. Mavor Moore hailed it as "the first Canadian play of real consequence, and the first demonstration of genius among us." It won five awards at the 1960 Dominion Drama Festival and a third Governor-General's Award for Reaney on its publication in 1962. The play's eclectic symbolist style, melodramatic plot and archetypal struggle between the forces of innocence and corruption signalled the shape of much of Reaney's work to come, including *The Donnellys*.

Reaney kept writing poetry—*Twelve Letters to a Small Town* (1962) and *The Dance of Death at London, Ontario* (1963)—but from now on most of his work would be in the theatre. *The Killdeer* was followed by *Night-blooming Cereus* and *One-man Masque* (1960), *The Easter Egg* (1962) and a series of fantastical plays for children commencing with the Manitoba Theatre Centre's 1963 production of *Names and Nicknames*.

With *The Sun and the Moon* (1965) at the London Summer Theatre, Reaney began his long association with Keith Turnbull, a key development in the evolution of his stagecraft. In *Listen to the Wind* (1966), produced by Turnbull and directed by Reaney himself, the young protagonist "dreams out" a play-within-a-play from his sickbed. The complex action unfolds on a bare stage with a props table, a few actors, and a chorus of children providing visual metaphors and sound effects. The presentational style reminds us that acting is merely formalized play, a revelation of the power of imagination to transform reality. Out of *Listen to the Wind* developed the Listeners' Workshop. Once a week for two years Reaney led groups of twenty-five or more local children and adults through elaborate play exercises designed to stretch their imaginations by, for example, improvising the Book of Genesis. From these workshops grew what he called the "embryonics" of *Colours in the Dark*, commissioned by the Stratford Festival in 1967. A Joycean epic revealing the macrocosm of all human history in the microcosm of an individual life, the play is described by Reaney as a theatrical experience "designed to give you that mosaic—that all-things-happening-at-the-same-time-higgledy-piggledy feeling that rummaging through a play box can give you."

The embryonics of *The Donnellys* also arose out of the Listeners' Workshop, though Reaney had been fascinated since childhood by this story that had occurred only twenty miles from where he was born. He began researching the project in 1967; and except for a major revision of *The Killdeer* in 1968, *The Donnellys* remained his sole dramatic concern for the next eight years.

In 1973 Reaney took what was by then a massive script to Halifax where Keith Turnbull and a group of actors that included Jerry Franken and Patricia Ludwick (the future Mr. and Mrs. Donnelly) put it through a series of workshops from which three separate plays emerged. Bill Glassco agreed to produce them at the Tarragon with Turnbull directing, and in November 1973, *Sticks and Stones: The Donnellys, Part One* opened in Toronto. Part Two, *The St Nicholas Hotel, Wm Donnelly, Prop.*, premiered in November 1974 and won the Chalmers Award. *Handcuffs: The Donnellys, Part Three* opened in March 1975. Later that year the newly christened NDWT Company—Reaney, Turnbull, et al—toured all three plays across Canada. *Fourteen Barrels from Sea to Sea* (1977) is Reaney's highly personal account of the tour.

Reaney continued to use the workshop-preparation method with the NDWT Company for his next series of plays, all based on local Ontario history or pseudo-history: *Baldoon* (1976), written with C.H. Gervais; *The Dismissal* (1977), featuring Mackenzie King as a scheming undergraduate; *Wacousta!* (1978) and its sequel *The Canadian Brothers* (1983), products of nearly two years' intensive workshops (vividly chronicled in the published text of *Wacousta!*); *King Whistle* (1979); and *Antler River* (1980). In *Gyroscope* (1981) Reaney returned to more personal dramatic material. And with his libretto for John Beckwith's opera *The Shivaree*, first performed in 1982, he was reunited with the composer for whose music he had written *Night-blooming Cereus* twenty years earlier. Reaney's recent publications include a ten-minute performance poem for two voices called "Imprecations" (1984), celebrating the arts of cursing and name-calling, a fitting celebration for a writer who has always held names to be as tangible as sticks and stones, only much more powerful.

The Donnelly story as Reaney tells it is very much about the power of names. To carry the Donnelly name is both a curse and a blessing, a sacrament and a doom. In *The St Nicholas Hotel*, Will Donnelly looks into the future and sees how his enemies "smeared our name for all time so that when children are naughty their mothers still say to them be quiet, or the Black Donnellys will get you." Historically, the Donnellys were Irish Catholic immigrants who settled in Biddulph Township near Lucan, Ontario, in 1844. James and Johanna and their seven sons and a daughter almost immediately became embroiled in conflict with their neighbours, and much of the violence that wracked the region—barn burnings, assaults, mutilations of farm animals—was attributed to the Donnellys. In 1857 James Donnelly killed a man in a fight and went to prison for seven years. In 1879 Mike Donnelly was stabbed to death in a hotel bar-room, his assailant imprisoned for only two years. Finally, on the night of February 3, 1880, a mob of vigilantes burst into the Donnelly home and murdered Mr. and Mrs. Donnelly, son Tom and niece Bridget, and later that night son John. Though an eyewitness identified many of the killers, no one ever went to prison for the crimes.

In researching the plays, Reaney discovered that his source material embodied two opposing views of the principals. First there were the evil Donnellys of popular history and local lore, incarnated in Thomas P. Kelley's 1954 best seller, *The Black Donnellys*, a potboiler that presented the family as "the most vicious and heartless bunch of devils that ever drew the breath of human life." In Kelley's version, the depraved family, led by the monstrous Johannah, terrorize the district for the sheer malicious joy of it and get only what they deserve in the end. A more objective and sympathetic treatment was Orlo Miller's book *The Donnellys Must Die* (1962). Miller argued that the Donnellys were essentially victims of a nasty feud that had carried over from Ireland where they had refused to join the secret anti-Protestant society of Whiteboys (or Whitefeet). As a result, in the largely Irish settlement of Biddulph they were branded with the hated name "Blackfeet," persecuted and made scapegoats for a great deal of local violence which was not of their doing. Reaney ultimately followed Miller's lead, but he went further than just exonerating the Donnellys. He celebrates them.

Part One, *Sticks and Stones*, covers the period 1857-67, opening with an expository flashback showing the Donnellys' stubborn refusal to bend to Whitefoot pressures in Ireland. We see them struggling to make a place for themselves in Biddulph, caught between the Roman (Catholic) and

Protestant Lines of settlers, uncomfortable with both. They lose half their farm in a bitter dispute with the Fat Woman and her husband, and Mr. Donnelly is goaded into fighting with the Fat Woman's brother, Pat Farl, who won't stop calling him "Blackfoot." When Mr. Donnelly kills Farl, only a heroic effort by Mrs. Donnelly gets her husband's sentence commuted to seven years in prison. At the end the Biddulph Whitefeet burn the Donnellys' barn and try to intimidate them into leaving the township, but Mr. Donnelly refuses, reiterating what he told them in Ireland: "Donnellys don't kneel." "It was at this time," Reaney writes, "that the Donnellys decided to be Donnellys."

To be a Donnelly in Reaney's portrayal is to be strong, proud, heroic, stubborn, forthright. It is to choose to be true to your own values no matter how much pain that may cause you. It is to stand up against the mob, the community, the church, even the law if they pressure you to be what you are not. It is to be intensely loyal to your own family and to be generous *as* a family to others whose own have rejected or betrayed them. To be a Donnelly, in short, is to have an integrity lacking in almost every character or institution that opposes them throughout the trilogy, from the corrupt magistrates George Stub and Tom Cassleigh in Part One to the churchmen who organize the vigilantes in Part Three, *Handcuffs*, and the jury that finds mob leader Jim Carroll not guilty of their murder. *Handcuffs*, focusing on the massacre itself and the few months in 1879-80 immediately preceding and following it, really just fills in the details of what Parts One and Two have already told us will happen. The Donnellys *must* die; their pride and stubbornness cannot be endured. They are tragic.

Whereas *Sticks and Stones* introduces the circumstances of the Donnellys' tragedy and *Handcuffs* presents its dénouement, the second play, *The St Nicholas Hotel*, poses the trilogy's key question: "Why did they all hate you so much?" Rev. Donaldson asks it of Will Donnelly in 1891 on the twelfth anniversary of Mike's murder, and Reaney gives us the events of 1873-79 as an answer. Superficially it is Mike's story. The play opens with intimations of his death and closes with his murder, his ghost, and his bloodstain that will never come out. But Mike doesn't die for anything that he as an individual has done; he dies because he is a Donnelly. The events that build inexorably to his death are part of the larger conspiracy that will culminate in the 1880 massacre.

One reason the Donnellys are so hated is their sheer zest for life which makes *The St Nicholas Hotel*, despite its tragic undertones, the most joyful and exhilarating of the three plays, full of stagecoach races, whirling tops, rousing music and dancing. Brimming with positive energy, the Donnellys provide a constant, unwelcome challenge to the negativity and complacency of their neighbours. Will and Maggie's romantic courtship in Act One is set against the calculated bargaining of Stub and Miss Maguire, and the loveless marriage bed of Bill and Mary Donovan. In Act Two young Tom Ryan tells how he ran away from his own brutal home to the Donnellys— making his humilated father another of their lifelong enemies—"because they're brave" and "they're handsome," and because "there's love there." The Donnellys themselves understand the double-edged nature of their condition. Mr. Donnelly acknowledges that they deserve the way they are treated: "for we're Donnellys." Like the spinning tops that symbolize their vitality, they are caught up in a momentum over which they have little control. They can't help being what they are. "Yes. It would be nice to stop, but we can't oh no we must keep on spinning and spinning," Mrs. Donnelly says. The context is Stub's proposal that they compromise their support of the Liberal candidate and back his Conservative opponent in exchange for a cessation of hostilities. Their rejection of this deal and the subsequent defeat of the Tory candidate add significantly to the enemies who will destroy them in Part Three.

The St Nicholas Hotel is by no means simply a whitewash of the Donnellys. Having exploded the myth of "the Black Donnellys" in Part One, Reaney seems willing in this play to admit to shades of grey. In Acts One and Two we see at times how pride and strength can turn to arrogance and bullying, playfulness to maliciousness, and energy to destruction. Will and Mike never hesitate to employ unfair business practices in running their Opposition Stage Line, even to the point of putting the competition's drivers in danger. Reaney intentionally leaves ambiguous their role in Ned Brooks' fatal accident, but there is little doubt about the responsibility of James Jr. for a variety of atrocities. By the third act, though, the balance of sympathy has swung back wholly in the Donnellys' favour as a result of the pettiness and cowardice of their enemies in the mob scene as well as in Mike's murder. When Will, Norah and Mrs. Donnelly face down the mob, we understand both the awe and the blind hatred this family could inspire. As Reaney's stage direction notes, "We should feel ashamed ourselves that we did not make a better showing against a lame man & two women."

The lame man, and really the central figure in the play, is Will, often called "Cripple" because of his club foot. He and Mrs. Donnelly are the two strongest characters in the trilogy and the ones at whom the most venom is directed. Will is also the most sensitive Donnelly, an artist of sorts, riding a horse called Lord Byron and opposing Jim Carroll with his handwriting and the music of his fiddle. But most of all he is a function of his name, very much the offspring of his father who is described in Part One as "a small square chunk of will"—the essence of Donnelly. The title of the play, *The St Nicholas Hotel, Wm Donnelly, Prop.*, locates Will outside Biddulph in a future beyond the massacre, a survivor, proprietor of his own fate and chief prop of a family name that endures as a curse, a legend, a stain on a bar-room floor, and now as a classic of Canadian drama.

•

The St Nicholas Hotel, Wm Donnelly, Prop.: The Donnellys, Part Two was first performed at the Tarragon Theatre on November 16, 1974, with the following cast: Ken Anderson, Nancy Beatty, Jay Bowen, Tom Carew, Peter Elliott, David Ferry, Jerry Franken, Rick Gorrie, Miriam Greene, Michael Hogan, Patricia Ludwick, Don McQuarrie, Keith McNair, Gord Stobbe and Suzanne Turnbull. It was directed by Keith Turnbull and designed by Rosalyn Mina.

Note: The punctuation of *The St Nicholas Hotel*—eccentric, inconsistent and often technically incorrect—has been left as Reaney intended it, to reflect the rhythms of his characters' speech. "Publishers beware: you rob the performers when you change Reaney's punctuation." (Patricia Ludwick, "One Actor's Journey with James Reaney" in *Approaches to the Work of James Reaney* [1983])—Ed.

THE ST NICHOLAS HOTEL, WM DONNELLY PROP. THE DONNELLYS, PART II

CHARACTERS

MR DONNELLY (James)
MRS DONNELLY (Johannah)
MIKE
WILL
JAMES JR
TOM } *their sons*
JOHN
BOB
PATRICK
JENNY, *their daughter*
BRIDGET, *their niece*
NELLIE, *Mike's wife*
NORAH (née Macdonald), *Will's wife*

JOHN MACDONALD, *Norah's brother*
MOTHER

BARTENDER (Frank Walker)
NED BROOKS, *a stage driver*
PATRICK FINNEGAN, *a stageowner*

REV. DONALDSON, *a traveller*

MISS MERCILLA MAGUIRE (later Mrs George Stub)
REV. DR MAGUIRE, *her father*
GEORGE STUB, *a merchant*

FAT LADY
JIM CARROLL, *her son*
BRIDGET, *her daughter (the Stubs' parlourmaid)*
WILL FARL, *her nephew*

MAGGIE DONOVAN, *her niece*
FATHER
AUNT THERESA
BILL DONOVAN, *Maggie's brother*
MARY DONOVAN, *his wife*
MOTHER SUPERIOR
NUNS

TOM RYAN
NED RYAN, *his father*
MRS RYAN

BAKER
BAKER'S APPRENTICE
McKELLAR, *a stage driver*
MR SCANDRETT, *a tollman*
MRS SCANDRETT
CHILD
CESSMAN

SQUIRE FERGUSON, *a Justice of the Peace*
CONSTABLE BERRYHILL
HUGH McCRIMMON, *a detective*
BAILIFFS
CONSTABLES
PRIEST
FIDDLER

TIMOTHY CORCORAN, *a Tory candidate*
ELECTIONS CLERK

CHAIRMAN (of the "Peace Society")
O'HALLORAN
DAN QUIGLEY, *a farmer*
SCHOOLMASTER

SID SKINNER (aka "Bill Lewis")
BILL LEWIS, *a trainer*
GREENWOOD
JIM MORRISON, *Mike Donnelly's workmate*

2 MAIDS

STAGE DRIVERS
STAGE PASSENGERS
TOLLGATE KEEPERS
TRAVELLERS
FARMERS
BOYS AND GIRLS
MOB
CHORUS

AUTHOR'S NOTE

The story of this play concerns a race, a race between the Donnelly boys and their enemies. The road the race takes place on has tollgates with signs on them saying: NO DONNELLYS ARE TO. . .run a stage line, marry my daughter, & c., & c. 'Helped' by their brothers, William & Michael Donnelly smash through most of the tollgates, but their victories only drive their enemies to build stronger & stronger barriers until, at last, Michael is suddenly & brutally murdered.

It is a tale of barrooms, wheels, horses, nuns, tops, convent yards, derailed trains, homeless boys, tavern brawls, refinements, squalors, wedding cakes, drunkards—and ghosts. In a certain hotel deserted for thirty years there is a stain on the floor no ordinary scrubbing brush can ever wash away.

James Reaney

ACT ONE

The barroom of the City Hotel, London; later on it will be the barroom of the Royal Hotel in Exeter, the St Nicholas Hotel (Wm Donnelly, prop.) in Appin, and Slaght's Hotel in Waterford. The barman seems always there; his somewhat skullish face and presence will remind us later on before we go to sleep that—this is the man who eventually killed Mike Donnelly. Behind the bar is a picture of Wm Donnelly's black stallion, Lord Byron. Passengers to the stages to the north slowly fill the benches at the sides of the room we too are waiting in; we see actors spinning tops (each one seems to have one) and hear them singing songs from the play. Like a cloud shadow the stage picture is slowly invaded now by the story of a road; the actors stop being actors and become fighters for the ownership of that road, a map of which goes all around the walls of the theatre from Crediton to Exeter to Clandeboye down to Lucan to Elginfield to London to St Thomas to Waterford, and advancing towards us comes the

STAGEDRIVER (NED BROOKS) *belching* Are there any passengers for Masonville, St John's, Bobtown, Ryan's Corners, Lucan, Flanagan's Corners, Mooretown, Exeter? Now loading at the front door please.

MIKE DONNELLY Are there any more ladies and gentlemen for Calamity Corners as tis sometimes called, St John's, Birr—my old friend Ned here calls it Bobtown, the more elegant name is Birr. Elginfield known to some as Ryan's Corners, Lucan that classic spot if it's not all burnt down, Clandeboye, Mooretown, Exeter *and* Crediton. If Ned here hasn't sawn it to pieces the coach is waiting for you at the front door and it pleases you.

STAGEDRIVER What does it matter if it's Bobtown or Birr; elegance be damned, Mike Donnelly, it's my team will get you there faster.

LADY *coming back in* Which stage is yours then? Louisa, there are no less than four stages out there all with different names. Sir wh—

STAGEDRIVER
The Favourite Line
Hawkshaw's Stage
Good Horses, Comfortable Stages & Fast Time.
Leaves the City Hotel for all points north at two o'clock, p.m.

WILLIAM & MIKE DONNELLY pass out announcement cards.

ANCIENT STAGEDRIVER *entering & flourishing a ragged whip* Come on everybody, Ho! for the North Uriah Jennings here, fifty years on the road, *coughing*

YET ANOTHER STAGEDRIVER Anybody here want a lift up north. You'll have to share the accommodation a little with

LADY TWO Martha, he's got six young pigs, two geese and a sack of flour in there already.

CHORUS *reading cards*
Notice
Exeter, Lucan & London Daily Stage: Change of Time.

WILL Leaves City Hotel at 2 p.m. and arrives Maclean's Hotel, Lucan at half past four

MIKE Twenty minutes ahead of all other stages.

Both halves begin together, but the first half pauses so the names are spoken after the second half has completed its speech:

HALF CHORUS	HALF CHORUS
Drivers	calling all places along the route for passengers

William and Michael
Donnelly

Into the bar comes a hard-driving Irishman who has as much force as the Donnellys but all as hard as grindstone.

FINNEGAN Just a minute there, Donnelly—whoa!! You boys aren't going to Lucan today.

WILL *with whip* It's Patrick Finnegan says we won't get to Lucan?

FINNEGAN Ah, yes, Will, because *to audience* good evening—don't you know my brother John Finnegan and myself, Pat, have bought out your boss and all his horses and wagons, so it's the Finnegan Stage now. Come along now, these passengers are mine, the road is mine, and the wheels. Give your whip to my driver, Will. Mr. Brooks, here's—he's driving for me, Will. I don't need you Donnelly boys. *trying to take whip*

MIKE Give that whip back to my brother. *grabbing it* No one ever lent us a whip.

WILL No, my father bought me that whip with the very first money I ever earned, on St Nicholas day—five years ago and that's how long we've been driving our stage.

FINNEGAN There you go, Will, it was never your stage. It belonged to Hugh McPhee and now it belongs to Pat Finnegan. We leave at two p.m. sharp, ladies and gentlemen, passengers to reach Lucan safely to connect with east and west trains to St Mary's and Sarnia.

MIKE Do you want to know, Mr. Pat Finnegan, how Will and Mike Donnelly will still beat you to Lucan today by a good half hour?

FINNEGAN It's my brother and myself here run a store and tavern up the road north of here—why the place is called after our father Finnegan's Corners, for God's sake, there were three hundred buggies at his funeral. Sure our father built the Proof Line Road these fellows say is theirs. So step up into my stage wagon and see whose road it is. Mike Donnelly, we'll run yous off it. Are there anymore passengers— *exit*

MIKE Look, we're starting our own line with our own equipment. Mr. Jennings, how much do you want for your vehicle that's been fifty years on the road. Will, just take a look at his beasts.

WILL We'll have to get new horses, fast ones, where we can get—

CHORUS William Donnelly, Groom.

The actors "melt" into a scene at the London races. They are held back from the track by a long rope. The BARTENDER jumps up on the bar and interprets the race through a megaphone. We only hear the drumming of invisible hooves and see on human faces the effect of the race.

MIKE
The horses for our stage line were bred from the winner of this race. We had the rights to a mare called Irish Girl whose mother you may recall was Billet Doux, grandmother to Sir Walter Scott. So, Will, is it let this race decide who'll sire the foal that is the nighhorse of our team on—what'll we call it.

Get a pool of extra silence around the naming of the line

WILL
The Opposition Stage

BARTENDER
The second day's meeting of The London Turf Club on the Newmarket race course attracted a large crowd yesterday afternoon. The weather was delightful and the track in good condition, except that it was a trifle dusty.

CHORUS
over & under Words blown away by the wind, dust & words in the stream of the time we all lie dreaming in

CHORUS
dreaming of horses and wagons going up the hill

This speech and the ones below go on simultaneously with WILL's "Opposition Stage" coming in just after the CHORUS's "dreaming in". The BARTENDER should blur his voice under and over the other levels so that we get the effect of a real racetrack where wind & distance play tricks with announcements; also it is a remembered racetrack where MIKE DONNELLY not only saw the horse they needed but also the first omen of his own death.

BARTENDER Dash of 1½ miles. Entries. Sleepy Jim, bay stallion & his colours are blue & yellow owned by Messrs Bookless & Thomas, Guelph. Florence Nightingale, grey mare. Scarlet & white.

CHORUS Down the hill

BARTENDER Lord Byron, full brother to Clear Grit out of Fleetwood the Second. He thus comes of good stock & will be heard of further.

CHORUS Long white road

BARTENDER Black & red, and *an actor runs around as Lord Byron—sometimes disappearing from view, then reappearing and followed avidly by all of the spectators' eyes* they're off! Although the delay in starting caused a good deal of impatience this, ladies and gentlemen, is an ex—citing dash. From the first it lies between Sleepy Jim, Nigger Baby & Lord Byron and, ladies & gents, as they first pass the string they are well abreast. On the turn, however, they're breaking up & now it's an open question. It's an open question, ladies & knights, which is going to win. It's Sleepy Jim, no it's Lord Byron—past the string slightly ahead of Finnegan who flashed up from behind with Nigger Baby third. Lord Byron ran, ladies & gentlemen, without his regular *gasp from the crowd who see the jockey's death before the barman does* trainer & his victory here today is therefore a greater tribute to his speed. Sorry to report. There seems to have been an accident there to Lord Byron's jockey among the oak trees there at the edge of the grove. A low branch.

CHORUS Words blown away by the wind, dust & words in the stream of

BARTENDER Time. Two minutes forty-nine & a half seconds.

Two human runners in singlets appear—one of them is DETECTIVE McCRIMMON whom Finnegan will one day hire to pursue the Donnellys.

BARTENDER Next ladies & gentlemen, it is calculated to have a foot race in addition, 100 yards, for a shake-purse. BANG!

The runners sweep toward us and then—whistles! and the actors all turn into a herd of horses in a Biddulph pasture; the Donnellys with their father have come to take out a team for evening training. Umbrella, fiddle.

MIKE Our father and another old man helped us to train the horses. Ploughboy! Pilot!

MIKE & CHORUS Farmer. Indian.

MIKE You see our horses came running to their names!

MIKE & CHORUS Manilla. Ginger.

A team comes up for training, umbrella thrown at them, horses shy, then calm. Slowly, all the horses grow used to umbrella & fiddle.

MR DONNELLY Throw the frightening old floppy thing at him again, Mike. And again. There my beauty. Again. There. Whisper to you. The fiddle, Will. *excruciating notes* There my beauty, my dove.

We return from the horse pasture to the tavern; crowd is a crowd once more.

MIKE Our brother Patrick had been apprenticed to a Carriage Works in town here. As a blacksmith. He helped turn the rusty old vehicle we bought from Jennings into a pretty smart, smooth road bird with new wheels for wings.

anvil in distance

FINNEGAN Are there any more passengers for London? Sure you'll want to see Mr Barnum's Circus that's in town today, and we've put on an extra stage just to accommodate the crowd.

WILL & MIKE On the sides of our stage what did we have painted?

CHORUS *with varying strength and texture*
The Opposition Stage.
Between London & Crediton
Through Exeter daily at 4 a.m.
First Rate Accommodation Prices Moderate
Proprietor, William Donnelly,
Driver, Michael Donnelly.
William Donnelly, Gentleman.

LADY Prices moderate, Mr. Donnelly? How much is a ticket to Lucan on your conveyance?

WILL Seventy cents, m'am.

TWO GIRLS Mr Finnegan, does your stage go into Crediton?

FINNEGAN Shure, and it can be induced to.

TWO GIRLS Are you entirely sure because your advertisement notes your destination as Exeter which is just four mile short of where Uncle Dan Philip lives.

FINNEGAN Girls, I'll get you there if I have to take yous on my back. *to LADY* Sixty cents.

A routine where she wavers between FINNEGAN & DONNELLY, running back & forth.

WILL Fifty

FINNEGAN Forty it is.

WILL & MIKE Thirty it is.

FINNEGAN Donnelly! Twenty, Madam.

WILL Sure that's nothing at all. We'll take you for a kiss and a penny. Michael, take the fare.

LADY *held on MIKE's arms and another's as in a cart, after being kissed* I prefer the Opposition Stage. A smooth ride with fast, evenly matched horses. Polite & skillful drivers. One hardly knows

where the time has gone when — the diligence stops, the driver jumps down . . .

But cows are faintly mooing, as if we had reached her farm, and the actors giggling under her effusiveness have crept around to confront her as embarrassing cows . . .

with firm hand takes yours and helps you across to your very gate.

CHORUS Her father's cows have come to meet her. *laughter*

FINNEGAN Allaboard for the circus excursion. *He or his driver blows a horn.* Here comes Finnegan. Here comes Finnegan.

WILL DONNELLY walks behind the bar and lights a candle as we slide into the next scene. Most of the tavern crowd depart. We hear them getting into the stage & driving off. More horn blasts & "Here comes Finnegan." "The Favourite Stage." Behind WILL DONNELLY there is a picture of a black horse. His wife NORAH brings in a tray of glasses and sets them behind the bar. The light changes. Fiddle. Wind.

CHORUS *a drifting voice* Yes, Bill Donnelly ran the St Nicholas Hotel down here at Appin. Was still running it when he died in the nineties. My father bought me some ice cream there in 1924.

And now we are at the St Nicholas Hotel, years after what we have just been watching.

NORAH Well, so our visitor will not stay the night, is that

WILL He'll come back. I put something in his cutter

NORAH It's too stormy a night for anyone to come out save the odd traveller like this reverend gentleman. But perhaps he's right. He should push on to Glencoe now rather than in the morning.

WILL No. He's going to stay here tonight. You'll see.

NORAH Are you that lonely, Will?

WILL Well, if he does not come back maybe we should call up the children and have a game of dominoes. *Pause.* Norah, you know the sort of travellers we get at the St Nicholas Hotel — grain-buyers and sewing machine agents, but — and neighbours into the bar here, but — it's seldom anyone comes down this road from the past, from up there.

The candle wavers.

NORAH Hsst! That blast came from Biddulph for sure. Sure there's water from there flows by here, in the river doesn't there. But the reverend gentleman did not seem Biddulphian to me, Will.

WILL We'll find out. I've met him somewhere in the seventies when Mike and me drove stage.

NORAH   So that's why you've lit the candle. I'd forgotten, forgive me, tonight's

WILL   Tonight's the night they murdered Mike, Norah. In a bar not unlike this one

Enter MINISTER with a block of ice in his hands.

NORAH   Sir, you've come back to us out of the storm?

DONALDSON   Who put this block of ice to my feet in my cutter?

WILL   I did, now I'll ask my son to put up your horse   *through a door*   Jack, we've a customer after all.

DONALDSON   I had to come back to find out why—

WILL   To keep your feet warm, you might as well stay with us, sir. What time is your appointment tomorrow in Glencoe?

DONALDSON   Sabbath School starts at nine. But how would that keep me warm?

WILL   By bringing you back to my St Nicholas Hotel instead of you driving seven miles on through a blizzard. It's warmer here than that.

He takes the ice block and puts it in a pail; all through the evening we watch it slowly melt till it is used by the scrubwomen at the end of the play to wipe MIKE DONNELLY's blood off the floor.

DONALDSON   Now, sir, I've met you somewhere before. The name of the hotel you are running is the St Nicholas Hotel, proprietor is—

WILL   My name is William Donnelly. *Pause.* Perhaps you'll want to hitch up your cutter again.

DONALDSON   Now why would you say that, Mr Donnelly?

WILL   Aren't you afraid of me?

DONALDSON   No. Quite the contrary. I remember you and your brother when you ran the stage between London and Lucan, excuse me *one* of the stages. The Opposition Stage.

NORAH   That must be a good many years ago, sir. Twenty years?

DONALDSON   More than that. I started visiting the Presbyterian Church in Lucan on appointments which I would receive, oh let me see now—the fall of 1875. I preferred your stage although people at the church wanted me not to patronize your line.   *to us*   Once I happened to come down to Lucan from Parkhill by train—hence to Irishtown by your rival's stage—The Finnegan Line. The Finnegan Line. I asked the driver how the new railway had affected the stage route between London and Lucan. What has become of the Donnellys?

STAGEDRIVER   *belching*   Ugh, the Donnellys've been run off the line at last.

DONALDSON   And what do they do now then?

STAGEDRIVER   Yes, what don't they do, sir. They're a bad lot and we're bound to get rid of them.

DONALDSON   Yes, Mr Donnelly. A small glass of wine would not go amiss. Thank you. Then I said   *to him*   It's strange that young men so good looking and so polite as I've always found the Donnelly boys to be, should be so much run down and set on by all parties, Romanists, Protestants and Secretists, when they are so very polite and strive so hard to live down all this opposition, by attention to business and kind treatment of all who favour them. He replied:

STAGEDRIVER   You do not know them, sir. They just put on appearances to deceive strangers. I once thrashed Mike and I will thrash him again.

DONALDSON   *pause*   Which son is Mike?

STAGEDRIVER   The second from the youngest. No sir, the people are bound to get rid of that family some way or another and that too before too long.

DONALDSON   We had reached the railway station and I told him what I thought as a teacher of the Gospel. I said: "You surely do not mean what you say, or you would not speak so to a stranger: there's room enough for the Donnellys and their opponents also in the world. Why, man, competition is the life of trade; we are all the better of the opposition lines."

STAGEDRIVER   *laughing*   You're too good yourself, sir, to understand what this family is like. *We* are bound to snuff out that family and we shall do it, so that it shall never be known how it was done.

DONALDSON   He turned on his heel and left. So, yes, I was never afraid of the Donnellys. William Donnelly. Mike Donnelly.

WILL   And when would that conversation be?

DONALDSON   In January of 1879. As early as that

WILL   As early as that then we were marked out for slaughter.

DONALDSON   Mike, what happened to Michael Donnelly?

WILL   Oh they got him first at the end of that year—just before Christmas, December the 9th, 1879.

DONALDSON   This is the 12th Anniversary of his death then? *Pause.*   I find it very pleasant to be sitting by such a warm fire after travelling through such a storm this afternoon. *They listen to the gale outside for a few moments.*   You have settled here, Mr Donnelly, in this peaceful place after a stormy journey far worse. Far worse.

WILL   Yes, I keep the inn here, I travel about in the spring with my stallion—True Grit out of Lord Byron and this may astonish you, but people are saying that I am the best constable this village ever had.

NORAH Sir, I am going upstairs with a warm brick for your bed. I promise you no more ice blocks. How soon do you wish to retire?

DONALDSON I may never drive this way again. Midnight. Until then Mrs Donnelly, I should like your husband to explain what lay behind the bloody statement of that young man at the railway station. Why did they all hate you so much?

NORAH Oh sir, that would take till the dawn itself. *passing out of the room*

WILL I'll tell you why the stage drivers for the other lines hated us so much. *taking a scissors from Norah's sewing basket* They blamed us for cutting the tongues out of their horses. Like this. *laughing & illustrating!* But at first it was something not quite so Sodom & Gomorrah we were blamed for.

Screams & curses offstage; some monumental collapse of Mr FINNEGAN's stage. Yes, a wheel has come off, for into the barroom it rolls. Passengers enter, shaken & muttering.

FINNEGAN Who in the mother of Hell's name loosened the bolts and cut the nuts off my wheels. Oh funny it is, Cripple, and one of my wheels skated right into your hands, and funny it is, Mike. Well it wouldn't be so funny if I'd been going down Mother Brown's Hill and they'd come off; we'd been all killed. *Pause.* Ladies & gentlemen, be patient for the twenty-minute delay there'll be while we fix up the wheels. You see what they done, don't go in his stage, you see what they done to me. Oh, Alec *to bartender* give me anything you got, oh

MIKE Now, are there any more passengers for St John's, Birr, Elginfield, Lucan, Finnegan's Corners, Mooretown, Exeter, and even Crediton.

He has been outside for a quarter of this; we hear his voice again outside and nearly the whole chorus eventually decide to follow the hypnotic elegance. Left now are only a maidservant (MAGGIE) and the FAT LADY.

MIKE Now leaving the City Hotel—the Opposition Stage.

MAGGIE Cousin Patrick, do me a pleasant thing and allow me to take the Opposition Stage out of town. They'll be put out with me I'm late to serve dinner.

In a necessary manoeuvre we can't see, the Donnelly Stage goes around the hotel, so that it circles the barroom and MAGGIE follows it inside in a circular, birdlike, trapped motion.

FINNEGAN Your father says, Maggie, you're to have no truck with the Donnellys, shun them and if you get on with them I'll drag you off of—I'll tell your father, miss.

MAGGIE No need to, Patrick Finnegan, I'll do that myself *pause, wavering* Some day. Well how long do I have to wait then, for the sake of heaven?

FINNEGAN How do I know, the blacksmith made no—but I swear I'll get them, for it's only them would do a trick like that, loosen my wheels *runs outside* I'll snuff them . . .

FAT LADY Maggie Donovan I'd wait a week, a year not to have to take that blackguard Donnelly's wagon. I'd walk up to Biddulph on my bare knees rather than use their coach.

MAGGIE Would you now.

FAT LADY Why girl, it's them and their mother cheated us out of half the farm that should've been ours. Don't you know how their old woman put a spell on my cows so they bear freemartens and my daughter is barren. Have you no ears?

FINNEGAN The wheels are back on, Maggie. We'll catch up to them. At Holy Corners. Why yes, why won't we. He's got the weight of all my passengers—

MAGGIE And you've got the weight of only one of his—Here comes Finnegan! Tootletee too!

FINNEGAN Onto the stage, girl. Don't you dare make mock of me.

MAGGIE I won't go. *FAT LADY & FINNEGAN chase her all over the barroom until he picks her up in his arms and carries her out.*

FINNEGAN Well, you will. You will even if I have to hitch you to the wagon and drag you to Lucan. *horn* The stage for Lucan, the Favourite Line. Here comes Finnegan. Aroint thee, ye jades, I'm after you, Donnelly.

Whip sounds &c., but also MAGGIE laughing. In the fading light the BARTENDER with his skullish face listens & thinks. He comes towards us and actors with tollgates mime the flow of the road against him.

BARTENDER Finnegan's stage and Donnelly's stage goes north on the road that goes north from here through crossroads and tollgates and Lucan until the road is outside the parsonage of the English priest.

The barroom clock strikes six. A decisive lady at the top of her youth, MISS MAGUIRE enters & rings a servant bell. She has managed the parsonage for her father ever since her mother's death ten years ago.

MAGGIE You rang, m'am.

MISS MAGUIRE That chamberpot needs emptying. Yes, I did ring and I have been ringing to no avail until now why?

MAGGIE Oh, Miss Maguire, the wheels fell off my cousin Patrick's stage.

MISS MAGUIRE   Very nice that must have been, was anybody hurt, were you?

MAGGIE   Not enough to mention, m'am.

MISS MAGUIRE   Your being so late puts me in half a mind to say you cannot go to vespers, but I suppose the priest would denounce me from the pulpit if I did so, could you finish up this room and be at the door till Mr Stub calls.

MAGGIE   Yes m'am.

MISS MAGUIRE   And did you leave the silk thread in your basket?

MAGGIE   Oh thank you, Miss Maguire, I was so afraid you'd keep me in for being late, just dump the basket out and you'll find the thread, never mind my things.

She goes out with the chamberpot; MISS MAGUIRE looks into the basket. Offstage we hear: "Good evening, Mr Stub. The upstairs drawing room, if you please sir." The REVEREND MAGUIRE enters first; an old, snowy vicar.

DR MAGUIRE   Daughter?

MISS MAGUIRE   Father? Mr Stub is coming to see me tonight.

DR MAGUIRE   Then I shall drop in later, Mercilla I've no intention of ruining your tête à tête with the foremost merchant of Main Street.

MISS MAGUIRE   Are you composing your sermon? I shall tell him that is why you are absent. I suppose you are wondering what I am doing in the maid-servant's basket.

DR MAGUIRE   Did she give you permission to rumple it out like that?

MISS MAGUIRE   Oh yes. You're always worrying about the servants, Father.

DR MAGUIRE   We are servants too, you know. Mercilla.   *He fades away.*

MAGGIE   *still with chamberpot*   Mr Stub to see you, m'am.

GEORGE STUB   *with nosegay for MERCILLA*   Good evening, Mercilla.

MISS MAGUIRE   Thank you, Mr Stub. I'd ask Maggie here to put these in some water in a vase, but I'm terrified what she might do. So. Do please be seated, Father is busy in his study with next Sunday's sermon, I'm finding the silk thread for the banner you're having me mend and so—what else?

GEORGE   I've bought the land for a house on what the villagers call Quality Hill.

MISS MAGUIRE   Is it going to be what size of a house, George Stub?

GEORGE   I want you to decide how big it should be, Mercilla.

MISS MAGUIRE   Because I'm to be the mistress of it, is that it?

GEORGE   *sweating*   Yes.

MISS MAGUIRE   And you're not married to someone else already?

GEORGE   I've been alone in my bed for a year & a half now, Mercilla.

MISS MAGUIRE   What a way you have of putting things. Why I've been alone in my bed ever since I was born. Well, seeing it's your second marriage and I'm older too than is usual, I feel that I ought to put some things in your way.

GEORGE   In my way?

MISS MAGUIRE   Yes, because I needn't get married. So—make it worth my while.

GEORGE   I've already mentioned the house I'm building.

MISS MAGUIRE   Glad you did because I'd not come to live above an old hardware store. Now, here are the rules. After all I'm mending your silly old Masonic banner for you, you do some promising for me.

GEORGE   Mercilla.

MISS MAGUIRE   Who are you anyway?

GEORGE   I've been a self made man. You know what a great thing I've made of the store, and I'm—

MISS MAGUIRE   One of the rules I might make tonight is that I expect the man I marry to be somebody, really somebody, like a Member of Parliament. What about that George?

GEORGE   It'll never come to pass. I'm far better behind the scenes. I get too excited in public.

MISS MAGUIRE   Didn't I hear you say once that you'd been promised a senatorship if you could get a Conservative candidate in in this riding?

GEORGE   Yes.

MISS MAGUIRE   Then that's the rules. It's some day to be Senator Stub, or else. I have depths of meanness, George. Don't ruffle them.

GEORGE   If I promise to obey the rules, I want things to be clearer.

MISS MAGUIRE   You mean when? I'll think it over tonight after you'll be gone.

GEORGE   I'd like something on—all this.

MISS MAGUIRE   Something on account. Here take my hand.

GEORGE   No.

MISS MAGUIRE   Oh, my mouth. Here, stop me from talking so much.

Her father enters.

MISS MAGUIRE   Remember sir, I am no widow. You may be a hot blooded widower, but my father has kept me in his parsonage, a chaste spinster, for many more years than Jacob served Laban for both Leah and Rachel. And I haven't minded that a bit.

GEORGE   Good evening, Doctor Maguire. It is a pleasure to see you looking so well.

DR MAGUIRE   Mr George Stub. How many faces of the poor did you grind in the main street of Lucan today?

GEORGE   Business is business, Doctor Maguire. I have to foreclose and get my money back sometimes twice in a month.

MISS MAGUIRE   Look what treasures I'm finding in the girl's basket. What are these strange lumps of metal, George, and here's a locket.   *a small bell rings*   Father, Maggie said I could "dump the basket out."

DR MAGUIRE   I don't think she meant you to open her locket.

MISS MAGUIRE   *tempted and walking about the room*   It's the one she's always wearing and she's had the catch fixed by a jeweller in town, why not here in Lucan, ah—George, open it for me.

GEORGE   These are the nuts off the axles of a wagon. Her father must have given her a list of things to bring him home on the farm out there. And this—I hate to tell tales on your servant girl, Doctor Maguire, but this is a picture of William Donnelly, William Donnelly Cripple.

DR MAGUIRE   Is there no other name you can call him then?

GEORGE   No, sir. I'll never call him anything else but that. He and his gang of cutthroats are one of the reasons that this riding often does not return a Conservative candidate.

MISS MAGUIRE   But George, he's devilishly handsome.

DR MAGUIRE   Mr George Stub, if I may venture an opinion in the face of your prejudice, I think he has a very sharp intelligent face. So that is Maggie's secret. Do you know I was asked to officiate at his brother Patrick's wedding not so long ago.

GEORGE   You would have met the whole monstrous family then.

DR MAGUIRE   Monstrous, not at all. They were a very handsome, unusual family with a—as if there was something there they weren't telling you. I disagree with you totally, Mr Stub, and here's the text for my sermon. Four wheels!   *picking up the nuts*   Now as I behold the living creatures, behold one wheel upon the earth by the living creatures, with his four faces. The appearance of the wheels and their work was like unto the colour of a beryl. . . .

GEORGE   Mercilla, I must leave. Please show me down.

MISS MAGUIRE   Follow me, Mr Stub. Father, George Stub is leaving, oh it is no use when he starts quoting scripture, no use at all.

They leave. As he goes on quoting from the Bible (Ezekiel I) he juggles the four nuts.

DR MAGUIRE   And they four had one likeness; and their appearance & their work was as it were upon a wheel in the middle of a wheel. When they went, they went upon their four sides; and they turned not when they went.

MAGGIE enters with a cup of tea. She collects the nuts, the locket, and begins to work at the banner with the coloured thread.

MAGGIE   Miss Maguire suggests, sir, that you take a drink of this camomile tea to calm your nerves. I have lit the lamp in your bedroom and changed your pillow case.

DR MAGUIRE   Ah, I have frightened him away. The Bible is a great help in getting me rid of people I don't like.

MAGGIE   Mr Stub is no angel of mercy, sir, but your daughter has to have some sort of life. Surely you don't expect her to be cooped up here in the parsonage by the river on this lonely stretch of the road all her livelong days.

DR MAGUIRE   I know what I know. He's the worst of a whole set of flinty hearted shopkeepers, just because my daughter comes from what he knows as an old family he wants her to be the lady in his new big house. You mark my words he'll call it Castle Stub—

MERCILLA enters and calmly slides into her father's flow.

MISS MAGUIRE   George Stub is not going to call his new place Castle Stub, Father. He's going to call it after me—Castle Mercilla, that is, if I marry him. Take heart, Father, I've put so many obstacles in his way.

DR MAGUIRE   The best obstacle is a firm "No." You've no idea what his set, the five families that consider themselves the aristocracy of the village, look like from the pulpit. I once dreamt their pale marble faces turned into sheep and I walked around with my crook—   *on his way to bed*   —until this exquisite pain around my ankles made me look down. There was George Stub, the biggest ram of them all, gnawing away at my leg. Blood.

MISS MAGUIRE   *also retiring*   Good night, Father. Maggie, clear up the teacups. Goodnight, I shan't get up for breakfast, nervous exhaustion, nervous *repeat this last phrase ad libato*

CHORUS   *singing*
Oh St Patrick was a gentleman
Who came of decent people
He built a church in Dublin town
And on it put a steeple . . .
No wonder that those Irish Lads
Should be so gay and frisky
For sure St Pat he taught them that
As well as making whisky . . .

MAGGIE clears the chairs of the previous scene, but leaves the Masonic banner MERCILLA has been mending in the centre of the floor; as members of the CHORUS light candles and kneel by their chairs we are changing from MAGGIE as a servant with a cap to MAGGIE remembering a world of power and love that might have been hers forever.

MAGGIE   As I go to my bed over the kitchen of the parsonage I think I see in the moonlight on the floor—a letter, an envelope coming up through the floor, but it is my sleepy brain remembering what many people would regard as a—the strange thing that happened to me in the church tonight at vespers. *The Vespers service in the background. There are other kneelers.*   Will Donnelly crawls under the floor of the church, the old wooden frame church, and he as I kneel is pushing the letter up to me through the cracks in the floor. My father and brother are so against me seeing him that it is only by letter or accident we can meet.

WILL   *lying down*   I sent her my picture which she had cut out to be placed in a locket.

MAGGIE   And I in turn pushed a letter down through the crack in the floor. *A letter comes down from above into WILLIAM's hand.*   I address you with these few lines hoping they will find you in good health as they leave me enjoying the same blessing at present. I thank you for your picture. Until my next birthday you will understand why I cannot wear it in public. Dear William, I was a long time about getting this picture for you. You can keep it now in hopes you think as much of me as I do of you.

WILL   In my next letter which she burnt to save it from their attention I proposed marriage and on April the 30th, 1873, my girl replied

MAGGIE   I now wish to inform you that I have made up my mind to accept your kind offer, as there is no person in this world I sincerely love but you. This is my first & only secret, so I hope you will let no person know about it. But I cannot mention any certain time yet.

They start rolling on the floor towards each other; this ends up with their standing back to back or kneeling back to back or with the banner veil between them. The rolling might be right over each other, but never so that their bodies coincide.

WILL   In our dreams we did this & wore the lockets although she was afraid to wear hers in the daylight.

MAGGIE   At night I am your wife; in the daytime I drudge for a woman who does not know whether she wants to be married or no. But although my hair is bound up for you and you alone to let down, Will, make no mistake, there was always something between us that summer—a fence, a veil, a muzzle on him, a wall about me, a floor between us. But I cannot mention any certain time yet. You can acquaint my parents about it any time you wish after the first of November next.

WILL fiddles. Since his letters are lost, we hear him play chords & enharmonics instead.

MAGGIE   Do not think that I would say you are soft for writing so often, for there is nothing would give me greater pleasure than to hear from you, but no matter now. I think soft turns is very scarce about you.

WILL fiddles.

MAGGIE   No, Will. Those who told you that I said I could never marry a lame boy are liars. If you have ever heard anything of the kind after me and it has given you pain, ask yourself if I have ever wanted that for you. If it does not suit you to wait so long, let me know about it, and I will make it all right.

WILL   You'll never know, Maggie, how much it's not like me to talk to a woman about that. Because my foot's deformed they think he's not a man. They'd laugh if they knew I write you a letter every day. But, Maggie, they'll come at you about the foot and what can you tell them? Why that he's not a cripple when he's on horseback, nor is he a thing soft when he has a pistol in his hand which makes all men equally tall;   *fiddles*   nor am I a Cripple when I'm driving or writing or riding I'm—our stage is a bird with wheels for wings and I'm free.

And the scene changes to early morning in Lucan with the two rival stages getting ready for the daily race to London. The convention for the stage wagons should involve at least one wheel each and a solid block of actors "inside" the coach; other actors are the sides of the road and move against the coaches to give the illusion of a journey; a sleepy TOLLGATE MAN with his gate is the first of a series of such gates which will keep stopping the stages as they gallop down to London. The drivers hitch up horses and check wheels and parcels; passengers.

CHORUS   The Opposition Stage

NED BROOKS   The Finnegan Stage. My name is Ed Brooks from Exeter. First carefully checking the wheels of my stage with a wrench I climb up determined to beat Donnelly this day, to beat him in the race to London even if it kills me.

A red haired boy makes his first appearance: TOM RYAN.

MIKE   Tom Ryan, you can't come with us today. You should be at home in your father's house. Why you've been sleeping all night in Pilot's manger lad, are you stage struck?

TOM   Mike Donnelly, ask your brother if I can go with yous again today. My old man won't let any of us come near the place right now and I watched the stable for you all night, Mike?

WILL   Mike, where's the bridle for the off-horse—Ploughboy. Tom Ryan, they sneaked that away on you when you were sleeping—sure you can come, but go up the street and get us a new bridle. Knock on the shutters till they open up. You don't want him along, do you Mike, is that it?

MIKE   It's his father I'm thinking of. "The Donnellys've stolen my only son away from me, work him to death on their stage line."

WILL   Pilot's shoe is loose, Manilla then. I'll let you drive her then, see if you can control her, my arms were out of their sockets the last time she's such a puller.   *Horn sounds.*   *TOM runs up with the new bridle.*

MIKE   Ah, but we're having a race today I see so maybe I won't hold him in.   *The Finnegan horn blows.*   Here comes Finnegan. Put those packages with me, Will. Haw, Ploughboy. Easy does it, Manilla, there girl, there . . .

CHORUS
Out from the yard of Levitt's Hotel
The Main Street of Lucan all quiet and still
Down the road between Goderich & London

The TOLLGATE KEEPER reaches up a cup on a stick; we hear seven pennies.

WILL   Down with that tollgate, Let us out of Lucan
Thank you, Mr. Kelly.

MIKE   Yes, we hope to surpass him
We'll win your wager,

CHORUS
a spark in each window,
people getting up

TOM   Mike Donnelly, I think the coach is a boat.

MIKE   Tom Ryan, it has wheels. Sit into the seat and you can feel the road coming up against our wheels. It's no boat you truant. Where's the sails?

TOM   I've heard Will call it a boat once and I see the sea all around us. Somehow I feel like jumping off into the water.

MIKE   Did you hear that, Will? On the way back we're putting you in a trunk for safety's sake and our own peace of mind. Where'd you buy the bridle, Tom?

TOM   At Mr Stub's store.

MIKE   Well, Will, do we turn back?

WILL   For a penny I would. That was a foolish thing to do, Tom. Don't you know who our enemies are yet? We'll take it off at Birr, the blacksmith will

have one there and, Tom, tonight you must take it back to Mr Stub and tell him it was a mistake.

TOM   Why was it a mistake?

MIKE   Because we never buy anything from Mr Stub and as you charged the bridle that means he'll be after us for a debt.

CHORUS
So early in the morning, shadows aren't yet and stars still out.
The big elm, St Patrick's, the taverns at Elginfield.

MIKE   Open up Mr. Scandrett, Let us out of Biddulph.

This chorus has several "tracks" and ribbons of sound and imagery rippling through it; there's an old doggerel song about the road; there's also a quiet voice naming the concession roads whose numbers get smaller as we get closer to London.

CHORUS
                                        concession 16
Proof Line Road straight down to London
Down the hill, whizzing down, down into the hollow
Rain in our faces, up the hill.

Two stages converge on one passenger.

FINNEGAN COACH   That's our passenger.

DONNELLY COACH   No, she's ours.

WOMAN   But I'm a Finnegan customer

MIKE   Too late now, ma'm, and we can't stop for we're in competition and—whree whurrah!! we're ahead of you now, Finnegan!

CHORUS
                                        concession 15
Proof Line Road straight down to London!
Sun's up. Travellers to where we come from
Gallop up to meet us. Up the hill down the hill
The four tavern corners. Holy Corners!   *singing*
The taverns they lined each side of the way.
As thick as the milestones in Ireland today.
And then the farmers all thought it was fine
If they once got as far as the London Proof Line.
                                        concession 14
Up to then any man that went for a load
                                        concession 13
Generally spent two days on the road;
                                        concession 12
And I hear that Sam Berryhill says to this day
That some took three—when he kept the Bluejay!
                                        concession 11

MIKE   Gate, Mr Walden, why so slow. Wait a minute, how'd he get through the check gate so fast

WILL   If he gets a pass, we get a pass. That's not fair.

CHORUS
          concession 8
Montgomery House, there, the bar goes east and west!

concession 6
Monaghan's, Talbot's—both bakes bread and brews beer.
concession 5
Up the hill, cross the creek, down the hill to the
concession 4
River valley: McMartin's and the last tollgate

TOM   Let us into London, Mr Murrow

CHORUS
                                    & over the river
concession 2
Past the mill, tree branch shadow, up Mount Hope
The Convent of the Sacred Heart

DONNELLY COACH
                    concession 1
We're turning out to pass him, he's going faster, watch yourself, Brooks, your front wheel, He's fallen down on his head. Horses run away. On his head. The front wheel came off.
At one end of our journey, we'll stop for a while
Watch your step, sir. Take my hand, m'am.
At the City Hotel. No, the Dead House for him.

In the conventions worked out for this accident, BROOKS should be held upside down so that his words come from an overturned face. CHORUS might try some upside down speech too.

MIKE   Oh for God's sake, Will, he's dying. Don't try to talk, Ned, we'll put you in our stage and take you to a physician. *Pause.* He wants to talk to you, Will.

BROOKS   I got the other one to come over just when life comes to the edge-place where you can see for ever and ever because you're neither alive nor are you dead. I said, Bill Donnelly, you done this to me and my wife and little ones will curse you and I'll tell you how your brother Mike's going to die. Fair play, neighbour. They'll never finish scrubbing up his blood. My God, neighbour, I'm gone. They'll never finish scrubbing up his blood.

His body is carried away and laid on the bar.

MIKE   What did he tell you, Will.

WILL   Nothing. Nothing that matters, Mike.

MIKE   Look at them looking at us. They all think we killed him.

WILL   Yes, Mike. Now how did we kill him? He tightened his wheel at Lucan, but still we managed. Maybe at Swartz's Hotel, or maybe at the Montgomery House at the eighth concession?

MIKE   Will. I don't want to drive stage anymore.

WILL   Why?

MIKE   Odd how there is always something happening when we're by. *Pause.* So how did his wheel come off then?

WILL   Get your head up, my brother. My brother what does it matter whether we killed him or Fortune did. We might just as well have, for they blame us anyhow. Get your head up and we'll turn and face them.

MIKE   The boy, did you get him to do it?

WILL   *with irony* Oh Yes! And Mike. I also got our father to train our horses so well that when Brooks' passenger that was riding beside him fell directly in front of us you were able to stop those horses on a penny, or he'd been cut to pieces instead of standing over there gawping at the Donnelly brothers whose same father failed to train one of his sons still to hold up his head though all the world is thinking you should crawl.

MIKE's face clears; he holds up his head and they turn to face a crowd that is growling at them.

CHORUS   We the undersigned jurymen summoned upon the inquest held upon the body of Edward Brooks do hereby agree that deceased came to his death from injuries received by being thrown from the Exeter Stage which was caused by the forewheel of said stage coming off and that the deceased came by his death
                                    accidentally

This scene dissolves into a bakeshop where a BAKER proudly shows off a wedding cake to an APPRENTICE.

BAKER   Isn't that the lovely object now?

APPRENTICE   Who ordered this cake, Pa?

BAKER   Why it's for John Finnegan owns the store up at Irishtown, he sent down for it as there is some farmer getting his daughter married in the vicinity. Now what did you find out about delivery?

APPRENTICE   Went to the Western Hotel. They say there'll be no Finnegan Stage today, the driver fell off this morning and got himself killed. So they said to send it with the Donnelly Line—it's the best anyhow for moving a cake and they leave the City Hotel at 2 o'clock.

BAKER   By golly, we'll start packing it right away then. Get me some straw. You know I sort of hate to see it get wrapped up in a mere brown paper box.

A city bell rings twelve; a street fiddler plays "Buffalo Gals"; distant sounds. A penny in his cup. The CHORUS illustrate the shadows changing of the buildings near the City Hotel.

CHORUS
Shadows of the buildings and the trees along the white road
Disappear at noon.
Sun, you golden stage, make our shadows
Passengers again to night, now longer and longer in the stream
We all lie dreaming in

BAKER   What can I do for you, sir.

McKELLAR   I'm the new stage driver for Finnegan's stage and I've come to collect the cake his brother ordered here.

BAKER   Well, golly, now, we were led to believe that The Finnegan Stage wasn't running today. But we found a way to send the cake.

McKELLAR   What way?

BAKER   The Opposition Stage. They're real good at carrying cakes. I've had good reports from customers whereas you people seem to sit on them or—it's too late. They'll have left town by now. With the cake.

McKELLAR   Look you old gossoon, do you not know there's a war on between them and us? I'll catch up to them and I'll get that cake back.   *The BAKER and his BOY run out of the shop after the STAGE DRIVER in protest.*

Already simply set up: MAGGIE'S FATHER washing feet in the coal scuttle containing the block of ice; his sister & MAGGIE. Plus another aunt waiting to take MAGGIE away.

FAT LADY   Ever since you came home, Maggie, from service at the English priest's you're so slow in doing things. You was two hours I swear looking for these eggs. Take this switch and keep the flies off your father while I finish packing your trunk.

MAGGIE   Packing my trunk, is it. Where am I going then?

AUNT THERESA   Maggie, you're welcome to come back with me to Limerick and stay as long as you like where that fellow won't be bothering you.

MAGGIE   What fellow won't be bothering me?

FATHER   Cripple. Whoever was playing that fiddle under your window last night till all hours, whoever wrote me a lawyer's letter asking for your hand, who came to my door and took me by the beard to tell me how old you are.

MAGGIE   And how old am I? Am I not of age All Souls' Day, Father?

FATHER   I don't know, maybe you'd better call Father Brennan to look it up, in the baptismal register, have you? *Pause.* But All Souls' Day doesn't change the spots on Cripple, he's a Donnelly and no girl of mine's of age who's thinking of marrying that Cripple. I'd rather see you going to your grave.

MAGGIE   Father, if only you'd speak a little faster. Faster! What have you got against Will Donnelly, tell me now, Father, you've never told me. Is it the father killing the man at the bee?

FATHER   Keep switching the flies off of me, will you? It's evidence not fit for the ears of either a young girl or an old one. He's been the mastermind of a gang in this neighbourhood and fleeces of wool, post offices, derailing a train have been some of that gang's amusements for the last four years until now high and mighty he starts his own stage line.

FAT LADY   Brother, this girl'll never understand I'm afraid and it's a secret place we'll have to put such a girl. Her brother is getting married to the proper sort, but no she has to cross battle lines. Have you no gratitude for your upbringing, girl?

MAGGIE   All the money I've ever earned as a servant girl you've received, Father. I emptied chamberpots so you could buy two new cows. Yes, look at what my brother's marrying. All Mary Egan talks about is cows. Will Donnelly's the only young man around here with brains in his head who didn't go into the priesthood, and no girl is to take a look at him, is it?

AUNT THERESA   A fine priest that lame devil would have made.

FATHER   Theresa, see if Martin's got the cart hitched up. Maggie, you're right. Will is a clever boy. Clever at getting the forewheel of a stage to roll off so the driver gets killed. Yes. But he is a Donnelly and they are to be left alone. They don't dig with the right foot. They always are digging with the wrong foot. Since Cripple's threatening to come and kidnap her—yes Maggie—Theresa, tell Martin to drive over to Finnegan's Corners, but when it gets dark to turn & take her down to Gallagher's. That's right by the Donnellys and they'll never think of looking there.

MAGGIE   I'll run to him now. Will! Will! Come and rescue me, take me away.

She is pursued; there is a struggle and we see her next taken away tied in a net. We are now moving closer to FINNEGAN's store at Irishtown; first to a tollgate house where a bag of pennies is poured out for counting. The counting of the money into a tin box goes under the dialogue like the road itself.

MOTHER   Come, children, help your father count the take at the tollgate today. The shadows are getting so long they're joining together anymore travellers up or down the road, Sam?

The privy cleaner or CESSMAN comes towards us; he is whistling "Buffalo Gals."

TOLLMAN   Just foot travellers. There's that old fellow makes a living cleaning out privies. Good night there, you look dusty.

CESSMAN   Oh I doesn't mind the dust, thank thee, Mr. Scandrett.

CHILD   He always whistles the same tune doesn't he.

MOTHER   Heading north down into Biddulph. What was all that racket today with the second stage that went through.

The tollgate scene begins to move forward and dissolve.

TOLLMAN They were chasing the Donnelly Stage. The Donnellys got away on them with something. A cake. A wedding cake.

We are in FINNEGAN's store up at Finnegan's Corners.

FINNEGAN No Donnellys are allowed on Finnegan premises ever again no, neither his store nor his tavern nor his very privy.

MIKE Even so, Mr. Finnegan, an express parcel from the Forest City Confectionery on Horton Street. Where shall I set it down?

FINNEGAN I said get out, Mike Donnelly.

MIKE Now, now, Mr. Finnegan, I do believe it is a cake. I'll just set it down on the floor here and that will be Cash on Delivery two dollars, twenty-seven and a half cents.

FINNEGAN Don't you dare tell me it had to be by your line that cake come, when I've got my own stage line, now get that bloody parcel out of here.

MIKE Well, it is a puzzle but the upshot of it was that our Opposition Stage was preferred. Twenty-seven and a half cents plus two dollars. Careful, Finnegan, it's a cake.

FINNEGAN Is it now, well it's a *He kicks it around the shop.*

MIKE I see how it is, Mr Finnegan. We have to pay for the cake, do we. You should know all about that, you're the bailiff of the Division Court up here, and another thing before I say Goodnight— don't take any more passengers to Crediton. We bought the rights there, you have not got them. Good evening, Mr. Finnegan.

FINNEGAN backs him out of the store with a gun. BILL & MARY DONOVAN come forward behind the dissolving FINNEGAN with a quilt which is their wedding bed.

BILL Come to bed, Mary. I'm told it's our wedding night.

MARY Well, you're the boss now, but it did just cross my mind.

BILL What crossed your mind?

MAGGIE'S FATHER is quietly washing his feet in the tub WILLIAM DONNELLY put the ice block in.

MARY Did you never hear of the custom of leaving the bride alone for three nights.

BILL Yes, I have, now why don't you get into the bed?

MARY It did just cross my mind that—they'll come looking here for Maggie.

BILL *yawning* Who'll come looking—

MARY Bill Donnelly and his gang.

BILL Well, they won't find her. She was in the cellar during the wedding, but she's crying in the garret at Gallagher's now. Father keeps moving her, and Will Donnelly just keeps missing her. You should of seen the letter he wrote Pa.

WILL Dear friend, my sole business last night (yes, I was in the crowd myself) was to have satisfaction for some of your mean low talk to your daughter that never deserved it. I want you to understand, dear sir, that I will have my revenge. You or your son will be prepared to receive me and my Adventurers before long again, and if old friend I want it impressed on your mind that if the business must be done on the way to church I can get any amount of men to do it so you may just as well stop getting yourself into trouble first or last.

MARY Sending his gang of scoundrels into your father's house and pretending it was a tavern and them constables was searching for a horse-thief when all the time it's Maggie they want.

BILL So come on then.

MARY Is she never to be married off then, or what is to be done with her?

BILL She'll either marry one of the Gallagher boys who's soft on her by next Saturday, or then it's Lent and it's too late to get married so I think Father plans to let the Sisters take care of her. If I were her—

MARY *getting into bed* Good, then this nonsense will be over. Galloping around the countryside trying to kidnap your lovely sister because he loves her. She doesn't really love that Cripple, does she?

BILL Mary, she does love him, and I don't blame her for it. I do blame her for not making a run for it, but I suppose she can't.

MARY Oh a woman can never do that. The man would never marry her then. How can you say she could really love him?

BILL Mary, she does. If ever I saw love. Not like us. Your mother and my father put us together like a pair of cattle.

Shivaree* serenaders gather in the shadows.

MARY Speaking of cows, Bill Donovan, what sort is your cows?

BILL Don't you like my cows?

MARY I never saw such miserable calves as them two you had in the yard today. Maybe it's late they were

BILL Cows, Mary, always cows.

MARY That's how the Egans and the Trehys got where they are now. Cows

---

*shivaree—a raucous mock-welcome for newlyweds.

BILL   And where might that be now?

MARY   Why I think one of them's in bed with a young bull, or is that not what you think you are sir?

BILL   Ah, Mary

MARY   Take it back then that your sister really loves Will Donnelly, that cripple and devil.

BILL   She never loves him, I was wrong, it's a lie.

MARY   That's better now— *knocking* Hark! There's somebody going to shivaree us.

VOICES   Shivaree!

MARY   Get them to go away. Give them some whiskey, Mother of God, it is the Donnellys, Bill.

MIKE   Tell us where Maggie is and we'll go away.

BILL   *at window*   Boys, she's not here now and if she were she'd say to leave her alone.

MIKE   Oh no you don't. We got a letter here from Maggie. She says she's being held against her will and to come and get her.

BILL   Mary, shall I tell them she's at Gallagher's and get them off our backs?

MARY   *running and stopping his mouth at the window*   You tell them where your sister's hidden & I'll withhold bed privileges. I'll ask for my dower third of the farm back and my red cow with the white ear back.

BILL   She's not here you blackguards. Off with you, Bill Donnelly.

Silence. Husband & wife return to bed. Then a blast of sound. Choose from buzzsaw sounds, guns firing, drums, horns, fiddles, maskers, circle of dancers around a bonfire, maskers entering bridal chamber and lifting up MARY.

MASKER   We found Maggie, Bill. She was under her brother's bed all the time. Is this her, Bill? Quick, for God's sakes, we can hardly lift her off the floor.

WILL'S VOICE   No, that's not Maggie, that's too fat for Maggie. That's probably Mary.

BILL & MARY crouch as the sounds melt into the newspaper's account.

MARY   Mother of God, there goes the chimney.

CHORUS
RURAL ROUGHS ON RAMPAGE
ATTEMPTED ABDUCTION IN BIDDULPH

MAGGIE   *in lay sister's working costume, with attendant nun*   I wasn't there of course. I was too much in love to unravel their cunning, and so—we lost sight of each other.

CHORUS
THE BIDDULPH   DISGRACEFUL
KU KLUX   CONDUCT OF
                      LOVE-SICK SWAIN

Newspaper boy, "extra, read all about it," bulletin readers in front of newspaper office, &c.

CHORUS
HOW HE WENT ABOUT IT
AND HOW HE FAILED TO SUCCEED

MAGGIE   And a needless enemy was my brother who before had been our ally as much as he dared, but after the serenade

BILL   Except to say hello I don't speak to that man. Speak to Will Donnelly—no, and Mary and me have the very next farm to the Donnelly place now, no, William Donnelly, no. No.

CHORUS
THE MIDDLE AGES REVIVED
LOVE'S LABOUR LOST EVIDENTLY

WILL   *with whip*   Read that cheap newspaper heading again.

CHORUS   THE MIDDLE AGES REVIVED

WILL   That's enough, thank you. Middle Ages Revived by whom? Me or them? We were hauled up in court, but I got off I suppose because Maggie had asked us to take her away. My God, I was never to see her again. And I'm not in the least sorry I tried to steal her away if that's what you call a life for a woman.   *to MAGGIE'S FATHER who is in bare feet at the tub*   And I'm not in the least sorry for any thing that happens from now on in that happens to those who try the same trick on me as you pulled on that girl that was once my sweetheart. I'll switch the flies off you you old fool.

He has taken MAGGIE'S FATHER up & is about to whip him, but then throws him down & chases him out of the theatre or attacks his feet with a toy whip & spins him out of the room.

HALF CHORUS   Question. The Convent of the Sacred Heart   *Sung; "incense" music as before.*
At Mount Hope on Richmond Street, why does the Opposition Stage always slow down?

HALF CHORUS   Answer. Oh I can answer that. When Will Donnelly is the driver

MAGGIE   He senses that I am drudging here in the kitchen of the Sisters' house. And when he is not the driver he has told the others to slow down at the chestnut tree because he knows that I wait each day for the sound. In the morning, in the evening— down the hill, past the mill and over Brough's Bridge until you can't hear the wheels or the hooves anymore. You hear the other stage. You hear your own heart. I scrub the stones of the convent yard as close to the gate as I can, but it is no use—the gate is locked. Someday, in the middle of the night, there will come such a knocking at that gate and it will be smashed open, and the nuns will run hither and thither screeching because my husband has come for me and in my wedding dress I will enter his coach to drive up his road forever. I love William Donnelly.

As MAGGIE lies dead before them, the MOTHER SUPERIOR confers with the sisters as to where she should be buried.

NUN   Mother Superior Finnegan, Maggie Donovan is dead. What shall we do with her?   *They kneel.*

MOTHER   What were the last words she said, Sister Feeny?

NUN   Her last words were

MAGGIE & NUN   I love William Donnelly.

MOTHER   Sister Feeny, where do you think she should be buried.

NUN   *pause, then crisply and swiftly*   By William Donnelly's grave up in Biddulph.

MOTHER   Sister Gallagher?

NUN   In the convent yard where the rest of us lie.

MOTHER   Sister Egan?

NUN   In the convent yard, Mother Superior, but close by the gate.

MOTHER   And that is where Maggie Donovan lies buried.

MAGGIE   I love William Donnelly.

WILLIAM DONNELLY sings a verse of "Buffalo Gals."

WILL
I asked her if she'd be my wife
Be my wife, be my wife
She'd make me happy all my life
If she stood by my side

CHORUS   End of Act One.

ACT TWO

Actors spin tops, dance, recite poems, until this recitation of poems slowly fades into TOM RYAN standing up on the bar and letting us see the story from a new angle.

TOM RYAN   And I'll recite you a poem I learnt once at school while we're waiting for the two o'clock stage to Lucan which I may have the honour of driving, young though I am, since the Donnelly boys have to put in a appearance in court.

Waiting for Pa

Three little forms in the twilight grey
Scanning the shadows across the way:
Six little eyes, four black, two blue,
Brimful of love and happiness too,
Watching for Pa

Soon joyous shouts from the window-seat
And eager patter of childish feet
Gay musical chimes ring through the hall
A manly voice responds to the call
"Welcome papa!"

The actor playing NED RYAN, TOM's father, now proceeds to growl drunkenly.

TOM RYAN   Well ladies and gentlemen, my home life wasn't like that quite, and since I'm said to be one of the reasons for the Donnelly Tragedy, you don't understand me unless you understand what waiting for my Pa was like. Tom Ryan is my name, this is my Pa, here's my Ma and a couple of my sisters. What are we doing? We are all waiting one cold winter morning for Pa—to get his rump off a chest that contains bread, cheese, tea and other necessaries of life which he refuses to let us have

TOM RYAN starts to saw a rail.

NED RYAN   They might cook it and poison me.

TOM RYAN   It's a cold day outside, but there's no fire in the stove because—

NED   You're ruining me with all this wasting of my substance. Stop the sawing, Tom stop sawing that rail! or I'll take this ax to you.

MRS RYAN   It isn't enough to be starving but we must freeze to death as well.

NED   Tell your son to stop sawing that rail and to clear out of here.   *starting to give chase*

TOM   Oh I admit I was pert and I should have stopped sawing, but I couldn't sit there and see my sisters and my mother shivering much longer.

NED   Get out of the house you bastard brat, talking back to your pa.

TOM   Don't hit me Pa. I was only. I will go and I will never come back, and I stepped out onto the road and looked in the snow for somebody to take me in: Who will take in the barefoot Ryan Boy?

The actors set up the Roman Line gamut of Part One as the road he will run up and down.*

Barry?	Trehy?	
Feeny?	O'Halloran?	*He is rejected by*
Cahill?	Cassleigh?	*everyone in*
McCann?	Flynn?	*various ways:*
Egan?	Marksy?	*backs turned,*
Quinn?	Farl?	*clubs, kicks &c.*
Gallagher?	Duffy?	
Clancy?	Donovan?	

Bell and jug sound for the tavern and the church; then MRS DONNELLY comes towards the rejected boy and accepts him.

MRS DONNELLY   Donnelly.

We see her at the end of a corridor of people. We renew her acquaintance now.

CHORUS   Yes, the Donnellys took him in.

JAMES DONNELLY, the Younger, sitting invalid in a chair by the stove should also register here. His mother has just finished giving him medicine.

MRS DONNELLY   Tom Ryan, climb up on the stove there and stop your shivering till I get these dry feet on you; here's a pair of Tom's pants to put on those you got on are drenched, what devil has your father got into that he drives you out barefoot in this weather or was there a reason, Tom?

TOM   I was only sawing a rail, Mrs Donnelly, to get a fire on so we would be warm.

MRS DONNELLY   Get behind the stove now and hide in the woodbox, your father I can see in the lid of my tea kettle coming in our gate. Can you not get the key to the pantry away from him while he's asleep?

TOM   He sleeps with it tied round his leg, Mrs Donnelly.

MRS DONNELLY   Well there are four of you and one of him, he's no giant, give him a clout and get the key some fine day Good day to you, Ned Ryan?

TOM   But he's always got the ax.

NED   Good morning, Mrs Donnelly. Have you seen my madcap, scapegrace harum scarum son Tom about?

MRS DONNELLY   No madcap, scapegrace, harum scarum son of yours has run in here, Ned Ryan.

NED   Then I just heard your stove say something about an ax.

---

*the Roman Line gamut of Part One—In Sticks & Stones Reaney frequently shows the Donnellys caught between the lines of their Catholic neighbours, two parallel rows of actors "like the line-up of a reel."

MRS DONNELLY   My stove talks a lot to itself, Ned Ryan, what with the kettle getting up steam and the wood crackling inside and the wind in the chimney. Do you not see my stove has a name? She's called Princess and she just saw the ax you're holding in your hand. I'd have said something myself at the strangeness of a father with an ax in his hand.

He backs up and slides off; MRS DONNELLY returns to sewing. TOM gets up on top of the stove (bar) and continues.

TOM   Pretty soon, he'd drag me back home again and say he'd try to be decent to us, but it didn't last and as I grew older if I could I helped the Donnelly boys with their stage, and if I couldn't I stayed home and caused trouble. Like—I set fire to the barn once with him—Pa—in it, he barely got out in time and he thought it was lightning, and I pissed in his whiskey after drinking half of it, oh my God was he mad at me.   *Violin screech—a poltergeist bottle flies through the air, disappears and we hear it smash.*   Yes, I can make things like that happen if I don't abuse myself for a month. It's like having a fit and I can will it that I'm going to have a fit. One day I asked my mother if it was true I had been born. And she said

MOTHER   Yes, Tom Ryan, you were born.

He starts to pack a carpet bag.

NED   And where might you be going, great high and mighty one with your clothes barely covering your thin little parsnip of a rump and your hair like a snipe's nest on fire, oh little runt of mine.

TOM   My mother here tells me it's St Bridget's Eve and tomorrow I'm old enough so I'm leaving forever.

MRS RYAN   Oh son, where will you stay?

TOM   *pause*   Donnellys.

MRS RYAN   Could you not pick a better place than that den of everything wicked.

TOM   If you want to know Mother, there's love there.

NED   Your poor father over here, Tom. Will you not give him a look, will you shame him before all our neighbours?

TOM   I'm not going to hang around here anymore and hear you say mean low things to my mother.

MRS RYAN   Would you live with people whose sons tried to carry a poor girl off, Tom?

TOM   Yes, because she wanted to be carried off from a house that was worse than this.

MRS RYAN   Could you not get a job in the town building the new lunatic hospital they're putting up?

TOM starts his speech now and walks into the GEORGE STUB scene.

NED It's into the lunatic hospital he should be going. *growling*

TOM But of course the first thing I did to the Donnellys was to bring them trouble in the shape of the bridle I bought for them on tick at Mr Stub's store.

STUB Tom Ryan, lad, just ask your boss William Donnelly, gentleman, when in the name of Heaven is he going to pay for the bridle you tapped on my shutters for last summer?

TOM Mr Stub, it was a mistake, and we brought it back.

STUB I know that, lad, but I didn't accept the return, it's used and I want my money.

TOM We paid for the use.

STUB Not by agreement, that's not the way I do business but I tell you, lad, I'm suing William Donnelly, gentleman, in Division Court next Tuesday so be warned.

TOM Aw, sue away. We'll never pay you for it, you old skinflint. But he kept summoning Mr Donnelly, sending summonses and we just wiped our ass with them. I used to ride up and down on the stage, they gave me a cap to wear. There was another lad hung around the Donnellys a lot—Will Farl. Some of the people were shocked that he got on with the Donnellys so well.

The two boys crouch by the Donnelly stove; MRS DONNELLY is sewing while JAMES DONNELLY JR sleeps in a rocking chair.

WILL FARL Why aren't you sitting still, Tom, does your shirt itch you?

TOM Old man beat me last night, my back's all welted up.

MRS DONNELLY Tom Ryan and Will Farl, what were we talking about just now—yes, you say that you'll help my sons against their enemies, what kind of help do my sons need against what kind of enemies?

TOM Oh—help.

MRS DONNELLY Wouldn't it be wise to consult us first before you go helping. *train whistle* What is the latest sample of your helping my sons, please tell their mother.

WILL FARL We've just put a log across the railway down at Granton.

MRS DONNELLY Now, just how does that help Will & Mike?

TOM Why don't you know George Stub, your Will's arch enemy, is coming back from the fair at St Mary's tonight. Most women would have screamed here but

MRS DONNELLY Is he coming back from the fair at St Mary's now, why Tom and Will Farl, my husband Mr Donnelly's at the fair too. You wouldn't want him to be train-wrecked, would you?

TOM There's lots of time, we'll take the logs off, Mrs Donnelly. See the welts, Will Farl?

WILL FARL You know I remember my father whaling me like that. And people ask me why I like to stay at the Donnellys' so much.

TOM *train whistle* We'd better get a move on. Will Farl there's the train. So why is it you like to stay at the Donnellys' so much then?

WILL FARL They killed my father.

They run off; train whistle; MRS DONNELLY turns to her patient and says:

MRS DONNELLY Were you listening, James Donnelly the Younger, or are you still asleep from the medicine the doctor gave you.

JAMES JR Oh mother, I'm still asleep from the medicine the doctor gave me.

MRS DONNELLY Good, because it's time you had another dose of it.

JAMES Mother, I won't take it. *Pause.* I won't take it unless

MRS DONNELLY Unless what, high and mighty.

JAMES Where's the saw? Let me hold it in my hand here. And I'll *She gets the saw. Gives him medicine. Sleepily he continues* I'll pull his beard out.

An actor sitting on the side benches with his fingers drumming on wood suggests the rain pouring down outside.

MRS DONNELLY Hsst. There's a whirlwind outside and the sky is dark. Your father's late home from the fair. Maybe he'll bring you something James though you're a trifle big and old for a bauble and did you pull his beard out in this big fight you had with him.

JAMES Ah, *in his sleep* it fell out of him. By God, I'll knock your brains out, there's no constable in Lucan able to take me.

MRS DONNELLY When I get you on your feet, my son, it's off to the priest and you're taking the pledge. It's either the water wagon or smash and when the smash comes your father and I won't be able to help you one little bit.

JAMES Where's Will and where's Mike?

MRS DONNELLY Where else would they be, but driving their stage up and down in this rain.

JAMES Where's John and Bob and Tom?

MRS DONNELLY   Out plowing. Tom went up to the blacksmith's.

JAMES   Why isn't Pat home helping us fight Finnegan?

MRS DONNELLY   Why isn't he? Have you asked him sure enough and get him into trouble. Is that why you came back from Michigan to get us all into trouble?

JAMES   No. No. I came to help Will and Mike smash Finnegan. Where's Father

MRS DONNELLY   He's just coming into the yard this very minute and if you're not quiet and good I'll tell him on you. Mr Donnelly I'm surprised to see you home from the fair at all.

MR DONNELLY   I am myself. There was a log across the rails. How'd you know about that? *Pause.* How's our first one?

MRS DONNELLY   Mr Donnelly, Doctor Quarry says—and he knows this himself for he was told— that even if we get him to stop the drink he's got only two more years to live.

MR DONNELLY   It's his lungs. And they're bad. How is he now then?

JAMES   Never felt better in my life. I'm going into Lucan.

MR & MRS DONNELLY   No, you're not. *They hold him down till he falls asleep.*

MRS DONNELLY   And what's that you've brought us home from the fair to give to a little one perhaps some time. *He gives her a top and she spins it. There is a whipstick that comes with it which she uses.*   I wonder how much longer they can all keep going, Jim?

MR DONNELLY   Stub was on the train.

MRS DONNELLY   And I knew that too. The things I've heard this afternoon, Mr Donnelly, and I was at no fair.

MR DONNELLY   Jim, says Stub, Jim—

STUB   *train whistle* Jim, thought I saw you back here coming back to see what in hell's holding up this train. Jim—if you and your boys get me Ward Three next election *Pause.* and you alone can do it—I don't care how, tell them not to vote or vote for my man who's going to be an Irish Catholic, Jim, yes—if you can promise me that, Finnegan will stop running his stage wagons tomorrow.

MRS DONNELLY   Yes, and my husband said—

MR DONNELLY   Nothing. We're promised long ago to Mr Scatcherd.

MRS DONNELLY   And you are so promised

MR DONNELLY   And yet

MRS DONNELLY   *whipping the top* Yes. It would be nice to stop, but we can't oh no we must keep on spinning and spinning, Mr Donnelly, because if we stop spinning we'll fall down and over and we hit them and they hit us and we—one day—our whip-arm's broke off. Go back to him and say yes!

MR DONNELLY   Never!

TOM   Mother and Father, wake Jim up will you? There's a fight up town and Will and Mike can't get the stage past Levitt's.

MRS DONNELLY   Your brother's not fit to go out anymore, Tom. Hush. . .

JAMES   No, Mother. The medicine worked. I'm well. Father. . . . Get my horse Tom.

MR & MRS DONNELLY   Get back in that chair.

JAMES   *escaping them* You heard what Tom said. Every man's needed, my brother's in a fight!

MR DONNELLY   Take your coat, Jim. At least put something on your back.

MRS DONNELLY   Take your hat, it's rain—he took the saw.

MR DONNELLY   Come back here, Tom and Jim. What's he got the saw for? *Exit*

FINNEGAN   Now I can explain the saw. Exactly a year ago, Thursday, September the 20th, 1874, someone took my stage wagon after dark and sawed it to hundreds of small pieces. I built a new stage. 1875. Today, Friday, September 20th—someone took that new stage out of my stable, dragged it up the road a piece and sawed it into even more pieces. There are to be no stages on the road, but Donnelly stages, are there? The Donnelly tribe is getting to be a terror to the neighbourhood.

JOHN MACDONALD approaches the bartender and buys a stage ticket. His MOTHER and sister, NORAH, approach for the same reason.

MACDONALD   A ticket, one way to Lucan please.

BARTENDER   Which line will you go on. . .

NORAH   Two tickets the same to Lucan please, for myself, sir, and my mother here. The Donnelly Line.

MACDONALD   Not the Donnelly Line for your brother, Norah, nor for your son, Mother, but the Finnegan Line, please.

NORAH   Please yourself, brother John, if you want your bones shaken to a jelly by Mr Finnegan's drivers. We'll be in Lucan before you.

MACDONALD   I want the two of you to get your money back and come on the same coach as your brother and son is going on. The wagon you're going on carries away more than my mother and my sister, for it bears away sister's reputation and any love for her son my old mother has ever had.

MOTHER   Will you lower your voice in a public place, my son John Macdonald. Why you've palled around with Donnellys ever since you can remember, what have you suddenly determined against them?

MACDONALD   Mother, you know and I know what Norah's up to with their Cripple now he's lost the Thompson girl.

MOTHER   Don't you dare call him a cripple, or there's people here standing'll see me haul off and give you the clout you so long for. Let Norah decide the man she'll marry, one thing, it can't be you, you get such rages into yourself about your sisters, it's the land you're worried about isn't it, that father likes William Donnelly a lot, not just that Norah does, is that not so?

MACDONALD   Your husband and my father make me wonder sometimes if I am his wife's husband's son.

As the quarrelling Macdonalds leave the barroom, the other actors form two coaches indicating that we have dissolved into the street outside the City Hotel, but just before this happens MRS MAC-DONALD raises her arms and says:

MOTHER   No wonder he likes Will Donnelly. At least Will Donnelly can talk straight when it comes to naming his relatives. I've even heard him call his mother his mother and his father his father, but with you John, your mother, why your mother is liable to be your grandfather's daughter and your sister, she's not your sister, she's your unborn grand-child's great aunt.

And out the Macdonalds go to immediately return as if we then saw them step out of the hotel and go to their respective coaches. We are getting ready for a decisive journey up the road, this time to some startling new developments.

MACDONALD   Mother, I'm sorry, but this wouldn't happen if Donnelly would just leave us and Norah alone.

They shout at each other through the windows of the stages, then the Finnegan horn, the tollgate and penny convention, the slight up and down movement of the two stages' passengers indicate that they're off!

NORAH   Brother, who's been at you? I'll tell you I'm proud he's in love with me, can you not remember the love you once felt for himself when you were always over there . . .

MOTHER   Mrs Donnelly had more to do with bringing you up than I did, now look at you. Sure, Father's given you one hundred acres already, he's not made of gold, leave him alone about his property.

MACDONALD   When I get home, Norah, I'm going to dig up all the potatoes in the front field you've been planting and I'll cut down the orchard mark

my words if I see you talking to him when we get to Lucan, it's lucky it is there's no Cripple driving today I suppose I'd see you both up on the driver's seat with him. There go the Cripple lovers, folks, my mother and my sister.

NORAH   Oh, Mother, give me the parcels, which one is the iron we bought I'll crack him one on his skull.

MOTHER   Pay no heed to him, darling, I just hope and pray he doesn't get up his courage at the taverns and try to drag us off at a tollgate, but we're outdistancing him I see, here we are shut up in a box with four wheels and the window blinds down for the heat and you can hear the drivers cursing each other through the roof. You have to pretend not to hear.

NORAH   A ride to Lucan is a sentimental education I can tell you. You'd hear Finnegan's driver say—
   trumpet   hold your ears. I guess only men would understand why they'd have to get down and fight about that, once a Donnelly said, "And your father wasn't married either, McKellar." To which came the reply: *trumpet* to which Mike Donnelly said:

NORAH & MIKE   "You'll not drive the stage another morning with your life, McKellar."

MOTHER   I don't mind hearing a good bout of swearing if they're really good at it, but it does slow up the journey which is somewhat more important, and that last remark by my future son-in-law.

NORAH   I think it was Mike said that, Mother

MOTHER   Well, whoever it was, that would lead to both stage drivers putting in an appearance at a local Justice of the Peace along the road called Squire Ferguson.

WILL   Squire Ferguson, I wish to lay a complaint against Peter McKellar re perjury in the information he laid against me and Mike last July the third, 1875.

SQUIRE   Mr Donnelly, I don't think you can do that.

WILL   Oh yes you can. Victoria, 1859, Chapter 1, subsection 6. Give me your manual, sir, and I'll show

NORAH   When Finnegan's witnesses would try to go down to the courthouse, Will Donnelly would get them arrested somehow at Birr for disorderly conduct. I bought him a couple of old law books for a Christmas box, and it was what we called the game of information and complaint or Legal Amuse-ments. And if two of the Donnelly boys got arrested why their mother had had the foresight to have seven sons, so it would be Tom or Bob or John would drive if they'd snared my Will or Mike into their clutches.

MOTHER   And they'd be at it again.

A brief horn and fiddle contest. Finnegan's horn taunts are returned with interest by Donnelly fiddle sounds.

MAN ON FINNEGAN'S STAGE   I used to ride both lines and turn about and you could see what was going to happen, sooner or later . . . oh, there were happy times too I observed in my going back and forth. I can remember the whole Donnelly family going down the road on their way to Bothwell to get Jennie married off. Or the day Mike all dressed up went down to London to get married to Ellen Haines, her father kept the City Hotel there. Mike didn't show up for a week after that, too tired, still abed at two in the afternoon his brothers said, stage drivers make good husbands, all that jouncing up and down. God knows, but sooner or later . . .

NORAH   Yes stage drivers do make good husbands. I was so proud of the way William drove and acted to his customers and I knew then that my life with him was like this journey. Through it all we would eventually come to the St Nicholas Hotel here off the road and out of the storm. My old mother's fallen asleep. Where does she dream she is?

LADY ON OTHER STAGE   Asleep!! Not me, I keep thinking when the wheels will they come off, when will the wheels come off, oh Mother, when will the wheels come have those Donnellys loosened the wheels?

CHORUS   fur hats in winter, straw hats in summer

MAN   our collar limp, our hat crushed, our watch stopped, our brain dizzy with vertigo, the elastic band of our wig snapped, our false teeth displaced in their setting, curses not loud but deep,

MIKE   Gee Ploughboy Gee Pilot

CHORUS   were carriers of passengers upon a stage or covered wagon from the City of London to the Village of Lucan

FINNEGAN   Hrup hrup there you slow beasts, don't try to beat me at the bridge, Donnelly, there's not room for the both of us.

MIKE   There's two sides to a road, Finnegan.

CHORUS   the defendant, William Donnelly, did not safely & securely carried upon the said on the said

MIKE   Oil your wheels, Finnegan.

The "coaches" are getting closer to each other & are blurring in outline just as things do before they collide.

FINNEGAN   Your half of the road's the ditch, Donnelly,   *horn & fiddle*

CHORUS
August the 31st, 1875
maliciously ran races with other stage coaches

MAN   I think that Finnegan kept as close as he could to the Hotel side to keep Donnelly from getting to the Hotel before him.

MIKE   The ladies wanted a drink of water at the hotel. He made a quick turn as quick a turn as ever I seen. I had ten passengers three in the driver's seat besides myself   seven inside

Using the whole team of actors, suggest the collision.

CHORUS   plaintiff was thereby wounded & injured in consequence on the said road and suffered great pain and expense in and about the cure of her wounds and injuries. And the plaintiffs—Mrs Louisa Lindsay & Miss Jennie Lindsay—claim five hundred dollars   *groaning*   damages.

MIKE   What did you do that for, Finnegan?   *whip*

FINNEGAN   *whip*   Mike Donnelly, I'd do it again like as not until and again till I've run you off this road.

The two stage drivers confront each other among a pile of coach fragments and accident victims slowly re-assembling themselves; but the scene is darkening, a bell rings, MIKE DONNELLY's face grows red from some fire he is looking at.

FINNEGAN   I said to myself under my breath why in God's name is Mike Donnelly's face turning so red.   *turning around*   He's thinking he's looking at my stables going up in flames with five horses alive in them.

FINNEGAN runs out into a blazing stable door as the tollgate between Birr & Elginfield is set up with the money pouring out for counting of the day's take.

FINNEGAN   Mother of God help me save my poor beasts from Donnelly's fire.

TOLLGATER   Guess that's all for today, let's count her up, sunset's hanging on there quite a while. Good night to you, sir. You're our last traveller for the day.

TRAVELLER   That's not the sunset by the way.

As this scene develops there should be well-spaced red glares that build till the Donnelly Boys in a photograph scene are surrounded by Hell with a mob of farmers in front of them with sharp hayrakes.

SOLO   *sings*   Patrick Finnegan's stables burning

CHORUS   Dies irae dies illa   *ecclesiastical*

SOLO   Solvet Finnegan in favilla

WIFE   Sam and me's been seeing quite a few red glows in the sky north of here lately every night.

TRAVELLER   Oh it's them Donnellys, another barn they've set fire to if it's a friend of Finnegan, burned down Pat Finnegan's stable last week with six horses in it burnt up alive.

TOLLGATER   That's one step up from loosening wheels and having you up in court for assault and battery, isn't it.

TRAVELLER   A considerable step indeed. I guess you see the Donnelly boys every day?

TOLLGATER   Twice a day regular as clockwork— their coach, Finnegan's coach down to town; except one day last week both the stages were awful late and then part of the Finnegan wagon limped by, and then two thirds of the Donnelly conveyance and then the rest of the Finnegan and then the hindwheels of the it was a Armageddon of a road catastrophe I can tell you.

WIFE   That night we saw our first red glow.

Three or more FARMERS come up to listen with hayrakes, big wooden spikes on them: lanterns.

TOLLGATER   And I can tell you ladies and gentlemen, when the other Finnegan stable got burnt up in Clandeboye why there was people said—what next?

WIFE	SOLO
What next indeed, Sam. The Maclean's Hotel where Finnegan ties up his stage, someone got into their kitchen and broke every dish and cup and teapot and soup tureen Mrs Maclean had to her name.	William Donnelly's stables burn too
	CHORUS
	Tuba Finnegan spargens sonum
	Per sepulchram regionum
	Coget Biddulph ante thronum

CHORUS
Oh them Donnellys

FARMER ONE   Is it all the members of the family, the mother and the father?

TOLLGATER   There's some say as that they called the oldest of the boys back from where he's been hiding out in Michigan—James Donnelly the Younger—and he drinks you see, and they just sort of let him loose at night

FARMER TWO   There's others say after the outrage at Walker's Hotel where they cut the tongues out of the stage horses there . . .

ALL   Cut the tongues out of the horses!

FARMER TWO   God yes, have you not heard— Finnegan went to hitch up on Monday morning and his horses were all—hacked open, dying or dead, and they had to be shot; the farrier said—put them out of their misery and there was a whole bunch in the village said—lynch Tom Donnelly or Will or Mike or Jim, yes, Jim he's the one and it's Bob who sets the fires and it's Will who plans it all.

WILL & MIKE drive up to the gate.

TOLLGATER   Toll there, travellers. Oh—it's you

WILL   Good evening, Mr Scandrett. Mrs Scandrett.   *Pause.*   I said Mr Scandrett—Good evening.   *Pause.*   Mr Scandrett, there's a lady passenger felt under the weather at Swartz's Hotel coming up from London today and she asked us if we could come and pick her up down there later in the evening.

WIFE   Sam, don't let them through, Sam. They're lying. They're out for night mischief.

FARMERS   Sam, we'll help you keep the firebugs out of our township. Nobody's going to cut our horses' throats.

MIKE	*A suspended moment in which we look at the Donnelly boys held back at the gate. They look at us still as a photograph. Who are they? What are they?*
Gate, Mr Scandrett.	
SOLO *sung*	
Donnelly's new stage sawn to pieces	

CHORUS   Confutatis maledictis

SOLO   Sawn to pieces Watson's horses

CHORUS   Flammis acribus addictis

The penny slides into the TOLLGATER's cup, a Donnelly penny.

WIFE   I saw blood on his sleeve I could swear. I was going to be sick then—

ANOTHER TRAVELLER   *from our side of the gate* Good night, Scandrett. Whoa. Guess we don't need to go any farther, Lila. There's Will and Mike waiting for you and I'm glad you feel more like completing your journey than you did at three o'clock there. *The gate finally comes down to let Mrs Shoebottom through.*   Good night, Bill, Mike.   *He turns around and goes back towards us.*

LADY   Thank you, Will Donnelly. Thank you, Mike. You're kind gentlemen both of you to put yourselves out so for an old woman like me.   *They depart with her.*

WIFE   But when their hands came down to help her up into their buggy the blood on their sleeves was gone.

Bar noise & scene. MIKE going through with trunk

MIKE   I heard what you said, sir. If you ever say again that my brother Tom robbed Ned Ryan of eighty dollars I'll kill you.   *Exit*

Voice of man who enters as MIKE leaves with trunk

SOLO VOICE   The Donnellys are coming, they're walking over from Levitt's.

A knocking, then a door-rending.

Lock up your doors, close the bar; hide everybody.

JIM, TOM & BOB enter to face a lone bartender, FRANK.

FRANK   No Donnelly gets a drink at this bar; I'll not serve you, James.

JAMES   I see. And it's a good bar you used to have too, Frank Walker.

FRANK   Used to have!

JAMES   Because you'll get a scorching inside of six weeks as it's laid out for you now, but I don't intend to have anything to do with it.

FRANK   What'll it be, Jim Donnelly, what'll it be?

JIM   Three gingerbeers for us lads here and a big bowl of porridge.

FRANK   Don't you mean three bowls?

JAMES   No, it's not for us. One big bowl of porridge and hustle it.

CONSTABLE BERRYHILL enters swaggering with his warrants in pocket

BERRYHILL   *with beard*   I can lick any man in this tavern, I can lick any man in Biddulph.   *He backs away from JIM DONNELLY.*   Jim Donnelly I've got twelve warrants for your arrest.

Out of range we hear a scream from BERRYHILL & he returns in the power of JAMES DONNELLY, JR.

MIKE   He had followed my brothers to Walker's Hotel.

BERRYHILL   They tore half my beard out.

JAMES   Oh—the beard fell out of him

MIKE   By the time I got there my brothers and their pals were throwing stones at home.

BERRYHILL   Several of the stones weighed five pounds each.

MIKE   That's a lie. Frank, how much does that one weigh?

FRANK   Got a bit afraid when I saw the stones flying through the air.   *weighing a stone in a balanced scale on bar*   It's three pounds?   *MIKE smiles.*

WILL   My brother Mike then hauled James and the others off and parted them.

BERRYHILL   But left me with them and you know what they made me do, that James Donnelly the Younger took the warrants out of my pocket and

They tear up the warrants, sprinkle them over the porridge and feed it to BERRYHILL.

FRANK   You're probably going to hit me, Jim, for asking you this, but why?

JAMES   I'm only feeding him the ones we didn't do, Frank. This one here—I'll eat myself, yes I did

beat that grocer up and I couldn't stand the way he whined and whoever is doing all those terrible things on these warrants will stop doing them, Frank, when the powers that be let my brothers have half of the road again. I started eating the paper and then it tasted bitter, I took it out of my mouth and saw Dr Quarry's signature why it was my death certificate and it was getting time to take the saw back to my mother and father.

Facing us a change comes over him: he dissolves from the bully into someone coughing blood on his sleeve and crawling toward us, towards his mother who waits for him.

MRS DONNELLY
Yes, my oldest son came home and after the doctor came it was time for the priest to come, but he did not come and we waited and he did not come so that it was I who had to lie down beside this grown man and lead him backwards and forwards through a life he had forgotten the deeds and maps to. As he whispered in my ear, yes, what do you want me to say, I could see life for him again some time. But for the first time I saw my own death. Just before he died I told him what I was to tell another son of mine not many years after.

Ritual walking confession, his back to us, she with her face as his life pours out. They are walking through his brutal life under some of the next scene, then he parts from her forever.

CHORUS
Nominations for North Middlesex
One of the Donnellys is Dead!
hilarious reaction

SOLO
Solvet Jacobus in favilla

CHORUS
Another diabolical outrage—a horse disembowelled with a scythe. Flammis acribus addictus
Fiendish outrage—a tree across the London, Huron & Bruce railway this morning. The trestles of the Grand

The CHORUS divide into those watching the news bulletin board where several are chalking up headlines, and others reading newspapers.

MRS DONNELLY's arm cannot keep her oldest son here anymore; she lets it drop to her side and walks across the CHORUS gossipers.

Trunk Railway bridge at Lucan Crossing sawn through by some fiend in human form. There is work for some clever detective in Lucan. Voca me cum benedictus, Dies irae, dies illa Dona eis requiem. The Detective. Our serial for the month of December. "A Detective's Diary," or

McCRIMMON *disguised as an old beggarwoman* How I brought the Donnelly Gang to heel. Gentlemen, are all the blinds down and the doors to Mr Stub's store room locked? Yes? Then I will resume my civilian garb. *flinging off his disguise* Mr Finnegan, I have been for some time engaged in ferreting out at your behest the perpetrators of certain crimes which have been committed in Lucan & its vicinity. Today is—I make this interim report to you on Thursday, February the 24th, 1876. Sunday —5th of December, 1875—we met here as you recall in camera.

FINNEGAN First of all, let me introduce you to Mr George Stub at the back of whose store we are hiding. Mr Stub, this is the private detective the town council gave permission to bring in. He's been here incognito already for about a month and I sure hope to hell he's going to tell us what we can do to prevent all our business affairs going bust. Gentlemen, Hugh McCrimmon.

CHORUS A giant in size, he was gentle as a child. Shy as a woman, his heart was bold as a lion's Modest as a maiden. . . .And in first place in the five mile dash! Hugh McCrimmon!

McCRIMMON Yes. For my athletic prowess in weight-lifting and footrunning alone I have won over a thousand gold medals both here and in Uncle Sam's dominions. You may remember how I asked you each to tell me your story and to tell me *all* of the story. Because there is a great detective up in the sky *all glance up* who does know and He'll make it known if you don't so I want all of the truth. My notes. This family—seven of them have done all these terrible things and they've been charged, but the constables can't arrest them. Too bad the one died and got away on us. You say no witnesses will dare to testify for fear of reprisal, in short they're running this town with a reign of terror, you want to run it and I'm here to help you. Chapter One, sirs, is to

STUB I'm having Will Donnelly arrested today if you must know—he's owed me a bill at the store in there for a bridle for over a year now and I'm having him arrested for debt.

McCRIMMON An arrest for a minor debt? Rather small potatoes, don't you think?

STUB He won't pay, his bowels hate me so much he won't pay that debt even though today is his wedding day, he won't pay it to keep out of jail.

CHORUS May the God of Israel join you together and may He be with you, who was merciful to two only children: and now, O Lord, make them bless Thee more fully. Alleluia, alleluia.

PRIEST William Donnelly, wilt thou take Norah Macdonald here present for thy lawful wife according to the rite of our holy Mother the Church?

WILL I will

PRIEST Norah Macdonald, wilt thou take William Donnelly here present for thy lawful husband, according to the rite of our holy Mother the Church?

NORAH I will *They hold right hands.*

PRIEST Ego conjungo vos in matrimonium, in nomine Patris, et Filii et Spiritus Sancti, Amen

He sprinkles them with water. Then he blesses the ring, gold & silver coins. BAILIFFS appear at the back of the church with staves.

Let us pray. Bless, O Lord, this ring which we bless in Thy Name, that she who shall wear it, keeping true faith unto her husband may abide in Thy peace and will, and ever live in mutual charity. Through Christ our Lord, Amen.

He sprinkles the ring with holy water in the form of a cross. The bridegroom receives from the PRIEST the ring and places it on the fourth finger of his bride.

WILL With this ring I thee wed, and I plight unto thee my troth. *silent Lord's Prayer*

BAILIFF Are you just about through. Because which one of you is William Donnelly; we've come with writ against him for debt.

PRIEST Look, O Lord, we beseech Thee, upon these Thy servants, and graciously assist Thine own institutions, whereby Thou hast ordained the propagation of mankind, that they who are joined together by Thy authority may be preserved by Thy help. Through Christ our Lord. Amen. Mr & Mrs William Donnelly, who are these men?

WILL Father Flannery, they are bailiffs for a debt I refuse to pay to a man you know well, Mother and Father, who used the ignorance of a child six months ago to snare me now on my wedding day. How many days?

BAILIFFS It says here—ten days in the jug, Bill.

WILL Norah. Meet me at Tom Ryder's wedding dance which is to be in ten days time at Fitzhenry's Tavern. Promise? We'll recommence there and no, Mother and Father, don't offer to pay, as a man I've decided not to. If George Stub wants me in jail he can have what he wants. And when I want him to lose this election that's coming up then I can have what I want. Got my fiddle there? I'll give you a tune as the bailiffs here march me off. Attention! March! *He goes off playing "Boney over the Alps." They listen to it dying away and then follow.*

NORAH   Mrs Donnelly, you gave Will that fiddle didn't you.

MRS DONNELLY   Are you thinking if I hadn't you might have your husband in your arms at this very moment, Norah, instead of his doing such a proud fool thing?

NORAH   No. I've never been so happy in my life to have married such a man.

McCRIMMON   Chapter One. January the twenty second, I wrote to my sweetheart. Chapter Two. I visit the outlaw's nest—in disguise.

Our attention focuses on JOHN washing himself at the Donnelly farmhouse. MIKE drives into the yard.

MIKE   What are we going to do, Jack? There's a detective on the way out here.

JOHN   He's already here. The boys brought him home with them.

MIKE   Do they know who he is?

JOHN   They think he's a pal, he stood up for them in some dispute at the Dublin House and slapped a man down. You should see him, he's all muscle. Should we tell them?

MIKE   No. It'd be too much for their minds to bear. Is he disguised?

MRS DONNELLY enters, kisses MICHAEL, and shows him a baby shawl she has knit.

JOHN   *whispering*   He's got an eye patch.

McCRIMMON enters & slouches around. BOB & TOM stand behind him.

MRS DONNELLY   Nellie was just showing me the baby, Mike, what shoulders he has already on him, and this is what I've knitted for Jenny's child and your father and me's off to the christening in St Thomas. Bob and Tom are you not going to say goodbye to your mother and father?

They come over to kiss her; she singles out the lounging pirate for a glance.

McCRIMMON   *vulgar voice*   Well, look at who it is. This must be your mother, boys. Old Johannah Donnelly herself. *He is hoping to provoke something.*

MRS DONNELLY   I always thought that gentlemen stood up when a lady came into the room.

McCRIMMON   I'm no gentleman, and this is no room. *laugh*

MRS DONNELLY   The yard of any house I live in, sir, has a very high blue ceiling called a sky, and I call it a room particularly if I say so and I step out into it.

McCRIMMON   *shambling & bowing*   Mrs Donnelly, I'm enchanted to meet you, met your two youngest ones while strolling through the village, and I gather you do not mind if they entertain a stranger at your high ceilinged residence. *glances up*

MRS DONNELLY   Strangers are always welcome here and I'm only sorry my husband and myself won't be here this weekend since we're going to St Thomas to visit my daughter and granddaughter there. Tom and Bob, why don't you take your friend to help father catch the driving horse. It seems to me I caught a glimpse of you earlier on looking at one of my son's shirts on the clothesline. *She comes over to him with a shirt & claps her hands together in front of his face.*   Well, if you're that interested in our laundry and linen out here, you can mend the big tear in that one yourself which was no doubt got in the sort of place my boys would meet you.

TOM   Mother, he stuck up for us. You and Will always do this to our friends.

MRS DONNELLY   Do what, this is the first one I ever caught pawing over my clothesline. Off to help with the horse now. *They exit.*   Mike and John, who is that man? Of all the orphans and has beens and poor lost souls you've brought home for me to take the edge of hunger off them, this is the only one I cannot seem to stand. How in Heaven's name can Tom and Bob not see that he's a rascal.

JOHN   Mother, you don't know what a dreadful comment this is on your character.

MRS DONNELLY   How so, is he really a good man?   *The boys laugh as she leaves.*

McCRIMMON   And with that she swept out. I took notes on all they said and done, but she breaks any pencil I have around me to describe. But I put them through their paces, and they never caught on. For instance, *vulgar voice again*   Bob. Which would you rather see—it burn, or put it out and have it cool in your pocket—a nice green dollar bill?

He sets fire to a dollar bill & floats it. BOB watches in fascination and fails the test utterly, squiggling as it burns and obviously "interested" in fire.

TOM   You know, Jake, you're not the only clever person around here and this is all among friends now.   *He sticks a lead pipe in his trousers & drops a penny from his nose into the pipe.*   Mike?

MIKE   I haven't the skill, Tom, but I bet your new friend can't do it either.

McCRIMMON *taking the pipe & sticking it in his trousers* Bender's the name, Mike, Jake Bender.

JOHN Ladies are present, Mr. Bender.

After making sure they're not, McCRIMMON balances the penny; TOM pours a dipper of cold water down the pipe. He roars & chases after them.

JOHN *with head to ground* What a runner he is, Mike. You can hear him pounding the earth like a giant. Where is he now?

MIKE Where the creek runs through. He's caught up to them. He's bringing them back, one under each arm. Look at the front of his pants!

McCRIMMON enters & modestly turns his back to us; STUB, FINNEGAN et al resume the backroom positions. The wedding party music strikes up.

McCRIMMON Yes, I was the first man to bring the Donnelly gang to heel. She got a pair of pants I had to leave out there, but I got all the sons save Mike into the jails and prisons they belonged in. Thursday February the 24th, 1876, Gentlemen, my constables are ready, I hear the dance about to start over at Fitzhenry's Hotel over there and we'll soon see some more wildcat action.

STUB Well, I hope so, the room we used to meet in got burnt down. What kind of a case have you made out against them?

McCRIMMON *going over to barrel* They've got about thirty friends. I'm going to select the weakest and dance him on a rope till he tells us what he knows about the Donnellys' activities, starting right here with this redhaired lad in the barrel. It's Tom Ryan the little sneaking spy it is. Chapter Three!

He closes the barrel & they roll TOM off as the wedding sweeps in. A FIDDLER jumps out over the bar; someone collects money in a hat to pay him; the bar in full flow, someone ladling out the punch, girls sitting on boys' knees.

BOY What will you dance?

GIRL Your will is my pleasure, Dan.

FIDDLER What'll you have?

BOY Barney, put your wrist in it or Kitty here'll leave us both out of sight in no time. Whoo! Success! Clear the floor. Well done, Barney. That's the go.

The dance: Polka, Schottische, Reel if time. Play WILL's march "Boney over the Alps" when he & JOHN enter, NORAH, Mr & Mrs Tom Ryder—the new bride & groom whose party this is.

CONSTABLE(S) *with staves* John Donnelly, we've come to arrest you for assault & battery of Joseph Berryhill. Read the warrant if you like. Come along now, John.

JOHN But it's dated a month ago, why have you waited till now when I'm at the dance?

CONSTABLE Come along with us to the lock-up.

WILL Come back here, John. Don't be dragged away by that fellow.

CONSTABLE Come back here, Jack Donnelly.

WILL Stay here, John. You're staying with me at this dance. I'm just out of jail and my brother's not going there and I'm not going back. Bob, where's Tom and Will Farl?

VOICE Give it to him. Will

CONSTABLE Hey you! Bring that man back here, he's my prisoner *grabbing*

JOHN What's this about, Bawden? When you arrested me before I went with you like a man.

CONSTABLE Yes, when you had to

He pulls at John, crowd pulls the other way.

VOICES *chanting* We won't let John go ever from this party oh

WILL Let him go, you son of a bitch. You couldn't have tried this at a more infuriating time I'll blow your heart out of you or any other man that'll try, just try to take him or any other of the family.

Melee, shots. All out save the hanging scene.

McCRIMMON Chapter Four! Tom Ryan, the militia are rounding up your friends and herding them into the lock-up so there's no one to gallop by and see you hanging up in this tree, so just tell us the answers please like a good lad.

CONSTABLES enter with JOHN & put him behind a ladder.

CONSTABLE The Queen versus John Donnelly. Assault and resisting arrest.

CHORUS Three months in the Central Prison.

STUB Three months! It should have been three years!

McCRIMMON You won't tell. No? Pull him up *Pause.* Now will you tell on the Donnellys?

CONSTABLES The Queen versus Tom Donnelly. Misdemeanour.

CHORUS Nine months in the Central Prison. The Queen versus Bob Donnelly

Again the two are brought in & placed behind ladders with clanking sounds.

CONSTABLES Shooting with intent, two years in the penitentiary

McCRIMMON Do you know anything about the burning & cutting up of those stage wagons? Do you know anything about the meat that's been stolen?

TOM   Listen, mister, if you'd let me see who you are I'd tell you everything.   *McCRIMMON motions to have his eyebandage removed.*   Ready?   *Pause.* I done them things. I stole the meat because I was hungry, I broke the dishes in the hotel. The Donnelly boys themselves would like to know who does half the things—   *He is pulled up.*

McCRIMMON   The young liar. If he wants to go to prison with those he loves so let him go.

CHORUS   The Queen versus William Donnelly.

RYAN comes to his ladder cell about the same time as WILL.

CONSTABLES   Shooting with intent. Nine months in the county jail.

McCRIMMON   Gentlemen, I'm ashamed of the brevity of their sentences, but we could not break the boy. I wish you'd warned me that he was subject to fits. Chapter Five!

TOM   Will, I'm so proud to be in jail with you. I love the jail.

WILL   Oh God, Tom Ryan. I hate the jail. Did Norah send anything along with you when you left Lucan now?

TOM   A bar of soap. Here.   *throws*   Has it got a saw in it, Will, you're eating it?

WILL   I know I am, Tom, and it's going to make me terribly ill.

McCRIMMON   But despite all that, gentlemen, I have rid your township of the vermin for some time and you Finnegan are again the King of the Road and you Squire Stub—can look forward to an election campaign where your candidate will meet only fair opposition, not the shears, clippers and torch he very well might have. Gentlemen, my pay.   *Just as they give him a bag—*

VOICE   *lady reading newspaper*   Well it says here that William Donnelly is very sick of a low fever in the jail and is not expected to live much longer—his wife is petitioning the Attorney General to let him off his sentence.

McCRIMMON   Chapter Six! Thank you. Thursday, August 22nd. Today I proposed to my beloved and was accepted. She will marry a man who has just been appointed Chief of Police for Belleville.

He exits into the audience with the quilt that is MIKE & NELLIE's bed held behind him.

CHORUS   Like a flower, Eunice found herself and her pink frilly dress swept into the powerful arms of the brave Detective, winner of many athletic events.

MIKE & NELLIE in bed.

NELLIE   Always seem to wake up before Mike. Listen for the children. Take a look at the newspaper. Think. The village has been quiet since they're all gone off to jail. Didn't get Mike though. In his dreams he's finally got off the stage, you can tell from his breathing. When he first wakes up there's a minute before he tenses up for the day on the road which goes by our window and in that moment you can tell him things that might get him too excited later on, apt to rush off and hit somebody. But there's something I've got to tell him before it's too late. When we first met at the dance—I broke off my engagement with a lad called Sid Skinner because I fell so in love with Mike. Sid and me'd been courting for a year, but I could not help it, Mike was the man for me, but Sid's been coming to my mother's house on Horton Street lately, tipsy from his work at the hotel and saying he's going to kill, you, Mike. Wake up, Mike, so I can put this to you. I've never told you but the man who tends bar at the City Hotel used to be in love with me. Mike?

MIKE   What time is it? Five o'clock by the light. Nellie?

NELLIE   Mike.

MIKE   Do you want to spend the rest of your life here in this house on Main Street of Lucan? Don't be afraid to tell me.

NELLIE   You know how happy I've been with you, Mike, wherever you are and whatever happens.

MIKE   I don't mean that, I know that, but have you ever thought you'd like to live another place?

NELLIE   Yes, oh God yes, Mike.   *Finnegan's stage horn*   Mike, there's Finnegan's stage—it's later than I thought, you'll be late for work.

MIKE   Nellie, I don't know why I've been ashamed to tell you, but yesterday was the last day I'll ever drive the Opposition Stage. They've won. Without my brothers beside me I can't go on. So I've got a job as a brakeman on the Canada Southern and we'll leave today for St Thomas. Do you feel ashamed of me?

NELLIE   God no, Mike. There was something else I wanted to tell you, but it's all right now we're moving so far away, what's the matter.

Stage passes with horn and shout.

MIKE   *shaking fist out window*   I'll drive over your grave yet, McKellar. Oh God, I loved driving that road.   *Pause.*   Nellie, there's smoke coming out of our kitchen window downstairs, they've set fire to our house, quick get the babies, Mother of God save us from Finnegan's Fire.

A red glare we have seen before. Viewpoint: roll on floor with baby dolls; scream from wife.

CHORUS
The Election of 1878
Then shout John A. forever boys,
That is the heading cry;
Every election we will win,

The time is drawing nigh,
The scheming Grits may bag their heads
That is if they've a mind,
Or go and dig up taters
With their shirts hung out behind.

STUB Gentlemen of Ward Three, it gives me great pleasure to see the Conservative Meeting at the Donnelly Schoolhouse so crowded tonight. As I see some of our Grit friends here I trust and hope that you will give our speaker a fair hearing. May I give a particularly warm welcome to Mr William Donnelly whom the Grit government of our fair province has seen fit to release from his chamber at the Queen's boarding house where he was reportedly deathly ill. Although looking quite recovered from his fever, I would ask as a special favour that he not overtax himself or it might bring on another—attack. As you all know the Conservative Candidate for this riding is an Irish Catholic nominated by his Irish Protestant brothers. Gentlemen, I have been requested to perform a very pleasing duty this evening and it is to introduce to you the next member for the riding of North Middlesex—Mr Timothy Corcoran. *applause*

CORCORAN *manipulating a puppet version of himself* Gintlemen farmers of Biddulph, yees are ruined by Mr McKinsey and his free trade. Ivery market in the country is filled with Yankee horses, cattle and hogs. Yees are losing fifteen cints on ivery bushell of barley ye sell, and yees can't get over half price for yees pays and oats, bekase millions uv bushels uv Yankee corn comes into the country not paying a cint of duty. You farmers have to pay tin cints more for yare tay and two cints more for yare sugar—Mr Chairman, I see a hand up at the back of the room.

MRS DONNELLY *who has been following the speech in a newspaper and has been reading along with the speaker for a bit* This is the same speech as he gave in Ailsa Craig a week ago. It's all printed down here in the *Advertiser*.

STUB Don't heed that hand, on and louder, Tim.

CORCORAN —two cints more for yare sugar, yes, Will Donnelly what did you want to ask?

WILL If, Mr Corcoran, you were elected to parliament next Tuesday and say in a year's time—say your party got in, Macdonald's party—and again there was a scandal about money and there came up a vote of confidence in the government how, Mr Corcoran, would you vote?

CORCORAN I don't know. When the time comes, Bill, I'd know by that time because I'd have studied it up you see.

WILL Although you are a Catholic the Orange Lodge supports your candidacy, Mr Corcoran. What is your vote likely to be when their Grand Master tries to ram a bill through Parliament for the incorporation of the Orange Lodge?

CORCORAN Oh, Will Donnelly, never fear I'd vote for such a thing.

WILL But Mr Corcoran, you would have to as a member of the Conservative Party.

CORCORAN Yes, I suppose I would. Mr Stub—

VOICE It's Mr Stub should be telling us instead of Tim

VOICE Sure, it's well known George Stub here gets a senatorship if Tim gets in

VOICE Sure, send him to parliament by voting for Tim. I say three cheers for the Grit Candidate Mr Colin Scatcherd who has one face under one hat. Hip Hip Hurrah.

In the cheers, objects fly at the speakers who withdraw. The newsclerk chalks up results on the bulletin board; a feeling of tension, torches, election night fever, close arithmetic.

CLERK Mr Scatcherd...the North Middlesex Riding has been won by the Grit Candidate in a tight race. Mr Scatcherd has won the seat by seven votes. *Cheers for Scatcherd led by WILL DONNELLY.*

STUB *in the drawing room* Seven votes. We lost by seven votes. We were supposed to win by four hundred! Where's my wife, Bridget?

BRIDGET *parlourmaid* Master Stub, your wife has gone back to live with your father-in-law. She said to tell you it might look like a Senator's house, but she read about the election results in the paper and you had not kept her promise to her.

STUB She's nervous and overwrought with the baby coming on. Bridget, what's your family's theory about why we lost. Is it not just the Donnellys?

BRIDGET Sir, my brother says, sir, it is the Donnellys. Without them and we'd have a Catholic gentleman in parliament this evening and maybe in Sir John A's cabinet, but no—it's the Donnellys don't want that.

STUB Could I speak to your brother some time, Bridget. How long has it been since he's back from the States?

BRIDGET Please, sir, not very long. He just arrived on the Finnegan Stage from town a good hour ago and sure I'm giving him a bit of supper in your kitchen.

STUB Tell him to come in here. *Pause.* What's your name?

CARROLL *wiping mouth* I told him what my name was.

STUB James Carroll. Did you leave here for the States because you were in any kind of trouble, Jim?

CARROLL No, sir. My father married again and I could not get along with my stepmother, after he died, she got his land away from us and I've come back to see about that and—

STUB   Your mother was a Farl, was she not, Jim?

CARROLL   How'd you know that?

STUB   Donnellys killed her brother, didn't they?

CARROLL   Yes. *to audience*   What this man was asking me to do was what my mother on her deathbed made me promise to do. To kill the Donnellys. But at first no one had the courage, no one except my poor dead mother, to say that. At first it was drive them out of the township, they were all out of prison more or less and all back on top of us so I was made a constable in Lucan and my aim was to find one victim of the Donnellys brave enough to stick to his story and fight it out in the courts and keep after them again and again until we had these Donnellys behind bars or out of the township or—out!

NED RYAN   *falling flat*   I've been robbed! Tom Donnelly robbed me of, he and Jim Feeney, robbed me of 85 dollars!

CARROLL   When did the robbery take place, Mr Ryan?

NED   Wednesday night, whatever night that was. About a year ago.

WILL   Mr Ryan, what did you have to drink at Walker's Hotel?

NED   Well, I do not get drunk often. I treated Tom and Jim to some whiskey, but I myself had some sherry wine and some ginger wine.

WILL   Is it true you were come into town that day for a spree, that you had been at the following hotels first: the Dublin House, the Queen's, the Royal, Fitzhenry's, the Western, Levitt's—

NED   Never at Levitt's, never darken his door, haven't got to Fitzhenry's, still haven't got there!

WILL   Is it true that you have several times lately entered my father's house and my own house in search of your son who has run away from you?

NED   My son! Waiting for his pa to come home with some food for the table and the Donnellys have stolen all his money away from him and I'm at home waiting for my son and he does not come to his pa and you want to know why—because the Donnellys've stolen him away from his dear pa and ma like the fairies used to steal little children away when you weren't watching.

WILL   Is it not true also that although you say that my brother choked you when you fell down, the inmates of the house who took you in could find no marks on your throat?

SQUIRE   I dismiss this case, Ned Ryan. I think one of the constables summed it all up when he said that you were so drunk that night you couldn't have known your mouth from your arsehole.

CARROLL   Your honour, may I as a friend of Ned Ryan's here and as a—may I say that I am not satisfied with the way my friend's case has been handled. We will bring it up before another magistrate.

WILL   Your honour, in view of Mr Carroll's statements, I would like the fact that the charges against my brother, Thomas Donnelly, have been dismissed, I would like a certificate made out to that effect.

CARROLL   Yes, and I could make you out a certificate about the way justice has been administered in this village so that his family and their ruffian friends can bully and terrify a township of three thousand inhabitants. You Donnellys say you're persecuted; ask the horses and cattle and the barns and the stables and the women and the men here like Ned Ryan who's lost his boy to you who is being persecuted. Is there anybody in this room who'll stick up for this gang of mad Donnelly dogs—look at his foot!—whom some of you think of as being so wonderful. And I hear one or two of yous thinking of renting my father's farm from my stepmother and there's some of you stopping at the Donnellys' for a drink of water at their well. There's a whole lot of you still doing that and if we hear of any such, or of any man or woman offering Mrs Donnelly a ride in their cart on the way to mass or

He menaces the whole theatre; we are afraid of him.

WILL   *lightly and suddenly entering*   Now is that you, Jim Carroll, sitting on that horse of yours, under the tree talking to yourself about us give me that whip of yours before you hurt yourself with it and come out of the shadow so we can get a look at you. Yes, you won. You smeared our name for all time so that when children are naughty their mothers still say to them

WILL & CHORUS   Be quiet, or the Black Donnellys will get you.

WILL   Isn't that what most of you in this room think of us as being? Because of him my mother was turned into a witch who rode around burning down sheds and barns, because of him . . . but there's one thing, Jim, that some people coming after will remark on. And that is—the difference between our handwritings. There is my signature. There is his. Choose. You can't destroy the way my handwriting looks, just as you can never change the blot that appears in every one of your autographs and the cloud and the smudge and the clot and the fume of your jealousy. There! the living must obey the dead! Dance the handwriting that comes out of your arm. Show us what you're like. Very well, I'll dance mine.

First WILL (fiddle) then CARROLL (trumpet) dance; the latter falls down in a fit. Placards displaying their signatures are held up for us to see.

WILL   Oh now Jim, I didn't mean you were to fall down in one of those fits you have now and again. Is it your heart sometimes, is it your mind sometimes, is it your great big feet sometimes, Jim, is it that you couldn't stand the way the Donnellys dressed, the way they looked right through you, the way my mother looked down at you. So you clubbed her to kneel at your feet, but you forget that our eyes don't kneel at your feet, but you forget that our eyes don't kneel and that her eyes will look down and through you until dies irae and beyond. Down and through the clown with blood on his sleeves they call James Carroll.   *Exit.*

CARROLL   It's true. I couldn't club down their eyes. After it was over I had to leave Biddulph. I never went back there. You people here'd used me like a piece of dirty paper to wipe the Donnellys off your backsides. I died out West alone. Grave whereabouts unknown. I hate William Donnelly. I hate William Donnelly.

CHORUS   End of Act Two.

ACT THREE

A gravel train with MIKE DONNELLY as brakeman backs into the audience. Three whistles for stop after MIKE has signalled this with his lantern. Switch light and the two red lanterns on the back of the train move accordingly. Song over and NELLIE to one side as commentary.

MIKE & CHORUS
I want to be a brakeman
And with the brakeman stand
A badge upon my forehead
A tail rope in my hand

With links & pins & bell cord
And signals red & white
I'd make a freight train back up
Or slack ahead all right.

When ere a train I shunted
At St Thomas so fair
I'd not forget my darling wife
But keep the crossing clear

NELLIE   My husband, Michael Donnelly, was a brakeman on a gravel train out of Waterford on the Canada Southern Line, division point St Thomas where I live with our children in a house on Mill Street—two nights he spends alone boarding at Waterford; tomorrow is his day off and he'll be home with us for four nights. But this is Wednesday, December 9th 1879. There's no snow yet. About

four o'clock it begins to rain. His mate afterwards told me this is the way it went with Michael and the train, I wanted to know every crossing they came to before when their work was over they walked into the barroom at Slaght's Hotel.

Two blasts. The journey establishes itself then goes under her speech.

That means the engineer is ready to go. From the hind end of the train Mike gives him the highball so he whistles two short blasts meaning "I understand." Yes, I understand—that in the months before my husband was murdered in that barroom at Slaght's Hotel—there was a train, there was another sort of train that started out just after that election of 1878 and every crossing it blew its whistle for was a crossing that was closer to my husband's death and I wish I could be clear in my own mind what that First Crossing was but I think I can see you there in cold blood talking about how you'll kill him and I run towards you to stop you but I meet the glass of mystery and time and trickery. I fall down and only know that I must listen for all the other four crossings Mike's train whistled for before the last time he walked out of the rain.

The barroom of the City Hotel fades in: CARROLL, SID SKINNER & a TRAINER (BILL LEWIS).

CARROLL   Well, shall we get started? We've got the job set up for you, Sid.

SID   That's good of you. And then what do I do?

CARROLL   What's the matter?

SID   It's a great thing I'm to do, kill a man and go to prison for God knows how long. All today, all tonight at this bar I've been thinking about it and I have to pinch myself to wake up—this is happening to me, this is happening to you, Sid. Sid is getting out of here.

CARROLL   Suit yourself, Sid Skinner. Maybe, and Bill here would agree with me, it'd just prove what Mike Donnelly said about you as he boasted about the girl he took away from you.

SID   I don't want to know what he said. Just the last few days I realized what a duck I was going to her mother and saying I was going to kill Mike Donnelly. I'm not a fighting man.

CARROLL   Then what kind of man was it who handled the bar in here tonight, eh Bill? That was a fighting man, but a fighting man that's not all just fight, but some brains in his head as well, eh? If Mike had seen you tonight he'd have had to eat his words—

SID   What words?

CARROLL   That you were a man of no prick. Yes, them's the dirty words he used about you, auh, he's a little fellow with no prick on him at all—*that* little fellow.

SID   Teach me how to kill him then. What dirt do I have to go through to wipe that off his mouth, yes, what's the false name you're giving me?

CARROLL   After the lesson tonight, Sid, if you learn it well, you'll have a new name. Now, you're lucky you don't have to deal with the whole tribe the way I have to up in Biddulph. I wish I just had the one desperate character to clean up, but I've got six or seven of Mike's relatives to deal with every day and do you know who's the worst?

SID   You're afraid of them?

CARROLL   The mother, she's the one I'm

SID   You're afraid of an old woman?

CARROLL   Well, what would you have done? If you can do it, maybe I can Sid, I don't know. On Monday morning last, Bill here saw me just after in Gallagher's yard and I was shaking like a leaf, for not an hour ago I'd took my life in my hands and dared to walk down the road past the Donnellys' place—was going to get some notes from a man I'd sold a fanning mill, Jack Donnelly was out plowing. Mrs Donnelly was milking a cow by the gate and Tom had just cursed me—Jack said—

JOHN   Now there's that fighting man, Mr Jim Carroll. Jim—I want to talk to you. What were you saying about Bob and our family at the sale last night?

CARROLL   I don't want to talk to you, Jack Donnelly. I've got too much respect for myself. Meet me this afternoon at Whalen's Corners.

JOHN   Let's have no mobbing at Whalen's Corners, Jim. I'll fight you, right now, I'll make your big head soft right there on that road. What business is it of yours how light a sentence Bob got?

CARROLL   Don't want much to fight, but if you'll meet me at Whalen's Corners I'll fight you. I'll lick all the Donnellys. Well, Jack drops his plow and he strode at me. I'm an inoffensive man. You come at me and I'll shoot you. Keep off

TOM throws a stone.

JOHN   Tom—get out on the road and thrash him—the coward, the thief.

CARROLL   Now listen to what she said.

MRS DONNELLY   You son of a bitch, you thief, you rogue. Give it to him, Tom, on his big head. Point a gun at an old woman milking a cow, would you, you bastard, you should be arrested, Jim Carroll, and when they arrest you they should put you back down into the devil with thirty tails you belong to.

CARROLL   Oh—the dirty names she called, calling my mother a dog and saying my father never married her, she made me feel so jumpy I just walked on, oh—I need someone to show me the way, I wouldn't dare shoot any of them now or ever. It's her, Sid, do you understand me, she's a witch and we'll never

get rid of any of them unless there's someone brave enough to just—But there isn't. The mad dogs have won.

SID   No, they haven't.

CARROLL   Oh, well then, Bill to the bar please and just let on that you're Michael Donnelly taking a drink. Now, Sid—

SID goes up to the TRAINER, hauls him around by the shoulder; they fight, but the TRAINER soon pins SID to the ground.

BILL   It's no use, Jim, all we've taught him doesn't put the weight on him Donnelly has and I'm doing just the things Donnelly does.

CARROLL   Let's add something. Sid, watch me. Bill. Stop shooting off your big mouth, Mike Donnelly.

BILL is stationed by the bar again. CARROLL draws a jackknife which he holds in his left hand; he hits BILL from behind and draws BILL into chasing him behind the bar. In the clinch, BILL has hold of CARROLL's shoulders but CARROLL holds him by the vest and with the other knife hand stabs him below the belt.

BILL   Do you want something from me. Holy name of God, Jim Carroll, go easy with that open knife. Do you want to try that now, Sid? And I think, Jim, the first few times with Sid here we'll have the knife closed.

SID   Stop shooting off your big mouth, Mike Donnelly.

BILL   Do you want something from me?

SID & BILL go through the new business. Exhausted but livened up & confident once more, SID leans back against the bar while CARROLL unlocks the bar and pours them all a drink . . . even for the privy cleaner who now comes forward with shaving mug & lather.

CARROLL   The mad dogs have lost.

SID   Who's he? He's been watching all this.

CARROLL   He's Mr Nobody, Sid, a retired barber, well semi-retired, he'd like to start shaving you just to rearrange your face whiskers a bit as well as your topknot.

SID   He smells!

CARROLL   Well, when you enter the world where you have two faces under the one hat, Sid, you can't be too choosy about your barber any more. Cleans out privies for a living now because the razor hand got rather unsteady there one famous time, oh nothing to fear, Sid, by the way we've got to start calling you by your new name.

SID   What's my new name.

CARROLL   You've got a new name with the new job you're going to take tonight—you'll be a navvy for the Canada Southern near Waterford where your friend from Biddulph is a brakeman on their gravel train right now and everything is fixed up, don't worry, remember borrow the jackknife a few days before from some chum at your rooming house, let's go back in here to shave him.

SID   What's my name.

BILL   Same as my name, Bill Lewis.

SID   But that's your name. I'm not a bit like you

BILL   Sure it is. Sure you're not, but look here don't start wanting some other name. Jim, he doesn't like my name. I'm getting sore.

CARROLL   Ah, darling, you like his name really don't you at heart. It's a stout little plain name for a stout little plain little—you'll be like St Patrick, "Bill Lewis."

Laughing, they both sing the St Patrick song as they escort him out behind the bar.

BOTH
When blind worms crawling in the grass
Disgusted all the nation,
He gave them a rise which opened their eyes
To a sense of their situation.

So, success attend St Patrick's fist
For he's a saint so clever;
Oh! he gave the snakes and toads a twist
And bothered them forever . . .

The toads went pop, the frogs went hop,
Slap-dash into the water;
And the snakes committed suicide
To save themselves from slaughter.

So, success &c.

The clock in the St. Nicholas Hotel strikes eleven: wind—establish this well before the other scene quite fades and we are back with the MINISTER & WILL.

WILL   Mr Donaldson, the next time the clock strikes, I know that I will have come to that part in my story I promised you—my brother Michael's death.

DONALDSON   You were telling me, Mr Donnelly, that the new priest formed a society against your family from among your fellow parishioners.

WILL   Oh he turned them against us. But the man who really worked at turning people against us, and you see we were not to be trusted because we had led the parish in not voting the way that Bishop and Sir John A would have had us vote—the man who really worked at it was a drifter named James Carroll. I'll show you, sir, how our family first met him. We became an obsession with him, I think he was hungry for land, our land, our eyes, our clothes, our mother. They'd just lost the election, we'd won and down the road he came and my mother was milking a cow by the gate.

JOHN   Oh I was on speaking terms with him. But he was a queer fellow.

CARROLL   Jack, what's this you were saying about me.

JOHN   Nothing yesterday, Jim Carroll, but what I could say today.

CARROLL   I wish you'd come out of that field and do it. You meet me at Whalen's Corners at two o'clock and we'll fight there.

JOHN   There's none here but the two of us. We'll have it out here, Jim Carroll, and have no mobbing about it.

CARROLL   *drawing a revolver* You son of a bitch. If you come one foot further, I'll blow your brains out.

TOM comes with stones.

WILL   Tom—throw the stones down, he wants law, not fight.

MRS DONNELLY   Go back, John, don't mind the blackguard or he'll shoot you.

CARROLL   I'd as leave shoot you as him.

MRS DONNELLY   *She rises, looks at him & turns her back on him.* Go away and mind your own business. I don't want anything to do with you.

CHORUS   The Queen against Julia Donnelly

CARROLL   Using abusive and insulting, grossly insulting language

MRS DONNELLY   And I was convicted of doing so and fined one dollar and costs. He dragged me into court and into one of the newspapers where it was printed that I had thrown stones at him. Why, sir, are you hunting me down. Yes, I must be a beast if you can draw a revolver and aim it at me and no one says no

CHORUS   The Queen against James Carroll

MRS DONNELLY   Making threats to use revolver with intent. *Pause.* Well, I see that we get nowhere with that charge so that next time he walks by our house it may be with a mob who will—Jim Carroll, when I looked into your eyes I could see your mother's eyes *FAT LADY's ghost crosses to her chair.* and I could see you hating me long ago because you were fat and we'd killed your brother, on your deathbed you must have sharpened his teeth for me. And if you have got some mud on the mother, the next crossing is to bring a mob to their father and mother's door, but first we have come to the *train journey up with crossing signal*

CHORUS   Third Crossing.

Actors form Roman Line leaving their chairs unguarded. TOM RYAN, TOM DONNELLY, JAMES CARROLL with cheesecloth over their faces play tricks, steal props from chairs, spin tops illegally, pick pockets, gallop up & down the road after they've gone asleep, snoring—whole Puck episode, ladies on their bums from chamberpots sort of thing.

WILL   *after a silent build*   Soon after this there began in the neighbourhood a whole parade of little mischievous things—Little, they began to get bigger and bigger and they told stories that my brother Tom took out horses, their horses at night and rode them up and down.

CHORUS   From tollgate to tollgate

FARMER   Until they're nigh dead and you know what Tom Donnelly's tied to her tail.

He holds up a placard saying "Vote Grit & Vote Right."

FAT LADY   *a scream of rage at this*   That's Cripple's beautiful handwriting.

WILL   There were stories that Tom Ryan in the middle of the night let people's cattle out of their fields and drove them up into Blanshard township.

VOICES IN SUCCESSION   Who stole my disk? Who stole my pig? My tea chest is gone. Who done that? I know who done that. Who shaved my horses' tails? Who put stones in my threshing machine and iron pins? We know who done that

WILL   Do you now and who done that?

CHORUS
Who? stole my disk and stole my pig
rode my horses and drove my cows
cut out their tongues and cut off their ears?
                                        repeat softly

The three mystery faces whip them like tops humming: Donnelly!

WILL   Until my father said one day: If a stone fell from heaven they'd say

WILL & CHORUS   Donnelly done it.

WILL   We were blamed for everything and people shunned us, *would* not talk to us. Three times Carroll arrested my brother Tom on the charge of stealing

NED   One hundred dollars from me—Ned Ryan—and three times the case fell through

WILL   But one fall night Carroll got a new warrant from the Grand Jury and he was out at our house at dawn to serve it

MRS DONNELLY   Yes, you should look behind the stove, Mr Carroll, and why not look right in the stove while you're at it.

CARROLL   I could not find him. I went over as far as Skinner's in Usborne and where Will lived at Whalen's Corners before I turned back.

MARY DONOVAN   I was spinning opposite the doorway in the house that day—could see the concession from where I was working. Saw Thomas Donnelly in his father's potato field picking potatoes. I went upstairs for yarn rolls and I saw William Donnelly drive into his father's place and signal to Tom in the field

CARROLL   I went over the fence into Mr Donnelly's field—went across a fall wheat field expecting to get in his tracks to follow him

MARY   When I saw Carroll & Thomas Donnelly running they were both near the stable. Saw John Donnelly come out with a horse. Tom Donnelly came up running, got on the horse and ran away.

CARROLL   If you'll stay away out of the county it's not particular if I catch you, Tom Donnelly.   *To JOHN*   I'll make it hot for you when I get to Lucan, John Donnelly. You'd no business giving him that horse to escape with.

JOHN   Jim, you never told me you had a new warrant for Tom.

CARROLL   What do you think I was running all over that wheat field for?

JOHN   Jim, Tom's not running away on you, sure he hardly seen you, he's going up to Kenny's blacksmith shop to get us some

CARROLL   I went over to Quigley's and stopped the thrashing. They got their horses and we chased Tom Donnelly into the bush all around the township from tollgate to tollgate all that night, but by the holy name of God could we   *helter skelter pursuit of TOM DONNELLY*

CHORUS
We've got him who stole my disk and stole my pig
rode my horses and drove my cows
cut out their tongues and cut off their ears

NED RYAN   It's my son, Tom, dressed up in Tom Donnelly's clothes. Tom, why would you play such a trick on us? Why would you side with the family that won't let the thrashing machine come to thrash at your father's farm and the crops are rotting in the field, why

TOM   You old ruffian—I'll tell you why I side with the Donnellys. And you clodhoppers and you drifter—trying to pull them down. Three reasons. Because they're brave. They're not afraid. They're so little afraid of living here among you that this morning they started sowing their fall wheat. Two. They're handsome. Look at your faces—your faces'd fit into the hoofprints of forty old cows hopelessly lost in a bog. Yes, high & mighty one with your dirty linen scarce covering your hippopotamus rump and your hair like—Third. When pa here took the ax to mother and Bridget and Sarah & me who was the only family on the whole road with enough sand to take us in?   *Pause.*   So that's why I side with them, Pa, and if you want to know who's doing all the mischief on this road it's him over there—Jim Carroll.

CARROLL   Is it Jim Carroll for sure now, Tom Ryan?

NED RYAN   Stand back from him all of you, let a father deal with his begetting. Come here my darling. I want you to be my boy again not the Donnellys' boy.

TOM   You're going to beat me, aren't you, Pa.

NED   No.   *pulling open his shirt*   Look at my heart in my chest now beating with love for you. Come to my heart—don't the rest of you lay a hand on him. Tom.

His arms are extended although we do see the club in his back pocket ready. TOM pauses, then runs at his belly with his head down and knocks him down, escapes. Everyone feels out of fuel; gawk listlessly, even CARROLL. All at wits' end then cowbell and spinning sound before it, leading up to

MARY   *ear-shattering*   My cow! The Donnellys have stolen my cow. On Sunday evening my cattle were all at my gate when I came home. On Monday morning I went to look for her. I cannot get a trace of her. Who's man enough here to come and help me look for my cow? My cow! They're skinning and eating and cooking my cow right this very minute now and you just sit on your backsides and gawp at me, you gomerils. My cow's hidden somewhere at the Donleys.

CHAIRMAN   Mary Donovan, Magistrate Stub says we can't have a warrant now because it's night time, but we are to keep watch and at dawn we can search. Will all members of the Peace Society who plan to visit the Donnelly homestead tomorrow come into the schoolhouse and take turns watching for dawn?

MARY   *whispering as she exits with the others*   It'll be too late by daybreak, they'll have eaten my cow all up, my cow! I had good reason to suspect the Donleys of taking my cow. The reason I suspected the Donleys is I had heard things spoke against them.

Silence as the night passes; crickets of early September, a bell rings matins, a wagon passes, train whistle, a clock strikes an early hour in the Donnelly house.

MRS DONNELLY   The air was hollow so that you could hear things far away that night. Or did I dream it that first I was on a coach and then a train and I was taking an empty coffin to a tavern where they were going to kill one of my sons. Their leaving the school and tramping down the roads towards our place must have wakened me, but as I lit the stove and went to wake up my niece Bridget they were quiet enough.

CHORUS   There's smoke coming up now from their chimney.

Whispers offstage under the audience. We are part of the mob.

MRS DONNELLY   The sun comes up, there's my shadow long—getting shorter already, turn earth another morning and noon and night I wish I could stop it Bridget take out the pail and pump us a fresh pail of water, yesterday I could hear Mary Donovan spinning in her doorway, watching us, I wonder

BRIDGET screams and runs in.

BRIDGET   Aunt Judith, where shall we hide, there's a mob in the yard with sticks in their hands.

JOHN sleeps behind the stove.

MRS DONNELLY   Augh! what has possessed them now. Go tell Mr Donnelly. John, get dressed. I stood behind the door and looked through the crack at them. Why is it getting so dark in our house. Because the light of each window is shut out by the people there.

BRIDGET   Uncle Jim, the yard is full of men with clubs. Johnny, you'd best get up.

MR DONNELLY, hitching up trousers, goes to the door and addresses a mob whose presence we feel rather than see.

MR DONNELLY   Good morning, boys, what's up with you?

CARROLL   We want nothing but to tell you Donnellys that we're not afraid of you

MRS DONNELLY   Look at the dark bunch of them and he alone, what is it, it's

VOICE   We're not afraid of you anymore, Donnelly.

MARY   I have lost a cow

MRS DONNELLY   A cow they say has been stolen from Mary Donovan's farm and we are suspected

VOICE   We're through being scared of the Donnellys.

MRS DONNELLY   Why 'tis only right the cow should be found. If you think the cow is here, Jim Carroll, don't leave one straw on top of another

JOHN   Turn the strawstack upside down. There's no stolen cow here, but I see the man who stole your cow in your crowd

Searching sounds, pails getting kicked, doors slammed &c.

VOICE   We'll make you keep quiet, Jack Donnelly.

JOHN   If you go up to the priest he'll curse the man who stole the cow and you'll find the cow before night.

CARROLL   How'd you like a good stiff kick in the ribs?

MR DONNELLY   And you can all kiss my backside. And I was a man, Jim Carroll, when you were not able to wipe your backside.

CARROLL We could break your bones at your door and you won't be able to help yourself.

MR DONNELLY I'll be here if the devil would burn the whole of you. I'm not in the least afraid of you. *He comes in the house.*

MRS DONNELLY They're kicking over hencoops and looking down the well, yes, fall down if you can, John Macdonald, what is it I hear him begging them to do, they're putting forks through the strawstacks we thrashed yesterday, he's saying—

MR DONNELLY I wish John would stay in closer to the house, do you see that?

MRS DONNELLY Yes, they've circled him and they're saying things like

CHORUS Who stole my disk

JOHN I don't know who stole your disk

CHORUS Who stole my pig

JOHN How the hell would I know

CHORUS
who stole my disk and stole my pig
rode my horses and drove my cows
cut out their tongues and cut off their ears
who shaved off my horses' tails

JOHN I don't know anything at all about your horses' tails, all I know is that you're trespassing and my father's farm has a fence, my father's land is enclosed, by the way you're acting you'd think it was a public path

MARY I have lost a cow.

CHORUS Don't you tell us to get out Jack Donnelly. We're not afraid of you I'll get satisfaction if it's for twenty years. This work'll be put down and it'll be put down by us.

A roar as they find TOM RYAN. They rush on stage with him & now we & the Donnellys look out at the mob.

CHORUS Here's one thing found.

CARROLL Sit up there in the wagon and don't you move

CHORUS Harbouring this young horserider and cattle driver, eh Donnelly.

MR DONNELLY I'd harbour your father's son, O'Halloran, if all the world said no

O'HALLORAN Little do you care Donnelly for my father's sons. Tie his hands, it's off to jail with this one.

TOM RYAN Mr Donnelly wasn't harbouring me, I slept in their strawstack last night, they didn't know I was there. *Pause.* And I sat up there on the wagon. She came out. I was handcuffed. She came out and looked across at me. Between me and her

was them with their clubs. What have I brought down on you, or would it have happened anyhow? Mrs Donnelly she was tall. If I could have I would have died for her. The wagon took me off to jail. I never saw her again.

Carrying TOM RYAN on their shoulders the mob circle and depart.

MRS DONNELLY Yes, I stood there and I watched them tie up that lad and cuff him and knock him about. They were leaving, they hadn't found Mary Donovan's cow, but I was so glad they were leaving that I didn't dare try to help the boy because for the first time in my life I felt old and small & afraid. There were so many of them. Is this not a pretty way we are treated Mr Donnelly?

MR DONNELLY But we deserve it, Mrs Donnelly.

MRS DONNELLY In the name of Heaven how?

MR DONNELLY For we're Donnellys.

MRS DONNELLY Yes, and I also heard Will's brother-in-law say they were going to his place at Whalen's Corners next. John, hitch up the driving horse for me, please.

There is a slight tug of war over the whip with MR DONNELLY.

Haven't they gone up the road by Keefe's, Mr Donnelly?

MR DONNELLY Yes. If you must go, Mrs Donnelly, then you can cut over on the sideroad.

MRS DONNELLY *pause* I must go.

What we have now is a bare stage with the bar as a place where MRS DONNELLY can coast up & down & around. A blacksmith should enter and stand near the bar which is going to be WILL DONNELLY's house. MARY DONOVAN should be sitting getting ready to spin & we need a girl who can simply fill in the choral replies to MRS DONNELLY, spin about perhaps supported by offstage voices. I'm in favour of a "Listen to the Wind" wheel & horse with MRS DONNELLY running behind. Simple & light.

JOHN Mother, what are you listening for? *triangle sounds*

MRS DONNELLY
I can hear the blacksmith who lives over at the village where Will & Norah live
Closer and louder the sound of his hammer
Wheels take me   Hooves draw me
Out of the yard of his father's house

GIRL
In the stream that I lie dreaming in I hear
A humming sound that fills me up with fear

MRS DONNELLY
My neighbour, Mary Donovan, cow lady,
I leave you behind me.

And MRS DONNELLY has done one circuit of the stage & vanished.

MARY   I heard a cow bawling over on Donley's place that sounded like my cow. I honestly believed the Donleys had my cow. The Donleys had my cow shut up. A great deal of pork & cattle stealing has been taking place in our neighbourhood. *A FARMER enters with two pails which he sets down.* Dan Quigley, did you hear I've lost my cow? The Donleys've stolen my cow.

FARMER   Mary Donovan, I just seen your cow.

MARY   Seen my cow? Impossible. Where?

FARMER   She's in our yard. I keep telling you the fence is down by McLaughlin's bush there and she strayed up to our yard with our cattle last night.

MARY kicks the pails & hits him off with either stick or spinning wheel or spindle.

MARY   Who the hell's side do you think you're on, Dan Quigley. Are you telling me I didn't hear her bawling over at Donley's?

anvil

MRS DONNELLY
Closer and louder the sound of his hammer
Wheels take me
Hooves draw me
Gee Pilot! round the corner of Marksey's farm
Down this road grown over with grass

Mob humming the tune of the St Patrick song & just about to burst out from beneath bar crossing down to us & meet SCHOOLMASTER.

GIRL
In the spinning I lie dreaming in I hear
A humming sound that fills me up with fear

MRS DONNELLY
Look not this way, Jim Carroll, my enemy.
I leave you behind me

Circuit ends & she disappears.

MOB
When blind worms crawling in the grass
Disgusted all the nation
He gave them a rise which opened their eyes
To a sense of their situation

SCHOOLMASTER   I was the schoolmaster at the Donnelly School. On the morning of September 3rd, 1879, I met 40 to 50 men at half past eight in the morning. They had clubs and bludgeons in their hands in the name of God, where are you all going to?

CHORUS   We are going away for a heifer that was lost.

SCHOOLMASTER   Did every one of you lose a heifer?

CHORUS   No, no.

SCHOOLMASTER   Then it's time to bid the devil good morning when you meet him.

CHORUS   Oh, we're a long time seeking him.

SCHOOLMASTER   Would you know the old lad when you meet him?

CHORUS   Would we know him, sure he's a cripple and lives near a forge.   *anvil*

MRS DONNELLY
Closer and louder the sound of his hammer
Wheels take me   Hooves draw me
Haw Pilot! turn north on the Cedar Swamp Line!
What is the matter with that field of grain?

GIRL   In the humming I lie dreaming in I wake and hear

MRS RYAN   Mrs Donnelly, have mercy on my children, tell your sons to please let the thrashing machine come harvest our wheat and barley. We'll starve this year if it rots away.

MRS DONNELLY   *the anvil gets louder & louder*
No! There's no time for the wife of Ned Ryan   *and louder as she enters Whalen's Corners.*
The first house, a shed, the second
A ditch, picket fence, gateway, a path, my journey is over
Will, Norah   *she knocks*   at my son's door.

But she has no sooner entered WILL's house than we hear the mob already at the blacksmith's; the anvil stops and there are sounds of hammers and forges being tossed down.

MOB   *offstage*   We'll visit you at all hours of the night when you least expect it.

Now WILL, NORAH & MRS DONNELLY come out. WILL can use either a fiddle or a gun—both are hanging behind the bar that represents his house.

WILL   Mother, Norah—I'll ask them for their authority to search either my house or its premises. Did they show father any warrant to search?

MRS DONNELLY   Nothing but their shadows

WILL   Well then, if they can't show me a warrant, I'll shoot the first man who comes in the gate.

MOB
Nine hundred thousand reptiles blue
He charmed with sweet discourses,
And dined on them at Killaloe
In soups and second courses

The mob now slowly come towards the backs of the Donnellys. They are afraid. It's not the same as at the other house. WILL's hand reaches up for his fiddle, he turns, tunes & then plays "Boney over the Alps" laughing at them. Some of them get into the audience by mistake. We should feel ashamed of ourselves that we did not make a better showing against a lame man & two women.

MRS DONNELLY   Are you looking for your mother Dennis Trehy? That you left to starve in the workhouse at Ballysheenan though you're rich here in Canada?

WILL   My mother's taken the hunger off a great many of you days gone by when your parents sent you to our school with no lunch.

MRS DONNELLY   And I wonder at Martin O'Halloran being with such a gang as his father's the decentest man in Biddulph.

WILL   Give them another, they're in full flight down the road.   *She turns sharply away.*   James Carroll fell down and there's others tripping about the proud Napoleons they are. Mother, Norah, do you remember I told you how mother gave me this fiddle?   *sings*

Then they sold me to the brewer
And he brewed me on the pan,
But when I got into the jug
I was the strongest man.*

And it's right what you told me then. If you're afraid you should be. If you're not you'll live. Today I thank you. One fiddle you gave me, a lame boy of twelve, has been worth forty men with rifles and clubs.

MRS DONNELLY   Yes, I've marked you with all my foolish words

WILL   Not foolish. You've been dreaming of a train. This fiddle stopped that train.

MRS DONNELLY   Yes. But only in the daylight. The night, Will and Norah, may have—the dark has shoulders they can stand upon. To reach our eyes and our minds at last. Hush!

They stand again with their backs to the vigilantes who enter with a sick CARROLL. It is as if MRS DONNELLY can hear them for she half turns. They stagger about as before. CARROLL is stretched on floor.

VOICE   What's the matter with him?

NED RYAN   They've made him ill.   *tends him with some restorative*

VOICE   He's having a fit if you ask me and I don't want to have anything more to do with this. I'm leaving.

They are all sitting down on their haunches.

CARROLL   How's your old mother, Dennis, back in the workhouse at Ballysheenan?

Then they sold me to the brewer . . . I was the strongest man—a verse from the Barley Corn Ballad which opens and closes Sticks & Stones and runs through the play as the Donnellys' theme.

NED RYAN   How'd she get there ahead of us so fast?

CARROLL   She's a witch, that's why. And she shall be burnt for a witch.   *relapses*

VOICE   Ned Ryan, I think he wants something. Bend over him and—

NED RYAN   *pause*   He wants you to bring him the Holy Bible out of the school cupboard.

It is brought & CARROLL uses it for a pillow.

CARROLL   Yes, Dennis, I ran like the rest of you. Now that's better. I ran like the rest of you—but there wasn't one of you behind me and there wasn't one of you I could keep up to—tell me, how many of yous are willing to draw lots—   *They all shy away.*   to see who will sue Jack Donnelly for perjuring himself when he says that we trespassed on his father's farm today. Because, you'll note the old man did tell us "If you think the cow is here, Jim Carroll, don't leave one straw on top of another."

They raise hands & come closer.

Well, who wouldn't dare to do that, but here's one more thing, and we'll just see who's man enough to raise their hands to this proposition. In this Bible someone has placed eight slips of paper each with the name of a Donnelly written thereon. Who is brave enough to come up and draw one of those slips of paper out?

VOICE   Jim, what does it mean if we do draw the piece of paper out?

CARROLL   It means that that Donnelly will be executed before the year is out. If it can be shown that one can be killed and the executioner get away with it how many of you are then willing to go on with me at your head against the rest of the family and I promise you there will be no risk involved.

VOICE   Sure if this one is killed and no one is punished, sure.

CARROLL   Let's take a vote then. Ned, take the vote will you?

NED   Yeas?   *hands are raised*   Nays?   *some hands go up*   Forty-one to seven, Jim.

CARROLL   The seven nays are to leave this room forever, and I dare them to speak. When the execution takes place remember—you must help or join the Blackfeets. Come up and swear.

VOICE   But, Jim, nobody's drawn the lot yet and I'm not.

NED   I'll draw it. She took away my son, I'll take back one of hers.

CARROLL   Remember what you're about to promise because yes a brave man has been found, not afraid of them, and he'll show us the way, the way I could not show you this shameful morning.

VOICE   Who's he going to kill then?

NED RYAN   Michael Donnelly.

MRS DONNELLY says the name too, screams "My son," train whistle, the train proceeds to the

CHORUS   Fourth crossing!

The BARTENDER at Slaght's Hotel slides a glass down the bar as MIKE & MORRISON, his mate, enter. "WILLIAM LEWIS" is waiting; an old man named GREENWOOD is standing at the bar, sometimes bending down to spin a top.

BARTENDER   Mike, Jim. You're off early tonight. Still raining outside?

MIKE   We both ordered hot whiskeys because we were cold & wet still. I could feel the heat of the drink coming through the glass into the flesh of my hand. There's that old fellow always in here spinning his top and going to make the same joke he always does about fighting dogs. My top against your top, Greenwood. You've been waiting for this all day, haven't you?

They both spin tops which fight each other.

GREENWOOD   How's your big bulldog you got, Mike Donnelly.

MIKE   Back home in St Thomas I've got a bulldog that can lick anything its weight in Ontario

GREENWOOD   I ain't got no dog, just this top, but I can whip any dog myself, I'll strip off my clothes and commence anytime.

MIKE   Ah, you couldn't beat my bulldog, you can't even beat my top with your old top it's got more than a few holes gnawed out of it, where do you keep it, old fellow, there's been rats biting away at this one.

GREENWOOD   Here, don't you insult my top. Those holes are for balance.

LEWIS   You don't want to hop on that man, Donnelly.

MIKE   No one is touching him, and it's none of your business if there was.

LEWIS   You are always shooting off your mouth, aren't you Donnelly.   *taking off his coat*

MIKE   Do you want anything of me.

MORRISON   Now look, you two, quit it. All he said, Bill Lewis, was that his top had holes in it. Turn around away from each other. Greenwood if that's your name, see if Mike'll do you a favour and have a return match with his top meanwhile where's the washroom around here?

A clock strikes six.

MIKE   You do want something from me.

"LEWIS" strikes DONNELLY from behind; as MIKE tries to pin him he leads him back behind the bar with the knife open & ready. Just as MORRISON returns from the washroom, MIKE is stabbed below the belt. LEWIS glides away; MORRISON catches MIKE just as he falls. Train whistle.

MIKE   My God, Neighbour, I'm gone   stabbed. Jim, that's our train!

The CHORUS comes—at the wake for MICHAEL at the Donnelly farm—with four poles which represent the fourposter bed he was laid on. Candles. People kneel by the bier, then retire to the sides of the room.

MRS DONNELLY   Yes, his bed is ready. Bring Michael in here boys. Bridget, bring me the clean shirt I've got ready for him.

She takes off his old shirt, washes him & puts on a white shirt.

MORRISON   We carried Mike to the washroom. I held his head for a while and saw him die.

CHORUS   He was under bonds to keep the peace, and he was considered a desperate character.

MORRISON   We were brakemen on that train together. I think he would fight if he was set upon, but as a bully I never saw him have a row.

CHORUS   The first named testified that the deceased was a quarrelsome bully and started the row, but the others testified that he was not a disorderly character—

MORRISON   I caught hold of Donnelly for the purpose of assisting him. I never heard anybody say anything against Donnelly, and I never saw him engaged in a row.

MRS DONNELLY   I then read in the newspaper that the respective lawyers and the judge then addressed the jury, after which they retired and returned in a short time with a verdict of manslaughter. Since there was no defence offered at all, one supposes that if the lawyer for this William Lewis had offered a defence why my son's murderer might have got off completely scot free, but as it was the judge sentenced this man whom Michael had never even met before that night, whom none of us knows—two years in prison. In this forest there is now a proclamation that the hunting season on my sons is open now. There are only five of them left, the breed is rare, but do not let that limit your greed for their hearts' blood.

Michael. I wish that as I spoke with your oldest brother as he lay dying last summer I could have been there with you this winter. I told him what I tell you now—to look straight ahead past this stupid life and death they've fastened on you—just as long ago your father and me and our firstborn walked up over the last hill in Ireland and saw, what you will see now—for the first time in our lives we saw freedom, we saw the sea.

MR DONNELLY Mrs Donnelly, the sleighs have come to take our son to the church.

Candles, four poster, all sweep out of the room. We are in a barroom again. Slaght's years after; two CHAMBERMAIDS have just been assigned to clean out the barroom; outside the sun is just getting up. The old tramp is whistling "Buffalo Gals" as he walks up the empty Main Street of Waterford; train whistle. The one MAID throws the pail of water over the floor and starts scrubbing. A clock strikes twelve. The ghost of MIKE DONNELLY stands behind the bar.

MAID ONE Ugh, clean the hotel from top to bottom would you. We won't be done in here till midnight, the old muck from their feet and mouths. What're you looking so pale for, it's only an old barroom, been closed up for thirty years till this fool thinks he can run it for a profit again.

MAID TWO I thought I saw someone standing by the end of the bar over there.

MAID ONE There's no one there I can see, Mary.

MAID TWO You don't know Waterford, this place, too well do you.

MAID ONE What's there to know? There's that old man sloping off into the dawn, I wish I were free to walk the roads, not tied down like this to a scrubbing brush.

MAID TWO I wish you wouldn't pick that place by the bar to scrub so, Sarah.

MAID ONE There you go with your ghosts again. I don't believe them.

MAID TWO Would you please stop your damn scrubbing at the same spot, Sarah.

MAID ONE Are you against clean floors or something? There's something on the floor here that won't come out.

MAID TWO He's looking right down at you

MAID ONE I'll wet his feet for him then. Give me that soap, I'll . . .

MAID TWO Don't you know there was a murder in this barroom about thirty years ago, one of the brakemen on the Canada Southern, was stabbed right there where you're scrubbing. That's the blood from his wound you're trying to wash out and my mother says . . .

MAID ONE Mary, go up and start the sitting room if this is too . . . what did your mother say?

MAID TWO That's the blood of Michael Donnelly on the floor there. No matter how hard you try it never comes out.

A top spins across the floor. Scrubbing of the remaining woman; Ghost still there. Whistling dies away. "Buffalo Gals."

CHORUS
The St Nicholas Hotel
        William Donnelly Proprietor
                The Donnellys, Part Two

THREE SONGS USED IN THE PLAY

ST PATRICK
(to the tune of *Pop Goes the Weasel*)

Oh! St Patrick was a gentleman,
    Who came of decent people;
He built a church in Dublin town,
    And on it put a steeple.
His father was a Gallagher;
    His mother was a Brady;
His aunt was an O'Shaughnessy,
    His uncle an O'Grady.

CHORUS
So, success attend St Patrick's fist,
    For he's a saint so clever;
Oh! he gave the snakes and toads a twist,
    And bothered them forever.

The Wicklow hills are very high,
    And so's the Hill of Howth, sir;
But there's a hill much bigger still,
    Much higher nor them both, sir.
'Twas on the top of this high hill
    St Patrick preached his sarmint
That drove the frogs into the bogs,
    And banished all the varmint.

So, success attend St Patrick's fist, &c.

There's not a mile in Ireland's isle
    Where dirty varmin musters,
But there he put his dear fore-foot,
    And murdered them in clusters.
The toads went pop, the frogs went hop,
    Slap-dash into the water;
And the snakes committed suicide
    To save themselves from slaughter.

So, success attend St Patrick's fist, &c.

Nine hundred thousand reptiles blue
    He charmed with sweet discourses,
And dined on them at Killaloe
    In soups and second courses.
When blind worms crawling in the grass
    Disgusted all the nation,
He gave them a rise which opened their eyes
    To a sense of their situation.

So, success attend St Patrick's fist, &c.

No wonder that those Irish lads
   Should be so gay and frisky,
For sure St Pat he taught them that,
   As well as making whiskey;
No wonder that the saint himself
   Should understand distilling,
Since his mother kept a shebeen shop
   In the town of Enniskillen.

So, success attend St Patrick's fist, &c.

Oh! was I but so fortunate
   As to be back in Munster,
'Tis I'd be bound that from the ground
   I never more would once stir.
For there St Patrick planted turf,
   And plenty of the praties,
With pigs galore, ma gramma's store,
   And cabbages . . . and ladies!

Then my blessing on St Patrick's fist,
   For he's a darling saint, oh!
Oh! he gave the snakes and toads a twist;
   He's a beauty without paint, oh!

HECTOR O'HARA'S JUBILEE SONG
(to the tune of *Perhaps She's on the Railway*)

Hark! the trumpets sounding
Proclaim this is the day,
With hearts so bright and bounding,
Thousands haste away;
To have a look on Salter's Grove,
The lads and lasses true
All thro' the day will shout hurrah,
For the Dominion's bonny blue.

CHORUS
Perhaps you've come to London
Upon this glorious day,
To Salter's Grove to have a lark,
You're sure to take your way.
The blues so true will stick to you,
So boldly they will stand,
The Grittish crew will never do,
No longer in the land.

The lads and lasses in their best,
Will ramble thro' the grounds—
The bands will play throughout the day,
In music's sweetest sounds;
The pleasant strains goes thro' the brains
Of each unhappy Grit,
It gives them all the belly ache,
And sends them home to—

From here and there and everywhere,
The folks have come today,
Darby and Joan have come from home
To see the grand display.
From east and west from north and south
There's people without end,
With frills and bows and furbelows,
They'll do the Grecian Bend.

Elgin girls and Biddulph swells,
Each other try to please,
By doing the lardy dardy dum,
All among the trees,
From Westminster the pretty girls
Are rolling in the hay.
Their mother's say they mustn't,
But their fathers say they may.

There's little Popsy Wopsy here,
From Ingersoll she has come—
She's doing the double shuffle
With the chap that beats the drum;
There's Bob and Jack, Sal and Pat
And Polly coming on,
Upon her head she carries a bed
And calls it her chignon.

Strathroy girls are here today,
So nicely dress'd in blue—
With chaps that come from Exeter,
The grand they mean to do.
Polly Strong, couldn't come on
For a nasty old tom cat,
Has got a lot of kittens in
Her Dolly Varden bat.

Then shout John A. forever boys,
That is the heading cry;
Every election we will win,
The time is drawing nigh,
The scheming Grits may bag their heads
That is if they've a mind,
Or go and dig up taters
With their shirts hung out behind.

BUFFALO GALS

CHORUS
Buffalo gals won't you come out tonight
Come out tonight, come out tonight
Buffalo gals won't you come out tonight
And dance by the light of the moon.

1.
As I was tramping down the street
Down the street, down the street
I chanced a pretty girl to meet
Oh, she was fair to view

2.
I asked her if she'd have some talk
Have some talk, have some talk
Her feet covered the whole sidewalk
As she stood close to me

3.
I asked her if she'd be my wife
Be my wife, be my wife
She'd make me happy all my life
If she stood by my side.

MICHAEL COOK

(b. 1933)

The particular power of Michael Cook's plays is the result of a fortunate congruence of writer and subject. Cook is not, like James Reaney, a poet by trade, but like Reaney he is a connoisseur of the spoken word. Raised on a diet of BBC radio in its Golden Age and gifted with the ability to articulate both the English and Irish traditions which are his heritage, Cook found in Newfoundland a culture bursting with linguistic vitality. The rich verbal flavour of his plays, redolent of Arden and O'Casey, is one result. At the same time he brought with him a Jesuit background and existential outlook in sympathy with what he calls the island's "obviously threatened ceremony of a way of life in which individuals struggle with the timeless questions of worth and identity against an environment which would kill them if it could." He sees himself as the chronicler of a traditional culture, language and spirit doomed to extinction, a situation rendered in *Jacob's Wake* with mixed feelings of sympathy and savage humour.

Cook was born in London, England, of Anglo-Irish parents. After a round of Catholic schools he joined the Army in 1949 and spent the next twelve years posted in Europe and the Far East. In addition to his regular duties Cook wrote, directed and acted in numerous troop entertainments. In 1962 he enrolled in a teacher-training course at Nottingham University, graduating three years later with a specialty in drama and a desire to emigrate. He began a new life in St. John's, Newfoundland, in 1966, at first directing plays for Memorial University. By 1970 he had been appointed Lecturer in English at Memorial and artistic director of the St. John's Summer Festival. Meanwhile he was writing a theatre column for the St. John's *Evening Telegram* and an average of two radio plays a year for the CBC.

All of Cook's first stage plays were performed by The Open Group, a local amateur company, before being professionally produced. *Colour the Flesh the Colour of Dust* was his debut, presented by The Open Group in 1971 under his own direction, then at the Neptune in Halifax in 1972. A Brechtian-style history play set in St. John's in 1762, *Colour the Flesh* was a preview of one direction Cook's drama would take. The other direction was established by *The Head, Guts and Soundbone Dance*, first staged in 1973. The play combined the naturalistic detail of a Newfoundland fisherman's "splitting room" with a Beckettian sense of absurdist isolation and futility as two old men play out their endgame, indulging in mad dreams of a romanticized past and an unlikely future while ignoring at great cost the realities of the present. Despite their obvious differences, Cook conceived of these plays as the first two parts of a "Newfoundland trilogy." The third part was *Jacob's Wake*, performed by The Open Group in summer 1974 and premiered professionally at Festival Lennoxville the following summer.

Cook moved from St. John's to the isolation of Random Island in 1975. The influence of that outport environment along with the continued pertinence of Beckett to Cook's view of the Newfoundland experience is evident in the two long monologues, "Quiller" and "Therese's Creed," presented as a double bill at the Centaur in 1977. He reached back again to historical material for *On the Rim of the Curve* (1977), a play about the extinction of Newfoundland's Beothuk Indians, and *The Gayden Chronicles*, his ambitious tale of a British seaman whipped through the fleet and hanged at St. John's in 1812 for revolutionary activities. Workshopped at Lennoxville and the O'Neill Centre in Connecticut, *Gayden* was first produced in Los Angeles in 1980. Cook has continued to write radio plays and to direct. He has served as an editor of *Canadian Theatre Review* and Chairman of Playwrights Canada. Since 1982 he has divided his time between Newfoundland and Stratford, Ontario.

Jacob's Wake is Cook's richest play, and the one generally acknowledged by academic critics to be his best. In contrast the play was critically panned by reviewers when it opened in Lennoxville. Perhaps that production failed to achieve the difficult balances *Jacob's Wake* demands. Like a wake it is both celebration and dirge, a mixture of moods and styles: by turns raucously funny, bitter, maudlin; intensely naturalistic for the most part but with a spooky, surreal quality that increases with the strength of the storm until it moves beyond realism altogether at the end. The play integrates elements of *Long Day's Journey into Night* and *Heartbreak House* with an overlay of *Endgame* and echoes of *The Homecoming*. At one level a domestic drama contained within the Blackburn family home, at another it adduces the spiritual malaise of an entire culture. Beyond that it mixes biblical allusions with a stark existentialism to climax in an apocalypse without salvation or resurrection. It is a play about Newfoundland battered by difficult social transformations and unrelenting Nature, and haunted by ghosts.

Maundy Thursday and Good Friday provide an ironic setting for the failed communion and multiple betrayals that mark the gathering of the Blackburn clan. Against the background of the hymn "Eternal Father Strong to Save" we see measure after measure of patriarchal failure. The Skipper has sent his son Jacob to his death, left his other son Winston a drunken welfare bum and his daughter Mary an embittered old maid. Winston's legacy has been the cynicism, madness and treachery of his own three sons. The women have done little better. Mary despises her father, her brother and the children she teaches. Even Rosie, the family glue and the ultimate nurturer, probably does more harm than good in her excessive mothering of Winston. Despite all attempts of the aptly named Rosie to put the best face on it, this family is a disaster. Its rituals, as Cook notes in a stage direction, have degenerated into "killing games."

Behind the bitterness hover the family's unexorcised ghosts. Cook has been criticized for bringing a literal ghost on stage at the end of the play, but he gives us ample warning. All three generations of Blackburns are haunted. For more than thirty years the Skipper has lain in bed crippled by guilt and remorse, holding his wake for Jacob and for the demise of the seal hunt that killed him. Winston is doubly haunted, living in the wake of his dead brother and unable to bury the memory of his own lost daughter Sarah. Brad is obsessed and finally destroyed by his ghosts, Mildred Tobin and her infant boy. Given the play's Easter Week setting we might expect the characters to discover meaning or redemption in these deaths. But ironically they see only emptiness and a future without hope.

The condition of the Blackburns reflects in extreme form Cook's view of contemporary Newfoundland itself: "somewhere in the transition between rural and industrial man they left behind a portion of their souls." In the old Skipper, relic of pre-Confederation days, the authority and self-sufficiency of the ship's captain and seal hunter are reduced to impotent ravings and an unhealthy fixation on the past. Winston's generation, the most painfully conscious of changing times, is unable to cope, caught "like rats in a trap, with the Welfare as bait." The future, such as it is, rests with Winston's sons, and their ascendancy marks the final overthrow of traditional values. The times of the seal are gone, Alonzo says. "It's the day of the dogfish now." If government, business and religion are represented by Wayne, Alonzo and Brad, they are in bad shape. Education is no better off with Mary.

Though Cook's prognosis is exceedingly gloomy, *Jacob's Wake* itself is not. The Blackburns don't just go blindly to their doom. Their Day of Judgement is tempered by significant moments of recognition and a pretty good showing when they are forced finally "to steer into the starm and face up to what ye are." Theirs may be a sinking ship capsized by their own turpitude and neglect, but they go down with the sort of theatrical élan that ought to keep us from judging them too harshly.

•

Jacob's Wake had its first professional performance on July 11, 1975 at Festival Lennoxville, with Griffith Brewer as Skipper, Roland Hewgill as Winston, Candy Kane as Rosie, Rita Howell as Mary, R.H. Thomson as Brad, David Calderisi as Alonzo and August Schellenberg as Wayne. Set and costumes were designed by Michael Eagan, lighting by Douglas Buchanan and sound by William Skolnik. The director was William Davis.

JACOB'S WAKE

CHARACTERS

SKIPPER ELIJAH BLACKBURN
MARY, *his daughter*
WINSTON, *his son*
ROSIE, *Winston's wife*
ALONZO ⎫
BRAD ⎬ *their sons*
WAYNE ⎭

THE DIALECT

I have taken a certain amount of dramatic licence in the presentation of dialect as spoken by the principals. Rosie, of all the characters, has been untouched by the wider world and her dialect is, as accurately as I am able to determine, authentic. Winston is a man of considerable experience and education, both of which he seeks to suppress. In consequence, whereas he retains most of the rich verbal inversions which are one of the great strengths of the Newfoundland dialect, I have resisted the temptation to localize his speech, i.e., the substitution of 'd' for 'th' and the dazzling varieties of the use of the aspirant which change from locale to locale about the Coast. As with both the Skipper and Alonzo, Winston occasionally broadens his dialect under stress or when the sound of the sentence requires it. Brad, Wayne and Mary have successfully suppressed their native speech and of the three only Mary, under pressure, sometimes reverts to the older and more satisfying use of the personal pronoun.

THE SOUND

It is essential if we are to believe and participate in the tragedy of the Blackburn family and, indirectly, the world that they inhabit, that the storm becomes a living thing, a character whose presence is always felt, if not actually heard, on the stage. Whereas this might make remarkable demands upon sound technicians, it is not so remarkable in reality. The fury of the North Atlantic is well known. Perhaps what is less well known is the elemental fury of that ocean in the early spring when snow and ice and hurricane combine to create a world in which nothing can live, save the creatures of the sea itself. The history of the early sealing tragedies has been well documented and the conditions that men struggled against, notably in Cassie Brown's epic account of one such disaster in *Death on the Ice* and Farley Mowat's moving testament, matched with David Blackwood's remarkable etchings, The Lost Party Series, in *Wake of the Great Sealers*.

I have, however, extended the known reality to encompass the possibility of an environment no longer responsive to the timeless bonding between itself and man which makes communion upon this earth possible, an environment with the will for destruction to match our own and a greater capacity to ensure that destruction, an environment which bred E.J. Pratt's *Titanic*-sinking iceberg, a vast neolithic structure created for just such a time when man's hubris had made him blind to nature, his own matching nature and that harmony which alone makes survival possible.

The storm then has a voice and a presence complementary to the voices and presences on the stage, but one which ultimately outstrips them, engulfs them, destroys them.

THE SET

The play can be staged in a variety of ways. The most obvious representation is one of total realism corresponding to the two levels of a typical Newfoundland outport house. The downstairs area is divided into two areas, although the room itself is one kitchen. The centrepiece is a large wood and oil stove, which must be totally functional. To the left is the eating area. A simple wooden table, with corresponding chairs will suffice, or a rather hideous chrome set. The sink is on the left wall. Water is piped in from a well during the summer. During the time of the play, however, it can be assumed that the ground is still frozen and that water is being brought in ten gallon plastic buckets. One or two full may be seen between the sink and the stove. There is a window behind the sink.

The area centre and left contains a rocking chair by the fire and at extreme left, beneath the second, matching window, a rather lumpy day bed stretches against the wall. Cupboards line the wall between the sink and the stove. One of these may be open to display various items of kitchen ware. There would be, on the walls, an oval picture of the SKIPPER and his wife in the heyday of their youth. One of those incredibly stiff, formal pictures in which the woman, often a sad-faced and beautiful wooden doll, is dominated by the glaring light eyes and the walrus moustache of the male. An illuminated prayer with a sorrowing Christ would confirm the family's Catholic origins, and perhaps a sepia tinted photograph of an old iron ship wallowing in a dead sea. The walls are papered, and should have that bulky consistency that comes from placing layer upon layer over the years upon wooden walls. At backstage centre is the one entrance, leading to the stairs and exterior. We should be aware of a small corridor leading offstage left and the stairs rising, fairly steeply, backstage centre. The dimensions should be contained so that at no time is it possible for anyone on stage not to be aware of, or have to move a great distance to, anybody else. There should be a sense of confining, of a claustrophobic intensity which washes against, and adds to, the emotional tensions built up during the play.

Upstairs, a landing runs centre, with two bedrooms right and left respectively. The rooms are small, low-ceilinged, with barely any room for physical movement other than walking around the beds, getting into them, or getting objects from the wall. In the SKIPPER's bedroom, right, there is a narrow pine highboy or chest of drawers. On it lies the SKIPPER's log book and on the wall behind, a barometer. Beneath the bed is a large chamber pot.

Both beds are old-fashioned, metal-framed. Each room contains a small window, backstage. The boys' room contains one chair, used for clothes; the SKIPPER's room, one chair used by visitors. Both beds are slightly raked and face the audience.

There are obvious small variations on the theme, but if staged for realistic presentation, then they must conform to our expectancy. It is, in fact, minute attention to realistic detail that heightens the progression towards symbolism and abstraction in the action of the play.

An acceptable alternative would be a stark, skeletonized set. The levels would have to remain essentially the same, but a structure as white as bone, stripped of formality, the house equivalent of a stranded hulk of a schooner, only the ribs poking towards an empty sky, would serve the play's purpose, and free the director for an existential interpretation of the play.

ACT ONE

Scene One

The stage is in semi-darkness. Sound of storm. A dawn light filters through the windows.

ROSIE is sitting in the rocking chair, sewing a patchwork quilt. MARY is at the kitchen table left, marking papers. There is no sound for a long minute, save the slight squeaking of the rocker as ROSIE sews, rocks, sews, rocks. MARY puts down a book and sighs wearily. She stands up, pushing a lock of hair from her eyes, looks at ROSIE, waiting for some comment. None is forthcoming. ROSIE rocks and sews. MARY goes to the stove and checks to see if the kettle is boiling. It is. She crosses to the cupboards left and takes a cup. She rummages again

and comes up with a teabag. She crosses to the fridge, pauses and sighs. She turns and puts the cup on the table. She turns back to the refrigerator, opens it and takes out a small bottle of lemon juice. Leaving the door open, she moves to pour a drop of lemon juice into the cup. She moves back and replaces the lemon, and shuts the door. She turns back to the table and sits. She picks up another book, then puts it down. ROSIE sews and rocks.

MARY   I just can't do any more.

ROSIE   What, dear.

MARY   I said . . . I can't do any more of this marking. It's like washing the same dirty dishes over and over again . . . without any results.

She sips delicately at her tea.

ROSIE   *resting her quilt in her lap*   Ye works hard at the teaching, maid. I knows. I wor talking to Sally Ivany t'other day. She boards dat new teacher, Mr. Farrell.

MARY   That one! She'd better watch herself then. The man has no principles. I don't understand how people like that ever get into the profession.

ROSIE   He got a powerful lot of degrees, Sally said. He's right clever. But he don't play uppity wi' her, she says. He's jest like one of the family. Eats his bit of fish and brewis. Jest loves a salt pork dinner. Sits down an 'as a beer afore dinner wid Rob when 'e's 'ome from the fishing. Right fond of him, she is.

MARY   I can imagine! Degrees don't necessarily make good teachers, Rose. Experience is the only teacher. Experience, common sense and a few good old fashioned virtues. There are too many Farrells about these days, walking into the best jobs, carrying on with their students. . . .

ROSIE   I said as 'ow ye was always at it an' Sally wor surprised. She said he don't ever bring no work 'ome.

MARY   *angrily*   Because he doesn't set any homework, that's why. I don't know what things are coming to. They all seem intent upon producing a generation of illiterates and I'm afraid the few of us who are left can hardly stem the tide.

A gust of wind shakes the house. There is a moan from SKIPPER upstairs. ROSIE looks up anxiously.

ROSIE   Skipper's not sleeping well dese days.

MARY   Has he ever? *sipping her tea*   I don't suppose I could either, with so much blood on my hands. . . . Some of it my own too. Ink, I suppose, has its advantages.

There is another gust of wind, and again SKIPPER moans.

ROSIE   I should go up to 'n.

She makes no move. MARY finishes her tea, gathers up her books and crosses towards the day bed. She bends down and pulls out a wooden chest from beneath it.

MARY Rose, I know you do your best, but don't you think Father should be in a place where he can be properly looked after?

ROSIE In the hospital. In St. John's, ye mean?

MARY Something like that. Yes.

She bends again and begins to stack the books into the chest. She lowers the lid and pushes it back underneath.

ROSIE No, maid. I'd never sleep a wink worrying about'n getting his drop o' rum, knowing 'e'd have no one to tend to'n or read from his book. Having no real voices to talk to. *rocking, reflective* Me own fader now, he were different. When his turn come to be took, he sent me mudder out. To spare 'er, he said. Then he begun to say the psalms. I wor young den. I minds me mother sent me in to look at'n. She reckoned he'd tolerate me where the sight of her would only irritate'n. It wor funny really. Me own fader. Shrivelled face, all yellow it were, an' a black hole for a mout'.... He had nar tooth left in his head...the words dribbling out. And...him wi' that old cap on his head like 'e always wore when 'e read the Book to us. I wanted to laugh, but was too afeard.

MARY Laugh? And your father dying?

ROSIE Ah, but he wor allus gone, maid, working at one t'ing or anudder. I nivir knew'n see. He wor jest somebody dying and I wor just a slip of a maid. Strange, I s'pose dat's why I likes to look after yer fader now. It's like he does for the both of'n.

A gust of wind. Another moan from SKIPPER. From inside the house, a clock strikes the half hour. MARY finishes stacking her books.

MARY There is a difference, Rose. I don't believe Father looked at the Bible once in his life unless it was to mumble a few words over the men he lost at the ice. And only then because the law required it.

ROSIE Ah well. I must go up to'n.

She puts her work down in the basket at her side, heaves herself up out of the chair and crosses to exit.

MARY *exasperated* For goodness sake, Rose. Leave him be. He's worse than a child.

ROSIE Yes, maid. I 'lows that 'e is. But den, I nivir could say no to none o' dem neither.

She goes out. Upstairs, SKIPPER mumbles something indistinct. MARY looks up. An expression of near hatred crosses her face.

MARY Why don't you just die and leave us alone.

A beam of light spills into SKIPPER's room as ROSIE puts the hall light on. He is sitting upright in bed, crying soundlessly. ROSIE bustles in, lays him back, smooths his forehead, then sits, holding his hand. A door bangs, loudly, off.

MARY Winston! Back already.

She makes for the door to get out before WINSTON arrives, but just as she reaches it, it is flung open and BRAD stands there carrying a suitcase. He has left his topcoat in the outer hall and is wearing a neat grey suit, surmounted with a clerical collar. Despite the traditional mode of his appearance, there is something wild about his eyes. His hair is dishevelled.

MARY Brad. Thank goodness, it's only you.

BRAD Hello, Aunt. *pushing unceremoniously past her, dropping his suitcase down by the wall* Where's Mother?

MARY Upstairs tending to your grandfather.

BRAD *moving out into the hallway* Mother! Mother!

MARY She's busy. Do you have to announce your arrival?

BRAD *coming back in* Yes. Yes, as a matter of fact, I do.

MARY Why? She knows you're coming. God knows, we all do. You always come on Maundy Thursday though why I've yet to find out. It's a time when most pastors choose to stay with their flock, isn't it? But then you always did make up your own rules.

BRAD Not any more, Aunt.

MARY What do you mean?

BRAD I...have been replaced. Thrown out.

MARY sits as the implications of his words sink in. With purposeful energy, as if laying some claim to the house, asserting his presence, he begins to make himself a cup of tea.

My ministry is ended...for the moment. But God's work doesn't end when one servant fails. Does it? Does it, Aunt Mary?

MARY What have you done now?

BRAD I challenged corruption. That is what I did, single handed. But what is one man against the Devil? One man against the armies of Cain? I wasn't strong enough, Aunt Mary.

MARY Still the same old delusions. Why are you wearing that collar?

BRAD The collar? *He wrestles with it, takes it off and holds it out.* The collar is a symbol. A link in the chain of pride. It chokes the soul. *throwing it to the ground* I am done with false images.

MARY   What are you going to do now?

She is confused, almost defeated. BRAD is an unbearable complication in an already intolerable situation.

BRAD   Stay here, of course. Wait to be called. Learn to be strong again.

MARY   No. No, Brad. You can't stay here.

BRAD   Why not? This is my house.

MARY   And so it is mine. I . . . your mother and I . . . we can't stand any more disruption, Brad. You know what it's like here.

BRAD meets her challenge without flinching. She turns from him in disgust.

You were always an emotional cripple. Of course you failed, as you put it. What made you think you could use God as a crutch for your fantasies?

There is still no response from BRAD.

Don't you think, at least, that your mother has enough to contend with? Or are you going to be content to just sit and add your weight to the rest pulling her down to an early grave?

BRAD   He was despised and rejected of men.

MARY   How dare you compare yourself to the Lord. You're sick, Brad. Sick. You need help.

BRAD   *taking her hands with a sudden movement* You're right, Aunt Mary. I do need help. Will you help me? Show me my faults?

MARY   *shaking him off*   We don't need you here, Brad. Will you get that into your thick head. Go. Go anywhere but here. There's a world out there waiting to be saved.

BRAD   But this is where I come from. This is where my work must be.

A door bangs off. ALONZO and WINSTON offstage stamp their boots, wheeze and laugh.

MARY   I think I hear your work coming now.

ALONZO and WINSTON appear in the doorway, arms round each other, singing, palpably the worse for wear. Like a travesty of an old music hall duo, they try to get through the door together and get stuck.

ALONZO and WINSTON   *singing*
In Dublin's city where I did dwell
Lived a butcher's boy I loved right well.
He courted me. . . .

The crescendo is broken as ALONZO staggers through the door first, nearly falling.

ALONZO   Christ, Father. You're getting as fat as a pig.

He spots BRAD and peers at him. WINSTON follows him in.

ALONZO   Well, well, well. It's the Reverend Blackburn. How are ye, Brad?

ALONZO slaps him on the back and nearly knocks both BRAD and himself over. He clutches BRAD for support. WINSTON crosses to the day bed as MARY rises and crosses to the door to escape.

WINSTON   'Tis the Prodigal himself, come fer to wish us a Happy Easter. A Happy Easter, son. *belching loudly*

MARY   It's Maundy Thursday. A few minutes from now it will be Good Friday.

WINSTON   Oh. 'Tis mauzy* Thursday, is it? I t'ought the weather were a bit queer.

ALONZO finds this very funny. MARY surveys the scene grimly and points to BRAD.

MARY   For once, Winston, your besotted brain has stumbled upon a truth. You should welcome Brad with open arms. That is, if you can open them. Your second mistake has come home. To roost.

She exits. WINSTON sits up, puzzled.

WINSTON   What did she say?

ALONZO   Dunno, boy. Something about a dicky bird.

BRAD   *crossing to his father and holding out his hand*   Hello, Father. I trust you're well.

WINSTON catches his hand and pulls him down on the day bed.

WINSTON   I think I wor, until I saw ye. Lonz. Lonz, b'y. D'ye hear that. He trusts I'm well.

ALONZO   That's what all them religious say when yer dying.

WINSTON   That's right too.

ROSIE enters and goes straight to the stove to fill a jug of hot water from the kettle.

ROSIE   Oh my. Yer all back. I jest bin sitting up wid yer fader, Winston. He's bin right upset tonight.

BRAD, disengaging himself from WINSTON, crosses to ROSIE.

BRAD   Mother. . . .   *He puts out his arms for an embrace.*

ROSIE   *turning towards him, holding the kettle* Why, Brad, I t'ought I heard ye when I wor upstairs. . . . How are ye? . . .

BRAD   Mother . . . I've come home.

ROSIE crosses to the kitchen area. BRAD follows her.

ROSIE   I knows, son. Ye allus comes to see us Easter. Yer a good boy.

---

*mauzy—hazy.

BRAD   No, Mother. You don't understand. You see, I've come home for good. I've. . .left the church.

WINSTON   That's what Mary meant! Well be the Lard Jesus, what have I done to deserve that?

ALONZO   I dunno, Father. It might do us all good to have the family conscience restored to the fold.

WINSTON   Family pain in the arse. That's what he is. Always wor, now I comes to think of it.

BRAD   *trying to maintain a semblance of dignity* Father. . .I've had a difficult day. . . .

ALONZO has found the collar on the floor and gleefully tries it on.

WINSTON   So have I, son, and ye've made it worse. . . .

BRAD   I don't expect you to understand. . . .I don't expect anyone to share my burdens. . . .But a little welcome. . . .

ALONZO   *prancing about the kitchen, the collar firmly fastened* How do I look, Mother?

ROSIE is pouring herself a cup of tea. She turns and laughs, the laughter of shocked delight.

ROSIE   Yer some shocking boy. Have ye no respect? Take it off.

ALONZO   *in a dreadful imitation of Garner Ted Armstrong* I'll take your bets now. . . .You're all gamblers. . . .We all gamble with our souls. . . .Yes, our souls. . . .So I'll take your bets now on the second coming. What's that, sir. . . . You haven't had one since you were eighteen. . . .

ROSIE   *putting down her tea and chasing ALONZO round the room, laughing* Lonz. Lonz! Now you give me dat.

He dodges round her. She pauses breathless and laughing at the table. WINSTON staggers to the fridge and gets a beer. He raises it and drains half the bottle in one gulp. Sighing with satisfaction, he wipes his face with the back of his hand. He belches loudly and begins to sing.

WINSTON   *singing*
Here's a health to ye, Father O'Flynn
Drink it in ginger or drink it in gin. . . .

BRAD   *anguished* Mother.

ALONZO   *sternly to WINSTON* Today's sermon will, yet again, be on the evils of drink. Last week. . .last week, the collection amounted to two dollars thirteen cents and one Japanese yen. And yet only the previous night many of you. . .yes, women too. . .spent triple, nay, quadruple, in fact, a hell of a lot more than that at that palace of sin. . .The Blue Flamingo. . . .

WINSTON collapses on a kitchen chair. ROSIE too laughs.

BRAD   Mother. Stop them.

ROSIE   Oh, don't mind them, b'y. Dey's only having a bit of fun wid ye. Now come on and I'll git ye a lunch. Ye must be starved come all dat way.

He stands uncertain. ALONZO capers round him.

ALONZO
Brad, Brad, wouldn't
Listen to his dad,
Went to be a preacher
Cos his folks they was all bad

Whooooo. . .eeeee.

ROSIE   And so ye are whooping and hollerin' and carryin' on. Set the table, the lot of ye. I'll get ye a cup o' tay.

WINSTON   Who needs tea? Rosie, get Brad a beer.

BRAD   No thank you, Father.

WINSTON   But ye've left the ministry. Ye said so.

BRAD   Yes. I have but. . . .

WINSTON   Then ye've no call not to be normal like the rest of us. Lonz, git a beer into him.

WINSTON hands ALONZO his beer. ALONZO stalks BRAD. ROSIE watches half shocked, half laughing.

ALONZO   Come on, Brad. Here, boy. Here. Ye've dropped yer collar now. It's jest like the ould days.

BRAD   I can't, Alonzo. It's not like that.

WINSTON   What is it like then, son? Ye comes home and tells us yer back wit' the family, so ye must takes what ye gets. Like the rest of us.

ALONZO has forced BRAD back onto the day bed. ROSIE is laughing outright. ALONZO forces the bottle to BRAD's mouth.

ALONZO   Come on, baby. Drink. . .drink. . . .

BRAD wrestles furiously. The beer pours all over him. WINSTON and ROSIE laugh aloud. BRAD, almost hysterical, succeeds in pushing ALONZO back. He falls on all fours. BRAD leaps up frenziedly wiping his mouth.

BRAD   *close to tears* Damn you. Damn you.

ROSIE   Alright, b'ys. 'Tis gone far enough.

WINSTON   Nice words from a man of the cloth.

ALONZO   And assault and battery.

BRAD rushes for the door, but WINSTON, sensing his move, blocks his way. BRAD moves round the room like a trapped animal.

ROSIE   *alarmed* Dat's enough now, Winston. Stop it.

BRAD   *screaming* I haven't given up anything. That's a symbol. A collar is just a symbol. . . .I haven't given up on God.

WINSTON *moving back away from the door* Stay around here long enough and He'll give up on ye.

BRAD Never. No. Never. He won't desert me.

Unnoticed, WAYNE has appeared in the door. He's immaculately suited and carries an executive overnight case.

WAYNE Well, well. The same old animal farm, I see.

ALONZO Welcome home, brother. Ye've missed the sermon, but yer just in time for the collection.

ROSIE *crossing to welcome him* Wayne. *He kisses her.* Yer father said ye'd not be coming dis year.

She takes his case and puts it behind the day bed. WAYNE comes on in.

WAYNE Well, Mother, I have to fight through the paper this high to get into the office, but it can wait another day or so. And I've some constituents with a few problems to see up this way. . . . So here I am.

ROSIE We're right pleased ye could come, aren't we, Winston?

WINSTON I'm overjoyed, maid.

ALONZO Who are ye trying to kid, Wayne. Seeing constituents on Good Friday! Ye're not that conscientious. There's something else in the wind. Wouldn't be anything to do with me, would it? A contract or two?

WAYNE Who knows.

WINSTON Come to see me, didn't ye, son? Unlike a few I could mention, he's proud of his father. Talks about me all the time in that House of Assembly . . . *chuckling* to the Minister o' Welfare.

WAYNE *ignoring him* Where's Aunt Mary?

ROSIE Oh, she's gone. Must've gone to bed while I wor upstairs wid yer grandfader. That wor afore Brad come. Poor Brad. They bin tormentin' 'im somethin' terrible.

BRAD has been standing stiffly by the window, trying to bring himself under control. WAYNE crosses to him and holds out his hand.

WAYNE Hi, Brad.

BRAD *turning, ignoring the hand, still dripping slightly* You!

WAYNE Good God. Have you been drinking?

WINSTON and ALONZO laugh.

BRAD Devil. You sent them. You did, didn't you?

WAYNE I don't know what you're talking about.

BRAD Oh yes, you do. Judas!

He rushes out.

ROSIE Dat's dem two, see. Nivir did take much to a ribbin', Brad didn't. I'd better go and see'n settled. *She makes for the door and turns.* He'll be sleepin' wid ye, Lonz. Ye don't mind, do ye?

WAYNE Why should he. Lonz has never been particular about who he slept with.

ALONZO Watch it, brother. Watch it.

ROSIE exits.

WINSTON Want a drink, son? *proffering a beer* Oh yis. I'm sorry, sir. *tugging his forelock* Beer's a working man's drink, i'n it?

WAYNE *mocking* Jesus, Fader. Then what are ye doing drinkin' it.

WINSTON goes to the dresser, opens a drawer, produces a bottle of moonshine, holds it up to the light and eyes it with great satisfaction.

WINSTON Now. . . .that's a good brew. One of the best I ever made, though I says it meself. *He puts the bottle on the table.* Lonz. Get a jug of hot water, boy. Wayne, me son. Git the mugs.

It's a traditional part of the family ritual. WINSTON gets sugar from the dresser and one teaspoon from a drawer. WAYNE gets three mugs. ALONZO pours hot water from the kettle into a substantial aluminum jug. All three deposit their burdens, pause and sit, almost simultaneously. The irony is that whereas the rules of the ritual have evolved into killing games, the unifying structure remains the same. WINSTON pours and mixes a drink.

WINSTON Now, boys. Let's celebrate the annual family re-union.

WAYNE What family? What union?

WINSTON eyes him steadily. WAYNE, unmoved, helps himself to a drink.

WINSTON Now, b'y. I knows ye've gone up in the world. Weren't nowhere else to go from here, was there? But ye still comes back every year. Or nearly every year. They must be something in it.

ALONZO The thrill of disaster.

WINSTON A good crack.

ALONZO No, b'y. Love. That's what it is. Love.

WINSTON I 'lows I nivir t'ought o' that.

They both laugh. WAYNE allows himself a grin. He knows the game, the rules, and showing emotion isn't one of them. ROSIE re-enters.

ROSIE Oh. Ye's all settled den. I bin talking to Brad, Winston. He's some upset. Seems like dey t'rew him out. Now, isn't dat shockin'? After all he done for dem too.

ALONZO About time they come to their senses. I heard stories about him, Mother, that ye wouldn't have been so proud of.

WAYNE   Me too.

WINSTON   Oh. What wor that then? I t'ought he wor incapable of sin.

WAYNE   He was becoming a damned nuisance. Moved one community from a decent fishing ground to a hole in the bog. Pestered us and Ottawa for grants of one kind or another. Even tried a little arson though we couldn't prove it.

ALONZO   So he was right. Ye got rid of him.

WAYNE   Did I say that?

ALONZO   Ye didn't have to. I can see I'll have to watch you, boy. Yer getting dangerous.

WAYNE   Thanks for the compliment.

WINSTON   Jesus. Politics! Let's get off the subject, afore I pukes. Rosie. . . Rosie, maid. Git the cards, will ye?

In the interior, a clock strikes twelve. ROSIE fetches a pack of cards.

ROSIE   Oh my. 'Tis twelve already. *yawning widely* Shall I go up and git the bed warm, Winston?

WINSTON   Ye can do what ye likes, maid. I 'lows it'll take more than warmth to dress me leg* tonight.

During the following speech, ROSIE exits and reappears with a handful of splits for lighting the fire in the morning. She lowers the oven door, places the wood in the oven and leaves the door down.

WAYNE   Father. For God's sake.

WINSTON   He allus wor squeamish, Lonz. I suppose that's what they calls sensitivity.

ALONZO   Is it? Jes', Fader. Ye're a walking encyclopaedia. I learns something every time I comes here.

ROSIE   Goodnight then, b'ys.

WAYNE   Goodnight, Mother.

ALONZO   'Night.

ROSIE exits. WINSTON picks up the cards.

WINSTON   First Jack deals?

They nod. He rapidly spins round the cards off the top of the pack. The first Jack falls to WAYNE.

Jesus, if he fell off a skyscraper, he'd land in a pile o' shit.

He throws the pack at WAYNE, who shuffles them and begins to deal. They are playing one hundred and twenties. The cards are dealt, five apiece, in blocks of two and three.

ALONZO   I blames Aunt Mary for Wayne, Father. Shoving all them books and morals into his head when he were young. Unhealthy, I says.

*dress me leg—have sexual intercourse.

All three examine their cards, WAYNE in particular making sure that no one can catch a glimpse of his hand.

WAYNE   Jealousy will get you nowhere. Anyway, you haven't done too badly out of me, one way or another.

WINSTON   Jealous! Of you! I'll go twenty. I wouldn't change me peace of mind fer all yer House of Assemblies.

ALONZO   Twenty-five. I make more money than he does anyway.

WAYNE   I'll take your twenty five. If you want to live by selling watered booze and importing prostitutes as strippers you're welcome to it.

ALONZO   There's more than one way of prostitution.

WINSTON   Make it, son.

ALONZO   And for me.

WAYNE   Diamonds!

WINSTON   I nivir told ye, Lonz, about the time we 'ad to get Wayne circumcised when he wor little. I'll take three.

ALONZO   No. Ye didn't. Two fer me.

WINSTON discards and accepts three cards from WAYNE. ALONZO, likewise. WAYNE goes through the discards, ignores them and takes two cards.

WINSTON   'Is mother wor some proud of his bird. It wor about t'ree inches long when he wor borned.

WAYNE   *rattled* Your down, Father. Your down!

WINSTON   *playing and continuing unperturbed* All the neighbours come in to look at'n. It wor the eighth wonder of the world, boy. Even yer Aunt Mary were excited, though she didn't know why.

WAYNE   For God's sake, Alonzo. Play, will you. Or pack it in.

ALONZO   *plays* What happened?

WAYNE   *plays* Can't you ever get your mind out of the gutter, Father?

WINSTON   It wor keeping yer cock out of the gutter that worried us. An' the doctors said if it wor real, ye'd nivir be no good to no one, 'cept an old ewe maybe. *He plays.*

ALONZO   *chuckling and beginning to sing*
Ewe take the high road
An' I'll take the low road. . . .

WAYNE   Play!

ALONZO plays.

WAYNE   You're just trying to beat this hand. It won't work. . . . *He takes the trick.*

WINSTON   Anyways, we took'n to St. John's. Yer mother took a photograph of 'n afore we left, just in case they cut'n right off.

WAYNE   Your card, Father. Your card. That's the Jack of trumps.

WINSTON   So it is. Well, I got nar' one.   *He throws away.*

ALONZO   What happened? The five of trumps, Wayne.

WAYNE   *shouting*   It can't be. I just played that.

ALONZO   You're mistaken, brother. I wondered why you took my twenty five in the first place.

WAYNE searches back through his tricks, finds the offending card and throws it in front of ALONZO.

ALONZO   You accusing me of cheating.

WINSTON   Like all politicians, Lonz. They can't bear to lose, even to family and friends.

WAYNE   I say you cheated.

SKIPPER   Jacob! Jacob!

WINSTON   There he goes. Slippin' out through the Narrows agin.

ALONZO   What happened?

WAYNE   You cheated.

SKIPPER   Jacob. . . .

WINSTON   It wor all skin. They was nothing there. Nothing at all. Smallest damn thing ye ever did see.

ALONZO collapses in hysterics. WAYNE, furious, strides round the table. Delves into ALONZO's pocket and comes up with a set of trump cards.

WAYNE   You disgusting, cheating pimp. No more favours, d'you hear. No more contracts. Not from me. Not from anybody in this government.

ALONZO   *unmoved*   Did it ever grow?

WINSTON   Never, b'y. Never. That's why he'd only let Aunt Mary give'n 'is weekly bath. An' that went right on 'til he wor thirteen or so.

ALONZO shrieks with laughter.

WAYNE   *shouting*   Stop lying. Stop lying, for Christ's sake.

MARY appears in the door, dressed in a voluminous nightgown.

MARY   What in the name of Christian charity is going on in this house? The noise is enough to wake the dead.

Coming forward, she sees WAYNE.

Wayne.

SKIPPER   I nivir sent the starm, Jacob. Ye can't blame me for that.

WINSTON   The dead arose and appeared to many.

WAYNE   I'm sorry, Aunt.

He attempts to recover composure, moves round the table, putting on his jacket which has been discarded at the beginning of the game. WINSTON watches him carefully, waiting for a further opportunity. ALONZO's chuckles punctuate the brief silence. MARY moves to WAYNE and puts her hand on his arm.

MARY   You shouldn't let them do this to you, Wayne.

WINSTON   That's right, maid. We shouldn't 'a let 'em do it to'n in the first place, I 'lows.

MARY   Do what? What drunken gibberish are you on with now?

WAYNE   For the love of . . . Shut up.   *to MARY* Each time I walk into this house, I lose my sanity. You'd think by now I'd know better.

MARY   You shouldn't come.

WINSTON   But he do, maid. He do. And we all knows why, eh, Lonz?

ALONZO   *sputtering*   For his bath.

WAYNE goes for ALONZO.

MARY   Wayne. Don't. That's just what they want.

WAYNE   *drawing back*   Don't worry, Aunt.   *to WINSTON and ALONZO*   This is definitely the last time, d'you hear? You've played your last game of cards at my expense, the pair of you.

He crosses to the day bed, picks up his case and walks out into the livingroom with MARY.

ALONZO   God, Father. That were worth coming home for. Father!

WINSTON slumps back on the chair, mouth open, and begins to snore. ALONZO shakes his head, gets up, moves as if to exit, but the old force of habit pulls him back. He closes the bottle, puts it back on the chest of drawers. He picks up the scattered cards and crosses, the cards in his hand, to the stair door.

Mother. Mother.

He goes back to the table, puts the cards in the box, and puts them away. He tries to lift WINSTON and gets him as far as centre, then the pair collapse. ALONZO gets up as ROSIE enters, tying her nightdress about her.

ALONZO   There ya are. Help me to git him upstairs, will ye?

The two manage to raise WINSTON and begin to drag him towards the door.

Jesus. He never used to be this heavy.

ROSIE   I knows, b'y. 'Tis all the beer, I suppose. What wor all the racket about?

ALONZO   *laughing*   Oh nothing, Mother. Jest a friendly game of cards. Jest like the old days. . . .

They exit. The lights dim, except upstairs on SKIPPER. He is listening intently. There is an ominous gust of wind, the beginnings of a storm. He nods and smiles. He folds his hands and lies back. The light fades.

Scene Two

The following morning. A cold dawn light filters through the windows. A savage gust of wind shakes the house, then subsides to a threatening moan. ROSIE bustles in with a kerchief tied about her head. Her first action is to turn on the radio before she lights the fire. As the radio fades in with a hymn, she hums and part sings along with it, putting in the splits, checking the oil burner, lighting the wood, filling kettles, making general preparations for breakfast. On the radio, John Beverley Shea sings.

VOICE   *singing*
There is a green hill
Far away beside a city wall
Where our Dear Lord was crucified
Who died to save us all.

MARY enters.

ROSIE   Good morning, Mary.

MARY   Is it? Have you looked outside?

ROSIE   What's dat, maid?

MARY   I asked, have you looked outside?

ROSIE   No, maid. Dis time of year I prefers not to do dat. 'Tis right depressing!

MARY crosses to the window. She looks out. She returns to the rocking chair. The hymn continues.

MARY   We're in for a storm it seems. It's snowing hard already. Just the excuse some people will be looking for, I suppose.

ROSIE   What for? Nobody's working today, girl.

MARY   I know that, dear. I really shouldn't myself. But I have so much to do before term begins.

She crosses and reaches under the day bed for the trunk with the exercise books in it.

ROSIE   Oh, dat's not work in dat way, Mary. Teaching is the Lord's work, dey say.

MARY   *settling down with some books on the day bed*   You're a good woman, Rose. Where's Winston? Although I should know better than to ask. Still sleeping it off, I suppose.

ROSIE   He'll be down in a minute, maid. Likes to come down to a warm kitchen, Winston do. It sets 'im up fer the day like. And when he's 'appy, we's all happy.

MARY   Are we? Winston's happiness spells disaster for those of us who don't enjoy alcohol or obscenity. Do you know what they did to Wayne last night?

ROSIE   Dey was only having a bit o' fun wid'n, maid. Dey allus done dat.

MARY   Fun is it.   *She corrects some mistakes and sighs.*   Rosie. Wouldn't it be nice, just for once, if you could stay in bed one morning and come down to a nice warm kitchen?

ROSIE   Stay in bed. Me.   *laughing*   I'd be lost in dat big bed all be meself, maid.

MARY   I've got my doubts about that. But you're probably right. Winston would set fire to the woodbox.

The last lines of the last verse of the hymn are heard.

VOICE   *singing*
Oh dearly, dearly has He loved,
And we must love Him too,
And trust in His redeeming blood
And try His works to do.

MARY   That's a lovely hymn, even if it is Anglican!

ANNOUNCER   Good morning, Newfoundland, on this Good Friday morning. The sponsors of our Sacred Music Hour would like to remind you that at the time of bereavement, their trained, dignified and sympathetic staff will attend to your personal needs with discretion. And now we continue with the stirring hymn, "Stand Up, Stand Up for Jesus". . .

There is an enraged roar from SKIPPER's bedroom upstairs.

SKIPPER   Fer Jesus sake, Mary. . . . Turn that damn thing off. . . .

The light goes up slowly to reveal SKIPPER in bed, struggling to prop himself up on the pillows and at the same time to retrieve his stick, a vicious looking piece of polished oak, from the side of the bed. Having done both things, he begins to thump loudly with the stick on the floor. The singing continues.

MARY   *angrily*   I'll drown him out.

She turns up the radio volume. SKIPPER renews his banging.

SKIPPER   And where's me rum? I wants me rum.

MARY   *shouting up*   It'll do ye no harm to hear a hymn or two on this one day of the year. And Dr. Barr said you were to have no more spirits!

SKIPPER   I don't give a tinker's cuss what the doctor said and if that thing isn't turned off this minute, I'll come downstairs and knock its brains out. . . .

He accompanies this with terrifying blows of the stick.

MARY   Don't be talking such nonsense. Ye haven't been out of that bed for thirty years, and what miracles will occur this day aren't likely to happen in this Godforsaken house.

SKIPPER   *hammering furiously* Ye bousy* ol' bitch. I'll. . . .

ROSIE, alarmed, scuttles to the radio and turns it off.

ROSIE   Now, Mary, ye knows how he is. And he's not much longer fer dis world, God rest his soul. . . .

MARY   I've got my doubts about that. . . .

ROSIE   What's dat, maid?

MARY   Whether God will rest his soul.

SKIPPER has been straining to hear this conversation. He leans back on his pillows and laughs, a ravaged, toothless laugh.

SKIPPER   Heh. She's turned it off anyways. Cantankerous as a starved gannet. Can't believe she ever sprung from these loins. Mustn't have known what I was about then, Mother. A poor substitute for Jacob, so she was.

He lolls back and pauses. The lights fade on the kitchen below. There is the sound of a storm building.

A man should be surrounded with ould friends in his dyin'. Ould shipmates. Not a bunch of harpies. All those brave boys. . .iced down. . .rolling in the Labrador current.

He sits up suddenly, staring straight ahead, and roars.

Over the side, lads. Over the side. Look lively, now. Gaff and sculp. Gaff and sculp.*

He sits back. The wind howls in his mind.

The ice and the sun and the brave boys.

He sits up roaring.

Git after them, damn ye. East. . .to the East. To hell wi' the starm. Ye can face into it. They must be East.

The sound of the storm increases in intensity.

De yer worst, ye howling black devil. I'm not afraid o' ye, nor me boys neither. Out of my way. I'll git

---

*bousy—grey-haired.

gaff—Sealer's saviour, now banned. A stout stick, heavily bound, with a two-pronged iron hook at the end. It was used for clubbing the seal; for drawing pelts across the ice; for surviving when the sealers fell through.

sculp—skin.

---

the men. Aye and the swiles* too. I defy ye. I defy ye.

He swings with his stick at the imagined but real enemy, the spirit of death, the spirit of the ice. The storm fades. He stares into the nightmare of the past then sinks back, exhausted. The lights fade on him and come up in the kitchen. WINSTON is warming his hands over the stove. MARY is sitting on the day bed, surrounded with books. ROSIE is laying the table.

MARY   First you and that insolent bar owner last night. And now Father. He does it deliberately. I'm sure of it. Every time there's a storm, roaring and blaspheming, damning us all with his tortured conscience. If I had my way. . . .

WINSTON   Ye'd have him in the Mental, along with the rest o' the family. And have the house to yerself then, eh? Or p'raps ye'd keep Rosie to look after yer ladylike needs. Go on wid ye. Give the old man his rum. It's a holiday.

MARY   Holiday is it. Every day's a holiday for some folk. And this the occasion of The Lord's death. I'll remind you, brother, that the origin of holiday is holy day.

WINSTON   Ye're not at school now, Miss! And I'm not one of yer students, thanks be to God.

MARY   Amen to that.

WINSTON   He's had his rum now every day since the day he wor borned. One drop, more or less, won't affect his chances of salvation.

MARY   And a day's work, more or less, won't affect yours. But that would be more of a miracle than getting old Lazarus up there to leave his room.

WINSTON   *exaggeratedly clutching his heart—on the wrong side* Now, sister. We've been over all that before. That murmur in my heart. . .I can hear it now.

MARY   If that's all we did hear from you, life might be easier in this house of useless men. I'm no feminist, but I swear to God I know why the movement was started.

WINSTON   Ye'd hardly qualify as a feminist, would you? Aren't they all women in that?

ROSIE   Now don't ye two start at it again. Come and sit down, Mary, whiles I gits yer breakfast. . . .

MARY   I'll be there in a minute.

MARY, glaring at WINSTON, crosses into the eating area and sits. ROSIE pours her a cup of tea, then scurries back to the stove where a variety of pots and pans are bubbling away.

ROSIE   It's some nice having all the family home for the holiday. Just like when dey was growing up!

---

*swiles—seals.

MARY   Wayne was down at Christmas.

ROSIE   Well, it's different at Christmas. Dere's so much to do. And den dere's all the visiting. Dere's hardly time to see yer own. But dis time, dere's no celebratin' to git in the way. What are ye doin', Winston?

WINSTON has crossed to the fridge. He opens it and rummages for a beer.

WINSTON   Getting meself a beer.

ROSIE   Before yer bit of bologna?

MARY   He's celebrating the family reunion, aren't you, brother?

WINSTON   Right, sister. Life is one long cele- bration.   *He opens the beer, takes a swig from the bottle and sighs with satisfaction.*   Never ye mind about me, Mary.   *belching loudly and crossing to the day bed*   Ye just get right on with all that marking ye've got to do. What is it this time?

He picks up one of the books, beer in one hand, book in the other.

MARY   *rising*   Leave those books alone, you savage....

WINSTON   *declaiming*   "Daffodils," by William Wordsworth. By Mary Freak for Miss Blackburn, Grade 6. "Daffodils is a poem all about yellow flowers called daffodils. The poet is flying in an aeroplane and looking down through the clouds, he sees..."

MARY rushes across to WINSTON and tries to seize the book. They struggle.

MARY   Give me that, you illiterate.... Give me that book....

The book is torn in half. WINSTON collapses on the day bed, laughing. MARY falls back centre, clutching the remnants of Mary Freak's book. She is nearly in tears. ROSIE rushes to comfort her.

ROSIE   Winston, ye shouldn't have.... Whatever will Mary say to the Principal.

WINSTON   *unrepentant*   Well, what's she doing bringing all that stuff home? Just does it to make us feel guilty, that's all. Ye can see the words like little balloons at the back of her head every time she picks up one of those poor kids' essays.... *mimicking*   Ye're all lazy and ungrateful and I've spent the best years of my life looking after ye and Father....   *He goes to the stove, lifts the lid, spits expertly into the flames and replaces it.*   Hell, if she'd taken the trouble to roll about in the grass a bit when she wor young, it might've made a dif- ference. Some foolish fella might've married'n. Too late now, I allows.

ROSIE   Winston! Now dat's enough, boy.

WINSTON   Who else would have her now except we?

ROSIE   I swear to God ye'd never know Mary wuz your sister! I'm not going to have the day spoilt afore it's even started. Ye had yer bit o' devilment last night wi' Lonz. Now give over, boy.

MARY has gone across to the day bed and is collecting the remainder of the assignments. She has recovered her composure and is icy.

MARY   It's alright, Rosie. It's all the thanks I can expect from him. He was always destructive of anything he couldn't understand. Even as a small boy. In fact, there was a time when everyone thought he was retarded.

WINSTON   *laughing*   And ye've nivir changed yer mind, have ye, sister?   *He fills his pipe. MARY stacks her books away.*   That's the one thing we have in common though, Mary. Neither one of us 'as changed a bit and we in't about to. Take me now...born retarded...dyin'...at least I thinks that's I'm doing...still retarded. And Mary...born a virgin. Getting ready to be laid out a virgin ... widout any of the benefits of an Immaculate Conception.

ROSIE   Winston! Dey's no call fer dat kind of talk.

MARY   Don't worry about me, Rose. I can look after myself. It's you I feel sorry for, dear. Plodding along after all these years with a man who's an expert at two things. Making moonshine and cheating the Welfare.

WINSTON   That's right, Mary. Haven't ye heard o' specialization? 'Tis what everyone has to do these days.

ROSIE   'Tis not as bad as dat, Mary.   *wistfully*   I wishes sometimes ye wouldn't fight so much. But den the two of ye nivir got on and dat's it, I suppose. An' I'm luckier dan me mother and dey whose men nivir spent a minute at home, traipsin' off to the Labrador or Toronto or such. I allus reckoned it wor his life to do what he would wit', providin' dey was a bit of food in the house and wood fer the stove....

WINSTON crosses to ROSIE and slaps her backside.

WINSTON   That's my Rosie. Fat and comfortable and mindin' her own business. Aye, and warm on a cold night too.   *He swings on MARY.*   But ye, ye frozen wharf junk. Ye wouldn't know anything about that part of life now, would ye?

MARY crosses to the table and sits down. WINSTON follows her, leans across at her, breathing into her face. She averts it in disgust.

WINSTON   Turn away ye might. I seed ya once. Through the winder of the school house. Strappin' some poor kid across the hand, and it a bitter morning, until he screamed fer ye to stop.

MARY slaps him across the face. For a moment, it looks as if WINSTON is about to spit in her face in reply, but ROSIE hurriedly intervenes.

ROSIE   Winston. . .   *pushing him away from the table*   Why don't ye take a drop of rum and sugar up to yer fader?

She hurriedly opens a cupboard, takes down a bottle of rum, pours a glass, shoves the glass into WINSTON's hand and hurries across to the stove, where she fills a jug with hot water.

Ye knows how he likes to talk to ye.

WINSTON   Doesn't talk to me. Talks to ghosts.

ROSIE   I know, dear.   *She crosses back with the jug and gives it to WINSTON.*   But 'tis good company for'n. Go on now.   *trying to shoo him out*   Go on, afore dere's any more trouble.

WINSTON   Who's good company, Rosie. Me? Or the ghosts?

He drains the glass of rum, collects the bottle and moves to exit.

Alright, alright. I'm going. And mind, woman, that there's a clean cloth on the table for the children when they finally haul their arses out of bed. We must make some effort to keep up appearances, eh, Mary?

MARY   We! You could turn Buckingham Palace into a beer parlour.

WINSTON chuckles and exits up the stairs.

ROSIE   My, my. Dey's always somet'ing, in't there? I'd better start the fish. The boys'll be down soon.

MARY   Boys! Rosie, they're all grown men, quite capable of looking after themselves. I'm sure Wayne, at least, wouldn't expect you to put yourself out.

ROSIE   I knows.   *with satisfaction*   But old habits dies 'ard.

In the boys' room, upstairs left, BRAD suddenly sits bolt upright.

BRAD   *shouting*   Fire. . . . Fire. . . . Mother. . . .

WINSTON pauses on the landing outside the room.

ROSIE   That's Brad having one of his dreams agin. The doctor said it wor on account of . . .

BRAD   Alonzo. Wake up. Wake up.

ALONZO   What. . . .

BRAD   I had a dream of fire. Everything burning . . .

ALONZO   *leaping out of bed*   Fire. . . . Where? . . .

MARY   On account of what?

ROSIE   H'imagination. Dat's what 'e said.

BRAD   Flames reaching up to the Heavens. And all the souls of the damned crying out. Yes. And you were there, Alonzo. And Father. Burning.

The lights go up in the boys' bedroom, as ALONZO, clad in a scanty pair of boxer shorts, releases the blind. BRAD is sitting stiffly up in the bed. He is wearing thick woollen combinations. WINSTON has stayed to listen at the door.

ALONZO   Oh, is that all? I thought it were something serious.   *shivering back to the bed and climbing in*   Mother. Mother.

MARY   If it's not one, it's the other.

ROSIE   *calling*   What is it, Lonz?

ALONZO   Would you get me a cup of tea, for the love of God. Brad's burning, but I'm near froze to death.

WINSTON moves into the doorway.

WINSTON   *disgusted*   Get it yerself. Jesus. I nivir saw the like of it.

ALONZO   Now now, Father. I learnt all me good habits from you, remember?

WINSTON   What I does is between yer mother and meself, and don't ye fergit it. Ye always were too damned saucy.

BRAD suddenly leaps out of bed. He rushes to the window and looks out.

BRAD   Damned. We were all damned.

He stares at WINSTON clutching the rum bottle. He rushes at him.

Father, I beg of you. Throw that evil away.

He wrestles for the bottle. WINSTON easily shakes him back onto the bed, where he is about to fall on ALONZO. ALONZO, as BRAD staggers, pushes him sideways.

ALONZO   Watch it.

BRAD   *pleading*   Father. Put that away.

WINSTON   *pointing at BRAD's crotch*   Ye put that away. I nivir knew ye'd got one.

ALONZO   *laughing*   The sword of the Lord out of its scabbard. A little rusty, but ready for action.

BRAD, embarrassed, discomfited, backs to a chair, covering himself, then turns and begins to dress with great speed. WINSTON and ALONZO watch with interest.

BRAD   Why won't you listen. Why will nobody listen to me. God.   *He drops to his knees.*   God. Is this your will. Give me a sign, Lord. A sign.

ALONZO   Who's he shouting at now?

WINSTON   God knows.

SKIPPER   I wants me rum. Me rum. Goddamn it, what's happenin' in dis house this marnin'.

ROSIE   *shouting up*   Winston's on his way, Mr. Eli.

WINSTON   Coming, Skipper. Coming.

He crosses to SKIPPER's bedroom, turns on the light and enters. The house is now ablaze. BRAD gets slowly to his feet and turns to face ALONZO.

ALONZO   Nar sign, eh, Brad? Well, me son. Keep on trying, that's my motto.

BRAD   I feel sometimes as if I'm wrestling with the Devil.

MARY   The goings on in this house. It's disgusting, Rose. What must people think.

ALONZO   *interested*   What's he like, Brad. I used to think he wor like a long lizard with a spiny tail.

ROSIE   *moving to the door with some tea*   I 'low it's too late to be t'inking of others now, maid.

BRAD   He's like you, Alonzo. You.

ALONZO   *shaken by BRAD's intensity*   Jesus. Yer as mad as the Skipper.

ROSIE arrives in the doorway.

ROSIE   *handing the cup to him*   Here you are, Lonz.

ALONZO   Thanks, Mother. Get me cigarettes, will ye. There . . . in me trousers. . . .

He indicates the place his trousers are hanging. ROSIE obediently fetches them.

ROSIE   Would ye like a cup of tea, Brad?

BRAD   I want nothing, thank you, Mother.

ROSIE   Ye got to eat and drink sometime, boy. Dey's hardly a t'ing to ye now. I got to fatten ye up.

ALONZO   The prodigal goose.

BRAD   Mother, no! I'm too upset. I have to pray. I feed on the Lord.

ROSIE   Well, if ye says so. Anyways I'll light the fire in the front room for ye. I knows how ye likes to be alone. . . . Allus did, even as a youngster.   *to ALONZO*   And ye leave off tormentin'n. Dey was quite enough o' dat last night!   *She turns to go.*

BRAD   Mother.

ROSIE   Yes, Brad.

BRAD   Could you fetch my Bible for me. I think I left it in the front room.

ALONZO   *echoing WINSTON*   Jesus. Git it yerself. Can't ye see she's run off her feet.

ROSIE   I'll get it the onct.

The lights fade in their bedroom. WINSTON, in SKIPPER's room, is pouring him a drink. SKIPPER takes it, drains it with immense satisfaction and holds the glass out for a refill.

SKIPPER   What were going on down there last night and this marnin'?

WINSTON   Oh nothing, Skipper. Celebratin' Good Friday, that's all.

ROSIE re-emerges at the top of the stairs and takes BRAD's Bible in to him. She comes out and rests wearily in the shadow, listening to SKIPPER and WINSTON, before going on down.

SKIPPER   Ah. That wor it then. I seen lots of 'em. Some good. Some bad. They's places in the world where 'tis jest a normal day.

He pauses and drinks. A gust of wind shakes the house. SKIPPER becomes intent, listening.

Tell me, boy, is the war over yit?

WINSTON   Not yet, Skipper. Not yet. Never will be, I reckon.

SKIPPER   Bloody Germans. Hampering the seal fishery. Lost me best barrelman* last week. . . . All the good hands gone to be soldiers. Foolishness.

WINSTON   Never mind, Skipper. Ye've still got a ship. And a crew.

SKIPPER   Crew. They's wet behind the ears, me son. Frightened o' me. Frightened o' wind and water, sick at the sight of blood. Jump when they hears a swile bark. I 'ad better eleven year old hands when I took me own schooner out of Trinity, conning through the gut,* the church rising and falling behind, the bells ringin'. . . . Women prayin' to God to send we back . . . but not too soon. . . . One-eyed Bugden at the lookout. Tough as gads in them days, boy! Are ye listenin'?

WINSTON   I hear ye, Father.

He pours SKIPPER and himself another drink. The old man drinks, then sighs deeply.

SKIPPER   That Kaiser. He must be some strange feller. Wears a gaff on his head I'm told.   *Pause.*   I tell ye, a man's enough to do fightin' nature. The rum, boy, the rum.   *WINSTON fills his glass again.*   You nivir did take to the salt water did ye, boy?

WINSTON   No, Father, I can't say as I did. Too much work. Nothing but living gales and fog and no fish.

SKIPPER   Fish. Who cares about fish. Oh, they was necessary. On account o' them, we took to the salt water. An' we shovelled them into our guts till our blood were colder'n theirs. That were schoolin' ye might say, but the hunt, that's different. Every man, once in a lifetime, has to know what it's like. To hunt. To kill. To risk yerself, yer ship. Yer sons. Aye, and to lose sometimes.

WINSTON   Ye can do that at war, Father. And ye can do it at 'ome, too!

SKIPPER   The hell ye can. It's not the same. Fightin' nature and fightin' yer brother. . . . How kin that be the same? How old are ye now, boy?

*barrelman—lookout.

 conning through the gut—steering through a narrow passage between two points of land.

WINSTON *scratching his head* Fifty-eight, I 'lows. Or is it fifty- nine? Ye should know.

SKIPPER Aye. I remembers. Two years afore yer sister. One afore yer brother, God rest his soul. *He pauses and drinks.* What makes a woman dry up like that...like an ould cod. *Pause.* Did I do wrong, boy?

WINSTON Ye didn't do anything, Skipper.

SKIPPER Aye. That's right. Not fer any o' ye.

He lies back on the pillow with his eyes closed.

Cold seas. Cold land. Nothing growing. Only the harp,* the whitecoat.* Rust and blood and iron. No place fer a daughter. Shouldn't a made one. No place fer me son, neither. Should we a made'n, Rachel? Should we?

Suddenly roaring.

I don't care if the wind has backed sou'east. Send the men over, damn you. Send them out. There's swiles to be killed. Ice to be trod. Out....Out....

He reaches for his stick and swings. WINSTON puts out a restraining hand.

WINSTON Easy, Skipper. Easy, now.

SKIPPER *glaring, then coming back to normal* Ach. Ye were always a disappointment to me, boy. But ye're human. Ye talk to me. Yer mother now ...wunnerful fine woman, a comfort in me kitchen, aye, and me bed too. But she never talked. Not after yer brother died that time. Blamed me fer turnin'n out on the ice and steamin' off. But as God is me witness, I couldn't move. When the starm came it wor like the Divil had the ship in his hand. He wor a good man on the water. Better still on the ice. But he's gone now, along wi' the rest. *Pause.* Where's me gran'children? They's in the house. I heerd 'em. Bawlin' and shoutin'.

WINSTON Aye. They's in the house, Skipper. They'll be schoolin' around like the dogfish by'n by, but I wouldn't expect too much from 'em if I was you. One of 'em pretends ye don't exist and the other wants to save yer black soul. *chuckling* And the third waits fer yer will.

SKIPPER And what do ye want, boy?

WINSTON Nothing, Skipper. Ye knows that. Nothing at all. Jest this. A place to come and have a quiet drink, away from the women, and look out at the sea.

He gets up, takes a barometer from the wall and hands it to the SKIPPER. He moves to the chest of drawers. The top is littered with the SKIPPER's medicine, old charts, a telescope. He picks up the

telescope and moves forward, looking out over the sea. The storm sounds rise.

SKIPPER What does she look like today, boy?

WINSTON Grey and ugly. Like an ould hag. They's some slob ice* by the look of it. But it's gittin' hard to see. They's a big starm brewing I'd say.

SKIPPER *tapping the glass and studying it* Aye. The bottom's gone out of her. Twenty-eight seven and still fallin'.

WINSTON They's a small boat runnin' in now. Crazy fools. Nearly too late too, be the look of'n. She's down at the stern and nearly awash. Jesus. ...She'll nivir get t'rough the Barracks wi' that sea runnin'.

SKIPPER Ice, boy. Any ice?

WINSTON I told ye. Some slob....Could be pack out there, but I can't see the sea from the sky now....Christ, boys, what are ye playin' at.... *turning* He's swinging back. *unbelieving* He's going back out to sea!

SKIPPER After the swiles, boy. This is swile weather.

WINSTON I'd say he's after a quick trip to Hell....

He comes back and pours another drink for himself and SKIPPER.

SKIPPER Swiles is bred and killed in Hell, boy. Dis is their starm! The starm fer the young swiles! Oh, they'll love it. Swimming up in their t'ousands, looking for the pack ice to breed on. Fierce mothers, boy. Fierce and proud, I tell ye....And the young, helpless, floundering. But we be the same, boy, plunging and stumbling on the floes. *starting to get excited* It's their element, boy. Not ours. Our gaffs is their enemy. The nor'easter and the ice is our enemy. I tell ye, boy...I tell ye....

WINSTON Yes, Skipper...ye tells me. All the time.

SKIPPER *sitting back, quiet* Ah, I thinks it's all gone at times. But ye never had anything to lose. Least, that's what ye thinks. And how could it be different when ye've done nothing but walk the shore all your life. But it isn't true for me, boy. They'll come back. The swiles'll come back in their t'ousands and when they do, I'll go greet 'em just like in the old days....

WINSTON What about yer legs, Skipper?

SKIPPER To hell wid 'em. I can crawl, can't I? That's what I did when I lost the use of 'em. When the ice took 'em. Is the house secure?

WINSTON Aye, Skipper. Mooring fast fore and aft.

---

*harp—the harp seal. Generally refers to the mother.

 whitecoat—baby seal.

*slob ice—ice formed in harbours by frost, as distinct from pack ice.

SKIPPER *to himself* But not fer much longer I allows. Let me know when she starts to drag. . . . How's the sea now?

WINSTON *going through the ritual again, crossing to the telescope and peering out* Worse. Can't see nar thing. Nothin' alive out there . . .

SKIPPER The boat . . .

WINSTON She must 'ave gone. Must 'ave.

SKIPPER Aye, that's the way of it. Let me know when we starts to drift.

He is getting drowsy. He leans back on the pillow, clutching the barometer. WINSTON goes to him and takes the empty rum glass from the bed.

Send Rosie to me, boy. She knows how to comfort an old man.

WINSTON Knows how to comfort any man.

SKIPPER Makes ye tolerable, boy. Ye learned something after all. Ye picked a good ship. Steers herself . . . makes no mind o' we and our foolishness.

He dozes. WINSTON begins to leave, quietly.

SKIPPER *calling from the depths of his bed* Wake me when we gits to the field, boy. Don't ye fergit, mind!

WINSTON Aye, aye, Skipper.

The sound of a hymn drifts up into the bedroom, "Eternal Father Strong to Save." SKIPPER sings the first two lines. The lights fade in the SKIPPER's room and go up on the kitchen as WINSTON comes down the stairs. MARY is sitting in the rocking chair and ROSIE is at the table, finishing her breakfast. The SKIPPER's voice, keeping broken time with the hymn, drifts down softly. WINSTON enters as the ANNOUNCER breaks in.

ANNOUNCER We interrupt our broadcast to bring you a storm warning, just issued from Environment Canada in Gander. A disturbance to the east has deepened rapidly in intensity and is expected to bring storm force winds and a heavy snowfall to all parts of the island by midday. Marine interests are advised that severe storm warnings are now in effect for all Newfoundland waters. And now, before returning you . . .

WINSTON *turning off the radio* According to the Skipper, 'tis the storm fer the young swiles.

He crosses to the day bed, lies down, stretches and yawns.

Rosie, love, fetch me a beer from the fridge, will ye.

MARY Can't you see that she's having her breakfast. The poor woman hasn't stopped since she got up.

WINSTON Neither have you. More's the pity.

ROSIE Here ye are, love. . . . *She hands him a beer and a hot bologna sandwich from the oven.* Now eat up yer baloney, boy. Ye've got to soak up the liquor wid somethin' else ye'll nivir git t'rough the day.

WINSTON I'll do me best, maid, but it's a kind thought.

With one hand he swigs at the beer and with the other he tries to get up ROSIE's skirt.

ROSIE Here you. Git your t'ievin' hands out of dat.

She swipes at him, pleased, and goes back to the table.

MARY Rose, I sometimes believe you encourage him deliberately to keep the peace.

WINSTON *exasperated* Shut up, woman, fer the love of God before I say something I might regret. I've had a hard mornin' . . . *MARY sniffs.* Oh yis. Sneer all ye want. Talking to me father is always hard work, like reading hist'ry backwards. Yer own. *leaning back, subdued* I wish sometimes that I could have been the son he wanted.

MARY *vindictive* Then you'd have been dead. Like Jacob.

WINSTON That's right, Mary. *He tips and drains the bottle.* That's absolutely goddamn right.

MARY moves as if to speak, thinks better of it, and exits towards the livingroom. WINSTON, visibly upset, crosses to the window and stares out. ROSIE keeps on eating, placidly.

Scene Three

The lights rise on the boys' bedroom. ALONZO is standing in his shirt and underpants looking out of the window, smoking. BRAD is sitting on a chair reading the Bible, his lips moving soundlessly.

ALONZO Hell of a day out there, Brad.

No response.

Bit like the night Mildred Tobin died.

No response.

I don't suppose ye'd care to remember that though. Always seemed to be able to block out things ye didn't want to remember.

No response. Disgusted, ALONZO comes down, stubs out his cigarette in the teacup and gets his trousers.

D'ye mind when we left ye in the woods that time, fer a joke. Then couldn't find ye. *laughing* That were the time of yer first vision, weren't it? Though as I recall it weren't God or the Virgin.... The headless horseman, weren't it?

He struggles into his trousers. Annoyed at the indifference to his baiting, he crosses and looks over BRAD's shoulder. He declaims:

"Many times have they afflicted me from my youth, yet they have not prevailed against me." Heavy stuff, Brad.

No response. ALONZO loses his temper.

Brad, for God's sake, put that away and talk to me as a brother should.

BRAD   Are you my brother, Alonzo?

ALONZO   Ah ha. A voice. Out of the depths. More! More!

With a sudden movement he grabs the Bible from BRAD and throws it to the floor. BRAD rises and makes as if to strike him. ALONZO adopts a boxer's stance and prances round him.

That's it, brother. That's it. Do it, fer Christsake. Let's hurt each other like real people.

BRAD   *sitting slowly, retrieving the Bible and dusting it off*   You're not a real person, Alonzo. There aren't any real people in my family, apart from Mother.

ALONZO   *crossing to him and willing BRAD into subjection*   Now listen, Brad. I've tolerated you ever since you were a snot-faced brat stealing quarters from me coat pocket. I remember you.

BRAD moves quickly to his feet, pushes past ALONZO with some force, and turns on him.

BRAD   You listen. All my life I've been jeered at. That's all I can remember. By stupid drunken men who were my fathers or my brothers. And when they weren't drunk, they hated me. Just for being alive. And now you jeer at me for saying God is my father. Don't you think that he's better than the one I've got?

ALONZO   You mind yer mouth.

BRAD   *in an ecstasy of rejection*   And everyone here fearful, afraid to call on Him. Catholic, Protestant, United.... They're all the same. Mumbling into prayerbooks. Sleeping in pews with obscenities carved in the back of them. Trying to keep God hidden. Like some dirty secret....

ALONZO   *shouting*   That's it. And that's all of it. I remember, God help me, when Mildred Tobin gave ye yer first and last piece of tail. That were it, weren't it? Slobberin' and crying on me shoulder, shouting out how ye was damned. Damned foolish, that's what ye was, too stunned to use the French safes I give ye. She, poor bitch, led ye to God, or whatever crazy thing it is ye've got in yer head.

BRAD   You're an open sewer, Alonzo.

ALONZO   Sewers are necessary, Brad. And don't fergit. It's your shit I carry to the landwash, as well as me own.

BRAD   You don't have to lecture me. I'm responsible for myself.

ALONZO   Then keep to yerself and leave us alone to burn or freeze as we wish.

BRAD   I can't Alonzo. I have to learn... to love you.

The words are a release, an orgasm. BRAD takes a pace towards ALONZO who backs away, unconsciously wiping his mouth with the back of his hand. BRAD recognizes a victory. He smiles. For a few moments his disintegrating soul is at rest.

ALONZO   You're sick, Brad. Really sick.   *recovering his composure and eyeing BRAD thoughtfully*   Tell me, what really happened up there? To yer flock? What did ye call yourselves.... Oh yes, the Church of the Revelations.

BRAD   In the age of the Apocalypse, we are afflicted by many beasts.

ALONZO   Jesus!

BRAD   My congregation were led astray.

ALONZO   They couldn't've been that dumb after all. Must've seen ye were leading 'em to a God of blind alleys. I heard ye burnt out Joel Miller.

BRAD   Miller tried to corrupt my congregation. He was one of them. An agent of the Devil.

ALONZO   He was an agent for Labatt's. Fer Christsake, he ran a bar, that's all. A bar. Even Noah was allowed moonshine on the ark. Give me the book and I'll find the place for ye.   *snatching the Bible*   Father taught me that, years ago.

BRAD   The fire was an act of God.

ALONZO   Ye don't say. Well, 'twas nearly an act of murder. He were lucky to get out with just his face and hands burnt, to say nothing....

BRAD   There's no point in continuing this conversation, Alonzo. I've nothing to say to you.

ALONZO   I've noticed. But one thing puzzles me. Ye've been fired from the only job, if I kin call it that, that ye've ever had and ye come running back here. Why? Nobody wants ye.

BRAD   This is my home. This is where I began. Where we all began. That's right, isn't it? You were born in this room. Probably on that bed. And this is where we're going to die. All of us. You too, Alonzo.

ALONZO   Spare yer thoughts for the Skipper. It's his house. He might not like the idea of it being filled wit' corpses.

BRAD   Yes. *Pause.* I must see him. I must pray with him. *crossing to the door and turning*

Alonzo, as it seems that we can't get on, would you leave me alone for the rest of the day. Please. For the sake of Mother, if no one else.

ALONZO   A pact, is it? Like when we were kids. Alright then. Here.

He holds out his little finger. BRAD, searching his face, slowly holds out his. Just before the fingers touch and hook, ALONZO grabs for BRAD with his free hand with the intention of twisting finger and arm around. BRAD is too quick for him.

ALONZO   Ah, ye little bugger. Ye haven't forgotten, have ye?

BRAD, after a second, leaves to cross the landing. ALONZO shouts after him.

I wouldn't make a pact with you if it were the Day of Judgement.

BRAD   It is, Alonzo. It is!

WAYNE emerges on the landing from the stairs.

WAYNE   Good morning, Brad. At it again, I hear.

BRAD ignores him and goes on into SKIPPER's room. The old man is, or appears to be, asleep. BRAD leans down, listens to his heart and nods.

BRAD   Grandfather. Grandfather. . . .

The old man doesn't stir. BRAD sits down by the side of the bed, opens the Bible and begins to read from the Book of Job. WAYNE has entered the boys' bedroom. ALONZO is at the window. He turns.

ALONZO   D'you think Brad's queer?

WAYNE   I don't know. I never slept with him.

ALONZO   I can see ye're looking for more than a game of cards. I thought ye were finished with us last night.

WAYNE   Look, Alonzo. Let's face it. We don't like each other. Never have.

ALONZO   It's a morning of revelations. Now tell me, ye're learning to love me.

WAYNE   *mocking*   I respect your ability.

ALONZO   And I respect your position.

WAYNE   I think you still owe me, Lonz.

ALONZO   *shaking his head*   Uh hunh. I deliver this district whenever it's required. That's worth a lot.

WAYNE   And so is my survival.

ALONZO   Check. What do ye want?

WAYNE sits on the bed, the sparring done.

WAYNE   It's about Grandfather.

ALONZO   You getting him committed.

WAYNE   It's possible.

ALONZO   What have I got to do with it?

WAYNE   I need your signature. Well . . . not yours.

ALONZO   Father's?

WAYNE   That's right.

ALONZO   That's dangerous.

WAYNE   You win some. You lose some.

ALONZO   You son of a bitch. Ye want me to forge the old man's signature in return for the motel contract.

WAYNE   I think I could guarantee it.

ALONZO   Think. Ye'd damn well better make sure of it if I'm going to forge the old man's signature. He'd kill the both of us if he ever found out.

WAYNE   He won't know. He'll never know.

ALONZO   *disturbed*   Aunt Mary's been at ye, hasn't she? She's behind this.

WAYNE   Look. We're all worried about Mother. How much more of this can she take.

ALONZO   The hell ye are. Christ!   *pacing in agitation*   Will ye guarantee that contract? No delays. No bits and pieces. The lot.

WAYNE   I will.

ALONZO   Christ! What a bunch of rats we are. Have ye got the forms?

WAYNE gets them from the inside of his coat pocket. ALONZO takes them, scans them quickly, not wanting to read what they contain. He flips to the last page, takes the form to the chair and kneels, using the chair for backing.

Pen.

WAYNE passes him a gold pen.

Shit. Look at this.

He begins to scrawl, then looks up.

It's a long time since I've done this.   *scrawling*   There. . . .

WAYNE takes the forms and puts them back in his pocket. ALONZO gets up.

WAYNE   Well, I suppose we'd better go and make the regulation visit. Get it over with. Are you coming?

ALONZO   *staring at WAYNE*   I don't believe it.

WAYNE   What?

ALONZO   Doesn't matter. We'll go and pay our last respects. My arm . . .

He proffers his arm to WAYNE. The irony is lost on him. They cross the landing into SKIPPER's room and stay in the doorway. BRAD is intoning softly.

BRAD
Yea the light of the wicked is put out
And the flame of his fire does not shine
The light is dark in his tent
And his lamp above him is put out
His strong steps are shortened . . .

SKIPPER *sitting bolt upright, roaring* Miserable Comforter. What the hell do ye know about it. Get out. I'm not dead yet. Get out.

BRAD *getting up a little hastily* How are you feeling, Grandfather?

SKIPPER How do I look, ye fool. Better than ye do, I hope.

BRAD You're fading, Grandfather. You should be . . .

SKIPPER I'm not fading. What do ye think I am? A goddamned flower? I'm dyin', ye pasty-faced pup. And I don't need ye for company. It's hard enough as it is. *Pause.* From the look o' ye, I judge ye to be 'Lonzo.

BRAD I'm Brad, Grandfather.

SKIPPER Ye all look and sound alike to me. *to himself* What happens to the roots? They isn't what they used to be. So much rotten timber. *calling out* Jacob . . . Jacob . . .

ALONZO, who has been delighted at this interchange, comes in.

ALONZO Well, Grandfather. Still around I see.

SKIPPER *coming out of it with a start* Ye're not Jacob. Get out.

ALONZO No, I'm not Jacob.

BRAD Jacob is dead, Grandfather. We must pray that he is with God.

ALONZO Brad. Who cares? Leave the old man with his nightmares.

SKIPPER Dead! Jacob, dead. *lost again* Eighteen thousand and the decks awash with blood. It's not enough, boys. Get over the side and to hell wid the glass. Gaff and sculp. . . . Gaff and sculp.

There is another great gust of wind and a menace in the silence that follows.

ALONZO Aren't ye coming in, Wayne? Join the wake!

WAYNE *advancing with his best politician's smile* Grandfather. It's so good to see you.

SKIPPER Is it?

WAYNE Indeed it is. And you're looking well too. You'll see the lot of us out, as I've always said.

SKIPPER *venomously* I don't give a damn what ye've always said.

He suddenly snatches up his stick and swings it viciously. ALONZO manages to get out of its path but it catches WAYNE squarely across the forearm.

WAYNE My God.

He backs away staring at SKIPPER as if he were looking at the Anti-Christ.

Grandfather. You've broken my arm.

SKIPPER I should have had ye to the ice. Just onct. *lashing out at the air with his stick* Living off me. Grandchildren. Crackies* more like. Not one o' ye a man. Not one of ye like Jacob. Ye've no God. And ye've no guts. Ye're nothin', the lot of ye. *shouting* Rosie . . . Rosie. . . . Come and git yer whelps out of here. Rosie.

The lights partially rise downstairs. ROSIE is sitting eating, her mouth full of toast. WINSTON is standing looking out the window.

ROSIE What is it, Fader?

WINSTON Fer the love of God, woman, leave him be. He's having a chat with the boys, that's all . . .

WAYNE We're going, Grandfather. We're going. Just came to pay our respects.

SKIPPER And that's about the only thing ye can pay.

WAYNE He doesn't know who I . . . who we are obviously.

ALONZO He knows, brother. He knows too well.

BRAD I'll pray for you Grandfather . . .

SKIPPER *roaring with rage* Curses, boy. I wants the curses of men. Not the piddlin' prayers of a mewlin' pup. I wants . . .

He glares about him in impotence, then sinks back, exhausted. BRAD leaves, clutching his Bible, and goes downstairs into the livingroom. WAYNE, holding his arm, turns to leave.

ALONZO You're not thinking of leaving.

WAYNE No.

ALONZO Good. I'd hate to be left without me thirty pieces of silver. I'll see ya later then.

WAYNE hesitates, then exits in the direction of his bedroom. ALONZO pokes about in the room, finds the bottle of rum and pours himself a stiff drink. He sits down at SKIPPER's bedside. The old man makes a gurgling sound. ALONZO raises his glass.

ALONZO I knows ye don't mind, Skipper. Ye nivir did when I were a boy. Used to come up and read to ye. D'ye minds that. An' fer me birthday, ye'd allus give me a gold sovereign from out your chest. I've often wondered who ye'll leave that lot to.

---

*crackies—mongrel pups.

Mother, I 'lows. And the old man'll kill himself with the proceeds. Here...

He props him up with an arm and holds the glass to his mouth. SKIPPER drinks. ALONZO almost gently lays him back on the bed. He sits staring, eyes open.

ALONZO   Ah, boy. Ye had your day. A good one too I allows if you're any recommendation. The times of the seal. But they've gone, Skipper. Gone, 'cept in your head and a few old log books. It's the day of the dogfish now.

He drains his glass and rises, placing the glass on the bureau. He goes out quietly. The lights fade and go up to full in the kitchen area. ROSIE is sitting having a cup of tea and toast, dipping her toast in the tea. WINSTON is standing downstage left looking out.

ROSIE   *with her mouth full*   What is it, love? What's the matter? Kin I get ye somethin'?

WINSTON   No, maid. No. Not just yet.

ROSIE   I knewed ye should have stayed in bed dis mornin'. Ye didn't look well...and yer stomach was grumblin' something awful...   *She dips more toast.*

WINSTON   *without turning, half to himself*   How long is it now?

ROSIE   What?

WINSTON   How long is it since we lost Sarah?

ROSIE   Oh my. Ye're t'inkin' o' dat again, are ye?

WINSTON   *crossing to table*   Every time I gits afflicted with me family I thinks of the one that might have been different. And Skipper don't help much.

ROSIE   *smiling*   Aye. She wor a bonny thing. Not like me or ye at all. More like Grandmother Penton. Same colour eyes she had...and dat cow's lick atop her head. What ever would she have done wid her hair I wonder?

WINSTON hasn't heard.

WINSTON   She might have had a chanct.   *turning to ROSIE*   I asked ye, Rosie. How long is it?

ROSIE   T'irty one years and two months. She'd have 'ad youngsters of her own be now. She wor borned in the February dark.   *She pauses, struggling with memories and affection.*   Ye minds how ye had to rush me to the hospital in the starm?

WINSTON   Aye, bundled ye up in the sled like an old walrus. And Trigger ploughing through drifts up to his chest. Like he knew...

ROSIE   I never seed ye like it. Ye were like a wild man. Like yer fader almost.   *proudly*   I believe ye'd 'ave faced the Divil dat night and gone on.

laughing   The pains wor comin' every five minutes and the sled were rearin' from side to side, but I still minds ye cussin'...trying to drive the snow away, I allow...

WINSTON   It wor never the same after she died. I doesn't know why. Once she'd gone, they wor...   *struggling painfully with the recollection*   I'd git into the woods and I'd see her, crouching in the snow, under the trees....And the damned foreman coming round charging ye five cents for every stump ye left in t'ree inches above ground. And me hacking away and not thinking, not thinking at all....Jesus!

ROSIE   I had to bind me breasts wit' oakum. I 'ad more milk for her and longer dan fer any of the boys. Still an' all, the Good Lord saw how much we loved'n, and so he got a mite jealous I suppose...

WINSTON   The Good Lord! What's he got to do wi' us livin' and dyin'? To Hell wid'n.

ROSIE   Winston!

WINSTON   They's nothin', Rosie. Nothin'. They's madness and they's death and they's some who work at it and some who wait for it.   *brutally*   Sarey's out there and they's nothin' left of her save a peck o' dust.

ROSIE   Winston...Winston....It wor thirty years ago....

WINSTON   And two months. But it weren't, Rosie. It were today.

He crosses to exit.

ROSIE   *upset and flustered*   Winston, don't ye be goin' now like dat. I'll get ye a beer....Ye're upset....

WINSTON   No!

ROSIE   I cares for ye, Winston.

WINSTON   *stopping by the entrance and looking at her*   I suppose ye do, maid. I s'pose ye do.

He laughs without mirth.

SKIPPER   Rosie! Rosie!

WINSTON   And when he thinks I'm Jacob, so do he....

The lights fade.

ACT TWO

ROSIE is attending the SKIPPER, tidying up the bed, rolling him from side to side with great speed and efficiency. Occasional curses spill from him, but they are not serious.

SKIPPER   Dammit, woman.... Ye've got hands like a squid. D'ye think I'm a barrel of flour?

ROSIE   Dere now, Skipper...all done.... How does dat feel?

SKIPPER   Terrible.

ROSIE   I knew ye'd feel better. Now it's time fer yer medicine.

SKIPPER   *roaring*   I won't take it. I won't take it.... I needs to capsize me cock.*

ROSIE   Ye've just done dat. 'Tis jest an excuse. Ye should be ashamed of yerself.

Impervious, she has gone to the chest of drawers, where she pours a liberal dose of evil-looking fluid into a small glass. SKIPPER struggles to slide down under the bedclothes, but thrashing and cursing is hauled up by ROSIE with one hand. He roars for the third time.

SKIPPER   Woman, I'm in charge of me own ship and she don't need none of that...

ROSIE seizes an opportunity when the toothless mouth is wide open and down the medicine goes. Sputtering and grumbling, SKIPPER swings at her with his stick, but she's already back at the cabinet and returns with a glass of rum.

ROSIE   I s'pose ye'll make me force dis down yer stubborn old t'roat too?

He glares, then chuckles and lays down the stick. He clutches the rum and lies back with a deep sigh of contentment.

SKIPPER   Ah, Rosie, Rosie. What a tumble we'd have had sixty years ago....

ROSIE   Ye'd have been tumblin' by yerself, yer badminded ould divil.... I weren't t'ought of den.

SKIPPER   Oh yis, maid. Ye wor thought of. We've all got our own courses prepared long afore us gits here.... The winds and currents waiting. The ships we meet. And the crews....

ROSIE   Well now, I don't know not'ing about dat and I don't t'ink I wants to.... If ye're all settled....

SKIPPER   No, Rosie. No. Don't go. Not yet. I wants ye to read to me.

ROSIE   *a little distracted*   Ye've chosen a bad day fer dat an' me wit' a houseful downstairs.

SKIPPER   They's old enough to look after theirselves.

*capsize me cock—urinate.

ROSIE pauses, irresolute, then she goes back to the chest of drawers. She opens a drawer, pulls out an old logbook, returns to the bed and sits in the rocker by the bedside.

ROSIE   What day d'ye want?

SKIPPER   *with eyes shut*   Aye, what day shall I have? There were that day in '19? 18th March it wor.... Lost the cook. Crew gaffed him. Swore he wor pissin' in the stew.   *He chuckles.*   Tasted like it too. 30th March.... No. That's not the day I'm lookin' fer...5th April. Try that....

ROSIE leafs through the ship's log and comes to the date. She begins to read.

ROSIE   Log of the S.S. Bonavista. Master, Captain Elijah Blackburn, Trinity, Trinity Bay. Day dawned a bit mauzy. Glass dropping but not'ing to indicate real bad wedder. Big patch of swiles to the sout'east. Barrelman spotted anudder herd to the north. Sent half the men over, wid Jacob Blackburn as Master Watch. We steamed on into the mist. Looked back once to see how dey was doing, a weak sun spilling t'rough a scad* of snow. The way dey was, so far away, dey seemed to form a t'in black cross on the ice. Den the ground drift swallowed dem up....

She stops reading and sits immobile in the chair. SKIPPER is crying great silent sobs that tear him apart. The light dims as we go downstairs to the kitchen. MARY is putting on her hat and coat, gloves, etc. She crosses to the bureau and takes down a Missal, checking herself in the mirror as she does so. Suitably impressed with her appearance before her Maker, she is about to depart when WAYNE comes through the door.

MARY   Wayne!

WAYNE   Good morning, Aunt.

He comes in and kisses her on the cheek.

MARY   Did you sleep well?

WAYNE   Like a baby. It was good of you to give up your bed.

MARY   Oh, that's nothing. It's warmer downstairs after all. And once your father had been dragged upstairs, it was quiet enough....

The events of the past twelve hours have undermined her reserves. She sits on the day bed, face averted, close to tears.

WAYNE   Aunt. Something's wrong.   *crossing quickly to her*   What's the matter?

MARY   *dabbing quickly at her eyes*   Oh, nothing. It's foolish of me to get so upset. Oh dear. I see you so rarely, Wayne. I'm not used to...kindness.

WAYNE   Father's been at you this morning?

*scad—a light shower.

MARY   He always is these days. *rising* I was just on my way to church.

WAYNE   You can't go like that. Sit down for a moment, come on. *He leads her, vaguely protesting, to the rocking chair.* Now. I'll get you a cup of tea and then we'll go together.

MARY   Oh, Wayne. Would you?

WAYNE   We always used to. *He gets her a cup of tea.* I still remember those summer mornings. We'd leave early, just the two of us. You stopping to point out the bank swallows, the terns. Steerings, we used to call them. And I'd grab handfuls of wildflowers and grasses from the roadside and you could identify every one.

MARY   Yes. Yes, I remember. There were some happy times then.

WAYNE   I owe a great deal to you, Aunt Mary.

MARY   Oh no, Wayne. You've repaid any debt a thousand times over.

WAYNE   It's not the kind of debt that can be repaid.

MARY   Wayne, I love to see you, you know that. But I wish you wouldn't come here. You don't belong here. That's what we worked for together, you and I, all those growing years. To free you from the cancer of this house, the horror of this place.

WAYNE   I know. But it disturbs me sometimes to think I've gained my freedom at your expense. Why don't you leave? Here am I, a bachelor with a huge apartment I can't run . . .

MARY   No, Wayne. I won't be a burden.

WAYNE   Burden? Aunt . . .

MARY   What could I do? I couldn't sit at home day after day waiting for you to get back. Oh, I know it's tempting. God knows, I lie awake at nights dreaming about it sometimes. But it would spoil, Wayne. I'd get to be like a nagging wife. I'm too old now. And I can teach here until I retire.

WAYNE   I could get you a job in the school system in town. There'd be no difficulty.

MARY   Allow me some pride, Wayne. I'm not qualified. I survive here because I'm something of an institution, I suppose. And no one has the nerve to fire me. You do help me you see, indirectly. Perhaps when Father goes. . . . *Pause.* It might seem petty, Wayne. But I'm entitled to something from here. After all these years.

WAYNE   I don't think justice is petty, Aunt. And that's all you're asking.

It is a moment of complete sympathy and bonding between them. She hands WAYNE her cup. He takes it and puts it on the table.

D'you know Grandfather hit me this morning.

MARY   What?

WAYNE   Well. You did warn me in your last letter. I got a bit too close to that stick of his, that's all.

MARY   The old savage. Are you all right?

WAYNE   Oh yes. Just a bruised arm. I think he'd like to have done more damage than he did.

MARY   I'm worried, Wayne. What if he struck your mother one day in one of his fits. He doesn't know where he is or who he's talking to half the time.

WAYNE after a moment checks the entrance to the stairs and pauses a moment at the livingroom door. He comes back to MARY and lowers his voice.

WAYNE   I've good news for you, Aunt. That's the main reason I'm here. I've spoken to the Health and Welfare people. We can get him into a home by making a case for psychiatric treatment.

MARY   Psychiatric treatment! *Hope flares up in her.* Wayne, there can't be any doubt. He's been living in the past for so long, I swear sometimes he believes that we're all crew members on his wretched boat. *Pause.* Will it take long?

WAYNE   I think we can get him off your hands within the week.

MARY   A week! Wayne. . . Wayne. I knew you wouldn't let me down. You've never let me down. But are you sure? What do we have to do?

WAYNE   Now don't you bother your head with the details. You've quite enough to worry about.

MARY   Oh, I'm so excited! I should be sorry—or ashamed—but all I can feel is relief. Oh, I do my best to keep up appearances but it's so difficult. And the people have got such a respect for him when it's you they should be proud of. I heard you were in line for a Cabinet post. Is that true?

WAYNE   *laughing* So much for Cabinet secrecy.

MARY   Then it is true.

WAYNE   Murdock's retiring next month on the grounds of ill health. He's really being fired for inefficiency. You're looking at the next Minister of the Environment.

MARY   Wayne. I'm delighted for you.

WAYNE   And I am delighted for you. With Grandfather in a place where he can be properly looked after things might change a little round here. Why, you might even be able to finish your marking. *He crosses to the day bed, picks up a loose book and thumbs through it, laughing at her gently.* Let's see if you've changed your style. No. No. Nothing has changed. Do you remember how you trusted me to mark the grades beneath mine. Severe but fair. Those were your instructions. I've never forgotten them.

236 / JACOB'S WAKE

MARY *crossing to him, taking his hands* You're right, Wayne. Things will be different. Perhaps I could come down for a weekend or two. Then you wouldn't need to come back here at all. *Pause.* Wayne. Can I ask you something?

WAYNE Surely.

MARY You're doing something for Alonzo again, aren't you?

WAYNE Well. . .it's something of mutual benefit, Aunt.

MARY Be careful, Wayne. Alonzo has designs upon you, I know it. He's clever. And without scruples.

WAYNE He's a bit of a crook, I know. But he does organize the party in this district and I have no choice but to work with him on occasions. . .

MARY moves to interject, but he cuts her off.

You're right, Aunt. But don't you worry. I can handle him. Now. . . *He proffers his arm.* Shouldn't we be going?

ROSIE bustles in.

ROSIE My, Wayne. You're the first down! Lord knows what the udders is doing. Have ye' 'ad somet'ing to eat?

WAYNE No, Mother. As a matter of fact, I'm just on my way to church with Aunt Mary.

ROSIE Ye can't go out in dis widout a bit o' somet'ing in yer stomach. And jest look at ye, ye're not dressed fer the Divil wettin' his mudder* an' it blowin' a livin' starm out dere. Now, ye sit down here. . . . *She bustles him protesting to the table.* An' 'ave a nice cup o' tay whiles I gits ye a bit o' fish.

WAYNE clutches his stomach.

Would ye like a drop o' rum in yer tay, das if yer fader's left any?

She scurries rapidly to the stove with a plate, dollops a handsome portion of fish and brewis on it and thrusts it in front of him just as he is trying to rise.

WAYNE Mother. Really, I couldn't. . . .

He turns an appealing face to MARY.

MARY I'm afraid your mother believes all men to be carbon copies of your father.

ROSIE Carbon or not, yer not goin' out widout somet'ing and dat's dat. Whatever would dey say in St. John's if ye got sick out here, an important man like ye?

WAYNE *desperately* Mother. Just the look of that makes me feel sick. Now take it away! Please!

_____
*Divil wettin' his mudder—a few spots of rain when the sun is shining.

MARY Wayne. . . . *taking one arm* We must be going. It will be a hard walk in this weather.

ROSIE Now, Mary. . . . *grabbing his other arm* He's not leaving until he's at least 'ad a cup o' tay.

MARY *tugging firmly* It's time our little church was honoured with the presence of its most famous son. Surely Rosie, you, his mother, would agree to that.

ROSIE *tugging him the other way* And what if he faints wid hunger as dey're taking up the collection. . . . Some proud we'd be den, I 'lows.

WAYNE *finally breaking clear of them both* Please. . .Please. . . .Both of you! *inspecting his suit for damage* Look, don't you think it would be better it we went in the car? I have studded snow tires. It shouldn't be too much of a problem.

MARY *pleased* Why, Wayne! How nice of you. It's a long time since I had a ride in a car. Well, in that case, you do have time for something.

WAYNE is about to protest, but MARY puts a restraining hand on his arm.

Rose. Stop fussing. You've got quite enough to take care of. Wayne, you sit down there. . . . *proferring the rocking chair* And here's your tea. . . .

She deftly evades ROSIE and gets the poured tea from the table.

Now. . .what would you like?

WAYNE Some lightly scrambled eggs please, with just a little milk. Doctor's orders, I'm afraid. . . .My ulcers.

ROSIE *taking the fish and brewis from the table and pouring it splashily back into the pot* My, Wayne, you got ulcers? Uncle Jim Tobin had one o' dem last year. Or wor it two? Just afore 'e died. Terrible pain 'e wor in. . .bleeding like a pig inside.

WAYNE winces.

Leastaways, dat's what Aunt Sadie said, but I always reckoned it wor 'is conscience dat killed'n fer driving poor Mildred out of the house. And her only one hour from borning the baby.

MARY has doffed her hat and gloves and Missal, putting them back on the bureau. She takes off her coat and, laying it on the day bed, starts to prepare WAYNE's scrambled eggs.

MARY Uncle Jim may have been severe, Rose, but he was morally right. *to WAYNE* His own niece now. Everyone knew. Carrying on on the day bed while he was upstairs praying for Winifred, God rest her soul.

ROSIE *stubborn* It were a wicked t'ing she done, I allow, dough God knows the fellers she done it wit' is alive and well enough to sing the Lord's praise on the Sabbath and nobody minds dat.

MARY   It's the girl's responsibility to keep herself pure. Until marriage at least. What do you think, Wayne?

ROSIE   What do he know about it. Men are all alike when it comes to dat an' I suppose dey's no harm in it in the long run.

MARY   That's a matter of opinion. I'm sure if Wayne had spent his college days running around after every loose girl he wouldn't be where he is now.

ROSIE   Jest the same, I wish I'd a knowed. It blowin' a starm jest like today and cold as a drowned man's breat'. And she desperate and shamed into crawling under Winston's old punt.

MARY   *grim*   Aye, and because of that bit of stupidity the tongue waggers pointing at Winston for the father as if we didn't have enough trouble already.

ROSIE   *reliving her emotions, her compassion struggling for expression*   I don't care if Winston wor or worn't. I doubts it dough, the liquor had him slowed down a bit even afore you, Wayne.

MARY   Rose. Does he have to be reminded of those things?   *handing him his scrambled eggs*   There you are, Wayne.

ROSIE   We all needs to be reminded of some t'ings, maid. And t'were a terrible way to die in a place where we're all kin. Baby boy it were. The pair of 'em frozen together until Winston found 'em when the ice cleared in the spring. If only she'd 'ave come 'ere. Ye was in St. John's den, Wayne. At the University. Ye minds dat? I wrote and told ye. Ye was sweet on her one time I remember, used to follow 'er home from school.   *laughing at the memory*   But she were a wild one dat, I remembers . . .

MARY   *getting irritated by ROSIE's reminiscences*   For goodness sake, Rose. Christian charity is one thing, sloppy sentiment is another. She got her just desserts.

As she speaks, there is a howl of wind, a door opening and slamming at the side entrance left. WINSTON appears carrying a dozen beer, stamping the snow off his boots and shaking himself. He is in by the last line.

WINSTON   Here, Rosie, get me coat, will ye?

She scurries across and helps him off with it. She disappears into the passage left.

Christ! The things a man has to do to get a dozen beer on a public holiday.   *He crosses to the fridge and begins to stack in the beer.*   Who got her just desserts, Mary? What poor soul are ye tormentin' this time?

ROSIE comes back on.

ROSIE   Mildred, dear. Mildred Tobin. . . . Ye remember.

WINSTON   I'm not likely to forget, am I?

He uncaps a beer and, still by the fridge door, takes a satisfying swallow.

And I suppose the baby did, too, eh? Breath enough for one cry before the air froze in his throat. I reckon he got his just desserts. Or should we be thankful that God took him back before more harm could befall the little bugger?

He has wandered into the main area and crosses in front of WAYNE.

Good morning, son. I hardly recognized ye. What in the name of God are ye eating?

WAYNE   Oh, good morning, Father. Scrambled eggs.

WINSTON is interested. He swivels around, grabs the plate and looks at the remains.

WINSTON   Scrambled. I thought that only happened with brains.   *handing WAYNE back the plate*   What do ye do? Smash 'em up with a fork and fry 'em? Looks like baby shit to me.

MARY   Do you always have to be so crude?

WINSTON   *shouting*   Yes, by God. Because I am crude. I drinks because it helps me to fergit where I am and I swears because I like it. It sounds good and it protects me from your kind of literacy. And I likes jokes about natural functions because they're funny and they're particularly funny when aired in front of ye. I suppose ye've never farted in yer life. What is it ladies do, break wind?   *laughing*   I can see ye now, catching it and bending it over yer knee and trying to tan its little arse off. . . .   *laughing again*   What do you think of that, son?

MARY   *taking WAYNE's plate*   If only the child were the father of the man.

WAYNE   Then I could wish my days to be bound each to each by natural piety.

MARY   *delighted*   You haven't forgotten.

WINSTON   Jesus, I've sired a book of sayings.   *taking a swig*   Well, son. . . . Now that ye've finished yer scrambled eggs I wants to ask you a question. How's the government?

MARY   Wayne . . .

She hurries to the chest of drawers and once again attires herself in her church accessories.

We really should be going now.

WAYNE   Right.

WAYNE rises from the rocker, but is suddenly thrust back as WINSTON turns and forces him down with one hand.

WINSTON   It's not alright. I'm asking ye a question, son, and I wants an answer. Don't see ye very often. Ye can talk to God any day of the week, like the

238 / JACOB'S WAKE

Virgin Mary there, but it's not often ye gets a chance to talk with yer father.

MARY   Thank God for small mercies, Wayne. I don't have such luck.

WAYNE   *rising again, and managing it, but keeping a wary eye on WINSTON*   I'm sorry, Father, but I promised Aunt Mary I'd run her to church. I'll be right back. . . . We can chat over lunch.

WINSTON   *staring at him in disbelief*   Chat! Over lunch!

ROSIE   Heard your name on the radio yesterday, Wayne. Just afore ye arrived. It said ye'd sold somet'ing to the Japanese.

WAYNE   *moving towards MARY*   That's right, Mother. The last fifty thousand acres of standing timber to the Nippon Match and Transistor Company. I don't mind telling you, it was tough going.

WINSTON   What're they going to use it for, matches or transistors?

WAYNE   That's only the name of the parent company. They're global now, oil, shipping, newsprint. This province is the only one in Canada whose economy is on the upswing.

WINSTON   I'm not interested, son.

He suddenly swings up and spins around WAYNE.

Whether you've sold yer arse to the Japanese. I am interested in the Welfare. Now. When is that crowd yer with going to do something about increasing it? Ye don't get my vote until ye do. And that would be a terrible thing, son, for the press to discover.

He reads from an imagined newspaper.

Mother and father vote for son's political opponent. "He's neglected us for years," said pale-faced Mrs. Rosie Blackburn, clutching a five-year-old to her empty dug. "Ever since we put him through college when me husband developed heart trouble from overwork!"

WAYNE   Father, I already send you a considerable allowance on top of your social assistance. And I'm taking a risk doing that.

MARY   Wayne. You know he's only goading you. Come along now. We're going to be late.

WINSTON   *dodging between WAYNE and MARY*   Ye do send us a piece of yer travelling expenses I know, and yer mother and I are very grateful, aren't we, Rosie?

ROSIE   Oh, yis, I don't know what we'd do widout it, the price of liquor being what it is.

WINSTON   Things is going from bad to worse in this house, son, because yer aunt hides all her money and try as I might, I can't find it. And I haven't got the heart to take any more from me father.

MARY   What I do with my money is none of your business, Winston Blackburn. I earn it, d'you hear. By work. It's mine. Mine! And I'm saving it to keep the rest of us alive when you've drunk yourself into a beery grave.

WAYNE puts a restraining hand on her arm.

I swear, Wayne, that if he could forge my signature at the bank, every penny of it would have been gone long ago.

ALONZO comes downstairs and through the centre door into the scene.

ALONZO   Good morning, all. What a lovely Good Friday this is.

He goes to his mother and gives her a swing which drops her breathless.

My God, Mother. You're getting broad in the beam.

ROSIE   Yis, boy, and ye helped make it dat way. Git on wid ye now.

She pushes him away and, taking a pot from the stove, moves into the pantry area. He follows her.

ALONZO   It's an amazing household ye run, Mother. Brad's been reading the Bible now fer the past hour. Skipper's loaded, and the rest of the family's plotting to send each other to the funny farm.

WAYNE   Alonzo!

ALONZO   Easy, brother. Don't strain yer ulcers. Ah Mother, if only I could begin to describe to ye the glow of goodness that fills me breast on this day of days. Ye see in me, Mother, a new man.

MARY   Mph. The Good Lord had better watch the patent.

ALONZO   *swinging round, advancing on MARY and grabbing her hands*   Aunt Mary, by all that's holy. You look as ravishing as ever. Why has no one ever sought to suck the honey from those sweet lips. Drown in those pools of blue, lay his tired head upon that gentle breast . . .

MARY   *throwing off his hands*   Wayne. I'm leaving this instant.

WAYNE crosses to MARY and takes her arm.

ALONZO   No ye don't, brother. Not yet. We've business to discuss and time is running out. I've got to be gone be dark.

WAYNE   We'll talk later, Alonzo. When I get back from church.

ALONZO   *reading his mind*   We'll talk now I think, Wayne. I knows what's on yer mind. Ye're aiming to slip off to church and then barrel off back to town or wherever it is you're going. Aunt Mary kin find her own way to Salvation. Ye stay put.

He grabs WAYNE by the arm, the bruised arm. WAYNE gives a yelp of pain and with a reflex action strikes out at ALONZO. ALONZO prances round him and hits him in the midriff, catching him off balance and knocking him down. He crouches in boxer style, both fists at the ready.

ALONZO   Come on then. If that's the way ye want it. Come on.

MARY   almost in tears   Wayne!

WINSTON   One, two, three, four, five.... Rosie, maid, this is better entertainment than TV.

WAYNE rises with murder in his soul. For an instant it looks as if he's about to give battle. ROSIE pushes between them.

ROSIE   Fer the love of God, boys, give over dis foolishness.

WINSTON   Sock it to 'em, Rosie.

WAYNE   There'll be no contract, Alonzo. I can promise you that.

ALONZO   Oh yes there will, brother. Haven't ye forgotten something? Father... I got something to tell ye.

WAYNE   reverting to origins   By Jesus, 'Lonz. I'll take you with me.

They square off. Again, ROSIE pushes them apart.

ROSIE   Nobody's taking nobody nowhere, 'cepting Wayne. Now, boy, ye take Mary off to church afore dere's any more trouble. And ye.   turning to ALONZO   Ye mind yer manners. Dis is still my house and I'm not above giving ye a tanned arse.

ALONZO   What about it, Wayne?

WAYNE   I'll be back.

He and MARY move to exit. ALONZO prances after them.

ALONZO   I've just lost me stripper down to the Blue Flamingo, Aunt Mary. Me and the boys was wonderin' whether ye was any good with a bottle.

MARY   Rose. I won't set foot in this house again until I have an apology from that brothel keeper there.

Mustering the remnants of dignity, she and WAYNE sweep out.

WINSTON   calling out   Is dat a threat or a promise?

A great gust of wind. The door slams. ALONZO, laughing, turns and shuts the door. He is greeted with a stinging slap on the face from ROSIE.

ALONZO   startled   Jesus, mam. What was that fer?

ROSIE   Ye knows. And ye'll git anudder if ye keeps up like dat. I'm well able fer ye and don't ye ferget it. Yer poor aunt. She's been driven right crazy dis

marnin' by yer fader. And ye spoils the one chanct she gits to see Wayne.   with unconscious irony   An' she been like a mudder to 'n.

ALONZO   a little subdued, going down into the pantry area and sitting   Oh come on, Mother. If Mary hadn't got anything to be disgusted about, she'd commit suicide.

WINSTON   Drive some poor kid in school to suicide more like.

ALONZO   beginning to examine the plates on the table   Mm! What have we here... fat back... fish and brewis, herring....My God, Mother, you've excelled yourself.... I can see I'll have to get married.

WINSTON   I heard ye had...widout the benefit of clergy. Several times....

ALONZO   sardonically   They's not too many women like Mother around any more, Father. They don't seem to want to put up wit' it somehow.

ROSIE   sadly   It'd be so nice if one o' ye would at least. I 'lows if Sarah 'ad been alive we'd a had some grandchildren of our own be now.

SKIPPER   Winston.... Winston.

WINSTON   impatient   What is it now?   under his breath   Jesus.

SKIPPER   Winston.

WINSTON   resigned   Aye, aye, Skipper.

SKIPPER   She's slipping her moorings, son. Git up on the bridge.

WINSTON   Don't be so foolish, Skipper. She's fine.

BRAD has entered silently.

SKIPPER   Be the Lar' liftin' Jesus. Haul yer arse up on that bridge afore I...

WINSTON   Alright, Skipper. Alright.

ALONZO   He's in a bad way this morning.

WINSTON crosses to the fridge for another beer. ROSIE bustles out through the door and leaves it open.

WINSTON   He's been in a bad way every morning this past twenty years.

He turns to go up, pausing to swig from the bottle He sees BRAD.

My God! It's the Second Coming. Again!

BRAD   You shouldn't do that, Father.

WINSTON   What?

BRAD   You shouldn't encourage him. It's not good for him.

WINSTON stares at him, amazed. BRAD gains courage.

BRAD   He's living in the past instead of getting ready to meet God. That's not good for anyone. He's dying and you're destroying his soul. With that.   *pointing at the bottle*   As well as your own.

WINSTON   Oh. I am, am I?

BRAD   Yes.

WINSTON   *advancing on BRAD*   Let me tell you something, son. I encourage him because it's all he's got. Because his dreams mean more to'n than what's left of his children. That's me and yer aunt, son, if you gits me meaning. And they mean a damn sight more to him than his grandchildren do, including ye, with or without yer collar.

He moves away and turns back.

And I'll tell ye something else. I encourage him because beneath that wrinkled old skull and those mad eyes I kin sometimes see a truth about meself which might make some sense out o' dying. D'ye understand. Killing him! Christ!

ROSIE appears in the doorway with an armful of splits. She puts them in the woodbox.

ROSIE   Ye see, Brad, for yer fader, it's a way o' getting out of the house.

WINSTON   *laughing*   Rosie, Rosie, wiser than us all. . . .

ROSIE   'E'll need a drop o' water now fer 'is toddy.

She gets a small jug and fills it.

BRAD   You're as bad, Mother.   *restraining her*   Can't you see that? Are you frightened of them? Are you? I'm not. Oh, they can humiliate me. They can laugh at me. But God . . . yes, God has made me strong this morning. He'll help me to make you strong.

ROSIE   *upset*   I doesn't know what ye're on about, Brad.

BRAD   What do you think is going to happen when Father and Grandfather, and yes, Alonzo too, stand before God in all His glory, stinking of rum. It is today, Mother. Today. Listen. Listen to the Voice of the Angels.

BRAD has worked himself up into a pitch of fervour. His is not true insanity, but the glorification of a mutilated ego as narrow as it is intense. Clothed in the richness of his fantasy, in the words of revelation, he becomes at this instant radiant, superior, his words imbued with an impact beyond his own fragile identity. He is The Messenger and even WINSTON and ALONZO are spellbound confronted by this immolation of the spirit.

Babylon is fallen, is fallen, that great city, because she made all nations drink of the wine of the wrath of her fornication. If any man worship the beast and his image and receive his mark on his forehead or in his hand, the same shall drink of the wine of the wrath of God which is poured without mixture into the cup of his indignation and he shall be tormented with fire and brimstone in the presence of the Holy Angels and in the presence of the Lamb. And the smoke of their torment ascendeth up forever and ever and they shall have no rest . . . day or night!

Hushed pause.

Mother. Come with me.

WINSTON   She won't be going, Brad.

ROSIE   *sensing an assault*   'Tis alright, Winston. He wor always like dis. Me fader wor much the same. There wor no one like God to his way o' t'inking.

WINSTON   *ignoring her*   I won't be there neither. In fact, I've no intention of going in front of Him at all if I kin 'elp it. I nivir took to the idea of bein' surrounded by a bunch o' damn fairies singing hymns day and night.

ALONZO   Heave it out o' ye, Father.

BRAD   That's blaspheming, Father.   *still riding the power of a few moments ago*   Your soul is burning.

WINSTON   Feels like heartburn to me, son. An' what ye calls blasphemy I calls common sense. Nivir could stand that nonsense, 'Lonz, even as a young feller. All them damned fairies bursting their little hearts out blowing the last trump. Like a Billy Graham revival hour. When I goes, I'll go wit' what I knows. An' that's nothing, boy. D'ye hear. Nothing.

BRAD   Ye see, Mother. He's lost. He's doing it deliberately.

WINSTON   You're damn right I'm doing it deliberately. Which is more I kin say fer ye when I spawned ye. Rosie, I half blames ye. Ye nivir fed me enough that night. Jesus. If I started to tell the Good Lord what I t'inks o' ye, 'twould fill the Book o' Judgement.

BRAD with a swift movement takes ROSIE's hands and slowly brings her to her knees.

BRAD   God, in your infinite kindness look down upon this wretched house and see that there is one yet who is pure of heart, whose sins are of omission only, Lord . . . of love. Spare her, Lord. Spare her!

ROSIE, confused and upset, is in tears. She struggles to release BRAD's grip, but WINSTON, outraged, moves swiftly and throws BRAD sprawling.

WINSTON   Ye leave yer mother be. An' if I wor ye, I wouldn't be so anxious to get to them pearly gates, because ye knows who'll be waitin' fer ye.

BRAD   *shouting, frightened at the violent intensity of WINSTON's anger*   God. God will be waiting.

WINSTON   God! No, b'y. Mildred Tobin. Wit' that poor little bastard of hers still froze to her tit. And what will ye say to that, ye snivellin' gospeller.

BRAD *wavering* That's between me and God.

WINSTON Oh it is, is it?

ROSIE Now, Winston. Ye don't know that he wor the fader fer sure.

WINSTON I've allus knowed. I heard a conversation between him an' 'Lonz the night after he done it. Book o' Judgement. *standing over BRAD* Ye might be a true disciple now me son, but don't fergit yer mother and I remember the shape and colour of yer arse.

He half lifts then throws BRAD across the room where he crashes into the wall.

ROSIE Winston!

WINSTON Git out. I don't want ye in my house. Git out.

BRAD God, help me. Help me.

In the brief silence, only the howl of the storm is heard.

ALONZO *softly* They's nobody out there, Brad. They's only us.

BRAD Mother... I've nowhere to go.

WINSTON Then go to Hell and keep a place fer me.

WINSTON moves as if to assault him again, but ROSIE gets between them.

ROSIE Don't be mindin' yer fader, Brad. Ye knows what he's like when 'e's 'ad a few. *wiping her eyes with her apron* I don't know what's happenin' in dis house dis day. Everyone at it like cats an' dogs. I wish... I wish we could all sit down like we used to an' sing a bit an' laugh....

WINSTON *savagely* We nivir laughed, woman. Stop coddin' yerself. And fer the love o' Jesus, will ye stop motherin' that. Let'n go and crawl out under me ould punt. Might be some justice in that.

BRAD I didn't know! Christ believe me. *sobbing* I didn't know.

WINSTON Well, ye knows now. And it's time ye kept that picture in front of ye, son. Instead of a God ye've invented to please yerself and a book ye don't understand. And when ye learns just what ye are, ye might be more of a man than ye've ever shown yerself to be in this house.

He crosses to the stove and picks up the jug of water where ROSIE has left it.

This water's cold, woman.

He exits upstairs. ROSIE kneels to comfort BRAD. He grabs at her.

ALONZO That's told ye, boy. Ye should have listened to me this marnin'.

ROSIE Ye keep yer big mout' out o' dis. Ye've done enough harm fer one day, God knows.

ALONZO Me?

BRAD He hates me.

ROSIE No, b'y. *comforting him* Yer fader don't hate nobody. He's a good man. 'E would've liked somet'in' better fer all of us, but dat's it, I suppose.

BRAD Do you love me, Mother?

ROSIE Dat's a foolish question.

BRAD No, it isn't. You never told me.

ROSIE *hurt and confused, releasing BRAD and getting up* Brad. Ye always makes me feel so guilty. I means, ye don't talk about what's dere.

ALONZO Leave her alone, Brad.

He moves protectively to ROSIE.

They was never any love here, sure. Not the kind o' thing you're looking fer anyways. We was too busy survivin' to put up with any o' that foolishness.

BRAD gets up and for one stricken moment looks from one to the other, then suddenly hurls himself from the room. There is the bang of the outside door.

ROSIE *rushing after him* Brad. Brad....Ye come back 'ere. Brad....

The storm shakes the house. ROSIE re-enters. She is at the breaking point.

'E's gone out now, widout not'in' on, no coat or boots, not'in'. He'll perish sure.

ALONZO *crossing to her and putting his arm about her shoulder* Don't worry about'n, Mother. He'll not do anything foolish.

ROSIE But it's so bad. It's so bad. *She crosses and sits in the rocking chair, closing her eyes.* 'Lonz. Git me a cup o' tay, will yer?

ALONZO *surprised* What...are ye sick, Mother?

Nonetheless he rapidly gets her a cup of tea.

ROSIE I dunno, b'y. Tell ye the trut'. The stomach's left me. Everyt'in' seems to be gone...or going... somehow. *She sips her tea and rocks.* Turn the radio on would ye, 'Lonz. Dere's a good boy. Dere might be a nice hymn or two playing to cheer me up.

ALONZO turns on the radio and the last verse of "Amazing Grace" played by the Pipe Band of the Royal Scots Greys swells out. It has the cadences and the implication of a dirge for the fallen.

ALONZO goes and sits in the pantry area, picking up a paper from the top of the cupboard as he does so. He sits and reads as the lights dim in that area.

They remain on ROSIE while the hymn plays. She is sitting back, eyes closed, rocking slightly. The tears fall down her cheeks.

The lights fade to black as the band falls silent. Suddenly, there is a crackle of static and into the blackness a rather panicky ANNOUNCER says . . .

ANNOUNCER   We interrupt our program to advise all listeners that a state of emergency has been declared and . . . *crackle of static*   All communications with the mainland have been disrupted and difficulty is being . . . *crackle of static*   RCMP advise that no vehicles may be operated except . . . *crackle of static*   Power disruptions may be expected and residents are . . . .

There is more static which fades off into a low hum and then out. From this moment on the radio remains on, fading off and on as the power flows intermittently. The lights go up slowly in the SKIPPER's room as WINSTON enters. They are at about half power.

WINSTON   Master Watch reporting for duty, Skipper.

SKIPPER   Master Watch. Jesus, b'y. Ye'd nivir have made second cook on my ship.

WINSTON   I wouldn't 'a made that on me own neither.

SKIPPER   Listen, boy. Listen.

The storm howls.

WINSTON   'Tis bad enough alright. Not fit fer man or beast . . . .

SKIPPER   Listen, I tell ye!

Silence. Again, the storm howls. It is very eerie . . . like a voice out of the elemental past.

Did ye hear it that time?

WINSTON   The wind, that's all.

SKIPPER   No, b'y. A swile. They's a swile out there.

WINSTON   Can't say as I heard him, Skipper.

SKIPPER   *sighing*   Are we fast, boy?

WINSTON   Aye. Fast enough. Couldn't shift her wi' dynamite.

SKIPPER   *sitting bolt upright*   I said that. Told yer mother, but she never did listen. Every bit of charge we had. Blow the goddamned ice apart, I says. We've got to get back. Oh, they sweated. I'll give 'em that. They laboured till their eyelids was weighed down wid ice and they couldn't see no more. I went down meself, boy, lined up on the ropes wid'n. But what's mortal man when nature sets her face agin him. Black as hell it wor. And the ice buckling and rafting beneath us, laughing, I swear. Laughing. . . . Hell isn't fire, boy. It's ice. Black, bitter, cold.

Empty. Filled with the frozen breath of fallen men. Tinkling over their dead hands like spoons in teacups. I saw Jacob in Hell, boy. Out there in the dark.

A great gust of wind seems to shake the whole structure. He grips WINSTON.

She's dragging, boy. Ye're lyin' to me. Lyin'. Like the glass. . . .

WINSTON   Skipper. We'se got to have this out. We're not at sea. We're not in a boat. I'm not Jacob. We might be in Hell, but they's probably better or worse ones. I don't know yit. Ye're at home, Father. Stuck in yer own bed without the use of yer legs just as ye have been for the last thirty years and yer daughter and grandsons are plotting to have ye removed to the Mental. A few more roars from the bridge and I allows ye'll be gone, being pushed in a wheelchair down a long corridor stinking of piss and antiseptic, to yer grave.

The old man clutches at him. He shakes him as if he were a puppy.

SKIPPER   Ye're a damn fool, boy.

WINSTON   Aye, I'm all of that.

SKIPPER   A house is a ship. Lights agin the night . . . some adrift . . . some foundered, some rotting old hulks full of the memories of men. . . . They's no difference.

WINSTON   *surprised*   I 'lows that's right enough.

SKIPPER   Then I tell ye, boy. This one's adrift.

He sits upright abruptly. He seizes WINSTON's shoulder with one hand and points out at the audience.

Look, b'y. Look. Kin ye see'n.

WINSTON   Can't see in front of me own eyelids, Skipper.

SKIPPER   Mark me. Look. 'Tis the shape of death, boy. I kin see'n jest like that first time, rising out of the drift, moving across the ice widout a sound, a man like a cross growing up into the sky.

WINSTON   Father, they's nothing there. Nothing. *peering into the SKIPPER's eyes*   It don't matter. When all's said and done, ye sees plainer than I.

SKIPPER   *relaxing as the vision fades*   Ah. It's time. *closing his eyes*   Ye'll check her moorings, son.

WINSTON   Aye. I will.

SKIPPER   That's good, Jacob b'y. That's good.

WINSTON draws the blanket about SKIPPER. The storm howls. He goes out softly and stands for a moment on the landing. The light remains on in the SKIPPER's room, but begins to change, narrowing in focus throughout WINSTON's next speech until there is only one white light on the SKIPPER's face giving us the distinct impression that the old man has died. WINSTON looks out of the window.

WINSTON   Jesus. They's something out there. Looks to be blowed agin the fence. 'Tis moving. *Pause.* 'Tis gone. *rubbing his eyes*   Ach, the old man's got me seeing things now.

The storm howls. There is the quality of an inhuman voice in the sound, an intense and savage fury.

But what if he's right? If we is a ship? Then we's as good as gone. She'll nivir ride this one out. And what's to become of you then, Winston Blackburn? Eh?

A door bangs downstairs. WAYNE and MARY are heard. The lights fade up on the kitchen.

WAYNE   *offstage*   Here, Aunt. Let me help you off with that coat.

MARY   *offstage*   Thank you, Wayne.

They stamp the snow off their boots and enter the kitchen, shivering, making straight for the stove. ROSIE is asleep. WINSTON has remained at the top of the stairs. ALONZO is reading yesterday's newspaper in the pantry area.

MARY   I don't remember ever seeing it as bad. Lord bless us, it's a miracle we got home. You were marvellous, Wayne.

WAYNE   I've driven in storms before, but I'll admit I wouldn't try that again in a hurry. Where d'you think Brad was going.

MARY   He seemed to be heading for the wharf.

ALONZO   *coming out of the kitchen area*   Did ye say ye saw Brad? Mother's worried about him.

MARY   She might well be. He was running and stumbling like a wild man, talking to himself.

ALONZO   Didn't ye stop?

WAYNE   Of course I stopped. But I'd hardly wound the window down before the ground drift swallowed him up. You can't see a thing out there.

ALONZO   I suppose he'll dodge in somewhere. Look at this, Wayne. *taking the newspaper up to him*   I've just bin reading the Provincial Report for this area. It's pretty bleak. Unemployment is up. Liquor sales is down. . . .

WAYNE moves away, averting his face. ALONZO follows him.

Fer God's sake, boy. What's wrong with you?

WAYNE   To put it bluntly, you stink of fish.

ALONZO   *mildly*   Oh, do I? I thought the brewis were a bit strong. Must've been some old leggies Father put down last year. Never gives 'em enough pickle, Father don't.

MARY   Wayne, don't forget what I told you. Please.

WAYNE   *slightly irritated*   Don't worry, Aunt.

The radio suddenly crackles and blasts on.

ANNOUNCER   And this reading from Psalm 69. "Save me, oh God, for the waters are come in even unto my soul. . . . I am come unto deep waters so that the floods run over me. . . ."

The radio breaks down to static and cuts out. MARY makes herself a cup of tea. ROSIE is still dozing in the rocking chair. WINSTON enters and crosses to the table.

ALONZO   Amen to that. Now, brother.

WAYNE   Alonzo. Can't it wait? From the look of things outside, I'm going to be here for days.

ALONZO   No. It can't wait. Fer me own peace of mind, I'd like to get the business settled once and for all. Where's the tenders.

WAYNE   I don't have them here. D'you think I'm a fool? *tapping his head*   But I can give you the details.

ALONZO   I don't trust you, Wayne. I want to see it in black and white.

WINSTON   Jesus. What have we here, a meeting of great minds. . . . Hang on to yer trousers, Wayne. Yer no match fer him.

ALONZO   Thanks, Father. Recognition at last.

MARY   I've always known what you were, Alonzo. The sins of the parents come home to roost.

WINSTON   And what sins would they be, Mary. What could Rose an' me have contributed to that. *pointing at ALONZO*

MARY   Moral ignorance. . . .

WINSTON   *enraged*   Moral ignorance. Ye mind yer tongue, woman. Ye can call me what you likes, but ye leave Rosie out of this, d'ye hear? Ye wouldn't recognize holiness if ye tripped in it.

MARY   Holiness. I'd prefer to call it childlike simplicity.

WINSTON hurls a bottle across the room. The glass splinters. The crash wakes ROSIE. WAYNE, who is shocked, hurries to MARY.

ROSIE   My. . . . What is it now? I were having such a strange dream . . . about when we shot Trigger. Do you remember, Winston, and had to push him over the cliff, on account of he wouldn't fall . . . Winston?

He is breathing hard, clutching his chest, and is palpably upset as he tries to suppress tears.

What is it, love? What's the matter?

WAYNE   After all this time, Mother. You still don't know? He's drunk.

WINSTON collapses into a chair.

ROSIE   He's not drunk. And if he was, what business is it of yours to be talking to your father so and shaming him? It's between him and me, so it is. *bending over him*   What is it, love, eh? Has the ould man upset you?

WINSTON raises a ravaged face and tries to smile, an awful smile.

WINSTON   Tell ye the truth, love. *gasping* I hardly knows meself. *suddenly gripping her hands* It's me heart . . . it really is. The real one this time. Ould bugger finally going to demand payment for services rendered. *He pauses, then faces her, anguished.*   What else could I ha' been Rosie? What else could I ha' done?

ROSIE   *gently*   Nothing, love. Ye was good enough for me.

WINSTON   *gritting it out*   It weren't good enough, Rosie. Not good enough. Seems as the times was wrong. Everything changed afore I knew what to do. The old ones so damned sure . . . and they . . . *nodding towards WAYNE and ALONZO*   So certain. Though what about, the Lord knows. And us, Rosie, us. . . . Like rats in a trap, with the Welfare as bait. I didn't know what to do, so I didn't try. There didn't seem any p'int. But Jesus, Rosie . . . Jesus. . . .

His inarticulate cry for meaning in life is wrenched from the gut. It is painful. There is only one antidote. There has only ever been one.

ROSIE   Here, love. . . . Here . . . have a beer. . . . It'll calm ye down.

ALONZO hands ROSIE an open bottle. She puts it in his mouth like a baby. He swigs, then has a clear vision of himself. He takes out the bottle and chokes with laughter.

WINSTON   Epitaph for a Remittance Man

Stranger, watch when ye're walking on this ground,
Fer Winston Blackburn, he wor drowned,
Not at sea, as ye might suppose,
But in a bottle, held by Rose.

He laughs, then drains the bottle and staggering to his feet, crosses to the rocking chair.

WAYNE   Mother of God, Alonzo. Did you see that?

ALONZO   Wayne, I'm impressed. Beneath that tailor's dummy there lurks a heart. You should watch that, brother. It could prove fatal. Now. When do I get that information.

MARY   Don't have anything to do with him, Wayne. Please.

WAYNE   *crossing to MARY and taking her hands* It's alright, Aunt. Trust me.

MARY   It's silly of me, but I have a premonition. . . .

WAYNE   Look. . . .

ALONZO   Come on, Wayne. Stop playing footsie with Aunt Mary and get to the point.

WAYNE hesitates a moment, then crosses back to ALONZO.

WAYNE   What point?

ALONZO   I want duplicate copies of those tenders.

WAYNE   You'll get them once I get out of here. Within forty-eight hours.

ALONZO   And how can I guarantee that once you've left here with that piece of paper. I was a little hasty there. The dying pains of conscience.

WAYNE   You have my word.

ALONZO   Oh Jesus! Your word. Come off it, Wayne. You're not talking to the voters now. It's me, remember. We know what we are.

WAYNE   *annoyed*   What else can I do, man? You're not prepared to accept what I can tell you. I've said you'll get the copies and you'll get them.

ALONZO   Alright. I'll have to be content with that, I suppose. But until I get them, I'll take that document back.

WAYNE   No.

WINSTON   Jesus, Rosie. Turn the radio on, would ye? I preferred 'em fightin' to talking.

ROSIE   'Tis on, Winston. The power keeps going or somet'ing.

ALONZO   Look, boy. Give me that paper else I'll blow the whole thing wide open.

He makes a grab for WAYNE's pocket, where the top of an envelope can be seen sticking out. WAYNE jumps back, taking the envelope from his pocket.

WAYNE   No. I'll tear the damn thing up first.

WINSTON, who has been watching the interchange keenly, suddenly bounds from the chair and snatches the envelope from WAYNE's hand.

MARY   Wayne.

ALONZO   Christ. Now we're in fer it.

WINSTON   Now I'll find out what in the name of God ye were muttering about.

WAYNE goes after WINSTON but he pushes him away, pulls out the document and begins to read.

My God. *turning to WAYNE*   You bastards. You black, scheming bastards.

WAYNE backs across the room.

Rosie, they've forged me signature. They've written me name to git the Skipper into the Mental. I allus knew they'd like to, but. . . .   *The words are ground out.*   My name! 'Tis all I've got left. *turning on MARY*   You, you bitch. Ye were in on this.

ROSIE   Now, Winston . . .

MARY   Wayne. You should have told me. I didn't want it that way.

WAYNE   *shouting*   It was the only way!

WINSTON moves at speed into the parlour. WAYNE shouts from the door.

Father. Look. It's for his own good. For the good of everyone in this house. He'd be well cared for, given the best medical. . . . My God.

WINSTON reappears carrying a shotgun and savagely shoves WAYNE out of the way as he proceeds towards the bureau, hauls out a drawer and produces two shells which he runs into the breech.

WAYNE   They could keep him alive for years, Father. Tell him, 'Lonz.

ALONZO   Ye keep me out of this. I jest wrote your name, Father, that's all. I bin doing that one way or another all me life, ye knows that.

ROSIE   Winston. Don't.

He turns and raises the gun. Everybody dives for cover. There's a mighty gust of wind and the lights go off as WINSTON fires.

ALONZO   Christ. Give over, Father.

MARY   *screaming and trying to pray*   Holy Mother of God, pray for us now and at the hour of our death, amen.

WINSTON curses and fires again.

WAYNE   You're mad, Father.

WINSTON   Yis. And I suppose ye'd like me to commit meself next. And suppose I goes, I'll go fer something worthwhile.

The lights go up. WINSTON looks about him.

Jesus. Nary one.

He throws the gun down in disgust.

First decent thing I ever wanted to do in me life and the power fails. To hell wid'n.

ROSIE hurriedly retrieves the gun and takes it back to the livingroom. There's a different sound added to the storm, as of a house straining at her shores. The radio blares.

ANNOUNCER   The Government has resigned. I repeat . . . the Government has resigned. . . .

The radio crackles and fades. WAYNE, forgetful of WINSTON, leaps to his feet and rushes to the radio. He beats at it furiously.

WAYNE   Did ye hear that? For God's sake, come on. . . . Come on. . . .

WINSTON   *breaking into roaring laughter*   Well, well . . . if that don't beat all.

ROSIE re-emerges and closes the door behind her.

Rosie . . . the Government has resigned. That takes care of 'em better than me old shotgun.

WAYNE   *still beating the radio*   Come on.

MARY   Wayne . . . don't get so upset. I don't like to see you like this.

WAYNE   Will you stop nagging me.

WINSTON   *roaring again and clapping his hands*   That's telling ye.

The lights go out again. There's a strange silence, then once again a fearful gust of wind that strains at the very foundations of the house.

WAYNE   Why in the name of God is everything so dark?

ALONZO   We're snowed in, b'y. Where the hell are ye going?

WAYNE   *making for the door*   I've got to get to a phone.

ALONZO   *shouting*   Ye won't git ten yards.

In the interior, a clock strikes three.

WINSTON   'Tis three o'clock. That's the hour, eh, Mary?

ROSIE   Winston. Kin ye get some candles.

WINSTON   I couldn't see afore the power went, maid. 'Tis worse now. 'Lonz. Ye get 'em.

ALONZO   How the hell do I know where the candles is?

ALONZO fumbles out.

ROSIE   *calling after him*   An' 'Lonz. Mind ye takes one to yer grandfather.

WINSTON   Rosie, me duck. Rosie. Come here. Come here, maid.

ROSIE finds WINSTON and sits with him on the day bed.

Has turned out to be a good day after all, one way or another. An' I suppose we shouldn't complain too much, eh? Life's bin as good as it could've bin to the likes o' we, I suppose.

ROSIE   *softly*   I nivir complained, Winston.

WINSTON   I knows, maid. And they was times I suppose ye should've done. *chuckling*   Does ye mind the time we wor desperate? I wor visiting your folks and we hadn't had it for a week or more.

ROSIE   Ye ould Divil.

She sighs. A light appears on the landing as ALONZO moves upstairs, crosses to SKIPPER's room and puts a lighted candle on the chest of drawers. As before, a light illuminates the SKIPPER's face. What is illuminated now, however, is a Death Mask, the actor playing the SKIPPER having left the room during the blackout and commotion downstairs. It is essential that the audience is left with the illusion that, though the SKIPPER is possibly dead, his corpse remains in the bed and it must be illuminated in the manner described until the end of the play. ALONZO, without checking on the old man, comes back down the stairs.

ROSIE   Ye took me out on the pint, and it cold, the snow hard on the ground. I nivir t'ought me backside'd ever git warm agin.

WINSTON   Ye minds, today I think it wor, when ye said ye cares fer me.

ROSIE   Yis.

WINSTON   Well . . . *struggling* I cares fer ye too. 'Tis hard to put it into words sometimes. That's all.

ALONZO enters with two candles.

ROSIE   Take one over to yer aunt, 'Lonz, and bring one 'ere.

He does so. WINSTON gets up, crosses to the pantry and gets down the remains of the bottle of moonshine. WAYNE, like a man in a trance, comes slowly back in.

ALONZO   Jesus, b'y. What's the matter with you?

WINSTON   Well. I don't know what's happening, boys. Or what's happened even. But as we is all here, we might as well take a little drink together. *pouring a glass and crossing to WAYNE* Here, boy. Ye lost after all. More than yer dignity, I allows. Ye've come home. *proffering the glass* Jine me in a drink?

WAYNE   *blankly* What? What's that?

ALONZO   Don't seem to have any choice, do we?

WINSTON   We nivir did have.

He crosses to MARY, who is sitting numbed and betrayed at the table. WINSTON puts an arm around her.

And ye lost too, maid. 'Twas wrong of me to laugh at yer. I . . . I don't suppose ye'd care to jine me, eh? Fer all the times we went down the road together to that same school ye teaches at now . . . hand in hand. . . . *to himself* Up over the hill, the bell ringing, the rivers running over our boots in the first thaw.

He holds out the glass to her. MARY looks at it and reaches for the glass slowly. Then, in a swift movement, she snatches the glass and throws the liquor in his face. He doesn't move. The liquid runs down his face.

They's tears, Mary. I'm crying. Ye've made me cry.

He leans sobbing against the wall. There is an upsurge of wind and storm and the sound of timbers straining, cracking. A distinct sense of catastrophe pervades the atmosphere. The light remains on the SKIPPER.

Into this mixture of fear and pain and expectancy come three loud, imperative knocks at the door. Everybody, appalled, looks fearfully in that direction. WINSTON raises his head. He looks aloft and, although not seeing, understands. He whispers . . .

'Tis his token.

He moves slowly to the door.

ROSIE   Winston!

He opens the door and falls back. The SKIPPER stands there dressed in his Master's uniform, his brass button coat and hat, seaman's boots. ROSIE crosses herself.

Blessed Virgin.

The SKIPPER strides into the room with the vigour of a man in his prime, inspecting the ship.

SKIPPER   Rosie. Rosie, woman. Git me a glass o' rum.

He pauses in front of WINSTON.

Take the wheel, boy.

WINSTON is confused.

The wheel.

He roars it out, indicating a position downstage. WINSTON stumbles to the spot.

Hold it steady, boy. Steady.

WINSTON reaches, feels for and then grasps the imaginary wheel. We must be in no doubt that for him it exists. He wrestles with it. ROSIE fearfully tenders the SKIPPER his rum. He drains it and gives her back the glass.

Forty years, it's been. Forty years, waiting to see if any o' ye could steer this ship. I give ye fair warning. Have ye anything to say? Good. Comes a time when things has to be brought together as best they kin. When ye has to steer into the starm and face up to what ye are.

He pauses in front of MARY.

Yer mother nivir did that, Mary. Turned her face to the wall and died like an old ewe. But what's lambs fer if they isn't to be sacrificed sometimes.

MARY   God help us.

SKIPPER
North Nor' East
And South South West
From the Round Head Isles
To Cape Bonavist,
Steer it clear

And steer it true
And the same will take ye
To Baccalieu.*

Did I teach ye that, boy?

WINSTON   Aye, Father. Ye did.

SKIPPER   Some damn use ye made of it.   *crossing to WAYNE and ALONZO*   Who are ye?

ALONZO   'Lonz Blackburn, Skipper.

WAYNE   Wayne Blackburn, Skipper.

SKIPPER   Fust voyage?

WAYNE and ALONZO   Aye, Skipper.

SKIPPER   Ach. That wor always the way of it. But 'tis a pitiful crew for an old haverbeen on his last voyage.   *roaring*   CREW TO STATIONS. Women, git below.

ROSIE and MARY exit, taking the candles with them. WAYNE runs right and grips an imaginary rope. ALONZO leaps upstairs and goes to the edge of the SKIPPER's room, peering out. The sound and

the process of disintegration have been building throughout the foregoing.

SKIPPER   What's the conditions?

ALONZO   *from aloft*   She's cracking up, Skipper. They's a lead up ahead. Wind East Nor' East....

SKIPPER   A lead. Then we'll blast her out. Are ye ready?

ALL   Aye, Sir. Ready.

SKIPPER   Listen.... Listen....

Above the storm sounds, very distinctly, comes a seal bark, then another.

Blood and fire and ice. A swile. A swile. I wor right, boys. They've come back. The swiles is back. Newfoundland is alive and well and roaring down the ice pack. A swile. A swile.

There is a moment when all are poised, a tableau, then there is a blackout and the sound of a cosmic disaster, a ripping and rending and smashing, the final release of the insensate fury of nature that has been building throughout the play. There comes a flash that lights up the stage. There is nobody there. Then again, a blackout, the storm dying. The lights go up again, intense, white light that illuminates the threadbare reality of the stage home. Upstairs, the Death Mask is still lit. All fades into the lone quiet crying of a bitter wind.

*North Nor East... To Baccalieu—The refrain chanted by the Skipper is part of a much longer poem by which schooner men of the East Coast of Newfoundland committed sailing instructions to memory. The Round Head Islands, Bonavista and Baccalieu are all critical landmarks on the voyage round the coast.

GEORGE F. WALKER (b. 1947)

George F. Walker has been called "the odd man out," "the untouchable enigma" and even "the Greta Garbo" of Canadian theatre. His reclusiveness has been partly responsible for these epithets, but so have the frequent obscurity and eccentricity of his dramatic work. Yet the fact that he has also been called our Marlowe, our Tom Stoppard and our Sam Shepard suggests the high regard in which his plays are held as well as a growing understanding of the way they operate. Avoiding the subjects and styles that have come to characterize the Canadian theatrical mainstream, Walker has staked out his own distinctive territory. It lies somewhere between satire and parody, but to call it either would be reductive. Drawn from the generic fringes of popular culture both present (cartoons, B-movies) and past (Jacobean revenge tragedy, gothic melodrama), it is peopled with obsessive characters living in perpetual extremity and given to philosophical musings about such things as the need to wrench order out of chaos. It exists, Walker has said, along "that fine line between the serious and the comic." No play of his occupies that black comic territory with greater stylishness or command than *Zastrozzi*.

Walker's personal turf was east end, working class Toronto. He was driving taxi in 1970 when he read a flyer on a lamppost soliciting scripts for Ken Gass' new Factory Theatre Lab. The play he submitted, *Prince of Naples*, was not only his first attempt at writing drama, but when he attended its opening in 1971 it was only the second play he had ever seen. Despite Walker's inexperience, Gass made him resident playwright from 1971-76, an invaluable apprenticeship and the start of an enduring association. Of Walker's sixteen plays to date, all but five premiered at the Factory Lab.

Prince of Naples and *Ambush at Tether's End* (1971) were basically absurdist exercises, more derivative of Ionesco and Beckett than original. With *Sacktown Rag* (1972) and *Bagdad Saloon* (1973) Walker began to find his own voice, planting increasingly exotic landscapes of the mind with pop icons like Gary Cooper and Gertrude Stein. This phase of his work climaxed with *Beyond Mozambique* (1974) and *Ramona and the White Slaves* (1976). The former features a B-movie jungle locale populated by a drug-addicted, pederastic priest, a disgraced Mountie, a porn-film starlet and a demonic ex-Nazi doctor whose wife thinks she is Olga in Chekhov's *Three Sisters*. *Ramona*, a murder-mystery-*cum*-opium-dream that marked Walker's directing debut, takes place in a Hong Kong brothel in 1919, opening with the heroine's rape by a poisonous lizard.

Walker took his next three plays to Toronto Free Theatre. *Gossip* (1977), *Zastrozzi* (1977) and *Filthy Rich* (1979) were all less obscure, more accessible and consequently more popular than his previous work. *Gossip* and *Filthy Rich*, heavily indebted to Humphrey Bogart and Raymond Chandler, were the first of his plays in the *film noir* style that has dominated the latter part of his career. Along with *The Art of War* (1983) they comprise a trilogy, published under the title *The Power Plays* (1986). All feature a character named Tyrone Power as either investigative reporter or private eye, equally cynical and shabby in both incarnations, reluctantly involved in sorting out political intrigue and murder. Related in theme and mood is the Chalmers Award winning *Theatre of the Film Noir* (1981), a bizarre murder mystery set in wartime Paris. Another Chalmers winner, *Criminals in Love* (1984), and *Better Living* (1986) take place in an east end Toronto of Walker's imagining.

Also among his later plays are *Rumours of Our Death* (1980), an anti-war parable first directed by Walker as a rock musical, and *Science and Madness* (1982), a turn-of-the-century gothic melodrama with links to *Zastrozzi*. Following its rave notices in Toronto, *Zastrozzi* itself has had productions in London, Seattle, Australia, New Zealand and Montreal (in French). It was also produced under the auspices of Joseph Papp at the New York Shakespeare Festival's Public

250 / GEORGE F. WALKER

Theatre in 1982 at the end of Walker's year as playwright-in-residence there. Currently Walker lives in Toronto.

Zastrozzi is the quintessential George Walker play. Typically trying to assert order or impose meaning in the face of chaos, his protagonists come in three basic kinds. First there is the artist who dreams up his own reality, but without much success, as in the "cartoon" plays *Sacktown Rag* and *Bagdad Saloon*. Verezzi is Walker's portrait of the artist as narcissist, a genuinely silly man who believes he is the messenger of God. Second there is the justicer: the detective-heroes of *Ramona* and the *film noir* plays who specialize in making things clear and putting them right. Victor, like them, is "an ordinary man" obsessed with symmetry and balance and committed to justice, playing superego to Verezzi's ego. But in *Zastrozzi* he is merely a foil for the much more potent forces of darkness embodied in the third of Walker's protagonists, the arch-criminal atheist. Assuming a metaphysical void in which, according to Zastrozzi, "life is a series of totally arbitrary and often meaningless events," he fills it with the unfettered self ("I am the absence of God," proclaims Rocco in *Beyond Mozambique*). Rather than trying to oppose the fundamental disorder at the heart of things, he makes himself its agent. For in a world defined by what Zastrozzi calls "negative spirituality," chaos is the natural condition, evil the most powerful motive force and crime the only meaningful action. As Rocco says, "there's something about committing crimes against humanity that puts you in touch with the purpose of the universe."

Zastrozzi is unique among Walker's protagonists in that he is not only the master criminal but also a justicer himself. Utilizing all the baroque conventions of Jacobean tragedy, Walker makes him the revenger, a man in obsessive pursuit of Verezzi for the murder of his mother. But revenge turns out to be only a secondary matter. Zastrozzi's real vocation is "making everyone answerable" to his own dark truth. As the self-appointed "Master of Discipline" he is both judge and executioner. Verezzi is singled out for special attention because of his facile religious optimism, his artistic impressionism, his smile—the incarnation of everything "pleasantly vague" that Zastrozzi abhors about the modern age relentlessly dawning in 1893.

Though Zastrozzi is a monster, we can't help feeling sympathy for him. Like a diabolical Don Quixote he is an anachronism caught in a time of transition and unwilling to adapt. He is a little reminiscent of Michael Cook's Skipper, a giant among pygmies and a dying breed with no obvious successor (his "student" Bernardo is just a thug without artistry or imagination). Weary, preoccupied and dogged by nightmares in which he is overwhelmed by goodness and weakness, he begins to show more and more cracks in his facade of invincibility, losing interest in his satanic soul-mate Matilda and falling in love with the purity and innocence of Julia. At the end, surveying his victories, he knows that he is only marking time. He has won another battle but will surely lose the war.

If all this sounds awfully solemn, it isn't. Like all good comedy *Zastrozzi* is at heart a serious play, but at the same time its inflated Grand Guignol style lovingly sends up a broad array of literary and theatrical sources: Shelley's overheated gothic romance; Nietzsche's philosophy; the stark dichotomies of melodrama; Artaud's theatre of cruelty. What these have in common is a dramatic excessiveness that tends toward self-parody. *Zastrozzi* celebrates their excesses—and its own—with elegant deadpan humour and a self-conscious inversion of values that rings of Oscar Wilde and Joe Orton, but ultimately can only be called Walkeresque.

•

Zastrozzi opened on November 2, 1977, at Toronto Free Theatre. It was directed by William Lane and designed by Doug Robinson with Stephen Markle as Zastrozzi, George Buza as Bernardo, Geoffrey Bowes as Verezzi, David Bolt as Victor, Diane D'Aquila as Matilda and Valerie Warburton as Julia.

ZASTROZZI:
THE MASTER OF DISCIPLINE
A MELODRAMA

AUTHOR'S NOTE

This play is not an adaptation of the novel *Zastrozzi* by Shelley. The author read a brief description of this novel in a biography of Shelley and that provided the inspiration for *Zastrozzi: The Master of Discipline*—something quite different from the Shelley novel.

CHARACTERS

ZASTROZZI, *a master criminal; German*
BERNARDO, *his friend*
VEREZZI, *an Italian, an artist, a dreamer*
VICTOR, *his tutor*
MATILDA, *a gypsy; a raven-haired beauty*
JULIA, *an aristocrat; a fair-haired beauty*

SCENE

Europe. Probably Italy. The 1890s.

SET

It should combine a simplified version of a Piranesi prison drawing with the ruins of an ancient city. There are interesting and varied chambers within and the walls are crumbling. The tops of several trees are visible and weeds are growing out of the stones.

PROLOGUE

Just before the storm. BERNARDO is looking up at the sky.

BERNARDO   It is not a passion. Passion will eventually reward the soul. It is not an obsession. Obsession will sustain you for a lifetime. It is not an idea. An idea is the product of an ordinary mind. It is not an emotion. It cannot be purged. It is not greed or lust or hate or fear. It is none of those things. It is worse. The sky is swelling. And all those with timid natures had better go hide. It will conspire with the sky and the air will explode and the world will break apart and get thrown around like dust. But it is not the end of the world. It is easily worse. It is revenge.

Blackout followed by a loud sustained volley of thunder. Deadly calm. ZASTROZZI lights an oil lamp and stands rigidly. His face is twisted with hatred.

ZASTROZZI   You are looking at Zastrozzi. But that means very little. What means much more is that Zastrozzi is looking at you. Don't make a sound. Breathe quietly. He is easily annoyed. And when he is annoyed he strikes. Look at his right arm.   *He holds it up.*   It wields the sword that has killed two hundred men. Watch the right arm constantly. Be very careful not to let it catch you unprepared. But while watching the right arm   *He suddenly produces a dagger with his left hand.*   do not forget the left arm. Because this man Zastrozzi has no weaknesses. No weakness at all. Remember that. Or he will have you. He will have you any way he wants you.

Lightning. A long pause. ZASTROZZI's face and body relax. He looks around almost peacefully. A long pause.

I am Zastrozzi. The master criminal of all Europe. This is not a boast. It is information. I am to be feared for countless reasons. The obvious ones of strength and skill with any weapon. The less obvious ones because of the quality of my mind. It is superb. It works in unique ways. And it is always working because I do not sleep. I do not sleep because if I do I have nightmares and when you have a mind like mine you have nightmares that could petrify the devil. Sometimes because my mind is so powerful I even have nightmares when I am awake and because my mind is so powerful I am able to split my consciousness in two and observe myself having my nightmare. This is not a trick. It is a phenomenon. I am having one now. I have this one often. In it, I am what I am. The force of darkness. The clear sane voice of negative spirituality. Making everyone answerable to the only constant truth I understand. Mankind is weak. The world is ugly. The only way to save them from each other is to destroy them both. In this nightmare I am accomplishing this with great efficiency. I am destroying cities. I am destroying countries. I am disturbing social patterns and upsetting established cultures. I am causing people such unspeakable misery that many of them are actually saving me the trouble by doing away with themselves. And even better I am actually making them understand that this is in fact the way things should proceed. I am at the height of my power. I am lucid, calm, organized and energetic. Then it happens. A group of people come out of the darkness with sickly smiles on their faces. They walk up to me and tell me they have discovered my weakness, a flaw in my power and that I am finished as a force to be reckoned with. Then one of them reaches out and tickles me affectionately under my chin. I am furious. I pick him up and crack his spine on my knee. Then throw him to the ground. He dies immediately. And after he dies he turns his head to me and says, "Misery loves chaos. And chaos loves company." I look at him and even though I know that the dead cannot speak let alone make sense I feel my brain turn to burning ashes and all my control run out of my body like mud and I scream at him like a maniac, *whispering* "What does that mean?"

Blackout.

I

A vicious series of lightning bolts flash, illuminating the entire stage. A bed chamber. ZASTROZZI is reeling about violently.

ZASTROZZI   Where is the Italian Verezzi? Tell him I have come to send him to hell. Tell him that Zastrozzi is here. Tell him I am waiting. He can hide no more. He can run no farther. I am here. And I am staying.   *He grabs a flask of wine and drinks.* Ah, Jesus, this wine tastes like it was made by amateurs. I hate amateurs. Death to all of them. Remember that.

BERNARDO bursts into the chamber. ZASTROZZI throws a sabre at him like a spear. BERNARDO ducks. The two men look at each other.

BERNARDO   It's Bernardo.

ZASTROZZI   Step closer. The light is tricky.

BERNARDO   It *is* Bernardo, sir.

ZASTROZZI   Ah Jesus!   *He turns and violently rips all the coverings from the bed.*   I thought I saw an Italian to be killed.

BERNARDO   Not this one I hope. Please be more careful.

ZASTROZZI   Don't worry, Bernardo. Of all the Italians worthy of killing I am interested in only one.   *He sits on the bed.*   But my mind is becoming clearer by the minute and unless I get some satisfaction I may come to the inevitable conclusion that all Italians are worthy of killing for one reason or another.

BERNARDO   Yes, I like your threats. They keep me alert.

ZASTROZZI   Learn to smile when you are being ironic. It might save your life some day.

BERNARDO   *smiling* The best advice is that of the best advised.

ZASTROZZI   Remind me to order you to say that again when I'm not preoccupied.

BERNARDO   It doesn't—

ZASTROZZI   Have you found him?

BERNARDO   He is here.

ZASTROZZI   Where?

BERNARDO   At least he was here. He has gone off into the countryside. But he is expected back.

ZASTROZZI   How soon?

BERNARDO   Eventually.

ZASTROZZI advances on BERNARDO.

That is what I was told. And that is what I am reporting.

ZASTROZZI   Told by whom?

BERNARDO   The innkeeper where he stays.

ZASTROZZI   Then you were at his rooms?

BERNARDO   Yes.

ZASTROZZI   How do they smell? What do they look like? Describe them to me. No, wait, first, are you sure it is the same man? Verezzi the poet.

BERNARDO   Now Verezzi the painter.

ZASTROZZI   Yes, yes. And before that Verezzi the dramatist. And before that Verezzi the dancer. His vocation makes no difference. Always changing. Always pleasantly artistic. But the man himself, Bernardo. A description.

BERNARDO   The innkeeper described the same man.

ZASTROZZI   Even so. Possibly a coincidence. But the important things.

BERNARDO   Those as well.

ZASTROZZI   A religious man?

BERNARDO   Very.

ZASTROZZI   Always praying?

BERNARDO   Before and after every meal. Often during the meal. Occasionally throughout the meal.

ZASTROZZI   And the ladies? Does he have a way with them?

BERNARDO   Many ladies have visited him in his room. Most come back again.

ZASTROZZI   What about the smile? The smile that I see clearly in my head even though I have never met the man who wears it. That smile is an unnatural thing, Bernardo. Empty.

BERNARDO   "He smiles an annoying much of the time." I quote the innkeeper directly.

ZASTROZZI   Then it is him. It is Verezzi the artiste. The Christian. The great lover. The optimist. I will have him soon. Are you happy for me, my friend?

BERNARDO   I have watched you wanting him for a long time. I have grown fond of the force behind the search for revenge. I think I'll miss it.

ZASTROZZI   At first I wanted him just for myself. For what he did to my mother. But what I have learned of this man, Verezzi, makes me want him for another reason. That smile, Bernardo, I will remove it from the earth. It is a dangerous thing. It raises a bigger issue than revenge.

He repeats this last sentence in German.

BERNARDO   Is this a new development?

ZASTROZZI   Actually, it is still revenge. But in a larger sense. In fact it is revenge in its true and original meaning. And, therefore, some other word is probably necessary. It is 1893 and language, like everything else, has become pleasantly vague.

BERNARDO   I'm not sure I understand.

ZASTROZZI   Naturally. Because if you did then there would be two of us and there is only need for one. No. Call it revenge, Bernardo. Tell everyone else to call it revenge. If it will make you happy, I'll even call it revenge.

Blackout.

II

The countryside, a light rain is falling. VEREZZI is sitting behind an easel, paintbrush in hand. VICTOR holds an umbrella over VEREZZI's head and examines the painting in silence for a while.

VICTOR   Always tell the truth. Except when under pressure.

VEREZZI   What does that mean?

VICTOR   How can you paint a German landscape when you have never been to Germany?

VEREZZI   My father was in Germany. He told me all about it.

VICTOR   That's silly. You present a false image.

VEREZZI   Perhaps. But my heart is in the right place.

VICTOR   Unsuspecting people will look at your art and think they see the truth.

VEREZZI   Perhaps my Germany is the real Germany. And if not, then perhaps it is what the real Germany should be.

VICTOR   What is that supposed to mean?

VEREZZI   I'm not quite sure. Yes, I am. Perhaps Germany is ugly. Or perhaps Germany is bland. What is the point of creating bland or ugly art?

VICTOR   To illustrate the truth.

VEREZZI   Art has nothing to do with truth.

VICTOR   Then what is its purpose?

VEREZZI   To enlighten.

VICTOR   How can you enlighten if you don't serve the truth?

VEREZZI   You enlighten by serving God.

VICTOR   Then God is not serving the truth.

VEREZZI   Is that a question or a statement?

VICTOR   Both.

VEREZZI   Then you are a heretic.

VICTOR   And you are a liar.

VEREZZI   A dreamer, Victor. A dreamer.

VICTOR   The same thing.

VEREZZI   Enough. I don't even remember asking your opinion.

VICTOR   If I waited to be asked you would never receive my criticism and, therefore, no education.

VEREZZI   You weren't hired as a tutor. You were hired as a servant.

VICTOR   That was before either of us realized how monumentally ignorant you are.

VEREZZI   Enough. What colours do you mix to make ochre?

VICTOR   Ochre is unnecessary.

VEREZZI   That hill should be shaded with ochre.

VICTOR   On some other planet, perhaps. On Earth it's green.

VEREZZI   Earth is boring.

VICTOR   Why don't you ask God to move you?

VEREZZI   Don't make fun of God.

VICTOR   I was making fun of Verezzi.

VEREZZI   The two are interchangeable.

VICTOR   That sounds slightly narcissistic to me.

VEREZZI   I am His messenger on earth.

VICTOR   What?

VEREZZI   *a revelation*   I *am* His messenger on earth.

VICTOR   This is a new development. Until recently you were His servant.

VEREZZI   Through devotion and regular prayer, I have attained a new position.

VICTOR   Then God encourages linear growth.

VEREZZI   I beg your pardon.

VICTOR   When will you be made messiah?

VEREZZI   Atheist. How do you sleep without fear?

VICTOR   A secret. Besides, I am not an atheist. I just have a more pragmatic relationship with God than you do.

VEREZZI   What is it?

VICTOR   It is based on reality, Verezzi. You wouldn't comprehend it.

VEREZZI   I should dismiss you. I think you mean to corrupt me.

VICTOR   Can I ask you a question?

VEREZZI   No.

VICTOR   Not even a sincere one?

VEREZZI   In all the time I've known you, you've never once been sincere on the subject of my religious experiences.

VICTOR   Be patient. At least I don't laugh in your face anymore.

VEREZZI   Ask your question.

VICTOR   How do you reconcile being God's messenger on earth with the fact that you find earth boring?

VEREZZI   That is my cross. I bear it.

VICTOR   *sadly*   Yes. Of course you do. You probably do.

VEREZZI   Besides, I am an artist. Even if I was not a religious artist I would be dissatisfied. That is the nature of an artist.

VICTOR   That is the opinion of a very silly man.

VEREZZI   Enough. I have to finish.

VICTOR   When are we going back to the village?

VEREZZI   When I have completed my painting.

VICTOR   And what will you do with the painting?

VEREZZI   It contains His message. I'll give it to someone.

VICTOR   Not sell it?

VEREZZI   His message should not be sold. It's a gift. Besides I have no need of money.

VICTOR   That's because your father was very rich.

VEREZZI   Yes. So what?

VICTOR   I was just wondering how a messenger of God would get by if he weren't independently wealthy.

VEREZZI   You are a subversive.

VICTOR   And you are a saint.

VEREZZI   Oh. Thank you.

VICTOR   No. It wasn't a compliment.

Blackout.

III

A dining chamber. Occasional thunder, lightning, and rain outside. On the table are the remnants of a meal. BERNARDO sits in a chair, munching a chicken leg, his legs on the table, and describes VEREZZI's room. MATILDA and ZASTROZZI are some distance apart preparing to fight. They cut the air with their sabres.

BERNARDO   The room smelled of lilacs, incense and mint tea. This Verezzi is an orderly fellow for sure. Nothing about the room was haphazard. Everything was neat and clean. In fact the place appeared to have been arranged by a geometrist, for all objects were placed at perfectly right angles to each other. And between the two halves of the room—one used for work and the other for play—there was a perfect symmetry.

ZASTROZZI   Then he has someone with him. A man like Verezzi is not capable of symmetry. *Pause.*   Balance. A dangerous opponent in regulated combat. But get him in an alley or a dark street and you have him disoriented. Nevertheless, out of respect for his inclination, I'll cut him up into thirty-two pieces of equal size. Are you ready, Matilda?

MATILDA   First I want to make one thing clear. I do not suffer from rapier envy. I just like to fight.

MATILDA and ZASTROZZI cross swords and begin to fight. As they progress it becomes clear that MATILDA is very good even though ZASTROZZI is not trying very hard.

BERNARDO   There were several of his paintings in the room. For the most part he is a mediocre artist but occasionally he exhibits a certain flair. It's naive but it's there. One painting in particular caught my eye. An informal unrecognizable series of swirls and circles in white, off-white and beige. He seems very fond of it himself. He has given it a title.

ZASTROZZI   What does he call it then?

BERNARDO   God's Stomach.

MATILDA   The man is a fool.

BERNARDO   I would tend to agree.

ZASTROZZI   Then how has he evaded us for three years?

BERNARDO   I've been thinking about that.

ZASTROZZI   Thinking?

BERNARDO   Perhaps he doesn't know we've been chasing him.

ZASTROZZI   Nonsense. He's a clever man.

BERNARDO   But surely there are none more clever than the guileless.

ZASTROZZI   Stop thinking, Bernardo. It causes you to have absurd poetic fantasies. I am clever. I am the most accomplished criminal in Europe. Matilda is clever. She is the most accomplished seductress in Europe. Do either of us seem guileless to you?

BERNARDO   No. But you, sir, are motivated by a strange and powerful external force and Matilda has certain physical assets which allow her activities a certain ease.

MATILDA   I also have a first-class mind, Bernardo. And it gives me self-confidence. But if I didn't and I heard that patronizing comment about my body I would take off your head.

BERNARDO   If I ever have my head taken off I hope you'll be the one who does it. But not with your sword. I would like you to use your teeth.

MATILDA   Are comments like that what you use to show sexual interest in someone?

BERNARDO   Excuse me.   *He stands and starts off.*

MATILDA   Don't be shy, Bernardo. Are you being shy, Bernardo?

BERNARDO   If you wish.

MATILDA   Actually all I wish is that men in general could perform with the same intensity that they lust with.

BERNARDO   I might surprise you.

MATILDA   You might. But I think we both doubt that.

BERNARDO   Excuse me. I think I'll go visit the inn again.   *He starts off.*   Oh, I forgot. Here is one of his drawings. I took it from his room.

ZASTROZZI   You stole it.

BERNARDO   Yes.

ZASTROZZI   Why?

BERNARDO   Zastrozzi asks why someone steals something. Zastrozzi, who has stolen more than any man alive.

ZASTROZZI   Put it back.

BERNARDO   Why?

ZASTROZZI   We are not thieves anymore.

BERNARDO   Then what are we?

ZASTROZZI   We are not thieves.

BERNARDO leaves.

MATILDA   I don't want to do this anymore.   *She throws down her sabre.*   Let's make love.

ZASTROZZI   I'm preoccupied.

MATILDA   With what?

ZASTROZZI   The image of Verezzi's painting.

MATILDA   You didn't even look at it.

ZASTROZZI   I saw it in my head. It is a colourful pastoral. An impression of a landscape. Impressionism. Distortion.

MATILDA   Very interesting. Great material for pre-occupation, I'm sure. But you were preoccupied the last time I came to you. And the time before that as well. We haven't made love in over a year.

ZASTROZZI   Then go somewhere else. Making love is not an accurate description of what we do anyway.

MATILDA   I realize that. I know what we do. We ravage each other. Nevertheless I miss it. Don't you?

ZASTROZZI   No.

MATILDA   Zastrozzi is hollow. I have come three hundred miles just to be reminded once again that Zastrozzi is hollow.

ZASTROZZI   Drink.

He picks up a flask and drinks.

MATILDA   Don't you ever get physically aroused anymore?

ZASTROZZI   No. All sexual desire left me the moment I realized I had a purpose in life.

MATILDA   So now you have a purpose. I thought you just wanted to make people suffer.

ZASTROZZI   Can't that be a purpose?

MATILDA   I don't know. But I do know it can't stop you from desiring me. There's something you're not telling me.

ZASTROZZI   Very well. I swore a vow of chastity.

MATILDA   To whom?

ZASTROZZI   The Emperor of Spain's mistress.

MATILDA   Nonsense. When would you have met her?

ZASTROZZI   When I robbed the Emperor's country estate. His mistress was there alone. One thing led to another and I raped her. Just as I was leaving she looked up and said, "I can live with this if you vow never to be intimate with another woman." I shrugged my shoulders, said "alright," and left.

Matilda laughs.

I knew you would understand.

MATILDA   I'm the only woman alive who would. We belong together. It would be delicious while it lasted. There's no one alive we couldn't victimize in one way or another. And when we're finally caught we can go to hell together.

ZASTROZZI   No, not hell. Some place less specific. Atheists don't go to hell. They don't know where it is. The Christians invented it and the only decent thing they've done is to keep its whereabouts a secret to outsiders.

MATILDA   Then forget hell. Let's go to Africa instead.

ZASTROZZI   Later. I have things to do.

MATILDA   Ah yes. This search for revenge on some God-obsessed Italian. You are letting it change your personality.

ZASTROZZI   He murdered my mother.

MATILDA   So find him. Then kill him. It's a simple matter. It should not be your purpose in life. Revenge is an interesting obsession but it isn't worthy of the powers of Zastrozzi.

ZASTROZZI   I know. But Verezzi represents something which must be destroyed. He gives people gifts and tells them they are from God. Do you realize the damage that someone like that can do?

MATILDA   Damage to what?

ZASTROZZI makes a dismissive gesture.

I don't understand.

ZASTROZZI   I don't need your understanding.

MATILDA   Yes. I know that. I haven't been coming to you all these years because I think you need anything from me. It's that I need something from you.

ZASTROZZI   Really. What?

MATILDA   The whore sleeps with the devil so she can feel like a virgin?

ZASTROZZI   Something like that. Yes. What a comfortable little solution to guilt. Except that your devil is unpredictable.

He hits her and knocks her down.

Get out.

MATILDA   Let me stay.

ZASTROZZI   Get out. Or your devil might slit your throat just to show the flaw in your argument.

MATILDA   If I crawl across to you and beg will you let me stay?

ZASTROZZI looks at her silently for a moment.

ZASTROZZI   First, let's see how you crawl.

She crawls slowly over to him, wraps her arms around his legs and rests her head on his boot.

MATILDA   Let me stay. Do what you have to. Go send this Italian Verezzi to hell and then let me stay forever.

ZASTROZZI   Shush.

He is thinking. He breaks away from her and begins to slowly pace.

Send this Verezzi to hell.   *chuckling*   Yes.

He paces some more, stops and looks at MATILDA.

I will. He is a Christian. He can go to hell. Or at least he thinks he can. And the pain. Such excruciating pain. Much, much more than if I were to merely kill him. He must be made to send himself in his mind to hell. By killing himself. The most direct route to hell is by suicide. Over a woman. The most desirable woman in the world. She will entrap him then destroy him. And his destruction will be exquisitely painful and it will appear to everyone to have happened naturally as if it were meant to be.   *Pause.*   You will do this for me, won't you, Matilda?

She looks at him. Stands. Straightens her clothes.

MATILDA   First, let's see how you crawl.

They stare at each other. Finally ZASTROZZI gets down and slowly crawls over to her. He wraps his arms around her legs.

ZASTROZZI   Entrap him. Then destroy him.

BERNARDO walks in. Sees them. Smiles.

BERNARDO   He's back.

Blackout.

IV

Street scene. A light rain is falling. JULIA is sitting on some steps. Holding an umbrella above her head. VEREZZI is standing centre stage, looking up smiling, hitting himself on the head with both his hands and moving about delicately.

VEREZZI   I'm so happy. Life has once again given me the giggles. What a surprise. In the ruins of an ancient city. On a foul, damp day in spring the soggy young artist, walking aimlessly about in search of something to draw, meets the most beautiful and sensitive woman alive.

JULIA   You are kind. But you flatter me.

VEREZZI   Not yet. But I will. I am growing silly with delight.

He reels around a few times.

JULIA   Good heavens. What's wrong with you? Why can't you just come sit down and have a pleasant conversation?

VEREZZI   You want me to be sober.

JULIA   If you'd just stay still for a moment. We only met a minute ago. All we said to each other was hello. And you started prancing about and giggling.

VEREZZI   Yes. A less perceptive person would think I was insane.

JULIA   Well you might be insane for all I know. Can't you even introduce yourself?

VEREZZI   *sobering*   Yes. Of course.   *He walks over.*   I am Verezzi.

JULIA   My name is Julia.

VEREZZI   *spinning around*   Of course it is! Could it be anything else? You are spectacular and your name is a song.

JULIA   Sir. You will sit down. You will stop talking like a frenzied poetic moron and will make rational conversation. It can be pleasant conversation. It can even be romantic conversation. But it will be rational or I am leaving.

VEREZZI   *sitting*   I am Verezzi.

JULIA   Yes, you've said that.

VEREZZI   Will you marry me?

JULIA   No.

VEREZZI   I am depressed.

JULIA   How old are you?

VEREZZI   Twenty-five.

JULIA   You have the emotions of a ten year old.

VEREZZI   That is often the case with a visionary.

JULIA   So you have visions.

VEREZZI   *a revelation*   I *am* a visionary.

JULIA   So you . . . have visions.

VEREZZI   Yes. But don't tell anyone. I'm not ready to meet my followers yet.

JULIA   Visions of what nature?

VEREZZI   Religious.

JULIA   Visions of God?

VEREZZI   Of God. By God. For God. Through God.

He smiles. She just stares silently at him for a while.

JULIA   You are the first visionary I have met. At least the first one who has told me that he was one.

VEREZZI   I hope you're not thinking I'm bragging.

JULIA   No, that's not what I'm thinking.

VEREZZI   Good. Because I worked hard to be what I am. At first I was just a person. Then a religious person, then a servant of God, then a messenger of God.

JULIA   And now a visionary.

VEREZZI   Yes.

JULIA   When did you have your first vision?

VEREZZI   I haven't had one yet.

JULIA   I don't understand.

VEREZZI   Neither do I. I suppose I'll just have to be patient.

Pause.

JULIA   But you told me you had visions. Of God. By God. For God. Et cetera.

VEREZZI   Yes. I was speaking hypothetically.

JULIA   I'm sorry. But I don't think that makes any sense.

VEREZZI   No. Then I was speaking metaphorically.

JULIA   That neither.

VEREZZI   Symbolically.

JULIA   No.

VEREZZI   Will you marry me?

JULIA   No.   *She stands.*

VEREZZI   Where are you going?

JULIA   Home.

VEREZZI   May I call on you?

JULIA   No.

She leaves.

VEREZZI   I love her. She is just the right kind of woman for me. She has no imagination. And she takes her religion very seriously. God is creating a balance.

VICTOR comes on.

VICTOR   Who was that woman?

VEREZZI   Her name is Julia. She lives here. She is very bright. She is an aristocrat. She thinks I'm insane. I gave her that impression intentionally by making fun of religious states of mind. It was a test. She passed. I'm going to marry her.

VICTOR   Shut up.

VEREZZI   I won't shut up. You are my servant. You shut up.

VICTOR   You're getting worse daily. You're almost insensate. There is danger here and you can't appreciate it.

VEREZZI   There is no danger here. There is only love here.

VICTOR   You are insane.

VEREZZI   Who says so?

VICTOR   I do.

VEREZZI   You are my servant. You are not to say I am insane. I say you are insane. Yes, Victor, you are insane. So there.

VICTOR   Shut up.

VEREZZI   You shut up.

VICTOR grabs VEREZZI by the throat and starts to shake him.

VICTOR   Shut up, shut up, shut up.

VEREZZI raises a hand and VICTOR lets him go.

Now are you ready to listen to me?

VEREZZI   You hurt me.

VICTOR   I'm sorry. You were in a daze.

VEREZZI   I was?

VICTOR   Yes. How do you feel now?

VEREZZI   My throat hurts.

VICTOR   But are you sensible?

VEREZZI   Of course.

VICTOR   I found out from the innkeeper that someone has been making enquiries about you. Do you know what that means?

VEREZZI   Yes. My followers are beginning to gather.

VICTOR   Shut up. You don't have any followers.

VEREZZI   As of last count my followers numbered 454. I can describe each of them to you in detail.

VICTOR   You've hallucinated every one of them. The man making enquiries about you was probably a friend of that man Zastrozzi.

VEREZZI   Zastrozzi. Zastrozzi the German? The master criminal? The man who seeks revenge upon me?

VICTOR   Yes.

VEREZZI   He does not exist! He is a phantom of your mind. For three years you have been telling me I have been hunted by Zastrozzi and yet I have never seen him.

VICTOR   Because I have kept us ahead of him. I have evaded him.

VEREZZI   As only you could. Because he is a phantom of *your* mind.

VICTOR   He was making enquiries about you.

VEREZZI   That was one of my followers.

VICTOR   Your followers do not exist. It was Zastrozzi.

VEREZZI   Zastrozzi does not exist! I have 454 followers. Follower number one is short and bald. Follower number two is tall with a beard. Follower number three is . . .

VICTOR   Shut up. You are insane. And you grow worse every day. But I promised your father I would take care of you so I will.

VEREZZI   You didn't know my father. I hired you. As a servant. You must be feverish in your brain. But I will save you. You are a challenge.

VICTOR   Very well. But let's move on. You can save me at some other place.

VEREZZI   I can't. The birds are here.

VICTOR   I beg your pardon.

VEREZZI   Look up. What do you see?

VICTOR   A flock of birds.

VEREZZI   Yes. They are the sign.

VICTOR   What sign?

VEREZZI   The one my followers will be able to see in order to know where I am.

VICTOR   I don't believe this.

VEREZZI   Try. Please.

VICTOR   I will not.

VEREZZI   Very well. But when my followers arrive you're going to feel very out of place. They all believe it.

VICTOR gestures in disgust and leaves. VEREZZI drifts off in his mind.

Follower number 54 is medium height but he limps. Follower number 101 is blind. Follower number 262 is . . . a Persian immigrant.

BERNARDO comes on dragging MATILDA by the hair. He is carrying a whip.

BERNARDO   Here's a nice quiet place for a beating. Strip to the waist.

MATILDA   No sir. Please forgive me. I won't do it again.

BERNARDO   For sure you won't. Not after this.

She tries to run away. He intercepts and throws her down. VEREZZI raises his hand.

VEREZZI   Excuse me.

BERNARDO   What do you want?

VEREZZI   A little human kindness, sir.

BERNARDO   Mind your own business.

BERNARDO raises the whip. VEREZZI approaches them.

VEREZZI   Leave her alone.

BERNARDO   You have been warned.   *He draws his sabre.*   Defend yourself.

VEREZZI   Do I look like an angel of God, sir?

BERNARDO   No.

VEREZZI   Then you are in for a big surprise.

VEREZZI draws his sabre. Swishes it about. Trying to impress BERNARDO with his style. BERNARDO laughs. They fight. BERNARDO allows himself to be disarmed. VEREZZI has his sabre at BERNARDO's chest. Suddenly VEREZZI drifts off in his mind.

No. This is violence, isn't it. I shouldn't be doing this. This is wrong. I am an artist. I am in touch with Him.

BERNARDO slips away. MATILDA goes to VEREZZI and seductively runs her fingers through his hair.

MATILDA   Thank you.

VEREZZI   You're welcome.

MATILDA   No. Thank you very, very much.

MATILDA smiles. VEREZZI smiles.

Blackout.

V

Evening. A secluded place. ZASTROZZI is sitting inert. JULIA comes on with a picnic basket.

JULIA   Excuse me sir. But do you mind if I sit here?

ZASTROZZI turns slowly toward her. Looks at her impassively for a moment.

ZASTROZZI   It would be best if you did not.

JULIA   But I always come here at this time on this particular day of the week to have my picnic.

ZASTROZZI   Without fail?

JULIA   Yes.

ZASTROZZI   Well today you have been broken of a very silly habit. Move on.

JULIA   Why should I?

ZASTROZZI   I want to be alone.

JULIA   Then you move on.

ZASTROZZI   I want to be alone. And I want to be alone exactly where I am.

JULIA   Well today you are not going to get what you want. I am sitting and I am eating.

She eats and ZASTROZZI watches her for a moment.

ZASTROZZI   You are an only child from a very wealthy family.

JULIA   Perhaps.

ZASTROZZI   You don't have a worry in the world.

JULIA   Perhaps not.

ZASTROZZI   You don't have a thought in your head.

JULIA   I have one or two.

ZASTROZZI   And you are a virgin? *Pause.* Well, are you or are you not a virgin?

JULIA   Why? Are you looking for one?

ZASTROZZI   Go away.

JULIA   In good time. Perhaps when I'm finished eating this piece of cheese. Perhaps after I eat my apple. In good time.

Pause.

ZASTROZZI   Do you know who I am?

JULIA   No. Who are you?

ZASTROZZI   I am the man who is going to take away your virginity.

JULIA   Many have tried. All have failed. It will never be taken away. It will be given. In good time.

ZASTROZZI   Yes. Before you eat your apple to be exact.

JULIA   I'll scream.

ZASTROZZI   If you scream it will be the last sound you ever hear.

JULIA   Then I'll go limp. You won't enjoy it.

ZASTROZZI   It is not important that I enjoy it. It's important that you enjoy it.

JULIA   Impossible.

ZASTROZZI   Look at me.

JULIA   No. I don't think I will.

ZASTROZZI   Why not? Don't you find me attractive?

JULIA   That's not the point. You've threatened to rape me.

ZASTROZZI   Surely you knew I was joking.

JULIA   You didn't sound like you were joking.

ZASTROZZI   I was only trying to hide the embarrassing truth.

JULIA   And what might that be?

ZASTROZZI   That like so many other men I have admired you from a distance and could never gather the courage to approach you.

JULIA   So you waited here knowing I was coming on this particular day?

ZASTROZZI   Yes.

JULIA   And you adopted an aggressive attitude to disguise your true and romantic feelings for me.

ZASTROZZI   Yes.

JULIA   Yes, I can believe that. Men have done sillier things for me. Do you still want me to look at you?

ZASTROZZI   No. I'm too embarrassed.

JULIA   I understand.

ZASTROZZI   Just look ahead.

JULIA   If you wish.

Pause.

ZASTROZZI   I hope you don't mind that I'm doing this?

JULIA   What?

ZASTROZZI   Running my hand through your hair.

He does nothing. He will do nothing.

JULIA   Oh. I don't feel anything.

ZASTROZZI   I am running my hand through your hair. Very softly.

JULIA   Well I guess it's alright.

ZASTROZZI   You have a very soft neck.

JULIA   Are you touching my neck?

She looks at him.

ZASTROZZI   Please just look ahead.   *He looks at her.*   Please.

JULIA   Alright.   *She turns away.*

ZASTROZZI   Very soft neck. Very soft shoulders too. And if I may just lower my hand a little.

JULIA   Please sir.

ZASTROZZI   I'm sorry you spoke too late. Yes, your breast is also soft. But firm.

JULIA   Please. No one has ever—

ZASTROZZI   Both breasts are so wonderfully firm. And my face so nice against your neck. If I could just reach down.

JULIA   No sir—

ZASTROZZI   You should have said so earlier. Your stomach. My God. This is such a wonderful feeling, isn't it?

JULIA   I'm not quite—

ZASTROZZI   That's it. Lean back a little.

JULIA   I shouldn't be doing this.

She does nothing. She will do nothing.

ZASTROZZI   Back a little farther. Lie down.

JULIA   All the way?

ZASTROZZI   Yes.

JULIA   But.

ZASTROZZI   Lie down.

JULIA   Like this?

ZASTROZZI   Yes.

JULIA   What are you doing now?

ZASTROZZI   Kissing you on your mouth.

Pause.

JULIA   Yes. And now?

Pause..

ZASTROZZI   Your breasts.

Pause.

JULIA   Yes. And now?

Pause.

ZASTROZZI   Relax.

Pause.

JULIA   Yes.

Blackout.

VI

The sky is rumbling again. ZASTROZZI is drunk. He is at the doorway of his bed chamber. He drinks the last of the wine in his flask and throws it on the floor.

ZASTROZZI   Where is my wine? I called for that wine an hour ago. I warn you it is in your best interest to keep me drunk. I am at my mellowest when drunk. Innkeeper?

A VOICE   Coming, sir.

ZASTROZZI grunts. Goes and sits in a chair near the bed. Picks up a book. Reads. Grunts. Grunts louder. Throws the book across the room.

ZASTROZZI   Liar!   *standing, pacing*   They're all liars. Why do I read books? What is this new age of optimism they're all talking about? It's a lie sponsored by the church and the government to give the people false hope. The people. I care less about the people than I do about the church or the government. Then what do you care about sin. I care that I should not ask myself questions like that. I care to be dumb, and without care. I care that I should not ask myself questions like that ever again.

He sits. Pause.

Sad.

He stands.   Wine!

He sits.   Sad.

VICTOR comes in with the wine.

ZASTROZZI   Who are you?

VICTOR   I own this inn.

ZASTROZZI   No. I've met the owner.

VICTOR   The former owner. I won it from him in a card game last night.

ZASTROZZI   Congratulations. Put the wine down and get out.

VICTOR puts the wine down.

VICTOR   You are the Great Zastrozzi, aren't you?

ZASTROZZI   I am a lodger in your inn.

VICTOR   Are you ashamed of being Zastrozzi?

ZASTROZZI   If you were to die in the near future would many people attend your funeral?

VICTOR   No.

ZASTROZZI   Then save yourself the embarrassment. Get out.

VICTOR   I heard that Zastrozzi once passed through Paris like the plague. Leaving the aristocracy nearly bankrupt, their daughters all defiled and diseased, the police in chaos and the museums ransacked. And all because, it is said, he took a dislike to the popular French taste in art.

ZASTROZZI   A slight exaggeration. He took a dislike to a certain aristocratic artist who happened to have a very willing daughter and one painting in one museum.

VICTOR   And did Zastrozzi kill the artist, rape his daughter and destroy the painting?

ZASTROZZI   The daughter was not touched. She had syphilis. Probably given to her by the father. The painting was not worth destroying. It was just removed from the illustrious company it had no right to be with.   *He takes a drink.*

VICTOR   But the artist was killed.

ZASTROZZI   Yes. Certainly.

VICTOR   Why?

ZASTROZZI   To prove that even artists must answer to somebody.

VICTOR   And what has Zastrozzi come to this obscure place to prove?

ZASTROZZI   Zastrozzi is starting some new endeavour. He is going to murder only innkeepers for a year.

VICTOR   I am not afraid of you.

ZASTROZZI   Then you are stupid. *Pause.* And you are not an innkeeper.

VICTOR   They say that all Europe has no more cause to fear Zastrozzi. They say that for three years he has been single-minded in a search for revenge on one man and that all the rest of Europe has been untouched.

ZASTROZZI   They think and say only what Zastrozzi wants them to think and say.

VICTOR   They also say that any man can cross him, that any woman can use him. Because the master criminal, the Great Zastrozzi, is in a trance.

ZASTROZZI   Ah. But then there are trances . . . *He draws his sword and does four or five amazing things with it.* . . . and there are trances.

He puts the sword to VICTOR's throat.

Now, who are you?

VICTOR *stepping back, afraid*   Your revenge upon Verezzi will be empty.

ZASTROZZI   Who is he to you?

VICTOR   I'm his tutor.

ZASTROZZI   His what?

VICTOR   Tutor. I teach him things.

ZASTROZZI   Is that so. And what, for example, do you teach him?

VICTOR   How to evade the man who wants to destroy him.

ZASTROZZI   You are the one responsible for stretching my search to three years.

VICTOR   Yes.

ZASTROZZI   Interesting. You don't look capable of having done it. You look ordinary.

VICTOR   I am.

ZASTROZZI   No. In your case the look might actually be deceiving. But we'll soon find out. Where is your weapon?

VICTOR   I don't have one.

ZASTROZZI   Then why the innkeeper disguise? You must be here to intervene for your student.

VICTOR   Intervention doesn't have to be violent.

ZASTROZZI   I'm afraid it does. Haven't you been reading the latest books? The world is in desperate need of action. The most decisive action is always violent.

He repeats this last sentence in German.

VICTOR   Interesting. But all I'm saying is that I didn't think killing you would necessarily have to be the only way to stop you. I thought I could try common sense with you.

ZASTROZZI   You were wrong. Try something else.

VICTOR   Verezzi is insane.

ZASTROZZI   I don't care.

VICTOR   But revenge on an insane man can't mean anything.

ZASTROZZI   Wrong. I don't share the belief that the insane have left this world. They're still here. They're just hiding.

VICTOR   But he thinks he is a visionary.

ZASTROZZI   Well, perhaps he is. I don't care about that either. That's between him and his God. This matter is between him and me.

Pause.

VICTOR   I know why you seek revenge on Verezzi.

ZASTROZZI   No one knows!

VICTOR   I know of the crime that he and his father committed upon your mother.

ZASTROZZI   Ah yes. The crime. What version have you heard?

VICTOR   The real one.

262 / ZASTROZZI

ZASTROZZI   Is that so?

VICTOR   I was a friend of his father. I was away studying. Hadn't seen him for years. Had never even met his son. A letter arrived. He said he was dying. And asked if I would protect his son who would probably be in danger.

ZASTROZZI   And the letter described what they had done?

VICTOR   Yes.

ZASTROZZI   What did you think?

VICTOR   It was horrible, of course.

ZASTROZZI   Describe exactly what you mean by horrible.

VICTOR   Bloody. Vicious. Unforgiveable.

ZASTROZZI   Wrong. Not even close. Horrible is when things proceed unnaturally. When people remain unanswerable for their actions.

VICTOR   But the letter also told me why they had done it. This woman's son had killed my friend's daughter. Verezzi's sister.

ZASTROZZI   No. It wasn't me.

VICTOR   Then who was it?

ZASTROZZI   Never mind. But even if I had killed her then the quarrel would be with me. Not my mother. That is usually the way with revenge, isn't it?

VICTOR   You couldn't be found.

ZASTROZZI   I was away. Studying. I was called back to examine my mother's corpse. And the father's letter actually did describe what they had done to her?

VICTOR   Yes.

ZASTROZZI   Imagine that. How could he bring himself to tell anyone. I thought he was a Christian.

VICTOR   It was a confession, I think.

ZASTROZZI   Are you a priest?

VICTOR   I was at the time.

ZASTROZZI   And you left the church just to protect Verezzi?

VICTOR   It doesn't matter why I left the church.

ZASTROZZI   Yes. That's correct. Only two things should matter to you. That Verezzi killed my mother in a horrible manner. And that I, her son, have a legitimate claim to vengeance.

VICTOR   But he has no memory of the crime. He never has had. He must have blocked it out almost immediately.

ZASTROZZI   I don't care. I seek revenge. Revenge is a simple matter. You shouldn't have turned it into such an issue by hiding him from me for all this time.

VICTOR   But there's something else, isn't there?

ZASTROZZI   I beg your pardon.

VICTOR   I think there's another reason altogether why you want to destroy Verezzi.

ZASTROZZI   What is your name?

VICTOR   Victor.

ZASTROZZI   No. You are not an ordinary man, Victor. But you would be wise to become one within the next few hours.

VICTOR   When are you coming to take him?

ZASTROZZI   I am here now. Are you going to run off again?

VICTOR   No. He won't leave. He's waiting for his followers. Listen. I don't care much for violence. But to get to him you will have to go around me.

ZASTROZZI   I have already done that. And I didn't even know you existed.

VICTOR   How?

ZASTROZZI   Never mind. Concern yourself with this. If what I plan doesn't work I will not be going around you or anyone or anything else. I will be coming directly at him. And if you are in the way you will be killed. Now go away. I'm tired. Tired of the chase. The explanation of the chase. Of everything. Of you specifically at this moment.

He turns around. VICTOR pulls a knife from inside his shirt, raises it to ZASTROZZI's back, and holds it there. Finally he lowers it.

ZASTROZZI   Go away.

VICTOR leaves. Passing BERNARDO who is coming in.

BERNARDO   He had a knife about six inches away from your back.

ZASTROZZI   Why didn't you stop him? He could have killed me.

BERNARDO   I doubt it.

ZASTROZZI   Did you arrange for the introduction?

BERNARDO   Yes.

ZASTROZZI   I wonder now if it is a good enough plan.

BERNARDO   Probably not.   *He starts off.*

ZASTROZZI   It doesn't matter. It's almost over. I sense it. One way or the other I have him. This way would be less violent but more satisfying. Where are you going?

BERNARDO   A young woman in the village smiled at me. She's very pretty. And obviously well-off. I think I'll seduce her and rob her blind.

ZASTROZZI   You know, Bernardo, that you don't have to do these things just to impress me.

BERNARDO   Thank you.

ZASTROZZI   You could try to become the nice young man you were before your one little mistake.

BERNARDO   And what was that?

ZASTROZZI   You murdered Verezzi's sister. Don't tell me you had forgotten.

BERNARDO   Yes, I had. I've murdered so many others since then.

ZASTROZZI   You really are a seedy little butcher, aren't you?

BERNARDO   Once you make your one little mistake, sir, you must continue or be destroyed. The insulation of evil is the only thing that makes you survive. I learned that from watching you.

ZASTROZZI   But sometimes your crimes are heartless enough to shock even me. Who is the dark personality here after all?

BERNARDO   You sir. But I strive hard to be your shadow.

ZASTROZZI   Good. That man with the knife to my back. His name is Victor. He is Verezzi's tutor. He looks harmless, doesn't he?

BERNARDO   Yes.

ZASTROZZI   He isn't. I give him to you. He'll probably present a challenge.

BERNARDO   Thank you.   *He starts off.*

ZASTROZZI   Oh, Bernardo.

BERNARDO   Yes.

ZASTROZZI   I don't expect you to understand why you are killing him. But I do expect you to do it with some imagination!!

BERNARDO leaves. ZASTROZZI takes a long drink.

Blackout.

Intermission.

VII

VEREZZI's room. VEREZZI and MATILDA are making love. He is delirious. We know they are finished when he makes an absurdly loud and sustained groaning sound. MATILDA gets out of bed and looks at him in disbelief. She is clothed. He is naked.

VEREZZI   I am in love.

MATILDA   So soon?

VEREZZI   I am enthralled. You were wonderful. What a new treat. Usually I am the one who is wonderful and the women are enthralled. Where did you get this strange power?

MATILDA   It's something I was born with.

VEREZZI   How do you know?

MATILDA   What else could it be? It's not something you get from practice. I'm not a whore.

VEREZZI   No. But you're not a saint either. I'd know if you were. Because *a revelation* I'm a saint.

MATILDA   Of course you are.

VEREZZI   Don't be intimidated. Saints are human.

MATILDA   Why should I be intimidated? Saint or no saint. You are the one who loves me.

VEREZZI   You mean you don't love me?

MATILDA   No. Of course not.

VEREZZI   I don't understand. Explain. Be kind about it.

MATILDA   I love someone else.

VEREZZI   Who?

MATILDA   You saw him earlier.

VEREZZI   That man who was going to beat you?

MATILDA   Yes. Bernardo.

VEREZZI   That's disgusting. How can you love someone that beats you?

MATILDA   It's not *that* he beats me. It's *how* he beats me.

VEREZZI   I don't understand. Explain. But be kind.

MATILDA   He beats me like he could kill me. And I love him for that.

VEREZZI   You should love me instead. I'm gentle. I'm an artist. I'm a saint. And I love you.

MATILDA   Could you kill me? If you could kill me I might love you.

VEREZZI   You're very strange. And you're very exciting. But I don't think you're very healthy. That's a challenge. I can help you. Stay with me.

MATILDA   I can't! I love someone else.

VEREZZI   Then why did you make love to me?

MATILDA   A part of me is gentle. It wanted to thank you. But a larger part of me is something else. It wants to be beaten.

She starts off.

VEREZZI   Stay. I could beat you. A little.

MATILDA   If you really loved me you could do better.

VEREZZI   But I'm a saint. I love things. I can't hurt things. How could I face my followers? They're coming soon. Some of them are very vulnerable. Some of them are swans. Some of them are tiny little caterpillars who have been crawling for weeks to get here. I can't disappoint them. How can I preach love and human kindness to all my followers, then go into the privacy of my bedroom and beat a woman unconscious?

MATILDA If you are a saint you can take certain liberties. People will understand.

VEREZZI But will the caterpillars? They are dumb. I love them. Honestly I do. But they are dumb. Crawl, crawl. That's all they do. Crawl. Life's dilemmas are multiplied for a saint. He has to deal with too many things at once. One of my followers is a Turk. I don't even speak his language. When he comes how am I going to give him the message? I keep waiting for the gift of tongues but it never comes. God is handicapping me. And now you want me to beat you. I abhor violence. It makes me retch. But I love you. I'll die if you leave me.

She starts off; he crawls out of the bed and over to her.

Please don't go. I know. You can beat me instead.

MATILDA That just won't do.

VEREZZI But won't you even try?

VICTOR comes in.

VICTOR What's this? Get up.

VEREZZI stands.

VICTOR *to MATILDA* Who are you?

VEREZZI She is the woman I love.

VICTOR And why were you grovelling on the floor?

VEREZZI Because she doesn't love me. What can I do, Victor? She's breaking my heart.

VICTOR It seems to me that I met the woman you love earlier. That virgin God sent for you.

VICTOR starts to pack.

VEREZZI Yes. Julia. That's right. I love her. I'd forgotten. Oh thank God. For a moment there I didn't know what I was going to do. It's alright, Matilda. You can go now.

MATILDA So you don't love me after all.

VEREZZI But I do. It's just that I also love Julia. And she's less of a challenge. She just thinks I'm insane. I can deal with that. But I don't know if I can ever deal with you, Matilda. You want me to want to kill you. That's unique. But it's not healthy. But I do love you. And if it weren't for Julia I would probably destroy myself over you. Or something to that effect.

MATILDA *with clenched teeth* Or something to that effect.

She starts off.

VEREZZI Oh. Say hello to Bernardo for me. I think he likes me.

She looks at him oddly, shakes her head and leaves.

VICTOR What was that all about?

VEREZZI One of the tests of sainthood, I imagine.

VICTOR Did you pass?

VEREZZI I don't know. Tell me, Victor, how do you suppose I can find out?

VICTOR Oh shut up. Get packed. We're leaving.

VEREZZI Why?

VICTOR Zastrozzi is here.

VEREZZI Who?

VICTOR Zastrozzi. Zastrozzi!

VEREZZI Oh yes. The phantom of your brain. You've dreamt him up again have you?

VICTOR I've seen him. I was at his rooms.

VEREZZI Oh really. And what does he look like? Does he have fangs? Does he have horns? Does he have eyes dripping blood?

VICTOR No. He's a man. Just a man. Calm. Purposeful. And very experienced. Just a man. But a very dangerous one.

VEREZZI Well then bring him along and I'll deal with him. A little human understanding should get him to leave you alone.

VICTOR You're no match for him.

VEREZZI Why not?

VICTOR Because he's perfectly sane. And you're a delirious lunatic.

VEREZZI And if I am, is it good and right for you to be telling me so? Would it not be more good and right for you to be more understanding? That's an hypothesis. Of a religious nature. I have decided that your degeneration has gone far enough. And I am commencing spiritual guidance with you immediately. *He sits on the bed.* Now come sit at my feet.

VICTOR Get packed.

VEREZZI Lesson number one. When the messiah speaks, listen.

VICTOR When did you become the messiah?

VEREZZI Did I say messiah? No.

VICTOR I heard you.

VEREZZI No. Not me. God said messiah.

VICTOR I don't understand. Are you God or are you the messiah?

VEREZZI I am Verezzi. I am whoever He wants me to be.

VICTOR You are exploring new dimensions of the

human mind, Verezzi. But I don't think the world is ready for you yet. Get packed. We're leaving.

VEREZZI   No.

VICTOR   Please! I promised your father. It's the only promise in my life I've ever kept. It keeps me sane. Please get packed!

VEREZZI   No. I have to go find Julia. I have to tell her that God is talking to me. I know she'll marry me now.

VICTOR   Let me try to explain it to you in a way you will understand.

VICTOR drops to his knees.

VEREZZI   Don't patronize me, Victor. I am not a moron. I am just a good and lovely man.

VICTOR   Well that could be a matter of opinion. But let us suppose you are in fact just a good man.

VEREZZI   And lovely.

VICTOR   Yes.

VEREZZI   And very tidy as well.

VICTOR   Yes. All those things. A good lovely tidy man. Who is gentle to all things living and dead, et cetera, and wishes only to carry about the positive uplifting spirit of God. Then doesn't it make sense that in order to do that you should become aware of the obstacles that lie naturally in your path. The forces of evil that wish to stop you. In effect, doesn't it make sense that a good man should also be a cunning man?

VEREZZI   No.

He leaves. VICTOR sits on the bed. Shakes his head.

VICTOR   I give up. Zastrozzi will get his revenge on the lunatic Verezzi. After three years he will finally destroy a vegetable. I don't know who to pity more. Zastrozzi, the poor vegetable, or whatever it was that created them both. Sad. *He shrugs.* No. I can't give up. I promised. I must save him. Even if I must hurt him a little.

He stands and searches the room for something heavy. He finds something, takes it, and runs out.

Blackout.

VIII

A lull in the storm. VICTOR is walking through a dark alley. Suddenly a torch is lit. It is held by BERNARDO. He is standing with sword drawn in VICTOR's way.

VICTOR   Excuse me. Did a man pass by here recently? A young man?

BERNARDO   Forget him. His time is almost here. You have business with me.

VICTOR   What do you want?

BERNARDO   I am from Zastrozzi.

VICTOR   And what does Zastrozzi want from me?

BERNARDO   Your life.

VICTOR   A bizarre request. Do you understand the reason for it?

BERNARDO   No. I am a more simple man than Zastrozzi. I can only understand simple reasons for killing a man. And very simple ways of going about it.

VICTOR   Interesting. What, for example, are the simple reasons for killing a man?

BERNARDO   To get his money.

VICTOR   I have none.

BERNARDO   If he has done some wrong to me.

VICTOR   I don't even know you.

BERNARDO   Or if he presents some kind of threat.

VICTOR   Surely you can tell just by looking at me that I'm harmless.

BERNARDO   Zastrozzi says you are not.

VICTOR   Zastrozzi flatters me.

BERNARDO   Zastrozzi sees things that others cannot.

VICTOR   Perhaps that is because he is insane?

BERNARDO   He is not the least bit insane.

VICTOR   Are you absolutely sure of that?

BERNARDO   Yes.

VICTOR   Oh.

BERNARDO   In fact, he is the sanest man I have ever met. He is also the most perverse. The combination makes him very dangerous. You do not upset a man like this. When he tells you to kill someone, you do it. Even though you personally have nothing to gain from it. When he tells you to do it with imagination you try to do so. Even though you do not know why or even how to go about it.

VICTOR   Poor fellow. You're in quite a fix.

BERNARDO   While you on the other hand are not, is that it?

VICTOR   I am probably going to die. That I can understand. You are going to spend the rest of your life fulfilling someone else's wishes that you do not understand. That, sir, is a state of mental chaos usually associated with purgatory. I pity you.

BERNARDO   Shut up.

VICTOR   I pity you like I would a diseased dog.

BERNARDO   I said shut up.

VICTOR   You are out of your element. Zastrozzi is the master of evil and you are just a thug.

BERNARDO   I am more than that, I know.

VICTOR   A thug. And a murderer. You cannot think of an imaginative way to kill me because you have no imagination. You stand there with a sword and threaten a man who is unarmed. That is the posture of a cheap murderer.

BERNARDO   I could use my hands. Would you feel better about that?

VICTOR   I am only thinking of you.

BERNARDO   *throwing down the sword*   It will take a little longer this way.   *approaching VICTOR*   I'm going to have to strangle you.

VICTOR   Well it's not exactly inspired. But it's better than just cutting me down with a sword. Congratulations.

BERNARDO   Thank you.

VICTOR   But before you start, I have a confession to make.

He quickly takes out the heavy object he has taken from the room in the previous scene and hits BERNARDO over the head. BERNARDO falls unconscious to the ground.

I lied about not being armed.

VEREZZI comes on. In a daze.

VEREZZI   Victor. I'm glad you're here. I can't find any of my followers. They must have gotten lost.

VICTOR   *pointing off*   No. There's one now.

VEREZZI turns and VICTOR hits him over the head with his object. VEREZZI falls unconscious. VICTOR picks him up under the arms.

A place to hide. Someplace quiet. I have to think about what is happening to me. That vacant prison I saw this morning.

He begins to drag VEREZZI away.

What's this? He's smiling. Even in pain he smiles.

Blackout.

IX

ZASTROZZI's room. ZASTROZZI is standing in the middle of the room. He has a blanket wrapped around him. He is shivering.

ZASTROZZI   I am having a nightmare. It involves the final battle over control of the world between the forces of good and evil. It is the most terrifying nightmare I have ever had. Something so extremely unusual has happened that my mind in all its power cannot even begin to comprehend it. I am in charge of the forces of good. And I am winning. I think there is just the slightest possibility that there might be something wrong with my mind after all. The nightmare continues. I lead the forces of good with their toothy God-obsessed smiles into the fortress of the commander of the forces of evil. We easily overcome the fortress and become gracious victors. Not raping or murdering or even taking prisoners. We just smile and wish goodness and mercy to rain down on everyone. And I am smiling and wishing out loud for goodness and mercy as well except that inside I am deeply ill and feel like throwing up. And then we are taken to meet the commander of the forces of evil and he walks through a large wooden door and I see that he looks familiar. And he should. Because it is Zastrozzi. And even though I know that I am Zastrozzi I cannot help but feel extremely confused. And he reinforces this confusion when he opens his mouth and says, I am Zastrozzi. At which point I feel myself smile even wider, so wide that I feel my skin tighten and I know that my face will become stuck forever like this in the widest, stupidest, most merciful and good smile ever worn by a human being. Then I die. But before I die I remember thinking. They are going to make me a saint. They are going to make me a Christian saint. The patron saint of smiles. The nightmare ends. I need a drink. I need to sit down. I need more than anything to stop having nightmares. They're getting worse every day. There might be something wrong with my mind.

He shivers.

The nightmare continues. Again.   *He smiles.*

MATILDA comes on dragging a whip along the floor. She is furious.

MATILDA   Zastrozzi!!

She swings the whip around above her head. Cracks it.

Zastrozzi! I'm going to whip you. I'm going to whip you for making a fool out of me. For sending me to entrap a man who is an idiot and feels nothing except idiotic things.   *Pause.*   The nightmares.

She sighs and starts off; she sees him shaking.

No.   *She turns back.*   Zastrozzi, I have failed. Whip me.

ZASTROZZI   I can't be bothered.

He turns to her. Smiling stupidly.

MATILDA   Zastrozzi, you have a stupid empty smile on your face. Just like the one the idiot wears. You are standing there shivering under a blanket like a sick old man. You don't look like Zastrozzi. You look like an ass.

ZASTROZZI   *trying to concentrate*   And now?

MATILDA   You are still shivering.

ZASTROZZI   *closing his eyes and concentrating*   And now?

MATILDA   You are still smiling like an idiot.

ZASTROZZI   *closing his eyes and concentrating*
Now?   *approaching her slowly*   Now?!

MATILDA   Now I feel like whipping you for threatening me.

She begins to whip him. He doesn't move.

Don't ever make a fool of me again. Don't ever threaten me again. Who do you think I am? I am not one of those who quiver when they hear your name. I am your match, sir. I am every bit your match.

She throws the whip down.

ZASTROZZI   Are you?

MATILDA   In every way.

ZASTROZZI   In every way?

MATILDA   Yes.

ZASTROZZI   Ah well. You must know. And if you know then I must agree. Correct?

MATILDA   Yes. So you will let me stay? We'll be together?

ZASTROZZI   I'm afraid that's impossible.

MATILDA   Why?

ZASTROZZI   We're too much alike. You've just said so. I am in love with someone else.

MATILDA   Impossible.

ZASTROZZI   Life is strange, isn't it? I met her just a short while ago. She is quite different from me. That is probably why I love her. She is pure and innocent and possesses a marvellous gentle sensuality that I have never experienced before. In fact, just thinking about her arouses me. I am thinking about her now and I am getting aroused now.

He grabs her.

MATILDA   What are you doing?

ZASTROZZI   I am going to make love to you. Haven't you wanted me to for a long time?

MATILDA   Not while you are thinking about another woman.

ZASTROZZI   I'm sorry. But that is the way it must be.

MATILDA   I couldn't bear it.

ZASTROZZI   But you are a match for me in all ways. And I could bear it. I could even enjoy it. In fact that is the way people like us should enjoy it. Try to enjoy it.

MATILDA   I can't.

ZASTROZZI   Try.

MATILDA   No.

ZASTROZZI   Are you crying?

MATILDA   No.

ZASTROZZI   You are crying, aren't you?

MATILDA   No.

ZASTROZZI   Are you sure?

MATILDA   Yes.

ZASTROZZI   Are you crying?

MATILDA   Yes.

ZASTROZZI hits her. She is propelled across the room and falls.

MATILDA   What are you doing?

ZASTROZZI   Making a point.

MATILDA   You treat me this way because I am a woman.

ZASTROZZI   Nonsense. Women, men, children, goats. I treat them all the same. I ask them to be answerable.

BERNARDO walks on. His head bandaged.

ZASTROZZI   *to MATILDA*   Here, I'll show you what I mean.

He walks over to BERNARDO.

I take it from your wound that you have failed.

BERNARDO   Yes, I'm sorry.

ZASTROZZI   That's not necessary. I don't want you to feel sorry. I don't want you to feel anything. Do you understand?

BERNARDO   I think so.

ZASTROZZI   Try to understand. Try to feel nothing. Are you feeling nothing now?

BERNARDO   I'm not sure.

ZASTROZZI   Try. Feel nothing. Are you feeling nothing?

BERNARDO   Yes.

ZASTROZZI   Good.

ZASTROZZI hits BERNARDO's face viciously with the back of his hand. BERNARDO staggers back, but doesn't fall.

Fall down when I hit you, Bernardo.

BERNARDO   Why?

ZASTROZZI   Because it makes it appear that you are resisting when you don't. And you have nothing to gain from resisting.

He hits BERNARDO again. BERNARDO staggers back but doesn't fall. He looks at ZASTROZZI and drops to his knees.

Some advice for both of you. Get to know your limitations. Then remember that as you go through life there are only two things worth knowing. The first is too complex for you to understand. The second is that life is a series of totally arbitrary and often meaningless events and the only way to make sense of life is to forget that you know that. In other words, occupy yourselves. Matilda, go seduce Verezzi and if he is preoccupied, remove his preoccupations. The plan to drive him to suicide is not the most inspired I have ever thought of but it will do to keep us occupied for a while. After you have done that come looking for me and if I am in the mood we can play your silly whipping games. And as for you, Bernardo, go do something you at least understand. Commit some foul meaningless crime. That village girl you mentioned earlier. Go abuse her and steal everything she values. And enjoy it as much as possible because eventually you will be made accountable. And now if you will excuse me. I am going to visit the local prison. It hasn't been used in years. But I'm sure it is still full of wondrous sensations. I do some of my best thinking in prisons. Did you know that?

MATILDA   Yes.

BERNARDO   No.

ZASTROZZI   It's true though. I've visited some of the best prisons in Europe. I find it invigorating. It helps to confirm my sanity. Only a sane person could function in those places as well as I do. Does that make sense?

BERNARDO   Yes.

MATILDA   No.

ZASTROZZI   You see I must visit these prisons. It is the only way to make myself answerable. I have never been apprehended and I never will be. So I have to voluntarily submit to a prison in order to make myself experience judgment. When I have experienced enough, I escape. Do you understand?

BERNARDO   Yes.

MATILDA   Yes.

ZASTROZZI   No you don't.   *He smiles and leaves.*

BERNARDO   He *is* crazy.

MATILDA   Of course he is. He has always been crazy.

BERNARDO   Not always.

MATILDA   How would you know? You are crazy yourself. For that matter so am I. For wanting him the way I do. I should find a more simple man.

BERNARDO stands and goes to MATILDA.

BERNARDO   I am a more simple man.

MATILDA   That's the problem. It is men like you who make me want men like him.

BERNARDO   I could surprise you.

MATILDA   You would have to.

BERNARDO   I would like to make love to you.

MATILDA   I know.

BERNARDO   May I?

MATILDA   I will be thinking of Zastrozzi.

BERNARDO   I might surprise you.

MATILDA   Well you can try at least.

He grabs her and kisses her.

MATILDA   Harder.

She grabs him savagely and kisses him.

Blackout.

X

For the first time the focus is on the full set. Stripped of all furnishings, it should appear like an old dungeon. BERNARDO comes on pulling JULIA, whom he has chained at the wrists. He takes her into one of the chambers.

JULIA   What are you doing this for?

BERNARDO   You smiled at me.

JULIA   It was just an invitation for polite conversation.

BERNARDO   What would that mean to me? What was I supposed to do after the conversation? Marry you? Settle into a wonderful lawful domestic life.

JULIA   I really had no plans beyond conversation, sir.

BERNARDO   You wouldn't. You spend too much time with civilized men. This will teach you never to smile at strangers.

JULIA   Have I offended you?

BERNARDO   No. I'm just accepting your invitation and using it in the only way I can.

JULIA   What are you going to do with me?

BERNARDO   Anything I please.

JULIA   What is this place? I've never been here.

BERNARDO   No, you wouldn't have. It's an old prison. It used to house the criminally deranged but now it's vacant. More or less. A friend of mine found it. He has a way of finding places like these. What do you think of it?

JULIA   It's horrible.

BERNARDO   Yes. It is, isn't it? It will do very nicely.

JULIA   For what?

BERNARDO   For whatever I please.

JULIA   You're going to rape me, aren't you? You're going to rape me and murder me.

BERNARDO   Not necessarily in that order, though.

JULIA   You appeared to be such a nice young man.

BERNARDO   *grabbing her hair*   Nice? What would I do if I was nice? If a pretty woman smiled at me and we had a polite conversation could I marry her and be lawful and decent? No, I wouldn't do that now. My mind would explode. Yet I am a man. When a woman smiles, I must do something. So I do what I am doing.

JULIA   You don't have to do this. Let me go. We'll start again from the beginning. We'll meet in the fresh air on a sunny day. Talk about healthy things. Develop a respectful attitude towards each other. Eventually fall in love on just the right terms.

BERNARDO   Impossible. You're not the woman I could be in love with.

JULIA   I could try.

BERNARDO   Impossible. I can tell from your smile. There is a woman I love, though, who could love me on the right terms. But she loves someone else. His name is Zastrozzi. Have you heard of him?

JULIA   I . . . I think so.

BERNARDO   He is the one they talk about in whispers in your circles. I am the one who follows him around like a dog.

He starts off.

JULIA   Where are you going?

BERNARDO   Back to your house. To rob it of everything of any value at all. And to kill your parents.

JULIA   Please don't.

BERNARDO   Why not? And give me a reason I can understand.

JULIA   They're dreadful people. You would only be putting them out of their misery.

BERNARDO   Not bad. That's interesting. So there is something else behind that civilized smile. I'll be back.

JULIA   If you leave me alone I'll scream 'til someone finds me.

BERNARDO   *walking to her*   You shouldn't have said that. That was a mistake.

He hits her. She falls. Unconscious. He unlocks the chain.

She doesn't need these now. And I might have to use them. *sadly* I might want to use them. I might love to use them.

He leaves. In another corner of the set VICTOR comes on carrying the unconscious VEREZZI on his shoulders. He takes him into a chamber, puts him down and examines his head.

VICTOR   Perhaps I hit you too hard. You're barely breathing. Well, you were doomed anyway. At least this way you have a chance. *He looks around.* This place is horrible. But he'll be safe here I suppose.

He sits.

Now what am I to do? The only way I can get him to run is to keep him unconscious and that's just not practical. I could leave him here and forget the whole matter. That's practical. Leave him here! Forget the whole matter! That's practical!! But I did make that promise. And it's the only promise I've ever kept. I certainly didn't keep my promise to God. But I don't feel so bad about that, having met this Zastrozzi. If he is one of God's creatures then God must be used to disappointment. On the other hand, I just don't like the man. Everything he does, everything he represents unsettles me to the bone. Zastrozzi decides that an artist must be judged by someone so he kills him. Zastrozzi is to blame for his own mother's death in a crime of passion but hounds a poor lunatic because he cannot accept the blame himself. Zastrozzi steals, violates and murders on a regular basis. And remains perfectly sane. Verezzi commits one crime of passion then goes on a binge of mindless religious love and becomes moronic. Something is wrong. Something is unbalanced. I abhor violence. But I also abhor a lack of balance. It shows that the truth is missing somewhere. And it makes me feel very, very uneasy. Uneasy in a way I have not felt since I was . . . Yes, Verezzi, I will restore a truth to your lunatic mind and your lunatic world.

He takes VEREZZI's sword.

Zastrozzi.   *He leaves.*

JULIA groans. She slowly regains consciousness and gets up. She makes her way around the dungeon, sees VEREZZI and goes to him. She kneels down and takes his pulse.

JULIA   What's happening to me? I go for a series of walks in the street. Smile at two young men. One of them tells me he is a visionary. The other abducts me and tells me he is going to rape and murder me, not necessarily in that order. Then he hits me like he would a man and knocks me unconscious. I wake up and find the young man who thinks he is a visionary lying on the ground bleeding to death from a head wound. What's happening to me?

MATILDA enters.

MATILDA   You must be the virgin. The one with the marvelous gentle sensuality.

JULIA   Who are you?

MATILDA   My name is Matilda. I am your competition. I have a sensuality which is not the least bit gentle.

JULIA   Really? What do you want?

MATILDA   I want to kill all the virgins in the world.

JULIA   Oh no. What's happening to me?

MATILDA   Unfortunately for you, we are both in love with the same man.

JULIA   *pointing to VEREZZI*   Him? I don't love him. I don't even like him.

MATILDA   Not him. Zastrozzi.

JULIA   I've heard of him. He's the one who is whispered about in polite society.

MATILDA   He is the evil genius of all Europe. A criminal. And I am a criminal too. We belong together. So we must fight and I must kill you.

JULIA   Why can't I just leave?

MATILDA   That won't do. Besides, I will enjoy killing you. It is women like you who make me look like a tart.

JULIA   Nonsense. It's the way you dress.

MATILDA   Stand up, you mindless virgin.

JULIA   *standing*   Madame, I am neither mindless nor a virgin. I am merely a victim of bizarre circumstances. A product of healthy civilization thrown into a jungle of the deranged.

MATILDA   Yes, get angry. You are better when you are angry. If I were a man I would seduce you on the spot.

JULIA   That's perverse!

MATILDA   *taking a knife from under her skirts*   Yes, get indignant. You are quite provocative when you are upset. Take off your clothes.

JULIA   Why?

MATILDA   We are going to make love.

JULIA   Oh no we are not.

MATILDA   Yes, get confused. You are quite ridiculous when you are confused. And it is exactly the way someone like you should die.   *She advances.*

JULIA   What are you doing?

MATILDA   We are going to fight. And we are only going to stop fighting when one of us is dead.

JULIA   I would rather not. I would rather discuss some other possibility. I'm only seventeen years old. People tell me I have so much to live for.

MATILDA   Oh? Name something worth living for and I might spare your life.

JULIA   But how could I? A woman like you could never appreciate what I think is worth living for. No offense. But take your dress for example. I would live to dress much better than that.

MATILDA   You mindless coy disgusting virgin!

MATILDA attacks and they struggle. The knife falls and JULIA scrambles after it. MATILDA leaps on her and somehow MATILDA is stabbed. She falls over dead. JULIA feels her pulse.

JULIA   Dead. Oh my God.

She stands.

What is happening to me? First a victim. Now a murderer! And I don't even know her. This is grossly unfair. I'm young. I've had the proper education. My future was a pleasant rosy colour. I could see it in my head. It was a rosy colour. Very pretty. This is truly grossly unfair.

BERNARDO comes in. He sees MATILDA's body and rushes to it.

BERNARDO   You killed her.

JULIA   I had no choice. She attacked me.

BERNARDO   She was the only woman I could have been in love with on the right terms. You have blocked out my future.

JULIA   I'm sorry. But she didn't love you anyway. She loved that Zastrozzi.

BERNARDO   You have closed off my life from my brain. It is exploding!

JULIA   Well if you'll pardon me expressing an opinion, I think she was not entirely a rational person. Not at all the kind of person you need. You are not a rational person either and you would be better off with someone who could tame your tendency toward violence. If you'll pardon my opinion, I mean.

He is approaching her.

What are you going to do?

BERNARDO   Stay still.

JULIA   *backing away*   No. This isn't fair. I shouldn't be involved in any of this. I didn't love him. I didn't hate her. I've only a strange and vague recollection of this Zastrozzi. And all I did was smile at you.

BERNARDO   Stay very still.

JULIA   Please.

BERNARDO strangles her. ZASTROZZI appears out of the darkness.

ZASTROZZI   Bernardo.

BERNARDO drops JULIA, who falls to the floor, lifeless. He turns to face ZASTROZZI.

ZASTROZZI   Another victim, Bernardo?

BERNARDO   She murdered Matilda.

ZASTROZZI   She was merely defending herself.

BERNARDO   You saw?

ZASTROZZI   I have been here for hours.

BERNARDO Why didn't you do something?

ZASTROZZI I was preoccupied.

BERNARDO Matilda is dead.

ZASTROZZI I didn't know you had such deep feelings for her.

BERNARDO It wouldn't have mattered to you. You only have one thought. Well there he is. Verezzi the Italian. Take him. I am going to bury Matilda.

ZASTROZZI Verezzi will wait. You are not going anywhere. You have to face your judgment.

BERNARDO It will come.

ZASTROZZI It has.

BERNARDO From you?

ZASTROZZI Is there anyone better at it?

BERNARDO Judgment for what exactly?

ZASTROZZI For all your crimes. All the people you have murdered have spoken to me in my nightmares and asked that you be made answerable.

BERNARDO I am just a student to the master.

ZASTROZZI And only the master is qualified to judge. Draw your sword, Bernardo. Let us have the formality of a contest. But know now that you are dead.

BERNARDO Sir. Let me go.

ZASTROZZI No.

ZASTROZZI draws his sword. BERNARDO draws his. They fight. Viciously. Expertly. BERNARDO is good. ZASTROZZI is the master though, and eventually he pierces BERNARDO's chest. BERNARDO drops to his knees.

BERNARDO Sir.

ZASTROZZI You are dead.

He knocks BERNARDO over with his foot. BERNARDO is dead. ZASTROZZI walks over to VEREZZI and stands silently looking down at him for awhile, then sits down and cradles VEREZZI's head.

Verezzi. Finally. Not dying at all. It's just a flesh wound. Your breathing becomes stronger. Soon you will wake up. I want you to be awake for this. It would have been more satisfying to have you destroy yourself. But you are too clever for that. Everyone thinks you are out of your mind. But I know you have just been hiding. Hiding from your crimes, Verezzi. Hiding from the crime of telling people you are giving them gifts from God. The crime of letting them think there is happiness in that stupid smile of yours. The crime of making language pleasantly vague and painting with distorted imagination. The crime of disturbing the natural condition in which the dark side prevails. Wake up,

Verezzi. Zastrozzi is here to prove that you must be judged. You can hide no more.

A VOICE FROM THE DARKNESS And what is Zastrozzi hiding from?

ZASTROZZI *standing* What do you want?

VICTOR comes out of the darkness carrying VEREZZI's sabre.

VICTOR Sir. Tell me. What is this about? *looking around* All this death.

ZASTROZZI It is a continuing process of simplification. I am simplifying my life. These people came here to be judged.

VICTOR By you?

ZASTROZZI Is there anyone better at it?

VICTOR Apparently not. Well then I too want to be judged by Zastrozzi, who judges for a profession.

ZASTROZZI Then step closer.

VICTOR Is there a fee?

ZASTROZZI Yes. But I take it from you quickly. You'll never even know it's gone.

VICTOR I have another idea. I think a man who enjoys his profession as much as you should be the one to pay the fee.

ZASTROZZI Perhaps. But I have never met anyone who would collect from me.

VICTOR You have now, sir.

ZASTROZZI I doubt it very much. You don't even hold your weapon properly.

VICTOR I have an unorthodox style. But it serves.

ZASTROZZI Let's see.

ZASTROZZI draws his sword. VICTOR begins a short prayer in Latin which ZASTROZZI finishes for him. VICTOR looks at ZASTROZZI. Pause.

ZASTROZZI *in German* Did you not know that I could see into your heart?

VICTOR *in any Romance language* Yes. But I can see into your heart as well.

ZASTROZZI *in the same Romance language* Then it will be an interesting battle.

Pause.

VICTOR So.

ZASTROZZI So.

They approach each other, cross swords and begin to fight. The fight will continue and move across the entire stage at least once. ZASTROZZI tests VICTOR. He responds well but his movements are very unusual. VICTOR will gradually get better by observing ZASTROZZI's moves.

ZASTROZZI   What are all these strange things you are doing designed for?

VICTOR   To keep me alive.

ZASTROZZI   Eventually I will find a way to penetrate your unorthodox style.

VICTOR   That might be difficult. Since I am making it up as I go along.

ZASTROZZI   You look silly.

VICTOR   But I am alive.

ZASTROZZI   Perhaps more alive than you have ever been. That is sometimes the way a person faces death.

VICTOR   I intend to live.

ZASTROZZI   Then you should have taken my advice and become an ordinary man.

VICTOR   Sir. The point is that I *am* an ordinary man.

ZASTROZZI   An ordinary man does not challenge Zastrozzi.

ZASTROZZI attacks him viciously. VICTOR defends himself well.

VICTOR   I am still alive. I am still waiting to be judged.

ZASTROZZI   And growing arrogant as well.

VICTOR   You talk about arrogance. The man who kills on a whim. Who kills an artist simply because he is mediocre. Who commits crimes against people because he believes he is the thing to which they must be answerable.

ZASTROZZI   They must be answerable to something.

VICTOR   There is always God, you know.

ZASTROZZI   I am an atheist. If a man who is an atheist believes that people must be answerable, he has a duty to make them answerable to something.

VICTOR   Answerable to your own demented personality.

ZASTROZZI   I am what they are. They answer to themselves.

VICTOR   Alright, forget God. A man is responsible to humanity.

ZASTROZZI   And I am part of humanity.

VICTOR   The irresponsible part.

ZASTROZZI   No. It is my responsibility to spread out like a disease and purge. And by destroying everything make everything safe.

VICTOR   Explain exactly what you mean by safe.

ZASTROZZI   Alive. Untouched by expectation. Free of history. Free of religion. Free of everything. And soon to be free of you.

ZASTROZZI attacks and VICTOR defends himself very well.

VICTOR   I am still alive.

ZASTROZZI   But you are totally on the defensive.

VICTOR   I don't have to kill you. I only have to survive. By merely surviving I neutralize you.

ZASTROZZI   You cannot neutralize something you do not understand.

VICTOR   We are approaching a new century. And with it a new world. There will be no place in it for your attitude, your behaviour.

ZASTROZZI   This new world, what do you suppose it will be like?

VICTOR   Better.

ZASTROZZI   Describe what you mean by better.

VICTOR   More humane. More civilized.

ZASTROZZI   Wrong. Better is when the truth is understood. Understanding the truth is understanding that the force of darkness is constant.

VICTOR   No, it is not. Your time is over.

ZASTROZZI   Wrong again.

ZASTROZZI attacks him viciously. VICTOR defends himself and is ebullient.

VICTOR   I am alive! Everything I said was true. You are neutralized. I am the emissary of goodness in the battle between good and evil. I have found God again.

VICTOR lunges forward wildly. ZASTROZZI plunges his sabre through VICTOR's heart.

I am alive.

He falls down and dies.

ZASTROZZI   Ah Victor. You understood what was in your heart. But you did not know your limitations.

ZASTROZZI throws down his sabre. VEREZZI groans and slowly wakes up. He sits, then stands, while ZASTROZZI watches him. VEREZZI staggers around looking at the bodies and slowly regaining his equilibrium.

VEREZZI   Look at all these dead people. What happened?

ZASTROZZI   A series of unfortunate accidents.

VEREZZI   Who are you?

ZASTROZZI   Zastrozzi.

VEREZZI freezes.

VEREZZI   I thought you didn't exist.

ZASTROZZI   Nonsense. You know me well.

VEREZZI   Are you responsible for all these dead people?

ZASTROZZI   No. You are.

VEREZZI   That's quite impossible. I am a servant of God.

ZASTROZZI has drawn a knife.

ZASTROZZI   You are dead.

VEREZZI   What are you going to do?

ZASTROZZI   Cut open your stomach.

VEREZZI   You can't. I'm immune. I am in touch with Him. Protected by Him. Loved by Him.

VEREZZI closes his eyes. ZASTROZZI approaches him.

You can't hurt me. I'll just wait here. Nothing will happen.

ZASTROZZI   Do you feel anything?

VEREZZI   Yes.

ZASTROZZI   Do you feel fear?

VEREZZI   Yes.

ZASTROZZI   Now who am I?

VEREZZI   Zastrozzi.

ZASTROZZI   And what is Zastrozzi?

VEREZZI   The devil.

ZASTROZZI   Nonsense. What is he?

VEREZZI   A man.

ZASTROZZI   What kind of man?

VEREZZI   I don't know.

ZASTROZZI   A sane man. What kind of man?

VEREZZI   A sane man.

ZASTROZZI   And what kind of man are you?

VEREZZI   I don't know.

ZASTROZZI   You feel fear when you are about to be murdered. And you are no longer smiling. You are a sane man too. From this moment on and forever. Do you understand? Perfectly sane and very, very afraid.

VEREZZI   Yes.

ZASTROZZI   Now get going.

VEREZZI   Where?

ZASTROZZI   You have to hide. I am giving you a day and I am coming after you. And do you know why I am coming after you?

VEREZZI   No.

ZASTROZZI   Because it will keep me preoccupied. Now leave. And hide well. I wish to be preoccupied for a long time.

VEREZZI slowly leaves.

ZASTROZZI looks at all the corpses.

smiling   I like it here. Sad. No. I like it here.

He takes a cape off one of the corpses and wraps himself with it.

I think I'll visit here again. It will help me stay sane.

Pause.

Yes. I like it here.

Blackout.

DAVID FENNARIO (b. 1947)

One of the distinguishing features of modern Canadian drama has been its tendency to give a stage voice to the dispossessed, those living outside or on the fringes of the Canadian mainstream. *The Ecstasy of Rita Joe*, *Fortune and Men's Eyes*, and *Creeps* draw their protagonists from worlds only marginal to the lives of the middle class majority. Salutin, Pollock and French have also written plays dramatizing the "other Canada." But no Canadian playwright has focused on a single sub-group as consistently as David Fennario. Fennario's world is "the Pointe," the primarily English working class district of Pointe St. Charles in Montreal. His characters are a politically disenfranchised urban proletariat doomed to a culture of poverty by socio-economic circumstances and their own sense of futility. Fennario's plays show them coping with the daily indignities at work and at home. And they show us what happens when these people are pushed beyond the point at which apathy, jokes or another beer are sufficient painkiller. In *Balconville* Fennario presents a vision of working class Quebec in microcosm, a sharply etched, richly human portrait of French and English divided by language though joined in every other significant way, still seemingly unable to recognize their common cause. In the process he has given us Canada's first truly bilingual play.

Fennario himself comes from the world he writes about. Born David Wiper in the Pointe, he was raised, as he explains in *The Work*, to be stupid: "That's about survival; if I think I'm stupid I'll be able to last forty years working at Northern Electric. . . . That was basic Pointe training." He dropped out of school at seventeen, took the name Fennario from a Bob Dylan song, and temporarily became part of the hippie sub-culture. In 1968 he went to work in a Montreal dress factory and then in a Simpson's warehouse—experiences he would use in his first two plays—meanwhile becoming an active member of the Socialist Labour Party.

Hoping to avoid the dead-end he seemed destined for, Fennario enrolled at Montreal's Dawson College in 1970. His English teacher recognized the astonishing raw talent shown in a journal he had been keeping, and she helped him have it published in 1972. *Without a Parachute*, Fennario's impressions of life in the Pointe from 1969-71, came to the attention of Maurice Podbrey, artistic director of the Centaur Theatre, and he commissioned Fennario to write a play. Like George Walker, Fennario had only seen one play before. So Podbrey helped get him a Canada Council grant to spend two years sitting in on rehearsals and learning theatre from the inside as writer-in-residence at the Centaur. He remained the Centaur's resident playwright for nearly a decade.

On the Job (1975), his powerful first play, brought Fennario theatrical success and personal notoriety. Gary, the young worker from the Pointe whose revolutionary politics initiate the wildcat strike in the dress factory shipping room, was obviously the playwright himself. Fennario became a media darling, the Canadian theatre's own angry young man, the artist as working-class hero. That had an effect on his next play, *Nothing to Lose* (1976), which is better in many ways than *On the Job* but suffers from the gross intrusion of autobiography. This time the workers are on a lunch break at a tavern. Job action is brewing when in walks Jerry, once a fellow worker but now a celebrity writer, back with tales from that other world. He's back yet again in *Toronto* (1978), Fennario's most self-indulgent and least successful play.

Balconville distilled the best of all Fennario's work. He wrote himself into the play only peripherally in aspects of young Tom; brought Jackie, the crazy worker and Pointe legend from the two early plays, into the foreground as Johnny Regan; increased the role of the French characters, an important but subordinate element in the earlier plays; and moved his setting from the workplace to the home, giving women a central role in his drama for the first time. But the real *coup de théâtre* was writing nearly a third of the dialogue in French. More than 50,000 Montrealers saw *Balconville* during its two runs in January 1979 and a year later. A revised version with a new ending broke attendance records at the St. Lawrence Centre in the fall of

1979, toured Canada, and won the Chalmers Award. In 1981 the Centaur took its production to Belfast, Bath and London, the first Canadian company ever to play the Old Vic.

Following *Balconville*, Theatre Passe Muraille produced an adaptation of *Without a Parachute* (1979), and from that developed *Changes* (1980), an autobiographical one-man show. Fennario was back at the Centaur for his next major play, *Moving* (1983), in which a single family becomes the battleground on which are fought the social and political wars of contemporary Quebec. Fennario has since deserted the middle class, professional theatre to devote himself to working with the Black Rock project, a cultural organization in Pointe St. Charles where he still lives. For it he wrote and directed *Joe Beef* (1984), a play about the local history presented by members of the community. His latest work-in-progress, *Neill Cream: The Mysteries of McGill* (1985), concerns the victimization of the working class in Victorian Montreal.

The rhetoric of Fennario's mouthpiece-characters and his own commitment to Marxism give the impression that his early plays are more ideological than they really are. The politics are mostly a veneer behind which the young workers act out their frustration and rage against the repressive system with wild releases of anarchic energy. *On the Job* and especially *Nothing to Lose* show us the last hurrah of sixties rebelliousness. With *Balconville* everyone has grown older. Elvis is dead and the sixties are just a dim memory. Johnny was "a rebel, a real teen angel," but he's grown up to be a drunk. The Parti Québécois is in power but nothing has really changed for the Montreal poor except that now the *maudits anglais* are in the same boat as the French. "That's one good thing now," Paquette tells Tom. "We're all equal. Nobody's got a chance."

This kind of bitter fatalism (the psychology of the poor, Fennario calls it) seems borne out in the play not only by Paquette's losing his job, but by the future apparently in store for the young people, Tom and Diane. Tom tries unsuccessfully to escape but can't get across the border. By the end he's on the treadmill, working at an unskilled job he already hates. Diane will help out her family by going to work as a waitress. But we see from Irene's life where that is likely to lead her: through the same bleak cycle of futility and despair.

Fennario dismisses "the myth of the happy poor," and indeed except for simple-minded Thibault his characters are not very happy. But they are funny and resilient in the tradition of what might be called "tenement naturalism" shared by playwrights like Tremblay and O'Casey. Like them Fennario finds great strength in his women. Although they all have desperate moments, they are not easily fazed. Cécile persists in feeding her "air force" and cultivating her plants no matter how often the cats piss on them. Irene never stops trying to rally her neighbours to political activism no matter how great their apathy.

And towards the end there are real signs of hope. Despite the heat making everyone irritable, despite the strong sense of two solitudes evoked by separate flags, separate languages, separate TV sets side by side, some progress is made. Johnny stops drinking and commiserates with Paquette *in French*. The broken step, the play's most conspicuous symbol of the disrepair in these people's lives, gets fixed. It can only happen one small step at a time, Fennario seems to be saying in this revised version of the play. The ending of the original production was a contrivance of wishful thinking: "the characters suddenly fall misty-eyed into each other's arms, ready to enter some nebulous franglophone workers' paradise," Fred Blazer reported in his *Globe & Mail* review. In rethinking the ending Fennario replaced his Marxist answer with a Brechtian question which the characters ask in their own separate languages. "I think maybe the other ending is more enjoyable," Fennario has said, "but this one seems more true."

•

A note on the text: Because the French dialogue is such an essential component of this play, the text has been presented here just as it was in production, intact and untranslated. Bilingualism is at the very heart of *Balconville*. The anglophone audience member who is unilingual or has only minimal French is in the same relationship to the play as an anglophone working-class Quebecker like Johnny Regan is to the francophone culture that surrounds him. He has to struggle to make sense of French speech. Thus the audience's experience of *Balconville* reiterates one of the things the play is about: language differences are a serious obstacle to communication, but can be overcome with effort. With its French passages translated it would be a different play. Of course a theatre audience has access to vocal inflection, gesture, facial expression and body language which can communicate eloquently even where words are not understood. The *reader* of a play, on the other hand, has only stage directions and his own imagination to help fill in the blanks. So the reader who knows little or no French will have to work even harder for a full understanding of *Balconville*. But the rewards are well worth the effort. — Ed.

•

Balconville was first performed at the Centaur Theatre in Montreal on January 2, 1979, with Jean Archambault as Thibault, Peter MacNeill as Johnny, Lynne Deragon as Irene, Marc Gelinas as Paquette, Cécile St-Denis as Cécile, Manon Bourgeois as Diane, Terry Tweed as Muriel and Robert Parson as Tom. Barbara Matis designed the production and Guy Sprung directed.

BALCONVILLE

CHARACTERS

CLAUDE PAQUETTE
CECILE PAQUETTE, *his wife*
DIANE PAQUETTE, *their daughter*
MURIEL WILLIAMS
TOM WILLIAMS, *her son*
JOHNNY REGAN
IRENE REGAN, *his wife*
THIBAULT
GAETAN BOLDUC

SET

The back of a tenement in the Pointe Saint-Charles district of Montreal. We see a flight of stairs leading up to two balconies which are side by side, the Regans' and the Paquettes'. Directly below the Paquettes' balcony is the ground floor balcony of the Williams'. [*Ed.*]

ACT ONE

Scene One

It is night. TOM is sitting on his back balcony trying to play "Mona" on his guitar. The sound of a car screeching around a corner is heard. The car beeps its horn. DIANE enters.

VOICE   Diane, Diane. . . .

DIANE   J'savais que t'avais une autre blonde.

VOICE   Mais non, Diane, c'était ma soeur.

DIANE   Oui, ta soeur. Mange d'la merde. Fuck you!

CECILE comes out of her house and stands on her balcony.

CECILE   C'est-tu, Jean-Guy? Diane?

DIANE   Oh, achale-moi pas.

The car screeches away.

MURIEL   *from the screen door behind TOM*   God-damn teenagers, they don't stop until they kill someone. Tommy, what are you doing there?

The sound of the car screeching is heard on the other side of the stage.

VOICE   Hey, Diane. Diane. . . .

DIANE   Maudit crisse, va-t'en, hostie.

CECILE   Diane, c'est Jean-Guy.

VOICE   Hey, Diane. Viens-t'en faire un tour avec moi. Diane?

The car beeps its horn.

DIANE   Jamais, jamais. J't'haïs, j't'haïs.

VOICE   Hey, Diane.

The car beeps its horn again.

PAQUETTE   *from inside his house*   Qu'est-ce qu'y a? Qu'est-ce tu veux, hostie?

VOICE   Diane, viens ici.

PAQUETTE   *yelling from the upstairs window*   Si tu t'en vas pas, j'appelle la police.

MURIEL comes out of her house, goes down the alley and yells after the car.

MURIEL   Get the hell out of here, you goddamn little creep!

The car screeches away. MURIEL returns to her house.

MURIEL   Tom you gotta get up tomorrow.

TOM   Yeah, yeah.

MURIEL goes into her house.

PAQUETTE   Maudit crisse, j'te dis que t'en as des amis toi. C'est la dernière fois que je te préviens. Cécile, viens-tu t'coucher?

CECILE   Oui, oui, Claude, j'arrive. Diane, Jean-Guy devrait pas venir si tard.

DIANE   Ah, parle-moi pu d'lui.

CECILE   Son char fait bien trop de train, y devrait faire réparer son muffler.

CECILE goes into her house with DIANE. JOHNNY enters. He is drunk and singing "Heartbreak Hotel." He finds that the door to his house is locked.

JOHNNY   Hey, Irene. . . . Irene, open the fuckin' door.

IRENE opens the door.

PAQUETTE   *from inside his house*   Hey! Ferme ta gueule, toi-là.

JOHNNY   Fuck you!

He goes into his house and slams the door shut. Blackout.

Scene Two

The next day. It is morning. THIBAULT enters wheeling his Chez Momo's delivery bike down the lane. TOM comes out of the house with toast, coffee, cigarettes and his guitar. When he is finished his toast and coffee, he begins to practise his guitar.

MURIEL *from inside her house* Tom, you left the goddamn toaster on again.

TOM Yeah?

MURIEL Yeah, well, I'm the one who pays the electric bills.

THIBAULT *looking at the tire on his delivery bike* Câlice, how did that happen? The tire, c'est fini.

TOM A flat.

THIBAULT Eh?

TOM A flat tire.

THIBAULT Ben oui, un flat tire. The other one, she's okay. . . . That's funny, eh? Very funny, that.

TOM Don't worry, Thibault, it's only flat on the bottom.

THIBAULT You think so? Well, I got to phone the boss.

He goes up the stairs and steps over the broken step.

TOM Hey, watch the step!

THIBAULT *knocking on PAQUETTE's door* Paquette, Paquette. . . .

PAQUETTE *from inside his house* Tabarnac, c'est quoi?

THIBAULT C'est moi, Paquette. J'ai un flat tire.

PAQUETTE Cécile, la porte. . . .

CECILE *from inside the house* Oui, oui. . . . Une minute. . . .

THIBAULT C'est moi, Paquette.

CECILE *at the screen door* Allô, Thibault. Comment ça va?

THIBAULT J'ai un flat tire sur mon bicycle.

CECILE Oh, un flat tire.

PAQUETTE Que c'est qu'y a?

CECILE C'est Thibault, Claude.

PAQUETTE Thibault? Thibault?

THIBAULT Oui. Bonjour.

PAQUETTE Es-tu tombé sur la tête, tabarnac? Il est sept heures et demie du matin, hostie de ciboire.

CECILE Claude a travaillé tard hier soir.

THIBAULT That's not so good, eh?

PAQUETTE Que c'est qu'y veut?

CECILE Y veux savoir c'que tu veux.

THIBAULT *yelling at PAQUETTE through the window* J'ai un flat tire. Je voudrais téléphoner à mon boss.

PAQUETTE Cris pas si fort, j'suis pas sourd. Cécile, dis-lui rentrer.

JOHNNY *from inside his house* What the fuck's going on?

THIBAULT C'est-tu, okay?

CECILE Oui, oui. Entre.

THIBAULT goes into PAQUETTE's house. JOHNNY comes out on his balcony.

JOHNNY What's going on?

TOM *from below* Thibault's got a flat tire.

JOHNNY Flat tire? Big fuckin' production!

He goes back into his house.

THIBAULT *inside PAQUETTE's house* Allô, Paquette. J'vas téléphoner à mon boss. C'est-tu, okay? C'est-tu, okay?

PAQUETTE *from inside his house* Ferme ta gueule! Tu m'as réveillé asteur. Fais ce que t'as à faire.

THIBAULT *on the telephone* Oui, allô, Monsieur Kryshinsky. . . . This is the right number? This is Monsieur Kryshinsky? . . . Bon. C'est moi, Thibault. . . . Oui. . . . Quoi? . . . Yes, I'm not there. I'm here. . . .

CECILE *from inside the house* Veux-tu ton déjeuner, Claude?

PAQUETTE Non, fais-moi un café. Ça va faire.

THIBAULT Un flat tire, oui. . . . Okay. Yes, sir. I'll be there. . . . Oui. I'll be there tout de suite. . . . Okay, boss. Bye. . . . Allô? Bye. *He hangs up the telephone.* Faut que j'm'en aille. C'était mon boss. Tu le connais, "I don't like it when you're late. When I get to the store, I want you there at the door. Right there at the door."

PAQUETTE *at the door, pushing THIBAULT outside* Salut, Thibault. Salut, Thibault.

THIBAULT Okay, salut.

Coming down the stairs, THIBAULT trips on the broken step and loses his cap.

TOM *from below* Watch the step!

THIBAULT Hey, that was a close one. Very close, that one.

THIBAULT exits on his bike.

PAQUETTE *on his balcony* Cécile, est-ce que Diane veut un lift pour aller à l'école?

CECILE *at the screen door* Diane?

DIANE *from inside the house* Non.

PAQUETTE Pourquoi faire?

DIANE Parce que j'aime pas la manière qu'y chauffe son char.

CECILE Elle a dit que. . . .

PAQUETTE J'suis pas sourd. Qu'elle s'arrange pas pour manquer ses cours, c'est moi qui les paye cet été.

DIANE Inquiète-toi pas avec ça.

JOHNNY comes out on his balcony again.

PAQUETTE *to JOHNNY* Hey, people gotta sleep at night, eh?

JOHNNY You talking to me?

PAQUETTE *pointing to the wall* No, him. Hostie.

CECILE Claude, j'pense que ce soir, je vais te faire des bonnes tourtières. Tu sais celles que t'aimes, celles du Lac St-Jean.

PAQUETTE Encore des tourtières?

CECILE Claude, t'aimes ça des tourtières.

PAQUETTE Oui, j'aime ça des tourtières, mais pas tous les jours.

DIANE *from inside the house* Maman, où sont mes souliers. . . mes talons hauts?

CECILE J'sais pas. Où est-ce que tu les as mis hier soir?

She disappears into the house.

PAQUETTE Cécile, j'm'en vas.

JOHNNY Watch the step!

PAQUETTE *coming down the stairs* C'est qui qui a encore laissé les vidanges en dessous des escaliers?

TOM *from below* Not me.

PAQUETTE It's me who got the trouble with the landlord, eh?

CECILE comes running out on the balcony with PAQUETTE's lunchbucket.

CECILE Claude, Claude. . . . T'as oublié ton lunch.

PAQUETTE C'est l'affaire de Thibault. . . . Pitch moi-la.

CECILE tosses him his lunch.

JOHNNY Baloney sandwiches again, eh, Porky?

PAQUETTE exits. IRENE comes out on her balcony to take the underwear off the clothesline.

JOHNNY What time is it, Irene?

IRENE *looking at him* You look a wreck.

JOHNNY You don't look so hot yourself.

IRENE You're beginning to look like a boozer, ya know that?

JOHNNY Hey, all I want is the time.

DIANE comes out on the balcony carrying her school books.

DIANE J'perds mon temps avec ce maudit cours stupide, surtout l'été.

CECILE Diane, est-ce que tu vas venir souper?

DIANE Peut-être.

CECILE goes back into her house. DIANE comes down the stairs. She is wearing shorts and high heels. JOHNNY and TOM both look at her.

JOHNNY Hey, Diane, ya look like a flamingo in those things.

DIANE makes a face at him and exits down the lane.

IRENE You like that, eh?

JOHNNY Just looking.

IRENE Well, no more meat and potatoes for you.

JOHNNY Eh?

IRENE You know what I mean.

JOHNNY What?

IRENE goes back into the house.

JOHNNY Fuck!

TOM She's mad, eh?

JOHNNY Ya ask her for the time and she tells ya how to make a watch.

He listens to TOM practising his guitar.

Hey, softer on the strings. Strum them, don't bang them.

TOM *trying to strum* Like that?

JOHNNY Yeah, sort of. . . .

TOM You used to play, eh?

JOHNNY Yeah. Ever heard of "J.R. and the Falling Stars"?

TOM No.

JOHNNY You're looking at "J.R."

MURIEL comes out of her house carrying a bag of garbage.

MURIEL *to TOM* What are you doing?

TOM The U.I.C. don't open till nine o'clock.

MURIEL Yeah, but there's gonna be a line-up.

TOM   It's a waste of time. They never get ya jobs anyhow.

MURIEL   Well, don't think you're gonna hang around here doing nothing.

TOM   Okay, okay. Ma, I need some bus fare and some money for lunch.

MURIEL   You can come home for lunch.

TOM   Ma. . . .

MURIEL   I'm not giving you any money to bum around with.

TOM goes into the house with his guitar.

MURIEL   And you leave my purse alone in there too.

TOM   *coming back out with her purse*   Ma, I want my allowance.

MURIEL   What allowance? You don't go to school no more.

TOM   I want my money.

MURIEL   Gimme that purse. Gimme that goddamn purse.

She snatches her purse away from TOM, opens it and gives him some bus tickets.

That's it. . . . That's all you get.

TOM   Fuck!

MURIEL   Don't swear at me. Don't you ever swear at me.

TOM exits.

JOHNNY   *singing*   "Hi-ho, hi-ho, it's off to work we go."

MURIEL   *to JOHNNY*   You're not funny.

JOHNNY   You're a little hard on the kid, aren't ya, Muriel?

MURIEL   Yeah, well, look what happened to you.

JOHNNY   Fuck! What's with everybody today? Is it the heat or what?

He goes into his house. CECILE comes out on her balcony. She notices MURIEL's wash hanging from the clothesline.

CECILE   It's so nice to see that, madame.

MURIEL   See what?

CECILE   To see you put up the washing the right way. First the white clothes, then the dark ones. The young girls, they don't care anymore.

MURIEL   Yeah, well, why should they?

CECILE   Having children is not easy today? Eh?

MURIEL   Ah, they don't know what's good for them.

CECILE   Oui, I suppose.

MURIEL   When I was a kid, you just did what you were told and that was it.

CECILE   Yes, I remember that too.

MURIEL   Everybody got along alright. Now, nobody knows their ass from their elbow.

CECILE   Elbow?. . .Yes. . . .

THIBAULT enters on his bike again. He is looking for his cap.

CECILE   Allô, Thibault. Comment ça va?

THIBAULT   Ma casquette. . . .

CECILE   Ta casquette?

THIBAULT   Ben oui, j'ai perdu ma casquette. Oh, elle est en bas.

He looks under the stairs and finds his cap.

J'veux pas la perdre. J'ai payé quatre dollars chez Kresge.

CECILE   Eh, Thibault, ton boss était pas trop fâché?

THIBAULT   Il a sacré un peu après moi, but so what, eh? Il est jamais content anyway. Qu'tu fasses n'importe quoi.

CECILE   C'est la vie, hein ça?

THIBAULT   Oh, oui. C'est la vie.   *He checks his transistor radio.*   Hey, thirty-two degrees. That used to be cold. Now, it's hot.

CECILE   Comment va ta mère? Est-ce qu'elle va toujours à Notre-Dame-des-Sept-Douleurs?

THIBAULT   Oh, oui. Tous les jours. Mes frères sont tous partis, mais moi, j'suis toujours avec.

CECILE   C'est bien ça. Ta mère doit être contente.

THIBAULT   J'fais toute pour elle. Toute. Dans un an, elle va recevoir sa old age pension et puis on va pouvoir s'payer un plus grand logement. On va déménager à Verdun.

CECILE   A Verdun. Ça va être bien ça. Thibault, ton boss.

THIBAULT   Oh, oui. Mon boss. I better go now.

THIBAULT exits. MURIEL's phone rings. She goes into her house to answer it. CECILE goes into her house.

MURIEL   *on the telephone*   Yeah, hello. . . .Who? . . .Bill, where the hell are ya?. . .On the docks. . . shipping out to Sault Ste-Marie. . . .Are you coming back or what?. . .Don't give me that crap. What's her name, eh?. . .Yeah, I'm getting the cheques. . . .Tom? No, he's not here. . . .Yeah. . . .Yeah. . . .Look, I'm busy. . . .Bye.

She hangs up the telephone.

Christ, I wish I knew for sure.

IRENE and JOHNNY come out on their balcony. JOHNNY is sipping a cup of coffee. IRENE is wearing her waitress uniform. She is on her way to work.

IRENE   I want to talk to you when I get back, Johnny.

JOHNNY   Yeah, yeah. *sipping his coffee* Agh! What are you trying to do, poison me?

IRENE   I used brown sugar instead of white.

JOHNNY   Shit.

IRENE   It's healthier for you.... You going down to the U.I.C.?

JOHNNY   Yeah.

IRENE   Today?

JOHNNY   Yeah, today.

IRENE starts to come down the stairs.

JOHNNY   Irene, what shift are you on?

IRENE   Ten to six this week.

JOHNNY   Why don't you quit that fucking job? Get something else.

IRENE   *stopping* Like what?

JOHNNY   Like anything except a waitress.

IRENE continues down the stairs and exits down the lane.

JOHNNY   *shouting after her* Pick me up a carton of smokes, I'm sick of these rollies.

Blackout.

Scene Three

TOM and JOHNNY enter from the alley. JOHNNY is carrying a case of beer.

JOHNNY   I'm telling ya, they're all fucking separatists at the U.I.C. If you're English, you're fucked.

TOM   The phones are always ringing and nobody ever answers them. Ever noticed that?

JOHNNY   Too busy having coffee breaks. *He hands TOM a beer.* Unenjoyment disappointment office.

JOHNNY sits at the foot of the stairs. TOM leans on the railing.

TOM   Hey, I went down to Northern Electric. I figured I've been breathing in their smoke all my life, so the least they could do is give me a job. Didn't get one.... They're automating.

MURIEL comes out of her house.

JOHNNY   Hi, Muriel.

MURIEL   *to TOM* What are you doing?

TOM   Standing up.

JOHNNY   Wanna brew, Muriel?

MURIEL   I told you to keep your goddamn beer to yourself. Tom, come here.

TOM   What?

MURIEL   Never mind what. Just come here.   *TOM moves towards her.*   So, did you go to that job interview?

TOM   Yeah.

MURIEL   So?

TOM   So, the guy didn't like me.

MURIEL   He didn't like you? How come?

TOM   I dunno.

MURIEL   What do you mean, you dunno?

TOM   He wanted to send me to some stupid joe job way out in Park Extension. Minimum wage.

MURIEL   Since when can you afford to be fussy?

TOM   I'd have to get up at five in the morning.

MURIEL   There's a lot of things I don't like either, but I do them.

TOM   Well, I don't.

MURIEL   Anyhow, your father phoned. He's not coming home.

TOM   I don't blame him.

MURIEL   What's that?

TOM   Forget it.

MURIEL   Don't you get into one of your moods, mister, 'cause I'll give it to you right back.

MURIEL goes into her house.

TOM   Fuckin' bitch!

JOHNNY   Hey, don't worry about it.

TOM   Just 'cause she's frustrated, don't mean she's gotta take it out on me.

JOHNNY   Let them scream, that's what I do.

JOHNNY leaves TOM and starts up the stairs for his balcony. TOM goes into his house to get his guitar. CECILE comes out on her balcony with a handful of breadcrumbs. She starts to feed the birds.

CECILE   Hi, Johnny.

JOHNNY   Hi, Cécile.

CECILE   Nice day, eh?

JOHNNY   Yeah, but it's too hot.

CECILE   Oh yes, too hot.

She continues feeding the birds.

JOHNNY   Feeding your Air Force?

CECILE   My what?

JOHNNY   Your Air Force.... Cécile's Air Force.

CECILE   Ah, oui. Air Force.

JOHNNY   Just kidding ya, Cécile.

He sits on his balcony with his beer.

CECILE   You just kidding me, eh, Johnny?

She throws some more breadcrumbs over the railing. They fall on MURIEL as she comes out of her house carrying a basket of washing.

MURIEL   Jesus Murphy!

CECILE   Oh, excuse me, madame. Excuse me. Hello!

MURIEL   Yeah, hello....

CECILE   Aw, it's so nice, eh?

MURIEL   What?

CECILE   The sun. It's so nice, eh?

MURIEL   What?

CECILE   The sun. It's so nice.

MURIEL   Yeah, I guess it is.

CECILE   It's so good for my plants.

JOHNNY   How are your tomatoes?

CECILE   My tomatoes? Very good. This year, I think I get some big ones. Last year, I don't know what happened to them.

JOHNNY   The cat pissed on them.

CECILE   The what?

JOHNNY   The big tomcat that's always hanging around with Muriel. He pissed on them.

CECILE   You think so?

JOHNNY   Sure.

CECILE sits on her balcony. TOM comes out of the house again and sits practising his guitar.

JOHNNY   *to TOM*   Too heavy on the strings....

PAQUETTE enters carrying his lunchbucket. He is coming home from work.

JOHNNY   Hey, the working man!

PAQUETTE   Somebody has to work, eh?

He starts to climb the stairs. JOHNNY stops him.

JOHNNY   Have a brew here.

PAQUETTE   Okay.

He takes a pint from JOHNNY and sits down on JOHNNY's balcony.

PAQUETTE   Hey, my car, it's not working again. That goddamn carburetor....   *to CECILE, on her balcony*   Cécile.... Hey, Cécile.

CECILE   Oui.

PAQUETTE   J'vas manger plus tard.

CECILE   Quoi?

PAQUETTE   *shouting at her*   J'vas manger plus tard.

CECILE   Tu vas manger plus tard?

PAQUETTE   Oui, tabarnac!

CECILE   T'as pas besoin de sacrer, Claude.

PAQUETTE   C'est correct. As-tu appelé Chez Momo pour faire venir de la bière?

CECILE   Oui, Claude.

JOHNNY   Hot, eh? Can't breathe in the fuckin' house.... Can't sleep.

PAQUETTE   Hey, don't talk about it. Today in work one guy, he faints.

JOHNNY   Oh yeah?

PAQUETTE   At the machine. Just like that. There's one way to get the day off, eh?

JOHNNY   Ya got no air conditioning?

PAQUETTE   No, the bosses say there's some energy crisis or something, so they stop the air conditioning in the factory, eh? Not in the office, of course.

JOHNNY   Tell the union.

PAQUETTE   Hey, the union. It's too hot to laugh, câlice.

JOHNNY   Another fire last night, eh?

PAQUETTE   Ah, oui. What street?

JOHNNY   On Liverpool.

PAQUETTE   Liverpool encore. Tabarnac.

JOHNNY   Fuckin' firebugs, man. This block is gonna go up for sure.

PAQUETTE   Oui, that's for sure.

JOHNNY   Soon as I get my cheque, I'm gonna pull off a midnight move. Fuck this shit!

PAQUETTE   Oui, midnight move, for sure. Hey, just like the Arsenaults en bas. Fuck the landlords! It's the best way.

JOHNNY   Yeah.... Whew, hot. Going anywhere this summer?

PAQUETTE   Moi? Balconville.

JOHNNY   Yeah. Miami Beach.

THIBAULT drives in on his Chez Momo's delivery bike.

THIBAULT   Chez Momo's is here.

JOHNNY   Hey, Thibault T-bone.

TOM   Hey, ya fixed the flat?

THIBAULT gets off his bike. He takes a case of beer from the bike.

THIBAULT   Oui, Hey, me, I know the bike, eh? I know what to do.

JOHNNY   Hey, T-bone.

THIBAULT   Chez Momo's is here.

Coming up the stairs, he trips on the broken step.

JOHNNY   Watch the step!

PAQUETTE   Watch the beer!

JOHNNY   You okay?

THIBAULT   Me? I'm okay. But my leg, I don't know.

PAQUETTE   Why don't you read the sign?

THIBAULT   Eh?

PAQUETTE   The sign. . . .

THIBAULT reads the sign on the balcony. It reads: "Prenez garde."

THIBAULT   Prenez garde. Okay, prenez garde. So what? Tiens, ta bière.

He puts the case of beer down next to PAQUETTE. PAQUETTE gives him some money for the beer.

PAQUETTE   As-tu fini pour à soir?

THIBAULT   Oui, fini. C'est mon dernier voyage. *shaking the change in his pocket*   Hey, des tips.

JOHNNY   Had a good day, eh?

THIBAULT   Hey, Johnny. Johnny B. Good. Long time, no see, like they say.

JOHNNY   Yeah.

THIBAULT   Bye-bye, Johnny B. Good. You remember that?

JOHNNY   Remember what?

THIBAULT   Hey, there in the park, when they used to have the dances. You used to sing all the time like Elvis. *He does an imitation of Elvis.*   Tutti-frutti, bop-bop-aloo, bop-a-bop, bam-boom. Like that, in the park.

JOHNNY   Yeah, yeah.

THIBAULT   C'était le fun. Me, I like that, but the girls grew up. They get old. You too. Paquette too. He's so fat now. Very fat.

PAQUETTE   Hey, hey.

JOHNNY   You remember all that shit?

THIBAULT   Me? Sure. I remember everything. Everything. Everybody forgets but me. I don't. It's funny, that, eh?

JOHNNY   Yeah.

THIBAULT   But you, you don't sing no more.

JOHNNY   No, I don't sing no more.

THIBAULT   Well, everybody gets old. It's funny, I watch it all change, but it's still the same thing. . . . I don't know. So what, eh?

PAQUETTE takes THIBAULT's nude magazine out of his back pocket and flips through it.

PAQUETTE   Hey, Thibault. You have a girlfriend?

THIBAULT   Me? Sure. I got two of them. Deux.

PAQUETTE   Deux?

THIBAULT   *taking back his magazine*   Sure. I got one on Coleraine and the other one, she lives on Hibernia. Two girls. It's tough.   *He comes down the stairs.*   English too. That surprise me. English, they do it too.

THIBAULT exits on his bike. PAQUETTE takes his beer and moves over to his balcony.

JOHNNY   *pointing to his head, referring to THIBAULT*   The lights are on, but nobody's home.

PAQUETTE   He might as well be crazy, eh? It helps.

JOHNNY   Thinking's no good, man. I wish I could have half my brain removed. Boom! No more troubles. Just like Thibault.

CECILE   Pauvre homme. He was such a good boy when he was young. Remember?

PAQUETTE   It's easy to be good when you're young.

CECILE   He should have become a priest.

PAQUETTE   Cécile, nobody becomes a priest anymore.

He bumps into one of CECILE's plants.

CECILE   Claude, fais attention à mes plantes!

PAQUETTE   Toi, pis tes câlices de plantes. Y'en a partout sur le balcon.

IRENE enters. She is wearing her waitress uniform. She is coming home from work. She stops at MURIEL's house.

IRENE   Hi, Tommy. Your mother home?

TOM   Yeah.

IRENE   *knocking on MURIEL's door*   Yoo-hoo, Muriel. It's me. . . . Pointe Action Committee meeting tonight at seven-thirty, eh?

MURIEL   *at the screen door*   I don't think I'll be going, Irene.

IRENE   It's an important meeting, Muriel. We're going down to the City Hall to demand more stop signs on the streets. Kids are getting hurt.

MURIEL   Yeah, I know.

IRENE   The more of us there, the better.

MURIEL   Yeah. I'm just not in the mood.

IRENE   You okay?

MURIEL   Yeah.

IRENE   Well, okay.

MURIEL goes back into her house. IRENE goes up the stairs, avoiding the broken step.

Shit, why doesn't somebody fix that goddamn step?

JOHNNY   I didn't break it.

PAQUETTE   Hey, if I fix it, the landlord will raise the rent.

IRENE   *at the top of the stairs, looking at JOHNNY and his beer*   Having fun?

JOHNNY   Just having a couple of brews, Irene.

IRENE   Yeah, sure.

JOHNNY   *offering her a beer*   Here, have one.

She pushes his arm out of the way.

Hey, don't get self-righteous, okay? I get bored, alright? Bored!

IRENE   *giving him his carton of cigarettes*   Did you go down to the U.I.C.?

JOHNNY   "The cheque's in the mail," unquote.

IRENE   They said that last week.

JOHNNY   They'll say it again next week, too. . . . Irene, relax. Have a brew.

IRENE   Let me by.

She goes into the house.

PAQUETTE   *from his balcony*   Hey, there's always trouble when a woman gets a job, eh?

JOHNNY   Yeah, fuckin' U.I.C. slave market, people lined up like sheep. I hate lines.

PAQUETTE   Me, I don't know what's worse, working or not working. Sometimes I wish they'd lay me off for maybe a month.

JOHNNY   Factory getting to ya?

PAQUETTE   Hey, I even dream of it at night, hostie. Click clack, bing bang, click clack, bing bang. It's bad enough being there in the day, but I see it at night too, hostie.

JOHNNY   Twelve weeks, I've been waiting for that cheque. . . four weeks penalty for getting fired, four weeks for filing the claim late, and another four weeks waiting for them to put the cheque in the fuckin' mail.

PAQUETTE   Hey, if they treat a dog like that, the S.P.C.A. would sue them.

DIANE enters, prancing along in her shorts and high heels.

JOHNNY   Love that walk, Diane.

DIANE   Fuck you!

PAQUETTE   Hey, watch ton langage, toi.

DIANE climbs the stairs. When she has passed PAQUETTE, she turns and mouths the words, "Fuck you too." She goes into the house.

JOHNNY   *shouting after her*   Hey, you're gonna break a leg in those things.

PAQUETTE   Maudit.

JOHNNY   She's starting to look good.

PAQUETTE   Oui. Too good.

JOHNNY   Lots of nice young pussy around the neighbourhood, man. Breaks my heart to see it all.

PAQUETTE   *reaching for his wallet*   Johnny, I have something. . . .

He comes over and shows JOHNNY a photograph from his wallet.

PAQUETTE   Hey. Look at that. . . .

JOHNNY   Who's that? Cécile?

PAQUETTE   Oui. . . . She was nice, eh?

JOHNNY   Yeah.   *looking at the photograph again*   Who's that?

PAQUETTE   That? That's me. Moi.

JOHNNY   You're not serious?

PAQUETTE   Hey. Okay, okay.

He snatches back his wallet and returns to his balcony. From DIANE's room, the record "Hot Child in the City" can be heard.

PAQUETTE   Hey, Cécile. . . . Cécile, dis à Diane de baisser sa musique de tuns.

CECILE   *shouting into the house*   Diane, baisse la musique juste un peu.

The volume goes down. The music fades away. IRENE comes out on her balcony to hang up her waitress uniform. JOHNNY goes over to her and starts to hug her.

IRENE   Stop it.

JOHNNY   Honey, don't be mad.

IRENE   I'm not mad, Johnny. Stop it. You smell of beer.

JOHNNY   Okay. I'll hold my breath, Irene.

IRENE   Johnny, you've got to do something . . . anything. . . . Keep yourself busy.

JOHNNY   Yeah, I'm gonna call up some people, try to get something together, as soon as I get my first cheque.

IRENE   That goddamn cheque!

JOHNNY   Well, I don't want to give up now. Those bastards owe me that money, Irene.

IRENE   Well, why don't you come down to our Unemployment Committee meetings?

JOHNNY   You know I don't like meetings.

IRENE   Yeah, yeah. Ya'd rather watch "Charlie's Angels."

JOHNNY   Irene, it's gonna be alright, okay? Say "okay." Say "okay."

IRENE   Okay.

JOHNNY   Alright.

IRENE   I don't know why I have to nag. I don't want to nag. Don't want to sound like my mother.

JOHNNY   Hey, what's the matter? *tickling her* You sensitive, eh? You sensitive?

IRENE   Johnny.

JOHNNY   Come on, a Québec quickie.

PAQUETTE   *from his balcony*   Hey, Jean. It's too hot for that, eh?

JOHNNY   Aw, the heat makes me horny. . . .

An election campaign truck passes by playing Elvis Presley music and broadcasting in French and English.

VOICE   Vote for Gaëtan Bolduc. Gaëtan Bolduc's the man for you. The man of the people. Bolduc is on your side.

JOHNNY   Fuck you, Bolduc!

IRENE   Bolduc is on *his* side.

VOICE   Remember, on the 6th, vote for progress, vote for change, vote for a winner. Vote for Bolduc, the man for you . . . available and dynamic. . . .

The sound fades away.

JOHNNY   Circus is starting early this year. A month away from the election and he's already doing his fuckin' number.

IRENE   Bolduc, the boss. Did ya see the size of his new house?

JOHNNY   Once a year, he buys hot dogs for the kids on the Boardwalk. Big fuckin' deal!

TOM   Yeah. . . . Stale hot dogs.

PAQUETTE   Those guys are all the same crooks.

IRENE   I don't know what's worse, Joe Who or René Quoi?

She goes and gets the mail.

PAQUETTE   Bolduc, he was okay . . . until he got the power. Then, that's it. He forgets us.

JOHNNY   Any mail for me?

IRENE   *looking through the mail*   No. Aw, shit. La merde.

JOHNNY   What?

IRENE   Water tax. Eighty-four dollars for water. Christ, it tastes like turpentine and they charge us like it's champagne.

JOHNNY   Hey, all the bills are in French anyhow, separatist bastards. Tell them we're paying in English.

PAQUETTE   Hey, I don't like that.

JOHNNY   What?

PAQUETTE   There's a lot of English bastards around too, eh?

JOHNNY   Yeah, but they're not forcing ya out of the province.

PAQUETTE   Learn how to speak French, that's all.

CECILE   You know, Irene, there was another fire last night.

IRENE   Another one?

CECILE   Oui. Last night. A big one.

IRENE   The Pointe Action Group thinks the landlords are setting the fires themselves.

PAQUETTE   The landlords? Burning down their own houses?

IRENE   For the insurance.

JOHNNY   Yeah, I believe that.

PAQUETTE   It's the punk kids that do it. They got no father. The mother, she drinks in the taverns. What do they care, eh? They should make them work. Stop all the welfare.

IRENE   There is no work.

PAQUETTE   There's jobs, if they want them. They don't try hard enough.

JOHNNY   Yeah, there's jobs, but who wants to be a busboy all their lives?

PAQUETTE   It's a job.

JOHNNY   Yeah, well, I'm no fuckin' immigrant. I was born here.

PAQUETTE   That's the trouble . . . too many people. Overpopulation, they call it. We need another war or something. Stop all the welfare and make the lazy bums work.

IRENE   How come people always blame the poor? They never blame the rich.

PAQUETTE   Hey you, tell me, who's got the money, eh? Who's got all the money?

JOHNNY   Not me.

PAQUETTE   It's the English and the Jews.

IRENE   Hey!

PAQUETTE   They control everything, the goddamn Jews. That's the trouble.

IRENE   Hey, my mother was Jewish, so don't give me that shit, okay?

PAQUETTE   Hey, I don't talk about the good Jews. . . .

JOHNNY   What the fuck's going on?

PAQUETTE   Hey, me, I work all my life. All my life, me. Since I was ten years old.

JOHNNY   Yeah, so why cry about it?

PAQUETTE   Hey, John, that's not what I'm talking about.

JOHNNY   Hey, fuck the politics!

CECILE   Who knows what is true, eh? What is the truth?

PAQUETTE   You, you go light candles in the church. Me, I know what is the truth. A piece of shit, câlice.

CECILE   Claude.

PAQUETTE   Ah, oui, Claude.

IRENE   Anyhow, forget it.

JOHNNY   Yeah, fuck the politics. Nobody has fun in the Pointe anymore. We should have a party or something.

IRENE   A party, on what?

JOHNNY   Next week, I get my cheque, right? We'll have a party, just like the old days. Invite everybody on the block. We'll have a ball.

IRENE   You'll have a ball. I'll clean up the mess.

IRENE goes into the house.

JOHNNY   Irene, fuck!

He exits after her.

MURIEL   *from inside her house*   Tom, your supper's on the table.

TOM   Yeah, yeah.

MURIEL   *coming out of the house carrying a pot of spaghetti*   Tommy, I'm not going to tell you again.

TOM   What is it? Spaghetti?

MURIEL   Yeah, spaghetti.

TOM   I'm not hungry. I don't want any.

MURIEL   You don't want it? You don't want it? Well, here, take it!

She dumps the spaghetti on TOM's head.

TOM   Ma! Shit!

He exits down the alley.

PAQUETTE   That woman, she's a little bit crazy, I think.

CECILE   T'as pas faim, Claude?

PAQUETTE   Y fait trop chaud. Fais-moi une limonade.

CECILE goes to get him a lemonade. DIANE comes out on the balcony and sits in the rocking chair. She is reading a magazine. PAQUETTE starts in on her.

PAQUETTE   Où est-ce que t'étais hier soir?

DIANE   Dehors.

PAQUETTE   Où ça dehors?

DIANE   Dehors. J't'ai dit dehors.

PAQUETTE   Dehors avec Jean-Guy pis toute la gang. Vous avez fumé, vous avez bu, vous avez fourré, vous avez eu du fun, hein?

DIANE   Oui, on a eu ben de fun.

PAQUETTE   Il est même pas pusher. Qu'est-ce qu'y fait pour vivre d'abord?

DIANE   Il travaille des fois. J'sais pas. Demande-lui si tu veux savoir.

PAQUETTE   Diane, tu vois pas que c'est un hostie de pas-bon.

DIANE   Parce que toi tu sais ce qui est bon pour moi. Tu t'es pas regardé.

PAQUETTE   Pis tu t'penses smart. Tu penses que t'as inventé le monde. Eh, Diane, regarde les femmes dans la rue. C'est ça que tu veux? Te marier, avoir un petit par année, devenir large de même, t'écraser devant la télévision, manger des chips et pis attendre le welfare et le mari. C'est ça que tu veux avec Jean-Guy?

DIANE   Tant qu'à ça pourquoi pas?

PAQUETTE   Bon. Ben tant que tu vas rester ici, tu vas rentrer à minuit. Tu vas à l'école. C'est pour te sortir de cette câlice de merde-là.

DIANE   Tu vas à l'école, pis y a même pas de job en sortant.

PAQUETTE   Diane, pense. Sers-toi de ta tête, pas de ton cul, crisse.

CECILE   *returning with a lemonade*   Claude.

PAQUETTE   Comment, Claude? Tabarnac, t'es sa mère, parles-y.

CECILE   Mais elle est jeune.

PAQUETTE   Oh. Oh, elle est jeune. Parce qu'est jeune, elle a droit de tout faire, pis quand elle va nous arriver en ballon.

DIANE   Fais-toi en pas, parce que j'prends la pillule.

She shows him her pill dispenser.

PAQUETTE   Maudit crisse.   *He comes down the stairs and exits into the shed.*   Va chez-toi.

CECILE   Tu l'as fait fâcher.

DIANE   Il est stupide.

CECILE   Mais, c'est ton père, Diane.

DIANE   Il est stupide pareil.

CECILE   Il essaye de t'aider. Y s'inquiète pour toi.

DIANE   Ça, Cécile, c'est ton problème. C'est pas le mien. J'suis pas obligée de l'endurer.

CECILE   C'est la job qui fait qu'y est fatigué. Y voudrait être fin avec toi des fois, mais il en peut plus, il est trop fatigué.

DIANE   Tu le gâtes trop, Cécile. C'est de ta faute. Tu le gâtes trop.

CECILE   Faut bien vivre.

DIANE   Dis-y donc non des fois, peut-être qu'il serait plus fin avec toi.

They hear a hammering noise coming from the shed. PAQUETTE is in there working on his car.

DIANE   Regarde, y passe plus d'temps avec son maudit Buick qu'il passe avec toi.

CECILE   Mon erreur moi-là, ça été d'avoir juste un enfant. Si tu te maries, Diane, arrange-toi pas pour avoir juste un enfant parce que tu vas te sentir bien toute seule.

DIANE   Maman, t'aurais dû rester au Lac St-Jean à la campagne avec ta famille. C'était là ta place, pas ici. C'est vrai, ça.

IRENE and JOHNNY come out of their house. IRENE is on her way to her Pointe Action Committee meeting.

IRENE   You wanna come to the meeting?

JOHNNY   No.

IRENE   Why not?

JOHNNY   'Cause they're boring.

IRENE   Boring?

JOHNNY   Yeah, everybody's sitting around with a long face.... Boring!

IRENE   We're planning our next action.

JOHNNY   Yeah, sure. Another demonstration. Big fuckin' deal!

IRENE   We gotta start somewhere.

JOHNNY   Yeah, well, they got a long fuckin' ways to go.

IRENE   *coming down the stairs*   If you're waiting for Superman, you're gonna wait a long, long time.

JOHNNY   If ya wanna fight politicians, go out and shoot a couple of them. All this talking drives me nuts.

He goes back into the house.

IRENE   *starting after him*   I'll be back at ten. There's some supper in the fridge.

IRENE sees MURIEL crying as she cleans up the spaghetti.

IRENE   Muriel, you okay? You alright, girl?

MURIEL   Oh, go away.

IRENE   What's wrong?... What's right? Guess that's an easier question, eh?

MURIEL   Oh, I feel stupid.

IRENE   Here, I got a kleenex.

MURIEL   Thanks.

IRENE   You're not pregnant, are ya?

MURIEL   Don't be crazy.

IRENE   Got the blues?

MURIEL   I'm worried about my stomach. It's acting up again.

IRENE   Maybe it's ulcers.

MURIEL   I don't know.

IRENE   Go to the hospital.

MURIEL   I'm afraid.

IRENE   You're afraid of what the doctor might say?

MURIEL   Yeah.

IRENE   Well, at least you'll know what you've got.... You'll feel better once you do.

MURIEL   I dunno.

IRENE   I'll go with ya.

MURIEL   Irene, you don't have to.

IRENE   Listen, I wouldn't want to go alone either. So, how about, uh, Tuesday?

MURIEL   I don't know. All they do is give ya pills, dope ya up and send ya back home again.

IRENE   Well, let them take a look at ya anyhow.

MURIEL   Tuesday?

IRENE   Yeah.

MURIEL   Sick or not, what's the difference?

IRENE   When is your old man due back from the boats?

MURIEL   Him? Oh, he's taking his time. Don't worry, he's in no hurry to come back. It's the perfect life for him. He can drink all he wants, screw around... and he gets paid for it.

IRENE   Well, still it'll be nice to have him back.

MURIEL   Come off it! And your old man isn't much better. I'd dump him so quick, it wouldn't be funny. You're too good for him, Irene.

IRENE   Oh, well, ya know how it is? Ya marry a prince and he turns into a frog.

MURIEL   Yeah, Bill was always great for a good time. But he was no good for nothing else.

IRENE   He still sends the cheques?

MURIEL   Yeah. Aw, it's nobody's fault . . . everybody's fault. . . . Ever think about what we'll be doing in ten years?

IRENE   Ten years? Ugh, I don't think about it. Maybe we'll win the Super Loto or something. . . . You know, you gotta get out of the house more. Ya make a lousy housewife. Try something else.

MURIEL   Like what?

IRENE   I don't know. School?

MURIEL   Jesus Christ, they threw me out of Grade 8 for punching out the teacher.

IRENE   Yeah, I remember that.

MURIEL   Yeah. Old man Breslin with the wandering hands.

IRENE   Pow, pow! Love it!

MURIEL   He had it coming.

IRENE   He sure did and you gave it to him. People still talk about it, eh? Sure.

MURIEL   Yeah, eh?

IRENE   Yeah. . . . Tuesday?

MURIEL   Yeah, Tuesday. . . . Thanks, Irene.

IRENE   Aw, us girls got to stick together, eh?

CECILE starts to water her plants. The water drips down on IRENE and MURIEL below.

IRENE   Aw, shit. When she's not feeding her Air Force, she's watering her jungle. . . . Bye.

IRENE exits. The broadcast VOICE is heard again.

VOICE   Gaëtan Bolduc, the man for you. The man of today, the man of the people, the man who cares. Vote for action, vote for a winner, vote for Bolduc. Gaëtan Bolduc . . . available and dynamic . . . the man for you.

FIRST VOICE   *from the truck*   Yeah, yeah. Bolduc, Bolduc, Bolduc. Câlice, how many more times do we have to drive around the block?

SECOND VOICE   *from the truck*   We got three more hours, hostie.

FIRST VOICE   *from the truck*   That shithead. Bolduc. Bolduc. Me, I'm so sick of his fuckin' name. Bolduc, Bolduc. Fuck you, Bolduc! You cheap son of a bitch.

SECOND VOICE   *from the truck*   Next time, we'll ask for forty bucks a day.

FIRST VOICE   *from the truck*   Hey, fifty. Fifty bucks a day.

SECOND VOICE   *from the truck*   Oui, fifty.

FIRST VOICE   *from the truck*   Crisse, François. The speaker is still on. They can hear us.

SECOND VOICE   *from the truck*   The speaker? What? The speaker!? Câlice.

The voices stop. Elvis Presley music comes back on. Blackout.

Scene Four

It is night. The sound of a record playing rock music is heard. DIANE, CECILE, IRENE, MURIEL, THIBAULT, and TOM are dancing in the street.

THIBAULT   Hey, look. I got one. The mashed potato duck.

IRENE   Hey. Come on, everybody, make a circle. Take turns in the middle. Come on.

DIANE steps into the circle and does a dance, then TOM takes his turn.

MURIEL   Move your feet. Move your feet.

THIBAULT   *stepping into the circle*   Hey, the duck. Look, I got one. The mashed potato duck.

They push him out of the circle.

IRENE   Hey, Cécile. Come on.

They push Cécile into the circle. She moves a bit. They applaud.

IRENE   Hey, shake that thing. Alright, Muriel. Come on, your turn. Come on.

MURIEL   Aw, that's kids' stuff.

IRENE   Come on.

Just as MURIEL starts to dance, the record ends.

MURIEL   Well, that's it.

THIBAULT   It's hot, eh? Hot . . . whew.

TOM   Hey. Where's Johnny?

IRENE   Him? He's always late. He's the star, right?

MURIEL   That's one word for him.

IRENE   Hey, Muriel. Tell that joke. The one you told me this morning.

MURIEL   Naw, naw. You tell it.

IRENE   Come on.

MURIEL   No. You tell it better.

IRENE   Okay. You ready? Okay, this guy is going to bed with a girl for the first time. . . .

THIBAULT   Oh, dirty joke! Hey!

MURIEL   Don't worry, Thibault. You'll never get it.

IRENE   Yeah, and he takes off his socks and shoes, and his feet are deformed, and she says, "What's wrong with your feet?" And he says, "Well, when I was a kid, I had toelio."

TOM   "Toelio."

IRENE   And she says, "You mean, polio." "No, toelio." And well, then, he takes off his pants. . . .

THIBAULT whistles.

MURIEL   Down, Thibault. Down.

IRENE   And. . .and his knees are all, you know, bulgy.

DIANE   C'est quoi ça, "bulgy"?

IRENE   Tout enflé. . . .And the girl says, "What's wrong with your knees?" "Well, when I was a kid, I had the kneasles." "You mean, measles." "No, kneasles." Then, he takes off his underwear. . . .

THIBAULT whistles again.

IRENE   And she says, "Oh, no, don't tell me you had smallcocks too." Small cocks.

They all laugh.

MURIEL   Thibault, ya got it now?

CECILE   Diane. "Smallcocks," c'est quoi?

DIANE   P'tite bizoune.

CECILE   Oh, bizoune. Oui.

MURIEL   Shit, it's been so long I forgot what they look like.

The girls all laugh.

THIBAULT   Hey, that's funny, that, eh?

TOM   Hey, ya wanna see my Elvis Presley imitation? Eh?

DIANE   Oui.

TOM   Ya wanna see it?

MURIEL   No.

IRENE   Sure.

TOM   Okay? Ya ready?

IRENE   Ready.

TOM   Elvis!

He bends his head back and crosses his arms like a laid-out corpse. They all groan.

DIANE   I like that.   *She copies his Elvis imitation.* Elvis!

THIBAULT   That's all?

TOM   Yeah.

DIANE puts another record on. It is "Hot Child in the City." THIBAULT grabs her and begins to dance.

THIBAULT   Cha-cha-cha, hostie.

DIANE   Hey, not so close, okay? Not so close. J'vas te puncher.

THIBAULT   Hey, let's dance. Dansons.

IRENE   *cutting in*   Here, Diane. You take Tom.

She grabs THIBAULT. TOM and DIANE dance.

IRENE   Come on, Thibault, you sexy thing.

THIBAULT   Cha-cha-cha, hostie.

IRENE and THIBAULT dance.

IRENE   *turning to MURIEL*   Christ, hey Muriel, look.   *referring to her and THIBAULT*   The last tango in the Pointe.

MURIEL   Careful. You'll get him so excited, he'll piss himself.

PAQUETTE and JOHNNY enter with their arms around one another's shoulders. They are drunk and singing.

PAQUETTE and JOHNNY   *singing*
Jesus saves his money at
   the Bank of Montréal.
Jesus saves his money at
   the Bank of Montréal.
Jesus saves his money at
   the Bank of Montréal.
Jesus saves, Jesus saves—
   Jesus saves.

IRENE   Shit, he's drunk already.

PAQUETTE   Hey, les femmes. Nous sommes ici.

DIANE mimics him.

THIBAULT   Hey, Paquette. Watch me dance.

JOHNNY   *singing with PAQUETTE*
Irene, goodnight,
Irene, goodnight,
Goodnight, Irene,
Goodnight, Irene,
I'll see you in my dreams.

PAQUETTE   Hey, les femmes. C'est moi.

JOHNNY   Hey, Irene. I'm a little late. Had a few drinks with what's his name.

PAQUETTE   Paquette.

JOHNNY   Pole-quette.

PAQUETTE   Naw. Paw-quette.

JOHNNY   Okay, tell the people your name *together.* . . .Paquette.

THIBAULT   Thibault. My name, Thibault.

PAQUETTE and JOHNNY start to climb the stairs. JOHNNY stumbles on the broken step.

PAQUETTE Eh, Johnny? Un autre p'tit step. La bière est en haut.

IRENE Fais attention à sa tête.

She goes to help JOHNNY up the stairs. She is followed by MURIEL, THIBAULT, DIANE and TOM.

PAQUETTE C'est sa tête carrée. C'est les coins qui accrochent.

When JOHNNY gets up the stairs, he grabs IRENE.

JOHNNY Irene, I love ya, love ya, love ya. . . .

THIBAULT We have fun, eh? Watch me dance.

JOHNNY Yeah, we're gonna rock this joint. Where's the beer?

MURIEL You've had enough.

PAQUETTE Hey, Johnny. Dansons, dansons.

He does a dance step.

JOHNNY Where *is* everybody?

IRENE This is it. We're all here.

JOHNNY What do ya mean? Where are they? Danny? Jerry?

IRENE Guess they couldn't make it.

JOHNNY I knew the fuckers wouldn't come.

IRENE Maybe they'll come later.

JOHNNY bangs into his house.

IRENE Johnny. . . .

PAQUETTE Put on some music. Hey, what's wrong? Put on some music. We'll have a good time.

He goes into his house and puts on the record "Hot Child in the City."

THIBAULT Tutti-frutti, hostie. Let's twist some more.

JOHNNY *inside his house* What's Jerry's number? What's his fuckin' number?

IRENE I dunno.

PAQUETTE Hey, Diane. C'est ta tune. *to MURIEL* Hey, let's dance. . . . Why not?

MURIEL Ask your wife.

PAQUETTE Come on. I don't bite.

MURIEL You're drunk.

They dance on the balcony.

PAQUETTE Eh? Not bad, eh? I dance good, eh?

MURIEL Yeah, sure. Terrific.

PAQUETTE Not bad for a peasoup, eh?

JOHNNY *inside the house, on the phone* Jerry, that you? What are ya doing home? You're supposed to be here. . . . What? . . . Hey, turn that fuckin' music down. . . . What? . . . Fuck that shit, man. This is

supposed to be a get together and nobody's here. Nobody! Just the Pepsi's next door. . . . What? . . . What? . . . . I don't want to hear that shit, Jerry. You coming? You coming? . . . Maybe later? Fuck you!

He slams down the receiver and bangs his way out onto the balcony.

IRENE Johnny. Johnny. . . .

JOHNNY The party's over. Fuck off! Everybody, fuck off!

PAQUETTE Hey, Jacques. We'll have a good time, eh?

JOHNNY *pushing PAQUETTE* Get on your own fuckin' side.

PAQUETTE Hey. Hey.

JOHNNY Fuckin' gorf. Pepper. Get on your own side.

PAQUETTE Hey, watch that, eh? Fais attention, okay?

JOHNNY We were here first, ya fuckin' farmer. Go back to the sticks.

PAQUETTE Hey, reste tranquille, eh?

JOHNNY Ya wanna fight? Wanna fight?

JOHNNY swings at PAQUETTE, but misses him. He falls down. IRENE and MURIEL push him towards the door of his house.

PAQUETTE Keep your garbage on your side.

JOHNNY *stumbling* The party's over. No more parties. No more.

IRENE Get him into the house.

MURIEL Stupid men.

They carry him into his house.

JOHNNY Jerry. Where's Jerry? Jerry?

MURIEL Good old days. . . . Never was any good old days.

They exit into the house.

THIBAULT Johnny, he gets a little drunk tonight, eh?

TOM Hey, a little.

DIANE It's fun for them. That's the way they have fun.

CECILE It's a full moon. That's why everyone is so crazy.

PAQUETTE What's wrong? Hey, what's wrong?

He puts the record back on. It is "Hot Child in the City" once again.

THIBAULT Away, Paquette. Let's twist some more.

TOM *to MURIEL, as she comes out of JOHNNY's house* Is he okay?

MURIEL   He's okay. You wanna end up just like him? That's the way you're going.

TOM   Yeah, yeah.

PAQUETTE goes over to MURIEL, who isn't interested in dancing, so he starts dancing with DIANE. He begins to slobber all over her. She pushes him away, goes down the stairs and exits down the lane.

CECILE   Diane. Diane.

PAQUETTE   Who wants to dance? Hey.

He heads towards MURIEL.

MURIEL   *pushing him aside*   Get lost. Beat it.

PAQUETTE   Quoi?

MURIEL   Ya make me sick.

PAQUETTE   Hey, parle-moi en français, eh? Parle-moi en français.

MURIEL   Go on. Hit me. Hit me. Try it.

PAQUETTE   Maudits anglais. How come I got to speak English, eh? How come?

MURIEL   'Cause you're stupid.

PAQUETTE   Maudits anglais. Throw them all out. Toute le gang. On est au Québec. On est chez-nous.

MURIEL   I was born here too, ya bigmouth Frenchman.

PAQUETTE   It's our turn now, eh? Our turn. And Ottawa, Ottawa can kiss my Pepsi ass.

MURIEL   Ferme ta gueule, toi.

THIBAULT   Fuck the Queen!

MURIEL   Fuck Lévesque!

MURIEL goes back into IRENE's house. PAQUETTE knocks over one of CECILE's plants by accident.

CECILE   Claude, fais attention à mes plantes. Claude.

PAQUETTE picks up one of her plants and throws it over the railing.

PAQUETTE   Tiens, ta câlice de plante.

CECILE runs into the house crying.

PAQUETTE   *opening another beer*   It's crying time again, eh? Crying time again.

THIBAULT   Me, I don't hate the English. I just don't like them, that's all.

PAQUETTE   Maudits anglais!

THIBAULT   They got funny heads. Square heads.

PAQUETTE   *to TOM*   You. Hey, you. Think maybe you got a chance, eh? No more. That's one good thing now. We're all the same now, eh? We're all equal. Nobody's got a chance. Nobody.

THIBAULT   Fuck the Queen!

PAQUETTE   Maybe you got dreams, eh? Me too. I had dreams. Thibault too. He had dreams.

THIBAULT   Oui, me too.

PAQUETTE   If you knew what I know, you'd go jump in the river right now. Tonight.

THIBAULT   Oui, tonight. The river. No joke, that.

PAQUETTE   *hugging THIBAULT*   Thibault, you're a bum . . . a bum and a drunk.

THIBAULT   Oui, a bum.

PAQUETTE   You know what? Me, I work all my life. All my life.

THIBAULT   That's too bad.

PAQUETTE   When I was young, I was going to do this and that, but the job, the fuckin' job, it took my life away. What can you do? Everybody says, "what can you do?" That's the way it goes.

THIBAULT   That's the way it goes.

PAQUETTE   You get old and ugly and you die . . . and that's all.

THIBAULT   That's all.

PAQUETTE   I try, but it don't help. No matter what you do.

TOM comes down the stairs and goes into his house to get his guitar.

PAQUETTE   No matter what you do.

THIBAULT   So what? That's what I say. So what?

PAQUETTE   So what? Maudits anglais.

THIBAULT   Oui. So what? *looking into the case of beer*   Hey. No more beer.

IRENE and MURIEL come out on the balcony.

THIBAULT   Eh, y a plus de bière?

PAQUETTE   On va aller en chercher en ville.

THIBAULT   Comment?

PAQUETTE   Ben . . . avec mon char.

THIBAULT   Ton char?

PAQUETTE   Ben oui. Mon char, hostie.

They come down the stairs.

THIBAULT   Ah, oui. Ton char dans le garage. Prenez garde. Watch the step.

They pick up some tools and exit for the shed, to fix the car.

IRENE   They're gonna get themselves killed.

MURIEL   Don't worry, they'll never get that car to start.

IRENE   Well, Johnny's out for the night. He'll wake up tomorrow, drink a bottle of Coke and ask me what he did.

MURIEL   He needs a kick in the ass. . . and fast.

IRENE   He told me he wants me to find another man. . . . Yeah. . . . Here I am, thirty-four years old, and he wants me to go find another man. Fat chance.

MURIEL   I dunno. You're still in pretty good shape.

IRENE   Aw, I'm no spring chicken anymore. . . . I'm a broiler.

MURIEL   You're better off without a man. Who needs them?

IRENE   Aw, I guess I love the creep.

MURIEL   Love? Love never got through the Wellington Tunnel.

IRENE   I had this guy who was nuts about me . . . always phoning me up, calling on me. He's a teacher now in N.D.G. . . . But I fell for Johnny. He was a rebel. A real teen angel, ya know what I mean?

MURIEL   Yeah, so they grow up to be drunks.

IRENE   I can't blame him. He's been trying.

MURIEL   No, guess you can't blame the poor ignorant stupid bastards.

IRENE   I'm scared for him.

MURIEL   It never pays to be too nice, Irene. I used to be nice, but it never got me nowhere.

IRENE   Yeah. . . . But why, Muriel? Why? How do you change it?

MURIEL   They're all the same, Irene. . . all of them.

IRENE   The doctor's still taking tests?

MURIEL   Yeah. . . . You know doctors. They never tell ya nothing. All they do is poke your stomach, take your blood, give ya some pills and tell ya to come in next week. Makes ya feel like a goddamn guinea pig.

IRENE   Yeah, well, meanwhile there's the late movie, eh? What's on anyhow?

MURIEL   I dunno.

IRENE   See ya. . . .

MURIEL   Yeah, Irene. . . . Don't let him walk on you. That's what I'm trying to say anyhow.

IRENE   'Night.

MURIEL   Yeah.

IRENE goes into her house. MURIEL comes down the stairs. She sees TOM sitting on her balcony with his guitar.

MURIEL   I'm locking the door at twelve o'clock.

TOM   Yeah.

MURIEL   I mean it.

TOM   Yeah, yeah.

MURIEL goes into her house.

PAQUETTE   *yelling at THIBAULT in the shed* Non, non. Le wrench. Donne-moi le wrench qui est sur la valise.

THIBAULT   La valise.

PAQUETTE   Oui, tabarnac.

THIBAULT   Y fait noir. Ouch!

PAQUETTE   Le hood. Fais attention au hood. Ta tête.

A slamming sound is heard.

Maudit, tabarnac de câlice de Sainte Vierge. Hostie, que t'es cave! Tiens la lumière.

THIBAULT   La lumière. Okay.

TOM   *playing his guitar and singing*
Tell you, Mona, what I'm gonna do,
Build a house next door to you,
Then I can see you in the summertime,
We can blow kisses through the blinds.
Come on, Mona, out in the front,
Listen to my heart go bumpetity-bump.

DIANE enters. When TOM has finished playing, she applauds.

TOM   Uh, hi. . . . Want some beer?. . . Go ahead, I got an extra bottle.   *DIANE takes a sip.*   The party's over, eh?

DIANE   The party? Oui.

TOM   Uh. . . everybody got drunk and crazy, eh?

DIANE   Quoi?

TOM   Drunk, crazy. . . . Like that. . . .

He mimes "drunk."

DIANE   Drunk? Ah, oui. . . . Mon anglais est pas tellement bon.

TOM   My French is, uh. . . comme ci, comme ça. . . . Like that. . . . So, uh. . . what's new?

DIANE   What's new?

TOM   Yeah, new.

DIANE   You tell me?. . . Bon?. . . Well?

She moves towards the stairs.

TOM   Hey, uh. . . where ya going?

DIANE   I don't speak the good English.

TOM   Look, finish your beer. I mean, uh. . . . Why not?. . .

DIANE   *stopping at the foot of the stairs* I don't want to go home.

TOM   Yeah. I know the feeling. You, uh. . . never look too happy.

DIANE   Happy? What's that?. . . Something on TV?

TOM   Yeah, well, I dunno.... You're so pretty. Ya should be happy.   *DIANE groans.*   That's a dumb thing to say, eh? Yeah.... So, uh...what do you do?

DIANE   Me? I still go to school.... I write poems sometimes.

TOM   Yeah, that figures.... Uh.... What kind of poems?

DIANE   Sad ones.

TOM   I'm asking 'cause, well...ya look like a girl who writes poems. Guess I could do it too, but I wouldn't know why. I flunked English. French too.... Babysitting, that's all school is....

DIANE   Do you like films?...Me, I like films. But they make me feel bad too. I don't want them to stop.

TOM   Hey, cinemascope. In living colour. Diane Paquette.

DIANE   No, I'll never use that name. Not Paquette.

TOM   Okay, Diane, uh....

DIANE   Diane Desmarchais. Why not Diane Desmarchais?

TOM   Yeah. Okay. Boulevard Desmarchais. Sounds good....

DIANE   So, you don't go to school no more?

TOM   Naw. I mean, I know my ABCs...most of them.... Looking for work.... I dunno, it's crazy. I mean, if someone wanted me to work for them, why don't they ask me. I mean, I don't know why I've got to go looking for work when I don't even want it.

DIANE   No job, no money. No money, no nothing.

TOM   Yeah, money.... Hey, uh.... Don't you ever blink?

DIANE   Never.

TOM   Once a year or what?...

DIANE   Your hair, it makes you look funny.

TOM   Funny? What do you mean?

DIANE   I think it's too short.

TOM   Oui, too short.

DIANE   I think you have to grow it longer....

TOM   Yeah, well, I'm getting out. I'm leaving. ...Ever think of doing that? Goodbye Pointe Saint-Charles.

DIANE   Where will you go?

TOM   I dunno...anywhere. New York City.

DIANE   New York City?

TOM   Yeah, sure.

DIANE   They got jobs down there?

TOM   I dunno.... It's a big place. Ya never know. I might find a job as a musician, ya know? Once I learn about, uh, major chords, minor chords. Shit like that....

DIANE   Well, salut. Bonne chance.

She starts up the stairs.

TOM   Hey, Diane. Wait. Attends peu.... You wanna come with me?

DIANE   Avec toi? Pourquoi?

TOM   Well, I figure you wanna get out too. ...Anyhow, forget it. It's stupid. Ya don't even know me.... I'm a bit stoned.... Well, see ya.

DIANE   Bye.... Write me a letter, okay?

She goes into her house.

TOM   Aw, forget it. It's stupid...stupid.

TOM exits with his guitar. PAQUETTE and THIBAULT are heard banging away in the shed.

PAQUETTE   Verrat de tabarnac de crisse de ciboire.

THIBAULT   J'pense que c'est pas le spark plug, eh?

PAQUETTE   Fuck you. Où est le pipe wrench?

THIBAULT   Le pipe wrench?

PAQUETTE   Oui, le pipe wrench. Je pense que j'l'ai laissé sur le balcon.

THIBAULT   Le balcon. Okay, okay, okay, okay. Okay, so what?

He comes in from the shed and goes up the stairs. While he is looking for the pipe wrench, he drinks some beer from some discarded beer bottles.

Le pipe wrench, le pipe wrench. So what? On se rendra jamais en ville.

PAQUETTE   Thibault.... Hostie....

THIBAULT   Oui, j'cherche. J'cherche.   *He takes a slug of beer from one of the beer bottles and gags on a cigarette butt.*   Agh. Touf. Une cigarette, hostie.

PAQUETTE gets the car started, guns the engine, then chokes it.

PAQUETTE   Tu veux pas partir. Tu veux pas partir. Ben. J'vas t'arranger ça.

PAQUETTE takes a hammer to the car. The sound of smashing is heard. CECILE comes out on her balcony.

CECILE   Mais, qu'est-ce qui se passe?... Claude?...

PAQUETTE comes out of the shed carrying a hammer. He throws the hammer to the ground and climbs the stairs.

THIBAULT   *to PAQUETTE*   You fix it?

PAQUETTE   *to CECILE*   Pas un mot s'a game. Pas un mot.

PAQUETTE and CECILE exit into their house, leaving THIBAULT standing alone on the balcony.

THIBAULT   Okay, on ira jamais en ville. So what? Thibault, he's okay. I go find my own beer. So what?

He comes down the stairs and exits. MURIEL comes out on her balcony.

MURIEL   Tommy, I'm gonna lock this door. Tommy?. . .Alright.

She shuts the door and bolts it closed. Blackout.

ACT TWO

Scene One

It is night. JOHNNY and THIBAULT enter singing. Both of them are drunk. JOHNNY is riding THIBAULT's delivery bike.

JOHNNY and THIBAULT   *singing*
We don't care about
All the rest of Canada,
All the rest of Canada,
All the rest of Canada.
We don't care for
All the rest of Canada,
We're from Pointe Saint-Charles.

MURIEL   *from inside her house*   Shut up out there!

JOHNNY   Fuck you!

THIBAULT   So what, eh? Get off my bike, you. . . .Away.

JOHNNY   *getting off THIBAULT's bike*   Hey, Thibault, you're not a separatist, are ya?

THIBAULT   FLQ, moi. Boom! I blow everything up.   *He kicks a garbage can.*   Boom!

MURIEL   *from inside her house*   Jesus Murphy.

THIBAULT   *taking a magazine out of his back pocket*   We have a good time, eh? Good time. Look, big tits.

He sits down on a bench. JOHNNY sits down beside him.

JOHNNY   You're my friend, eh, Thibault?

THIBAULT   Sure, if that's what you say.

JOHNNY   You're my only, only friend.

THIBAULT   I'm your only friend. . .and I'm not even your friend.

JOHNNY   So whose friend are ya?

THIBAULT   I don't know.

JOHNNY   You wanna know whose friend you are? You're my friend.

THIBAULT   Sure. . . .My mother, once she takes me to the Oratoire, because I got the polio. So, she takes me there. She prays to Saint Joseph, but the polio, it don't go away. . . .

JOHNNY   Fuck off.

THIBAULT   Eh, so what?

JOHNNY   What, so what?

THIBAULT   What so what?

JOHNNY   Yeah, you say, "So what?" and I say, "What so what?"

THIBAULT   You crazy, you.

JOHNNY   Fuckin' right, I'm crazy.   *yelling*   I'm trying, Irene. I'm trying. . . .I'm dying.

THIBAULT   Hey, Johnny. Do Elvis. Do Elvis. . . ."I'm all shook up."

JOHNNY   *snapping into an Elvis imitation*   "I'm all shook up."

IRENE comes out on her balcony.

IRENE   Johnny.

JOHNNY   Irene, remember me when I was eighteen? *He does his Elvis imitation*   "Be-bop-a-lula."

IRENE   Come on up to bed, Johnny. I've got to work tomorrow.

JOHNNY   Tomorrow? Fuck tomorrow! Everybody's worried about tomorrow. I'm worried about right now.

THIBAULT   Hey, do Elvis. Do some more Elvis. . . ."You ain't nothing but a hound dog."

JOHNNY   Elvis is dead, ya dumb Pepsi. He's dead. Don't ya understand that? He's dead.

He goes to the stairs and starts to climb them. He collapses.

IRENE   Come on, Johnny.

She comes down and tries to get him up the stairs. He grunts.

IRENE   Shit. La merde. . . .Muriel? Muriel?

MURIEL   *from inside her house*   I'm asleep.

IRENE   Muriel, give me a hand, will ya?

MURIEL   *from inside her house*   Leave him there, it'll do him good.

CECILE   *coming out on her balcony*   Madame, you need some help?

IRENE   Thanks.

CECILE comes down the stairs. Together, she and IRENE carry JOHNNY up the stairs and into his house.

JOHNNY   Irene, I love you. . . . Gonna buy ya a house, Irene.

CECILE comes back out. She sees THIBAULT sitting on the steps looking at one of his magazines.

THIBAULT   Paquette, Paquette, tu t'souviens? Toi et moi à la Rodéo? Big Fat Babette. . . . "Please Help Me I'm Falling in Love with You." Big tits . . . big tits.

CECILE   Shhhhhh, Thibault. Claude dort.

THIBAULT   *looking at his magazine* Tits . . . big tits.

He rips a page out of the magazine. He goes and sits on his bike. IRENE comes out on the balcony carrying two Cokes.

IRENE   Veux-tu un Coke, Cécile?

CECILE   Yes, that would be nice.

CECILE sits down on her rocking chair. IRENE comes and sits down beside her.

CECILE   It's so quiet, eh? This is my favourite time, when it's quiet.

IRENE   Yeah.

CECILE   Look, there's the Big Dipper.

IRENE   Oh yeah?

CECILE   Right there. Right next to that shed.

IRENE   You know, I haven't looked at the sky in years.

CECILE   When I was a little girl in Lac St-Jean, I knew the names of all the stars . . . the Great Bear, the Swan, the Hunter. . . .

IRENE   They've got names, eh?

CECILE   Of course. Everything has a name.

IRENE   How did you met Paquette? Uh . . . Claude?

CECILE   He had a truck. He was a truck driver. . . . So handsome. . . . At first, we thought he would marry one of my older sisters, but she didn't want him because he was too loud. . . . And my mother too, she didn't like him. But . . .

IRENE   You liked him.

CECILE   I was a young girl. . . .

IRENE   So was I. . . . I had a dream last night. . . .

CECILE   A dream? Tell me. I love dreams.

IRENE   I . . . I dreamed I saw Jacob wrestling the angel. Imagine that.

CECILE   Jacob?

IRENE   Yeah, you know? Jacob . . . in the Bible.

CECILE   Jacob. Ah, oui.

IRENE   Anyhow, I woke up feeling good. . . . Well, it's been one of those years, eh?

CECILE   Johnny and Claude, right now . . . they not getting along so good?

IRENE   Well, they're both being stupid. But Johnny started it. He's such a goddamn redneck sometimes.

CECILE   It's strange. . . . Before, Claude, he wants to be like the English . . . and now, he puts everything on them.

DIANE enters.

CECILE   Diane, il est passé minuit. Ton père va être fâché.

DIANE   *coming up the stairs* Irene, I have something. . . .

IRENE   Oh?

DIANE   Une lettre de Tom.

IRENE   Tom? He wrote you?

DIANE   Oui, but I can't understand all the words.

IRENE   Let me see it. *She takes the letter and looks at the postmark.* Ormstown? What's the silly bugger doing in Ormstown? . . . You want me to read it?

DIANE   Oui.

IRENE   "Hi, Diane. . . . Took me a day hitchhiking to get this far so far. Tomorrow, guess I'll reach the border and cross over into the land of Jimmy Carter and Mickey Mouse."

DIANE   *laughing* Mickey Mouse.

IRENE   "I can feel New York City down there, pulling me like a magnet." Tu comprends? Magnet?

IRENE mimes "magnet," banging the fist of one hand into her other hand.

DIANE   Oui.

IRENE   "Pull at him." Shit, it's gonna hit him on the head.

DIANE   Quoi?

IRENE   Uh . . . okay. "I don't have no money, but a faggot bought me a meal." Faggot? C'est un tapette.

DIANE   Oui.

IRENE   "I'm glad we had that talk, even if I did sound kind of crazy. . . . I think you're beautiful. I mean, how do you say something like that? But, it's true." Wow! Hot stuff!

DIANE   *taking back the letter* It's okay. . . . I understand the rest.

IRENE   Hey, sounds like Tom really likes ya, girl.

DIANE   Hey, I know what he wants.

IRENE   Yeah, so is he gonna get some?

DIANE   He's cute. . .a bit.

IRENE   New York City.

DIANE   Me, I want to go there.

IRENE   Yeah?

DIANE   Sure. Go there and live like in the movies. It would be fun, eh?

IRENE   Yeah. . .like the movies. Poor Muriel.

DIANE   His mother?. . .What for?. . .She was going to throw him out anyhow.

IRENE   Well, I've got to work tomorrow. Bye.

DIANE   Bye.

CECILE   Goodnight, Irene.

IRENE exits into her house.

Diane, viens-tu te coucher?

DIANE   Non.

CECILE exits into her house. DIANE sits at the top of the stairs. THIBAULT is still sitting on his bike at the bottom of the stairs.

THIBAULT   Diane. Diane.

DIANE   Va-t'en chez-vous, Thibault.

THIBAULT   Eh, Diane? J'vas m'acheter une Honda 750. C'est vrai, Diane. Brammmmm, brammmmm. Honda. J'vas m'en acheter une.

DIANE   Oui, oui.

THIBAULT   J'vas t'faire des rides, eh?

DIANE   Va-t'en chez-vous, Thibault.

THIBAULT   C'est vrai, Diane. Une 750. Brammmm, brammmmm.

He exits on his bike. DIANE remains at the top of the stairs looking at her letter. Blackout.

Scene Two

The next day. It is a very hot Sunday afternoon. JOHNNY, PAQUETTE and DIANE are on the balcony watching the ballgame on TV—on separate TVs. MURIEL is sweeping her balcony.

JOHNNY   *watching TV*   Aw, shit. . .bunch of bums!

PAQUETTE   *watching TV*   Maudits Expos!

IRENE enters yawning. She is coming home from work, wearing her waitress uniform. She sees MURIEL sweeping her balcony.

IRENE   Boy, this heat. . . .

MURIEL   Couple more days of this and we'll be having riots.

IRENE   Yeah.

MURIEL   Sorry about last night. . . .I was in one of my moods.

IRENE   Aw, forget it. Hey, Diane got a letter from Tom, eh?. . .Yeah.

MURIEL   He writes to her, but he doesn't write to his mother?

IRENE   He's in Ormstown.

MURIEL   Ormstown? Where's that?

IRENE   Somewhere in the bush.

MURIEL   Well, as soon as he gets hungry, he'll come home. . . .Just let him try to get through the door.

IRENE   Aw, don't worry. Young guys are like tom-cats. They always land on their feet.

MURIEL   Who says I'm worried?

IRENE   Okay.

PAQUETTE   *watching TV*   Away, away. . .câlice.

JOHNNY   *watching TV*   Aw, shit! Le merde! Move your ass! Move your ass!

PAQUETTE   *watching TV*   Il est temps, tabarnac!

JOHNNY   *seeing IRENE coming up the stairs*   Hey, did ya pick me up some smokes?

IRENE dumps a pack of smokes in his lap and goes on into the house. CECILE enters. She is wearing her church clothes. She comes up behind MURIEL.

CECILE   Bonjour, Madame Williams.

MURIEL   *jumping in fright*   Oh God, don't creep up on me like that.

CECILE   How are you?. . .Nice day, eh?

MURIEL   Too hot.

CECILE   Ah, yes, too hot. . . .It's so nice to see people together in the church. Being together makes people feel so good.

PAQUETTE and JOHNNY   *together*   Grimsley, ya bum!. . .Aux douches!

MURIEL   Yeah. . . .   *looking at where CECILE is standing*   Move. . . .

CECILE moves and MURIEL continues sweeping. CECILE goes up the stairs. DIANE notices her hat.

DIANE   Maman, les femmes n'ont plus besoin de porter de chapeau pour aller à la messe.

CECILE   Je sais, Diane, mais je suis habituée de même.

PAQUETTE and JOHNNY both react to something on the baseball game on TV.

CECILE   Diane, tu devrais venir avec moi dimanche prochain.

DIANE   C'est toujours le même show. Quand ils changeront le programme, peut-être que j'irai.

PAQUETTE   *to CECILE and DIANE*   Tabarnac, y a-tu moyen d'écouter ma game tranquille? Ça fait une semaine que j'attends après ça. Cécile, va me chercher une bière.

CECILE   Oui, Claude....

She goes to get him a beer.

JOHNNY   Hey, Irene?... Irene?...

IRENE   *at the screen door*   Yeah?

JOHNNY   Get me a Coke.

IRENE   What's the matter, you break your leg?

JOHNNY   It's too hot to move.

IRENE   I'm moving.

PAQUETTE   *watching TV*   Merde!

JOHNNY   *watching TV*   Shit!

PAQUETTE   Un autre foul ball, hostie!

CECILE   *bringing PAQUETTE a beer*   Claude, veux-tu un sandwich?

PAQUETTE   Quoi?

CECILE   Un sandwich?

PAQUETTE   *watching TV*   Away...away là!

She goes to get him a sandwich.

JOHNNY   *watching TV*   Faster! Get under it! Get under it!... No, fuck!

PAQUETTE   *watching TV*   Shit! La merde!

CECILE comes back and puts a sandwich in one of PAQUETTE's hands and a beer in his other hand.

DIANE   Paquette est assez grand pour se mouvoir tout seul, Cécile.

PAQUETTE   Cécile.... C'est ta mère que t'appelles Cécile. Tu vas me faire le plaisir de l'appeler Maman.

DIANE   *to PAQUETTE*   You are a piece of shit.

She throws a bag of potato chips at him and stomps off into the house.

PAQUETTE   Voyons. Qu'est-ce qu'y lui prend?

CECILE   J'sais pas. J'pense qu'elle s'est chicané avec sa chum.

JOHNNY   *watching TV*   Go, go, go!

PAQUETTE   *watching TV*   Vite, vite, vite!... Bonne. That's it.... Oui.

JOHNNY   *watching TV*   About time....

Inside the house, DIANE puts on a record. It is "Hot Child in the City."

PAQUETTE   Cécile, dis-lui de baisser sa câlice de musique de hot child in the city, hostie.

CECILE goes into the house. The music fades away. IRENE comes out and hands JOHNNY a Coke.

IRENE   Johnny, I want to talk to you.

JOHNNY   Yeah, yeah.

IRENE   What happened last night?

JOHNNY   Last night?... Hey, I'm watching the game.

IRENE   When does it end?

JOHNNY   Eh?... Ten minutes.

IRENE   I want to talk to you before I go out.

JOHNNY   Yeah, yeah...talk. Okay.

IRENE   I mean it.

JOHNNY   Don't do the martyr, okay? Not the martyr, please.

IRENE exits into the house. THIBAULT enters on his bike. He starts putting "Gaëtan Bolduc...available and dynamic" campaign posters all over the walls.

MURIEL   *watching THIBAULT*   What's this?

THIBAULT   Dix piastres pour la journée....Me and four other guys are putting them up all over. Bolduc, he wants to win this time, eh?

MURIEL   *ripping down one of the posters*   Not on my wall....

THIBAULT   Eh? Not on your wall?

MURIEL   No.

THIBAULT   No?

MURIEL   No, you stupid little jerk.

She crumples up the poster and throws it at him.

THIBAULT   No?...Okay, no.

He goes up the stairs with his posters and sees PAQUETTE and JOHNNY watching TV. He sits beside PAQUETTE.

THIBAULT   Hey, c'est quoi l'score? What's the score?

PAQUETTE   Huit à cinq.

JOHNNY   *shouting across at them*   The Expos got five.

THIBAULT   Hey. Good game, eh?... Hot, eh? Hot ...very hot. Très chaud....Agh...hard to breathe. *He coughs.*   Agh, my throat....Hot....

PAQUETTE   *calling to CECILE*   Cécile, apporte-moi deux autres bières.

CECILE   *at the screen door*   Deux?

PAQUETTE   Oui.

THIBAULT   Ah, oui. . . . Good game, eh?

PAQUETTE   Ferme ta gueule, toi. Okay?

THIBAULT   Hey, regarde.

He shows PAQUETTE a poster.

PAQUETTE   Ote-toi d'là. C'est quoi ça? Bolduc?

THIBAULT   Oui. Prends-en une.

PAQUETTE   Tu vas laisser tes cochonneries ailleurs.

He crumples up the poster and throws it over the balcony.

THIBAULT   Eh, tu votes pas Libéral cette année?

MURIEL   *from downstairs*   Hey. . . . Watch the garbage, okay?

CECILE   *bringing out two beer*   Ah, bonjour, Thibault. Comment va ta mère?

THIBAULT   Oui, ça va bien.

JOHNNY   *watching TV*   Slide, for fuck's sake! Slide!

PAQUETTE   *watching TV*   C'est pas un coursier, c'est un cheval de labo!

CECILE   Claude, j'aurais besoin de cinq piastres.

PAQUETTE   Cinq piastres, pourquoi? Diane? Dis-y de venir les demander à sa piece of shit, okay?

CECILE exits into the house.

THIBAULT   *looking at both TVs*   Hey, hey, it's the same game! The same game!

The broadcast VOICE is heard again.

VOICE   N'oubliez pas dans deux semaines, votez Gaëtan Bolduc. Bolduc est sur votre côté, toujours disponible et dynamique. . . . Bolduc. . . .

The broadcast truck plays Elvis Presley music. The music fades away.

THIBAULT   *referring to the broadcast VOICE*   Oui, that's him right there.

PAQUETTE   *watching TV*   Maudit, même pas capable de regarder sa game tranquille.

THIBAULT   *watching TV*   Trois hommes sur les buts.

PAQUETTE   *watching TV*   Y sont capables, si y veulent.

IRENE comes out on the balcony.

IRENE   Can we talk now?

JOHNNY   Shit, it bugs me when goofs like Bolduc use good Elvis music.

IRENE   Johnny, you got drunk again last night.

JOHNNY   Yeah. . . .

IRENE   Four nights in a row. . . . You said you were gonna stop. I thought we had all that settled.

JOHNNY   Listen. . . . This is not the right time.

IRENE   It's never the right time. I'm tired of waiting for the right time. Let's talk now. . . . Let's try to talk.

JOHNNY   Talk. . . . Look, I just need one more night to straighten out.

IRENE   Straighten out what?

JOHNNY   I'm not working, so you think you can pick on me, is that it? Is that it?

IRENE   This is not a contest.

JOHNNY   I got a hangover. . . . I'm in a bad mood.

IRENE   So, you're gonna go out tonight too?

JOHNNY   Yeah, that's right. . . . Yeah.

IRENE   Well, don't count on me being here to wipe up your puke forever.

JOHNNY   Nobody's asking you to.

IRENE   I'm tired of being the wife in your life, Johnny. I'm not gonna hang around here and watch you wreck yourself. . . . No thanks.

JOHNNY   I don't want to hear this.

IRENE   From now on, every time you get drunk, that's one more step towards goodbye. . . . Not tomorrow or next week, but soon, because it's not doing either of us any good.

JOHNNY   Irene, it's too hot to get mad.

IRENE   Wish I was mad. Can't even cry about it anymore.

JOHNNY   Look, I'm going up to hospital next week. There's a pill they got, it makes ya sick every time ya take a drink.

IRENE   Johnny, you got to do it yourself.

JOHNNY   Okay, that's it for now. Okay? . . . You're right, but it's the wrong time, okay? Okay?

IRENE goes into the house.

JOHNNY   *shouting after her*   Hey, Irene, is there any more Coke in the fridge? Irene? . . . Fuck!

CECILE comes out to water her plants.

CECILE   Mes plantes. They get thirsty too.

JOHNNY   Eh?

CECILE   *holding up a plant*   See? . . . They're smiling.

JOHNNY shrugs and gets up and turns off the TV. CECILE goes back into her house.

JOHNNY   Goddamn bums don't know how to win. . . .

THIBAULT   *to JOHNNY*   They're losing in French too.

PAQUETTE *watching TV* Nos champions! L'ont encore dans le cul, hostie.

JOHNNY *to PAQUETTE* So, Paquette, what do ya think of the game? Eh?

THIBAULT He don't speak the English no more.

JOHNNY Oh yeah?

THIBAULT Oui, and me too. I don't speak the English since last week. Maybe a few times, but that's all.

JOHNNY Yeah, well, fuck the both of yas!

He goes into his house and comes out with a Canadian flag which he starts nailing up above his window.

THIBAULT *looking at JOHNNY's flag* As-tu vu ça, Paquette?

PAQUETTE Tu t'as pompé là, hostie!

PAQUETTE dashes into his house and comes out with a huge Québec flag, which THIBAULT staples to the wall.

PAQUETTE Tabarnac! Tu m'en spotteras pas avec ça. Thibault, viens m'aider, prends ton bord.

THIBAULT goes over to help JOHNNY staple his flag above the window. When JOHNNY turns around, he sees PAQUETTE's huge Québec flag.

JOHNNY Fuck!

He exits into his house. PAQUETTE and THIBAULT laugh. They turn off their TV set and exit into PAQUETTE's house.

The broadcast VOICE is heard again.

VOICE Gaëtan Bolduc, the man for you . . . available and dynamic. . . . Gaëtan Bolduc, the man for you . . . available and dynamic. . . .

The sound fades away. GAETAN BOLDUC enters and knocks on MURIEL's door.

MURIEL *coming to the door* Yeah, yeah. Hold your horses. *She opens the door and sees BOLDUC.* Holy shit!

BOLDUC Ah, bonjour. . . . Tu parles anglais? English?

MURIEL Yeah.

BOLDUC Ah. . . . I'm Gaëtan Bolduc, your Member of Parliament. We all know that something is wrong with Québec right now, eh?

MURIEL You're goddamn right.

BOLDUC Well, I would like to help fix it. . . . Bon. Here's my card with information. . . . Don't be afraid to call, eh?

MURIEL Yeah, yeah.

BOLDUC Don't forget me on the 6th.

MURIEL Don't worry, I will.

She slams the door shut in his face. He goes up the stairs and knocks on JOHNNY's door.

IRENE *inside the house* Johnny. . . . There's someone at the door, Johnny. I'm in the tub.

JOHNNY *inside the house* Shit! *He opens the door.* You!

BOLDUC Ah, bonjour. . . . Tu parles anglais? English?

JOHNNY Yeah.

BOLDUC Ah, I'm Gaëtan Bolduc, your Member of Parliament. . . .

JOHNNY Oh, "Gaëtan Bolduc, the man for you . . . available and dynamic." So, what can I do for you?

BOLDUC No. . . . What can *I* do for you?

JOHNNY You mean, what can I do *to* you?

BOLDUC Bon. Here is my card with information. Don't forget, a vote for Gaëtan Bolduc is a vote for me. . . . Bonjour.

JOHNNY Hey! Wait a minute. . . . I'm not finished yet. I only get to see you once every four years.

BOLDUC Is there something you'd like to know?

JOHNNY Yeah. . . . Houses are still burning down, there's no jobs. . . . What happened to all them promises?

BOLDUC It takes time. . . . We're working on it. . . .

JOHNNY Yeah? Eh, well, you got a lot of nerve walking around here . . . and quit using Elvis music, okay? What's the matter, you got no respect for the dead?

JOHNNY exits into his house.

IRENE *from inside the house* Johnny, what's that all about?

JOHNNY *from inside the house* It's fuckface, Bolduc.

IRENE *from inside the house* Bolduc?

BOLDUC knocks on PAQUETTE's door. DIANE answers the door.

DIANE Oui?

BOLDUC Etes-vous la femme de la maison?

DIANE Moi? Jamais. . . . Paquette? Paquette, c'est Bolduc.

PAQUETTE Quoi?

THIBAULT sneaks out the window and goes downstairs where he starts putting up more Bolduc posters. PAQUETTE comes to the door.

BOLDUC Bonjour. Je suis Gaëtan Bolduc, votre député au parlement.

PAQUETTE   Salut, Gaëtan.

BOLDUC   Allô?

PAQUETTE   Tu me reconnais? Claude Paquette?
. . . Ecole de Notre-Dame-des-Sept-Douleurs?

BOLDUC   Ah, oui. . . . Oui. . . .

PAQUETTE   Claude Paquette. . . .

BOLDUC   Claude Paquette?. . . . Oui, c'est ça. . . .

PAQUETTE   Tu sais que t'as l'air de pas t'arranger,
mon Bolduc.

BOLDUC   Je travaille fort, tu sais. . . . On fait ce
qu'on peut. . . .

PAQUETTE   Moi aussi. . . . J'travaille fort. Tu sais
qu'j'ai jamais été sur le welfare. Moi, jamais. Les
jeunes y se câlicent de ça, mais y faut que quelqu'un
paye les taxes. Ces crisses de jeunes-là, y devraient
toutes les câlicer dans l'armée. Comme ça, y travail-
leraient.

BOLDUC   Alors, tu vas voter pour moi, eh, Claude?

PAQUETTE   Fuck you! Tu me poigneras pas une
deuxième fois!

JOHNNY comes out and goes down the stairs. When
he reaches the bottom of the stairs, he turns around
and throws some eggs back at BOLDUC. They miss
him and hit PAQUETTE.

PAQUETTE   Hey!

BOLDUC   C'est un joke, ça? Tu vas entendre parler
de mes avocats, toi.

BOLDUC comes down the stairs and exits hurriedly.
JOHNNY hands the eggs to THIBAULT to make it
seem as if he had thrown them. He exits after
BOLDUC.

PAQUETTE   Qu'est-ce que c'est ça? Qu'est-ce que
c'est ça?

CECILE comes out. She looks at PAQUETTE.

CECILE   Claude, c'est quoi? Un oiseau?

THIBAULT starts coming up the stairs.

PAQUETTE   to THIBAULT   Thibault, est-ce que
t'as qu'que chose sur la toiture?

THIBAULT   La toiture?

PAQUETTE   Oui. . . la toiture.

THIBAULT   looking up at the roof   Non.

PAQUETTE sees the eggs that JOHNNY has given to
THIBAULT.

PAQUETTE   C'est quoi ça?

He takes the eggs from THIBAULT and starts throwing them at him. THIBAULT runs down the stairs.

THIBAULT   Hey! Hey!. . .

PAQUETTE   Ah, mon petit, tabarnac. . . .

JOHNNY enters and goes up the stairs to his balcony.

THIBAULT   C'est pas moi. C'est pas moi. . . .   He
points to JOHNNY.   C'est lui. C'est lui.

JOHNNY stands on his balcony laughing.

PAQUETTE   C'est toi ça, eh? Big joke, eh? Big joke.

He throws an egg at JOHNNY.

JOHNNY   You watch yourself. . . . Okay?

JOHNNY crosses to PAQUETTE's balcony.

PAQUETTE   Hey, keep on your own side! Keep on
your own side!

JOHNNY   You and Bolduc, eh? Ya suck!

PAQUETTE   Hey, c'est toi qui vote pour les Libérals,
eh? Pas moi.

JOHNNY   Yeah, eh?

They start shoving each other. IRENE comes out
and she and CECILE try to break up the fight.

CECILE   Claude. . . .

IRENE   Johnny, stop it. . . .

IRENE starts hitting JOHNNY with a towel.

JOHNNY   What are ya hitting me for?

IRENE exits into the house with JOHNNY in tow.
DIANE laughs at PAQUETTE from inside the house.

PAQUETTE   La petite crisse, elle trouve ça drôle?
Ça t'fait rire? Ça t'fait rire?

DIANE   from inside the house   Oui, je trouve ça
drôle. . . . Lâche ça. . . . Lâche ça. . . .

PAQUETTE goes into the house, takes one of
DIANE's records and throws it out the window.

PAQUETTE   Est-ce tu trouves ça drôle?

DIANE   from inside the house   Sors de ma
chambre. . . . Va-t-en d'ici. . . .

TOM enters and knocks at MURIEL's door.

MURIEL   coming to the door   Yeah, yeah.   She
opens the door.   You're back.

TOM   Yeah.

MURIEL   Well, you better wash up. . . . There's some
food in the fridge.

TOM   Ma?

MURIEL   Yeah?

TOM   Uh. . . nothing. . . .

He walks into the house. DIANE comes out of the
house and sits in the rocking chair. She is crying.
JOHNNY comes out of his house and sits on the
balcony. CECILE comes out on her balcony.

CECILE   J'ai hâte qu'il fasse froid. Ton père peut pas dormir quand il fait trop chaud. Ça le rend de mauvaise humeur. *She checks her plants.* C'est vrai. Il y a de la place ici. Je pense que je vais déménager mes plantes sur le balcon d'en avant.

She sees that DIANE is crying.

Diane. . . . Diane, qu'est-ce qu'y a?

DIANE   Y a rien.

CECILE   Tu vas voir, ton père va être malheureux de ce qu'il a fait, il va être gentil avec toi.

DIANE   Oui, mais j'suis pas un jouet, moi, maman.

CECILE   Diane. . . .

DIANE   Laisse-moi tranquille. . . .

CECILE goes back into her house.

JOHNNY   Irene? Hey, Irene?. . .

IRENE   *coming to the screen door*   Yeah?

JOHNNY   Lend me a few bucks. I wanna go uptown. . . .Yeah, yeah, I know. . . .Look, why don't you just tell me to leave. Ya know, tell me to leave and it's all over.

IRENE   You're so weak.

JOHNNY   Just tell me it's over and I'm gone.

IRENE   I have to be strong for the both of us.

JOHNNY   It's so easy for you. You do this because of that. You do that because of this. It's not that easy for me.

IRENE   *throwing him five dollars, yelling*   I hate you. . . . I hate you. . . .

She goes back into the house and slams the door.

JOHNNY   One more night, Irene. . . .

He exits. MURIEL comes out and throws a pair of boots in the garbage can. TOM follows her out. He has nothing on his feet.

TOM   Hey, Ma. . . . What are ya doing?

MURIEL   You're not wearing these. They stink.

TOM   What do ya mean?

MURIEL   They stink and I'm throwing them out.

TOM   Ma, it's the only pair of boots I've got.

MURIEL   You're not wearing them in the house . . . and just because your father is a bum, doesn't mean you have to be one too.

She goes back into the house. TOM takes the boots out of the garbage can and puts them back on.

TOM   She's nuts. I mean, she's clinical. . . .

DIANE   You?. . .You're back again?

TOM   Yeah. Did a circle. . . .

DIANE   Why did you come back here?

TOM   I had no choice. . . . Same old shit, eh?

DIANE   They drive me crazy, all these people. . . .

TOM   I know what you mean.

DIANE   They're not happy, so they want everybody else to be the same way.

TOM   Yeah. . . .

DIANE   Me? I want to get out. . . . But how? Where do you go?

TOM   Not to Ormstown, I'll tell ya that. . . . Bunch of farmers. . . .

DIANE   You don't like New York City?

TOM   Never got there. . . . Wouldn't let me cross the border. . . . No money.

DIANE   You need money, eh?

TOM   Yeah.

DIANE   Always the same thing. . . .

TOM   Yeah. They don't make it easy for ya.

DIANE   They?. . .Oui. . .they.

TOM   You, uh. . .get my letter?

DIANE   Oui.

TOM   So. . . . What do ya think?

DIANE   Why do you worry about what I think?

TOM   I don't know. . . .

DIANE   The letter was. . .okay.

TOM   Oh yeah? I meant what I said, ya know?. . .in the letter.

DIANE   I'm not beautiful.

TOM   I don't know. . . . Girls that never blink turn me on.

DIANE   That's too bad for you.

TOM   Hey, uh. . . . I'm gonna look for work here and when I got some money, maybe I'll try New York again.

DIANE   What for? It's the same thing everywhere.

TOM   Hey, uh. . .you're in a good mood, eh?

PAQUETTE comes out carrying some pop bottles down the stairs.

PAQUETTE   Hey, Diane. Je m'en vas au magasin. As-tu besoin de qu'que chose?

DIANE   Je veux rien qui vient de toi.

PAQUETTE   Tu pourrais au moins être polie, câlice, apart de ça. J't'ai pas dit que j'voulais pas que tu t'tiennes avec les têtes carrées.

DIANE   You don't tell me what to do.

PAQUETTE   Crisse, parle-moi en français, par exemple.

DIANE   Fuck you!

PAQUETTE   *to* TOM   Et toi-là. Keep on your own side.

He exits.

TOM   Good to be home again. . . .

DIANE   Nobody tells me what to do. . . . Nobody.

TOM   All those French guys over thirty. . . . Grease!

DIANE   Et toi, tête carrée. What do you look like, eh?

TOM   Don't know. . . . Have to wear a box for a hat, I guess.

DIANE   That's right. . . . Aw, it's so hot!

TOM   You, uh, want to take a walk? . . . No, eh?

DIANE   A walk?

TOM   Yeah, a walk.

DIANE   Where?

TOM   I don't know. . . the Boardwalk? I always walk there.

DIANE   Okay.

TOM   Uh . . . which way?

DIANE   I don't care.

TOM   This way. . . .

They begin to exit. MURIEL comes out of the house.

MURIEL   Tom?

TOM   Yeah?

MURIEL   Just look at you. . . . You're a mess!

TOM   We're going for a walk.

MURIEL   Tom, come here. . . . I want to speak to you. . . .

TOM   What?

MURIEL   Do you think this is fair to me?

TOM   What?

MURIEL   All of this? . . .

TOM   I guess not.

MURIEL   You guess not?

TOM   Look, I had nothing to do with this. I was just born here, that's all.

MURIEL   Listen, don't think you can start in all over, hanging around here daydreaming, 'cause I won't have it. Either you get a job or you get out. It's one or the other. . . .

TOM   Job! Job! Job! I'm gonna get a job!

MURIEL   I've heard that one before.

TOM   This time I'm gonna look.

MURIEL   Sure . . . and then, you'll move out with your first cheque.

TOM   Ma?

MURIEL   Don't you "Ma" me.

TOM   Ma? I don't wanna fight with ya, Ma.

MURIEL   So, don't fight. . . .

MURIEL exits into her house.

TOM   Home, sweet home. . . .

He bangs a garbage can and exits down the lane with DIANE. Blackout.

Scene Three

The sound of sawing is heard offstage. JOHNNY is in the shed working. CLAUDE enters carrying his lunch bucket. He is coming home from work early. CECILE is watering her plants on the balcony.

CECILE   Claude, t'es de bonne heure. Qu'est-ce qui arrive? Es-tu malade?

PAQUETTE   Non, je ne suis pas malade.

CECILE   Qu'est-ce qu'y a qui va pas?

PAQUETTE   J'ai perdu ma job. Je suis revenu à pied.

CECILE   Veux-tu une chaise, Claude?

PAQUETTE   Pas une crisse d'avertissement. Je suis allé voir le boss en haut. Il a dit que ça lui faisait ben de la peine, mais il pouvait rien faire. Là, je suis allé voir le gars de l'union. Tu sais ce qu'il m'a dit, le gars de l'union, eh? "There's nothing we can do. The company is stopping their operation in Montréal. They're going to relocate it in Taiwan." . . . Taïwan!

CECILE   Taïwan? C'est au Vermont, ça?

PAQUETTE   Treize ans de ma vie. . . . Treize ans de ma câlice de vie. . . .

CECILE   Quatorze, Claude. Je me souviens. Quand t'as eu ta job, c'était en octobre.

PAQUETTE   J'ai quarante-deux ans, tabarnac. J'peux pas recommencer à zéro. Qu'est-ce que j'vas faire?

CECILE   Tu l'aimais pas ta job de toute façon.

PAQUETTE   J'sais que j l'aimais pas, mais y faut ben manger.

CECILE   Oui.

PAQUETTE   Les crisses y sont ben toutes pareils. Les tabarnacs. Y s'servent de toi pis quand y'ont pu besoin de toi, y te câlicent dehors comme un vieux torchon sale. Pis, fuck you! Mange d'la merde. Pis si tu meures, c'est encore mieux. Y'ont pu de welfare à payer.

CECILE   Welfare? Mais on a jamais été sur le welfare, Claude.

PAQUETTE   Cécile, c'est pas de ma faute. C'est pas de ma faute.

CECILE   Je sais que je dis des choses stupides, mais je sais pas quoi dire.

The broadcast VOICE is heard.

VOICE   Don't forget tomorrow. Voting day.... Re-elect Gaëtan Bolduc, the man for you... available and dynamic....

The sound fades away. DIANE and TOM enter together.

DIANE   *Apocalypse Now?* C'est quoi, *Apocalypse Now?*

TOM   It's a film about that war there in the States.

DIANE   What war?

TOM   Uh...China.... Somewhere over there. ...Wanna go? Tonight?

DIANE   Okay.... Salut....

She goes up the stairs.

TOM   See ya....

He goes into his house.

DIANE   *at the top of the stairs*   Allô, Maman. Ça va?

PAQUETTE   Diane, tu peux oublier ton école.

DIANE   Qu'est-ce qu'y lui prend lui?

CECILE   Ton père a perdu sa job.

DIANE   Sa job?

CECILE   Oui, Diane.

DIANE   Bon. Y a pas d'quoi se plaindre.

CECILE   Ah, Diane.

DIANE   C'est bien mieux de même. Comme ça, on l'entendra plus chicaner. Cette job-là, nous a toutes rendus fous. C'est vrai.

CECILE   Elle est jeune, Claude.

PAQUETTE   Laisse-la faire.

DIANE   Je vais m'en trouver une job, moi. Inquiète-toi pas. C'est facile. Ils ont toujours besoin de waitress cute. Puis moi, je suis cute. Je vais en parler avec Irene, okay?

PAQUETTE   Moi, il faut que je fasse quelque chose.

DIANE   Va quelque part avec Cécile. Vous êtes libres, là. C'est le temps ou jamais. Oubliez ça pour un bout de temps.

PAQUETTE   Oh, non.

CECILE   Mais où est-ce qu'on irait?

PAQUETTE   Diane, tu te souviens quand tu étais petite, petite de même, on montait en haut sur la montagne, eh? On regardait les beaux arbres, les beaux oiseaux. C'était beau, hein? Diane, j'ai toujours voulu ce qu'il y avait de mieux pour toi. Je suis fatigué. Je ne sais plus quoi dire.

CECILE   Viens t'allonger, Claude. Viens t'allonger.

CECILE helps PAQUETTE to the door.

DIANE   Papa.

They exit into the house. DIANE sits on a chair on the balcony. MURIEL and IRENE enter.

IRENE   So what did they say this time?

MURIEL   Ah, you know doctors.... They just try to scare ya....

IRENE   Hey, you're going to be okay.

MURIEL   Nope. They said it was serious.

IRENE   Yeah? How serious?

MURIEL   I'm gonna have an operation.

IRENE   Oh no, Muriel.

MURIEL   Yeah.... On the stomach. Ulcers.

IRENE   Oh no.

MURIEL   Aw, now that I know what they're gonna do, I'm not worried about it. It's just thinking about it that drives ya nuts.

IRENE   Ulcers.... Hey, so I was right, eh?

MURIEL   Yeah. Now, I'm gonna have to drink lots of milk.... Yuk!

IRENE   Does Tom know?

MURIEL   Yeah, he seems worried about it.

IRENE   Well, of course....

MURIEL   Ya know what those bastard doctors told me? Told me, I had to stop being so nervous. ...Yeah, there's this fat pig making $80,000 a year, living in Côte Saint-Luc, telling me not to be a nervous wreck.... Well, I got so mad, I tell ya.... I got so mad, I couldn't talk.

IRENE   I can't blame ya.

MURIEL   It makes ya wanna kill yourself just out of spite.

IRENE   Ya oughta go to the clinic in the Pointe. The doctors there treat ya like a human being.

MURIEL   I dunno.... I heard they're all Commies or something.

IRENE   So what?

MURIEL   Yeah, well, guess they couldn't be any worse.... Oh, Irene, wait... I wanna show ya something. *She takes a small box out of her purse and opens it.* Look.

IRENE   A brooch.... That's beautiful.

MURIEL   Tom bought it for me with his first pay.

IRENE   It's beautiful.

MURIEL   Yeah.... Stupid kid. Now, he doesn't have enough money for car fare.

JOHNNY enters from the shed carrying some lumber and some tools. He has built a new step for the stairs.

IRENE   Does he like his new job?

MURIEL   Well, he's lasted a month. That's some kind of record. *She sees JOHNNY and the step.* Holy shit! Hey, watch your thumbs!

JOHNNY glares at her.

MURIEL   Just a joke....

She goes into her house.

JOHNNY   Irene, gimme a hand with this.... Yeah, I know, officially, we ain't talking, but I need a hand....

IRENE   I don't believe it.

She goes over to help JOHNNY put the new step in place.

JOHNNY   So, what's new?... How are ya?

IRENE   I don't know.... Haven't been talking to myself lately.

JOHNNY   I've been off the sauce for a week now, right?

IRENE   Yeah.

JOHNNY   Yeah....

IRENE   You want a medal or what?

JOHNNY   Irene.... It's not easy, okay?

IRENE   Try being a woman for a while....

DIANE   *from upstairs*   Oui, that's right.

JOHNNY   *taking IRENE over to one side*   Irene, all that crap about you being strong for the both of us....

IRENE   It's not crap.

JOHNNY   Yeah, okay.... It's true, but I didn't make up the rules of the game, okay? I mean, it wasn't me.

IRENE   It wasn't me.

JOHNNY   I'm sorry, Irene. You know that?... I'm sorry.

IRENE   I was worried....

JOHNNY   About what?

IRENE   I've never seen you that bad before....

JOHNNY   Hey, I don't melt in the rain.... I don't get diarrhea in the snow. I'm a survivor.

IRENE   Yeah.... *They embrace.* So, what are ya gonna do?

JOHNNY   Maybe I can get back into music.

IRENE   You've been miserable ever since ya quit playing....

JOHNNY   You're the one who nagged me to quit.

IRENE   All I wanted you to do was stop drinking and screwing around so much.... Music had nothing to do with it.

JOHNNY   What do you know about the nightlife, Irene?

IRENE   Yeah, well.... Anyhow, no matter what happens, we'll always be friends, eh?

JOHNNY   Is that a threat?

IRENE   Yeah.

TOM comes out with his guitar and starts to play a song.

IRENE   Hi, Tommy.

IRENE goes up the stairs and into the house. JOHNNY comes over to talk to TOM.

JOHNNY   So, how's the new job?

TOM   Aw, Troy Laundry.... What can I say? Some guys been there twenty years and I'm there twenty days and already going nuts.

JOHNNY   Bad news, eh?

TOM   Hey. Can't talk to anybody.... They're all deaf from the noise.

JOHNNY   They probably got nothing to say anyhow.

TOM   Ya don't get a watch when ya retire, ya get a hearing aid.

CECILE comes out on her balcony to speak to DIANE.

CECILE   Tu sais, Diane, j'ai vu ton père pleurer juste une fois. C'est quand t'étais petite puis bien malade.

DIANE   Je ne me souviens pas de ça.

CECILE   Ça fait longtemps. On restait sur la rue Joseph.

TOM plays a tune on his guitar.

TOM   *to DIANE*   Hi, Diane.... You like that?...

DIANE   No.... Know any disco?

TOM   Disco!... Disco duck.... I don't got the right buttons on this thing.

MURIEL   *from inside the house*   Tommy?

TOM   Yeah?

MURIEL   I'm gonna need a hand in here.... I'm moving out your old man's junk into the shed.

TOM   You're moving it out?

MURIEL   Yeah.... He's never here and we can use the room.

TOM   Okay.

He goes in to help her move the things out to the shed. IRENE comes out of her house and goes down the stairs.

IRENE   All the trouble that step caused us over the last year and look at that, it's fixed.

JOHNNY   Yeah, I'm gonna send Giboux the bill.

DIANE   *to IRENE*   Irene, is there any jobs at your place?

IRENE   What?

DIANE   I have to find work. My father, he lost his job.

IRENE   He lost his job?

CECILE   Yes. The company is going to Taiwan, but they don't want to take Claude.

IRENE   The bastards.

JOHNNY   He got the axe, eh?

IRENE   How is he?

DIANE   Not so good.... Maybe you can talk to him, Irene.

IRENE   Be better if you talk to him, Johnny.

JOHNNY   What the fuck am I gonna say? He don't even want to speak my language.

IRENE   *shouting*   Hey, Muriel. Paquette lost his job.

MURIEL comes out of her house.

MURIEL   What? Another one for your Unemployment Committee. *to CECILE*   Sorry, madame. I really am.

IRENE   We can get him out on our next demonstration.

JOHNNY   Another one?

IRENE   We're gonna march in front of the U.I.C. building. Let them know we don't like the forty percent unemployment down here.

JOHNNY   Demonstration in the Pointe? That's not news.

MURIEL   We should do it in Westmount. That's where all the money is. Go up there and sit on their goddamn front lawns.

DIANE   Oui. Go right up there and let them know what we look like.

TOM   Yeah.

CECILE   It's very nice up in Westmount.... It's very nice.

JOHNNY   Yeah, you can take Thibault and leave him up there.... Boom! Into the woodwork. ...Westmount's infested....Thousands of little Thibaults running around....Boom! Another Pointe Saint-Charles!

MURIEL   Thibault...our secret weapon.

TOM   So secret, he don't even know.

IRENE   Johnny, talk to Paquette....

JOHNNY   You talk to him....

IRENE   Johnny?

JOHNNY   Look, it's the principle of the thing....

IRENE   Principle of what?

JOHNNY   Well, he started it, right?

IRENE   Started what?

DIANE   Maudit crisse, Johnny!

JOHNNY   Alright. Ya want me to be the nice guy.... Why do I always got to be the nice guy?

He goes up the stairs and knocks on PAQUETTE's door.

Hey, Porky.... Peace in the valley, okay?

PAQUETTE   *from inside his house*   Quoi?

JOHNNY   Let's kiss and make up.

PAQUETTE   Quoi?

IRENE   Tell him you're sorry he lost his job.

JOHNNY   Look, I'm sorry you lost your job....

IRENE   Tell him in French.

JOHNNY   I don't know how.

IRENE   Try.... J'ai de la peine....

JOHNNY   J'ai de la peine....

IRENE   J'ai de la peine que tu as perdu...que tu as perdu....

JOHNNY   J'ai de la peine que tu as perdu....

IRENE   Ta job.

JOHNNY   Ta fuckin' job.... He's not talking.

IRENE   He's upset.

JOHNNY   Diane, how do you say, "Together, we can fuck Bolduc"?

DIANE   "Ensemble on peut fourrer Bolduc."

JOHNNY   Hey, Paquette...."Ensemble..."

PAQUETTE   *at his screen door*   Hey, you go away with the bullshit, okay? Take it somewhere else. ...It's just another Pepsi who loses his job. T'es content.... Alors, viens pas m'écoeurer avec ça.

He slams the door shut.

JOHNNY   Irene!

He goes into his house and slams the door shut.

IRENE   Oh boy!

She goes up the stairs to PAQUETTE's door and knocks on it. There is no answer.

MURIEL   Talking's easy, Irene, but try to get people together.... Ppphht?

IRENE   What does it take to move you guys?... We gotta help ourselves. That's easy to understand, isn't it?

DIANE   They don't want to understand.... It's easier to eat shit.

IRENE   I don't know why I bother.

MURIEL   Ah, we can still do the demonstration without them.

CECILE   We need the government to help us.

MURIEL   What are you talking about? Bolduc *is* the government!

IRENE   Well... I'm tired....

THIBAULT enters on his bike. He has a case of beer for PAQUETTE.

THIBAULT   Chez Momo's is here.

TOM   Hey, Thibault. How's the girls?

THIBAULT   Oh boy, don't talk to me about that. ...Trouble all the time....

He goes up the stairs and discovers the new step.

Hey! *He dances on the new step.* Où est Paquette? *He puts the case of beer down on the balcony.*

CECILE   Claude est pas bien aujourd'hui. Il a perdu sa job.

THIBAULT   Il a perdu sa job? Aw, everybody's got trouble now, eh? Me, last week, I got hit by a Cadillac.

MURIEL   By a what?

THIBAULT   A Cadillac, oui.... Big car, eh?... So, I phone the boss and he says, "How's the bike?" "How's the bike?" hostie.... Hey, me, I know the boss. Sometimes he talks nice, but he's still the boss, eh?

MURIEL   Aw, bosses.... They're all the same, Thibault.

THIBAULT   Sure, I know that.... Maybe I'm crazy, but I'm not stupid, eh?

MURIEL   They do what they want, the bastards. They always do what they want.

She starts ripping down Bolduc posters.

THIBAULT   Hey, Bolduc won't like that....

MURIEL   Ppphht on Bolduc.

THIBAULT   Okay.... He won't like that, that's all.

DIANE   Irene, do you smell something?

IRENE   Yeah....

TOM   Probably someone burning garbage.

MURIEL   Do you see any smoke?

IRENE   Yeah, but I don't know where it's coming from.

CECILE   C'est un feu.

THIBAULT   Un feu? Où ça un feu?

IRENE   *to JOHNNY, inside the house*   Johnny, go down the lane and take a look.

JOHNNY   *coming out of his house*   Why do I always have to do everything around here?

He dashes off down the lane, followed by TOM and DIANE. They all yell, "Fire!" JOHNNY comes running back on.

JOHNNY   Irene, call the cops! It's a big one! Just a few houses down....

He runs back down the lane.

CECILE   Claude? Claude, y a un feu!

IRENE   I can't get the cops. The lines are busy....

PAQUETTE comes running out of his house.

CECILE   Claude, dis à Diane de ne pas aller trop proche....

He exits down the lane.

IRENE   It's a big one.

CECILE   Oh, yes... a big one....

MURIEL   Those old houses go up like matchsticks....

PAQUETTE   *yelling offstage*   Ça s'étend aux sheds d'à côté!

CECILE   Mon Dieu!

MURIEL   What did he say?

IRENE   It's spreading....

MURIEL   Where the hell are the firemen?

IRENE   If this were Westmount, there wouldn't be a fire.

MURIEL   Yeah, right....

PAQUETTE comes running back on.

PAQUETTE   Ça continue à s'étendre!

MURIEL   What's he saying?

PAQUETTE   Cécile, on va sortir les meubles!

JOHNNY comes running back on, followed by TOM and DIANE.

JOHNNY   Hey, Irene, start moving our stuff out!

There is general running around and shouting. THIBAULT gets in everyone's way. JOHNNY and PAQUETTE carry down their TV sets and their beer first. CECILE carries down her plants.

MURIEL   Tom, move your ass!

TOM   Aw, we're insured anyhow. . . .

MURIEL   Move it!

PAQUETTE   *to CECILE* C'est pas le temps toi et pis tes hostie de plantes.

MURIEL   Thibault, get your bike out of the way!

THIBAULT   Hey, don't touch my bike!

MURIEL   Then get it out of the way!

THIBAULT   Eh, Madame Paquette, y a un gros feu là-bas! Hey, good thing we fix that step, eh?

JOHNNY   *to PAQUETTE* Keep your shit on that side. . . .

PAQUETTE   Va donc chier, câlice!

JOHNNY and PAQUETTE collide at the top of the stairs. They start pushing and shoving each other to see who will go down the stairs first.

PAQUETTE   Ote-toi de là, hostie!

JOHNNY   Get out of my way!

IRENE, CECILE and DIANE rush in to break up the fight.

IRENE   Don't be so stupid. . . . Now, get out of the way . . . both of you. Come, you guys. . . . Hey, Muriel, Tom. . . . We'll do a relay. . . . We'll move them out upstairs, then we'll do you.

MURIEL   Why upstairs first?

IRENE   Muriel, come on!

The relay begins. They all start passing stuff down. It comes at them through the windows and through the doors. PAQUETTE calls JOHNNY over to give him a hand with the sofa.

PAQUETTE   Lève-toi. . . . Lève-le. . . .

JOHNNY   Irene, he's speaking French!

IRENE   Lift it!

PAQUETTE   Tourne-le. . . . Tourne-le. . . .

JOHNNY   Yeah, yeah . . . tour-ney. . . .

PAQUETTE   A droite. . . .

IRENE   To the right.

PAQUETTE   Laisse-le slyer sur la rampe . . . la rampe. . . .

JOHNNY   What???

IRENE   Slide it down the banister!

They slide the sofa down the banister. JOHNNY hurts himself when he and PAQUETTE put the sofa down at the foot of the stairs.

PAQUETTE   Okay, allez, Johnny. . . . We go move ton sofa. . . .

He helps JOHNNY up the stairs. When they get halfway up, a huge crashing noise is heard.

TOM   There goes the roof!

CECILE   Mon Dieu!

IRENE   Here it comes. . . .

MURIEL   Christ, we're next!

The broadcast VOICE is heard once again.

VOICE   Citizens of Pointe Saint-Charles, we live in a time when we need a strong government, a just government, one that is not afraid to deal harshly with disrupters, sabotage, corruptions and criminals. Remember a vote for Gaëtan Bolduc is a vote for security, for justice, for law and order . . . and for the future. Le futur. . . .

JOHNNY, IRENE, MURIEL and TOM *turning to the audience* What are we going to do?

PAQUETTE, CECILE, DIANE and THIBAULT *turning to the audience* Qu'est-ce qu'on va faire?

Blackout.

DAVID FRENCH (b. 1939)

If a single playwright can be said to epitomize the success of modern Canadian drama, it would be David French. From his apprenticeship with the CBC and his early identification with alternate theatre in Toronto to the current status of his plays as a mainstay of the regional theatres and a cultural export, his career has coincided with the growth and maturation of Canadian theatrical art. French has written broadly popular, commercially appealing plays while remaining true to his roots and his craft. His Mercer family trilogy and the phenomenally successful *Jitters* are painful, funny, affectionate and incisive examinations of conditions that are universal yet at the same time emphatically Canadian.

French was born in Coley's Point, Newfoundland, but moved to Toronto with his parents and four brothers when he was six. After finishing high school in 1958 he studied acting for two years in Toronto and Pasadena, California, and from 1960-65 worked as an actor, mostly for CBC-TV. Meanwhile he was also writing. In 1962 CBC bought his first play, "Behold the Dark River," and over the next decade broadcast seven more of his half-hour television scripts. Through the late sixties French supported his writing by working at a variety of jobs including a two-year stint in the Regina Post Office.

While summering on Prince Edward Island in 1971, he decided to try writing a stage play about his family's experience of adjusting to life outside Newfoundland in the late 1950s. By autumn he had a one-act which he offered to Bill Glassco after seeing Glassco's production of *Creeps* at the Tarragon. Expanded to full length, *Leaving Home* opened in May 1972 and immediately made French a star. The play has since enjoyed more than seventy productions. It also marked the start of a rich collaboration that has seen every one of French's plays premiere at the Tarragon under Glassco's direction.

At the end of *Leaving Home*, young Ben Mercer sets out on his own after a terrible row with his father, Jacob, leaving the rift between them as unresolved as Jacob's own sense of manhood and feelings of cultural alienation. *Of the Fields, Lately* (1973) picks up two years later with Ben's temporary return to his parents' home in Toronto, ending with Jacob's death. The play is gentler and more elegiac, but also slighter than its predecessor. It won the Chalmers Award for 1973 and has been very successful in its own right with more than forty productions to date including a brief Broadway run in 1980.

After a number of abortive attempts to write a third Mercer play, French altered his focus to the sleazy underworld of cheap hoods, hookers and con men, but *One Crack Out* (1975) was a disappointment. Glassco then suggested that he try translating Chekhov, and French's version of *The Seagull* (1977) did seem to get him creatively on track again. Now inspired to write a full-out comedy, he returned to a subject he knew well, this time the wonderful world of Canadian theatre itself. *Jitters* (1979) was an unadulterated smash, running for four months in Toronto followed by productions in nearly every regional theatre across Canada. In late 1979 it had a good run at the Long Wharf Theater in New Haven, and was headed for Broadway in 1981 when it closed prematurely in Philadelphia. *Jitters* is French's most highly praised play and his most popular, already having had over a hundred productions. The version printed here was newly revised in 1985.

The Riddle of the World (1981), a comedy of ideas about the sexual and spiritual lives of urban sophisticates, is probably French's least notable play. But in 1984 he finally completed his Mercer trilogy. *Salt-Water Moon* is a lyrical two-character "prequel," flashing back to Newfoundland in 1926 for the courtship of Jacob and Mary. It has proven almost as substantial a success as the earlier plays about the Mercers, and French has indicated that he may go back to their story again for as many as two more plays.

The Mercer plays are driven by archetypal energies: father-son conflict, the passage into manhood, the dynamics of family. But what make them special are the cultural circumstances that shape those energies, particularly the confrontation in the first two plays between the father who still considers himself a Newfie and the son who is a fully assimilated Canadian. Similarly, *Jitters* is both a conventional genre play—"an almost perfect comedy of its kind," the *New York Times'* Mel Gussow called it—and a comic rendering of a uniquely Canadian experience. Its kind is "backstage comedy," which lays bare for our amusement the insanities common to show biz people everywhere while hooking us into caring whether they will succeed in the face of all their adversity. But again, *Jitters* doesn't chronicle backstage life just anywhere. Because everyone involved in the production of the play-within-the-play is Canadian, they suffer, in addition to their standard fears and insecurities, those peculiar to a culture in which "success is like stepping out of line."

Jitters is set in a small, low-budget Toronto theatre that suspiciously resembles the Tarragon, and the play being performed sounds very much as if it could have been written by David French. In fact Robert Ross' *The Care and Treatment of Roses* has a lot in common with *Of the Fields, Lately*. Both are second plays following smash-hit theatrical debuts. Both are domestic dramas with four characters in corresponding relationships. And the review read at the end of *Jitters* is a delicious parody of the kinds of notices French's play received. Robert's fainting at the opening of his first play is also an only slightly exaggerated version of French's own experience on opening night of *Leaving Home*.

Jitters' other links to French's early plays are less pointed but even more germane. Its characters constitute their own "family" with all its attendant crises and rivalries, loves and disappointments. They too wrestle with the difficult question of leaving home, in their case for the wider professional world of New York, the pinnacle of theatrical success American-style. Jessica, like Ben Mercer, has gone for two years and now returned; Patrick, like Jacob, resents her bitterly for going. To the Canadian theatre professional, New York is something like what Canada is to the old Newfoundlander, both a promise and a threat. "Down there they embrace success." That's the myth anyway. Down there you can be a star. But you can also find out that you're not as good as you think you are. Here at home success is resented or punished or simply ignored ("Where else can you be a top-notch actor all your life and still die broke and anonymous?" Patrick asks). But here at home at least you're safe and relatively secure. Patrick is actually terrified by the prospect of going to Broadway. And his mixed feelings are shared to varying degrees by the other members of this all-Canadian company trying to cope with the "normal" jitters involved in opening a new show.

Overseeing all the comic chaos *in loco parentis* is George, the director, who has to calm fears, soothe bruised egos, placate, mediate, encourage, and maintain discipline like any head of a family. But he's not immune to errors in judgement. "Can't we all sit down and discuss this like adults?" he asks, and Jessica snaps back, "We're not adults, we're actors." They *are* childish, and their childishness is exasperating (as well as hilarious). Like James Reaney, David French clearly loves the theatre for just that quality—and perhaps the young Canadian theatre especially for having it in abundance. *Jitters* is his tribute to the quirky, childish vitality that makes it go.

•

Jitters was first performed at the Tarragon Theatre in Toronto on February 16, 1979, directed by Bill Glassco and designed by David Moe. Patrick was played by David Calderisi, Jessica by Charmion King, Phil by Les Carlson, George by Miles Potter, Robert by Matt Walsh, Tom by Jim Mezon, Nick by Morrison Bock, Susi by Amanda Lewis, and Peggy by Sheilah Currie.

JITTERS

CHARACTERS

PATRICK FLANAGAN
JESSICA LOGAN
PHIL MASTORAKIS
GEORGE ELLSWORTH
ROBERT ROSS
TOM KENT
NICK
SUSI
PEGGY

ACT ONE

An afternoon in May.

The set of the play-within-the-play, although the audience is as yet unaware of this. The set is the living-room of a middle-class home. There is a sofa, armchair, hi-fi, hanging plants and a Christmas tree. In the hallway a staircase leads up to the second floor. The front door is offstage.

The time of the play-within-the-play is winter. This particular scene takes place at night.

At rise, JESSICA is seated on the sofa, knitting with the sort of concentration that is an attempt to hide anxiety.

At the table, PHIL and TOM have just finished a hand of gin. While TOM shuffles the cards, PHIL pours himself a glass of Scotch.

JESSICA   What time is it?

PHIL   It's almost midnight. I don't think he'll be back.

JESSICA   I keep thinking I hear his car.

Slight pause.

PHIL   Can I get you something?

JESSICA   I'm fine.

PHIL   You sure, Sis? It's no trouble.

JESSICA   Eric, I said no. I'm in no mood to drink. Just leave me alone.

TOM   Oh, for Christ's sake, Mom!

He hurls the cards down on the table, rises, and crosses to stage left where he stands shuffling his feet.

JESSICA   Watch your temper, you. I won't have that sort of language in this house.

TOM   That's funny, coming from you.

JESSICA   When have you heard me talk like that? I have never used that sort of language. Ever.

PHIL   Come on, you two. Haven't we had enough for one night?

TOM   He's making a fool of you, Mom, and you're the only one who can't see it. Frank's only out for what he can get.

JESSICA   Aren't we all?

TOM   Haven't you ever wondered where he goes every Thursday afternoon? Or do you prefer not to know?

PHIL   Please, Jimmy, this isn't the time.

JESSICA   *to TOM*   What are you getting at?

TOM   He goes to 438 Duncan Street. He takes a key from under the mat and lets himself in.

JESSICA   How do you know?

TOM   I followed him.

PHIL   Jimmy, you promised you wouldn't . . .

TOM   *cutting in*   You want to know who lives at 438 Duncan Street? An eighteen-year-old girl who waits on tables at the Horse's Ass.

PHIL   The what?

JESSICA   I think he said the Horse's Ass.

They all break up.

GEORGE   *from his seat in the audience*   All right, cast, we'll stop there. We'll run it from the top now in costume.

TOM   Sorry, George. I know it's the Horse's Head. I don't know why I said the Horse's Ass.

GEORGE   Just don't say it tonight, Tom.   *calling out*   Patrick, we're not going on. We won't be needing you.

PATRICK   *entering*   I could've told you that weeks ago. From now on I'll phone in my part.

PEGGY enters from backstage and begins to set up for the top of the play.

GEORGE   How was it that time, Jess? Did the knitting help?

JESSICA   It's perfect. Exactly what a woman might do if she's anxious.

GEORGE   You sure, love?

JESSICA   Absolutely. I know what I do: I clean the oven or wax the floor.

PATRICK   Just don't get too excited when you rush out to greet me. I don't want a knitting needle in my eye.

He sits.

JESSICA   Worry more about the critics, Flanagan. They go straight for the jugular without dropping a stitch.

PATRICK   I'd rather worry about my acting, if you don't mind.

JESSICA   I can understand that. I'd be worried, too, if I were you.

PATRICK   Exactly what does that mean?

JESSICA   Not now, darling. I know a good exit line when I hear it.

She exits.

TOM   How's my position, George? It always feels . . . you know . . . like I'm too far stage left.

GEORGE   No, I want the distance. Only don't shuffle your feet. It looks like you're doing a soft shoe.

TOM   I'm expressing my anxiety.

PATRICK   Why don't you have him clean the oven or wax the floor?

GEORGE   Tom, it's better to remain still. Especially when Jess is speaking. At that moment the focus should be on her and you take it away if you move.

PATRICK   *to TOM*   In other words, you're up-staging our Star. Cut it out.

TOM   *to GEORGE*   I won't do it again. I promise.

He exits. GEORGE starts down the aisle.

NICK   *over the PA*   A run-through of the show will begin in twenty minutes. Please be ready to go at four o'clock. Peggy, be set as soon as you can.

PHIL   George, old buddy, have you seen my costume? My so-called costume?

GEORGE   *stepping onstage*   What's wrong with it?

PHIL   It's hideous. I'm insulted. Deeply offended.

GEORGE   Put it on, Phil. Let's have a look.

He sits at the table and takes a sandwich out of his lunch bag.

PHIL   George, you're a wonderful man, a sweet-heart. I'd do anything for you. Anything. Even take my shirt off on stage. But don't ask me to be more ridiculous than that.

He exits backstage.

PATRICK   I'm waiting. And don't tell me again she didn't mean it. That's the second time in two days.

GEORGE   *eating the sandwich*   I still think it was an accident.

PATRICK   Don't give me that. That apron is sup-posed to hit my chest, not my face. She threw it so hard it knocked my hat off.

GEORGE   That part I don't like. But your reaction was marvellous.

PATRICK   What reaction?

GEORGE   The way you raised your fist.

PATRICK   That was my own reaction, not the character's.

GEORGE   Keep it. And I loved that little dance you did. Like you were holding the lid on a volcano.

PATRICK   That wasn't *acting*, mate. I wanted to punch her in the mouth. Knock her right on her twelve-carat arse.

GEORGE   Patrick, the tension was terrific. I wasn't sure whether you were going to hit her or not. Believe me, the audience will feel that, too.

PATRICK   I'll let you in on a little secret. You listening? If she throws that apron in my face one more time, I won't leave you or the audience in any doubt. Is that too subtle for you?

SUSI   *entering*   George, treasure, I hate to inter-rupt but since I'm such a good sport I've volunteered to work on my tea-break.

GEORGE   What is it, Susi?

SUSI   The sofa cushion needs mending. Would you mind if I did it now? I'm in a hurry.

GEORGE   Now or later, love. But it has to be done by tonight.

PATRICK rises and crosses to the table.

GEORGE   Sorry. Where were we?

SUSI sits on the sofa and mends the cushion.

PATRICK   We were talking about that prima donna. Canada's Own Jessica Logan. God, that kills me. She's been in the States half her life, she comes home to do one play for six weeks, and suddenly she's a national resource.

GEORGE   Blame the press, not her. You know what they're like.

PATRICK   I've been a name here for twenty years, I can't even get a bank loan.

GEORGE   You want a sandwich?

PATRICK   Even in that Albee piece she played herself. That's all she can do, bitches.

GEORGE   I made it myself. Cheddar cheese on pumpernickel.

PATRICK   Bitches and tarts. That's her forte. Middle-aged bitches and sleazy tarts.

GEORGE   Pat, she's not playing a bitch. This is a very sympathetic role.

PATRICK   And smaller than mine. And for that she gets top billing. I have to squint to read my name on the posters.

GEORGE   Look, I know you two aren't exactly hitting it off, but your work together is sensational. I'm very happy. So is Robert.

PATRICK   Well, he has a funny way of showing it, our playwright. Most days he slinks in here and broods. His silences are right out of Pinter.

GEORGE   He's just shy. It's only his second play.

PATRICK   Today's the first time he's spoken to me all week. Come to think of it, I prefer his silences. No, really, he has no tact, that kid. So keep him away from me. As far as possible.

PHIL   *off*   George, I'm dressed. Are you ready for this?

GEORGE   Just a minute, Phil.   *to PATRICK*   Look, we'll talk about this later, okay?

PATRICK   I'm a damned fine actor, and he ought to consider himself lucky to get me. Instead he picks away at my confidence. Well, this's the last play of his I'm ever going to do, and you can tell him that for me.

He exits backstage.

SUSI   *still mending the cushion*   He's really on the warpath, isn't he? I'm glad I kept my mouth shut.

PEGGY   That's the first time he's attacked Robert. I'm surprised.

GEORGE   Well, it's the first preview tonight. That might have something to do with it.

PHIL   *off*   George, I'm still here. I haven't got all day.

GEORGE   Whenever you're ready, Phil.

PHIL enters, dressed as a priest.

PHIL   Well?

GEORGE   You look great. What's the problem?

PHIL   Are you kidding? Look how tight the pants are. The man's a priest, not a flamenco dancer. What priest wears tight pants? Not only is it sacrilegious, it's worse—it's ludicrous.

GEORGE   They don't look that tight.

PHIL   No, not if I'm dancing *Swan Lake*. George, old buddy, this is a contemporary play. You want me in this costume? Fine. Give me a rapier and change my lines to iambic pentameter.

GEORGE   How is it otherwise?

PHIL   See for yourself. Not only are the pants tight, they're shiny. Is this man so poor he has to iron his own pants?

GEORGE   Is that it?

PHIL   No, this clerical collar's too small. My neck's 15½, this collar's 14. We've got four previews, George. Four previews starting tonight. By the opening my eyes'll bug out so much they'll think I have a thyroid condition.

GEORGE   What else, Phil?

PHIL   Isn't that enough?

GEORGE   All right, I'll see what I can do. Thanks.

PHIL   *as he starts to exit*   I won't even mention the shoes.

GEORGE   What's wrong with the shoes?

PHIL   *stopping*   The right one pinches.

GEORGE   Why just the right?

PHIL   My right foot's one inch longer than my left.   *He points at SUSI.*   And no jokes.

GEORGE   All right. I'll talk to Wardrobe, they must've forgotten. We don't want you mincing in this role.

PHIL   And one last thing, George. Bear with me on this.

GEORGE   What?

PHIL   Believe me, I don't want to be difficult. I hesitate to even mention it, it's the hairpiece. I ask you, what priest wears a toupée?

SUSI   A priest with tight pants.

PHIL   *to GEORGE*   You see that? From the mouth of babes, George. From the mouth of babes.   *to SUSI*   Thank you, sweetheart.

GEORGE   Listen, I was against the hairpiece from the start. It was your idea.

PHIL   Okay, so I changed my mind. It looks tacky. Besides, who the hell needs a rug? I can *act* hair!

He exits backstage.

SUSI   He's making the girls in Wardrobe rich. They've never had so much overtime.

GEORGE   *to the control booth*   Nick, did you get all that?   *then*   Nick?

PEGGY   He may have gone for a coffee.

GEORGE   Then tell Wardrobe to take Phil's pants away for the run-through.

PEGGY   There's nothing wrong with his pants.

GEORGE   I know that, but let him think they've been worked on. He'll drive us crazy, otherwise.

He has finished eating. He crumples the paper bag and tosses it off the stage.

Enter TOM.

TOM   Susi, do you think I could have two comps for tomorrow night? My Dad can't make the opening.

SUSI   No problem. I'll leave two tickets at the box office in your name.

TOM   Great. Thanks.

SUSI   And next time you want a favour, Tom, drop by my apartment. We'll talk about it in the shower.

TOM   Is she kidding, George? I never know when she's kidding.

PEGGY   She's not kidding, Tom. Her water bill's higher than her rent.

GEORGE   Let's skip hygiene for now, Tom. Sit down.   *TOM does.*   Tell me, how's Jess?

TOM   Oh, I think she's fabulous. She's so generous. So easy to work with . . .

GEORGE   No, I mean how's she holding up? It's hard to know with Jess. Did she say anything at lunch?

TOM   She's not showing it, George, but she's really upset. Like, she kept dropping her knife and fork. Things like that.

GEORGE   What else?

TOM   She wouldn't eat her sandwich. Luigi made it with mayonnaise and she made him take it back. Jess never complains like that, even when the toast is burnt.

SUSI   Is Patrick still calling her at three in the morning?

TOM   Yeah, he is. I told her she should take her phone off.

SUSI   And did she?

TOM   Yeah, she did. And two nights running he called the guy next door. He said it was an emergency, her phone was off the hook, and could he run next door and tell her.

GEORGE   *rising*   Jesus, he's impossible.

TOM   I know. Now the guy next door has *his* phone off the hook. So like, last night, guess what happens?

GEORGE   What?

TOM   Around three or four in the morning, she said, a pizza truck pulls up in front of her house.

GEORGE   A pizza truck?

TOM   She says if he gets any more smart ideas and sends an ambulance, she'll go him one better and take it. Then he'll be up a creek.

SUSI   Won't we all?

GEORGE   Okay, thanks, Tom. You better finish dressing.   *TOM is staring at SUSI.*   Tom.

TOM   Oh. You bet.   *He exits.*

NICK   *over the PA*   Peggy, have you finished your preset?

PEGGY   George, is that where you want the armchair? You better double check. Yes, Nick, we're all set.

GEORGE   *to PEGGY*   That's perfect. Would you tell the cast I want to speak to them onstage before the run-through? And tell Jess and Patrick to come out as soon as they're ready.

PEGGY   I'll hurry them up.

GEORGE   One more thing. Any sign of a bottle? *PEGGY shakes her head.*   Well, keep checking the dressing-room. If you find anything, let me know.

PEGGY   Actors who drink make me nervous.

SUSI   Actors who drink and make phone calls at three a.m. make me glad I'm front-of-house. I wouldn't want to be on stage with one.

PEGGY   I like Patrick, though. I know he's a bastard, but he's very sensitive.

She exits backstage.

SUSI   Oh, God, not one of those types. Is she in the right business.

PEGGY   *returning*   Besides, I don't think Patrick even remembers those calls. If he did, how could he look anyone in the eye?   *She exits.*

SUSI   I bet she picks up stray puppies. There. I'm finished, George. Anything else I can do?

GEORGE   Yes, I want you on book for the run-through. Robert's been bitching again. He's worried about the text.

SUSI   George, I don't have all that much time. I still have to clean the lobby and washrooms.

GEORGE   Get one of the other girls to do that. This is more important. The actors really are getting sloppy. Phil is the worst.

SUSI   I can believe that. I've been running lines with him. I know them better than he does.

GEORGE   How's the house?

SUSI   We're sold out. A waiting list of thirty-five, last time I checked. And the word from New York is good. Bernie Feldman is definitely coming.

GEORGE   His office confirmed it?

SUSI   This morning. He'll be here for the opening. So cheer up, treasure. We'll be making headlines.

She exits.

GEORGE   *to the control booth*   Nick, are you in the booth?

NICK   *over the PA*   I'm here.

GEORGE   Good. I want to make a change in the sound level at the top of the show. It's too loud. What is it now?

NICK   It's at four.

GEORGE   Bring it down to three and a half. You got that?

NICK   Yeah, I got it.

GEORGE   And I want the music in faster. As soon as the house goes to half, bring it in and up. Don't wait.

NICK   I wish you'd make up your mind. This morning you told me to go to black before I bring in the music.

GEORGE   That's what run-throughs are for, Nick. So I can change my mind. I may even change it again before we open. Now did you get that? *then* Nick?

NICK   What? The new cue or the sarcasm?

ROBERT enters down the aisle, carrying two cups of coffee in styrofoam cups.

GEORGE   Oh hi, Robert. I thought you'd left.

ROBERT   *suspiciously* Why? Did you want me to?

GEORGE   No, of course not. Listen, did you say anything to Patrick today? Anything that might upset him?

He takes a coffee.

ROBERT   I said hello, that's all. Why? Did he say I upset him?

GEORGE   No, but he's got this idea in his head you don't like what he's doing. I thought maybe you knew why.

ROBERT   Jesus, I think it's the best thing he's ever done. I couldn't be more pleased. I love to come in here and just watch him work.

GEORGE   Don't tell me, tell him.

ROBERT   I couldn't.

GEORGE   Why not?

ROBERT   I couldn't say things like that to his face, I'd be too embarrassed. Besides, it's Jess I'm worried about. She was terrible today.

GEORGE   I know. All of a sudden she's playing emotions instead of objectives.

ROBERT   What're you going to do about it?

GEORGE   Well, it's only been the last couple of days. I'll see what happens in the run-through. Meanwhile, do me a favour: stay out of his way; don't even look at him.

ROBERT   Yeah, and then he'll think for sure I don't like him.

GEORGE   Now you know what I go through. If I spend too much time with Jess, he says I'm neglecting him. If I do give him special attention, he gets insecure and says, "Why don't you work with her? She's the one who needs it."

ROBERT   Be firm. You're the director. Either he gets his act together—

GEORGE   *cutting in* Or what? If I lay down the law, he might quit. It's four days to opening. You want that? *ROBERT says nothing.* He knows damn well we can't replace him. He thinks he can pull any stunt now and get away with it.

ROBERT   That's even more reason to be firm, isn't it? What if Jess decides she can't take any more? What then?

GEORGE   She won't.

ROBERT   How do you know?

GEORGE   Robert, listen to me. She chose this play. It was her idea to do it in Toronto and get a New York producer up.

ROBERT   So?

GEORGE   So, she's not about to let Patrick botch her chance to take this show to Broadway.

ROBERT   Yeah, but how much can she put up with?

GEORGE   A lot. He may be difficult but he's worth it. The best scenes in the play are the ones they have together.

ROBERT   They also happen to be the best-written.

GEORGE   I'm not saying they're not. All I'm saying is he gives her a lot to work with. In other words, he's good for the *play*. And what's good for the play is good for her, for me, and for you. *You*, Robert.

Enter JESSICA followed by PATRICK. She is now wearing a curly blond wig.

JESSICA   George, I want your unbiased opinion. Does this wig look funny?

GEORGE   It doesn't look funny. It looks stunning.

PATRICK   *to JESSICA* I never said the wig looked funny. I said you looked funny in the wig. Hello, Robert. Still waiting to see if I improve?

JESSICA   He'll have a helluva long wait if your talent's as limp as your wit. *to GEORGE* What can we do for you, darling? Peggy said you wanted to see us.

NICK   *over the PA* Top of Act One in five minutes, please.

GEORGE   I want to go over a moment in the second act. There seems to be a slight problem.

JESSICA   What moment's that?

GEORGE   The bit with the apron.

PATRICK   Oh, *that* moment.

JESSICA   I thought that moment worked quite well for me.

PATRICK   I think that's the problem.

GEORGE   I don't want anyone to get hurt. So let's take a look at it. Jess, are you hitting your mark?

JESSICA   I always hit my mark.

PATRICK   Notice how she looks my way? Try to be a little more subtle, love. In the trade we call that "indicating."

JESSICA   Yes, I know. I saw your Shylock.

GEORGE   What about you, Patrick? It seems to me you were a little too far upstage of the table.

PATRICK   Well, I hate to contradict the director, but I was standing exactly where I always stand.

GEORGE   Okay, let's see your positions. That way I can judge for myself.

He goes up the aisle. PATRICK and JESSICA take their positions upstage of the table.

PATRICK   Here it is. I haven't budged since we blocked it.

GEORGE   Are you in position, Jess?

JESSICA   I am.

TOM rushes on, dressed in yellow polo pajamas.

TOM   Do you need me, George? Peggy said you were doing the apron scene.

GEORGE   No, I don't need you, Tom. Thanks anyway.   *TOM exits.*   Patrick, maybe if you moved a step or two closer she'd be more certain of her aim.

PATRICK   If it's a question of aim, I'd prefer to stand in the wings, if you don't mind.

JESSICA   Aren't you being paranoid? It was an accident.

PATRICK   Listen, that was no accident. Once is an accident. Twice is assault with intent to wound. Is that the best you could dream up, an apron in the face?

JESSICA   No, but then it's not four in the morning, is it? Which reminds me. Next time you order pizza, make it a small without anchovies.

PATRICK   What're you talking about?

JESSICA   And call the same place. I adored that curly-haired delivery boy.

PATRICK   I don't know what she's talking about. She's crazy.

GEORGE   Please, Jess, Patrick, the moment's not that important.   *to JESSICA*   From now on just toss the apron at his feet. That'll make the same point.

ROBERT reacts to this.

PATRICK   Fine, but I won't pick it up.

GEORGE   I'm not asking you to. Tom's in the scene, I'll have him pick it up.

ROBERT   Wait a minute, George. Don't you think that weakens the moment? It's much stronger if she hits him.

PATRICK   Listen, boyo, one moment's not going to make or break your precious play, so don't get defensive. I don't care what the script says, I'm not getting an apron snapped in my face. Is that understood?

He exits.

JESSICA   Adamant, isn't he? That's what I like, a man who knows what he doesn't want.   *to ROBERT*   Give me a cigarette, darling.

ROBERT does, and lights it for her.

JESSICA   *as GEORGE comes down the aisle*   Don't worry: no more aprons in the face. I've gotten it out of my system. But God, it felt good. I could've done that all day.

ROBERT   I don't blame you.

JESSICA   *sitting at the table*   What was he like in your first play, Robert? Was he much trouble?

ROBERT   No, but in *Murphy's Diamond* he had top billing. Besides, he always gets along much better with . . .   *He stops, realizing he's almost put his foot in his mouth.*   . . . you know . . . with . . .

He looks desperately to GEORGE for help.

JESSICA   With what? Young actors?

GEORGE   *quickly, as he steps onstage*   I don't think that's what Robert meant. I think he means actors like Tom. Kids he doesn't feel threatened by. You know.   *He gives ROBERT a throat-cutting gesture.*   Pat better watch out, though. He's getting a reputation for being temperamental.

JESSICA   Don't kid yourself. Any actor as good as Flanagan always works. But right now I want to talk about me, not him. How'm I doing, George? I can't tell any more. I feel I'm not doing justice to the woman.

GEORGE   It's coming along beautifully. Isn't it Robert? God, the improvement today in the second act was phenomenal. It's not quite there, granted, but you have no need to worry.

JESSICA   I've been away two years, George. I'm rusty. I can't seem to relax and enjoy it.

GEORGE   You tell her, Robert. She's wonderful, isn't she?

ROBERT   It's a much tougher role than Flanagan's. He has the far more colourful character.

JESSICA   Oh? You think so?

GEORGE   I think what Robert means is that you're very close to this character, and that's hard to play. Whereas Patrick's role is a character role. Isn't that what you meant, Robert?

JESSICA   George, the last two directors I worked with didn't have the guts to level with me, and one was my ex. I would've been better if they'd been more honest.

GEORGE   I'm being as honest as I know how.

JESSICA   I want this play to work for me. I'm counting on it. What I don't need is to be told I'm marvellous when I'm not.

GEORGE   Jess, you're one of the best actresses this country's ever produced. Look at the work you've done in London and New York. My God, most actors would sell out their country to have worked with Olivier.

JESSICA   Is that what you think I've done? Sold out?

GEORGE   No, no. Look, we've all been under a strain the past few days. Once we get in front of an audience Patrick will start to behave himself.

JESSICA   Patrick? Well, if you think Patrick's affecting my performance you better do something about it and damn quick.

Enter PHIL and TOM.

PHIL   Here we are, friends. "The brief abstracts and chroniclers of our time."

TOM   What's that from?

PHIL   *Hamlet.*

TOM   Did you do *Hamlet?*

PHIL   Are you kidding? I've done all the classics.

TOM   Who'd you play, Osric?

PHIL   No, the grave-digger.

GEORGE   Don't believe him. He did the Player Queen and he was damn good, too. He only did the grave-digger one night. Where's Patrick?

PATRICK   *entering* Coming.

PATRICK sits at the table. PEGGY enters and also sits at the table. JESSICA and TOM sit on the sofa. PHIL moves to the armchair and ROBERT to the window seat. GEORGE remains on his feet.

NICK   *over the PA* George, we have two and a half hours to have this run. If you want the actors to have a proper dinner break, we have to start right away.

GEORGE   *to the control booth* This'll only take two minutes.

NICK   We don't have two minutes.

GEORGE   Then we'll make two minutes, won't we?. . .Okay, let's settle down. I just want to say a few words. First, I think you'll all agree we made enormous progress today with Act Two. Some exciting things were beginning to happen. I know you all felt that. *Slight pause.* You did all feel

that, didn't you? I thought the last scene was stupendous. It still needs toning down, but it was really beginning to cook.

PHIL   George, I still don't have the new shoes. Have you spoken to Wardrobe?

GEORGE   No, I haven't had time. I promise you'll have them for tonight. Peggy, make a note of that. Phil has to have new shoes. *to the control booth* Nick, did you hear that?

NICK   *over the PA* What size?

PHIL   A nine and a ten.

NICK   Come again.

GEORGE   He needs two different sizes. One foot's a bit longer than the other. *to PHIL* Actually, you only need one shoe, don't you? The left foot?

PHIL   No, the right. *to NICK* A size ten for the right foot, sweetheart. And make sure they match. I don't want the audience staring at my feet.

GEORGE   Okay, let's go on. Where was I?. . .Oh, yeah. Right now the show's running at least ten minutes too long. We can slash five minutes off tonight by just picking up cues. But don't rush it. Take your beats, take your pauses, but come in sharp on the cues. That's especially true at the beginning. It's important that we get off to a fast start with this play. A lot depends on your energy to drive it forward. Now, you've got four previews. Start working with the audience. By the time we open you'll have the right pace.

PATRICK   Speaking of openings, what's the word from Mecca? Is Feldman coming?

GEORGE   He'll be here for sure, Pat. We just had word today.

PHIL   Beautiful!

TOM   Hollywood, here I come!

PATRICK   God, we're such a bunch of hicks. Let a Yankee producer notice and we all sit up and wag our tails. Well, he's not going to pick all of us. We know who'll get the word and it won't be the men.

JESSICA   Nonsense. If Bernie likes the production, he'll move it intact.

TOM   Why wouldn't he like it? It's a super show.

PHIL   It's an incredible show. He'd have to be a Philistine.

PATRICK   With any luck, he'll give my role to George C. Scott.

NICK   *over the PA* Forgive me, cast, but can't we do that on the dinner break?

PATRICK   Which is fine by me. Not that I have anything against George C. Scott. It's just I'd rather work in Canada. Where else can you be a top-notch actor all your life and still die broke and anonymous?

PHIL   I can't even get arrested in this country.

GEORGE   Okay, people, that's all for now. Are there any questions?

PATRICK   Just one. *indicating PHIL* Does he really have one foot longer than the other?

PHIL   I don't find that amusing.

PATRICK   I doubt if your mother does, either, sweetheart. Must cost her a fortune to keep you in footwear. *He exits.*

PHIL   God, he's ridiculous. My mother hasn't bought my shoes in years.

NICK   *over the PA* Top of Act One in five minutes, please.

JESSICA   *rising and crossing to GEORGE* Interesting, isn't he?

GEORGE   Who?

JESSICA   Flanagan. I've never seen an actor so afraid.

GEORGE   What? Afraid Feldman won't want him?

JESSICA   No. Afraid that he will.... Come along, Tommy. We've got work to do.

TOM   *as he exits with JESSICA* Jess, you know the first scene in Act Two? Does it sound funny the way I laugh? I find it hard to laugh on stage. Way harder than crying....

They exit. GEORGE stands there, thinking about JESSICA's remark. PHIL is still seated in the armchair.

PEGGY   Phil, places have been called.

PHIL   One second, sweetheart. I want a word with George. Be right along.

PEGGY exits backstage.

GEORGE   What's the problem?

PHIL   *crossing to GEORGE* I didn't want to bring this up in front of the others. Not around Flanagan.

GEORGE   What is it?

PHIL   I'm almost afraid to ask.

GEORGE   Don't be silly. What?

PHIL   Will there be a prompter for this show?

He peers eagerly into GEORGE's face.

GEORGE   No. From tonight on you're all on your own out there. If you get in trouble, you'll just have to rely on each other.

PHIL   George, tell me you don't mean it. Tell me it's just your gallows humour. I can take a joke.

GEORGE   I'm sorry. We just don't have the staff. Besides, the theatre's too small. A prompter would be heard in the last row.

He starts up the aisle.

PHIL   I'll tell you what else can be heard in the last row. An actor with his mouth open and no words coming out. Is that what you want? With Bernie Feldman squirming in his seat? I ask you?

ROBERT   *to GEORGE, quickly* I could prompt.

PHIL   God bless you.

GEORGE   *returning to the stage, to ROBERT* I wouldn't let you within ten feet of the stage on opening night. Look what happened at *Murphy's Diamond*.

ROBERT   Anyone can faint.

GEORGE   Before the curtain goes up?

ROBERT   What do you expect? It was my first play.

GEORGE   That's right, and they weren't expecting anything. This time they'll be waiting to see the whites of your eyes.

ROBERT   Did you have to say that?

GEORGE   I just don't want you crashing onto the set in a dead swoon, so forget it. Look, Phil, you'll be great. I realize you have a problem with the odd line, but by opening night...

PHIL is pacing, rubbing his stomach.

What's wrong?

PHIL   It's nothing, nothing.

GEORGE   Come on. What is it?

PHIL   I don't want to burden you, George. It's nothing. *He winces.*

GEORGE   Phil, will you tell me what it is? Maybe I can help.

PHIL   I think it's my ulcer.

GEORGE   I never knew you had an ulcer.

PHIL   Neither did I. Oh, the pain, the pain. Like a kidney stone.

NICK   *over the PA* Should I get him a doctor?

PHIL   No, a prompter!

GEORGE   You don't need a prompter. That's all in your head. You just got off book this morning. The other actors've been off book for two weeks.

PHIL   Sure, rub it in.

GEORGE   I'm not. I'm just saying that's why you're a little unsure of the lines still. We've got four previews. By the time we open you'll be word perfect.

PHIL   What if I dry?

GEORGE   Why should you?

PHIL   I always dry.

GEORGE   That doesn't mean you will this time. Stop thinking that way.

PHIL   George, I have long speeches in this play. Words coming out my ears. If I stumble, I could skip ten pages and not know it. You want ten minutes off the running time? I could easily slash twenty minutes off and still take all my beats and pauses.

ROBERT sits on the sofa and puts his face in his hands.

GEORGE   Phil, you worry too much. You expect to dry, so you dry. Forget about the lines. I don't care if you get it word perfect. Neither does Robert. Isn't that so, Robert?

ROBERT nods, his face in his hands.

PHIL   George, take part of my salary. Pay some kid to stand in the wings with a book. I'll buy the flashlight. Only don't take away my safety net. Look at me. Knots in my stomach, it's only a preview. Think how I'll be opening night. My throat tightens. My heart, George. My heart hammers so loud in my ears I sometimes miss my first cue.

GEORGE   Calm down.

PHIL   It's so bad I once thought of taking lip-reading.

GEORGE   You're working yourself into a stew.

PHIL   I know. And to look at me you'd think I had nerves of steel, right? "Phil," they say, "Phil, you're so relaxed on stage." Oh, if they only knew, George. If they only knew inside I'm twenty different flavours of Jello and a pulse rate of one hundred and forty.

NICK   *over the PA*   George, if Phil has recovered sufficiently I would like to get this show on the road. All actors should be in position. I would like the stage cleared.

ROBERT steps off the stage.

GEORGE   Sorry, Phil. We'll have to do this another time. Just don't underestimate yourself. You're a pro.

He takes his seat on the aisle.

PHIL   You bet your life I'm a pro. You think a novice like Tom would stand here pleading? Begging and grovelling? He hasn't had the experience. I know what it's like to be terrified: I'm a seasoned veteran. So bear that in mind when I implore you not to make me face the audience cold. Would you ask a man afraid of heights to jump from a plane without a parachute? God bless you, but there's a limit, George. A limit to what a man can do for Art. I'm only human. And don't hand me that crap you can't afford it. If you can afford to buy me shoes, you can afford a prompter.

NICK   *over the PA*   For the last time, can we please clear the stage? We'll be starting in one minute. That's sixty seconds.

Lights begin to dim and music starts.

PHIL   I see I'm wasting my breath. Okay, have it your way, old buddy.   *He starts to exit.*   Just don't say I never warned you. I love this play, and if I botch it, I'll never forgive you.

He exits backstage, only to poke his head out the window.

Look, George, hear me out. I can't afford to screw up. Feldman's my only hope: he's an American.

NICK   Thirty seconds.

PHIL   Down there they embrace success. Up here it's like stepping out of line.

NICK   Twenty seconds.

PHIL   Don't you see? I may never get a break like this again. That's all I'm saying.

NICK   Fifteen.

PHIL   You're all heart, Nick!

He exits. ROBERT starts up the aisle and SUSI starts down.

SUSI   *to GEORGE*   Sorry, treasure, I was cleaning the lobby.

She sits in the aisle.

GEORGE   Now remember: underline anything they get wrong, no matter how small. And if Phil needs a line, give it to him.

The theatre is in blackness, except for the light of the flashlight.

ROBERT   Hey, George.

GEORGE   What?

ROBERT   Why do you think they're waiting to see the whites of my eyes?

GEORGE   Robert, please! That was just a figure of speech!

Lights up onstage. JESSICA is alone onstage, watering the hanging plants. After a moment, PATRICK comes down the stairs. He is shirtless, and is doing up his belt. He glances at JESSICA, who ignores him. He crosses to the table and pours himself a cup of coffee.

PATRICK   *with an Italian accent*   Why'd you get so upset for, Lizzie? All I asked is how long is he going to stay?

JESSICA   He's home for the holidays. That's all I know. What do you want me to do, tell him to go to a hotel? He's my son.

PATRICK   I don't like the way he looks at me. Like I'm not good enough to sit on the furniture. He'd better not start that today, because if he does, he'll wish like hell he didn't.

JESSICA   I don't want trouble, Frank.

PATRICK *sitting at the table* Then put his nose back in joint or I'll do it for him.

The doorbell rings.

JESSICA That's Eric, now.

She sets down the watering-can and switches off the hi-fi.

PATRICK Where the hell are my shoes?

JESSICA Honestly, you're worse than Jimmy.

She stands behind his chair and strokes his chest.

Your shoes are upstairs. And would you please put on a shirt?

PATRICK Lizzie, I'll give the kid two weeks. Either he's gone or I go. Make up your mind. *He rises.*

JESSICA Don't threaten me.

PATRICK Two weeks, Lizzie.

He exits upstairs. The doorbell rings again. JESSICA crosses into the hallway out of sight. We hear the door open and close.

PHIL *off* Hello, Elizabeth.

JESSICA *off* Hi, Eric. Come in. You look half-frozen.

PHIL and JESSICA enter, PHIL taking off his overcoat. He glances into the living-room. He seems quite relieved to find it empty.

JESSICA Here. Let me take your coat. *She hangs his hat, coat, and scarf on the hat rack.* I appreciate this, Eric. I wouldn't have called if it wasn't important.

PHIL I know that. That's why I'm here. *He crosses near the sofa.* What is it? Frank?

JESSICA No, it's Jimmy.

PHIL Oh?

JESSICA Sit down. I just made a fresh pot of coffee. Have you eaten?

PHIL Nothing for me. I had breakfast at the rectory.... What's happened, Sis?

JESSICA He's quit school.

PHIL Jimmy quit school?

He sits on the sofa, near the arm.

JESSICA He says he's had all he can take of university and wants to stay here until he figures out what he's going to do. *She sits on the arm of the sofa.* I'd hate to see him make a mistake, Eric. I don't want him to do something he'll regret later on.

PHIL Well, maybe university isn't what he needs right now.

JESSICA *putting her hand on his knee* Please, I want you to talk to him. You're the only one who can. He won't listen to me.

PHIL And how's Frank feel about all this?

JESSICA He doesn't know yet. All he knows is Jimmy's home for the winter break.

PHIL nods. And nods. Clears his throat.

GEORGE Patrick, that was your cue.

PATRICK *off* I beg to differ. My cue is Phil's line, "I see." I didn't hear it.

PHIL I didn't say it.

GEORGE Did you forget?

PHIL No. I thought I'd try not saying it. Don't you feel the silence is more telling?

PATRICK *off* The only actor I know who likes to cut his lines.

PHIL That's because I can *act* them.

PATRICK *off* Act all you want, mate, only don't act my cues. I'll be up here all night.

GEORGE What do you think, Robert?

ROBERT Cut the line. He doesn't need it.

PHIL There. The author.

GEORGE Okay, Patrick, take your cue from Jessica's "Jimmy's home for the winter break." Jess, take it back to "Let me take your coat."

PHIL George, can I look away when she starts that crap about Jimmy? I did this time. It felt better.

GEORGE *angrily* Look, we can't have these interruptions! We have a preview tonight! Let's just get on with it! When you're ready, Jess. Thank you.

PHIL gives GEORGE a look. Then he and JESSICA get into position. He takes his overcoat off the hat rack and glances again at GEORGE.

JESSICA Here. Let me take your coat.

PHIL thrusts it at her.

JESSICA I appreciate this, Eric. I wouldn't have called if it wasn't important.

PHIL *irritably* I know that. That's why I'm here. *He crosses near the sofa.* What is it? Frank?

JESSICA No, it's Jimmy.

PHIL Oh?

JESSICA Sit down. I just made a fresh pot of coffee. Have you eaten?

PHIL Nothing for me. I had brunch at the rectory. . . . What's happened, Sis?

JESSICA He's quit school.

PHIL Jimmy's quit school?

He sits on the sofa, near the arm.

JESSICA He says he's had all he can take of university and wants to stay here until he figures out what he's going to do. *She sits on the arm of the sofa.* I'd hate to see him make a mistake, Eric. I don't want him to do something he'll regret later on.

PHIL   Well, maybe college isn't what he needs right now.

He sneers out at GEORGE.

JESSICA   *putting her hand on his knee* Please, I want you to talk to him. You're the only one who can. He won't listen to me.

PHIL   And how's Frank feel about all this?

JESSICA   He doesn't know yet. All he knows is Jimmy's home for the winter break.

PATRICK comes down the stairs, laughing.

PHIL   *rising* Hello, Frank.

PATRICK   *to JESSICA* You ought to see that kid of yours. He can't even get his socks on. What, they don't teach him to drink in college? *to PHIL* So how's it going, Father? You still dipping into the poorbox?

JESSICA   Frank, you're awful. *to PHIL* He's just pulling your leg.

PHIL   Is he?

PATRICK   Did she tell you? The kid took a swing at me last night.

PHIL   *putting a cigarette in his mouth* No, Elizabeth never mentioned it. . . .

He fishes in his pockets for matches.

PATRICK   He thought he could drink me under the table.

He brings out his lighter and lights PHIL's cigarette.

PHIL   Thanks. . . . He's going through a very difficult period, Jimmy.

PATRICK   Well, he better get over it fast or he'll get his ass kicked.

JESSICA   Frank, please.

PATRICK   I mean it, Lizzie.

PHIL   He needs understanding right now, not brute force.

PATRICK   Is that so?

He sits on the sofa and stares at PHIL.

JESSICA   *moving behind PATRICK* Honey, let Eric handle it. He knows how to talk to Jimmy. Okay?

She leans over to kiss the top of his head, but as she does so, PATRICK ducks and leaps to his feet. He stares at GEORGE, grimacing.

GEORGE   *moving to the stage* What's wrong?

PATRICK   I don't like that kiss, I've never liked it, I can't do it.

GEORGE   Patrick, we can't keep starting and stopping like this. We'll never get through the play.

PHIL   How come *he* doesn't get hell? I notice you don't say he's interrupting. With him it's starting and stopping.

GEORGE   *to PATRICK* What's wrong with the kiss?

PATRICK   I don't believe her.

JESSICA   Listen, you, I was doing leading ladies when you were failing to get through adolescence. So don't tell me how to act.

PATRICK   I forgot: she's worked with Mike Nichols. Let's all curtsy.

JESSICA   At least I've got the guts to work outside this country.

PATRICK   The truth is your last two Broadway plays died in the first week. You haven't acted in theatre for two years. You're living in the past, lady.

GEORGE   Okay, take it easy. Let's just solve the problem and get back to work. We're running behind. *to PATRICK* What is it about the kiss you don't believe?

PATRICK   First of all, the priest hates my guts. He resents the fact we're living together, and here she is kissing me after I've just insulted him. Not only is it unbelievable, it's maudlin.

JESSICA   It's not maudlin, it's tender. And perfectly in character.

PATRICK   Well, it's not in character for me to let you. At that moment Frank doesn't want to be touched. It makes his skin crawl.

JESSICA   We all make sacrifices, don't we? Personally, I would rather kiss a monkey's ass. Now let's get on with it.

GEORGE   Yes, we're wasting time. Maybe there's another way to make the same point. *He looks out at ROBERT.* What do you think, Robert?

ROBERT   I don't see the problem. I think it works.

PATRICK   How predictable.

ROBERT   It's worked all along, hasn't it? Why does it suddenly not work?

PATRICK   Why? Because I've never questioned it before. I've always done it because those were the stage directions. *Your* stage directions.

ROBERT   I see.

PATRICK   That's Phil's line. It's been cut.

ROBERT   Why're you so hostile? What did I do?

He starts down the aisle.

PATRICK   I criticize his masterpiece, and suddenly I'm hostile.

ROBERT   That's not what I meant, and you know it. If you've got a beef, tell me.

GEORGE   *to ROBERT*   Okay, don't get hot under the collar.   *to PATRICK*   Let's just cut the kiss and get on with it.   *to JESSICA*   Put your hand on his shoulder. That'll make the same point.

ROBERT   *stepping onstage*   No, goddamnit!

GEORGE   Look, Robert—

ROBERT   *cutting in*   What the hell is this? That's a very significant and subtle moment. She's letting Eric know if it comes to a choice she'll choose Frank over him and the son. That's what the kiss means.

PATRICK   *to GEORGE*   Look, mate, get him out of here. He's done his work, now let the actors do theirs. We have enough on our hands without him on our backs.

JESSICA   He's not on your back.

PATRICK   *in a rage*   He's here every goddamn day, isn't he? I wouldn't mind if he cringed in a corner somewhere. But no, he paces around like a condemned man. Even when I can't see him I can *feel* him. He's out there wringing his hands, sighing and wincing, leaping to his feet every time we drop a monosyllable, every time we change a bit of business. Christ, what's more important, George? That we observe every arbitrary stage direction or nail down a character?

GEORGE   He has a point, Robert.

PATRICK   And on top of that, he has the bloody nerve to tell me I'm incompetent.

ROBERT   I never once said that.

PATRICK   One hit play to his name, and he thinks he's hot stuff. A play that I helped create, by the way. And I've got the reviews to prove it.

ROBERT   I never said you were incompetent.

PATRICK   Maybe I've never played Washington or Dallas or New York, but I've been from one end of this country to the other.

JESSICA   So has the railroad. Get to the point.

PATRICK   *to ROBERT*   I've done it all, too, from the Greeks to Beckett. I even had the misfortune to be in two one-acters called *Lay of the Land* and *Giving Head*. But not even the author of those two epics had the audacity to walk into a theatre, as you did today, and say to me, "Are you getting any better?" She had a little more class than that.

ROBERT   So that's it.

PATRICK   And don't try to wriggle out of it.

ROBERT   That was a joke. You ought to know me better than that. That's just my sense of humour.

PATRICK   Sense of humour? Mate, if that's your idea of a joke, don't ever attempt comedy.

ROBERT   I was being ironic. I thought you knew that.

PATRICK   Try flattery next time. Irony belongs in plays. Irony makes me insecure. Irony makes me think you don't like what I'm doing.

ROBERT   Nothing could be further from the truth. I think you're a superb actor. One of the best actors I've worked with.

PATRICK   He calls that flattery. He's done two plays and the first had a cast of two, including myself.

JESSICA   *exasperated*   George, when you have things under control, let me know. I'll be in the dressing-room.

She exits backstage.

PATRICK   *to ROBERT*   In the future, if you have a future, don't come bouncing into rehearsal and slap an actor on the back and get cute. Just tell him he's fantastic and bite your tongue.

ROBERT   Go to hell!

NICK   *over the PA*   George, I realize how little respect you have for stage managers, but I feel I have the right to know what's going on. Are we having a run-through or just a rehearsal? And either way, could we please carry on?

GEORGE   Oh, get off my back!

NICK   Fine. I only hope you realize that after six-thirty we'll be into overtime.

GEORGE   I could replace you with a recorded announcement.

NICK   At the rate you pay, you just might have to.

PHIL   Friends, I've been patient up to now. I've stood here and not said a word. Now I'm annoyed. No, incensed. Outraged that one member of this company is allowed to waste valuable time with his petty, childish behaviour. Not only that, he doesn't get reprimanded.

PATRICK   And who might that be, may I ask?

GEORGE   *angrily*   Okay, okay, this is getting out of hand.

PHIL   *to PATRICK*   If the shoe fits, old buddy. If the shoe fits.

PATRICK   Well, at least we know he's not talking about himself.

GEORGE   Goddamnit, let's stop it!   *to the control booth*   Nick, let's take it from the top. As soon as you're ready.

NICK   *over the PA*   This is a recorded announcement. Places for the top of Act One. Stand by to go in three minutes. Peggy, could you come out and put the coffee back in the pot? And reset the chairs.

PEGGY enters and does her job.

PATRICK   *to PHIL*   That was quite a speech. More than twenty words in a row and you never dried once. 'Course it was off the cuff, wasn't it?

He smiles and exits backstage.

PHIL   *to GEORGE*   Did you hear that? He wants to undermine my confidence. Well, he doesn't know it yet but the laugh's on him. I don't have any!

He exits backstage.

GEORGE   Robert, I could've handled him, if you'd just let me. Next time stay out of it.

ROBERT   Like hell I will. He's not pushing me around. And I'm not losing that moment.

GEORGE   Stop worrying. I'll have that moment back before we open. I promise.   *ROBERT doesn't seem convinced.*   I give you my word. Trust me.

ROBERT   George, don't say "Trust me." Any time I hear "Trust me" I know I'm about to be screwed.

GEORGE   What're you saying? That you don't trust me? That hurts, Robert.

ROBERT   Listen, you know how long it took me to write *The Care and Treatment of Roses*. I never thought I'd finish.

GEORGE   You had a big success with your first play. That made the second that much harder to write.

ROBERT   So what if it gets panned? What'll I have to show for three years of my life? What?

GEORGE   It won't get panned.

ROBERT   No?

GEORGE   It's a beautiful play.

ROBERT   Yeah, I know. Every play's a beautiful play. Then it gets knocked, and suddenly everyone has second thoughts. Instant hindsight.

NICK   *over the PA*   Two minutes to curtain.

GEORGE   I'm doing my best, okay? I want this to be bigger than *Murphy's Diamond*. Robert, this theatre's done four turkeys in a row. We need a hit or else.

ROBERT   George, they're waiting to see the whites of my eyes. I know it.

GEORGE   Forget I said that, will you?

ROBERT   No, it's true. They hate success in this country. They punish you for it. I mean, if I get slaughtered I want it to be my own fault. They don't know an actor wouldn't do a moment. He's not the one they'll blame.

GEORGE   All right, if I don't get you that moment back, I'll call every critic in town and let them know.

NICK   *over the PA*   One minute to curtain. Clear the stage, please.

GEORGE   *leading ROBERT to the edge of the stage*   Look, do me a favour. Go away. Go to a movie.

ROBERT   I hate movies.

GEORGE   Then get drunk.

ROBERT   I can't drink. I'm not supposed to.

GEORGE   Go home then. Take a Valium and sleep until the preview.

ROBERT   I already took two Libriums. That's why I'm not supposed to drink. What're you trying to say, George? You don't want me around?

GEORGE   I don't think it's wise, do you? For the sake of the play, Robert. The *play*.

ROBERT   Okay, I'll go. . .   *He steps off the stage.* But only because you asked me, not because of Flanagan.   *He starts up the aisle.*   Boy, some day I'd like to get that bastard in an alley. . .

He smashes his right fist into his palm.

GEORGE   Robert.

ROBERT   What?

GEORGE   Take another Librium, it wouldn't hurt. Or better still, work on your new play.

The stage lights are dimming and the music has begun.

ROBERT   Jesus, what a business. When you're unknown and fall on your face, they pity you. When you're successful and take a beating, they say you deserved it.

GEORGE   Forget the critics, will you?

ROBERT   Who's talking about critics? I meant my writer friends. They're far more vicious.

He exits. GEORGE steps off the stage and takes his seat on the aisle. The theatre is now in blackness.

GEORGE   Stay on book, Susi, but forget what I said before. At this stage of the game, harping on lines would only demoralize them more.

Lights up onstage. JESSICA is alone onstage, watering the hanging plants. After a moment, PATRICK comes down the stairs. He is shirtless, and is doing up his belt. He glances at JESSICA, who ignores him. He crosses to the table and pours himself a cup of coffee.

PATRICK   *with an Italian accent*   Why'd you get so upset for, Lizzie? All I asked is how long is he going to stay?

JESSICA   He's home for the holidays. That's all I know. What do you want me to do, tell him to go to a hotel? He's my son.

PATRICK   I don't like the way he looks at me. Like I'm not good enough to sit on the furniture. He'd better not start that today, because if he does, he'll wish like hell he didn't.

JESSICA   I don't want trouble, Frank.

PATRICK   *sitting at the table*   Then put his nose back in joint or I'll do it for him.

Slight pause.

JESSICA   Did you hear the doorbell?

GEORGE leaps to his feet and glares at the control booth, jabbing his finger in the direction of the front door. Suddenly there is a knocking on the door. GEORGE sits and shakes his head.

JESSICA   That's Eric, now.

She sets down the watering-can and switches off the hi-fi.

PATRICK   Where the hell are my shoes?

JESSICA   Honestly, you're worse than Jimmy.

She stands behind his chair and strokes his chest.

Your shoes are upstairs. And would you please put on a shirt?

PATRICK   Lizzie, I'll give the kid two weeks. Either he's gone or I go. Make up your mind.

He rises.

JESSICA   Don't threaten me.

PATRICK   Two weeks, Lizzie.

He exits upstairs. A second knock on the door. JESSICA crosses into the hallway out of sight. We hear the door open and shut.

PHIL   *off*   Hello, Elizabeth.

JESSICA   *off*   Hi, Eric. Come in. You look half-frozen.

PHIL   *as he enters*   Not half as frozen as that doorbell.

NICK   *over the PA*   Sorry.

JESSICA   Here. Let me take your coat.

She hangs his hat, coat, and scarf on the hat rack.

I appreciate this, Eric. I wouldn't have called if it wasn't important.

PHIL   I know that. That's why I'm here.   *He crosses near the sofa.*   What is it? Jimmy?

JESSICA   No, it's—Yes, it *is* Jimmy, as a matter of fact.

PHIL   Oh.

JESSICA   Sit down. I just made a fresh pot of coffee. Have you eaten?

PHIL   Nothing for me. I just had a snack at the rectory. . . . What's happened, Sis?

JESSICA   He's quit school.

PHIL   Jimmy quit school?

He sits on the sofa, far from the arm.

JESSICA   He says he's had all he can take of university and wants to stay here until he figures out what he wants to do.   *She sits on the arm of the sofa.*   I'd hate to see him make a mistake, Eric. I don't want him to do something he'll regret later on.

PHIL   Well, maybe university isn't what he needs right now.

JESSICA   *leaning and stretching to put her hand on his knee*   Please, I want you to talk to him. You're the only one who can. He won't listen to me.

PHIL   And how's Frank feel about all this?

JESSICA   He doesn't know yet. All he knows is Jimmy's home for the winter break.

PATRICK comes down the stairs, laughing.

PHIL   I see.

PATRICK's laughter stops, then starts again.

PHIL   *rising*   Hello, Frank.

PATRICK   I see. I see, I see, I see . . .   *to JESSICA*   Well, you ought to *see* that kid of yours. He can't even get his socks on. What, they don't teach him to drink in college?   *to PHIL*   So, Father, I see you, I see you. How's it going? You still dipping into the poorbox?

JESSICA   Frank, you're awful.   *to PHIL*   He's just pulling your leg.

PHIL   I see!

PATRICK   Did she tell you? The kid took a swing at me last night.

PHIL   *putting a cigarette in his mouth*   No, Elizabeth never mentioned it. . . .

He fishes in his pockets for matches.

PATRICK   He thought he could drink me under the table.

He brings out his lighter to light PHIL's cigarette. PHIL bends to accept the light, and as he does so, a tall flame shoots up like a blowtorch from the adjustable lighter. PHIL recoils instinctively. He reaches for the vase of red roses on the coffee table and hurls the roses and water into PATRICK's face. PHIL dashes around the table, and with a wild look of outrage, PATRICK starts after him. GEORGE rushes down the aisle to the stage. Pandemonium ensues.

GEORGE   Cut! Cut! Cut!

Blackout. Music.

ACT TWO

The dressing-room, four days later. It is 7:45 on opening night. The dressing-room contains a make-up table with mirror and four chairs, a clothes-rack, and all the usual odds and ends. On the table in front of PATRICK's chair are a shoebox and an electric razor. Downstage are two chairs separated by a small wooden stand. On the stand are a newspaper and an ashtray. Stage right is the wash-room. Upstage is the door that leads into the backstage area. Next to the dressing-room, stage left, is the Green Room. It is small and contains a fridge, sofa, end tables, a telephone, and a coffee percolator on a small table. A door leads into the Green Room from the street.

At rise, JESSICA is dressed in costume, except for her wig which is still on the wig-stand. She stands near the make-up table, buttoning her blouse. Then she crosses and looks at herself in the mirror on the washroom door.

In the Green Room, PATRICK reclines on the sofa, wearing glasses to read his script. He is dressed in bathrobe and pants. He glances at his silver pocket watch and goes back to the script.

PEGGY enters from the street door, carrying a stack of styrofoam cups, a box of sugar cubes, and a pair of pants on a wooden hanger. She sets down the cups and the sugar, then enters the dressing-room and hangs up the pants.

PATRICK   Any sign of the others?

PEGGY   Not yet, Pat.

PATRICK   What about George?

PEGGY   He still hasn't come back from dinner. I told Susi you wanted to see him.

She comes back into the Green Room and pours herself a cup of coffee. PATRICK watches her a moment.

PATRICK   God, you're lovely, Peg. A Yeats poem made flesh. Did I try to get fresh last night?

PEGGY   Not at all.

PATRICK   I've drawn a blank, you know.

PEGGY   You were a perfect gentleman.

JESSICA   *into the mirror*   Watch him, Peg.

PATRICK   I was very fond of a girl once who looked like you.

PEGGY   I know. You told me last night.

PATRICK   I did?

PEGGY   You said I reminded you of your ex-wife. I thought that was very sweet.

PATRICK   What actually happened after we got back to my place?

PEGGY   You want the truth?

PATRICK   Not if you put it like that.

PEGGY   *entering the dressing-room*   It's just that I've never put a man's teeth in a glass before.

PATRICK   Was it you who did that? Good God.

PEGGY   I had to. You were so drunk you might've choked in your sleep.

She goes to the box with the actors' valuables in it.

PATRICK   Do you know how hard I searched this morning? I tore the house apart. For God's sake, girl, don't you know you never put teeth in a fridge?

JESSICA   *to PEGGY*   Darling, you just made my day.

PATRICK   Listen, you two, don't spread that around. You know how malicious the gossip is in this town. "Reputation," Peggy, "is an idle and most false imposition; oft got without merit, and lost without deserving."

JESSICA   *sitting at the make-up table*   That wasn't from the Scottish play, I hope.

PATRICK   *Othello*. And I'm not in the least super-stitious.

He removes his glasses, rises, and wanders into the dressing-room, aimless, restless, distracted. PEGGY smiles, blows him a kiss, then exits into the backstage area.

JESSICA   *after a moment*   It must be late . . .

PATRICK   Quarter to eight.

He takes his shirt off the hanger, examines it, then takes a needle and thread from his shoebox. He sits and sews the shirt, singing a few lines from an Irish folk song.

Must be an easier way to make a living.

JESSICA ignores him. She is flattening out her hair with bobby pins in preparation for the wig.

PATRICK   You know, the day I left Ireland was the day after I got married. The old man called me a lazy, shiftless sonofabitch and said I'd never do an honest day's work in my life. Imagine that.

JESSICA   How prophetic.

PATRICK   I know, and I wasn't even an actor yet.

JESSICA turns and looks at him.

JESSICA   How do you feel?

PATRICK   Why do you ask?

JESSICA   In case you haven't noticed, you only shaved on one side of your face.

PATRICK   Did I?   *He looks in the mirror.*   So I did.

JESSICA   Your good side, naturally.

PATRICK   Instinct.   *He leans close to the mirror.*
Jesus H. Christ. . .

JESSICA   What is it?

PATRICK   The lines around the eyes. Laugh lines.
No, they are. And speaking of laugh lines, I wish I
had a few more in this friggin' play.   *He shaves.*

JESSICA   Tell me, Flanagan. Will you go to New
York if Bernie wants you?

PATRICK   *clicking off the razor*   Why wouldn't
he want me?

JESSICA   Oh, I'm sure he will. . . . The cast works
so well together. Not a single weak link. Don't you
agree?

*PATRICK clicks on his razor and goes back to
shaving.*

JESSICA   Why? Who do you think's the weak one?
Phil? Tommy? . . . Well, that just leaves the two of
us, doesn't it?

She turns and goes back to fixing her hair.

PATRICK   Between you and me, I think we should
leave well enough alone. I think Broadway's had
enough domestic dramas.

JESSICA   I don't believe you can second-guess an
audience any more than you can the critics. All you
can do is a play you believe in.

PATRICK   The critics there would laugh us out of
town.

JESSICA   They could do the same here, couldn't
they?

PATRICK   New York's tougher.

JESSICA   That's never stopped anyone. We take
risks all the time, don't we? New York's just a larger
arena. Higher stakes.

PATRICK   Well, I'm a Catholic and Catholics are
against suicide. Besides, I don't think we should
judge success by New York. No, really. I've never
felt that or I'd be there, wouldn't I?

JESSICA   Flanagan, haven't you ever imagined yourself on Broadway? Believe me, it's the most exciting
feeling in the world, bar none. And you know what's
the nicest part? You feel you deserve it.

PATRICK   Yes, but how does it feel to get clob-
bered?

JESSICA   I wouldn't know.

PATRICK   You were in two flops.

JESSICA   The plays were; I wasn't.

PATRICK   Well, I'd feel I deserved it.

JESSICA   *into the mirror*   Our sense of ourselves
is so tentative, isn't it? Maybe that's the real risk we
take.

PATRICK   What's that?

JESSICA   Facing our own sense of failure.

PATRICK   Look, I make a damn good living here. I
have my pick of roles. I might not be a Star, but
who is in this country? And not everyone feels that
compulsion to outshine.

JESSICA   You don't need to get defensive. If you
don't want to go, that's your problem.

PATRICK   Christ, you sound like my ex-wife. All
she ever wanted was Success with a capital *S*. The
old Bitch-Goddess, to quote William James. As if
there's something wrong with not wanting to work
your butt off for agents and accountants and Internal
Revenue.

JESSICA   Maybe she thought you were settling for
too little.

PATRICK   Well, I've seen the Bitch-Goddess up
close. I've had a sniff or two up her skirt, I know
what she's like, she's insatiable, a parasite, a cancer.
She gets on your back like the Old Man of the Sea
and won't get off.

JESSICA   The trick is to ride success and not let it
ride you.

PATRICK   Well, I'm the one who has to go out
there and be good. She never understood that, my
wife. She. . .   *Then, as if he has said too much
already*   Look, let's drop it, shall we? And before I
forget: I don't appreciate being upstaged. You did it
again last night.

*He enters the Green Room and pours himself a
coffee. PEGGY returns.*

JESSICA   When?

PATRICK   You know when.

JESSICA   I haven't the foggiest.

PATRICK   The supper scene.

JESSICA   Oh, is that why you looked so upset? I
thought you had gas.

PATRICK   And while we're at it, don't cross your
legs onstage. Last night you sat on the sofa working
your legs like a pair of scissors. Freud would have
had a field-day with that gesture.

JESSICA   I was simply working up a breeze. Didn't
you find it stifling out there?

PATRICK   The first three rows don't have to know
you're wearing black lace panties.

JESSICA   I bet you were the only one who noticed.
Did you also notice the bruise on my left thigh?

PATRICK   No, I didn't. And it was your *right* thigh.
God knows how you got that.

Enter NICK from the street door.

NICK Peggy, have you finished your preset? I want to open the house.

PEGGY Nick, that was done ages ago.

NICK How about Patrick? Does he have his new prop?

PATRICK I do, and I bloody well resent the implication.

He removes a small Ronson lighter from his pocket and flicks it to produce a small, weak flame.

To cover myself I should have two of these. If they both fail, I can rub them together to get a light. *to PEGGY* That reminds me, love. Could you please put a little more tea in the whiskey bottle? There's only one thing worse than having to drink that vile stuff and that's not having enough. Last night I had to squeeze the bottle.

JESSICA I thought he was being cheap with his shots.

NICK Oh, and before I forget, Jessica, you still haven't signed the callboard. Some stage managers don't mind, but I'm very, very strict about that.

JESSICA You can see I'm here. Sign it yourself.

NICK I'd rather you did. I don't want to start getting into bad habits. *to PEGGY* What about the cue light? Phil was late last night on his second entrance.

PEGGY There's nothing wrong with the cue light. He's been taking a verbal cue from Pat and he missed it.

PATRICK He was too busy giving himself the last rites.

NICK *to PEGGY* Well, tell him I'll cue him in. I don't want that to happen again.

PEGGY I'll remind him.

She exits into the backstage area. NICK starts into the Green Room. He stops suddenly and turns.

NICK *Now*, Jessica, please.

He exits out the street door.

JESSICA Did you hear that? Who does he think he's ordering around?

PATRICK What do you expect, reverence? I find him refreshingly democratic. He treats us all with equal contempt.

GEORGE enters from the backstage area. Dressed in a navy-blue suit, he carries a bouquet of long-stemmed red roses and a shopping bag containing wine and presents.

GEORGE Hello, Jess, Patrick.

JESSICA Oh, George, am I glad to see you. Don't you look handsome.

GEORGE *setting down the shopping bag* You look wonderful yourself, love. *He kisses her cheek.* Radiant.

He hands JESSICA the flowers.

These are for you, Jess. I hope you like roses.

JESSICA I adore roses. Oh, aren't they lovely. *She embraces him, kissing his cheek.* Thank you, darling.

PATRICK *into his newspaper* What's in the bag, a vase?

GEORGE Oh, God, I completely forgot.

JESSICA That's okay. I'll find one.

GEORGE Stay where you are. I'll get one in Props.

JESSICA No, I insist. Besides, I have to sign the callboard or Nick'll report me to Equity.

She exits out the street door.

PATRICK *to himself* Roses. How cliché.

GEORGE takes a box tied with ribbons from the shopping bag and crosses to PATRICK.

GEORGE For you, Pat.

PATRICK For me? You're kidding.

GEORGE tosses him the box, and PATRICK flicks off the ribbon and lifts the lid. He laughs.

GEORGE You recognize it?

PATRICK *removing a catcher's mask* The catcher's mask from *Murphy's Diamond*. Thanks, mate, I'm touched. No, really. That play meant a lot to me. When it closed, there was more of a hole in my life than when I got divorced. Then again, I had more fun in the play. Did Susi give you my message?

GEORGE *taking two bottles of champagne from the shopping bag and crossing to the fridge* Yeah, what is it? She said it was urgent.

PATRICK It's crucial. Did you speak to Phil about last night?

GEORGE Yeah, I did. And believe me, he's upset enough already.

PATRICK He ought to be. He botched the entire first act.

GEORGE Look, it wasn't that serious. The audience didn't even notice.

PATRICK How could they help but notice? There we are, our big scene at the breakfast table. He's right in the middle of his long speech and suddenly he gets this strange look in his eye. "Excuse me, Frank," he says, and walks offstage.

GEORGE He dried. He ran back to get his line from Peggy.

PATRICK I know, and left me alone on stage. No dialogue, no business, nothing to do but sit there and eat my bacon and eggs. He was gone so long I had a second cup of coffee.

GEORGE It didn't seem that long. I'm telling you, no one noticed.

PATRICK George, you've never been an actor. Long doesn't begin to describe it. Now I know what they mean by a pregnant pause. By the time he came back I was in labour. And then he sits back down as though nothing has happened and says, "So as I was saying, Frank . . ."

GEORGE Pat, it won't happen again. Next time he'll just ad lib.

PATRICK Next time?

GEORGE If it does happen, I mean.

PATRICK There better not be a next time, mate. Because if he walks offstage tonight, I'm walking off behind him. And I don't care if Feldman *is* in the audience.

GEORGE Forget Feldman. I wish I'd never heard of Feldman. He's probably so jaded he won't like the show anyway.

PATRICK That's what Jess thinks.

GEORGE What do you mean?

PATRICK She's heard he's had second thoughts about the play. That's between you and me.

GEORGE That's ridiculous. Feldman's crazy about it. Why do you think he's coming tonight?

PATRICK If you ask me, she's getting cold feet. Oh, she puts up a good front, but underneath it all she's terrified. I think she's into the sauce.

GEORGE You think so?

PATRICK I know so. It's those New York critics. She's convinced they're out to get her.

GEORGE The thing to remember, Patrick, is no actor is under any obligation to this show after it closes here. That goes for Jess or anyone. Even you.

PATRICK Oh, I couldn't go if I wanted to. Didn't I tell you? I'm already committed to another play.

Enter JESSICA carrying a vase.

JESSICA No sign of Phil or Tommy? It's almost eight.

GEORGE They may be in the theatre. I'll check with front-of-house.

JESSICA carries the vase and roses into the washroom, leaving the door ajar. She runs the water. GEORGE closes the door quickly and takes PATRICK aside.

GEORGE What do you mean you can't do the play? That's not what you told me six weeks ago.

PATRICK Sorry, mate, you misunderstood.

GEORGE You knew the whole production might move to New York. I made that clear.

PATRICK I already gave my word. The director's an old, old friend of mine. I can't let him down.

GEORGE Who is it?

PATRICK I'm not in a position to say at the moment. Just a dear, dear friend.

GEORGE What play are you doing?

PATRICK What's that matter? The point is I have a commitment which I don't intend to break. I gave my word, and that's it.

GEORGE Well, the most important thing right now is that we do the play here and do it right. I don't care what happens after that.

He starts for the backstage door.

PATRICK George. *GEORGE stops.* I'm sorry.

GEORGE It's okay, Pat. I understand.

PATRICK And speak to Mastorakis again, will you? By now he's probably forgotten.

GEORGE Relax. Stop worrying. Just go out there tonight and have fun.

He exits to the backstage area.

PATRICK Relax, he says. That's easy for him to say. His work's done. He can sit in the dark now and chew his cuticles. I've got to go out there with a kid fresh out of Theatre School and a forty-four-year-old Greek with a mind like Rip Van Winkle.

The doorknob rattles.

JESSICA *off* This damn door's stuck again. Give us a pull, Flanagan.

PATRICK One second.

He removes a bottle of whiskey from the shoebox on the make-up table and takes a good drink.

JESSICA *off* Flanagan!

PATRICK Hold your horses.

NICK *over the PA, as PATRICK crosses to the washroom* Good evening, ladies and gentlemen, this is your half-hour call. If you are in the theatre and have not signed the callboard, would you please do so now?

PATRICK pulls the door open. JESSICA strides out.

JESSICA If he mentions that friggin' callboard one more time, I'll ram it up his nose.

She sets the vase on the table and arranges the roses. SUSI enters from the backstage area with telegrams.

SUSI Telegrams for Jessica. And Patrick. And for Tom and Phil.

PATRICK   Did you say *for* Tom and Phil? Or *from* Tom and Phil?   *He rips open a telegram and scans it.*   "Best luck with *Roses.* Break your legs, Edna."

SUSI   Shouldn't that be "break a leg"?

PATRICK   Not if you knew my ex-wife. She's very precise.

JESSICA   This one's from Innerkip. "Knock 'em dead." Signed "Percy."

SUSI   Who's Percy?

JESSICA   I haven't the foggiest. Where the hell is Innerkip?

PATRICK   Never mind Innerkip. Where the hell is Tom and Phil?

GEORGE enters from the backstage area.

GEORGE   Susi, Nick's looking for you. He wants to open the house.

SUSI   He's gotta be kidding. It's like a sauna in there.

GEORGE   Speak to him. That's between the two of you.... Can I see you a moment, love? The Green Room...   *to PATRICK and JESSICA*   I'll be right back.

He guides SUSI into the Green Room. PATRICK and JESSICA continue to read their telegrams.

SUSI   I know. Keep my voice down.

GEORGE   I don't want them to know I'm worried. Nick's trying to locate the others. Did Tom say what he was doing today?

SUSI   How should I know?

GEORGE   I thought he was at your place last night.

SUSI   George, give me a break. I know Phil was shooting a film this afternoon. Some industrial film.

GEORGE   Where?

SUSI   In the garment district, I think.

GEORGE   Would his girl-friend know?

SUSI   Gloria? She might. His mother would know for sure. He has to call in once a day or she phones Missing Persons.

GEORGE   You have her number?

SUSI   She's in the lobby.

GEORGE   Great. Ask her where he's working and have Nick call them.

SUSI   Right.   *She starts out, then turns.*   What about Feldman? Should I bring him back as soon as he picks up his tickets?

GEORGE   No, keep him out. I don't want him around Patrick. Where's Robert?

He sits on the sofa.

SUSI   Where he always watches the show. From the booth.

GEORGE   Well, tell him to get his ass down here on the double. The least he can do is put in an appearance.

SUSI   Gotcha.

She exits. In a rage GEORGE hammers his fists on the sofa and stamps his feet. PATRICK and JESSICA exchange a glance.

GEORGE   *to himself*   Jesus Christ, tonight of all nights!

Enter PHIL from the street door. He's out of breath and visibly upset. He wears sunglasses and a beret. Under his arm is a much-worn copy of the script.

PHIL   Forgive me, people. I apologize. It's inexcusable. George, old buddy, don't look at me like that. I'm not to blame. I swear to God.

He puts down his script and kicks off his shoes.

GEORGE   Where have you been?

PHIL   *crossing to the clothes-rack and removing his shirt*   They ran overtime. They knew I had an opening tonight. They still lied about the time. I will never buy my mother another Singer sewing machine. Oh, George, do you know if Gloria's picked up her ticket?

GEORGE   She's in the audience.

PHIL   I wasn't sure she'd come.

JESSICA   Don't tell me you two are still fighting.

PHIL   Can you blame us? Every time we discuss marriage my mother goes to bed and refuses to eat.

He removes his pants. He's wearing a pair of bright red bikini briefs.

PATRICK   Well, look at *her.* Red bikinis. Very, very smart, love. A gift from Mother? Or a pair of Mother's?

PHIL   *putting on the priest's pants*   I always wear red opening night. I feel like a bullfighter. It's gore or be gored.

PHIL removes his sunglasses. He leans forward to examine his left eye in the mirror. JESSICA glances his way, does a double-take, then stares.

JESSICA   Oh, my God, he's got a black eye.

PHIL   It's nothing, nothing.

GEORGE   Let me see.   *He inspects the eye.*   Phil, how did you do that?

PHIL   I can't tell you. I'm too ashamed. Please, I'm okay. Don't be alarmed.

JESSICA   I'll get some ice.

GEORGE   Forget the ice. There isn't time. Phil, you'll have to hide it with make-up. How's your vision?

PHIL   Twenty-twenty, old buddy. I just can't feel my cheekbone. But compared to my hand, George. My hand.

GEORGE   What's wrong with your hand?

PATRICK   He's been hitting himself again. I told you to stop doing that.

PHIL   Just what I'd expect from you. I'm in exquisite pain, and he laughs.

GEORGE   Let's see.   *PHIL holds out his hand.* Looks fine to me.

PHIL   I think it's broken. The index finger. Look: blue. A hairline fracture, at least. Oh, God, God. Why tonight?

He continues getting dressed.

GEORGE   So what happened?

PHIL   Incredible, huh? Phil Mastorakis. I abhor violence. I'm squeamish. That dumb film. That's what did it. Take after take after take. And to lie to me, to deceive me about the time. A rage, George. I was in a rage when I left. Stormed out. Two blocks later, it happened.

GEORGE   What happened?

PHIL   The fight. The fist fight. How do you think I got this shiner?

GEORGE   *exasperated*   Phil, that's what I'm trying to find out!

PHIL   These two musclemen, right? They're strolling towards me. I.Q. tattooed on their biceps. With a penknife. I go to pass, one points to my beret and says, "Artiste!" I went berserk, George. I saw red. I ran back and took a swing at the guy. Next thing I know I'm sitting on the sidewalk, my beret in my lap, some guy walks by and drops in a quarter.

He tosses the beret on the make-up table.

JESSICA   That was a crazy thing to do, Phil. You could've been killed.

PHIL   Don't remind me. And you know what's even crazier? For twenty years I've wanted to be called an artist in this country and the first guy who says it I *punch* him.

Enter NICK and PEGGY from the street door.

NICK   George, the house is in. I've been calling— Oh, hello, Phil, you're here.   *to GEORGE*   Thanks for letting me know.

JESSICA   Obviously you never checked the call-board.   *to PHIL*   Did I tell you? Nick is very, very strict about that.

NICK   All kidding aside, I haven't been able to reach Tom. Does anyone know where he went today?

PHIL   *shocked*   He's late?!

NICK   Take it easy, Phil. There's no need to panic.

PHIL   Fine. Great. Fantastic. We go up in twenty minutes, and there's no need to panic?

GEORGE   Nick's right. Maybe he got held up in traffic.   *to NICK*   Did you call his new number?

NICK   Naturally I called his new number. There was no answer. If I'd called his new number and spoken to him, I wouldn't be here now asking the cast if anyone knew where he was, would I?

GEORGE   Listen, you pompous ass . . .

PHIL   *cutting in*   I think he mentioned a wedding. Yeah, he did. He had a wedding to go to.

JESSICA   A wedding?

PHIL   His father was getting married again. That's why he came to a preview.

NICK   What church? Do you know?

PHIL   Wasn't in a church. He was getting married in his back yard. Weather permitting.

NICK   Do you know where he lives?

PHIL   Let's see. I wasn't paying that much attention. . . . No, I'm sorry. I can't . . . . I can't . . .   *He shrugs.*

PATRICK   The word is remember.

PHIL   Hey, look, Flanagan . . .

JESSICA   *cutting in*   Phil, it might help if we knew his father's name. Did Tom ever mention it?

PHIL   His first name, huh? Let's see. I'm lousy with names. God, it's right on the tip of my tongue.

GEORGE   Think hard.

PHIL   Okay, but don't stand over me like that. I have to do this my way. . . . Tom and I had lunch at Luigi's on Tuesday. He ordered french fries and a cheeseburger with the works . . .

GEORGE   *cutting in*   We don't care what he ate, just his father's name.

PHIL   I'm working up to it. . . . And I ordered an egg salad sandwich on brown and a chocolate milk shake. We got our order and Tom said he had to go to a wedding the afternoon of the opening.

GEORGE   What did you say?

PHIL   I said "Who's getting married?"

GEORGE   And he said?

PHIL   His old man.

GEORGE   *exasperated*   Phil, we know that!

PHIL   Only he didn't say his old man. They call each other by their first names. How often do you hear a father and son . . . ?

GEORGE   *cutting in, grabbing PHIL by the front of his shirt*   The name, Phil! Just the name!

PHIL   Percy.

JESSICA   Percy? Oh, my God, Tommy's in Innerkip.

GEORGE   Innerkip?

JESSICA   See for yourself. *She hands him the telegram.* It must be his. There must've been a mix-up.

GEORGE   Where's Innerkip?

JESSICA   Listen, until a second ago we never knew who Percy was.

NICK   *taking the telegram*   I'll get on it right away.

He enters the Green Room and uses the phone, quietly ad-libbing his phone calls. PEGGY, who has been sitting on the sofa, rises and wanders into the dressing-room. She and GEORGE exchange a worried look.

JESSICA   What time is it?

PEGGY   Exactly 8:12.

JESSICA   8:12. Almost time for, "Ladies and gentlemen, this is your fifteen minute call." So help me, if his voice comes over that box, I'll throttle him.

NICK overhears this remark and makes an obscene gesture. ROBERT, pale and somewhat nervous, enters from the street door, carrying a magnum of champagne. GEORGE notices his entrance and enters the Green Room, putting his finger to his lips to silence him.

PHIL   Anyone have a cigarette?

JESSICA   I thought you quit.

PHIL   *as JESSICA passes him a cigarette*   Seven years ago, but now and then I get the urge. Right now I need a cigarette.

NICK hangs up. Looks grimly at GEORGE.

NICK   No answer.

GEORGE   All right then, I want to talk to the two of you, and I don't want hysterics. *to ROBERT*   Is that understood?

ROBERT   What is it?

GEORGE   Tom still hasn't shown up and there's a real possibility that he might not. The question now is what to do.

NICK   What choice do we have?

GEORGE   We can't cancel, Nick. There are eighteen members of the press out there. They have openings every night this week. If we cancel, we may not get reviewed till the middle of next week, if then.

NICK   So?

GEORGE   Besides, Feldman's out there. We can't assume he'll just cool his heels till tomorrow night. Bernie's a busy man, and for all we know Tom might've been in a serious accident.

ROBERT   What are you saying, George?

GEORGE   What I'm saying, Robert, is that I need someone to go on for Tom. Now there are only three people who can do it. You, me, and Nick.

NICK   Me? I can't do it. I'm running the show.

GEORGE   Exactly.

ROBERT   Then I guess it's up to you, George.

GEORGE   Robert, you want me to stumble through your beautiful play with a script in my hand? Playing a college student in polo pajamas?

ROBERT   George, I am not an actor!

GEORGE   You used to be.

ROBERT   That was eight years ago, and you know why I quit? Because I was terrified. I made Phil Mastorakis look confident.

GEORGE   I heard you were a wonderful actor.

ROBERT   Who told you that?

GEORGE   Phil. He said you played the juvenile lead in his first TV show, "Six Mangoes to Morocco."

ROBERT   George, you can't expect me to just step into the role at a moment's notice. I'm not prepared. I don't even know the lines.

NICK   You wrote them, didn't you?

ROBERT   That doesn't mean I *know* them.

GEORGE   Ad lib what you don't remember.

ROBERT   Like hell I will. I worked over those words like a blacksmith. It's a tightly-written play. If I left out certain lines, the rest of the play wouldn't make sense.

GEORGE   Look, that's the best thing we have going for us, the play. The *play*, Robert. It's so strong that even Phil can't screw it up. And if you're worried about being nervous, don't be. Just go out there and *be* nervous. Don't try to hide it. Let it show, and before you know it . . .

ROBERT   *cutting in*   No!

GEORGE   There's something else I want to say, and I've never said this before. In some ways you would have been a better choice for this role than Tom.

ROBERT   Get serious.

GEORGE   It's true. Tom has to *act* the part, you've lived it. Robert, you *are* Jimmy.

ROBERT   I'm not. I'm all those characters. I'm Frank and Eric. George, I'm even Elizabeth. Jimmy's just one facet of myself.

GEORGE   Fine, but right now the facet of yourself that is Jimmy can save the show, if you'll just do it. Don't think of Jess and Phil and all they have invested in tonight. Don't think of me, either: our friendship doesn't matter. Do it for yourself, Robert, because you're the one who's got the most at stake here. You're the one who'll have to live with yourself if you chicken out now and let Feldman go home empty-handed.

ROBERT   You're a real bastard, George. You know that?

GEORGE   *to NICK* He'll do it. *to ROBERT* Just one word of advice: look each actor in the eye when you're talking to him. That's very important.

ROBERT   If I look Phil in the eye, he'll forget his lines for sure.

GEORGE   All right. Look them all in the eye except for Phil. With Phil, look over his shoulder or above his head.

ROBERT   One more thing: I'm not going on in those stupid polo pajamas.

GEORGE   Nick, go up to Wardrobe. Get Robert another pair of pajamas. Meanwhile, I'll talk to the cast.

NICK   No problem.

He exits. GEORGE gives ROBERT the thumbs-up sign and enters the dressing-room.

JESSICA   *as she puts on her wig and turns to GEORGE* There. How do I look? Don't tell me: ghastly. Cheap and ghastly.

GEORGE   You look gorgeous. It's perfect.

JESSICA   Liar. It's horrid, and you know it. I look like a Barbie doll for octogenarians.

She returns to the mirror and begins to comb her wig. ROBERT enters the dressing-room.

PATRICK   Oh-oh, just what we need: Banquo's ghost. *to JESSICA, quietly* And I didn't quote the Scottish play.

JESSICA   No, but you came damn close. Chin up, Robert. This is your big night. Peg, be a dear and take that bottle. If he holds it any tighter, he'll pop the cork.

PEGGY   *taking the bottle* I'll put it in the fridge.

GEORGE   One second, Peg. I have something important to say to the cast and I want you to hear it. This concerns us all.

PHIL   I hope it's about these new shoes you got me, George, because they squeak.

JESSICA   Is that what that was last night, your shoes? I thought we had a loose floorboard.

PHIL   *to GEORGE* There. You see.

GEORGE   Phil, I've got more on my mind right now than new shoes. I promise you'll have another pair for tomorrow.

PHIL   Can't Nick oil them?

PEGGY   Phil, you don't oil shoes, you oil a hinge. Shoes you wear in.

GEORGE   All right, let's get down to business. . . . Now folks, we still haven't been able to locate Tom. I'm sure he'll arrive any second, but just in case . . .

PHIL   Incredible. Stalin tracked down Trotsky in Mexico and put an axe in his head and we can't locate one lost actor.

GEORGE   Look, Phil, I need the full co-operation of every member of the cast. It's very close to curtain, so time is precious. This show, cast, is going on tonight, with or without Tom.

PATRICK   Really?

JESSICA   What do you have in mind, George?

NICK enters, holding the bottoms of a pair of striped pajamas against himself.

NICK   *to GEORGE*   How do these look?

JESSICA   Oh, no! If you think I'm going onstage with that little martinet playing my son, you've got another think coming!

NICK   These are not for me, they're for him.

JESSICA   Robert?

PATRICK   Oh, Jesus.

GEORGE   Look, either Robert gets ready to go on right now or we cancel tonight's show and kiss Broadway goodbye. It's up to you.

PHIL   The kid can act, George, I've seen him. He's dynamite!

GEORGE   Now I've already discussed this with Robert, and he's more than willing to jump into the breach. Aren't you, Robert? *then* Aren't you? *ROBERT nods, sickly.* Besides, Pat, he's close to the right age and he knows all the lines. In fact, he knows all the parts and all the blocking.

PATRICK   I know. And he'll stand out there tonight and correct all our grammar. This show could run till morning.

GEORGE   What's more, I intend to make an announcement. I'll go up on stage and explain that something has happened to the actor playing Jimmy and that tonight the playwright will step in. They'll love it.

PATRICK   You overestimate their good will.

GEORGE   Are you kidding? Remember *Murphy's Diamond*? The night the lights went out in the middle of Act One? I walked calmly down the aisle and up on stage and told the audience we were starting over. Remember what they did?

PATRICK   Distinctly. A mad crush for the exits.

GEORGE   They cheered is what they did. They felt they were sharing in a crisis. Half of them come here anyway expecting the set to fall on the actors' heads, and when it does, they adore it...

PATRICK   That's comforting to know, George.

JESSICA   Well, I, for one, Flanagan, think it's quite courageous of Robert. I certainly wouldn't want to be in his shoes. I think he deserves our full support.

PHIL   Bravo, Robert!

GEORGE   Besides, you've all been through a lot worse than this, I'm sure. I know this is difficult, but you're all professionals, and I know you can rise to the occasion and turn this crisis into a triumph.

PHIL   Hear, hear!

JESSICA   And let's not forget Bernie. He flew all this way to see a show, so let's give him one. Let's give him the best damn performance he's ever seen!

PHIL   Three cheers for Robert! Hip, hip, hurrah!

ALL except PATRICK   Hip, hip, hurrah! Hip, hip—

TOM rushes in, dressed in a suit and tie, the tie loose, the jacket in his hand.

ALL including PATRICK   Hurrah!!!

TOM   Oh, Jeez, I'm sorry. Honest. I'm sorry, everybody. Don't be mad.

JESSICA   Thank God.

TOM   I know: I'm late. I'll get dressed.

He rushes to the clothes rack and begins to tear off his clothes.

GEORGE   Slow down, Tom. Don't get yourself in a state.

TOM   My first part, and this happens. I can't think straight. It's like a nightmare.

He rips off his shirt, popping the buttons.

PHIL   He thinks *he's* distraught? My whole career just flashed before my eyes. Can you imagine going onstage with Robert?

ROBERT wanders into the Green Room and stretches out on the sofa.

NICK   *to TOM*   If it's not too much to ask, where the hell have you been?

JESSICA   Never you mind. The thing is he's here and all is forgiven. Just take those pajamas back to Wardrobe and sign Tommy in. I wouldn't want you remembering your precious callboard right in the middle of a sound cue.

NICK exits, glowering.

TOM   *removing his pants*   My Dad got married, George. He would've been hurt, I hadn't gone. Like, I didn't want to go. It's forty miles outside the city.

JESSICA   Innerkip?

TOM   How'd you know?

JESSICA   Tell you later.

TOM   *putting on his pajama top*   The cab had a flat on the way back. I never knew that cabs got flats. I thought they weren't like other cars.

JESSICA   Shouldn't it only take a few minutes to fix a tire?

TOM   Sure, if you got a spare. Like, he had no spare. I mean, there we were trying to flag down the highway on another cab. Jeez, you can never get a cab when you want one. Oh, yeah, I forgot. Like, could someone play the driver? I'm a little fixed for cash.

PHIL   Play the driver?

JESSICA   Fixed for cash?

PEGGY   I'll take care of it.

GEORGE   And tell Nick to get back down here. On the double. Tell him to bring back the pajamas.

PEGGY exits. GEORGE enters the Green Room.

On your feet, Robert. We might need you after all. Tom is pissed.   *He re-enters the dressing-room.*

PATRICK   Jesus H. Christ.

He turns away in disgust. PHIL buries his face in his hands.

TOM   No, really, I'm fine. Look: I'm fine.

He tries to stand on his head.

GEORGE   What'd you have to drink, Tom?

TOM   Punch.

PHIL   Punch?

TOM   Pineapple punch.

GEORGE   What was in it?

JESSICA   Need you ask? Look at him.

PATRICK   He can't go onstage like that, George. He'll fall asleep on the sofa. Stick his head in the sink.

He rushes into the Green Room, glancing at ROBERT, and pours a coffee. PHIL puts on his scarf and overcoat.

PHIL   Wait till my shrink hears about this. And he thinks *he* has problems!

JESSICA is helping TOM who is struggling to get his pajama bottoms on over his slippers.

JESSICA   Here we go. One leg at a time. That's it.

TOM   Know what Percy thinks? He thinks I got drunk because I hate the bitch he married. That wasn't the reason. I just didn't know the spike was punched.

JESSICA   *to GEORGE*   And he has to make it through a four-page monologue.

She returns to the make-up table.

TOM   Jesus H. Christ.

PATRICK   *returning with the coffee*   That's my line, cocky, get your own. Here, drink this.   *TOM does.*   More. More. . . . Okay, George, he's all yours. Just don't drown him.

GEORGE   Come on, Tom.

He leads TOM into the washroom, leaving the door ajar.

PATRICK   Just remember, Thomas, no matter how much you ache to go to the can, don't walk offstage before intermission. I already had one actor pull that.

PHIL   Then don't cross your eyes in the middle of my speech. That's why I dried.

PATRICK   I never crossed my eyes.

PHIL   No? What would you call it?

PATRICK   I might've winced a little.

PHIL   Winced?

PATRICK   And no bloody wonder. There was enough garlic on your breath to peel the paint off a Pontiac. How's he doing, George? Is he sober and repentant?

PHIL   I'm warning you, Flanagan. Don't ever do what you did last night. If you ever call me up again at three a.m. . . .

PATRICK   I was sound asleep.

PHIL   Accusing me of walking offstage just to spite you. Using that filthy gutter language.

PATRICK   You dreamt it.

PHIL   I suppose my mother dreamt it, too? She has her own extension. She heard every word.

GEORGE and TOM come out of the washroom, TOM drying his head with a towel. He squirts water from between his teeth.

PATRICK   I wish I found that amusing.

Enter NICK, with pajamas.

NICK   How is he? Can he go on?

GEORGE   I need time to sober him up. Make an announcement. Tell the audience there's been a delay. Meanwhile, get Robert into those pajamas. Just in case.

NICK   We can't hold much past 8:45. Nine at the latest.

GEORGE   Listen, we'll hold as long as it takes. We're not cancelling this show unless the actors want to. Is that understood?

NICK   Perfectly.

GEORGE   If I can just get him to the point where he can say, "The punch is spiked."

TOM   *looking up*   I don't say that, do I?

GEORGE   Let's take a walk, Tom. Better still, let's jog. On your mark, Tom. Go.

He starts off with TOM trailing behind, the towel draped around his neck. They exit.

PATRICK   The late-comers are in for a treat. Wait'll they see George and Tom jogging around the block.

Pause.

JESSICA   What time is it?

NICK   Five minutes to curtain.

JESSICA   This is what happens when you don't have understudies.

PHIL   Understudies? They're too cheap to hire a prompter.

He reacts, turns and sits at the make-up table. Takes his script and runs lines.

Pause.

PATRICK   The intangibility of the stage. A few remembered moments that add up to a life. Like pissing into the wind.

PHIL   God, you're contemptible.

NICK enters the Green Room. Tosses the pajamas to ROBERT.

NICK   Here. George wants you to get into these and be ready to go.

ROBERT   Screw off.

NICK   I'm not asking you, I'm telling you. George may treat you with kid gloves, but right now you're just another actor. So get dressed.

ROBERT   Like hell I will. I'm not wearing these stupid striped pajamas.

NICK   Suit yourself. Go on in your jock-strap for all I care.   *He starts to exit.*

ROBERT   I'm not wearing make-up, either!

NICK   Wear what you want. I just don't want you upsetting the actors. You get it?

He exits.

JESSICA   Fascist!

ROBERT enters the dressing-room and hurls the pajamas on the table.

ROBERT   It's not fair, Jess. Why should I have to go out there tonight and butcher my own play? That's what actors get paid for.

He sits at the make-up table.

JESSICA   Don't fret, my heart. I worry more when a show goes too smoothly. I've been in Broadway shows that barely made it to curtain.

PATRICK   I beg to differ. I happened to star in his first play and the only crisis we had was the one he wrote in the second act.

PHIL   That's not what I heard.

PATRICK   Then again, his first work was called a play. This one's being touted as a vehicle. A vehicle for Miss Jessica Logan. From Art to Mechanics at one fell swoop.

JESSICA   *springing to her feet*   All right, you son-ofabitch, *that* was from *Macbeth*.

PATRICK   What? "One fell swoop"?

JESSICA   Hurry up. Walk backwards out of the room, turn around three times, and beg permission to come in.

PATRICK   If I walk out of this room, I won't be coming back.

JESSICA   If you have no respect for yourself, at least have some for tradition. Right now we need all the luck we can get. Or don't you want this show to go on?

PATRICK   Look, how can we miss? We have a Star in the cast. It's not like *Murphy's Diamond*, is it, Robert? We have a real Star. A Star who can lure Bernie Feldman up to the boondocks.

JESSICA   It also helps if the play is good.

PATRICK   By the way, I loved your interview in the *Globe*. *He holds up the newspaper.*   Isn't it noble of Miss Logan to act in a new play at a two-hundred seat theatre? No dressing-room of her own. No star on her door. Working for scale with local character actors.

PHIL   Hey, get off her back, why don't you?

PATRICK   That's from the play, isn't it? Are you talking to me or just running lines?

PHIL   I've had it up to here with you and your sick jokes. This is a real lady here, and that's more than I can say for you.

JESSICA   Why don't you save your nastiness for Act One and just let the rest of us get into character?

PATRICK   Don't pull rank on me.

JESSICA   I'm not pulling rank. I'm simply telling you to shut your mouth. I don't want to hear about Bernie Feldman or being a Star or anything else you dredge up to cover your own fear.

PATRICK   *My* fear?

JESSICA   And as for New York, Buster, I wouldn't want you in the cast anyway. After this show closes here, I'll be quite happy to read your obituary!

NICK   *over the PA*   Ladies and gentlemen, may I have your attention, please. Due to technical difficulties, the curtain will go up a few minutes late. We're working on it, so please bear with us. Thank you.

ROBERT   Jess, I feel weird. I'm dizzy. My ears are ringing . . .

JESSICA   Quick. Put your head between your knees. *He does.*   Phil, get your smelling salts.

PHIL   Here.

JESSICA   Sit up, Robert.   *He does.*   Now breathe in.   *She holds the bottle under his nose.*   That's it. Again.

ROBERT   Jess, I think I'm going to be sick . . .

He bolts up, covers his mouth, and lurches out the street door.

PATRICK   What was wrong with the washroom? Be just our luck if he brings up all over a critic.

He picks up the shoebox and starts for the washroom.

PHIL   Get them first. That's what I always say.

JESSICA   *to PATRICK*   Where do you think you're going? Stop him, Phil. He's got a bottle.

PHIL   A bottle?

He bounds from his chair and gets between PATRICK and the washroom.

Okay, old buddy, I'll take that.   *snapping his fingers*   Hand it over.

PATRICK   Do that again, I'll break your arm. Now get out of my way.

PHIL   Did you hear that? He threatened the Equity deputy!

JESSICA   What the hell do you think you're doing, drinking before an opening?   *as PEGGY returns*   Where's Nick? I won't step on that stage tonight if this sonofabitch takes a drink!

Enter GEORGE and TOM, both gasping for breath. GEORGE now has the towel draped around his neck. TOM appears to have sobered considerably. He halts at the coffee percolator and pours himself a black coffee.

GEORGE   Peggy, what time is it?

PEGGY   8:40.

PATRICK replaces the shoebox on the make-up table. GEORGE puts on PEGGY's headset which is on the wall in the Green Room.

GEORGE   Nick, are you in the booth? . . . Okay, we can go any time you're ready. Is Robert there? . . . Tell him to relax. Tell him we won't be needing him. . . . Yeah, Tom's much better, he'll be fine . . .

He replaces the headset. TOM exiles himself in the Green Room and stares at the floor.

NICK *over the PA* Okay, cast, we'll be starting in exactly five minutes. So stand by beginners for Act One. Have a good show.

PATRICK, JESSICA and PHIL each sit and give last minute attention to themselves in the mirror. GEORGE crosses to JESSICA.

GEORGE *kissing her cheek* Good show, love. I'll see you later.

JESSICA Are you watching the show?

GEORGE No, I'll be in the lobby.

JESSICA Would you have your wife sit near the front?

GEORGE Why?

JESSICA I want to know if she can see up my skirt. Tell her to sneeze once for yes.

GEORGE crosses to PATRICK who is running a lint brush over his pants.

GEORGE What can I say, Pat?

PATRICK A simple "Thank you" would suffice. "You're a helluva great actor" would be even better.

GEORGE How about both?

PATRICK Terrific, mate. Only next time think of it yourself.

GEORGE *moving to PHIL* Phil.

PHIL *staring into the mirror* Oh, gentle Jesus, my eye, George. My eye's closing. See.

GEORGE We'll have it looked after at intermission. I have to go, Phil.

PHIL How do I explain this to my mother?

GEORGE Phil, listen. Just tell me one thing: can you go on? That's all I need to know.

PHIL *leaping to his feet* Oh, God, George, if that isn't pathetic. You have to ask Phil Mastorakis whether or not he can go on. And you want to know what's even more pathetic? I don't think I can!

PATRICK *crossing to TOM* Hey, what the hell you doing? This's your baptism here tonight. Hold up your head, you're an actor. *TOM does.* It's not the end of the world. I don't hold it against you. Neither do the others. You know what happened to me my first opening?

TOM What?

PATRICK Nothing. It went like clockwork. I got a rave review.....Here. *He takes out his pocket watch.* Take this.

TOM I can't take your watch.

PATRICK I want you to have it. *dropping the watch into TOM's hand* Think of it as a baptism present. My old man gave me that as a talisman the day I went into show business. He was so proud, the old bugger.

TOM Thanks, Pat.

PATRICK *lifting TOM to his feet* Besides, Tom, it could've been worse. We might've gone on tonight with Robert in the part. Perish the thought.

He sends TOM into the dressing-room.

TOM *to GEORGE, showing him the watch* My Dad didn't give me anything.

GEORGE Have a good show, Tom. Everyone.

As the actors make ready to go, GEORGE crosses into the Green Room to exit but is met by SUSI coming in; she puts her finger to her lips.

Don't tell me. If it's bad news, I don't want to hear.

SUSI The baby-sitter just called. Your wife's in the hospital. She tripped on the way down the steps and broke her leg.

GEORGE *leaning against the door* Oh, God, I thought you were going to tell me Feldman couldn't make it.

SUSI You never let me finish. He just called from the airport. His plane was late getting in. Soonest he could be here, he said, was forty minutes.

GEORGE We can't hold the curtain that long. I don't care who he is. *Beat.* Can't he get here any faster?

SUSI He's just as upset as you are.

GEORGE Well, he'll have to see it another time. He can't judge the show on the last act.

SUSI Tomorrow's fine with him, he said. He sounded very nice.

GEORGE The actors won't like it. The second night is always a let-down.

The actors, aware that something is going on in the Green Room, are all staring in that direction.

SUSI Should I tell them? I don't mind doing your dirty work.

GEORGE Don't you dare or we'll have the let-down tonight. I wouldn't mind telling Patrick, only he'd never keep his mouth . . .

He puts a finger to his lips and crosses into the dressing-room. All four actors are staring at him.

Good show, everyone.

He raises his arm in a salute. Slowly all four actors raise an arm, almost in perfect unison.

GEORGE *to SUSI, as they exit* What hospital's she in? . . .

NICK *over the PA* Peggy, are beginners in place? It's two minutes to curtain.

JESSICA   Two minutes? Oh, my God, what am I doing here? I could be home, knitting.

PEGGY   *into her headset*   No, they're not, Nick. Not quite.

NICK   *over the PA*   Actors, places have been called.

PEGGY gets her flashlight and crosses to the door that leads into the backstage area. She holds open the door and waits.

JESSICA   I could crochet a better wig than this.

PATRICK   Peggy, did someone turn the fan off? I'm not shouting above that racket.

JESSICA   I think brushing only brought out the shine.

PHIL   *putting on his shoes*   A pair of shoes that don't squeak. Is that a lot to ask?

PATRICK   *flicking his lighter repeatedly*   I ought to tell George to stick this. What's he think I'll do, burn down the theatre? I'm bloody well insulted.

JESSICA   I could've bought a wig myself. Why didn't I?   *to PEGGY, plaintively*   Oh, Peggy . . .

PHIL   *pacing*   With these shoes, they'll hear us going on in the dark.

JESSICA   With this on my head, they'll probably see us.

By now all three actors are lined up at the door. PEGGY flicks on her flashlight and exits. TOM is seated at the make-up table, applying make-up between sips of coffee.

JESSICA   *about to exit*   I don't know why she needs a flashlight. I give off enough light for all of us.

She pats her wig and exits.

PATRICK   Spoken like a true Star.

JESSICA   *poking her head back in*   Bet your ass.   *She exits.*

PATRICK   *to PHIL*   Listen, mate, would it throw you too much if I use matches instead?   *He exits.*

PHIL   *to TOM*   He doesn't even wait for an answer.

He notices the shoebox. He snatches it up and rushes into the washroom, leaving the door ajar.

TOM   Phil, what're you doing?

PHIL   *off*   Dumping his courage down the sink. That'll teach him a lesson.

TOM closes the door so as to be able to inspect himself in the full-length mirror on the door.

NICK   *over the PA*   Okay, here we go. Have a good show everyone. Stand by. House to half. Light cues one through four. Preshow out and sound cue one.

The doorknob rattles.

PHIL   *off*   Tom! Tom!

TOM   What?

PHIL   *off*   I'm locked in! Oh, Jesus, Sweet Saviour, I'm locked in!   *He kicks and pounds on the door.*   Get me out!

TOM rushes over and struggles to pull open the door. PEGGY darts back into the room.

PEGGY   What's going on? Where's Phil?

TOM   In the can . . .

At that moment, the doorknob comes off in his hand and he goes backwards head over heels and knocks himself out. PEGGY rushes to TOM, sees that he's unconscious, and grabs her headset.

PEGGY   Nick, don't go on light cue one. Phil's locked in the washroom and Tom's out cold. . . . Okay, I'll tell them we're holding.   *She rushes to the washroom.*   Phil, don't panic. We'll have you out in a jiffy.

PHIL   *off*   I'm too moved to speak.

PEGGY exits into the backstage area, closing the door behind her.

PHIL   *off*   Tonight was just not in the cards, Peggy. I know it now. To have the critics predisposed against you is one thing. To have Providence is quite another. He's in this door, sweetheart. I believe that, within an inch of my life. The God of the Old Testament. "Vengeance is mine, sayeth the Lord."

As PHIL's speech continues, ROBERT rushes on and tries to revive TOM. First, he shakes him and then slaps his face, and then he applies the smelling salts. When this proves unsuccessful, he grabs the vase of red roses on JESSICAS's make-up table, but in his panic he gets the sequence wrong: with his right hand he hurls the roses at TOM, at the same time tipping the vase with his left hand so that the water spills to the floor. Frantically, he sits TOM up, trying to pull off his pajama top, at which point he notices the pair of striped pajamas on the make-up table. He lets TOM drop back to the floor and frantically tries to change into the striped pajamas. At the same time he has a script open on the floor, leafing through it in panic.

PHIL   *off*   The world is torn by chaos and strife. Nation against nation. Race against race. Religion against religion. Critics against actors. . . . My people created the theatre, bless their souls. Two thousand years ago. To celebrate life. . . .

What is He trying to tell us here tonight? I wonder, I wonder. Is He telling us we've strayed too far in the wrong direction? Telling us in His own inimitable fashion to get back to the celebration of life? If He is, amen to that. Amen. . . .

Because Peggy, the human spirit is sacred and holy, a shining light in all of us. Disregard the nay-sayers, the cynics, the Philistines. The human spirit is alive and deserves to be uplifted and enshrined!

ROBERT has one leg in the pajama bottoms and one foot on his script to keep it open as he scans the lines.

ROBERT   Phil, will you shut up! I can't think!

PHIL   *off* You can't think? I'm only talking to keep my spirits up! You're not the one who has his foot stuck in the toilet!

TOM begins to stir and sit up as NICK rushes on carrying a fire-axe. ROBERT notices TOM and reacts. NICK takes in the scene and grimaces with exasperation.

Blackout. Music.

ACT THREE

The set of the play-within-the-play, the next after-noon around 1:30. The stage still remains set for the last scene of the play from the previous night. At rise, GEORGE and ROBERT sit at the table, working on the script, while PEGGY moves about setting up for the top of the play.

ROBERT   Page sixty-five. Jessica's first line. I think it's weak.

GEORGE   I like it.

ROBERT   Wouldn't it be more effective to say nothing? That would make Phil work harder to reach her.

GEORGE   *wearily* Cut it, cut it.

ROBERT   Not unless you agree.

GEORGE   I agree, for Christ's sake. *He strokes out the line.* But if it doesn't work, I'm putting it back in.

ROBERT   Page seventy-three. Middle of the page. Patrick's second speech.... George, the line is, "I went *towards* her and she began to cry." That's much better than what he's been saying.

GEORGE   What's he been saying?

ROBERT   "I went *to* her and she began to cry."

GEORGE   "To" instead of "towards"?

ROBERT   The rhythm is better.

GEORGE   That might be tricky. He's gotten used to saying "to."

ROBERT   You mean changing a preposition is going to blow his performance?

GEORGE   No, but it won't make that much difference, either.

ROBERT   George, let a character use one word he wouldn't normally say and I stop believing him.

GEORGE   Listen, I've got to consider morale. If I keep harping on such minor points...

ROBERT   *cutting in* Minor points?

GEORGE   Yes, minor points.

ROBERT   To you it may be minor; to me it makes me cringe in my seat. And don't you think you ought to tone down his performance? It was way too big last night. I'm surprised he didn't get slammed by the critics.

GEORGE   Robert, please. I've got enough on my mind right now. Give me a break, will you?

He picks up his script, crosses to the sofa and sits, exasperated. Just then, TOM rushes down the aisle. He carries a small brown bag containing coffee.

TOM   *thrusting the bag at GEORGE* I'll never go to Luigi's again. That's the last time, George. He embarrassed me so much I went cross-eyed.

ROBERT   Cross-eyed?

TOM   Yeah, whenever I feel ridiculous I cross my eyes. To unfocus the world. You know.

GEORGE   Why? What happened?

TOM   He wanted my autograph.

GEORGE   *sipping his coffee* Tom, you've just had your first taste of success. Learn to live with it. It's when they stop asking, you start to worry.

TOM   I don't mind autographs, George. I hate actors who treat their fans with contempt.

GEORGE   Why're you so upset then? I don't understand.

TOM   He had nothing to autograph, so you know what he gave me?

GEORGE   What?

TOM   You know what he gave me, George?

GEORGE   What did he give you?

TOM   A menu. Like, he took a menu off the table and had me sign it. He even told me what to say.

GEORGE   Well, to him it's a big deal. He'll take it home and show his kids.

TOM   No, he won't. He put it back on the table. George, I know dozens of people who go in there every day for lunch.

GEORGE   What did you write?

TOM   "Hugs and kisses from the world's greatest actor, Tom Kent." I'll never live it down, George!

He starts to exit.

GEORGE   Tom, wait a minute. Come here. I want to talk to you.   *TOM returns.*   Forget Luigi. Listen, what I'm about to tell you, I don't want you to mention it to Jess until I tell her myself. Okay?

TOM   Bernie Feldman had a heart attack.

GEORGE   Worse. He went back to New York this morning. One of his shows is in trouble. The way things look he may not make it back before we close.

ROBERT   Two-faced little creep.

TOM   Who does he think he is, the President of the United States? Even the President can spare a night at the theatre.

GEORGE   I know.

TOM   Doesn't he realize how much this means to Jess? Doesn't he care how hurt she'll be?

GEORGE   I know, I know.

TOM   Bernie Maple Leaf Feldman. He comes up here as if he's doing us all a big favour, and then pulls out.

ROBERT   Coitus interruptus.

TOM   He probably knocked up some showgirl and has to run back to get her an abortion.

GEORGE   I know, I know, I know.

TOM   Jesus, George. Jesus, Jesus, Jesus.   *He starts to exit and turns.*   Well, there goes my film career!

He exits backstage.

GEORGE   He's going to make a wonderful actor, that kid.

ROBERT   I know. He's got the right combination of empathy and self-absorption.

GEORGE   *to PEGGY*   Are the others here yet, love?

PEGGY   It's only twenty-five after. They'll be trickling in soon. Robert, are you going to be long? I'll need you to move.

GEORGE   We're almost finished, Peg. Just say the word.   *to ROBERT*   We *are* almost finished, aren't we?

ROBERT   One more and that's it. Page ninety-eight. Bottom of the page. Phil's line. We don't need the line. It's subtext. Phil can act it.

GEORGE   Great. His lines I don't mind cutting.   *He strokes out the line.*

ROBERT   He's been screwing it up anyway. Last night his excuse was he had a hair in his coffee.

Enter PATRICK down the aisle. He carries a small thermos bottle and cup. He looks slightly hungover.

PATRICK   *sipping from the cup*   I take back what I've always said about critics. We're finally getting a few discerning ones.

GEORGE   Congratulations. That was a helluva rave the *Star* gave you.

He indicates the newspaper on the coffee table.

PATRICK   So Susi tells me. I've not read it myself. I just crawled out of bed.   *He steps onstage.*   Hello, Robert. What're you up to? Don't tell me, you've rewritten the entire first act.

ROBERT   Have you really not read the reviews?

PATRICK   Listen, sometimes I don't read them till the run's over. No, I mean it. I don't like to gloat. Irish coffee, anyone?

GEORGE   Too early for me.

PATRICK   Don't blame you, mate, it's bitter. Maybe I put in too much coffee. Oh, well.   *He sits at the table.*   Speaking of last night, didn't you think that was a strange audience? A bit subdued? I think the house was papered with academics looking for meaning. Either that or Nick's entire family was here.

GEORGE   I thought the audience was marvellous. Very attentive.

PATRICK   Attentive is fine for a funeral. For the theatre I prefer wildly enthusiastic. And did you notice what happened to my only laugh in the play? Some old lady coughed right on the punch-line. I could've strangled her.

ROBERT   That was Phil's mother. She was chewing her worry beads.

PATRICK   I might've known. I notice she never coughed once on *his* lines.   *GEORGE passes the newspaper to PATRICK.*   That's it, is it?   *He begins to clean his reading glasses.*   Too bad Feldman wasn't here last night. He missed a good show. The cast was in top form.

GEORGE   Listen, Pat, about Feldman . . .

At that moment, NICK comes out from around the set, and SUSI starts down the aisle to the stage.

NICK   Excuse me, George. I just did an equipment check. The Christmas tree lights aren't working.

GEORGE   How long will you be?

NICK   A few minutes. It's probably just the plug. *He sits in the window seat and repairs the plug.*

SUSI   *sitting on the arm of the sofa*   George, Phil just called. He said to tell you he's just leaving. He might be a few minutes late.

GEORGE   We'll wait. I can't start without him. I need all four actors.

SUSI   You'll never guess where he's been all morning. At the hospital.

GEORGE   The hospital? Don't tell me his eye is worse?

SUSI   I was afraid to ask. I figured he'd never get off the phone.

GEORGE   How did he sound?

SUSI   Hysterical.

PATRICK   Listen, he's at the hospital more than the doctors. He's on a first-name basis down there. They set their watches by him.

SUSI   This was different. I've never heard him act so strange.

GEORGE   How do you mean?

SUSI   I could hear his mother in the background. And get this: he kept telling her to shut up and leave him alone.

GEORGE   Oh, Christ, they've pumped him full of sodium pentathol.

SUSI   It's out of character, isn't it? Let's hope he's not having a nervous breakdown.

She starts back up the aisle.

GEORGE   That woman's going to be the death of him yet, I swear.

SUSI   You think so? I have a hunch he'll get her first.

She exits.

PATRICK   *finding the review* Don't you just love this? "*Roses* Author Has Green Thumb." Oh, that's cute. *to GEORGE* I don't know why but I always expect to get knocked by this fellow.

GEORGE   Didn't you make a pass at his wife?

PATRICK   Maybe that's the reason. No, really, he always gives me a rave, but in each one he manages to get in these little digs. Remember *Murphy's Diamond*? "Mr. Flanagan plays the baseball coach with a lustful twinkle in his eye and the smirk and leer of a perverted Peter Pan."

He glances at PEGGY.

PEGGY   No comment.

PATRICK   Okay, Patrick, settle down. Quiet on the set, please. The modest actor will now read his glowing good fortune, brief though it be. . . *reading* "Last night a remarkable new play burst on the scene at the small but prestigious Leicester Street Playhouse. Entitled *The Care and Treatment of Roses*, it is the much-awaited second play by Robert Ross, the young author of *Murphy's Diamond*, the baseball play of three seasons past."

ROBERT   Baseball play? It wasn't about baseball. It was a play about a father and son.

GEORGE   It was set on a baseball diamond.

ROBERT   So what? Is *Hamlet* about castles?

PATRICK   "The new work is old-fashioned in the true sense of the word: well-written and well-structured, observing at least two of the classical unities of place and action. The play spans three days in the lives of its characters, and the outcome is moving indeed." *to GEORGE* I can see this is going to be boringly good. "Elizabeth Thompson (Jessica Logan), newly-widowed, has taken a lover (Patrick Flanagan), a violent and irascible bartender, a widower who is haunted by the spectre of his dead wife. With this simple situation the playwright weaves a seamless fabric of passion and renewed hope that threatens to unravel when her son, a college student, decides to remain at home during the winter break. The boy bitterly resents his mother's cohabitation with this man and is intent on destroying the relationship. He fails to understand her needs and the new lease on life that this vulgar opportunist symbolizes." *to himself* Well, I suppose that's better than "perverted Peter Pan." *back to the newspaper* "The play opens with Elizabeth and her lover, Frank, awaiting the arrival of her brother, Eric (Philip Mastorakis), a parish priest who has been summoned to persuade the son to remain in school. If there is a flaw in this play, it is simply that it begins too quickly. We leap at once into the conflict."

ROBERT   What does he want, Ibsen? Two maids telling each other things they already know?

PATRICK   "A more gradual build-up, it seems to me, would have worked much better."

ROBERT   The nit-picking is just to prove he's doing his job. He can't just come out and say it's perfect.

PATRICK   Right. "Enter the son (Tom Kent), the catalyst, who sets off the powder keg of conflicts. From the moment Mr. Kent staggers onstage, hung-over from the prevous night, the stage is set for a classic battle of wills, refereed by the priest—a battle that rages almost unrelentingly until the final curtain." *to himself* Ah, now comes the good bit. "The cast for the most part is superb. Patrick Flanagan as Frank, in the most impressive performance of his career, gives a tone and texture to his character that is truly breath-taking. There is not a false note in it. His final reconciliation with Elizabeth in the last moments of the play is the most genuinely moving moment of the night." *to GEORGE* I thought I was better in the last preview, didn't you? "Tom Kent in the pivotal role of the son, Jimmy, manages to strike the right balance between awkward youth and groping aspirations. A fine debut for a young actor in his first professional role." *to GEORGE* Oh, that should please Tom. I'm glad he got that. "But by far the most memorable performance of the night. . . *He pauses, his expression turning from incredulity to outrage.* . . .goes to

Philip Mastorakis as the priest, brother of the much-put-upon Elizabeth." *to GEORGE* "The most memorable performance of the night"! We carried him the whole night, the three of us. *He tosses the newspaper to GEORGE.* Here, you read it. I can't read that garbage.

GEORGE *reading* "But by far the most memorable . . ."

PATRICK *cutting in* Must you repeat that? That's only one man's opinion, remember?

GEORGE "In a brilliant stroke the playwright has paralleled and contrasted the groping of the son against the loss of faith of this most human of all priests."

PATRICK He was so out of it before we went on I had to remind him to check his fly.

GEORGE "Mr. Mastorakis, vulnerable in an almost painfully childlike manner, fumbling for words that seem constantly to elude his grasp, makes the inner struggle seem all the more urgent and adds a dimension of humanity that endears him instantly to the audience."

PATRICK You sure his mother didn't write that?

GEORGE "The only disappointment in the cast is Jessica Logan as the doleful Elizabeth."

PATRICK You're kidding.

GEORGE No, he hated her.

PATRICK She was wonderful. No, I mean it. I wouldn't say that to her face, mind you. Christ, and he liked Mastorakis. Well, that just proves what I've been saying all along about critics. By the way, what does he mean, "the doleful Elizabeth"?

ROBERT Melancholy.

PATRICK That'll piss her off. All along she thought she was archetypal. What else does he say?

GEORGE "Perhaps Miss Logan has been absent from the theatre too long. Perhaps she misjudged the intimacy of the small theatre. The fact remains that her performance is by far too large for such an intimate space, almost wildly extravagant, reducing the character at times to caricature. She starts off at such a high emotional pitch she has nowhere to go except into the upper ranges of hysteria."

PATRICK God, that's dreadful. She'll be devastated.

Slight pause.

NICK *still working on the plug* Don't stop there, George. Read the rest.

GEORGE "For this, the director, George Ellsworth, must in part be faulted, although, otherwise, his handling of the cast is exemplary. Mr. Ellsworth has demonstrated in the past . . ."

PATRICK *cutting in* Don't tell me. "A fine and delicate touch."

GEORGE ". . . a fine and delicate touch, an unobtrusiveness that is the hallmark of a first-rate director. Perhaps Miss Logan was simply too strong a personality to control. That aside, *The Care and Treatment of Roses*, quite simply, is the best new play to arrive all season. And if it does not become the hottest ticket in town, this reviewer for one will eat his hat."

He tosses the paper on the coffee table.

PATRICK Eat camel dung.

PEGGY Typical. He didn't mention the set, costumes or lighting.

GEORGE *to PATRICK* The other papers are in the front office. You want to read them?

PATRICK What do they say?

GEORGE Basically the same thing.

PATRICK The answer is no. And to think I crawled out of bed for *that*.

He crosses to the armchair with his thermos and cup. He picks up a magazine and begins to leaf noisily through it.

PEGGY George, I'm almost through. I need the table now.

GEORGE It's all yours, Peg. And thanks. *He crosses to the table with his script.* Robert, give it a rest. Peg needs the table.

ROBERT I can take a hint.

GEORGE Why don't you use my office? Type some of these pages. *He hands ROBERT his script.* Only don't fuss with my desk. I like disorder. I'll never find a thing if you straighten up.

ROBERT Yeah, well, that clutter drives me crazy. At home I can't even work if the bed's not made.

He exits up the aisle. GEORGE sits down on the sofa and sips his coffee.

PATRICK *turning pages* Phil Mastorakis?!

GEORGE I know. That should throw him into a tailspin. He's grown to expect the worst.

PATRICK I thought he was much better in *Titus Andronicus*.

GEORGE Are you serious? He was *dreadful* in that.

PATRICK I know.

Enter JESSICA from backstage. She is bristling. As she strides on, she is swinging her wig. PATRICK buries his face in the magazine, and NICK, who is on his feet checking the Christmas tree lights, darts back into the window seat and pretends to be fixing the plug.

JESSICA Where's George? Ah, there you are. Stand up. I want a word with you.

GEORGE *springing to his feet* How are you, love? What can I . . .?

JESSICA *cutting in* Have you been in the dressing-room this morning? I use the term loosely. Black Hole of Calcutta's more like it. Even my roses wilted.

GEORGE What's wrong with the dressing-room?

JESSICA What's wrong? It *reeks* back there, that's what's wrong. The wallpaper's starting to peel from the smell of popcorn and cigarettes.

GEORGE Popcorn?

JESSICA Yes, popcorn. I know what popcorn smells like. Like a roomful of dirty socks. I defy anyone to go back there and not gag. Poor Tommy is face down on the sofa muttering "Jesus, Jesus, Jesus."

PEGGY *to GEORGE* I haven't cleaned it yet. I was just about . . .

JESSICA *cutting in, to GEORGE* What do you take us for, a pack of degenerates? As if it wasn't bad enough before, being herded into a sweatbox, now you deny us a door on the WC. It's disgraceful.

GEORGE Nick, hasn't that door been replaced?

JESSICA No, it has not. Are you calling me a liar? And I want a fan back there to circulate the dust. You have one in *your* office, I notice.

GEORGE *to PEGGY* Leave that for now. Clean the dressing-room. Get someone to repair the door. And bring down the fan from my office. Right away.

PEGGY exits quickly backstage.

JESSICA *to GEORGE* Don't look at me like that. I won't be pitied or patronized. These are legitimate complaints, not the whimsy of some delinquent child.

GEORGE Sorry, love. I wasn't aware that I . . .

JESSICA *cutting in and brandishing the wig* And I won't wear this one more night, do you understand? Would you wear it? Yet you have the nerve to dress me up in a wig that any little street tart would think in bad taste. Well, I won't wear it. *She tosses it to him.* Take it back to the zoo where you found it. I play a housewife in this play, not Harpo Marx in drag.

She turns and strides over to PATRICK and knocks away his magazine.

And don't you ever hang up on me again, you hear? Don't you ever!

PATRICK Was that you this morning? I thought it was an obscene call.

JESSICA You're just lucky you took the phone off.

PATRICK Had I known it was you, love, I wouldn't have been that rude. I don't have any real friends. Only fans and enemies.

JESSICA *starting to exit* If I were a man, I'd take you outside and pummel you.

PATRICK If you were a man, I wouldn't go.

JESSICA Coward!

She exits.

PATRICK A rather weak exit line, I thought. Even Robert can do better.

GEORGE *to NICK* Why the hell wasn't the door put back on the washroom?

NICK The reason it wasn't put back yet is because we weren't supposed to have this illegal rehearsal, that's why.

GEORGE This rehearsal is not illegal.

NICK According to the Equity rulebook we need twenty-four hours to call a rehearsal after an opening.

GEORGE *angrily* You know what I'd like to do with your Equity rulebook? *He tosses the wig to NICK.* The same thing I'd like to do with your friggin' callboard.

JESSICA comes storming back on. NICK exits quickly around the side of the set.

JESSICA *to GEORGE* I suppose you think I'm being a bitch, don't you? Just because I demand to be treated like a human being.

GEORGE Jess, I don't think you're a bitch. I don't think that at all.

JESSICA Well, I am a bitch, and you know why? I have to be to get treated like a human being. So there.

GEORGE I see your point.

JESSICA What point?

GEORGE About being a bitch.

JESSICA So you think I'm a bitch, do you?

GEORGE No, no . . .

JESSICA *cutting in* I knew you did.

GEORGE No, I meant demanding.

JESSICA Oh, really?

GEORGE Yes, I think you're demanding.

JESSICA Why? Because I demand to be treated fairly?

GEORGE No, because . . . *He pauses.* Jess, I think I'm lost . . .

JESSICA What was I saying?

GEORGE Don't you know?

JESSICA Did you change the subject?

GEORGE What was it?

JESSICA   I don't remember...

She sits on the arm of the sofa and lights a cigarette.

PATRICK   *rising*   Excuse me, I have to call my agent. I'm the only one who ever does. It cheers him up.

He exits up the aisle. Pause.

JESSICA   Oh, George, I have the mark of Cain on me. In this racket that's worse than leprosy and twice as contagious. Aren't you worried you'll catch it?

GEORGE   Listen to me. You are not a failure. Far from it. You're just finding your level, that's all.

JESSICA   *pacing*   What's the circulation of the *Toronto Star*? You have any idea?

GEORGE   Half a million?

JESSICA   That many? Oh, God, half a million people who don't know my work now believe Jessica Logan to be "wildly extravagant."

GEORGE   Jess, you were the one who asked for this rehearsal. Didn't you say last night you thought you were too big?

JESSICA   It's one thing for *me* to say it, it's quite another to wake up in the morning and find it in print.

GEORGE   I think you're overreacting.

JESSICA   You can afford to be generous. They all *loved* you.

GEORGE   What do you care about one or two critics? The audience adored you. They gave you a standing ovation.

JESSICA   Be serious. Most of that audience was made up of relatives and well-wishers. They still hadn't read the papers to find out what they were supposed to think.

GEORGE   That's a bit cynical, isn't it?

JESSICA   I'm feeling cynical. My own brother saw the show and raved about me. This morning I showed him the *Star* review. You know what he said? "I didn't think you were *that* bad." George, I wasn't that bad, was I?

GEORGE   You have never been bad in your life.

JESSICA   *still pacing*   To be the only one singled out. And to be drawn and quartered so brutally. "She has nowhere to go except into the upper ranges of hysteria." Anyone who didn't know better would think it was an opera.

GEORGE   Jess, listen to me. The phone hasn't stopped ringing. The answering service is threatening to raise our rates.

JESSICA   I'm not surprised. Opera is very popular.

GEORGE   In fact, this show could be the biggest hit we've ever had.

JESSICA   Do you know what I find so contemptible? The pomposity, the incredible arrogance. I thought only the Pope was infallible; at least with the Pope it's a Divine Right.

GEORGE   Forget what he said, will you? You're too good to take that garbage seriously.

JESSICA   I don't take it seriously, George, and I don't give a damn *what* he thinks. It still hurts. We spend weeks, months on a play to be carved up by someone on a free pass who rushes home to scribble off six or seven hundred words in sixty minutes that affects our livelihood and reputation. I don't know about you, but I can't even write a letter in that length of time. And oh, his writing style, let's not forget that. He writes like he needs a good enema. His sentences are so tight-assed, if he ever left out a period he'd run right into Classified Ads.

GEORGE   That's all the more reason not to take him so seriously. Who in his right mind would want to be praised by that man?

PATRICK   *off*   Phil Mastorakis.

JESSICA   *as PATRICK comes down the aisle*   I thought you were calling your agent.

PATRICK   The phones in the office are busy.

JESSICA   Well, don't you disparage Phil. At least he has respect for his fellow actors. He'd never deliberately make someone look bad.

PATRICK   *stepping onstage*   I agree. By comparison he makes us look better.

ROBERT starts down the aisle.

JESSICA   Is that why you got raves?

PATRICK   Which makes me wonder why you didn't. Maybe in New York you should play the Met.

Pause.

JESSICA   *quietly*   That's it. I quit. I quit, I quit, I quit.

GEORGE   You quit?

JESSICA   As of right now. You have my resignation. Effective this very second.

ROBERT sits on the edge of the stage and puts his head in his hands.

GEORGE   *in a panic*   Could we clear the theatre, please? Everybody out in the lobby. I want to talk to Jess alone.

JESSICA   Save your breath. I won't work with someone whose tongue is sharper than his wit. Out of my way, Flanagan. I'm in a very dangerous mood.

PATRICK steps quickly out of her path as she exits backstage.

GEORGE Dammit! *then* What're you doing here, Robert? Why aren't you up in the office?

ROBERT It's your wife, George. She just called from the hospital. She asked me to give you a message.

GEORGE *angrily* What does she want now?

ROBERT A visit.

GEORGE Can't you see what's happened? I'm busy. I'll see her tomorrow.

He exits.

ROBERT *yelling after him* That's it for me. I'm writing novels.

He steps onstage and sits on the sofa and taps his foot.

Pause.

PATRICK What're you trying to say, Robert? Get it off your chest. I never did learn Morse code.

Pause.

So I'm the villain of the piece, am I? Is that it? Well, don't forget: I made you what you are, you little bugger.

Pause. PATRICK sits at the table.

I was only kidding. I don't know why I even said it. I'm just talking to hear myself. I've never liked being alone.

Pause.

How's your new play coming? You got a title yet?

Pause.

Funny you should mention it, but I've been meaning to ask about *The Care and Treatment of Roses*. What precisely is the difference between "care" and "treatment"?

Pause.

Listen, she was just looking for a way out. You know that, don't you?

ROBERT Then why'd you give her one? Jesus, you're an actor. You know how vulnerable she is right now.

Pause.

PATRICK What'd you stop for? You have more to say when I leave out a comma. Give me hell if you want. I know you hate my guts.

Pause.

Listen, where do you get off blaming me? I'm the one who should be angry here. I'm the one she used.

ROBERT You?

PATRICK She baited me. You heard her. All I did was react like any good actor. Goddamn prima donna. I can act circles around her or anyone else in this country.

ROBERT Is that why you stay here?

PATRICK Just what does that mean? On second thought, keep your mouth shut. I don't like what comes out. *He stands and begins to exit.* And if you think you're such hot stuff, maybe New York's just what you need.

ROBERT Maybe it is.

PATRICK *turning back to ROBERT* How would you like to find out you're not as good as you think you are? As good as everyone says? Can you take that? Having your nose rubbed in your own worst doubts?

ROBERT I'm not afraid of it, if that's what you mean. *He turns to face PATRICK.* Listen, I want that experience. I want to be put up against the best. Otherwise, how am I going to grow, Flanagan? How do I develop?

Just then, JESSICA comes storming back on, carrying her make-up kit. Desperately, GEORGE runs ahead of her.

JESSICA No, I've taken all I care to take from that imbecile. I won't demean myself further. So goodbye.

She attempts to leave the stage but GEORGE blocks her way.

GEORGE Jess, wait, wait. Let's not be rash. I know you're upset, but can't we all sit down and discuss this like adults?

JESSICA We're not adults, we're actors. If you haven't learned that yet, you have no business in the theatre. Now get out of my way.

GEORGE Jess, without you in the cast this show will fall apart. I could never find a replacement.

JESSICA That's not true. I can think of any number of actresses who could do this part and better.

GEORGE Name one.

JESSICA Offhand I can't, but that's beside the point.

GEORGE Jess, this part was *made* for you. Robert practically wrote it with you in mind. Didn't you, Robert?

ROBERT Practically.

JESSICA *indicating PATRICK* I can't work with that man. He's the worst excuse for a human being that I've ever run across.

PATRICK *to ROBERT* I'll let that one go by.

JESSICA He's had my stomach in knots from day one. Oh, I can forgive his ill manners and his ill temper. I can forgive his vicious sense of humour. I can even forgive his alcoholic phone calls and his caravan of pizza trucks.

PATRICK How am I doing, Robert?

JESSICA But what I can't forgive is unprofessionalism. His behaviour last night on this stage was nothing short of atrocious.

PATRICK *angrily* And what was that, may I ask? Unless you're referring to my damn fine performance. In which case I stand justly accused.

JESSICA And you attack Robert for being ironic. My God, if that isn't ironic.

ROBERT How was I unprofessional?

JESSICA You know damn well what I'm talking about. *She sets her make-up kit on the table.* From the moment you strutted down those stairs you pulled out every stop. You snorted and bellowed like a wounded moose.

PATRICK I did like hell! *to GEORGE* Did I?

GEORGE turns and walks up the aisle.

I know I was rushing, but. . .

JESSICA *cutting in* Rushing? You were *charging*. The rest of us could barely keep up.

PATRICK Look, it was opening night. We were all nervous. Anyway, it's your own fault. You're the one who invited Feldman up here.

JESSICA He wasn't in the audience.

PATRICK Did I know that? Every time I looked out I thought I saw him glowering. So maybe I was bigger than usual. A touch.

JESSICA Bigger?

PATRICK Must you repeat every word I say?

JESSICA The word is shrill. Shrill as in frightened silly. Shrill as in Irish soprano. And in half those scenes I'm supposed to top you.

PATRICK If we were both shrill, then how come only you got panned?

JESSICA Because I am the Star, darling. I am the Star of this goddamn show, and don't you ever forget it!

TOM rushes on from backstage. He sees what he thinks is the apron scene being rehearsed.

TOM Sorry, George. I fell asleep. You want me to get the apron?

GEORGE I don't think so, Tom. And I don't need you, either. We haven't started yet.

TOM Oh, I thought. . . . Like, I thought. . . you know. . .

GEORGE I know, I know.

PATRICK *to JESSICA* Go ahead, tell the kid why there won't be a show tonight. I think he deserves an explanation. And don't use me as a scapegoat.

TOM There's no show?. . .

PATRICK Your mother just quit.

JESSICA I'm sorry, Tommy.

PATRICK The papers'll say, "For reasons of health." But we all know the real reason, don't we?

GEORGE *from up the aisle* That's enough, Patrick. Stop it.

PATRICK *to GEORGE* Then why didn't she quit last night? Why did she wait for the reviews? And why walk out the same day as Feldman is coming? Answer me that.

JESSICA Stop badgering him. What do you think this is, *Inherit the Wind*?

GEORGE Forget Feldman, the both of you. He's not coming tonight. He's gone back to New York.

PATRICK What?. . .

JESSICA I don't believe it. . .

GEORGE It's true. Ask Robert. Some crisis came up and he left.

ROBERT He has no class, either. He left the message with the answering service.

JESSICA *to GEORGE* Was this before or after the reviews came out?

GEORGE *running down onto the stage* Jess, for God's sake, stop believing the critics.

JESSICA Well, I don't believe there was a crisis. He just didn't want to face me, the coward. I'm supposed to be the draw in New York and I was the only one to get panned.

GEORGE Jess, this show's a hit. He'd be crazy not to take it.

JESSICA Oh, he'll want the show, he just won't want me.

GEORGE In that case, we'll find another producer. This play doesn't go to New York unless you go with it. Am I right, Robert? *ROBERT turns away.* I just don't want you believing you were bad.

JESSICA Bad? I was dreadful last night, and you know it. Godawful.

GEORGE You were not godawful, you were wonderful. All we have to do now is get it back to the right size. That goes for Patrick as well.

PATRICK Me?

GEORGE *firmly* Yes, you!

NICK rushes down the aisle. He is barely suppressing his indignation. He puts one foot on the stage.

NICK   Excuse me, George. I'd like to speak to the cast, if I may. Well, may I?

GEORGE   Oh, be my guest.

NICK   *stepping onstage*   Now I'm not accusing anyone, I want you all to understand that. But someone in this theatre has taken a hammer and ripped the callboard off the stairwell.

JESSICA   Someone stole the callboard?   *laughing*   Oh, God, there is a God after all. Wait'll I tell Phil.

NICK   I'm sorry, Jessica, but I fail to see the humour. That callboard is there for a purpose. I want it replaced.

JESSICA   Well, I'd like to take the credit. Believe me, I would.

NICK   I'm not accusing you. I'm just saying I want it nailed back up by eight o'clock tonight.

JESSICA   Don't you take that tone with us. You're lucky we don't nail *you* to the wall. Now trot back to the control booth and pull in your horns.

NICK   Don't tell me what to do. You're no longer with this show.

JESSICA   *crossing slowly to NICK*   Listen, you, I have never walked out of a show in my life. The day I decide to let down my fellow actors I guarantee you will be the first to know. Now stop wasting our time. We've got a rehearsal to get through.

She looks over at GEORGE. Pause.

GEORGE   Well, you heard the lady. We'll be starting as soon as Phil arrives.

NICK   Eight o'clock, George, or find yourself another stage manager.   *He starts up the aisle and turns.*   And I resent being made an ogre!

He exits.

GEORGE   *crossing over and hugging JESSICA*   Thanks, Jess.

JESSICA   God love the sonofabitch who stole that callboard.

She glances at ROBERT, then at TOM, who shakes his head vigorously. Slight pause.

Thank you, Flanagan.

PATRICK   Me?

JESSICA   It was you, wasn't it? Who else is perverse enough to think of it, let alone do it?

PHIL rushes down the aisle. His eye is swollen and badly discoloured. He is wearing an ascot, beret, and Hawaiian shirt.

PHIL   I'm sorry, boys and girls. I got here as fast as I could.

GEORGE   How are you? How'd it go at the hospital?

JESSICA   The hospital?

PHIL   *stepping onstage*   Ah, friends, you don't know what I've been through. No possible idea. I can't begin to describe it. Sheer torture.

PATRICK   What were you doing, paying a bill?

PHIL   That's exactly what I'd expect from you. No, I was not paying a bill. I was getting my stomach pumped.

JESSICA   What!

PHIL   *nodding grimly*   Incredible, huh? Fantastic.

GEORGE   Are you serious?

PHIL   Would I kid about a thing like that? You ever had your stomach pumped? It's murder.

JESSICA   No wonder you're pale. That must've been an ordeal.

PHIL   Tubes down the throat, needles, the works. I figured I was a goner. Food poisoning.

TOM   Food poisoning?

GEORGE   How'd you get that?

PHIL   George, that's not the worst of it. I just buried my cat, Gus.

GEORGE   Gus is dead?

PHIL   May he rest in peace.

PATRICK   Let me get this straight. You ate your cat?

PHIL   Very funny. No, my cat ate the tuna salad.

PATRICK   Then who ate your cat?

PHIL   Nobody ate the cat. What's wrong with you? Don't you ever listen?

JESSICA   Phil, start from the beginning. We'll unravel it together.

She sits him in a chair at the table.

PHIL   Okay. This's what happened. It's early this morning. Around seven. My cat's making noises. A wonderful cat. Like a brother. He's into the medicine chest, knocking pills in the sink.

PATRICK   Does he do that often?

PHIL   Every morning. That's how he gets me up. Intelligent, huh? I hurry down to the kitchen. I hunt around. No cat food. Nothing in the fridge but a bowl of tuna salad my mother made. I give Gus some and make myself two toasted tuna salad sandwiches on rye. To keep him company. Okay, he's finished. I put him outside on the porch and go back to bed. Around nine I get up, make myself coffee, and go out to get Gus.   *He chokes up.*   There he is, George. He's lying stretched out on the porch . . .

GEORGE   Dead?

PHIL   Stiff as a board.

JESSICA   Darling, I'm sorry.

PHIL   I panic. My first thought: food poisoning. I call an ambulance and in no time I'm at the hospital. The rest you know.

JESSICA   Phil, that's terrible. What a trying day.

PHIL   You think that's bad? Wait till you hear the finish. I go home. I'm depressed, wiped out. My mother comes back from shopping. "Oh, Phil, Phil," she says, "I'm so miserable." "You think *you're* miserable?" I say. "Yes, I'm wretched. I have a terrible confession to make. This morning I backed out the driveway and ran over Gus. I didn't want to ruin your sleep so I put him on the porch." *He shakes his head incredulously.*   And she wonders why I'm mad.

PATRICK   Phil, do you ever feel that life is making you the butt of some vast practical joke?

PHIL   Hey, what're you trying to do, make me paranoid?

PEGGY enters and continues her preset of the table.

JESSICA   Yes, you leave my Phil alone. He got the best notices in the show. Didn't you, my heart?

PHIL   I was fortunate. Very fortunate, I must say. And what they said about you, Jessica, is disgusting. I intend to write a letter to the editor. Better still, I'll cancel my subscription to the *Star.*

JESSICA   That's sweet of you darling, but let's not get drastic. I'll tell you what you can do, though. Be brilliant tonight. We'll all be brilliant. To hell with Bernie Feldman.

NICK   *over the PA*   George, the rehearsal was called for two o'clock. It's now 2:05.

GEORGE   *to the cast*   Okay, let's settle down. This'll only take a minute. What we'll do today is start from the top. We'll run each scene individually and then work on it.

TOM   Costumes?

GEORGE   No, just props. I also want to work some light and sound cues. Does anyone object to that? No? Okay, then let's get this show on the road.

NICK   *over the PA*   Top of Act One in two minutes, please.

JESSICA   *taking TOM's arm*   Your mother doesn't have to wear her funny hair. Isn't that good news?

They both exit backstage.

PHIL   George, I've been thinking. Maybe I should go back to the hairpiece.

PATRICK   George, if Phil's getting his rug back, I want my adjustable lighter.

He exits.

PHIL   George, can I have tinted glasses for tonight? It doesn't look right, George, a priest with a black eye.

He exits.

ROBERT   *rising from the sofa*   What about the changes?

GEORGE   Later. We'll work them in during the run. Now is not the time.

He fusses with the set.

PEGGY   *to the control booth*   I'm all set, Nick.

She exits.

ROBERT   Did you really mean that, George? You think we can still get this play done in New York?

GEORGE   If not this play, Robert, your next. You've got your whole life ahead of you.

NICK   *over the PA*   He hasn't got that long. He has exactly sixty seconds unless he gets the hell off my stage.

PHIL rushes back on.

PHIL   George, what's this I hear about Feldman? Are they kidding me or what?

GEORGE   I'm afraid not, Phil.

PHIL   Beautiful. Just beautiful. First the black eye, then Gus, and now this.

GEORGE   What about that wonderful review?

PHIL   A lot of good it does. I have to walk on tonight in those creaky shoes and shiny pants, knowing my future's back in New York with his feet up on his desk.

GEORGE   Phil, we're running behind.

PHIL   Look, couldn't Robert write me a line to explain the shiner? Maybe I got hit with a snowball on the way to the house.

NICK   *over the PA*   Forty seconds.

NICK   Incredible. I'm bleeding to death here, and that Turk is counting the seconds.

SUSI rushes down the aisle.

SUSI   George, there's a call for you on line two.

GEORGE   Not now, Susi. I'm busy.

SUSI   It's Bernie Feldman.

GEORGE   Feldman? What's he want now?

JESSICA   *off*   Tell him to go to hell!

PHIL   Let's not be rash. Maybe he's had second thoughts.

SUSI   He wants to know if you and Jessica can have dinner with him tonight after the show.

GEORGE   Tonight? What do you mean?

SUSI   I mean he's still in town! He's at the hotel!

JESSICA   *entering*   He's not in New York?

SUSI   No, and he says he has no idea who left that message on our service. Should I tell him yes?

PHIL   Yes! Tell him yes! Tell him I'll personally invest in the Broadway show!

GEORGE   Just tell him we'd love to have dinner. I'll call him back within the hour.

SUSI   Gotcha.   *She starts up the aisle.*   Oh, and he says for the cast not to worry about the reviews. He never reads the local critics.

She exits.

PHIL   Terrific. The best reviews of my life, and the sonofabitch has principles.

JESSICA   I knew Bernie would never desert us. George, I think we all owe that dear, sweet man an apology.

GEORGE   I don't get it. Who would want to play a stupid sadistic joke like that?

NICK   *over the PA*   The same dumb shit who vandalized my callboard.

All eyes turn towards the top of the stairs.

JESSICA   Flanagan, that was your cue.

PATRICK minces down the stairs, wearing an apron and JESSICA's wig, and carrying a red rose.

PATRICK   *mimicking JESSICA*   Honestly, you're worse than Jimmy. Your shoes are upstairs. And would you please put on a shirt?

JESSICA   Why, you miserable, rotten—

She snatches the bouquet of roses from the vase and starts after PATRICK, beating him with the bouquet as he flees about the set. Pandemonium ensues.

GEORGE   Jess! Patrick! Please! Please!

Blackout. Music.

ERIKA RITTER (b. 1948)

In a very funny essay in her book *Urban Scrawl,* Erika Ritter imagines a group of single women trying to talk their friend Sarah out of getting married. But citing a long catalogue of the indignities singles have to suffer, Sarah goes ahead and does it anyway—even while admitting that Elmer is hardly her ideal man, what with his annoying habits like reading movie credits out loud and keeping his money stapled to his undershirt. The essay ends not long after the wedding with Sarah's friends barely resisting the temptation to say "I told you so."

The characters in Ritter's plays occupy the same precarious comic ground, though their stakes are much higher. Each play features a marriage in which a woman is victimized by her husband's inadequacies and has to learn to cope with her own. As in the essay, these women are torn by a dual impulse: hang on to the security of marriage—even a bad one—or follow the painful path of independence. The singles life after a separation means guilt, insecurity and confusing new codes of sexual behaviour. But, like marriage itself in Ritter's cosmology, it has to be faced as one of the rites of passage of the contemporary urban female. When the woman is a professional writer or performer, her relationship to her work is an additional complication. In *Automatic Pilot* Ritter attacks this material with sizzling wit, creating one of the finest comedies in the Canadian repertoire.

Born in Regina, Ritter left for Montreal and McGill University in 1965, graduating with a B.A. in drama in 1968. She went on to an M.A. at the University of Toronto Graduate Centre for Drama in 1970, married, and was back in Montreal from 1971-74 teaching at Loyola College. Her first play, *A Visitor from Charleston*, was staged at Loyola in 1974. Eva, its main character, refuses to deal with the emotional wreckage of her life which includes an actor ex-boyfriend and a would-be novelist ex-husband, opting instead for the fantasy of *Gone with the Wind* which she has seen forty-eight times. Though not a good play, *A Visitor from Charleston* provides interesting indications of the better things which were to come.

In 1974 Ritter moved to Toronto where she has lived ever since. For the next few years she wrote articles and stories for magazines such as *Chatelaine*, and in 1976 a writers' workshop at Tarragon Theatre sent her back to playwriting. By now separated herself, she wrote a hard-edged comedy about marital collapse and the need for emotional and artistic integrity. *The Splits* centres on Megan, a script writer who finally finds the strength to get her life together and "split" from all the dependencies that diminish her as a human being: the ex-husband who bleeds her, the producers who want to turn her serious drama into a sitcom, and most of all her own fearful refusal to let things die when their time has come.

After the popular success of *The Splits* at both Toronto Free Theatre and Actors' Theater of Louisville in 1978, *Winter 1671* was produced by Toronto Arts Productions in 1979. An ambitious historical drama set in seventeenth century Quebec, it is also a play about marriage and the still timely problems of three women. The central character, Renée, is a lot like Megan in period dress. But neither the costume-drama style nor the solemn tone of the play really suited Ritter's talents, and for her next project she returned to the sexual follies of our day. In preparation for dramatizing one of her own stories about a female stand-up comic recently estranged from her husband, Ritter spent the summer of 1979 performing stand-up routines at Yuk Yuk's, a Toronto comedy club. The story "You're a Taker" (published in *Saturday Night* in December 1979) became the play *Automatic Pilot*. It opened in January 1980 at Toronto's Adelaide Court, moved to Toronto Free in February and reopened in the summer for an extended run, subsequently playing in seven regional theatres from Thunder Bay to Victoria. When it won the Chalmers Award for 1980, Ritter split the $5000 cash prize with director William Lane, explaining that "marriage is a comparatively trivial undertaking beside finding a good director."

Since 1980 Ritter has done one further stage play, *The Passing Scene* (Tarragon, 1982), a look at the shaky marriage and ethical turmoil of a pair of journalists. Much of her writing has been for radio, including an adaptation of *Automatic Pilot* that won the 1982 ACTRA Award for radio drama. In addition to *Urban Scrawl* (1984), a collection of comic essays, she continues to publish short fiction and also writes a regular column for *City Woman* magazine. Ritter has been writer-in-residence at Montreal's Concordia University and the Stratford Festival, and since 1985 has hosted *Dayshift*, a popular daily radio show on CBC.

Automatic Pilot is a comedy that explores the potential dangers of a comic approach to life. Charlie is a compulsive comedienne. Onstage and off she responds to nearly everything with a joke, an avoidance mechanism that establishes safety through ironic distance. She uses humour as protective colouration, deflecting real feeling and ultimately impeding her own emotional growth. It is one of the regular manifestations of her "automatic pilot" syndrome, the switch she pulls whenever she can't bear to confront reality head-on.

Charlie has good reason to be a little gun-shy. Her ego has taken a terrible beating in the aftermath of her marriage. To have your husband leave you for another woman is bad enough; to have him leave for another man, as Alan has, can reduce a fragile self-image like Charlie's to mush. Her reactions are characteristically compulsive. She won't let go of Alan, hanging on in the desperate hope that it will all prove just a horrible misunderstanding. She naturally seeks sexual approval from other men, but uses sex "like a drug" as if it might cure her of whatever drove Alan away. On the other hand she denies her sexuality, wearing male clothing to perform a self-deprecating comedy routine that presents her as unfeminine and unattractive. Charlie seems able to operate only at extremes. She is either monogamous or promiscuous, drunk or on the wagon, funny or maudlin. She cleans the fridge either incessantly or not at all. She writes soap opera fantasy or exaggeratedly cynical comedy, but somehow misses the reality in between. The choices she makes available to herself inevitably exclude the healthy middle ground.

Charlie's taste in men shows a similar design. In some ways the fey Alan and the macho Nick couldn't be more different. Yet in other respects they are almost doubles. Both call her "babe" and both are self-serving "seventies people," always keeping their options open. Nick is the more straightforward of the two, a bastard but refreshingly honest about it, and extremely perceptive about Charlie's need to self-destruct. Alan comes off as an unsympathetic manipulator at first. But by the end he faces up to his own identity crisis more honestly than Charlie does to hers. Neither man is particularly good to or for her, but neither is finally to blame for Charlie's condition. In *The Work* Ritter says of her female characters that "their oppression is largely a product of their own mentality and their attitude about themselves. . . . It's not what people are doing to them; it's what they're doing to themselves."

That certainly is Charlie's case, as we see through her relationship with Gene. Ritter has described him as "a man of the Eighties because he combines the kind of commitment of the Sixties with the individualism of the Seventies." He is as naturally funny as Charlie but knows when to be serious. He is a writer like Charlie but uses his writing for genuine self-discovery. His perspective dominates the second act as the emotional centre of the play shifts, along with our sympathies, from Charlie to Gene. Ritter leaves the ending ambiguous, suggesting that rejecting him may be a trade-off necessary for Charlie to pursue her creative life in comedy. But Charlie's inability to accept the sanity and stability Gene offers her may be the ultimate measure of her failure. In either case, as her closing monologue makes evident, it is one of those painful choices of adult life that no amount of wisecracking can make easy.

•

Automatic Pilot was first performed on January 17, 1980, produced by New Theatre at the Court Theatre, Adelaide Court, in Toronto. Fiona Reid played Charlie, Geoffrey Bowes was Gene, John Evans was Nick and Patrick Young played Alan. The director was William Lane, the designer Roderick Hillier.

AUTOMATIC PILOT

CHARACTERS

CHARLIE, *30*
GENE, *23*
NICK, *35*
ALAN, *30*

SCENE

Toronto, time present. The action takes place over approximately two months in the late summer and early fall.

ACT ONE

Scene One

Lights come up on the area of the stage designated as The Canada Goose, a comedy club, suggested by a mike on a stand and a spotlight. CHARLIE, dressed simply in a blouse and jeans, and without her glasses, stands nervously at the mike, speaking awkwardly into it without daring to remove it from the stand.

CHARLIE   *to the audience*   I decided to try my luck as New Talent tonight, because at my age, it's an accomplishment to appear as new *anything*. This is my first time. You'd never know it, but I'm scared to death. I can't imagine why. What could be more natural than this, standing up in front of a room full of total strangers, attempting to give them the time of their lives? Actually, I'm accustomed to making a fool of myself. In real life, I'm the head writer for a soap opera. Many people ask me exactly what a head writer *is*. The fact is, the head writer is responsible for the characters only from the neck up. We have hand and foot writers, too. Even elbow writers, if the script calls for a lot of nudging. People ask me how I can waste my talent writing for *Land of Dreams*—that's the name of the soap. What I tell them is writing soap opera is a valuable community service. After a few afternoons watching *Land of Dreams*, even the chronically unemployed run out and get jobs. In case you're one of them, and wonder what's new on my show, I'll tell you. Not much. Tommy's cystic fibrosis has flared up again; Sue's abortion didn't take. And Sarah's *still* hoping no one will notice that peculiar smell coming from the basement. . . . Soap opera's what you call sit-down comedy. They told me the difference with stand-up was that the audience would rise if they liked a joke. So? . . . Does this mean I'm bombing? Too bad. I was planning to give up soap and get into this full-time. Not that TV hasn't been good to me. I live

in a real classy part of town—the chic Carlton-Sherbourne area? Also known as the Heart of Darkness? You know, Yorkville Avenue has nothing on my neighbourhood. . . .

Blackout on CHARLIE. In the black, a tape of her voice takes over and continues the story. The taped voice is surer, brisker, more experienced, and there is audience laughter on the tape.

CHARLIE   *on the tape*   I mean, my neighbourhood has exclusive high-priced shops, too. They're called variety stores. In variety stores they look at you as though you're out of your mind if you ask for something really exotic—like a lemon. But they're great for staple items. . .if your idea of a staple item is a plaster-of-Paris cheetah. And say it's after six, and the other stores are closed and you run out of fluorescent yo-yos. . . .

Lights now come up on the area that is CHARLIE's apartment, as the tape continues to run. CHARLIE, wearing her glasses, is slumped wearily in an armchair, with a cigarette, a drink and a wrist-watch. She also has a notebook and a pen. To suggest that there has been progress in her stage "style" she wears a too-large suit jacket, a long aviator scarf, and a gaudy brooch or artificial flower. Her voice comes from a small cassette recorder on a nearby table.

Still, you gotta watch those stores or they'll rip you off. I bought one of those litre-and-a-half bottles of Coke the other day? Damn thing *refused* to explode. It was a dud—

CHARLIE snaps off the tape, scribbles a note to herself.

spoken   Fifteen-thirty. Too fucking long.

She looks down at the notations on the pad for a moment, then loses interest, slumps back in the chair, sips her drink. Finally, after some indecision, she reaches for the phone, dials a long-distance number.

into phone   Hi, sweetheart, I— *pause, then coldly*   Oh. Is Alan there? *Pause.*   That's right, it's Charlie. *Pause.*   Yes, I know it's you, Jackie. *quickly*   Jimmy, I mean. Sorry, Jimmy. *Pause.*   Look, I said I was sorry. A simple mistake. Is Alan there? *Pause.*   Thank you so much. *a longer pause, then her tone becomes warmer*   Hi, sweetheart. I just thought I'd call and— *Pause.*   Jimmy, right. Okay, okay, I won't get it wrong again. *Pause.*   Alan, I don't want to discuss my attitude. I'm lonesome and I need to talk to you. *Pause.*   Yeah, I'm still doing it. I was up tonight, in fact. Fifteenth triumphant performance at The Canada Goose. But I'm getting better. It would be nice if you'd come up to Toronto sometime and catch me. *pause, trying for lightness* That's right, I work without a net. Look, is there any chance of you coming to town? *pause, then with some asperity* Uh huh. Well, when you have an audition here then. When it's worth your while to make the trip. *Pause.* I know you didn't mean it that way, Alan. You never mean it that way. Look, I've got to get some sleep here. *Pause.* Yeah, fine. Just fine. Don't worry. Bye, bye, sweetheart. Goodbye, *Jackie.* I can hear you breathing on the extension. *slamming down the phone* Fuck it.

She pours herself another drink, ponders for a moment, then her expression relaxes and a sardonic smile crosses her face. She connects the mike to the tape recorder, pushes the record button.

into the mike Jackie, Jimmy, what's the difference? I mean, they've all got names basically suitable for embroidering on the front of a pair of coveralls, right? Names they swiped off the Mouseketeers. Aw, but they're great guys, the Jackies and the Jimmies and the Bobbies. I figure God invented gay guys so there'd be people around to remind us of how good the Bette Midler special was. If it weren't for gay guys, who'd buy bean-bag frogs? Or dimmer switches for the chandeliers? Most important, if there were no gay guys, who'd point out the smudged glasses in restaurants and send them back? Gay guys are terrific at sending back smudged glasses. It's weird, though. How they'll pick up some stranger at the baths, no questions asked, and end up on penicillin for six months. But they won't go near a smudged glass at Bemelmans. *pause, then wearily* Take my life— please.

Blackout.

Scene Two

Lights come up on GENE, in shirt and jeans, sitting at the desk in the area that serves as his room. He speaks into the mike of a cassette recorder.

GENE *improvising* Deathless Prose, by Eugene Bolton, is simply that. This daring, tough, tender, compassionate, evocative first novel by a breath-taking new talent makes *Crime and Punishment* look like a cakewalk; towers head and shoulders over anything Thomas Pynchon ever dreamed of writing, and would have *killed* Faulkner, were he not already dead. The young Canadian author . . . law student, bon vivant, and sometimes employee of the Hudson's Bay Department Store—

An alarm clock on the desk rings. GENE breaks off, shuts off the alarm and then the tape.

Shit. *staring at the clock* Now, what the hell? Oh. *leaning back, shouting* Nick? Nick!

No response. GENE puts on his glasses, rises, and leaves the desk area which is then plunged into blackness. As he moves into NICK's bedroom area, lights come up there to reveal an anonymous form asleep alone in a large rumpled bed. GENE approaches the bed without really looking at the contents.

Come on, tiger. You order wake-up, you get wake-up. Ohh, say can you seee, By the—

CHARLIE, startled, sits up, clutching the sheet around her.

CHARLIE What the fuck??—

She and GENE stare at each other uncomprehendingly.

GENE Oh. Sorry. *starting to leave* As you were. As you were.

CHARLIE Wait!

She locates her glasses, puts them on, gazes around again, but with no more comprehension. GENE watches as her glance falls on her own clothes, strewn on the floor.

GENE *kindly* What's the matter? Don't you know where you are?

CHARLIE Of course I do. *with a hopeful smile* At your place.

GENE Lucky shot.

CHARLIE Don't be silly. I . . . *infusion of warmth* I had a wonderful time.

GENE Good. You must get it into your diary. Before it fades. *as she continues to stare at him* What's wrong?

CHARLIE You . . . look different, somehow.

GENE No way. I've looked the same since I was sixteen. I can show you my high school yearbook. *He sits companionably on the bed.* Come on, admit it. You don't remember a goddamn thing.

CHARLIE I wish you wouldn't say that. *rubbing her temples* So loudly.

GENE Oldest story in the world. You have a couple too many, it feels like somebody slipped you a Mickey Finn. Strange guy brings you home, practises a little necrophilia on your comatose body. You wake up with a big headache and a big blank where your memory used to be. . . .

CHARLIE You've got a great way with words. Have you considered cheap detective fiction?

GENE *bleakly* Right now I'm considering the monastery.

CHARLIE What?

GENE I might as well. I mean, usually a night with me is something a woman remembers all her life, tells her grandchildren about when they're old enough to hear.... But look at the impression I made on you. El Blanko.

CHARLIE   Bullshit. Total recall. It was great.

GENE   Don't try to spare me. Besides, I wasn't too bowled over either.

CHARLIE   Oh now, look, maybe the earth didn't pitch violently for either of us, but you don't have to be like *that*.

GENE   No, as far as I'm concerned, it never happened.

CHARLIE   Of all the insulting.... Look, we both made a mistake, that's all.

GENE   *grinning* Uh-uh. *You* made a mistake, honey—

NICK enters through the doorway, dressed only in slacks and socks, towelling his slightly damp hair.

Now, does *this* guy ring a bell?

CHARLIE   *glancing rapidly from NICK to GENE* Why, you son of a bitch!

NICK   *mildly* Hey, babe...

CHARLIE   *indicating GENE*   I mean him.

GENE   You sure now? We all look alike in the dark.

NICK   I see you two have met.   *kissing CHARLIE* Hiya, babe.

CHARLIE   *faintly*   Hi.

GENE   *to CHARLIE*   His name is Nick.

CHARLIE   *quickly*   I know. Nick. I *know*.

NICK   *to CHARLIE*   Gene's my kid brother. But I guess you know that.

CHARLIE   I didn't. But your awful secret's safe with me.

NICK   *laughing*   That's what you get, Geno. For sneaking in and trying to make time with my chick.

GENE   You set your clock in my room. I assumed you wanted a wake-up.

NICK   I did? Guess I was a little hammered last night.

GENE   *smiling at CHARLIE*   Lot of that going around.

NICK   Anyway, I woke up early. And went down for a swim.

CHARLIE   Swim?

NICK   Yeah, this building has everything. Pool. Sauna. Squash.

GENE   Elevators. The rent's six-ten a month.   *to NICK*   I thought I'd save you the trouble of telling her.

NICK   Five-twenty. Fuck off, little brother.

GENE   And as a struggling student, I can only afford to give him one-twenty-five. He'll tell you that, too.

CHARLIE   Well, I'll try to act surprised.

NICK   I said fuck off. There's coffee in the kitchen.

GENE exits.

CHARLIE   Is he always like that?

NICK   Just lately. He's working at the Bay for the summer. It gets him down.   *putting a robe around her shoulders*   He's going to make one sharp lawyer, though. Hey...   *warmly*   You were really good last night, babe. Did I tell you that?

CHARLIE   *pleased*   Thank you. You weren't so bad yourself.

NICK   How do you think that stuff up?

CHARLIE   Well...I just lie there, and it comes to me....

NICK   Goddamn, that bit about lottery tickets—

CHARLIE   Oh. The *act*.

NICK   I'm telling you, you'd be great in a movie with that stuff.

CHARLIE   Oh, come on, now....

NICK   Seriously. You'd go. I've got an instinct for what goes. Every film I've put money in, I've made back at least double.

CHARLIE   You're involved in movies?

NICK   The financial end. And you'd go. But I told you that. Last night.

CHARLIE   Nick, to tell you the truth, I'm just a little vague about last night. I mean, I guess we met at the club, and—

NICK   You guess. You're cute. Christ, we sat there talking till they cleared all the glasses off the table—   *Pause.*   You don't remember that? Jesus.

CHARLIE   It's just.... After the show, I—check out sometimes. Especially if I drink.

NICK   Well, you certainly can drink. Hey, you were bombed? No shit?

CHARLIE   I wasn't bombed. Did I act bombed?

NICK   No. Believe me, I'm not in the habit of dragging home drunken women.

CHARLIE   And I wasn't drunk. I just have—gaps sometimes. My body keeps going after my mind quits....   *softly*   Hey, I remember some things. And I had a wonderful time.

NICK   You sure now? I guess I could tell you it was the greatest sexual experience of your life and you'd have to believe me.

CHARLIE And how did it rate for you? *quickly* Forget it. It was a dumb question.

NICK Real dumb. *He kisses her.*

CHARLIE You have a certain backhand way with compliments.

NICK My forehand's pretty good too.

CHARLIE Well, sure. Squash courts right in the building.

NICK *laughing* You're great. Hey—

He kisses her.

CHARLIE Hey what?

NICK Hey, where have you been all my life?

CHARLIE Waiting under the clock at Grand Central. What kept you?

NICK You want coffee or something?

CHARLIE *seductively* Something. If I have the choice.

NICK I'll get you some coffee.

CHARLIE *disappointed* Oh.

NICK It's just that I have a meeting this morning.

CHARLIE On Sunday? What are you, a Quaker?

NICK I have to see a man about a restaurant. That's my main weakness, restaurants. But I told you that.

CHARLIE This seems to have been a very open relationship. Too bad I missed it.

NICK What do you take in your coffee?

CHARLIE Cream and sugar. But I told you that.

NICK Smartass.

NICK exits. Humming happily, CHARLIE locates her purse among the rubble of her clothing, takes a compact from it, looks at herself and abruptly stops humming. She starts scrubbing the smudged makeup on her face with a kleenex.

CHARLIE Jesus Christ. Gone for coffee, my ass. He's gone to call a plastic surgeon.

GENE appears at the doorway with a mug of coffee.

GENE You look ravishing.

CHARLIE *turning in surprise* Where's Nick?

GENE He's running late. Cream and sugar, right?

CHARLIE You mean he left?

GENE You know Nick. He hates emotional good-byes. *He puts the coffee in her hand.* But he wanted you to have this. Don't worry, I'll drive you home.

CHARLIE You don't have to do that.

GENE Oh, I'm used to it.

CHARLIE What kind of crack is that—you're used to driving Nick's girls home?

GENE I don't want you to feel alone. As though you'd bombed somehow.

CHARLIE Thanks.

GENE Actually, I don't usually drive his girls.

CHARLIE Aha, I did bomb.

GENE No! It's just that most of them have cars.

CHARLIE I liked it better when I just felt alone. Gene, if you don't mind, I'd like to get dressed. Before you tell me how many other girls you've seen in this robe.

GENE Very few. It's mine.

CHARLIE Oh—I'm sorry.

GENE No sorrier than me. It looks good on you, though. That'll give me incentive.

CHARLIE Thank you. If you'll let me get dressed, you can have it back.

GENE You know, you shouldn't take Nick personally. He's got the manners of a forklift.

CHARLIE *brightening* You mean it was nothing I did?

GENE Boy, you are really something. You meet the guy—what, last night? And take the blame for the habits of a lifetime. *as she says nothing* Do you always assume everything's your fault?

CHARLIE I suppose this is a course in law school. Badgering the Witness.

GENE Law school's Nick's idea. Actually, I'm a writer.

CHARLIE Ah, you writers. Nothing much gets past you, does it? I'd really love to read your work. I think I've got an old sales slip from the Bay. Maybe it's one of yours?

GENE *starting for the door* The car's in the underground garage. Come down to the front door when you're dressed.

CHARLIE Gene! *as he turns around* I'm sorry. I make a lot of crummy jokes. Ask Nick. He saw my act.

GENE Nick liked your act. He told me.

CHARLIE Did he—mention anything else?

GENE *smiling* He'll call you. Sometime this evening.

CHARLIE You wouldn't kid me about that?

GENE No. I'm sorry I gave you such a hard time, when I woke you up.

CHARLIE Oh, what the hell.... Talk to me when you're my age, sonny. We'll see if *you* get all the names straight in the morning.

GENE   Bullshit. You're the type who puts "Sleep Around" on her Things To Do list.

CHARLIE   Now, what the hell is that supposed to mean?

GENE   I just don't think you've got a lot of experience with this kind of thing. What are you, married or something? Divorced? Or—separated? Yeah, I like separated. Very half-assed. Very seventies.

CHARLIE   Lucky shot.

GENE   Naw, a lot of Nick's ladies are separated.

CHARLIE   *sinking down dispiritedly on the bed* Just the ones without cars, I hope. I'd hate to fuck up the demographic profile.

GENE   *sitting down beside her*   I'm sorry. I really am.

CHARLIE   So am I. About everything. Particularly the invention of alcohol.

GENE   How much do you remember about last night?

CHARLIE   Not much. Pretty funny, eh?

GENE   I'm not laughing.

CHARLIE   Neither am I. Say something hilarious.

GENE   Want to get married?

CHARLIE   *with a startled laugh*   What?

GENE   See? I knew that would raise a smile.

CHARLIE   I can't marry a man with prospects. It's against my religion.

GENE   I'm thinking of quitting law school.

CHARLIE   Aw, that's what they all say.

GENE   No, seriously, I am.

CHARLIE   Even so, you can't marry me, sonny. I'm old enough to be your mother.

GENE   Bullshit. You're only as old as you feel.

CHARLIE   *looking into her compact mirror wearily* I know. Christ, look at this. First runner-up in the René Lévesque Look-Alike Contest.

GENE   Stop that. But I am going to quit. Don't tell Nick.

CHARLIE   When am I going to tell him? I'll probably never see him again.

GENE   Oh, you'll see him. If you want to.

CHARLIE   You make it sound like I shouldn't.

GENE   You make it sound like you want to. Get dressed and I'll drive you home.

CHARLIE   I told you, I can get home myself.

GENE   Okay. Whatever you like.

He moves to the door.

CHARLIE   Gene—   *as he stops*   Thanks—for the use of the robe.

GENE   Anytime. I know—that's what they all say.

He gives her a smile and exits on a blackout.

Scene Three

A couple of weeks later. Lights come up on the area that is CHARLIE's apartment. The room is empty, but there is the sound of someone rattling at the door. The rattling continues until a credit card slides through the lock, then the door opens and ALAN enters, with a small suitcase. He is obviously pleased with himself for pulling off the credit card stunt, shuts the door and tenderly replaces the card in his wallet. He puts down the suitcase, goes immediately to the phone and dials.

ALAN   *into the phone*   Hello, Deborah? It's Alan. *Pause.*   Alan Merrit. The actor? One of your clients? *laughing*   Right. That explains why you never get me any work. You have no idea who I am.   *Pause.*   Yeah, slow season, I know. Funny how it's always slow season when I'm in town and Audition City when I'm away. . . .   *Pause.*   Skip it, Deborah. I'll be in town a couple of days at— *checking phone dial*   967-1313. I'll check back with you before I leave.   *Pause.*   Alan, that's right. Alan Merrit.

He hangs up dispiritedly, lights a cigarette, looks up an address in his book, then dials again, singing quietly, "I really want this job, I really need this job. . . ."

ALAN   *into the phone*   Hello, Grant Austin, please. It's Alan Merrit calling.   *Pause.*   Hello, is he in? It's Alan Merrit.   *Pause.*   Hello, Grant, it's—   *Pause.* Oh. Well, *could* he come to the phone? It's Alan Merrit. He's expecting my call.   *Pause.*   Look, I made a special trip into town to see him. Couldn't he—?   *Pause.*   Thank you. I appreciate it.   *longer pause, then*   Grant! Hi! You said to call Tuesday and it's—   *Pause.*   Alan Merrit? You said—   *Pause.* Alan, right. The actor? We met at the Molière opening and—   *Pause.*   No, I wasn't exactly *in* it, but we talked at the bar after and—   *Pause.*   Yeah, I guess I might have been in a red shirt.   *Pause.* Thank you, it's one of my favourite colours too. . . . Look, Grant, you said Tuesday would be a good day to call, so I came in from Stratford and—   *Pause.* No, I'm not exactly *in* the Stratford company, but— *Pause.*   Oh, *next* Tuesday. I guess I misunderstood. But I did come into town to see you, and— *Pause.* Well, how be if I call back in the morning? Just to see if your schedule's cleared? I'd really like five minutes of your—   *Pause.*   Okay, Grant, fine. I'll call back in the morning.

He hangs up, speaking bitterly to himself.

ALAN   Any special colour you'd like me to wear?

The phone, which is in his lap, rings. He starts violently, picks it up.

into the phone   Hello?   *Pause.*   Look, I said not to call here. You know how she—   *Pause.*   Yeah, I just got off the phone with Austin. He's delighted I'm here and wants to see me tomorrow.   *Pause.* Oh, it's not such a big deal. If you know the right strings to pull.   *Pause.*   I don't know. Tomorrow night, maybe, or Thursday. Depends.

Unnoticed by ALAN, CHARLIE has come in the open door and stands in the doorway. She has a paper bag of liquor in her arms.

ALAN   *into the phone*   Yes, I miss you, too. But I—

As CHARLIE rattles the bag angrily, ALAN turns and sees her.

ALAN   *into the phone*   Look, I've got to go, okay? Call you tomorrow.

He hangs up, turning to CHARLIE with a bright smile.
Hiya, babe!

CHARLIE   Well, surprise, surprise!   *allowing him to kiss her*   Who was that on the phone?

ALAN   Nobody. Casting people.

CHARLIE   Who miss you? Shucks, I bet they say that to *all* the actors. It was him, wasn't it?

ALAN   He's got a name, you know.

CHARLIE   "Casting people." Why do you keep lying? Force of habit?

ALAN   I just got here. Can't we save the cracks for later?

CHARLIE   How'd you get in?

ALAN   Credit card.

CHARLIE   That's amazing.

ALAN   *self-effacing*   Oh, I wouldn't go that far. . . .

CHARLIE   That *you* were actually issued a credit card? That's nothing short of miraculous.

ALAN   Actually, it's Jimmy's.

CHARLIE   Good old Jimmy. Say it with plastic. So what are you doing in town?

ALAN   You've been after me to come up and see you.

CHARLIE   Uh-huh. And—?

ALAN   And. . .I've got some people to see.

CHARLIE   Yeah, I figured.

ALAN   Grant Austin, for one. I hope that's okay.

CHARLIE   Well, if it's okay with Grant Austin, it's okay with me.

ALAN   I mean, it's all right to stay here.

CHARLIE   Here? In my apartment? It's out of the question.

ALAN   Charlie, I'm your husband. Who's going to object?

CHARLIE   My boyfriend. To name one.

ALAN   I didn't know you had a steady boyfriend.

CHARLIE   I figured if you had one, I should too. Alan, Nick will be here in a minute. We're going to The Canada Goose.

ALAN   You're on tonight? Terrific. Can I join you?

CHARLIE   You want to come along? You won't feel a little weird about Nick?

ALAN   Should I? I mean, is there something organically wrong with him?

CHARLIE   I give up. You can't crash here. That's all there is to it.

ALAN   That's nice. That's very nice. After eight years of marriage, this is what I get?

CHARLIE   *quiz show voice*   This, Alan, and much much more! During your marriage, you received: four million loads of clean laundry; the keys to a car your wife never got to drive; leftovers no more than twice a week; plus sex available at several convenient locations in your own home!! Yes, Alan, these are only some of the prizes you won playing Eight Years of Marriage!

ALAN   Charlie, don't be that way. I thought we'd got past all the bitterness.

CHARLIE   I hope not. I mean, when that's gone, what's left?

ALAN   I don't know. A new start, maybe?

CHARLIE   As what? I admit, I've always *wanted* a sister, but—

ALAN   Knock that off.

CHARLIE   Then *you* knock it off.   *pouring herself a drink*   Oh, Alan, don't tell me you're having doubts about your femininity again.

ALAN   I should know better than to expect to be taken seriously.

CHARLIE   Oh, I took you seriously, all right. The last two years of our marriage when you said you were working late all those nights. I took you seriously when you told me I was crazy to think any different. And I took you very seriously indeed when you disappeared into the pages of *Christopher Street*, never to emerge again. Now, I'd say there was a limit to just how long a person can go on taking you seriously. Or any way at all. Wouldn't you?

ALAN   If that's how you feel, why do you keep asking me to come and see you?

CHARLIE   I don't know.

ALAN   Neither do I. Can you pour me one too?

CHARLIE   On one condition. That you refrain from referring to homosexuality as a "phase." You always make it sound like teenage acne.   *She gives him a drink.*

ALAN   I know what you've been through. But it's not easy on me, either. Especially when you phone me up, late at night—

CHARLIE   There won't be any more calls. Not that kind. I'm feeling much better now.

ALAN   Thanks to Nick?

CHARLIE   What's the matter? Don't you believe someone could be interested in me?

ALAN   Oh, I believe it. Do you?

CHARLIE   I don't have this adverse effect on everybody, you know. I don't drive all men to gay bars.

ALAN   Did I ever say you did?

CHARLIE   Yes.

ALAN   *after a pause*   I'm sorry. I guess I had to blame somebody.

CHARLIE   I wish you'd picked your mother, like everybody else. She lives six hundred miles away. It wouldn't have fucked *her* up.

ALAN   You're not fucked up. Not any more. Thanks to Nick.

CHARLIE   So it does bother you a little?

ALAN   We've been split up almost a year. I know there've been guys. . . .

CHARLIE   Oh dear, and I thought I was so discreet!

ALAN   Come on. You always made sure I knew.

CHARLIE   *after a pause*   Most of those guys were clunkers.

ALAN   And Nick isn't a clunker? *Pause.* Okay, it bothers me.

CHARLIE   *gently*   It's just this phobia you've got. About closed doors. Most people think of the world as their oyster. In your mind, it's one big telephone exchange. With everyone on Hold.

ALAN   Only you, babe. Come here, and let me put you on Hold.

He hugs her. There is a knock on the door.

CHARLIE   That's Nick. I guess he forgot his credit card.

She opens the door. NICK enters and gives her a bottle of champagne.

NICK   Hiya, babe. Bubbly to the bubbly. In honour of your performance.

CHARLIE   I perform twice a week. Champagne is for special.

NICK   Then be specially good. Dom Perignon, kid. Don't give me no domestic-bubbly performance.

He kisses her, then sees ALAN.

Oh. Hi.

CHARLIE   Nick, this is Alan.   *as the men shake hands*   My late husband.

NICK   *dropping the hand like a hot rock*   Charlie! Je-sus.

ALAN   Charlie's little joke. And it's little.

NICK   *backing toward the door*   Look, I didn't know you were double-booked here. And if you two have things to straighten out—

CHARLIE   *quickly*   No, Alan's just dropped in from Stratford.

ALAN   *also quick*   Just to say hello.

CHARLIE   *even quicker*   Not even that, practically.

ALAN   Don't mind me.

NICK   *shrugging sheepishly*   If you'd had as many husbands sprung on you as I have. . . . Now, whenever I hear the word, I automatically check the exits.   *to ALAN*   In from Stratford, eh?

ALAN   Couple of business things.

NICK   Ball bearings?

ALAN   I beg your pardon?

NICK   *innocently*   That's what they do up in Stratford, isn't it?

CHARLIE   Nick's little joke. He grew up there. He knows goddamn well there's a theatre there.

NICK   She's right. Saturday nights, our idea of a hot old time was driving into town to bash a few faggot actors.

CHARLIE   *quickly*   Have a drink, Nick.   *producing a bottle from the bag*   I got some Scotch, just for you. Alan?

ALAN   *campily*   No thanks. I'll stick to Shirley Temples.

NICK   *laughing*   Hey, that's good. So, you're with the Festival. Watch your ass, that's all I can say.

ALAN   *very macho*   I'm not with the Festival yet. You think I'm watching my ass *too* closely?

NICK   Could be. What do you think, Charlie? You're the resident expert on the gay scene.

ALAN   *to CHARLIE*   Do tell.

NICK   Babe, how does that bit go, about the faggots in the restaurant?   *to ALAN*   They're always sending back dirty forks, right, then they pick up some stranger and get the clap.

ALAN   That's very funny, Charlie. Not very insightful, but funny.

CHARLIE   I do a whole bunch of different stuff. You'll see.

ALAN   Some other time, maybe.

CHARLIE   I thought you wanted to come tonight.

ALAN   I've changed my mind. *picking up his suitcase* Have a good show. I'll call you tomorrow.

CHARLIE   Alan—

ALAN   *more conciliatory* Look, I've got a heavy day tomorrow. I have to be on the phone early to Grant Austin and—

NICK   Grant? You working with him?

ALAN   *stiffly* I'd like to.

NICK   *to CHARLIE* Grant was on that picture I told you about. Christ, I more than tripled on that one.

ALAN   *setting down his suitcase* Lupercal? You had money in that?

NICK   Lucky me. You see the numbers on that fucker?

ALAN   No, but I saw the fucker. It was great.

NICK   Grant's dynamite. Camp as a row of tents, but a hell of a director. You seeing him tomorrow?

ALAN   He's not sure what his time is like.

NICK   Well, he starts casting next week. You better catch him before the big rush.

ALAN   You don't happen to know what the film is?

NICK   Another blockbuster, I hope. I've got money in this one too.

ALAN   *avidly* No kidding? You haven't seen a script, by any chance?

NICK   I know where to get one. Why?

ALAN   *to CHARLIE* Listen, maybe I *can* join you at the club. Once I dump the suitcase. . . .

CHARLIE   I thought you had such an early day ahead.

ALAN   *artificially sweet* I thought you wanted me to see your act.

CHARLIE   *the same* A minute ago, my act rated slightly below trench-mouth.

ALAN   I haven't got any idea what you're talking about.

CHARLIE   Haven't you? I mean it's just amazing how the atmosphere in this room has warmed up since Grant Austin dropped in.

ALAN   *to NICK* You don't mind if I join you later at The Canada Goose? And maybe talk about this new script?

NICK   I don't mind. I like to talk. Charlie knows that.

ALAN   *picking up his suitcase* See you later, then. Bye, babe.

He exits. CHARLIE takes a long sip of her drink.

NICK   Nervous kind of guy. He any good?

CHARLIE   I don't know. He never gives himself a chance to find out. He's too busy making useful contacts.

NICK   You should talk. Soon as you found out I backed movies, you couldn't get your clothes off fast enough.

CHARLIE   Nick! You don't believe that.

NICK   Come on, you're entitled to your self-interest, like everybody else. It doesn't detract from the quality of the sex.

CHARLIE   I'm telling you, I'm not in it for the fringe benefits. I want to get that clear, Nick.

NICK   You people with "pure motives". You make me nervous.

CHARLIE   Oh, I'm not so pure. . . . *putting her arms around him* Let's not talk about work. You've already got Alan prepared to lay down his life for you because you might be useful to him. Isn't that enough?

NICK   I don't get it. If I can get him in to see Austin, why shouldn't I? If I can do you a favour too, why not? What is it, you've got your life in ledger columns? "Business." "Romance."

CHARLIE   That's right. Just don't mix me in with business, that's all. This town is one giant office. Casting done in bars. Contracts ratified on waterbeds. People sucking up to power because it might rub off. Those macrobiotic people had it all wrong. Around here, you are *who* you eat.

NICK   You don't know a goddamn thing about it. Work, sex, dinner, dealing—it's all the same. I don't even try keeping them apart. And I like people who do the same. No questions asked.

CHARLIE   *pouring herself a drink* That's a tall order.

NICK   *indicating drink* Hey, you're working tonight. Were you always such a little lush? Even when you were married to what's-his-name?

CHARLIE   Lush. You make me sound like a golf course. This is only my second. And anyway, what's it got to do with what's-his-name?

NICK   That's what I wonder. What broke you two up? You never told me.

CHARLIE   You never asked. I like that arrangement. *kissing him* I don't want to talk about it. I want to fool around.

NICK You always want to fool around. What did you do, wear the guy out?

CHARLIE *sharply* Will you forget about Alan?

NICK No, I want to know. What was the problem?

CHARLIE *exasperated* Isn't it obvious? My frigidity!

NICK Hey, How come you always act like you'll never get laid again?

CHARLIE Right now, I'd settle for a really decisive kiss.

NICK sighs, then kisses her very decisively. She pulls away finally, hesitates for a moment before speaking.

Nick. . . . Do you think I'm attractive?

NICK You haven't figured that out?

CHARLIE I mean—do you like being with me?

NICK Hell, no. When you stop giving green stamps, I'm gone.

CHARLIE *urgently* Nick—please?

NICK *pause, then with slight distaste* Okay. Of course I like being with you. Very much.

CHARLIE Yeah, I figured.

She pulls him to her, kisses him.

NICK Hardcore comes later. It's almost show time.

CHARLIE How be if I skip the club? We could have a nice evening—just you, me and Dom Perignon.

NICK You can't just back out.

CHARLIE Sure I can. There's always someone hanging around who'll take over my spot.

NICK You expect to get ahead with an attitude like that?

CHARLIE It was just a thought.

NICK What's the problem?

CHARLIE I just don't feel very funny tonight.

NICK No? Well, you goddamn well better be. Unless you want to sleep alone.

CHARLIE *mock terror* Oh, shit. *quickly* Say, did I ever tell you the one about the lady comic, her bullying boyfriend and the vat of cold vichyssoise? Funny? You bet. Seems the comic was walking over the vichyssoise on a tightrope and—

NICK Okay, okay. You don't sleep alone. Now let's get the fuck out of here.

She picks up her purse and he slaps her on the ass on the way out the door on a blackout.

Scene Four

Later that night. Lights come up on The Canada Goose. CHARLIE wears the now habitual uniform of her performance—her glasses, jacket, scarf and brooch.

CHARLIE *bounding down to the mike, removing it from stand, addressing the audience* Hi, how is everybody tonight? Come on, it's not a trick question. How about you, sir? How are you? *if the audience doesn't answer* It's all right, sir. I read lips. *if audience member does answer* Who asked you?

Hey, I'm in a great mood tonight. I just got my Mensa card. *taking a card from her pocket, showing it* You know what that means? It means I'm insured against ever skipping a period.

So. . .how do you like my hair? Mr Doug did it. That's my hairdresser—Mr Doug. Ever notice what flamboyant names Canadian hairdressers have? Mr Doug. Mr Glen. Mr Garth of North Bay. Mr Doug told me he was just going to "shape the hair." Notice how they never refer to it as YOUR hair? This is so they can wreck it without either of you feeling personally affected by it.

But I trust Mr Doug. Implicitly. I mean, he doesn't charge an arm and a leg like those trendy uptown places, where you pay for the decor and the cute little cover-up robe. Mr Doug works out of an auto body shop. He keeps his costs down that way. Although I notice the Turtle Wax IS doing strange things to my hair. And there was this mix-up one day where a lady came in for a cut and set and wound up getting a ring job. *to an audience member who is laughing* Hey, that's not funny. It's tragic. I suppose you laughed when Ben Hur's mother and sister got leprosy.

You know, I have what people in showbusiness describe as a great RADIO face. Actually, it's not mine. It comes attached to the glasses. It's part of a disguise. See, when you look like Bo Derek, everybody mobs you. Okay, okay. . .so I don't look like Bo Derek. But I am a Ten. I'm what they call a Canadian Ten. Which means they don't even accept me at par in Buffalo. *indicating audience member* This man is laughing. He has no idea what I go through. Great shirt, sir. How long do you have to wear it before you win the bet?

Oh, by the way, a note was slipped to me backstage. But I intend to go on with the act anyway. No, seriously. . .I have a note here. *producing note from her pocket, reading from it* Mrs. D of Erin Mills writes: "Dear Charlie, Where do you get your ideas for the characters on *Land of Dreams?*" Oh, in case you don't know, *Land of Dreams* is the name of this soap opera I write for. Where do I get my ideas for characters, Mrs D? I steal them from American soaps and change their names to Glen and Doug. Any more questions? *without waiting for a reply* Fine.

Hey, you know, I always wanted to be one of those teensy little girls. You know the kind I mean? The kind of girl whose nickname is Bitsy? The kind of girl I lend a bracelet to, and she wears it as a belt. Helpless. That was always my goal in life. To be helpless. Helpless and sweet and quiet. Like Bitsy. Bitsy never has to talk. She's mastered one simple basic sentence—"How was your day, honey?"—and the world's beating a path to her door. I meanwhile am lucky if a guy ventures up my walk to read my meter. See, men just don't come on to big, capable girls—girls who speak English as if it was their native language. Especially when your voice sounds like Full Alert in the London Blitz. I ask a guy if he wants to come to bed, and it sounds like a threat. Now, Bitsy has this tiny, feminine, whispering voice, right? Put her on a phone, man, and she gets results. *imitating* "Hello? Oh, hi, Brad. Dinner? No thanks. I just ate half a soda biscuit and I couldn't touch another thing."

When Bitsy goes shopping for clothes, the clerks always advise her to try the Petite Section, right? The Petite Section. It even sounds elegant, doesn't it? So what do they call the large section? You guessed it. The Large Section. And I so much as even try walking into the Petite Section and they throw a cordon around the entire department and get on the bullhorns— *imitating* "Attention all staff. Large person attempting entry. Large person attempting entry." Then they send some little Munchkin over to reason with me, right? *imitating* "Listen, honey, nothing personal, but you're built like a Maytag, all right?"

You notice how tiny all the clerks are in the Petite Section? The manager of the department wears a point-zero-six dress. I'm not kidding. And when I won't go quietly, the entire staff rushes to the barricades. It looks like a convention of jockeys. They all swarm around my kneecaps chanting— *imitating* "Follow the yellow brick road. Follow the yellow brick road . . ."

Hey, you've been a great audience. Thank you and goodnight!

Blackout.

Scene Five

Later that night. Lights come up on a table in The Canada Goose where Alan sits alone with a full drink. CHARLIE, dressed as in Scene Four, hurries breathlessly to the table. She stops short, glances around.

ALAN   *rising, kissing her*   Babe, that was dynamite.

CHARLIE   Where's Nick?

ALAN   He said he's sorry he missed the act. Something—

CHARLIE   *joining in*   "Something came up." Fuck.

She sits down.

ALAN   He went to make a call about that script, and when he came back he said he had to leave.

CHARLIE   You had to have that goddamn script, didn't you?

ALAN   Since you ask, yes. It would be very helpful. *Pause.* He said he'd try to make it back to your place later.

CHARLIE   White of him. I want a drink.

ALAN   *pushing the drink over to her*   Here. I ordered it for you.

CHARLIE   Thanks.

ALAN   Babe, you were wonderful. The fact that Nick missed it doesn't change that.

CHARLIE   You think that's all I care about? Whether he saw the fucking *act*?

ALAN   I figured you'd care. Nick says he'd like to back a film with you in it.

CHARLIE   I'm not in it to get ahead! I don't quaff cocktails with people I hate just to get a script.

ALAN   Is that how you think I operate?

CHARLIE   I *watched* you operate with Nick.

ALAN   *bitterly*   All right, so what? The guy's a redneck, but his money's the same colour as anyone else's. If Grant Austin can put up with Nick's faggot jokes, I guess I can too. *Pause.* You don't understand, Charlie. You can stand up in front of a roomful of people without anybody's help and run your own show. I can't.

CHARLIE   Oh, I know how to get love from groups of twenty or more, all right. But one to one? You could give me some tips in that area. I mean, at least you've got Jackie—

ALAN   *mechanically*   Jimmy—

CHARLIE   —Jimmy, to keep the home fires burning while you're out knocking on doors. I come out of the spotlight, and find the bastard's taken a powder.

ALAN   Charlie, it's not easy. For anybody. But as long as you've got the spotlight, you're way ahead. I wish I could do what you do—dress up in a costume and act out my worst fears about myself.

CHARLIE   It's not a costume!

ALAN   Come on. You look like an out-take from *Annie Hall*. All the years I knew you, you were too vain to wear your glasses, even.

CHARLIE   *snatching off her glasses*   There are no glamorous lady comics. It doesn't work.

ALAN   You dress like that because you think it's how you really look. I admire you for that. I wouldn't have the nerve to go up there—or anywhere else—and try to be myself.

CHARLIE   *taking his hand*   Sweetheart, what's the matter?

ALAN   It's—confusing, that's all. I think I've got my priorities straight—or bent, or something. Then I see you, and you're telling stories about queers picking up tricks—

CHARLIE   *quickly*   I didn't use any of that stuff tonight.

ALAN   But you tell the stories all the same. And I don't recognize myself in them.

CHARLIE   Of course not. Alan, that isn't *you*.

ALAN   Then what is? What do you see, Charlie?

CHARLIE   I don't know. What do you want me to see? What do you want me to do?

ALAN   I don't know. I had some idea when I decided to come into town that maybe . . .   *He shrugs.*

CHARLIE   That maybe what?

ALAN   Of course, I didn't know about Nick. I hadn't counted on that.

CHARLIE   *urgently*   Alan, you can't *do* this to me. If you want something, tell me.

ALAN   I guess there's nothing you can do.

CHARLIE   Not if you're going to be so goddamn cryptic.

ALAN   Charlie, what difference does it make now? Nick's in the picture, and all bets are off.

CHARLIE   You mean it's safe to make overtures, now that I'm hooked on someone else?

ALAN   Yeah. I guess maybe that's it. You are hooked, aren't you?

CHARLIE   Yes, I'm afraid so.

ALAN   That's all right, then.

CHARLIE   Not from where I sit. God, I wish I knew how he felt about me.

ALAN   And if the verdict's favourable? You might decide you're fit to live?

CHARLIE   Isn't that what it means when you're hooked?

ALAN   No! There's a big difference between caring about him and building your life around the idea. I mean, when do you stop expecting other people to supply you with self-respect?

CHARLIE   You make me sound like a backward nation.   *travelogue voice*   "Here in Charlieland, the natives try to find enough self-esteem to power even one generator."

ALAN   That's not funny, babe.

CHARLIE   Neither is venereal disease. But you know, it's a sure-fire laugh?

Blackout.

Scene Six

A few days later. Lights come up in NICK's bedroom. NICK is asleep. GENE comes in, begins stealthily dialing the phone. NICK stirs, raises his head.

NICK   *annoyed and sleepy*   What? Gene, what the fuck are you doing?

GENE   *hanging up the phone*   Sorry, but the one in the kitchen is temporarily out of service.

NICK   *rubbing his eyes*   This is just an extension, you asshole. It won't work either.

GENE   Sure it will. It's out of the war zone. Mustard gas attack in the kitchen.   *German accent*   It's dat Sharlie again, mein Kapitan. She shtrikes mitout varning.

NICK   Charlie?   *looking at the empty side of the bed*   What's she doing up?

GENE   Cleaning the fridge.

NICK   Oh fuck. This is too much. Yesterday she made blueberry pancakes.

GENE   Last week she washed the windows.

NICK   Next thing I'll wake up to find my goddamn room re-papered.

GENE   I think you should nip this thing in the bud. Remember your stewardess? Almost six feet of stunning blonde stooped over the bathtub, scouring away with Spic and Span?

NICK   If that's how you feel, why don't you tell Charlie to knock it off?

GENE   Because it's not *my* fault she thinks the way to your heart is through your stinking refrigerator. Nick, you owe it to her to straighten her out.

NICK   No way. A woman's determined to dig her own grave, I'm not going to hide the shovel.

GENE   Christ. Maybe you should just tell her you don't *have* a heart.

NICK   Come on, it's too early in the morning for that crap.

GENE   It's eleven-thirty, and there's a woman in your kitchen *humming*, if you'll believe it, while she dungs rotted matter out of the fridge whose stench would turn the stomach of a wart hog. Christ, there are carrots covered in blue fuzz and mutated leftovers that the Special Effects Department at Universal should only take a look at. And yet she is out there humming, Nick—I swear it's God's honest truth—because those noxious vapours emanate from *your* fridge, *your* kitchen, *your* apartment, and as far as she's concerned, anything that pertains to *you* is strictly Chanel Number Five. No, I don't think it's at all too early in the morning for that crap. And either you go out there and tell her you love what she's doing, or advise her she's spelling out her own destruction in moulded spuds. But either way, wear a gas mask, I'm warning you.

NICK   I don't need advice on women from you. I wrote the book.

GENE   I know. It's the one with the large print and the small words. You won't help her, will you? You won't help her at all.

NICK   All this sudden concern for Charlie. What's the matter, you fumble the ball with that great-looking cocktail waitress? Sure you did, I can tell. I fix you up on Saturday night, and here you are on Sunday morning, all by yourself. Unless Donna is out in the kitchen battling bacteria with good old Charlie.

GENE   Donna would be better off if she *were* into fridges. Something. Anything. What do you talk about to someone whose idea of a moral dilemma is whether hot pink clashes with green?

NICK   You took Donna out to *talk*?

GENE   I had it in mind as an option.

NICK   Christ, what am I going to do with you? I fix you up with a beautiful girl who borders on genius, sexually speaking, and you complain because she isn't a Rhodes scholar in the bargain. What is it, they haven't invented a woman good enough for you?

GENE   Once in my life, I'd like a shot at a woman you haven't slept with first. Although I realize such women are hard to find.

NICK   Too bad you feel that way. Otherwise, you could take Charlie off my hands.

GENE   Oh, sure, we'd both go for that. I mean, her glasses are almost as strong as mine. Lasting relationships have been based on less. *with distaste* Nick, Jesus Christ. . . .

NICK   You're right, it's not much of a thought. She's cute, but she's nutty as a fruitcake. And she acts like she's mainlining Spanish Fly.

GENE   That doesn't sound so bad.

NICK   Don't kid yourself. That woman doesn't just *like* to screw. She needs it. Like a drug.

GENE   Like a drug, eh? Wow. Of course, you're in your thirties. I keep forgetting. No longer the ideal . . . drug pusher?

NICK   You know who puts out that crap—about men beginning to decline at age nineteen? Hostile women put it out, that's who. It's all part of a plot to discredit us. *Pause.* Anyway, Charlie's too old for you.

GENE   I'm twenty-three.

NICK   And she's thirty. That's exactly what I mean.

GENE   No, that's exactly what *I* mean. Charlie and I would be the ideal combination.

NICK   Bullshit. Sexual peaks have nothing to do with Charlie.

GENE   I wonder. I mean, here you are, so impressed with Donna's sexual prowess. A younger woman, not yet in her prime, not so difficult to keep up with. . . .

NICK   Good, Geno, you're doing fine. You'll be looking for a new apartment by lunchtime.

GENE   Hey, Nick, for Christ's sake. I'm only kidding.

NICK   *sulkily*   I'm telling you, that stuff about peaks is crap. I'm as hot as I ever was. With the right woman.

GENE   You mean you really don't want Charlie any more?

NICK   For Christ's sake, I just woke up. How the hell do I know what I want? I want to be a millionaire before I'm forty, I want a cup of coffee. I want a woman for a change who doesn't turn into Betty Crocker on a moment's notice.

GENE   So what are you going to do? Order the perfect one out of the catalogue? Relationships have to be worked on, haven't you heard?

NICK   I work hard all day long. Why should I work when I come home, too? Either it clicks with a woman or it doesn't, and all the heart-to-heart talks in the world never fixed anything. Take it from Nicky. Nicky knows. Gene, on the other hand, knows zip.

GENE   *quietly*   Poor Charlie.

NICK   Will you cut it out? Anyway, it's not like we're a couple or anything.

GENE   What would you call it? A string quartet?

NICK   It was just for—fun, that's all. But when the fun goes. . . . Well, I just don't have that much enthusiasm for it any more.

GENE   Big brother, you haven't had much enthusiasm for anybody since about 1968. Since then, it's been painting by numbers.

NICK   You know, this interest you take in my relationships is downright unhealthy. Why don't you find a project of your own—like losing your virginity?

GENE   You think anybody whose little black book comes in fewer volumes than the *Britannica* is a virgin. I've been around. But unlike you, I can remember *where*.

NICK   Yeah? When was the last time you got laid? I mean, here you are, so hot to be a writer. What the hell are you going to write about?

GENE If you're still pissed off about law school, why don't you just admit it?

NICK Me, pissed off? Hell, no. Why, I've got the First Lady of Show Business into some heavy defrosting out in my kitchen. And in the bedroom, the kid I staked through two years of law school who's decided on a permanent career at the pen counter of the Bay instead. By God, I'm a lucky son of a gun. I think my life would make great musical comedy, don't you?

GENE I'm sorry, I'm just not cut out for law school. Besides, I won't be at the Bay forever. Look at Charlie. She makes a living writing.

NICK Charlie! Is *she* the inspiration behind this? God, it was a dark day when I let her and her arsenal of cleaning products in here.

GENE Don't be so melodramatic. It was my own idea.

NICK Yeah? Well, at least you're right about one thing. If you're going to be a writer, make a full-time career out of it. I know people who'd be interested in you.

GENE I don't think I want to write menus.

NICK Not restaurant people, you asshole. Movie people.

GENE I've got to do it my way. Me and Sinatra.

NICK First you let somebody get you in the door. Then you do it your way.

GENE Nick, it's bad enough I live here at the Club Med with you and pay one-twenty-five in rent. I'm not going to use your connections too.

NICK You're my brother. I feel responsible.

GENE *Italian accent* Eh, Niccolo, listen to your brother, eh? Alla time, you give, give, give. But never nothing outa yourself. Capisce?

NICK Jesus, it's as bad as talking to Charlie. Worse.

GENE All my life—fastest cheque book in the West, favours done while you wait. And champagne always on ice.

NICK I never bought anybody in my life.

GENE I've seen you buy a few people *off*. Tell me, when Charlie gets her pink slip, will she get the bouquet of roses that traditionally goes with it?

NICK Jesus, I wish you'd get off that. Or go after her yourself, if you're so concerned.

GENE And break Jane Fonda's heart?

NICK *grinning* Don't lie to me, you little fucker. You'd do it, wouldn't you? You'd do it just for spite.

GENE Not for spite. But maybe to jazz up her sex life a little.

NICK *laughing* Get the fuck out of my room. And don't touch my phone either.

GENE goes.

You little wise-ass, you're twenty-three years old and a law school drop-out. *wearily* And I'm a hundred and twelve. Easy.

Blackout.

Scene Seven

Two days later. Lights come up on CHARLIE on the phone in her apartment. There are a couple of empty wine bottles beside her and she has a glass in her hand. She is drunk, but not inarticulate. A bouquet of roses is bundled conspicuously in a wastebasket.

CHARLIE *into the phone* No, I'm not drinking. Alan, you sound like my mother, except your voice is higher. *quickly* I'm sorry, I didn't mean that. Don't hang up, please. *Pause.* I know there weren't going to be any more calls, but this is important. Maybe I've been too categorical about things. Maybe we *could* get back together someday. Stranger things have happened, right? And until everything went crazy, we were happy together. *pause, then firmly* Goddamn it, we *were*, until you took this notion to emulate the late Oscar Wilde. I think it's a fad, Alan, just a trendy fad. In the sixties, everybody went back to the land. In the seventies, they went gay. *pause, then wearily* I know. I still love you, too. But we sure have a funny way of showing it. *Pause.* Yes, okay, I'm drinking. Maybe I'm drunk. *Pause.* I don't know why. See, there was this bottle here and I— *pause, then bitterly* No, Nick is not here. *beginning to cry* How the hell do I know where Nick is?

She listens into the phone, nods corroboration, and when she can manage it, speaks.

Yes, finished. As far as I knew, everything was going fine. Then today I get the kiss-off, and tonight these roses arrive. He sends roses and a note that Kahlil Gibran must have ghosted. "No regrets. No bitterness. No blame." What the hell does that *mean*? After all this, he buys me off with cryptic platitudes. And a lunch. I knew there was going to be trouble when he asked me to lunch. Never, never go to lunch. It's always the bad-news meal. Everytime I— *Pause.* Nick has nothing to do with this call. I told you, I love you. And you said that you— *pause, then angrily* Wait and see? How the hell do you expect me to wait and see? You were a beautiful boy when I met you and now you're nothing but a—goddamn—faggot! *Pause.* I *can't* get past it. Can you get past it? Eight goddamn years, Alan. How the hell do I get that back? There's just nowhere to go from here. *Pause.* I don't *know* what I mean by that!

She slams down the phone and pulls the jack out of the wall on a blackout.

Scene Eight

A few hours later. Lights up in CHARLIE's apartment. The scene is unchanged except for an added empty bottle or two. CHARLIE sits on the bed, more sober, singing into the mike on her tape recorder.

CHARLIE
"When the tires are humming,
And the engine purrs,
And your car is eager,
And the thought occurs:
It's good to be alive in this land of ours,
It's good to drive in this land of ours—"

Unnoticed by CHARLIE, GENE has entered, and as CHARLIE falters, he sings the next line of the song.

GENE
"What a great, great feeling,
What a wonderful sense—"

CHARLIE, with no hint of surprise, turns to him and they continue the song together, building to a strong and zesty finale.

CHARLIE and GENE
"Of sheer enjoyment,
And of confidence.
There's something you're aware of,
Your car's been taken care of,
At the Esso sign of confidence,
At the Happy Motoring Sign!"

CHARLIE and GENE salute each other simultaneously and bark "Happy Motoring" Murray Westgate-style, then laugh uproariously.

CHARLIE   How do you know that? You weren't even born back then.

GENE   Don't you believe in the collective unconscious?

CHARLIE   Oh sure. It's the collective *conscious* I have doubts about.

GENE   Aren't you going to ask me how I got in?

CHARLIE   Chargex, American Express—what's the difference?

GENE   The door's open, that's how. Charlie, it's late. Don't you ever lock it?

CHARLIE   Is that what brings you here? A survey on the Imprudent Habits of Single Women?

GENE   They missed you down at The Canada Goose tonight.

CHARLIE   What were you doing at the club?

GENE   I knew you were on tonight.

CHARLIE   Yeah? How did I do?

She laughs, but he doesn't join in.

GENE   When I got there, Mel was trying to get you on the phone to find out where the hell you were.

He goes to the phone, examines the disconnected jack.

Out, I see.

CHARLIE   In a manner of speaking.

GENE   Anyway, I was worried.

CHARLIE   And you rushed right over, in the hopes of being the first to say, "I told you so." *indicating wastebasket*   Congratulations. You made it.

GENE   Roses. Jesus.

CHARLIE   You want to look at the card?

GENE   *looking her in the eye*   "No regrets. No blame. No bitterness." Something along those lines?

CHARLIE   *after a pause*   Say, did I ever tell you the one about the dumb broad, the professional bastard and the professional bastard's know-it-all younger brother?

GENE   Let me tell you one. Nick never promised you anything. So you've come out ahead. If you count the flowers as a bonus.

CHARLIE   Don't you stick up for him.

GENE   He's my brother, Charlie. He has his faults, and I'm sorry if he hurt you. But he tried to play it straight with you and you know it.

CHARLIE   Am I supposed to thank you for pointing that out?

GENE   No, but you could offer me a drink.

CHARLIE   Not if you've come here to gloat.

GENE   No.

CHARLIE   In that case, have a drink   *She unscrews the top from the last bottle of wine.*   Care to smell the cap?

GENE   Where did all these bottles come from?

CHARLIE   The liquor store sends their empties over. I'm too young to drink, of course. But I like my garbage to look adult.

GENE   *taking a swig of wine*   My favourite. Melted cough drops.

CHARLIE   If you don't like the house wine, don't blame me. I stole it from my neighbour. He's out of town and I'm feeding his cat. Of course, we can always try our luck with the neighbour on the other side. I'm watering her plants.   *shaking a key ring*   The keys to the kingdom, baby.

GENE   How much of this did you drink tonight?

CHARLIE   All of it.

GENE   All of it? Holy shit. Charlie, are you all right?

CHARLIE Never better. Oh, the day's had its ups and downs, I don't deny it. But I'm feeling better now. I had a good cry, I guess, and a little nap, and now I'm even working on the act.

She switches on the tape, sings into the mike.

"You can trust the products at the Esso sign—"

But as GENE regards her steadily, she switches off the tape.

Oh well, a little later, maybe. *close to tears* After a cigarette. You got one, by any chance?

GENE *handing her a cigarette* You're in no mood to work on the act now.

CHARLIE I know. But maybe that's no excuse.

GENE Charlie, that doesn't make much sense.

CHARLIE I don't know. I was thinking tonight, about this comic they brought up from L.A. one time to headline at The Canada Goose. There was this one night, the show hadn't gone very well at all. And he invited three or four of the comics—young guys and me—back to his hotel room. He said he wanted to smoke dope and forget about the way the act had gone. But you know what happened when we got back to the hotel room?

GENE What?

CHARLIE The headliner brought out the dope all right, but while the rest of us smoked it and watched the gangsters on the Late Late Show, the comic just sat in a corner, all alone, and played the tapes of his act. The room was a mess—dried up old pizza crusts and coffee cups and cigarette butts. But the comic just sat there in the mess, with a stop-watch and a notepad, and played the tapes.

GENE So what did the rest of you do?

CHARLIE What could we do? He *was* the headliner from L.A. So after every line, somebody would say, "That's a funny bit, man. That's very funny." And gradually the headliner began to pay attention to the fact that we were there, and he started throwing out new lines he'd spun off from the stuff on that tape. And after every line, he'd stop and ask, "What about *that*? Could *that* be funny?" Some of it was funny and some of it wasn't, but we told him it was dynamite and he wrote it down. I think that he was afraid that if he stopped, he'd die. You know, the way a shark has to keep moving or die? I think he was afraid that if he stopped, he'd be consumed by the garbage in the hotel room, or the ambition of the young comics coming up behind him, or the brutality of the Late Late Show.

GENE But he was the one who messed up the room. He was the one who invited you in, and turned on the TV.

CHARLIE That's right. *Pause*. I wonder. Maybe he actually *needed* the awfulness around him for

incentive. Maybe he needed some place like that, that he *had* to be funny in or die.

GENE Could be.

CHARLIE So, maybe this is no time for *me* to stop. Maybe I've got to keep going now, or die.

GENE clicks on the tape recorder and speaks into the mike.

GENE Charlie, you're not going to die. Not tonight, anyway. *clicking it off* There. Now you've got it on tape. Play it back whenever you need reassurance.

CHARLIE That's the worst part of being a comedian. Everybody just laughs at you. *as GENE laughs* See what I mean?

GENE You're priceless. You really are.

CHARLIE You're not so bad yourself. I've always liked you, Gene.

GENE Now, there's a case of revisionist history.

CHARLIE After that first morning, I mean. And you were right. To give me a word of warning.

GENE It could be worse. You could be in love with him.

CHARLIE Who says I'm not?

GENE I do. What do you say?

CHARLIE *after a pause* No. I toyed with the possibility while we were in the restaurant today and I realized he was looking for a way to kiss me off. I came very close to being in love with him, out of pure spite. But I'm not. It's more of a fascination, I guess. How anybody with so many connections can be so unconnected to anything. Women fall for stuff like that.

GENE Yeah? I'll make a note of it.

CHARLIE No, don't. Don't you turn into one of those half-assed seventies people. There are enough of them already. I guess we used up our quota of commitment in the sixties. Now we always keep our options open, as my late husband would say.

GENE And what does he mean by that?

CHARLIE Someday, sonny, when you're older, you'll understand.

GENE Do you?

CHARLIE No.

GENE Then you're not one of those people either, are you?

CHARLIE Gene, why did you come here tonight?

GENE I never miss a chance to sing the Happy Motoring Song.

CHARLIE Is that all?

GENE I like you, Charlie. I always have.

CHARLIE   Now, there's a case of revisionist history.

GENE   Seriously, from the first minute I saw you. I said to myself, "Now there's a woman I could quit law school for."

CHARLIE   Bullshit. You quit law school to become the greatest novelist the world has ever known. You told me so yourself.

GENE   Charlie, you've got to learn to take a compliment.

CHARLIE   I want to know why you came here.

GENE   You mean did Nick send me? No.

CHARLIE   You mean he's not in the habit of passing along his old girlfriends? Like hockey skates? I wouldn't put it past him.

GENE   You ought to think a little better of me.

CHARLIE   I'm sorry.

GENE   So am I.

CHARLIE   Are you?

GENE   Sorry. *He kisses her.* Sorry. *He kisses her again.* Sorry. *And again.*

CHARLIE pulls away.

Uh...that's not exactly how I planned my move.

CHARLIE   This isn't quite how I saw today shaping up either.

GENE   Charlie, this may come as a surprise to you, but you're not a pair of hockey skates.

CHARLIE   Is that one of those compliments I'm supposed to learn how to take?

GENE   If I'd wanted wisecracks, I'd have stayed at The Canada Goose.

CHARLIE   And if I'd wanted to save my sanity, I'd have stayed away from the Bolton boys.

GENE   I'm not one of the Bolton boys. I'm Gene. And what went wrong with you and Nick has nothing to do with me.

CHARLIE   You mean, don't throw out the baby with the bathwater? *suddenly laughing* Oh God, I'm sorry.... *still laughing* I just realized what I said.

GENE   *sharply* Charlie, I said cut the cracks. I'm not a baby and I'm not the relief pitcher, or any other goddamn thing you think. And if you had any kind of decent opinion of yourself, I wouldn't have to tell you that.

CHARLIE   *staring at him uncertainly* Gene....Do you want to sleep with me?

GENE   It's crossed my mind. From time to time. To time.

CHARLIE   Why?

GENE   What kind of a question is that?

CHARLIE   I mean, why am I not a pair of hockey skates?

GENE   *earnestly* Listen to me. I don't make a habit of chasing around after the recently broken-hearted, knocking on the door—

CHARLIE   You *didn't* knock—

GENE   Knocking on the door and offering myself as the consolation prize. You attract me, all right? You always have. In spite of your neuroses and your bad taste in men and your habit of calling me "sonny." And right now, I can't think of anything nicer than being in bed with you. I can't see how it can fail as a bright idea.

CHARLIE   But?

GENE   I didn't say but.

CHARLIE   You were thinking but. I saw it, in one of those balloons, over your head.

GENE   But I'm not like Nick and all the open-option people. Gene. The name is Gene. I want you to have that straight in the morning. And the morning after. And the morning after that. What do you say, Charlie?

CHARLIE switches on the tape, picks up the mike.

CHARLIE   *into the mike* Gene. I have it straight. And I'll have it straight in the morning. *She clicks off the tape.* There. Now you've got it on tape. Play it back when you need reassurance.

She takes off her glasses.

Your turn. Fair is fair.

GENE takes off his glasses, then picks up CHARLIE's, looks through them.

GENE   You're as blind as I am.

CHARLIE   This could be the beginning of a beautiful friendship.

She leans towards him, and he kisses her on a blackout.

ACT TWO

Scene One

A day or two later. Lights come up on GENE at his desk, speaking into his tape recorder.

GENE   *Deathless Prose* by Eugene Bolton. Chapter One. It came as a surprise to him to realize that this was what being in love felt like. He'd imagined the feeling many times, of course, and it had been different. Better circumstances, more exotic locations, a different kind of woman. For he wasn't so caught up in emotion that he couldn't admit that to himself. He'd simply never expected to fall, when he fell, for a woman like her. She was taller than what he'd had in mind, she smoked too much, and she was absolutely nothing like Jane Fonda. And she was older than he was. Most of all, she was older. And while it was nice to be around someone imbued with the kind of wisdom that only comes with age—like knowing all the lyrics to old Everly Brothers songs, and understanding more than he would ever know about how to fold a fitted sheet—while it was nice to have a shortcut to that kind of knowledge, it was also true that she'd had more time to accumulate bad memories. They'd talked about that, of course. They'd talked about it exhaustively, until sometimes it seemed to him that was what new relationships mostly consisted of—performing autopsies on relationships from the past. *breaking off* Hey, that's not bad. I wonder if it's true? *back to business* Anyway, the more they talked, the more often he caught himself wishing that he'd inherited a prize somewhat more intact, emotionally speaking. Because almost from the first moment, a terrible suspicion had begun to form in him that, in the relationship game, you could actually be held accountable for debts run up long before you appeared on the scene. That he would be punished somehow, for having turned up too late.

Blackout.

Scene Two

A day or two later. Lights up on CHARLIE's apartment. An anonymous figure is under the covers of the bed. There is a knock on the door, a pause, another knock. Finally a credit card comes sliding through the lock, the door opens and ALAN enters, carrying his suitcase. He puts down the suitcase and approaches the bed.

ALAN   Charlie. Baby, wake up.

GENE starts, sits up.

GENE   Who the hell are you?

ALAN   *startled*   I could ask you the same question.

GENE   You don't know who you are? *coming to*   Oh, right. I see.

ALAN   Look—I'm sorry.

GENE   It's okay. I know the feeling.

ALAN   Where's Charlie? You do know who Charlie is?

GENE   She was here.... Holy shit. I have to be at work at twelve!

ALAN   *consulting his watch*   It's eleven-o-six.

GENE   Oh, lots of time.

He lies back down in the bed, pulling the covers over himself.

ALAN   Look, is she okay?

GENE   Charlie? *smiling*   She's fantastic.

CHARLIE, fully dressed except for her glasses, appears from the kitchen with two cups of coffee. She stops short when she sees ALAN.

CHARLIE   Alan! What are you doing here?

ALAN   *indicating GENE with chagrin*   Charlie, for Christ's sake....

CHARLIE   Alan, this is Gene.

GENE   Oh, you're Charlie's late husband. *shaking hands*   Nice to meet you. Gene Bolton.

ALAN   *to CHARLIE*   Bolton?

CHARLIE   Nick's brother. You remember Nick.

ALAN   Better than you, evidently. Well, isn't this just jolly?

GENE   We think so. *indicating the coffee*   Is that mine?

CHARLIE hands him a coffee, proffers the other to ALAN.

CHARLIE   Coffee, sweetheart? Or should I break out the digitalis?

As he takes the coffee, she peers at his suitcase.

Why, Alan, I didn't know you had a dog.

ALAN   Put on your glasses, will you? It's my suitcase.

CHARLIE   My God. I hope you boys have name tags sewn in your clothes. *as no one laughs*   I wasn't expecting to see you.

ALAN   Evidently.

CHARLIE   Will you stop saying "evidently"? You sound like you've dropped in from Scotland Yard.

ALAN   I dropped in from Stratford, Charlie. A mere three hours on a very slow train. Because I thought you needed me.

CHARLIE   *puzzled*   That's very sweet of you. But I'm just fine.

ALAN   You didn't sound fine when you called me the other night.

CHARLIE   The other night?

ALAN   Christ, after that conversation, I rushed down here expecting to find you in a coma, not in flagrante delicto.

CHARLIE   Sorry to disappoint you. Besides, nobody's in flagrante anything. Gene, put your clothes on.

ALAN   I bet you don't remember a goddamn thing about that call, do you?

CHARLIE   Sure I do. I—I guess it was about Nick?

ALAN   You guess. Your heart was broken, I'd let you down too, and when I tried to call you back—

CHARLIE   Oh God. The jack.

She goes to the phone and plugs it in.

ALAN   I've been calling on the hour, and wondering if I could get here before the ambulance.

CHARLIE   Oh, sweetheart. I'm sorry.

GENE   It took you three days to come a hundred miles? Were you really that concerned?

CHARLIE   Gene. . . .

ALAN   Under the circumstances, it's a good thing I didn't run out to the highway and flag down a police car, isn't it?

GENE   But there's no point carrying on as though you had, is there? I mean, I assume you were coming to Toronto anyway.

ALAN   Well, there are people— *angrily* Look, what the hell business is this of yours?

GENE   Charlie's business is my business now.

ALAN   Well, good luck. Now that you've checked into the Hotel California, you'll need it.

CHARLIE   Thanks for the glowing reference. I am sorry about the call. But I was drunk and—

ALAN   *joining in*   —And don't remember a thing about it. Charlie, when is this stuff going to stop?

CHARLIE   I think it's stopped. This time I really think it has.

ALAN   *glancing at GENE*   I see. That's good, then. *getting up* Pardon the intrusion, as we say at Scotland Yard.

CHARLIE   Where are you going?

ALAN   Where do I usually go from here? To see if there are any other inns in Bethlehem. *pause, then defensively*   I mean, since I came all the way to town, I might as well stay for a day or two.

CHARLIE   *smiling* You might as well. If you *do* have people to see, I'd feel a lot less guilty.

ALAN   I can drop in on Grant Austin.

CHARLIE   Good. Don't run away. I'll put on more coffee.

She exits.

ALAN   Anyway, Grant will put me up, probably.

GENE   If not, you could stay here. It's not like I'm moved in officially. I can go back home for a day or two.

ALAN   No thanks.

GENE   I don't mind. I mean, it's not like—

He stops short, busies himself tying his shoes.

ALAN   It's not like what? It's not like having another man staying here?

GENE   I didn't say that.

ALAN   You don't have to. I'm a mind reader. So Charlie's told you all about me?

GENE   The subject's come up. Look, Alan, I only meant everything's in the past with you and Charlie.

ALAN   Everything's in the past? Did she say that?

GENE   No, I'm a mind reader too. I see a couple separated for a year, I'm enjoying a gorgeous relationship with the lady, the guy's living with some other *guy*—I just had a wild hunch.

ALAN   *after a pause* Coming out, you know, it's not like having a personality transplant. Some part of me is still her husband.

GENE   *gently* That must be confusing.

ALAN   It is. *smiling ruefully* As you point out, it takes me three days to show up after one of her calls, but I show up.

GENE   Well. . . . A wife in your past. Maybe it's comforting in a way?

ALAN   Maybe it is. But maybe it's time to stop.

GENE   Maybe it is.

ALAN   Yeah. *Pause.*   I'm glad about you and her. I honestly am. It simplifies things a little.

GENE   From the byzantine to the merely baroque?

ALAN   *smiling* Something like that.

CHARLIE returns with a coffee pot and her own cup.

CHARLIE   I knew there was more mileage in those grounds. Gene?

GENE   Sounds irresistible, but I have to get to work. A salesclerk's life isn't his own.

CHARLIE   You won't forget to call me on your break?

GENE   Not likely. The one time I forgot, I got calls all afternoon in different accents. From women claiming to be customers I'd seduced and abandoned.

CHARLIE   *innocently* No kidding?

GENE   No kidding. You do a lousy Russian, by the way.

CHARLIE   *Russian* Pah, ees stinking lie. *in her own voice* Smartass.

GENE   Bitch. *kissing her* Alan—nice meeting you.

He exits.

CHARLIE   *pouring ALAN more coffee* Well.

ALAN Well, what can I say? You hit the jackpot this time.

CHARLIE You really think so?

ALAN Come on, he loves you. Anybody can see that.

CHARLIE He's very young.

ALAN Obituaries in advance? It won't work with him.

CHARLIE You don't think it's a bit silly—working my way through Nick's family?

ALAN Babe, it has nothing to do with me. It's time we both admitted that.

He rises.

CHARLIE There's a tone of finality there I don't like. *quickly* I poured you more coffee. You can't leave.

ALAN Someone's got to tell you: your coffee's not worth hanging around for. *kissing her* Be happy.

CHARLIE *nervously* There's that tone again.

ALAN Why are we so stubborn? The sun goes down, and we still won't call it a day.

He picks up his suitcase.

CHARLIE Alan—

ALAN Bye, Charlie.

He exits, leaving CHARLIE a little startled on a blackout.

Scene Three

Four weeks later. Lights come up on CHARLIE's apartment, where she sits typing desultorily, and x-ing words out repeatedly. The phone rings.

CHARLIE Thank God for interruptions. *picking up phone* Hello? *pause, Italian accent* Yeah, whatchoo want onna pizza? *Pause.* Yeah. *Pause.* Yeah. *Pause.* No. No anchovies, we no got today. Gino, he still out inna boat. Ciao.

She hangs up. GENE has come in from the kitchen during the conversation, wiping his hands on a dish towel tied around his waist.

GENE They want Tower of Pizza?

CHARLIE Who else? Since they opened, nobody ever calls for us. *unplugging the phone* This time, I'm leaving it off. Until one of us gets a new number. I wouldn't mind if people didn't get so ugly about the anchovies.

GENE Guy called earlier, wanted orange sections. On a pizza. It's enough to make you want to get out of the catering business all right.

CHARLIE Speaking of which, how's dinner coming?

GENE Later. I'm still working on the fridge. Haven't you ever heard of defrosting?

CHARLIE You live here too, you know.

GENE I've only been here a month. I won't say how long it's been since that fridge was touched, but there's a hunk of frozen fish in there wrapped in newspaper. Headline says: "White Sox Throw World Series." *as CHARLIE laughs* Anyway, there's no rush on dinner. Nick isn't even coming till eight.

CHARLIE At this point, I'm ready to start without him. Any excuse to drop this.

She picks up a piece of her writing and reads:

"It's no use, Jerry. We can't get married as long as Alison's ghost stands between us. After all, if she hadn't killed herself because you left her for me, it would be her you'd be taking to the altar Wednesday morning."

GENE She.

CHARLIE What?

GENE It would be *she* you'd be taking to the altar Wednesday morning. There's your problem right there.

CHARLIE The problem *is*, Alison's suicide has nothing to do with Jerry. Alison was carrying Leonard Casey's child, and somehow, I've got to tip off Ruth and Jerry to that. Otherwise nobody goes to the altar Wednesday morning.

GENE Well, Wednesday is a stupid day for a wedding anyway.

CHARLIE It happens to be Jerry's day off. He works Saturdays. At the Bay.

GENE Yeah? How come the bastard didn't invite *me* to the wedding?

CHARLIE They're keeping it small. In deference to Alison. And there isn't going to *be* any wedding. Not unless I can get the truth out to somebody.

GENE Leonard Casey might have a word with Jerry.

CHARLIE He might—if they hadn't croaked him at the last story conference. On Thursday's show, Leonard's brakes will fail. On Friday, the actor goes into rehearsal in New York.

GENE It just goes to show. How fleeting is death.

CHARLIE Look, we can't all be novelists, sonny.

GENE They called again from The Canada Goose.

CHARLIE What do they want on their pizza?

GENE Mel called to find out if he could book you for a night next week.

CHARLIE What's the point? I haven't got any new stuff.

GENE   There's old stuff, isn't there?

CHARLIE   I have to feel that I want to be there, that's all. Otherwise, it might as well be soap opera.

GENE   Well, wait until you feel like it then.

CHARLIE   Easy for you to say. How many chapters have you knocked out in the last few weeks?

GENE   A couple.

CHARLIE   Only a couple. On top of a full-time job. While I don't know what comes after, "Hi, everybody, and welcome to The Canada Goose."

GENE   Charlie, what's the matter? I thought you were happy.

CHARLIE   It's always hard to cope with the new and bizarre.

GENE   Is that why you asked Nick to dinner? Out of nostalgia for the bad old days?

CHARLIE   Do you think it's a bad idea?

GENE   You, me and Nick? It smacks of such modernity, that's all. "Have Your Ex Over to Dinner to Meet Your Current." It would make a great story for *Toronto Life.*

CHARLIE   Toronto Life is a contradiction in terms.

GENE   Don't change the subject.

CHARLIE   Why should there be hard feelings between you and Nick and me? Everybody's got what they want.

There is a knock on the door.

GENE   Christ. Eight o'clock I told the asshole. It's five to. Some people have no consideration whatso— *opening the door to admit NICK* Nicky! Good to see you. Champagne! You finally off the penicillin?

NICK presents the champagne to CHARLIE along with a kiss.

NICK   Hiya, Charlie. Bubbly to the bubbly.

CHARLIE   The usual bottle of Baby Bear, I see.

NICK   If you don't like Dom Perignon, there are plenty who do.

CHARLIE   It's just that every time you turn up, I feel I should have an unlaunched ship on hand.

NICK   I bought it to launch the new picture. But now it looks like shooting's postponed. So I figured you two could use it.

GENE   Second-hand champagne. How tacky. I'm sorry about the film, Nick.

NICK   *indicating GENE's dish towel* I'm sorry I missed the drag show, little brother.

GENE   I was cleaning the fridge.

NICK   Well, no need to ask what brought you two together.

GENE   The screwdrivers I made froze solid. It was time for a little defrosting.

NICK   Okay, but you know what the fridge-cleaning syndrome leads to.

CHARLIE   Nick, we didn't get you over here to reminisce. We're all familiar with the past and presumably none of us is too wild about it.   *taking the champagne*   I'll get you a screwdriver popsicle.

She exits.

GENE   *firmly* I'm making the dinner. We might as well have that out in the open too.

He exits. CHARLIE returns momentarily with a frozen pitcher of screwdrivers and two glasses.

CHARLIE   *prodding at the pitcher* One lump or two?

NICK   However it comes. I only see two glasses.

CHARLIE   I'm not drinking these days, Nick. And you know something? I thought sobriety would be awful. It's not. It's hideous.

NICK   Then you might as well have a drink.

CHARLIE   Later.

NICK   Later?

CHARLIE   A week Thursday. That'll be a month. I promised myself a month on the wagon.

NICK   But babe, you were always such a fun drunk.

CHARLIE   Such a load of laughs that you dropped me.

NICK   Aw now, don't be that way. I felt rotten that day in the restaurant.

CHARLIE   Your pain showed. As I recall it, you said, "We're through, Charlie. I wonder if the artichokes are any good today."

NICK   Bullshit, I did not.

CHARLIE   You're right. But I've never let the truth spoil a good story yet.

NICK   No brother of Gene's can be that bad. After all, I raised that kid practically single-handed. If he didn't learn decency from me, where did he learn it?

CHARLIE   He probably had to pick it up in the streets.   *There is a knock on the door.*   Are they coming to take *out* pizzas here now?

She opens the door as ALAN, harried, steps in.

Well! The gang's all here.

ALAN   So you *are* home. I've been calling and calling and—

CHARLIE   Oh, right. We get all these wrong numbers, so I've been leaving it off.

NICK   Hi, Alan.

ALAN   Oh, hi, Nick.   *bewildered*   How are you?

CHARLIE   *plugging the phone in*   There. Now try your call again.

ALAN   I don't know why you bother having a phone, Charlie.

CHARLIE   Who are you? A field worker from the Telephone Appreciation Society?

NICK   What this man needs is a drink. And a glass.

He exits.

ALAN   I don't have time for—   *but NICK is gone*   Charlie, do you still have that metal box we kept all the valuable papers in?

CHARLIE   I've got the box, but you took all your papers out, remember? When we split up.

ALAN   Can you look? I think I must have left my passport. I've got to have it.

CHARLIE   Why? Where are you going?

ALAN   I won't be going anywhere if you don't look in the goddamn box!

CHARLIE doesn't budge.

Spain.

CHARLIE   Spain? What with? I mean, I hear it's cheap there, but it can't be free. Or—*who* with? Maybe that's more to the point?

ALAN   Grant Austin.

CHARLIE   You're kidding.

ALAN   Now that I've answered the skill-testing question, can I have my passport?

CHARLIE   You and Grant Austin. So good old Jackie's out in the cold?

ALAN   Charlie, please! Just find my passport, and I'll tell you anything you want to know.

CHARLIE   *bitterly*   It never stops with you, does it?

ALAN   It has now. This time it's stopped.

CHARLIE stares at him for a moment, then exits swiftly. ALAN lights a cigarette. NICK comes back with a glass, pours ALAN a screwdriver from the slightly-melted batch.

NICK   That kid. I never saw him so much as heat up a can of soup, and now he's out there up to his eyebrows in soufflé. Soufflé, for Christ's sake. *handing ALAN a screwdriver*   Here you go.

ALAN   Thanks.

He gulps it, checks his watch.

NICK   You in a hurry to get somewhere?

ALAN   Yeah. Spain.

NICK   Spain? Lot of that going around. Remember Grant Austin? The fucker's walked off the picture to go to Spain.

ALAN   Is that a fact?

NICK   Jesus, I should have known. The guy may be a cinematic genius, but he goes down the road of life using *True Confessions* as a driving manual. I call him up and ask him what the hell he thinks he's doing to me, and you know what he tells me? He's in love.

ALAN   *coldly*   It happens.

At this moment CHARLIE comes back to the doorway with the passport, unnoticed for the moment.

NICK   Yeah, Grant's in love with some cute little fruit. And after some little faggot wedding ceremony they're honeymooning in Spain.

CHARLIE   A wedding?   *to ALAN, with deep distaste*   A gay wedding?

ALAN   *reaching for the passport*   You found it. Great.

CHARLIE   *slamming it into his hand*   I found it all right.

NICK   Yeah, how about that, Charlie? There's material there for you. Can you see the wedding cake? Two little guys in tuxes under a flowered arch!

ALAN   Why don't you just fuck off?

CHARLIE   Why should he? It's pretty funny at that, Alan. I wish I'd been there to see you go down the aisle. Why wasn't I invited to the wedding? But of course, how *do* you seat the groom's wife? Or is it the bride's wife? I guess Amy Vanderbilt doesn't cover that one.

NICK   Oh Christ. Charlie, I didn't know. Alan. . . .

At this moment GENE enters from the kitchen.

GENE   My soufflé just fell. Who did it?

NICK   *quietly*   I did it. I put my foot in it.

CHARLIE   My God, if you wanted a divorce, you could have said so. Or would you rather conduct secret ceremonies behind my back? Just to make sure I'm *really* out of the picture?

ALAN   What do you care what I do now? Why should it matter to you? You're living with him, for God's sake—   *indicating GENE*   He drops in for drinks—   *indicating NICK*   You think you can hold onto everybody?

CHARLIE   You do it, don't you? That's always been your stock in trade.

ALAN   Not any more! It's a day, Charlie. Why can't we just call it that?

CHARLIE   Because it isn't! You need me, Alan. If only to trot out for state occasions.

ALAN   Not any more. If anybody wants to think of me as a fruit, or a faggot or a fucking queer, they can go ahead. I've made my peace with it. And I'm not taking the blame any more for the tragedy of poor little Charlie, victim of the Evil Homosexual Conspiracy. There were a hundred things wrong with our marriage and if I'd stayed as straight as Charles Bronson, we'd have fallen apart anyway.

CHARLIE   That's not true.

ALAN   It's true and you know it. But now you've got someone who loves you and so do I. So let's let go. Before we guilt each other to death. Let me go, Charlie.

ALAN touches her arm briefly, pockets the passport and leaves. GENE and NICK stare warily at CHARLIE, as if she were a bomb about to explode.

GENE   *at last*   Charlie? . . .

CHARLIE   He's going all the way to Spain. And he didn't even say goodbye.

GENE   He said goodbye. You know it.

NICK   Christ, Charlie, I didn't know. You never told me anything about it.

CHARLIE   I know. Look, why don't you guys go ahead with dinner? I'd like to take a walk.

GENE   Now? Come on, why don't you—

CHARLIE   *snatching up her purse*   I need this walk, Gene. I really do.

She hurries out, slamming the door.

GENE   Oh, Christ. *to NICK*   What the hell did you do?

NICK   I mentioned Austin walked off the picture to marry some little fruit. How did I know it was Alan? Come on, kid. Relax. A week from Thursday has probably come a little early, that's all.

GENE   She was through getting drunk over him. That was all behind her.

NICK   Then you don't have to worry about her, right?

GENE   You don't know a goddamn thing about it.

NICK   You will pardon me, but I do have some experience of the lady. And a few others just like her.

GENE   She's not just "some lady"—some back number in your little black book. She's Charlie, Nick, and you've got no idea. I mean, you didn't even know Alan was gay.

NICK   Maybe not. But I know one thing, Geno, and you'd better deal with it. She just jumped at the chance to go to pieces tonight. And if she's looking for ways to be unhappy, there's nothing you can do about it.

GENE   Stop right there, Nick, because I'm not going to take it. Some underdone theory on another woman you scratched at the gate. I live with her, for Christ's sake. I've taken responsibility. And on that subject, I'm the big brother.

NICK   Listen, you little wise-ass. I'll take a lot from you, but not a lecture. Talk to me about responsibility! I put clothes on your back and a roof over you—

GENE   And you felt virtuous as hell because I needed you! But not anymore. Now I've got someone who needs *me*. And a life of my own. Do you get that, Nick?

NICK   Sure, sure. You're running your own show now—and making a real class job of it. Sitting at the door like a spaniel and whining because she's left you all alone.   *moving to the door*   No, you don't need me. Not much. Because all I ever gave you was cash and connections and everything you're too goddamned good for, right? But when I try to give you anything else—like some sound advice— you tell me to fuck right off. Okay, kid, you've got it. I'm gone.

GENE   Nick! I—don't want you to go.

NICK   Why? Because you're afraid to be here all alone?

GENE   No. I—   *slowly*   I think maybe—I need some—advice.

NICK   Could be. Could be I've considered a few angles you haven't. About having a life of your own.

GENE   She's better off with me, Nick. Better off than she's been in her whole life. And she knows it.

NICK   I don't deny it for a second. Anybody who can't be happy with you ought to have her head read.

GENE   *laughing weakly*   Yeah. That's what I think, too.

NICK   Okay. But I got to thinking the other day. I was down at The Canada Goose, with some people who want to shoot a film. I asked after Charlie, and what do you know? Seems she hasn't shown up there in almost a month.

GENE   I know. She hasn't felt like working lately.

NICK   Why? Because she's up to her armpits in domestic bliss? Sure, I'll buy that. But it's funny how she only feels like performing when she's got a beef. Inconvenient, too.

GENE   What do you mean?

NICK   Well, she's got nothing to complain about now. With you on the premises—tossing up soufflés and, I trust, keeping her happy in the sack the way only you undergraduates can. I mean, it's the ideal arrangement all down the line. But what can someone like Charlie do with that?

GENE   She can enjoy it, can't she? She's earned it.

NICK   Right. Now she's better off. But does she want to be better off? Does she even know how to be? You're a good kid, Geno, and it's too early in the game to get tied to a losing situation. She wants to be a loser, she can be a loser without you.

GENE   Either it clicks with a woman or it doesn't, is that it? No point in trying to talk about it?

NICK   Oh hell, talk if you want to. But if you're bright, you'll make *her* do the talking. She's the one with the problem. And if you don't like what you're hearing, hit the road.

GENE   Just like that.

NICK   Just like that. There's only one way to go if you're going—fast.   *gently*   Hey, don't look like a house just fell on you. Nothing's happened yet. Relax, and drink your screwdriver before it melts.

He raises his glass to GENE on a blackout.

Scene Four

The next morning. Lights up on CHARLIE's apartment where GENE is listlessly tidying up from the night before. The door unlocks, and CHARLIE, tired and dishevelled, enters. She starts a little when she sees GENE.

GENE   That was some walk.

CHARLIE   It was a little longer than I'd planned.

GENE   Fourteen hours. What did you do, jog out to the airport and back?

CHARLIE   I'm sorry if you were worried. You didn't skip work on account of me?

GENE   It's my day off. Wednesday. Remember? *Pause.*   Are you okay?

CHARLIE   I . . . didn't expect to find you here, that's all. I planned to just crawl in and sleep and sleep.

GENE   You can do that. You can do whatever you want.

CHARLIE   You're not mad at me for staying out? I'd be mad. I'd be mad as hell.

GENE   *after a pause*   The soufflé didn't fall after all. It just buckled at the knees a little. Nick was impressed, in spite of himself.

CHARLIE   What?

GENE   Last night's dinner. You missed it.

CHARLIE   Oh, right. . . .

GENE   I tried to save you some. Except once the fridge got the knack of defrosting, it went hog wild. The butter started melting. A few eggs hatched.

CHARLIE   *absently*   That's too bad.

GENE   Yeah. I think the fridge is fucked. But Nick said—

CHARLIE   Gene, don't you want to know where I went?

GENE   Not unless you want to discuss it. Anyway, Nick said if we were in the market for a new fridge, he knows some guy—

CHARLIE   I went to a bar and I started drinking. That's the last thing I remember until this morning—

GENE   So you fell off the wagon.

CHARLIE   *relentlessly*   Until this morning when some guy I'd never seen before shook me awake and told me he'd drive me to the subway because he had to be at work by nine.

GENE   Okay, so now you've told me.

CHARLIE   For Christ's sake, is that all you've got to say?

GENE   What else do you want me to say?

CHARLIE   What the hell kind of question is that? What do you *feel* like saying? I mean, you are entitled to get mad, you know. At the very least you're entitled to raise your voice!

GENE   Why? Because you've got this little trick switch in your mind that allows you to check out whenever you feel like behaving like an asshole? Charlie, it's not worth getting mad about. It's stupid and it's sad, but beyond that it doesn't mean a thing.

CHARLIE   I don't know. . .

GENE   Yes you do, and if you want to tell me, let's get it over with.

CHARLIE   Gene, I wouldn't hurt you, not for the world. . . .

GENE   I know that line. It's what you say just before you hurt someone.   *lightly*   So what's the story? You fell in love with this guy on the way to the subway station?

CHARLIE   No. It was when I saw Alan, Gene. I realized it's not over for me.

GENE   Well, it's over for him. And I love you. Why the hell do you want to louse it up?

CHARLIE   I don't want to louse it up. . .

GENE   But? But what? Come on, I can see it. In a balloon right over your head.

CHARLIE   Sonny, this just isn't working.

GENE   It's working for me. Sorry to be so uncooperative, but there it is.

376 / AUTOMATIC PILOT

CHARLIE *exasperated* Look, you're seven years younger than I am, and sooner or later you're going to want to play with girls your own age. Then you'll walk out on me and—

GENE Oh no you don't. You're the one walking, don't try to pull that switch. I've told you I love you, and you've got no reason to think any different. So if you want to walk, fucking do it. But at least admit it's your own idea.

CHARLIE *exploding* How the hell can you want this? I'm screwed up and I drink too much and you're way too good for me.

GENE That's not the problem. You want to know what the problem is? The fact that I love you. You just can't deal with that. Because any club that would have you as a member just isn't good enough to join.

CHARLIE You don't know what you're talking about.

GENE Don't I? You think you want Alan. It's only because he doesn't want you. That's his entire attraction. All somebody has to do is dump you, and you'll follow them anywhere.

CHARLIE It has nothing to do with what I *want*.

GENE It has everything to do with it, because this time *you're* calling the shots. It's not as easy as being the victim, is it? And I have no intention of making it easy for you. Come on—go or stay? What do you want me to do? It's not enough to get loaded and pick up some guy in a bar and hope that'll turn me off.

He snatches up her tape recorder, switches it on and puts the mike in front of her.

You're going to have to tell me. Once and for all.

CHARLIE *at last* Gene, you'll be better off without me.

GENE *snapping off the tape* I asked for an answer, not bullshit! *more calmly* But I guess it's an answer all the same.

He reaches under the bed for his suitcase.

CHARLIE I love you. I don't care if you believe it.

GENE You know what I believe? That this moment is the closest you've come to it since I first met you. And by the time I go through that door, you'll be there. Now tell me that isn't true.

CHARLIE I— *covering her face with her hands* I never wanted to hurt you, Gene. You're the best man I've ever met.

GENE I know. I only hope someday you'll find it in your heart to forgive me for it. *as she touches his arm* Let go of me. I need two arms to pack. In that respect I'm no better than any of the others.

His perfunctory packing done, he closes the case and moves to the door.

CHARLIE Gene . . .

GENE Do me a favour. Don't send roses, okay?

He leaves. Lights hold on CHARLIE for a moment, then blackout.

Scene Five

Some weeks later. Lights up on The Canada Goose, where CHARLIE is on stage in her customary gear plus a feather boa, with the mike in her hand.

CHARLIE Hey ladies, there's a big vogue now in younger men. You noticed that? I don't know about you, but I don't want to go out to dinner with someone who has to ask the waiter to bring him the Child's Menu. Okay, okay, so the kid CAN come ten times in a single night. So what? It's always over so quickly, right? It's like getting ten episodes of *Leave It to Beaver*—right in a row.

It beats the old guys, though. A session with your average older man is like a screening of *The Sorrow and the Pity*. Only longer and sadder. You nod off two or three times and wake up, and he's STILL at it. "I almost came that time," he says. Eventually, you start trying to outfox him, right? "You came," you tell him. "You definitely came. It's just been so long you've forgotten what it's like. But that was it. Trust me. Now, can we get some sleep?"

But the real bitch about younger men is how goddamn earnest they are. One roll in the hay, and they're ready to move in— provided you're willing to help them with their algebra. And when you say, "Hey, wait a minute, sonny—"

She falters on the name, breaks off for a moment, and then, almost to herself:

Sonny.

Long, baffled pause, then she plunges on, almost desperately.

No, no, I prefer to stick to single guys my own age. Hey, has anybody SEEN any single straight guys lately? You know they're an endangered species. *gradually regaining composure* In fact, I heard recently a woman was picketed on Bloor Street by the Greenpeace people for wearing a coat made of the pelts of single straight men.

But I actually met a single guy once. First thing he said to me was, "Babe—" He called all women Babe. I guess it eliminated the problem of learning names he'd only have to forget. "Babe," he said, "I'm not into involvement." And you know something? He wasn't. In fact, if you called him up when he was out, there was this message on his answering machine. "Hi, I'm not home right now. And I'm not into involvement." But I did manage to go out with him—once. And he said to me, "Babe, you chicks are all the same. You're takers." Some taker. We'd been out to dinner, where we split the tab. We split a taxi to the movie—where I paid my own way, plus sprang for his popcorn. Now we're back at my place, doing it in my bed, drinking my Scotch and smoking my cigarettes—and I'm a taker? What do I have to do to be a giver? Donate my kidneys?

Blackout on CHARLIE. Lights up on GENE at his desk speaking into his tape recorder.

GENE   *into the mike*   In fiction when people split up, they never see each other again. Their farewells are conveniently followed by a blank page or a closing credit roll. In real life, it works a little differently. For a while he avoided anything or any place that reminded him of her, because fiction had taught him that was the right thing to do. But in the end, real life won out, and he went down to the club where she performed and watched her unobtrusively from the back. And while he considered the things that she said to be specious and exaggerated, he did have to concede that she seemed happier up there, telling stories that featured her as the perpetual underdog, perpetually disappointed.

And as he watched her it occurred to him for the first time that perhaps he'd got what he wanted too. That losing not only makes for better prose but is, in the long run, safer than winning. Safe being a relative term, of course. There were, for instance, people who considered it unsafe to set foot in an airplane. And yet he knew for an absolute certainty that it was a hell of a lot more dangerous down on the ground.

Blackout.

JOHN GRAY
with ERIC PETERSON

(b. 1946)

(b. 1946)

In a theatrical context the term "musical" usually evokes visions of Broadway extravaganzas like *Oklahoma* or *Annie*. But the musical tradition in Canadian theatre, with the possible exception of *Anne of Green Gables*, has been more modest and generally more offbeat. Its highlights include satire (*Spring Thaw*), sociology (*Ten Lost Years*) and a country and western adaptation of *Othello* set in Saskatchewan (*Cruel Tears*). In recent years the dominant figure in Canadian musical drama has been John Gray. As writer, composer, director and performer, Gray has created literate and immensely entertaining plays that bridge the gap between the "legitimate" stage and the musical. By any criteria *Billy Bishop Goes to War* is one of the two or three most successful Canadian plays ever written.

Gray was born in Truro, Nova Scotia, one of three brothers who all became professional musicians. From 1965-68 while attending Mt. Allison University, he played organ and trumpet with The Lincolns, a local rock'n'roll band. After graduating in 1968 with a B.A. in English, Gray headed for Vancouver where he studied directing at the University of British Columbia, emerging in 1971 with an M.A. in theatre. Over the next four years, as a founding member of Tamahnous Theatre, he directed eight of the plays that established Tamahnous as one of the most exciting experimental companies in the country. Gray moved to Toronto in 1975, joining Theatre Passe Muraille as a composer and sometime director. From 1975-77 he wrote music for a half dozen Passe Muraille shows including *1837: The Farmers' Revolt*.

Gray's first play, *18 Wheels*, was produced by Passe Muraille and then Tamahnous in 1977 under his own direction. Its all-night truckers and truck-stop waitress tell their stories in country and western song. With its simple set, witty lyrics, affection for the ordinary guy, and keen sense of Canadian identity, *18 Wheels* established Gray's musical and dramatic signature, including its dark existential streak. The trucker, like Billy Bishop, rides out alone, "Where the night is all around, as thick as clay, / And death is riding shotgun all the way."

Billy Bishop Goes to War made its first appearance in November 1978, co-produced by the Vancouver East Cultural Centre (VECC) and Tamahnous, after a workshop earlier in the year at Passe Muraille. Its genesis goes back to 1971 when Gray and Eric Peterson first met. Peterson, Saskatchewan-born, had spent two years in British repertory theatre before arriving on the West Coast. After two years with Tamahnous he preceded Gray to Toronto in 1973 and quickly gained a reputation as one of Passe Muraille's most imaginative actors, playing, among other parts, Mackenzie and Lady Backwash in *1837*. It was Peterson who discovered Bishop's autobiography, *Winged Warfare*, in 1976, and co-researched the show with Gray over the next two years. Though Gray is the writer of record, Peterson's skilled character development and virtuoso acting have been essential ingredients in the play's success.

After their initial Vancouver run, Gray and Peterson took *Billy Bishop Goes to War* on a sixteen-month Canadian tour. Then in 1980, with Mike Nichols as co-producer, they opened in Washington as a prelude to four months on and off Broadway where Peterson won the Clarence Derwent Award for Most Promising Actor in the New York theatre. Later that year the show went to the Edinburgh Festival, then to Los Angeles where it won both Best Play and Best Actor awards. In 1982 the published play won the Governor-General's Award for drama.

Gray's third consecutive hit musical, *Rock and Roll*, opened under his own direction in 1981, co-produced by the VECC and National Arts Centre. In this semi-autobiographical play about a sixties Nova Scotia dance band, Gray once again tells an exuberant comic tale of small-town Canadian boys who look back slightly disillusioned and nostalgic at their coming of age. Two children's plays followed, *Bongo from the Congo* (with Eric Peterson) and *Balthazar and the Mojo Star*. Halifax's Neptune Theatre has since premiered Gray's only non-musical, *Better Watch Out, Better Not Die* (1983), a farcical thriller, and *Don Messer's Jubilee* (1985), Gray's homage to the legendary Maritime folk band and his fourth successive musical smash. In 1984, Gray scripted and co-directed a prize-winning video version of *Rock and Roll* and published his first novel, *Dazzled*, a comic saga about growing up absurd in the seventies. He currently lives in Vancouver.

Billy Bishop Goes to War is first and foremost a *tour de force* for one actor. Apart from the Narrator/Pianist who provides mostly musical support, the actor playing Bishop is alone on stage telling his story, doing all the other characters without changes of costume or makeup, and nearly all the sound effects (the pianist does the rest). He works on a bare set except for the piano, and is equipped with a minimum of props. Perhaps the essence of the play is to be found in the extraordinary scene where Bishop describes his first solo flight, accompanying his narrative with his own vocal effects and only a hand-held model airplane for illustration. This is theatre pared down to its essentials: a skilled actor on a bare stage creating a world before our eyes. As always, *reading* the play demands an imaginative reconstruction on the reader's part. Of great help in this case is the original cast recording, available on Tapestry Records (GD 7372).

Hearing *Billy Bishop Goes to War* also makes one aware of the subtle modulations of tone effected by Gray's music and songs. Most of the criticism directed at the play concerns Bishop's attitude towards war and his own part in it, as well as the play's attitude towards Bishop. Does Gray celebrate war by glamourizing Bishop and his bloodlust, or trivialize war by showing it as a game? Does Bishop have any doubts about his own cold-bloodedness? Gray insists in his preface that the play "does not address itself to the issue of whether or not war is a good thing or a bad thing." But colouring Bishop's ascendancy to the status of war hero is the terrific melancholy of the opening song in Act One, "We Were Off to Fight the Hun," which resonates through the play, belying his naive idea that war would be "lots of fun." Many of the songs share that tone. The play's most beautiful song, "In the Sky," is as much a poignant lament as a romantic celebration of aerial warfare; and "Friends Ain't S'posed to Die" makes blatant, in melody and lyrics, the shame Bishop felt in surviving when "most of us never got old."

Of course there are also the spirited anthems that reflect Bishop's joy in his work. He did love flying and he makes us share in his exhilaration. But he came to love killing, too. We watch the comic innocent of Act One develop into the icy professional of Act Two who stays "as calm as the ocean" and goes up even on his days off because he likes it so much. Gray never allows Bishop to be totally unconscious of the ironies in his situation. The fact that the "Survival" song at the top of Act Two is sung by Bishop in the voice of a French *chanteuse*, "the Lovely Hélène," gives it an edge of self-mockery; maybe Bishop is even a little embarrassed about his new-found cynicism. "The Dying of Albert Ball" is Bishop's indirect response to his manipulation by Lady St. Helier and the rest of the British ruling class who "like their heroes / Cold and dead." Finally, the rousing "Empire Soirée" provides a bitter counterpoint to the celebrations of victory. The personal heroism and sacrifice of the brave men dancing and dying in the sky is superceded by the pointless and impersonal "dance of history" as one war is followed by another.

"Makes you wonder what it was all for," Bishop mutters in 1941. Though he is not a very introspective man, he is far from blind to the insanity of war. His visions of No Man's Land and of the two German flyers falling out of their plane are among the most chilling moments in the Canadian theatre. But ultimately, Billy Bishop's reminiscence is not so much about his experience of horror and death as it is about being young and the most intensely alive he ever felt. "One thing's for sure," he sings. "We'll never be that young again." He sings not only for himself but for a world that would never be the same.

•

Billy Bishop Goes to War opened on November 3, 1978, produced by the Vancouver East Cultural Centre in association with Tamahnous Theatre, and designed by Paul Williams. Eric Peterson played Billy Bishop and all the other characters. John Gray was the Narrator/Pianist and director.

BILLY BISHOP GOES TO WAR

PREFACE

Billy Bishop Goes to War was born out of a nasty case of the Three B's of Canadian Theatre—Broke, Bored and Branded. Broke, because it was 1976 and there was not much work. Beating a trail from one one-hundred seat theatre to another is the usual lot of the Canadian theatre artist. Consequently, he is always broke. Bored, because our leaders, the Old Warriors of Canadian Nationalism, were in a rut. Audiences were getting ugly and scarce. But being Broke and Bored did not prevent us from being Branded as Canadian Nationalists, and therefore, unfit for the more cosmopolitan world of the Regional Theatres. And so, we come full circle again, back to Broke—and the landlord turns off the heat.

It was at this time that Eric Peterson lent me a book called *Winged Warfare*. We were in Ottawa at the time, performing for Theatre Passe Muraille. Ottawa is one of the few Canadian cities in which the all-Canadian bookstore is a major entertainment resource. *Winged Warfare* was written by a twenty-one-year-old pilot named Billy Bishop and it contained a cool account of his first six kills during World War I. A little research indicated that before the war was over, he had upped his total to seventy-two. As representatives of a generation of Canadians who had never been anywhere near a war, we regarded the man with apprehension and curiosity. Was he a homicidal maniac? What was going on in that war? What was it like to be a Canadian then? Why were more top aces Canadian than any other nationality? As citizens of a relatively pacifist country, what was it about our nature that made us bold and daring whenever we became involved in a foreign war? What did all this have to do with our colonial heritage, our sense of inadequacy when it comes to our position in the English-speaking world? What was the experience of two generations before us whose lives were defined and shaped by war? Eric and I talked about these things for about a year in our favourite snooker halls and beer parlours—in between trips to the Military Archives to do research.

In January, 1978, I started writing and by March, I had a draft of a play that was almost as long as the war itself. Eric read it and approved. The Old Warriors of Canadian Nationalism read it. They approved. Theatre Passe Muraille gave us some workshop money, and Tamahnous Theatre got a commitment from the Vancouver East Cultural Centre for a production in the fall. With dreams of steady employment to inspire us, we set to work.

One choice we made: *Billy Bishop* would take its narrative form from a phenomenon I noticed while playing the barn circuit of Southwestern Ontario. Playing on stages where you had to kick the cowpies aside while crossing the boards, I noticed that Canadians don't much like listening in on other people's conversations. They think it's impolite. This plays havoc with the basic convention of theatre itself, so what do you do? Well, you drop the fourth wall and you simply talk to the audience. They tend to relax a bit because they are in an arena whose aesthetics they understand: the arena of the storyteller. A dogfight can be a tricky number to stage, and the sky is a hard thing to evoke with a roof over your head. But to a good storyteller anything is possible, and Eric is a wonderful storyteller.

Another choice: only two of us would do it. Eric would play all the parts and I would play the music; Eric would be the mouth and I would be the hands. That way, we got to keep all the money. Besides, one-man shows were all the rage in those days, times being what they were.

Billy Bishop Goes to War opened in Vancouver around Remembrance Day in 1978. The fact that there was a newspaper and a postal strike on didn't make November the best month for a premiere, but response was good and we were held over for two weeks. We seemed to have tapped a well of experience that had been hidden for years. Veterans from both wars came backstage to tell us stories, to talk about the ironic position of being a colonial in a British war; to express their ambivalence about their own survival in a war where so many of their friends died. This response was a source of tremendous relief to Eric and me. Our one fear was that someone would come backstage and say to us, "You're wrong. You got it all wrong. That's not the way it was at all."

Sometime during the holdover in Vancouver, a tall stranger came backstage. He was an American and he was smoking a cigar. He wore a sheepskin coat, had grey hair and the smile of a country doctor. His name was Lewis Allen. He was a producer; then, the co-producer of *Annie*. *Annie* was making the profit of an oil sheikdom at the time and he said that he thought *Billy Bishop* deserved to go to Broadway too. He would get his partner Mike Nichols to look at it. That's a good one, we thought. We entertained the fantasy for a few minutes, then left for the bar and forgot all about it.

We were feeling good. The Cultural Centre had arranged a two-week run in Saskatoon, a tour of Southwestern Ontario and a run at Theatre Passe Muraille. Even the Regional Theatres were beginning to nibble. We might work until the spring. Maybe buy a car. We were as happy in December of 1978 as any Canadian theatre artist can be. We had work; we had a show that didn't bore us; we had audiences who wanted to see our play, who gave us standing ovations. We were being paid.

Touring Canada in mid-winter, one encounters a lot of snow. A lot of snow and a lot of viruses. Every acting school in the country should teach a course entitled "Performing While Sick" because their students are going to be doing a lot of that. In Saskatoon, we learned how to perform with a bad cold. In Owen Sound, it was the flu. In Listowel, Ontario, it all came together in a kind of winter fugue. Eric had the flu; I had a cold—and there was a blizzard so bad that traffic from Kitchener had been stopped. This meant that the risers which the audience were to sit on didn't arrive, nor did the stage. And we were performing in an old railway station. We looked bad. That is, we looked bad if you could see us at all. Watching the show was like trying to get a peek at the scene of an accident. Those who did get a glimpse recoiled at the sight of two broken men croaking their way through a play, accompanied by a piano with six important keys missing. It was an evening to remember. But we got through the show. Once you're out there, it seems there's no alternative, so you go on. The audience applauded sympathetically and left. We collapsed backstage, calling for the antibiotics we had come to know and love.

In walked Mike Nichols. How he had got from New York to Listowel in a blinding snowstorm was a mystery to us. Perhaps he hired a personal snowplough. But there he was, looking just like he did on the cover of *Time*. He said that he liked the show. He said that he intended to bring it to New York. When he left, the snow swirled around his vicuna coat like fog around a genie. We stared after him, wondering if the fever was worse than we thought. But Mike left something behind with us: the idea that we might become rich and famous. It was winter. It was Canada. What were the odds?

In theory, we all belittle the coarser rewards of life, but it's usually sour grapes. When the prospects of riches and fame are actually dangled in front of us, we are in there like rats up a drainpipe. I've seen New York or Hollywood bring on many a pair of sunglasses in my life. We were no exception. Visions of limousines, handsome West Side suites, Piaget watches, dinners at Elaine's and smart Italian suits came to mind. Before you pass judgement, let's face it, most of us get into theatre for childish, silly reasons. You start out thinking that being in the theatre will make you an interesting person. I myself got interested in the theatre in the belief that women there would be looser than the general female populace. But after you have been working for a while, you find yourself just as boring as ever and your chances of scoring remain the same. So you replace an improbability with a complete absurdity: you dream about becoming a star. It is a rare person who knows that working in the theatre will not make you anything other than what you already are. And so you plod on, hoping against hope that one morning you'll wake up, read the reviews and realize that you've become glamorous and witty and cosmopolitan and rich. And you accomplish little, because when a dream of *being* takes hold, there is little room for thoughts of *doing*.

By the time we hit Toronto, we had become Top of the Pops. It's really amazing the extent to which Yankee acceptance affects Canadian prestige. Suddenly, *Billy Bishop* had become the show that Mike Nichols liked. This was the Canadian show that was going to Broadway. Overnight, a modest little work by and for Canadians had become a Hot Property. Newspaper articles, reviews, interviews all centred around the fact that we were going to Broadway. Were we excited? Would our play be a hit? Would it fail? How would we feel if it failed? There was never a word about the show itself; no interest in what it meant, what it was trying to say about war, about heroes, about Canada, about life. All that mattered was that we were going to Broadway. Would it make us rich and famous? It was as if we'd suddenly switched careers. We were no longer Canadian performers. We were athletes on our way to the Olympics. Would we win or lose? Would we cure or confirm the National Inferiority Complex?

Canadians have long existed with the suspicion that we have something missing in our chromosomal make-up when it comes to art; that there is some wishy-washy component in our gene structure that makes us incapable of strong artistic statement. This is our colonial heritage at work. We export natural resources and we import culture. That is our lot in life. When a Canadian work goes abroad, it is a little like an Indian running for Prime Minister. Our cultural inadequacy makes the odds for success rather long.

Still, I must say, the whole thing was very good for business. Interest from the Regional Theatres blossomed. Neither Eric nor I had worked in a Regional Theatre before. A tour of Regional Theatres was arranged for the following fall and winter. You see, government cutbacks and the demand for more Canadian plays had come at the same time. And what could be cheaper than a Canadian play with two actors? Then we were to go to Washington, D.C., for a tryout at the Arena Stage. Then we were to go to Broadway. Over a year's worth of work for us; we who had never run a show for more than six weeks of our lives. And a carrot on the end of the stick as well: New York.

I don't want to appear ungrateful for the opportunities that were presented to us, but we really weren't ready for this. We had barely got used to the idea of steady work when suddenly we were an international property with Canada's theatrical self-esteem in our care. For us, the future was full of peril. Terrible images came to mind: an anvil suspended above our heads ready to fall at any moment. We were like straight men in some monstrous slapstick comedy, for if there is such a thing as success, then there must be the opposite. Would we be heroes—or would we be bums? In the world in which we found ourselves, there was no middle ground, for Canadians reserve their greatest contempt for artists who fail abroad.

However, one adapts. One evolves. Some new plumage; an extra toe, but you cope. And cope we did—on a six-month tour of the Regionals where we were to find what we had been missing all those years: the audience that goes to a hit show because it's the thing to do. It's a souvenir hunt. The fact that you saw such and such will make wonderful dinner conversation for days to come. "I saw *Billy Bishop Goes to War*. It's going to Broadway, you know."

The winter went by. We played Ottawa, Montreal, Halifax, Kingston, Hamilton, Kitchener, London, St. Catherines, Edmonton and Calgary. More snow fell on our heads; more viruses passed through our systems. Perhaps human beings were invented to transport viruses from one place to the next? Then there were the interviews. How does it feel to be a success? What's it like to be finally working in the bigtime? We never told them the truth. It wasn't newsworthy. We were being educated and education is expensive. We were learning that there was no such thing as easy money; we were learning just what kind of a meatgrinder you had to go through to get your sausage.

In March, 1980, we headed for the Arena Stage in Washington, D.C. Mike Nichols filled us in on the difference between the Canadian and the American aesthetic. To begin with, our little set with its roll drop and miniature plane simply would not do. For Canadians, this set gave the play a comic and human perspective in keeping with the hero. For Americans, the set was puny. When your American spectator pays upwards of twenty bucks a ticket, he wants to see equally conspicuous consumption on the part of the play. Our toy plane became a full-sized plane. The roll drop went and was replaced by a hydraulic lift, a smoke machine and triple the number of lighting instruments. Instead of forty thousand dollars, the budget was now three hundred thousand dollars. But we were still a modest little show.

We opened well. We received raves from the Baltimore and Washington papers, and, wonder of wonders, from *The New York Times*. Success seemed near at hand. However, we wondered just what it was audiences were seeing when they saw the show. I mean, these were Americans we were playing to, not Canadians. The difference between the two audiences was never so apparent as the night we were sitting in our underwear after the show when in walked the heads of the F.B.I., the C.I.A., the Joint Chiefs of Staff, the Air Force, along with Hodding Carter, the President's Press Secretary. These guys can make you feel real small, particularly when you're half naked. In any case, they pumped our hands, slapped our backs and said that they loved the show—without reservation. This gave us pause. We had been hoping for a little more appreciation of irony, but Americans, it seems, aren't into irony. In America, when you address a subject such as War, you're either for it or agin it. And when your hero is a military man, he is either a good guy or a bad guy. So when it came to *Billy Bishop*, which does not address itself to the issue of whether or not war is a good thing or a bad thing, we became pro-war by default. As a result, to the liberal press, we were bad guys, a disturbing harbinger of violent things to come. And to the conservative press, we were good guys, reassessing the military man without simplistic sixties judgements. Because popular mythology at the time had it that America was turning right, it was thought that we had hit just the right note for the times. For us, we were never sure whether or not we had hit the note that we wanted to hit. This was our first encounter with the American penchant for obscuring an issue by simplifying it beyond belief. As Canadians who tend to be paralyzed by the complications of life, we found all this a little strange.

But then again, who really cares about the content? How many people leave a play asking what it meant? Isn't it more important whether or not it was fun, whether or not it was skilfully produced, whether or not it was a hit, whether or not it was going to make its participants rich and famous? With no serious discussion of content among either audiences or press, an artist finds himself in a vacuum where ideas have no power. In a society where ideas are effectively robbed of their power, either by disinterest, greed, ignorance or decadence, an artist abandons his pursuit of an idea in favour of the pursuit of money. He is woven into the fabric of the capitalist system. By the time we reached New York, our little play, despite its original meaning, had become an expression of our desire to become rich and famous. *Billy Bishop Goes to War* had become an expression of the American Dream.

A Canadian never feels more Canadian than when he is in the United States. And these two Canadians were beginning to weary of the American Dream. In fact, we had taken to flying to Canada for a few days now and then, like divers coming up for air. And, to continue the metaphor, it seemed we were in a whirlpool that began to spin faster and faster. We were introduced to a great many rich and famous people in those months and we learned something about them. First of all, rich and famous people tend to come in pairs. The only way a rich and famous person can *feel* rich and famous is by hanging around with other rich and famous people. Rich and famous people tend to be very frightened of *not* being rich and famous. They are constantly looking over their shoulders to see if their riches and fame have decreased any. Another thing: only a certain number of people can be rich and famous. Somebody has got to fail. The whole thing is now in perspective. In the search for riches and fame, you will either succeed or fail. If you fail, you will be disappointed. If you succeed, you will be frightened. Take your pick.

Billy Bishop Goes to War opened at the Morosco Theatre on May 29, 1980. It received a standing ovation and rave reviews from eighty percent of the critics. The party at Sardi's was a huge success, with glittering people everywhere, and Andy Warhol, the Samuel Pepys of Gotham, snapping Polaroids of everyone for posterity. When we walked back to our hotel at four o'clock in the morning, New York wasn't a city of filth, decay, bag ladies, derelicts and junkies. It was a magic city—a magic city where childish and greedy dreams come true.

The next morning, our producers were talking about closing the show. Nobody was buying tickets. "What happened?" the anguished Canadian press wanted to know. Was it a muddy review from the *Times*? Was it that the show was too small for the Broadway stage? Was the show not as good as we had thought? Was there really something missing from the Canadian chromosomal make-up? Were Canadians really inferior? Canadians take failure on Broadway much more seriously than Americans do. Americans know that hardly anything ever succeeds on Broadway—maybe about one show in a hundred. And we Canadians have put far less than one hundred shows on Broadway. It's a tremendous longshot. But this explanation is far too simplistic and pragmatic for the Canadian press. It doesn't address itself to the National Inferiority Complex. We still have interviewers asking, "What happened?" as though we were two runners who had failed to post their best times at the Olympics, and so had let their country down.

What had happened was that our American producers had made a miscalculation. They were betting that rave reviews and the name of Mike Nichols, tastemaker to Broadway, would be enough to draw the huge grosses that were necessary to survive on a Broadway stage. They had thought that if they loved a play, Americans would love a play—even a Canadian play. They were wrong. Of course, if *Billy Bishop* were a British play, the job of selling it would have been tough, but possible. America has long had a love-hate relationship with Britain. Britain is the country it fought to achieve its independence; it was the country it eventually replaced as muscleman of the Western World. And Americans have a National Inferiority Complex too. They are afraid that even with all their technological, financial and military achievements, they have still not become a civilized country. Americans are afraid they are Rome to Britain's Greece. And admiration, envy and fear can combine to make a British success in America possible.

But a Canadian play? Forget it! Americans don't want to see two unknown Canadians perform a play about an unknown Canadian war hero who fought in a war that America did not win. Not with *Barnum* across the street. How good the play was was irrelevant, as were the reviews and the awards. Americans simply weren't buying it. It took our producers a few months and an unprecedented move to off-Broadway, where we should probably have been to begin with, before they admitted defeat. Rich and Famous, those two sirens, were finally silent.

When we left New York in August for the Edinburgh Festival, which was another story entirely, our parting was amicable. We have friends in New York and Mike Nichols jokingly offers to mis-produce anything I write. I sometimes think that education has more to do with the loss of illusions than with the acquisition of knowledge. If that is true, we received more education in four months in New York than in seven years at university. The tuition was high, but the school gave good value. Our experience in New York has given me the suspicion that, in fact, it may be better to give than to receive; that perhaps it is more difficult for a rich man to enter the kingdom of heaven. It seems that the greater our so-called international success became, the more we longed for audiences like those first few thousand souls who braved strikes, snow, viruses and lousy sightlines to see our little play about Billy Bishop. Perhaps theatre is a very simple activity in which a group of people get together to focus on what is best about themselves.

Eric and I would like to thank all those who helped along the way. Some of the names that would fill a small telephone directory are Lewis Allen, Martin Bragg, Col. Dode Clark, CP Air, Ross Douglas, Haig Farris, David Gropman, Beverlee Larsen, George Miller, Mike Nichols, Lorna Gail Peterson, Jay Presson-Allen, Cedric Smith, Ken Smith, Tommy Smith, Kay Staley, Ronald Stern, Paul Thompson, Jennifer Tipton, Paul Williams, Jackie Willis-O'Connor and Chris Wootten and all his colleagues at the Vancouver East Cultural Centre.

Billy Bishop Goes to War is dedicated to all those who didn't come back from the war, and to all those who did and wondered why.

John Gray
Vancouver, B.C.
December 1981

CHARACTERS:

NARRATOR/PIANIST
BILLY BISHOP, *who also plays*
  AN UPPERCLASSMAN
  ADJUTANT PERRAULT
  AN OFFICER
  SIR HUGH CECIL
  LADY ST. HELIER
  CEDRIC, *her butler*
  A DOCTOR
  GENERAL JOHN HIGGINS, *Brigade Commander*
  A TOMMY
  THE LOVELY HÉLÈNE
  ALBERT BALL
  WALTER BOURNE, *Bishop's mechanic*
  A GERMAN
  GENERAL HUGH M. TRENCHARD
  AN ADJUTANT
  SECOND OFFICER
  KING GEORGE V

ACT ONE

The lights come up slowly on BILLY BISHOP and the PIANO PLAYER, who sits at the piano. They are in an Officers' Mess.

BISHOP and PIANO PLAYER   *singing*
We were off to fight the Hun,
We would shoot him with a gun.
Our medals would shine
Like a sabre in the sun.
We were off to fight the Hun
And it looked like lots of fun,
Somehow it didn't seem like war
At all, at all, at all.
Somehow it didn't seem like war at all.

BILLY BISHOP speaks to the audience. He is a young man from Owen Sound, Ontario. His speech pattern is that of a small town Canadian boy who could well be squealing his tires down the main street of some town at this very moment.

BISHOP   *to the audience*   I think when you haven't been in a war for a while, you've got to take what you can get. I mean, Canada, 1914? They must have been pretty desperate. Take me, for instance. Twenty years old, a convicted liar and cheat. I mean, I'm on record as the worst student R.M.C. . . .Royal Military College in Kingston, Ontario . . .I'm on record as the worst student they ever had. I join up, they made me an officer, a lieutenant in the Mississauga Horse. All I can say is they must have been scraping the bottom of the barrel.

BISHOP and PIANO PLAYER   *singing*
We were off to fight the Hun,
Though hardly anyone

Had ever read about a battle,
Much less seen a Lewis gun.
We were off to fight the Hun
And it looked like lots of fun,
Somehow it didn't seem like war
At all, at all, at all.
Somehow it didn't seem like war at all.

BISHOP   *to the audience*   Yeah, it looked like it was going to be a great war. I mean, all my friends were very keen to join up, they were. Not me. Royal Military College had been enough for me. Now the reason I went to R.M.C. is, well. . .I could ride a horse. And I was a great shot. I mean, I am a really good shot. I've got these tremendous eyes, you see. And R.M.C. had an entrance exam and that was good because my previous scholastic record wasn't that hot. In fact, when I suggested to my principal that, indeed, I was going to R.M.C., he said, "Bishop, you don't have the brains." But I studied real hard, sat for the exams and got in.

He imitates an R.M.C. officer.

Recruits! Recruits will march at all times. They will not loiter, they will not window shop. Recruits! Recruits will run at all times when in the parade square. Recruits! Recruits will be soundly trounced every Friday night, whether they deserve it or not.

As himself.

I mean, those guys were nuts! They were going to make leaders out of us, the theory being that before you could learn to lead, you had to learn to obey. So, because of this, we're all assigned to an upperclassman as a kind of, well. . .slave. And I was assigned to this real sadistic S.O.B., this guy named Vivian Bishop. That's right, the same surname as me, and because of that, I had to tuck him into bed at night, kiss him on the forehead and say, "Goodnight, Daddy!" I mean, it's pretty hard to take some of that stuff seriously. One of my punishments: I'm supposed to clean out this old Martello Tower by the edge of the lake. I mean, it's filthy, hasn't been used for years. Now I do a real great job. I clean it up real well. This upperclassman comes along to inspect it.

UPPERCLASSMAN   What's this in the corner, Bishop?

BISHOP   That?   *He has another look.*   That's a spider, Sir.

UPPERCLASSMAN   That's right, Bishop. That's a spider. Now you had orders to clean this place up. You haven't done that. You get down on your hands and knees and eat that spider.

BISHOP   *to the audience*   I had to eat that spider in front of all my classmates. You ever have to eat a spider? In public? I doubt it. Nuts! Now, whenever I'm not happy, I mean, whenever I'm not having a really good time, I do one of three things: I get sick,

I get injured or I get in an awful lot of trouble. My third year at R.M.C., I got into an awful lot of trouble. This friend of mine, Townsend, one night, we got a bottle of gin, eh? And we stole a canoe. Well, we'd arranged to meet these girls on Cedar Island out in Dead Man's Bay. Well, of course, the canoe tips over. Now, it's early spring, really cold. We get back to shore somehow and we're shivering and Townsend says to me, "Bish, Bish, I'm going to the infirmary. I think I got pneumonia." And I'm sitting there saying, "Well, whatever you do, you silly bugger, change into some dry clothes." Because we couldn't let anybody know what we'd been doing. I mean, we were absent without leave, in possession of alcohol and we'd stolen a canoe. What I didn't know was the officer on duty had witnessed this whole thing. Townsend goes to the infirmary and is confronted with these charges and he admits everything. I didn't know that. I'm rudely awakened out of my sleep and hauled up before old Adjutant Perrault.

At attention, addressing the Adjutant Officer.

Sir! I've been in my bed all night. I really don't know what you're talking about, Sir.

PERRAULT   Come on. Come on now, Bishop. We have the testimony of the officer on duty. We also have the full confession of your accomplice implicating you fully in this. Now, what is your story, Bishop?

BISHOP   *to the audience*   Well, I figured I was in too deep now to change my story.   *to PERRAULT* Sir, I still maintain. . . .

PERRAULT   Bishop! I'm going to say the worst thing that I can say to a gentleman cadet. You are a liar, Bishop!

BISHOP is sobered briefly by this memory, but he quickly recovers.

BISHOP   *to the audience*   I got twenty-eight days restricted leave for that. It's like house arrest. Then they caught me cheating on my final exams. Well, I handed in the crib notes with the exam paper! And that's when they called me the worst student R.M.C. ever had. They weren't going to tell me what my punishment was until the next fall, so I could stew about it all summer, but I knew what it was going to be. Expulsion! With full honours! But then the war broke out and I enlisted and was made an officer. I mean, for me, it was the lesser of two evils. But everyone else was very keen on the whole thing. They were.

BISHOP and PIANO PLAYER   *singing*
We were off to fight the Hun,
Though hardly anyone
Had ever seen a Hun,
Wouldn't know one if we saw one.
We were off to fight the Hun
And it looked like lots of fun,

Somehow it didn't seem like war
At all, at all, at all.
Somehow it didn't seem like war at all.

The PIANO PLAYER raps out a military rhythm.

BISHOP   *to the audience*   October 1st, 1914, the First Contingent of the Canadian Expeditionary Forces left for England. I wasn't with them. I was in the hospital. Thinking of Margaret. . . .

The PIANO PLAYER plays the appropriate "Dear Margaret" music under the following speech.

BISHOP   *As if writing a letter.*

Dear . . . Dearest Margaret. I am in the hospital with pneumonia. I also have an allergy, but the doctors don't know what I'm allergic to. Maybe it's horses. Maybe it's the Army. The hospital is nice, so I am in good spirits. Thinking of you constantly, I remain. . . .

The PIANO PLAYER raps out a military rhythm once again.

BISHOP   *to the audience*   March, 1915, the Second, Third, Fourth, Fifth and Sixth Contingents of the Canadian Expeditionary Forces left for England. I wasn't with them either. I was back in the hospital . . . thinking of Margaret.

As if writing a letter.

Sweetheart. Please excuse my writing, as I have a badly sprained wrist. Yesterday, my horse reared up and fell over backwards on me. It was awful, I could have been killed. My head was completely buried in the mud. My nose is, of course, broken and quite swollen, and I can't see out of one eye. I have two broken ribs and am pretty badly bruised, but the doctor figures I'll be up and around by Monday. The hospital is nice, so I am in fine spirits. Thinking of you constantly, I remain. . . .

The PIANO PLAYER raps out a military rhythm once again.

BISHOP   *to the audience*   June, 1915. The Seventh Contingent of the Canadian Expeditionary Forces left for England. I was with them. Now, this was aboard a cattle boat called the *Caledonia*, in Montreal. There was this big crowd came down to the pier to see us off. I mean, hundreds and hundreds of people, and for a while there, I felt like the whole thing was worth doing. It's pretty impressive when you look out there and you see several hundred people cheering and waving . . . at you. I mean, when you're from a small town, the numbers get to you. And you're looking out at them and they're looking back at you, and you think, "Boy, I must be doing something right!"

The PIANO PLAYER strikes up "God Save the King."

And they play "God Save the King," and everybody is crying and waving and cheering, and the boat starts to pull out, and they start to yell like you've never heard anybody yell before. I mean, you feel

388 / BILLY BISHOP GOES TO WAR

good. You really do! And we're all praying, "Please, God, don't let the fighting be over before I can get over there and take part...."

He becomes carried away and starts yelling.

"On the edge of destiny, you must test your strength!"

He is suddenly self-conscious.

What the hell am I talking about?

The music changes from heroic to the monotonous roll of a ship.

BISHOP   The good ship *Caledonia* soon changed its name to the good ship Vomit. It was never meant to hold people. Even the horses didn't like it. Up, down, up, down. And they're siphoning brandy down our throats to keep us from puking our guts up on the deck. It was a big joke. Whenever anyone would puke, which was every minute or so, everyone would point to him and laugh like it was the funniest thing they had ever seen. I mean, puke swishing around on the deck, two inches deep, har, har, har! You couldn't sleep, even if it was calm, because every time you closed your eyes, you had a nightmare about being torpedoed.

He demonstrates a torpedo hitting the ship.

Every time I closed my eyes, I could see this torpedo coming up through the water, through the hull of the ship and...BOOM! And we were attacked, too, just off the coast of Ireland. I was scared shitless. All you could do was stand at the rail and watch the other ships get hit and go down. Bodies floating around like driftwood. But we made it through. The Good Ship *Caledonia*, latrine of the Atlantic, finally made it through to Portsmouth, full of dead horses and sick Canadians. When we got off, they thought we were a boat load of Balkan refugees.

BISHOP and PIANO PLAYER   *singing*
We were off to fight the Hun,
We would shoot him with a gun.
Our medals would shine
Like a sabre in the sun.
We were off to fight the Hun
And it looked like lots of fun,
Somehow it didn't seem like war
At all, at all, at all.
Somehow it didn't seem like war at all.

BISHOP   *to the audience*   A few days later, we marched into Shorncliffe Military Camp, right on the Channel. You know, on a clear night, you could see the artillery flashes from France. I took it as a sign of better things to come.... It wasn't.

As if writing a letter.

Dearest Margaret...Shorncliffe Military Camp is the worst yet! The cold wind brings two kinds of weather. Either it rains or it doesn't. When it rains, you've got mud like I've never seen before. Your horse gets stuck in a foot and a half of mud. You get off and you're knee deep. The rain falls in sheets and you're wet to the skin. You are never dry. Then the rain stops and the ground dries out. What a relief, you say? Then the wind gets the dust going and you have dust storms for days. The sand is like needles hitting you, and a lot of the men are bleeding from the eyes. I don't know which is worse, going blind or going crazy. The sand gets in your food, your clothes, your tent, in your...body orifices. A lot of the guys have something called desert madness, which is really serious. As I write this letter, the sand is drifting across the page. Thinking of you constantly, I remain....

To the audience.

Being buried alive in the mud....I was seriously considering this proposition one day when a funny thing happened.

He demonstrates with a chair.

I got my horse stuck in the middle of the parade ground. The horse is up to its fetlocks; I'm up to my knees. Mud, sweat and horse shit from head to toe.

The music becomes ethereal and gentle.

Then, suddenly, out of the clouds comes this little single-seater scout. You know, this little fighter plane? It circles a couple of times. I guess the pilot had lost his way and was going to come down and ask for directions. He does this turn, then lands on an open space, like a dragonfly on a rock. The pilot jumps out. He's in this long sheepskin coat, helmet, goggles...warm and dry. He gets his directions, then jumps back into the machine, up in the air, with the mist blowing off him. All by himself. No superior officer, no horse, no sand, no mud. What a beautiful picture! I don't know how long I just stood there watching until he was long gone. Out of sight.

He breaks the mood abruptly.

I mean, this war was going on a lot longer than anyone expected. A lot more people were getting killed than anyone expected. Now I wasn't going to spend the rest of the war in the mud. And I sure as hell wasn't going to die in the mud.

The PIANO PLAYER strikes up a new tune. BISHOP drunkenly joins in.

BISHOP and PIANO PLAYER   *singing*
Thinking of December nights
In the clear Canadian cold,
Where the winter air don't smell bad,
And the wind don't make you old.
Where the rain don't wash your heart out,
And the nights ain't filled with fear.
Oh, those old familiar voices
Whisper in my ears.

Chorus

Oh, Canada,
Sing a song for me.
Sing one for your lonely son,
So far across the sea.

The piano continues with a popular dance tune of the period. BISHOP's reverie is interrupted by a Cockney OFFICER, who is also drunk, and who is slightly mad.

OFFICER   You don't fancy the Cavalry then, eh?

BISHOP   What?!

OFFICER   I say, you don't fancy the Cavalry then, eh? It's going to be worse at the front, mate. There, you got blokes shooting at you, right?. . . With machine guns.

He imitates a machine gun.

DakDakDakDakakaka. Har, har, har. It's a bloody shooting gallery. They still think they're fighting the Boer War! Cavalry charges against machine guns. DakDakDakak. Har, har! It's a bloody shooting gallery with you in the middle of it, mate.

BISHOP   This is awful. Something's got to be done. Jeez, I was a casualty in training.

OFFICER   Take a word of advice from me, mate. The only way out is up.

BISHOP   Up?

OFFICER   Up. Join the Royal Flying Corps. I did. I used to be in the Cavalry, but I joined the R.F.C. I like it. It's good clean work. Mind you, the bleeding machines barely stay in the air and the life expectancy of the new lads is about eleven days. But I like it. It's good clean work.

BISHOP   Just a minute. How can I get into the Royal Flying Corps? I'm Canadian. I'm cannon fodder. You practically have to own your own plane to get into the R.F.C.

OFFICER   Au contraire, mate. Au contraire. The upper classes are depressed by the present statistics, so they aren't joining with their usual alacrity. Now, anyone who wants to can get blown out of the air. Even Canadians.

BISHOP   Well, what do I have to do?

OFFICER   You go down to see them at the War Office, daft bunch of twits, but they're all right. Now. . . you act real eager, see? Like you want to be a pilot. You crave the excitement, any old rubbish like that. Then, they're not going to know what to ask, because they don't know a bleeding thing about it. So, they'll ask you whatever comes into their heads, which isn't much, then they'll say you can't be a pilot, you've got to be an observer.

BISHOP   What's an observer?

OFFICER   He's the fellow who goes along for the ride, you know? Looks about.

BISHOP   Ohhh. . . .

OFFICER   So, you act real disappointed, like your Mum wanted you to be a pilot, and then, you get your transfer. . . .

BISHOP   Just a minute. So, I'm an observer. I'm the fellow that goes along for the ride, looks about. So what? How do I get to be a pilot?

OFFICER   I don't know. Sooner or later, you just get to be a pilot. Plenty of vacancies these days. Check the casualty lists, wait for a bad one. You've got to go in the back door, you know what I mean? Nobody gets to be a pilot right away, for Christ's sake. Especially not bleeding Canadians!

BISHOP   *to the audience*   Did you ever trust your future to a drunken conversation in a bar? Two days later, I went down to see them at the War Office.

The PIANO PLAYER plays some going to war music. In the following scene, SIR HUGH CECIL interviews BISHOP at the War Office. He is getting on in years and the new technology of warfare has confused him deeply.

SIR HUGH   So. . . you wish to transfer to the Royal Flying Corps? Am I right? Am I correct?

BISHOP   Yes, Sir. I want to become a fighter pilot, Sir. It's what my mother always wanted, Sir.

SIR HUGH   Oh. . . I see. Well, the situation is this, Bishop. We need good men in the R.F.C., but they must have the correct. . . er. . . qualifications. Now, while the War Office has not yet ascertained what qualifications are indeed necessary to fly an. . . er . . . aeroplane, we must see to it that all candidates possess the necessary qualifications, should the War Office ever decide what those qualifications are. Do you understand, Bishop?

BISHOP   Perfectly, Sir.

SIR HUGH   That's very good. Jolly good. More than I can say. Well, shall we begin then?

BISHOP   Ready when you are, Sir.

SIR HUGH   That's good, shows keenness, you see. . . . And good luck, Bishop. *to himself* What on earth shall I ask him? *There is a long pause while he collects his thoughts.* Do you ski?

BISHOP   Ski, Sir?

SIR HUGH   Yes. . . do you ski?

BISHOP   *to the audience*   Here was an Englishman asking a Canadian whether or not he skied. Now, if the Canadian said he didn't ski, the Englishman might find that somewhat suspicious.

To SIR HUGH.

Ski? Yes, Sir.

To the audience.

Never skied in my life.

SIR HUGH   Fine, well done . . . thought you might. *Pause.*   Do you ride a horse?

BISHOP   I'm an officer in the Cavalry, Sir.

SIR HUGH   Doesn't necessarily follow, but we'll put down that you ride, shall we? *Pause.*   What about sports, Bishop? Run, jump, throw the ball? Play the game, eh? What?

BISHOP   Sports, Sir? All sports.

SIR HUGH   I see. Well done, Bishop. I'm most impressed.

BISHOP   Does this mean I can become a fighter pilot, Sir?

SIR HUGH   Who knows, Bishop? Who knows? All full up with fighter pilots at the moment, I'm afraid. Take six months, a year to get in. Terribly sorry. Nothing I can do, old man.

BISHOP   I see, Sir.

SIR HUGH   However! We have an immediate need for observers. You know, the fellow who goes along for the ride, looks about. What do you say, Bishop?

BISHOP   *to audience*   I thought about it. I wanted to be a pilot. I couldn't. So, in the fall of 1915, I joined the Twenty-First Squadron as an observer. That's what they were using planes for at that time. Observation. You could take pictures of enemy troop formations, direct artillery fire, stuff like that. It seemed like nice quiet work at that time and I was really good at the aerial photography. I've got these great eyes, remember? And to fly! You're in this old Farnham trainer, sounds like a tractor. It coughs, wheezes, chugs its way up to one thousand feet. You're in a kite with a motor that can barely get off the ground. But even so, you're in the air. . . . You're not on the ground. . . . You're above everything.

The PIANO PLAYER plays some mess hall music.

It was a different world up there. A different war and a different breed of men fighting that war. . . . Flyers! During training, we heard all the stories. If you went down behind enemy lines and were killed, they'd come over, the Germans, that is . . . they'd come over under a flag of truce and drop a photograph of your grave. Nice. If you were taken prisoner, it was the champagne razzle in the mess. Talking and drinking all night. It was a different war they were fighting up there. And from where I stood, it looked pretty darn good.

PIANO PLAYER   Can you be a bit more specific, please?

BISHOP and the PIANO PLAYER sing a song of champagne and vermouth.

BISHOP and PIANO PLAYER   *singing*
I see two planes in the air,
A fight that's fair and square,
With dips and loops and rolls

That would scare you (I'm scared already).
We will force the German down
And arrest him on the ground,
A patriotic lad from Bavaria (Poor bloody sod).

But he'll surrender willingly
And salute our chivalry,
For this war is not of our creation.
But before it's prison camp
And a bed that's cold and damp,
We'll all have a little celebration.

Chorus

Oh, we'll toast our youth
On champagne and vermouth,
For all of us know what it's like to fly.
Oh, the fortunes of war
Can't erase esprit de corps
And we'll all of us be friends
'Til we die.

PIANO PLAYER   Can you go on a bit, please?

BISHOP and PIANO PLAYER   *singing*
Oh, we'll drink the night away,
And when the Bosch is led away,
We'll load him down with cigarettes and wine.
We'll drink a final toast goodbye,
But for the grace of God go I,
And we'll vow that we'll be friends (Cheers—ping)
Another time.

Chorus

Oh, we'll toast our youth
On champagne and vermouth,
For all of us know what it's like to fly.
Oh, the fortunes of war
Can't erase esprit de corps
And we'll all of us be friends
'Til we die.

BISHOP   You want chivalry? You want gallantry? You want nice guys? That's your flyer. And Jeez, I was going to be one! January 1st, 1916, I crossed the channel to France as a flyer. Well, an observer anyway. That's when I found out that Twenty-First Squadron was known as the "suicide squadron." I mean, that awful nickname used to prey on my mind, you know? And the Archies? The anti-aircraft guns? Not tonight, Archibald! I mean, you're tooling around over the line, doing your observation work, a sitting duck, when suddenly you are surrounded by these little black puffs of smoke. Then . . . wham-whizz! Shrapnel whizzes all around you. I was hit on the head by a piece of flak, just a bruise, but a couple of inches lower and I would have been killed. And we were all scared stiff of this new German machine, the Fokker. It had this interrupter gear, so the pilot could shoot straight at you through the propeller without actually shooting the propeller off. All he had to do was aim his plane at you! And casualties? Lots and lots and lots of casualties. It was a grim situation. But we didn't know how grim it could get until we saw the RE-7 . . . the Reconnaissance Experimental Number Seven. Our new plane. What you saw was this mound of cables and wires, with a thousand pounds of equipment hanging off it. Four machine guns, a five hundred pound bomb, for God's sake. Reconnaissance equipment, cameras. . . . Roger Neville (that's my pilot), he and I are ordered into the thing to take it up. Of course, it doesn't get off the ground. Anyone could see that. We thought, fine, good riddance. But the officers go into a huddle.

imitating the Officers Mmmmum? What do you think we should do? Take the bomb off? Take the bomb off!

as himself So we take the bomb off and try it again. This time, the thing sort of flops down the runway like a crippled duck. Finally, by taking everything off but one machine gun, the thing sort of flopped itself into the air and chugged along. It was a pig! We were all scared stiff of it. So they put us on active duty . . . as *bombers*! They gave us two bombs each, told us to fly over Hunland and drop them on somebody. But in order to accommodate for the weight of the bombs, they took our machine guns away!

as if writing a letter Dearest Margaret. We are dropping bombs on the enemy from unarmed machines. It is exciting work. It's hard to keep your confidence in a war when you don't have a gun. Somehow we get back in one piece and we start joking around and inspecting the machine for bullet and shrapnel damage. You're so thankful not to be dead. Then I go back to the barracks and lie down. A kind of terrible loneliness comes over me. It's like waiting for the firing squad. It makes you want to cry, you feel so frightened and so alone. I think all of us who aren't dead think these things. Thinking of you constantly, I remain. . . .

PIANO PLAYER *singing*
Nobody shoots no one in Canada,
At least nobody they don't know.
Nobody shoots no one in Canada,
Last battle was a long, long time ago.

Nobody picks no fights in Canada,
Not with nobody they ain't met.
Nobody starts no wars in Canada,
Folks tend to work for what they get.

Take me under
That big blue sky,
Where the deer and the black bear play.
May not be heaven,
But heaven knows we try,
Wish I was in Canada today.

Nobody drop no bombs on Canada,
Wouldn't want to send no one to hell.
Nobody start no wars on Canada,
Where folks tend to wish each other well.

The music continues as BISHOP speaks.

BISHOP Of course in this situation, it wasn't too long before the accidents started happening again. It's kind of spooky, but I think being accident prone actually saved my life. I'm driving a truck load of parts a couple of miles from the aerodrome and I run into another truck. I'm inspecting the undercarriage of my machine when a cable snaps and hits me on the head. I was unconscious for two days. . . . I had a tooth pulled, it got infected and I was in the hospital for two weeks. . . . Then Roger does this really bad landing. I hit my knee on a metal brace inside the plane so hard I could barely walk. . . . Then I got three weeks leave in London. None too soon. On the boat going back to England, we all got into the champagne and cognac pretty heavy, and, by the time we arrived, we were all pretty tight and this game developed to see who would actually be the first guy to touch foot on English soil. I'm leading the race down the gangplank. I trip and fall! Everyone else falls on top of me, right on the knee I hurt in the crash! Gawd, the pain was awful! But I was damned if I'd spend my leave in the hospital, so I'd just pour down the brandy until the thing was pretty well numb. I had a hell of a time! If the pain got to me in the night and I couldn't sleep, I'd just pour down the brandy. But around my last day of leave, I started thinking about the bombing runs, the Archies, the Fokkers, and I thought, Jeez, maybe I better have someone look at this knee. The doctor found I had a cracked kneecap, which meant I'd be in the hospital for a couple of weeks. They also found I had a badly strained heart, which meant I would be in the hospital for an indefinite period. As far as I was concerned, I was out of the war.

BISHOP and PIANO PLAYER *singing*
Take me under
That big blue sky,
Where the deer and the black bear play.
It may not be heaven,
But heaven knows we try,
Wish I was in Canada today.

I'm dreaming of the trees in Canada,
Northern Lights are dancing in my head.
If I die, then let me die in Canada,
Where there's a chance I'll die in bed.

BISHOP The hospital is nice. People don't shoot at you and people don't drop things on you. I thought it would be a nice place to spend the rest of the war. I went to sleep for three days.

Distorted marching music is heard.

I had this nightmare. A terrible dream. I am in the lobby of the Grand Hotel in London. The band is playing military music and the lobby is full of English and German officers. They're dancing together and their medals jingle like sleighbells in the snow. The sound is deafening. I've got to get out of there. I start to run, but my knee gives out underneath me. As I get up, I get kicked in the stomach by a Prussian boot. As I turn to run, I get kicked in the rear by an English boot. Then I turn around and all the officers have formed a chorus line, like the Follies, and they are heading for me, kicking. I scream as a hundred black boots kick me high in the air, as I turn over and over, shouting, "Help me! Help me! They are trying to kill me!"

He wakes up abruptly.

LADY ST. HELIER   My goodness, Bishop, you'll not get any rest screaming at the top of your lungs like that.

BISHOP   *to the audience*   In front of me was a face I'd never seen before. Very old, female, with long white hair pulled back tightly in a bun, exposing two of the largest ears I had ever seen.

LADY ST. HELIER   You'd be the son of Will Bishop of Owen Sound, Canada, would you not? Of course you are, the resemblance is quite startling. Your father was a loyal supporter of a very dear friend of mine, Sir Wilfred Laurier. It was in that connection I met your father in Ottawa.

She zeros in on BISHOP.

A gaping mouth is most impolite, Bishop. No, I am not clairvoyant. I am Lady St. Helier. Reform alderman, poetess, friend of Churchill, and the woman who shall save your life.

BISHOP   *speechless*   Ahh...oh...mmmm. Ahh....

LADY ST. HELIER   Enough of this gay banter, Bishop. Time runs apace and my life is not without its limits. You have been making rather a mess of it, haven't you? You are a rude young man behaving like cannon fodder. Perfectly acceptable characteristics in a Canadian, but you are different. You are a gifted Canadian and that gift belongs to a much older and deeper tradition than Canada can ever hope to provide. Quite against your own wishes, you will be released from this wretched hospital in two weeks' time. Promptly, at three o'clock on that afternoon, you will present yourself before my door at Portland Place, dressed for tea and in a positive frame of mind. Do I make myself clear? Good. Please be punctual, Mr. Bishop.

BISHOP   *to the audience*   Well, jeez, that old girl must have known something I didn't, because, two weeks later, I'm released from hospital. Promptly, at three o'clock, I find myself in front of her door at Portland Place, in my best uniform, shining my shoes on my pants. The door is opened by the biggest butler I have ever seen.

He looks up and speaks to the butler.

Hi!

The butler looks down at him with distaste, turns away and calls to LADY ST. HELIER.

CEDRIC   *calling*   Madam, the Canadian is here. Shall I show him in?

LADY ST. HELIER   *from a distance*   Yes, Cedric, please. Show him in.

CEDRIC   *turning his back to BISHOP*   Get in!

BISHOP   *to the audience*   I'm shown into the largest room I've ever seen. I mean, a fireplace eight feet wide and a staircase that must have had a hundred steps in it. I'm not used to dealing with nobility. Servants, grand ballrooms, pheasant hunting on the heath, fifty-year-old brandy over billiards, breakfast in bed...shit, what a life!

CEDRIC   Madam is in the study. Get in!

BISHOP   The study. Books, books...more books than I'll ever read. Persian rug. Tiger's head over the mantle. African spears in the corner. "Rule Britannia, Britannia rules the...." I stood at the door. I was on edge. Out of my element. Lady St. Helier was sitting at this little writing desk, writing.

LADY ST. HELIER   Very punctual, Bishop. Please sit down.

BISHOP   I sat in this chair that was all carved lions. One of the lions stuck in my back.

CEDRIC   Would our visitor from Canada care for tea, madam?

LADY ST. HELIER   Would you care for something to drink, Bishop?

BISHOP   Tea? Ahhh, yeah.... Tea would be fine.

LADY ST. HELIER   A tea for Bishop, Cedric. And I'll have a gin.

CEDRIC   Lemon?

BISHOP   *disappointed*   Gin! I wonder if I could change.... No, no. Tea will be fine.   *to the audience*   Tea was served. I sip my tea. Lady St. Helier sips her gin. And Cedric loomed over me, afraid I was going to drool on the carpet or something. Lady St. Helier stared at me through her thick spectacles. Suddenly, her ears twitched, like she was honing in on something.

LADY ST. HELIER   I have written a poem in your honour, Bishop. I can but hope that your rustic mind will appreciate its significance.

She signals to the PIANO PLAYER.

Cedric!

LADY ST. HELIER   *spoken to music*
You're a typical Canadian,
You're modesty itself,
And you really wouldn't want to hurt a flea.
But you're just about to go
The way of the buffalo.
You'd do well to take this good advice from me.

I'm awfully sick and tired
Being constantly required

To stand by and watch Canadians make the best of
   it,
For the Colonial mentality
Defies all rationality.
You seem to go to lengths to make a mess of it.

Why don't you grow up,
Before I throw up?
Do you expect somebody else to do it for you?
Before you're dead out,
Get the lead out
And seize what little life still lies before you.

Do you really expect Empire
To settle back, retire,
And say, "Colonials, go on your merry way"?
I'm very tired of your whining
And your infantile maligning.
Your own weakness simply won't be whined away.

So don't be so naïve,
And take that heart off your sleeve,
For a fool and his life will soon be parted.
War's a fact of life today
And it will not be wished away.
Forget that fact and you'll be dead before you've
   started.

So, Bishop, grow up,
Before I throw up.
Your worst enemy is yourself, as you well know.
Before you're dead out,
Get the lead out.
You have your own naïveté to overthrow.

to the PIANO PLAYER Thank you, Cedric.

To BISHOP.

Do I make myself clear, Bishop? You will cease this
mediocrity your record only too clearly reveals.
You will become the pilot you wished to be but
were lamentably content to settle for less. Now this
will take time, for you must recover the health you
have so seriously undermined. To that end, you will
remain here, a lodger at Portland Place, top of the
stairs, third floor, seventh room on the left. Cedric,
be kind to Bishop and ignore his bad manners. For
cultivation exacts its price. The loss of a certain
. . . vitality. Beneath this rude Canadian exterior,
there is a power that you will never know. Properly
harnessed, that power will win wars for you. Churchill
knows it and I know it too. Good day, Bishop.

BISHOP *to the audience* Now there are one or
two Canadians who would have taken offence at
that. Not me. Staying at Portland Place, I found out
some things right away. For example, life goes much
smoother when you've got influence. Take this pilot
business, for example. Lady St. Helier was on the
phone to Churchill himself, and, the next day, I was
called down to the War Office. The atmosphere
was much different.

Going to war music is heard once again.

SIR HUGH Bishop, my boy. Good to see you,
good to see you. Well, well, well, your mother's
wish is finally going to come true.

BISHOP Really, Sir?

SIR HUGH Yes, yes. You are going to become a
pilot. No problem, pas de problème. Medical examination in two days time, then report for training.

BISHOP *to the audience* Medical examination!
What about my weak heart? What about the fact
that three weeks ago I was on the verge of a medical
discharge?

DOCTOR *addressing BISHOP, but seldom ever
looking up from his desk* Strip to the waist, Bishop.
Hmnmnmnm? Stick out your tongue and say ninety-
nine. . . . Good. . . . Cough twice. . . . That's good,
too. . . . Turn around ten times. . . . Eight, nine, ten.
. . . Attention! Still on your feet, Bishop? You're fit
as a fiddle and ready to fly!

BISHOP *singing*
Gonna fly. . .
Gonna fly so high,
Like a bird in the sky,
With the wind in my hair,
And the sun burning in my eyes.
Flying Canadian,
Machine gun in my hand,
First Hun I see is the first Hun to die.

Gonna fly. . .
In my machine,
Gonna shoot so clean,
Gonna hear them scream
When I hit them between the eyes.
Flying Canadian,
Machine gun in my hand,
First Hun I see is the first Hun to die.

Chorus

Flying. . .
What have I been waiting for?
What a way to fight a war!
Flying Canadian,
Machine gun in my hand,
First Hun I see is the first Hun to die.

Gonna fly. . .
Gonna shoot them down
'Til they hit the ground
And they burn with the sound
Of bacon on the fry.
Flying Canadian,
Machine gun in my hand,
First Hun I see is the first Hun to die.

Chorus

Flying. . .
What have I been waiting for?
What a way to fight a war!
Flying Canadian,

Machine gun in my hand,
First Hun I see is the first Hun to die.

The song ends abruptly.

BISHOP   I'll never forget my first solo flight. Lonely? Jeezus! You're sitting at the controls all by yourself, trying to remember what they're all for. Everyone has stopped doing what they're doing to watch you. An ambulance is parked at the edge of the field with the engines running. You know why. You also know that there's a surgical team in the hospital, just ready to rip.

The PIANO PLAYER calls out the following. BISHOP repeats after him.

PIANO PLAYER   Switch off.

BISHOP   Switch off.

PIANO PLAYER   Petrol on.

BISHOP   Petrol on.

PIANO PLAYER   Suck in.

BISHOP   Suck in.

PIANO PLAYER   Switch on.

BISHOP   Switch on.

PIANO PLAYER   Contact!

BISHOP   Contact!

During the above, BISHOP does all the sound effects vocally, much as a small boy would do during such a demonstration.

The propellor is given a sharp swing over and the engine starts with a roar . . . coughs twice, but soon starts hitting on all cylinders. You signal for them to take away the chocks. Then you start bouncing across the field under your own power and head her up into the wind.

He checks the equipment.

Rudder.

Click, click.

Elevator.

Click, click.

Ailerons.

Click, click.

Heart.

Boom-boom! Boom-boom!

I open the throttle all the way . . . and you're off! Pull back on the stick, easy, easy.

He demonstrates the plane bumping along, then rising up into the air.

Once I was in the air, I felt a lot better. In fact, I felt like a king! Mind you, I wasn't fooling around. I'm

flying straight as I can, climbing steadily. All alone! What a feeling!

He looks about.

I've got to turn. I execute a gentle turn, skidding like crazy, but what the hell. I try another turn. This time, I bank it a little more. Too much. Too much! . . . All in all, I'm having a hell of a time up there until I remember I have to land. . . . What do I do now? Keep your head, that's what you do. Pull back on the throttle.

The engine coughs.

Too much! I put the nose down into a steep dive. Too steep. Bring it up again, down again, up, down . . . and in a series of steps, kind of descend to the earth. Then I execute everything I remember I have to do to make a perfect landing. Forty feet off the ground! I put the nose down again and do another perfect landing. This time, I'm only eight feet off the ground, but now I don't have room left to do another nose down manoeuvre. The rumpty takes things into her own hands and just pancakes the rest of the way to the ground. First solo flight! Greatest day in a man's life!

PIANO PLAYER and BISHOP   *singing*
Flying . . .
What have I been waiting for?
What a way to fight a war!
Flying Canadian,
Machine gun in my hand,
First Hun I see is the first Hun to die,
First Hun I see is the first Hun to die.

BISHOP   In the early part of 1916, I was posted back to France as a fighter pilot. Sixtieth Squadron, Third British Brigade. I worked like a Trojan for these wings and I just about lost them before I really began. I was returning from my first O.P., Operational Patrol, and I crashed my Nieuport on landing. I wasn't hurt, but the aircraft was pretty well pranged, and that was bad because General John Higgins, the Brigade Commander, saw me do it. Well, he couldn't help but see me do it. I just about crashed at his feet!

HIGGINS   I watched you yesterday, Bishop. You destroyed a machine. A very expensive, a very nice machine. Doing a simple landing on a clear day. That machine was more valuable than you'll ever be, buck-o.

BISHOP   Sir, there was a gust of wind from the hangar. I mean, ask Major Scott, our patrol leader. It could have happened to anyone.

HIGGINS   I was on the field, Bishop.

BISHOP   Yes, Sir.

HIGGINS   There was no wind.

BISHOP   No wind? Yes, Sir.

HIGGINS   I have your record here on my desk, Bishop, and it isn't a very impressive document. On the positive side, you were wounded. And you score well in target practice, although you have never actually fired upon the enemy. The list of your negative accomplishments is longer, isn't it, much longer? Conduct unbecoming an officer. Breaches of discipline. A lot of silly accidents, suspicious accidents, if I may say so. A trail of wrecked machinery in your wake. You are a terrible pilot, Bishop. In short, you are a liability to the R.F.C. and I wish to God you were back in Canada where you belong, or failing that, digging a trench in some unstrategic valley. In short, you are finished, Bishop, finished. When your replacement arrives, he will replace you. That is all.

BISHOP   That was the lowest point of my career. Then came March 25, 1917.

The following is performed on microphone with BISHOP creating the sound effects. The PIANO PLAYER joins him. The mike should be used as a joy stick and the aggression implied in the story should be transferred to the microphone.

March 25, 1917. Four Nieuport scouts in diamond formation climb to nine thousand feet crossing the line somewhere between Arras and St. Léger. Our patrol is to crisscross the lines noting Heinie's positions and troop movements.

The sound of an airplane engine is heard.

RRrrr. I'm the last man in that patrol, tough place to be, because if you fall too far behind, the headhunters are waiting for you. It starts out cloudy, then suddenly clears up. We fly for half an hour and don't see anything, just miles and miles of nothing. RRrrr. Suddenly, I see four specks above and behind us. A perfect place for an enemy attack. I watch as the specks get larger. I can make out the black crosses on them. Huns! It's hard to believe that they are real, alive and hostile. I want to circle around and have a better look at them. Albatross "V" strutters, beautiful, with their swept back planes, powerful and quick. RRrrr. We keep on flying straight. Jack Scott, our leader, either hasn't seen them or he wants them to think that he hasn't seen them. They are getting closer and closer. We keep on flying straight. They are two hundred yards behind us, getting closer and closer. Suddenly, RRrrr! Jack Scott opens out into a sharp climbing turn to get above and behind them. The rest of us follow. Rrrr! RRrrr! RRrrrr! I'm slower than the rest and come out about forty yards behind. In front of me, a dogfight is happening, right in front of my very eyes. Real pandemonium, planes turning every which way. RRRrrr! Machine gun fire. Suddenly, Jack Scott sweeps below me with an Albatross on his tail raking his fuselage and wing tips with gunfire! For a moment, I'm just frozen there, not knowing what to do, my whole body just shaking! Then I throw the stick forward and dive on the Hun. I keep him in my Aldis sight 'til he completely fills the lens. AKAKAkak! What a feeling, as he flips over on his back and falls out of control! But wait, wait....Grid Caldwell warned me about this. He's not out of control, he's faking it. He's going to level out at two thousand feet and escape. Bastard! I dive after him with my engine full on. Sure enough, when he comes out of it, I'm right there. AKAkakakaka! Again, my tracers smash into his machine. Gawd, I've got to be hitting him! He flips over on his back and is gone again. This time, I stay right with him. EEEeeeee! The wires on my machine howl in protest. Nieuports have had their wings come off at 150 miles per hour. I must be doing 180. I just don't give a shit! I keep firing into the tumbling Hun. AKAKaka! He just crashes into the earth and explodes in flames. BAA-WHOOSH! I pull back on the stick, level out, screaming at the top of my lungs, I win, I WIN, I WIN!

The sound of wind is heard—no engine, no nothing.

Jeezus, my engine's stopped! It must have filled with oil on the dive. I try every trick in the book to get it going again. Nothing. Oh God, I'm going to go in! Down, down.

The sound of gunfire is heard.

Gunfire! I must still be over Hunland. Just my luck to do something right and end up being taken a prisoner. Lower and lower. I pick out what seems to be a level patch in the rough terrain and I put her down.

The sound of a bouncing crash is heard.

I got out of the plane into what must have been a shell hole. I took my Very Lite pistol with me. I wasn't exactly sure what I was going to do with it.

TOMMY   *in a "Canadian" accent*   Well...you're just in time for a cup of tea, lad.

BISHOP   *surprised*   ARrghgh...you spoke English! Hey, look, where am I?

TOMMY   You're at the corner of Portage and Main in downtown Winnipeg. You want to keep down, lad. Heinie is sitting right over there. Well, goll, that was a nice bit of flying you did there! Yep, you're a hundred yards our side of the line.

BISHOP   OOhhh, look...can you do me a favour? I'd like to try and get the plane up again.

TOMMY   Not tonight, lad, nope....You're going to have to take the Montcalm Suite here at the Chateau.

BISHOP   I spent the night in the trench in six inches of water! The soldiers seemed to be able to sleep. I couldn't.

The sound of shelling gets progressively louder.

Next morning at first light, I crawled out to see how my plane was. Miraculously, it hadn't been hit. And that's when I got my first real look at "No Man's Land." Jeezus, what a mess! Hardly a tree left standing. And the smell! It was hard to believe you were still on earth. I saw a couple of Tommys sleeping in a trench nearby.

He goes over to the Tommys.

Hey, you guys, I wonder if you could give me a hand with . . . ?

He takes a closer look. The Tommys aren't asleep. He backs off with a shudder.

The PIANO PLAYER sings and BILLY BISHOP joins him.

BISHOP and PIANO PLAYER   *singing*
Oh, the bloody earth is littered
With the fighters and the quitters.
Oh, what could be more bitter
Than a nameless death below.
See the trenches, long and winding,
See the battle slowly grinding,
Don't you wonder how good men can live so low.

Up above, the clouds are turning,
Up above, the sun is burning,
You can hear those soldiers yearning:
"Oh, if only I could fly!"
From the burning sun, I'll sight you,
In the burning sun, I'll fight you.
Oh, let us dance together in the sky.

Chorus

In the sky,
In the sky,
Just you and I up there together,
Who knows why?
One the hunter, one the hunted;
A life to live, a death confronted.
Oh, let us dance together in the sky.

And for you, the bell is ringing,
And for you, the bullets stinging.
My Lewis gun is singing:
"Oh, my friend, it's you or I."
And I'll watch your last returning
To the earth, the fires burning.
Look up and you will see me wave goodbye.

Chorus

In the sky,
In the sky,
Just you and I up there together,
Who knows why?
One the hunter, one the hunted;
A life to live, a death confronted.
Oh, let us dance together in the sky.

ACT TWO

The lights come up, as in Act One, with the PIANO PLAYER and BILLY BISHOP at the piano.

BISHOP and PIANO PLAYER   *singing*
Oh, the bold Aviator lay dying,
As 'neath the wreckage he lay (he lay),
To the sobbing mechanics beside him,
These last parting words he did say:

Two valves you'll find in my stomach,
Three sparkplugs are safe in my lung (my lung),
The prop is in splinters inside me,
To my fingers, the joystick has clung.

Then get you six brandies and soda,
And lay them all out in a row (a row),
And get you six other good airmen,
To drink to this pilot below.

Take the cylinders out of my kidneys,
The connecting rod out of my brain (my brain),
From the small of my back take the crankshaft,
And assemble the engine again!

The music changes to a theme reminiscent of a French café. Time has gone by and BISHOP has changed.

BISHOP   Survival. That's the important thing. And the only way to learn survival is to survive. Success depends on accuracy and surprise. How well you shoot, how you get into the fight and how well you fly. In *that* order. I can't fly worth shit compared to someone like Barker or Ball, but I don't care. If I get a kill, it's usually in the first few seconds of the fight. Any longer than that and you might as well get the hell out. You've got to be good enough to get him in the first few bursts, so practice your shooting as much as you can. After patrols, between patrols, on your day off. If I get a clear shot at a guy, he's dead. You ever heard of "flamers"? That's when you bounce a machine and it just bursts into flames. Now, I don't want to sound bloodthirsty or anything, but when that happens, it is very satisfying. But it's almost always pure luck. You hit a gas line or something like that. If you want the machine to go down every time, you aim for one thing: the man. I always go for the man.

The music stops. The PIANO PLAYER becomes a French announcer.

ANNOUNCER   Ladies and Gentlemen . . . Mesdames et Messieurs . . . Charlie's Bar, Amiens, proudly presents: The Lovely Hélène!

BISHOP   *as the Lovely Hélène, singing*
Johnny was a Christian,
He was humble and humane.
His conscience was clear,
And his soul without a stain.
He was contemplating heaven,

When the wings fell off his plane.
And he never got out alive,
He didn't survive.

George was patriotic,
His country he adored.
He was the first to volunteer,
When his land took up the sword,
And a half a dozen medals
Were his posthumous reward.
And he never got out alive,
He didn't survive.

Chorus

So when you fight, stay as calm as the ocean,
And watch what's going on behind your shoulder.
Remember, war's not the place for deep emotion,
And maybe you'll get a little older.

BISHOP   *as himself*   Come into a fight with an advantage: height, speed, surprise. Come at him out of the sun, he'll never see you. Get on his tail, his blind spot, so you can shoot without too much risk to yourself. Generally, patrols don't watch behind them as much, so sneak up on the last man. He'll never know what hit him. Then you get out in the confusion. Hunt them. Like Hell's Handmaiden. If it's one on one, you come at the bugger, head on, guns blazing. He chickens out and you get him as he comes across your sights. If you both veer the same way, you're dead, so it's tricky. You have to keep your nerve.

BISHOP   *as the Lovely Hélène, singing*
Geoffrey made a virtue
Out of cowardice and fear.
He was the first to go on sick leave,
And the last to volunteer.
He was running from a fight,
When they attacked him from the rear.
And he never got out alive, (no)
He didn't survive.

BISHOP   *as himself*   Another thing is your mental attitude. It's not like the infantry where a bunch of guys work themselves up into a screaming rage and tear off over the top, yelling and waving their bayonets. It's not like that. You're part of a machine, so you have to stay very calm and cold. You and your machine work together to bring the other fellow down. You get so you don't feel anything after a while . . . until the moment you start firing, and then that old dry throat, heartthrobbing thrill comes back. It's a great feeling!

BISHOP   *as the Lovely Hélène, singing*
Jimmy hated Germans
With a passion cold and deep.
He cursed them when he saw them,
He cursed them in his sleep.
He was cursing when his plane went down
And landed in a heap.
And he never got out alive, (no)
He didn't survive.

Chorus

So when you fight, stay as calm as the ocean,
And watch what's going on behind your shoulder.
Remember, war is not the place for deep emotion,
And maybe you'll get a little older.

BISHOP   *as himself*   Bloody April? We lost just about everyone I started with. Knowles, Hall, Williams, Townsend, Chapman, Steadman, shot down the day he joined the squadron. You see the Hun has better machines and some of their pilots are very good. But practice makes perfect, if you can stay alive long enough to practice. But it gets easier and easier to stay alive because hardly anyone else has the same experience as you. Oh yeah, another thing. You take your fun where you can find it.

The music and mood change.

He has noticed the Lovely Hélène. She has noticed him. They meet outside. Without a word, she signals him to follow. Silently, they walk down an alley, through an archway, and up a darkened stairway. They are in her room. He closes the door. He watches her light a candle. She turns to him and says: "I should not be doing this. My lover is a Colonel at the front. But you are so beautiful and so, so young." An hour later, they kiss in the darkened doorway. She says: "If you see me, you do not know me." She's gone. He meets his friends who have all enjoyed the same good luck. It's late, they've missed the last bus to the aerodrome. Arm in arm, they walk in the moonlight, silently sharing a flask of brandy, breathing in that warm spring air. As they approach Filescamp, they begin to sing, loudly: "Mademoiselle from Armentières, parlez-vous. Mademoiselle from Armentières, parlez-vous" . . . as if to leave behind the feelings they have had that night. In an hour, they will be on patrol. They go to bed. They sleep.

There is an abrupt change of mood. BISHOP is flying and shooting once again.

As if writing a letter.

Dearest Margaret. It is the merry month of May, and today, I sent another merry Hun to his merry death. I'm not sure you'd appreciate the bloodthirsty streak that has come over me in the past months. How I hate the Hun. He has killed so many of my friends. I enjoy killing him now. I go up as much as I can, even on my day off. My score is getting higher and higher because I like it. Yesterday, I had a narrow escape. A bullet came through the windshield and creased my helmet. But a miss is as good as a mile and if I am for it, I am for it. But I do not believe I am for it. My superiors are pleased. Not only have I been made Captain, they are recommending me for the Military Cross. Thinking of you constantly, I remain. . . .

BISHOP and PIANO PLAYER   *singing*
You may think you've something special
That will get you through this war,

But the odds aren't in your favour,
That's a fact you can't ignore.
The chances are, the man will come
A-knocking at your door.
And you'll never get out alive,
And you won't survive.

Chorus

So when you fight, stay as calm as the ocean,
And watch what's going on behind your shoulder.
Remember, war's not the place for deep emotion,
And maybe you'll get a little older.

The music stops. There is a blackout.

BISHOP talks to ALBERT BALL.

BISHOP   Albert Ball, Britain's highest scoring pilot, sat before me. His black eyes gleamed at me, very pale, very intense. Back home, we would have said he had eyes like two pissholes in the snow. But that's not very romantic. And Albert Ball was romantic, if anybody was.

BALL   Compatriots in Glory! Oh, Bishop, I have an absolutely ripping idea. I want you to try and picture this. Two pilots cross the line in the dim, early dawn. It is dark, a slight fog. They fly straight for the German aerodrome at Douai, ghosts in the night. The Hun, unsuspecting, sleeps cosily in his lair. The sentries are sleeping. Perhaps the Baron von Richt-hofen himself is there, sleeping, dreaming of eagles and . . . wienerschnitzel. It is the moment of silence, just before dawn. Suddenly, he is awakened from his sleep by the sound of machine gun fire. He rushes to his window to see four, maybe five, of his best machines in flames. He watches as the frantic pilots try to take off and one by one are shot down. The two unknown raiders strike a devastating blow. Bishop, you and I are those two unknown raiders.

BISHOP   Jeez, I like it. It's a good plan. How do we get out?

BALL   Get out?

BISHOP   Yeah. Get out? You know, escape!

BALL   I don't think you get the picture, Bishop. It's a grand gesture. Getting out has nothing to do with it.

BISHOP   Oh! Well, it's a good plan. It's got a few holes I'd like to see plugged. I'd like to think about it.

BALL   All right, Bishop, you think about it. But remember this: Compatriots in Glory!

BISHOP   Quite a fellow.

He turns to the audience and announces.

"The Dying of Albert Ball"

The following is performed like a Robert Service poem.

BISHOP
He was only eighteen
When he downed his first machine,
And any chance of living through this war was
    small;
He was nineteen when I met him,
And I never will forget him,
The pilot by the name of Albert Ball.

No matter what the odds,
He left his fate up to the gods,
Laughing as the bullets brushed his skin.
Like a medieval knight,
He would charge into the fight
And trust that one more time his pluck would let
    him win.

So he courted the reaper,
Like the woman of his dreams,
And the reaper smiled each time he came to call;
But the British like their heroes
Cold and dead, or so it seems,
And their hero in the sky was Albert Ball.

But long after the fight,
Way into the night,
Cold thoughts, as dark as night, would fill his brain,
For bloodstains never fade,
And there are debts to be repaid
For the souls of all those men who died in vain.

So when the night was dark and deep,
And the men lay fast asleep,
An eerie sound would filter through the night.
It was a violin,
A sound as soft as skin.
Someone was playing in the dim moonlight.

There he stood, dark and thin,
And on his violin
Played a song that spoke of loneliness and pain.
It mourned his victories;
It mourned dead enemies
And friends that he would never see again.

Yes, he courted the reaper,
Like the woman of his dreams,
And the reaper smiled each time he came to call;
But the British like their heroes
Cold and dead, or so it seems,
And their hero in the sky was Albert Ball.

It's an ironic twist of fate
That brings a hero to the gate,
And Ball was no exception to that rule;
Fate puts out the spark
In a way as if to mark
The fine line between a hero and a fool.

Each time he crossed the line,
Albert Ball would check the time
By an old church clock reminding him of home.
The Huns came to know
The man who flew so low
On his way back to the aerodrome.

It was the sixth of May,
He'd done bloody well that day;
For the forty-fourth time, he'd won the game.
As he flew low to check the hour,
A hail of bullets from the tower—
And Albert Ball lay dying in the flames.

But through his clouded eyes,
Maybe he realized,
This was the moment he'd been waiting for.
For the moment that he died,
He was a hero, bonafide.
There are to be no living heroes in this war.

For when a country goes insane,
Obsessed with blood and pain,
Just to be alive is something of a sin.
A war's not satisfied
Until all the best have died,
And the devil take the man who saves his skin.

But sometimes late at night,
When the moon is cold and bright,
I sometimes think I hear that violin.
Death is waiting just outside,
And my eyes are open wide,
As I lie and wait for morning to begin.

Now I am courting the reaper,
Like the woman of my dreams,
And the reaper smiles each time I come to call;
But the British like their heroes
Cold and dead, or so it seems,
And my name will take the place of Albert Ball.

The PIANO PLAYER sings a sad song. BISHOP joins in.

BISHOP and PIANO PLAYER   *singing*
Look at the names on the statues
Everywhere you go.
Someone was killed
A long time ago.
I remember the faces;
I remember the time.
Those were the names of friends of mine.

The statues are old now
And they're fading fast.
Something big must have happened
Way in the past.
The names are so faded
You can hardly see,
But the faces are always young to me.

Chorus

Friends ain't s'posed to die
'Til they're old.
And friends ain't s'posed to die
In pain.
No one should die alone
When he is twenty-one,
And living shouldn't make you feel ashamed.

I can't believe
How young we were back then.
One thing's for sure,
We'll never be that young again.
We were daring young men,
With hearts of gold,
And most of us never got old.

In an abrupt change of mood, a loud pounding is heard: CEDRIC is knocking on BISHOP's door.

CEDRIC   Wakey, wakey, Bishop. Rise, man! Rise and shine!

BISHOP   *hung over*   Ohhh, Cedric. What's the idea of waking me up in the middle of the night?

CEDRIC   It's bloody well eleven o'clock and Madam has a bone to pick with you.

BISHOP   All right, all right, I'll be right there. *Pause.*   Good morning, Granny.

LADY ST. HELIER   Bishop! Sit down. I have a bone to pick with you. Cedric, the colonial is under the weather. Bring tea and Epsom salts. Where were you last night, Bishop?

BISHOP   I was out.

LADY ST. HELIER   Good. Very specific. Well, I have my own sources and the picture that was painted for me is not fit for public viewing. Disgusting, unmannered and informal practices in company which is unworthy even of you, Bishop. But what concerns me is not where you were, but where you were not. To wit, you were not at a party which I personally arranged, at which you were to meet Bonar Law, Chancellor of the Exchequer. What do you have to say in your defence?

BISHOP   Look, Granny....

LADY ST. HELIER   I'll thank you not to call me Granny. The quaintness quite turns my stomach.

BISHOP   Look, that was the fourth darn formal dinner this week! First, it's General Haigh, then what's-his-name, the Parliamentary Secretary....I want to have some fun!

LADY ST. HELIER   Bishop, I'm only going to say this once. It is not for you to be interested, amused or entertained. You are no longer a rather short Canadian with bad taste and a poor service record. You are a figurehead, unlikely as that may seem. A dignitary. The people of Canada, England, the Empire; indeed, the world, look to you as a symbol of victory and you will act the part. You will shine your shoes and press your trousers. You will refrain from spitting, swearing, gambling and public drunkenness, and you will, and I say this with emphasis, you will keep your appointments with your betters. Now, tonight you are having dinner with Lord Beaverbrook, and tomorrow night, with Attorney-General F.E. Smith. Need I say more?

BISHOP   No, no. I'll be there.

LADY ST. HELIER   Good. Oh, and Bishop, I had occasion to pass the upstairs bathroom this morning and I took the liberty of inspecting your toilet kit. There is what I can only describe as moss growing on your hairbrush and your after shave lotion has the odour of cat urine. I believe the implications are clear. *addressing the butler* Cedric, a difficult road lies before us. Empire must rely for its defences upon an assemblage of Canadians, Australians and Blacks. And now, the Americans. Our way of life is in peril!

BISHOP   *slightly drunk and writing a letter* Dearest Margaret. I'm not sure I can get through this evening. In the next room is Princess Marie-Louise and four or five Lords and Ladies whose names I can't even remember. I drank a little bit too much champagne at supper tonight and told the Princess a lot of lies. Now I'm afraid to go back in there because I can't remember what the lies are and I'm afraid I'll contradict myself and look like an idiot. Being rich, you've got a lot more class than me. They'd like you. Maybe we ought to get married. Thinking of you constantly, I remain. . . .

The PIANO PLAYER and BISHOP break into song.

BISHOP and PIANO PLAYER   *singing*
Breakfasting
With Queens and Kings,
Dining with Lords and Earls;
Drink champagne,
It flows like rain,
Making time with high class girls.
Just a Canadian boy,
England's pride and joy,
My fantasies fulfilled;
Ain't no one
Asks me where I'm from,
They're happy for the men I killed.

Chorus

Number One is a hero,
Number One's the hottest thing in town!
While I'm in my home
Away from home,
Nobody's gonna shoot me down, oh no,
Nobody's gonna shoot me down.

I'm a hired gun,
Gonna shoot someone,
But England's gonna stand by me;
And if I die
You can't deny
They're gonna call it a tragedy.
I'm quaint company,
From the Colonies;
Their love is so sincere.
And when the war is done
And the battle won,
I've got friends as long as I stay here.

Chorus

Number One is a hero,
Number One's the hottest thing in town!
When I'm in my home
Away from home,
Nobody's gonna shoot me down, oh no,
Nobody's gonna shoot me down.

The music changes to a more sinister note. The following story is half-told, half-acted out, the overall effect being of an adventure story being told in the present tense. It is done as a boy might tell a story, full of his own sound effects.

BISHOP   I woke up at three o'clock in the morning. Jeez, was I scared! Very tense, you know? I mean, Ball said you couldn't do it with just one guy and Ball was a maniac. But I figure it's no more dangerous than what we do every day, so what the hell. I mean, it's no worse. I don't think. The trouble is, no one has ever attacked a German aerodrome single-handedly before, so it's chancy, you know what I mean? I put my flying suit on over my pyjamas, grab a cup of tea and out I go. It's raining. Lousy weather for it, but what can you do? Walter Bourne, my mechanic, is the only other man up. He has the engine running and waiting for me.

BOURNE   Bloody stupid idea if you ask me, Sir. I would put thumbs down on the whole thing and go back to bed if I was you, Sir.

BISHOP   Thanks a lot, Walter. That's really encouraging.

BOURNE   It's pissing rain, Sir. Bleeding pity to die in the pissing rain. I can see it all now. Clear as crystal before me very eyes. First, Albert Ball snuffs it. Then, Captain Bishop snuffs it. It's a bleeding pity if you ask me, Sir. I mean, it's a balls-up from beginning to end. Why don't you take my advice and go back to bed like a good lad, Sir?

BISHOP   Why don't you shut up, Walter? Ready?

BOURNE   Ready, Sir!

The plane takes off.

BISHOP   God, it's awful up here! Pale grey light, cold, lonely as hell. My stomach's bothering me. Nerves? Naw, forgot to eat breakfast. Shit, just something else to put up with. RRRrrrr. I climb to just inside the clouds as I go over the line. No trouble? Good. Everybody is asleep. Let's find that German aerodrome. RRrrr. Where is it? Should be right around here. RRRrrr.

He spots something.

All right, a quick pass, a few bursts inside those sheds, just to wake them up, and then pick them off one by one as they try to come up. Wait a minute, wait a minute. There's no planes. There's no people. The bloody place is deserted. Well, shit, that's it, isn't it? I mean, I can't shoot anyone if there is nobody here to shoot. Bloody stupid embarrassment, that's what it is. RRrrr. Feeling really miserable now, I cruise now looking for some troops to shoot them. RRrrrr. Nobody! What the hell is going on around here? Is everybody on vacation? Suddenly, I see the sheds of another German aerodrome ahead and slightly to the left. Dandy. Trouble is, it's a little far behind the lines and I'm not exactly sure where I am. But, it's either that or go back. My stomach is really bothering me now. Why didn't I eat breakfast? And why didn't I change out of my pyjamas? That's going to be great, isn't it, if I'm taken prisoner, real dignified? Spend the rest of the bloody war in my bloody pyjamas. RRRrrrrr. Over the aerodrome at about three hundred feet. Jeezus, we got lots of planes here, lots and lots of planes. What have we got . . . six scouts and a two-seater? Jeez, I hope that two-seater doesn't come up for me. I'll have a hell of a time getting him from the rear. It's a little late to think about it now. RRRRrrrrr.

Machine gun fire opens up.

AKAKAKakakakak. RRRRRRRRRrrrr. AKAKAKakaka.

On the ground, GERMANS are heard yelling.

GERMANS Ach Himmel! In's Gelände! In's Gelände! Hier sind wir alle tot!

BISHOP I don't know how many guys I got on that first pass. A lot of guys went down; a lot of guys stayed down. I shot up a couple of their planes pretty bad.

The sound of ground fire is heard.

I forgot about the machine gun guarding the aerodrome, bullets all around me, tearing up the canvas on my machine. Just so long as they don't hit a wire. Keep dodging. RRrrr. RRRrrr. I can't get too far away or I'll never pick them off as they try to come up. Come on, you guys, come on! One of them is starting to taxi now. I come right down on the deck about fifteen feet behind him. AKAKAkakaka. He gets six feet off the ground, side slips, does this weird somersault and smashes into the end of the field. I pull her around as quick as I can . . . RRRrrr . . . just in time to pick up another fellow as he tries to come up. AKAKAKAakaka. My tracers are going wide . . . AKAKAKA . . . but the guy is so frightened that he doesn't watch where he is going and smashes into some trees at the end of the field. I put a few rounds into him and pull back on the stick. RRRrrrrrr. I'm feeling great now. I don't feel scared, I don't feel nothing. Just ready to fight. Come on, you bastards, come on! Wait a minute, wait a minute. This is what Ball was worried about. Two of them are taking off in opposite directions at the same time. Now I feel scared. What do I do now? Get the hell out, that's what you do! One of them is close enough behind me to start firing. Where's the other one? Still on the ground. All right, you want to fight? We'll fight! I put it into a tight turn, he stays

right with me, but not quite tight enough. As he comes in for his second firing pass, I evade him with a lateral loop, rudder down off the top and drop on his tail . . . AKAKAKAKAKAKAKAK . . . I hit the man. The plane goes down and crashes in flames on the field. Beautiful! The second man is closing with me. I have just enough time to put on my last drum of ammunition. I fly straight for him, the old chicken game. I use up all my ammunition . . . AKAKAKAka . . . I miss him, but he doesn't want to fight. Probably thinks I'm crazy. I got to get out of here. They will have telephoned every aerodrome in the area. There will be hundreds of planes after me. I climb and head for home. RRRrrrrrr. All by myself again, at last. Am I going the right way? Yeah. Jeezus, my stomach! Sharp pains, like I've been shot. Nope, no blood. Good, I haven't been shot, it's just all that excitement on an empty stomach. Being frightened. Jeez, I think I'm going to pass out. No, don't pass out!

He looks up.

And then I look up and my heart stops dead then and there. I'm not kidding. One thousand feet above me, six Albatross scouts, and me, with no ammunition. I think I'm going to puke. No, don't puke! Fly underneath them, maybe they won't see you. RRRrrrrr. I try to keep up. . . . For a mile, I fly underneath them, just trying to keep up. RRRrrrrrr. I got to get away. They're faster than me and if they see me, they got me. But I got to get away! I dive and head for the line . . . RRRRRRRRRRR! . . . I can feel the bullets smashing into my back at any second, into my arms, into my legs, into my. . . .

He looks up again.

Nothing! Jeez, they didn't see me. RRRRrrr. Filescamp. Home. Just land it, take it easy. RRRR. I land. Walter Bourne is waiting with a group of the others.

BOURNE I'm standing around, waiting for him to be phoned in missing, when there he comes. Like he's been out sightseeing. He lands with his usual skill, cracking both wheels, then comes to a halt, just like usual, except there is nothing left of his bloody machine. It's in pieces, bits of canvas flopping around like laundry in the breeze. Beats me how it stayed together. Captain Bishop sits there, quietlike, then he turns to me and he says: "Walter," he says, "Walter, I did it. I DID IT! Never had so much fun in me whole life!"

BISHOP That was the best fight I ever had. Everyone made a very big deal of it, but I just kept fighting all summer. My score kept getting higher and higher and I was feeling good. By the middle of August, I had forty-three, just one less than Albert Ball. And that's when the generals and colonels started treating me funny.

Going to war music is heard once again.

402 / BILLY BISHOP GOES TO WAR

TRENCHARD   Bishop! Yes, we have lots of medals for you, eh? Lots and lots of medals. And that's not all, no, no, no. You will receive your medals, then you'll go on extended Canada leave and you won't fight again.

BISHOP   What did you say, Sir?

TRENCHARD   Do I have a speech impediment, Bishop? I said you won't fight again.

BISHOP   Not fight again? But I've got to fight again. I've got forty-three; Ball had forty-four. All I need is one more of those sons of . . .

TRENCHARD   Bishop! You have done very well. You will receive the Victoria Cross, the Distinguished Service Order, the Military Cross. No British pilot has done that, not even Albert Ball, God rest his soul. Leave it at that, Bishop. You have done England a great service. Thank you very much. Now you don't have to fight any more. I should think you'd be delighted.

BISHOP   You don't understand, Sir. I like it.

TRENCHARD   Oh, I know you like it. But it's becoming something of a problem. You see, you have become a colonial figurehead.

BISHOP   I know, a dignitary.

TRENCHARD   A colonial dignitary, Bishop. There is a difference. You see, Bishop, the problem with your colonial is that he has a morbid enthusiasm for life. You might call it a Life-Wish. Now, what happens when your colonial figurehead gets killed? I'll tell you what happens. Colonial morale plummets. Despair is in the air. Fatalism rears its ugly head. But a living colonial figurehead is a different cup of tea. The men are inspired. They say: "He did it and he lived. I can do it too." Do you get the picture, Bishop?

BISHOP   I believe I do, Sir.

TRENCHARD   Good lad. You shall leave Squadron Sixty, never to return, on the morning of August 17th. That is all.

BISHOP   Well, that still gives me a week. A lot can be done in a week.

To the audience.

In the next six days, I shot down five planes. I really was Number One now. And the squadron, they gave me a big piss-up on my last night. But something happened in that last week that made me fairly glad to get out of it for a while. It was number forty-six.

Music is heard.

It's dusk. Around eight o'clock. I'm returning to Filescamp pretty leisurely because I figure this is my last bit of flying for a bit. It's a nice clear evening and when it's clear up there in the evening, it's really very pretty. Suddenly, I see this German Aviatic two-seater heading right for me. It's a gift. I don't even have to think about this one. I put the plane down into a steep dive and come up underneath him and just rake his belly with bullets. Well, I don't know how they built those planes, but the whole thing just fell apart right before my very eyes. The wings came off, bits of the fuselage just collapsed, and the pilot and the gunner, they fall free. Now I'm pretty sure I didn't hit them, so they are alive and there is nothing I can do to help them or shoot them or anything. All I can do is just sit there and watch those two men fall, wide awake . . . to die! It's awful. I know I've killed lots of them, but this is different. I can watch them falling down, down. One minute, two minutes, three minutes. It's almost like I can feel them looking at me.

He stops for a moment, perplexed by unfamiliar qualms, shrugs and then goes on.

So when I leave for London the next day, I'm pretty glad to be going after all.

The scene changes to London.

LADY ST. HELIER   Bishop, today you will meet the King. This represents a high water mark for us all and you must see to it that you do not make a balls-up of it. I understand the King is particularly excited today. It seems this is his first opportunity of presenting three medals to the same gentleman. Furthermore, the King is amused that that gentleman is from the colonies. The King, therefore, may speak to you. Should you be so honoured, you will respond politely, in grammatically cogent phrases, with neither cloying sentimentality nor rude familiarity. You will speak to the King with dignity and restraint. Do you think you can manage that, Bishop? Is it possible that the safest course would be for you to keep your mouth shut?

Music is heard.

BISHOP   I arrive at Buckingham Palace, late. It is very confusing.

ADJUTANT   Excuse me, Sir, but where do you think you're going?

BISHOP   Oh, look, I'm supposed to get a medal or something around here.

ADJUTANT   Oh, you're way off, you are, Sir. This is His Majesty's personal reception area. You just about stumbled into the royal loo!!!

2ND OFFICER   What seems to be the trouble around here?

ADJUTANT   Good Lord! Well, the colonial here wants a medal, but his sense of direction seems to have failed him.

2ND OFFICER   Come along, Bishop. We've been looking all over for you. Now, the procedure is this: ten paces to the centre, turn, bow.

The PIANO PLAYER strikes up "Land of Hope and Glory."

2ND OFFICER   It's started already, Bishop. You're just going to have to wing it!

The music continues as a processional. BISHOP enters stiffly into the presence of the KING.

BISHOP   Here comes the King with his retinue, Order of St. Michael, Order of St. George, and here I am. The King pins three medals on my chest. Then he says. . . .

The KING's voice is booming, echoing. It is spoken by the PIANO PLAYER and mimed by BISHOP.

KING GEORGE   Well, Captain Bishop. You've been a busy bugger!

BISHOP   I'm not kidding. I'm standing here and the King is standing here. The King talks to me for fifteen minutes! I can't say a word. I've lost my voice. But after the investiture comes the parties, the balls, the photographers, the newspaper reporters, the Lords and Ladies, the champagne, the filet mignon and the fifty-year-old brandy. And here's me, Billy Bishop, from Owen Sound, Canada, and I know one thing: this is my day! There will never be a day like it! I think of this as we dance far into the night, as we dance to the music of . . . the Empire Soirée.

The PIANO PLAYER and BISHOP sing soto and sinister.

BISHOP and PIANO PLAYER   *singing*
Civilizations come and go (don't you know),
Dancing on to oblivion (oblivion).
The birth and death of nations,
Of civilizations,
Can be viewed down the barrel of a gun.

Nobody knows who calls the tune (calls the tune),
It's been on the Hit Parade for many years (can't you hear).
You and I must join the chorus,
Like ancestors before us,
And like them, we're going to disappear.

Chorus

You're all invited to the Empire Soirée,
We'll see each other there, just wait and see;
Attendance is required at the Empire Soirée,
We'll all dance the dance of history.

Revolutions come and go (don't you know),
New empires will take the others' place (take their place).
The song may be fun,
But a new dance has begun,
When someone points a gun at someone's face.

Alexander and Julius had their dance (had their chance),
'Til somebody said: "May I cut in?" (with a grin).

All you and I can do,
Is put on our dancing shoes,
And wait for the next one to begin.

Chorus

You're all invited to the Empire Soirée,
We'll see each other there, just wait and see;
Attendance is required at the Empire Soirée,
We'll all dance the dance of history.

At the end of "The Empire Soirée," BISHOP does a little dance of victory for the audience, ending with a final salute.

Blackout.

A spotlight hits the PIANO PLAYER, who sings a narration summing up BISHOP's career and building to a reprise of "We Were Off to Fight the Hun." The song has a bitter edge now, for it is World War II we are talking about.

PIANO PLAYER   *singing*
Billy went back home again,
But still, he was not done;
Seventy-two planes did their dance,
To the rhythm of his guns.
And in twenty years, he was back again,
A new war to be won;
And the hero calls to new recruits in 1941.
The hero calls to new recruits in 1941.

And they were off to fight the Hun,
They would shoot him with a gun.
Their medals would shine,
Like a sabre in the sun.
They were off to fight the Hun
And it looked like lots of fun,
Somehow it didn't seem like war
At all, at all, at all.
Somehow it didn't seem like war at all.

The lights come up slowly on BISHOP. Twenty years have gone by and he is much older and very tired. He is wearing an astonishing array of medals and they seem to weigh him down a bit. BISHOP addresses the audience as though they were fresh World War II recruits. His voice has the tone and melody of war rhetoric.

The PIANO PLAYER plays "God Save the King."

BISHOP   I have seen you go and my heart is very proud. Once again, in the brief space of twenty years, our brave young men rush to the defence of the Mother Country. Once again, you must go forward with all the courage and vigour of youth to wrest mankind from the grip of the Iron Cross and the Swastika. Once again, on the edge of destiny, you must test your strength. I know you of old, I think. God speed you. God speed you, the Army, on feet and on wheels, a member of which I was for so many happy years of my life. God speed you the Air Force, where in the crucible of battle I grew from youth to manhood. God speed you and God bless you. For, once again, the freedom of mankind rests in you: in the courage, the skill, the strength and the blood of our indomitable youth.

BISHOP's recruitment speech ends on a grand note. He stops and stares at the audience for a while with a certain amount of bewilderment. The PIANO PLAYER plays a haunting and discordant "In the Sky." BISHOP speaks, but this time it is quiet and personal.

You know, I pinned the wings on my own son this week. Margaret and I are very proud of him. And of our daughter. Three Bishops in uniform fighting the same war. Well, I guess I'm on the sidelines cheering them on. It comes as a bit of a surprise to me that there is another war on. We didn't think there was going to be another one back in 1918. Makes you wonder what it was all for? But then, we're not in control of any of these things, are we? And all in all I would have to say, it was a hell of a time!

BISHOP sings a cappella.

Oh, the bloody earth is littered,
With the fighters and the quitters.
You can hear the soldiers yearning:
"Oh, if only I could fly!"
From the burning sun, I'll sight you,
In the burning sun, I'll fight you,
Oh, let us dance together in the sky.

The PIANO PLAYER joins him in the chorus.

BISHOP and PIANO PLAYER *singing*
In the sky,
In the sky,
Just you and I up there together,
Who knows why?
One the hunter, one the hunted;
A life to live, a death confronted.
Oh, let us dance together in the sky.

BISHOP Goodnight, ladies. Goodnight, gentlemen. Goodnight.

Blackout.

A SELECTIVE BIBLIOGRAPHY OF SOURCE MATERIAL

I. Backgrounds, Surveys and General Studies

Anthony, Geraldine, ed. *Stage Voices: Twelve Canadian Playwrights Talk about Their Lives and Work.* Toronto: Doubleday, 1978.

Bessai, Diane. "Documentary Theatre in Canada: An Investigation into Questions and Backgrounds." *Canadian Drama*, 6 (Spring 1980), 9-21.

Brissenden, Connie, ed. *Spotlight on Drama: A Teaching and Resource Guide to Canadian Plays.* Toronto: The Writers' Development Trust, 1981.

Canada on Stage: Canadian Theatre Review Yearbook. Ed. Don Rubin. Toronto: CTR Publications, 1974-82.

"Canadian Theatre Before the 60s" Special Issue. *Canadian Theatre Review*, 5 (Winter 1975).

Conolly, L.W., ed. *Modern Canadian Drama: Some Critical Perspectives*, in *Canadian Drama*, 11, no. 1 (1985), pp. 1-229.

Contemporary Dramatists, 3rd ed. Ed. James Vinson. New York: St. Martin's Press, 1982.

"Contemporary Dramatists & the Art of the Theatre" Special Issue. *Canadian Literature*, 85 (Summer 1980).

Gould, Allan M. "Act II." *Toronto Life*, 16 (November 1982), 56-57, 108-12.

Hendry, Tom. "The Canadian Theatre's Sudden Explosion." *Saturday Night*, 87 (January 1972), 23-28.

Kinch, Martin. "Canadian Theatre: In for the Long Haul." *This Magazine*, 10 (November-December 1976), 3-8.

Lister, Rota. "Recent Canadian Drama: Passion in the Garrison." *English Studies in Canada*, 1 (Fall 1975), 353-62.

Mallet, Gina. "Canadian Playwrights: In Demand and Broadway Bound." *Chatelaine*, 53 (October 1980), 42-44, 110-13.

Mays, John Bentley. "Taking It on the Road." *Maclean's*, 92 (4 June 1979), 60-64.

Moore, Mavor. *4 Canadian Playwrights.* Toronto: Holt, Rinehart, 1973.

Nardocchio, Elaine. *Theatre and Politics in Modern Quebec.* Edmonton: University of Alberta Press, 1986.

New, William H., ed. *Dramatists in Canada: Selected Essays.* Vancouver: Univ. of British Columbia Press, 1972.

The Oxford Companion to Canadian Literature. Ed. William Toye. Toronto: Oxford Univ. Press, 1983.

Parker, Brian. "Is There a Canadian Drama?" in *The Canadian Imagination: Dimensions of a Literary Culture.* Ed. David Staines. Cambridge, Mass.: Harvard Univ. Press, 1977, pp. 152-87.

Parkin, Andrew, ed. *Stage One: A Canadian Scenebook.* Toronto: Van Nostrand Reinhold, 1973.

Perkyns, Richard, ed. *Major Plays of the Canadian Theatre, 1934-1984.* Toronto: Irwin, 1984.

Profiles in Canadian Literature, Series 4. Ed. Jeffrey M. Heath. Toronto: Dundurn Press, 1982.

Ripley, John. "Drama and Theatre, 1960-73," in *Literary History of Canada*, 2nd ed. Ed. Carl F. Klinck. Toronto: Univ. of Toronto Press, 1976, III, 212-32.

Rubin, Don. "Celebrating the Nation: History and the Canadian Theatre." *Canadian Theatre Review*, 34 (Spring 1982), 12-22.

—————. "Creeping Toward a Culture: The Theatre in English Canada since 1945." *Canadian Theatre Review*, 1 (Winter 1974), 6-21.

—————, and Alison Cranmer-Byng, eds. *Canada's Playwrights: A Biographical Guide.* Toronto: CTR Publications, 1980.

"Stage Canada" Special Section. *The Globe and Mail* (Toronto), 28 November 1983.

Stuart, E. Ross. *The History of the Prairie Theatre.* Toronto: Simon & Pierre, 1984.

—————. "Song in a Minor Key: Canada's Musical Theatre." *Canadian Theatre Review*, 15 (Summer 1977), 50-75.

Tait, Michael. "Drama and Theatre, 1920-1960," in *Literary History of Canada*, 2nd ed. Ed. Carl F. Klinck. Toronto: Univ. of Toronto Press, 1976, II, 143-67.

Usmiani, Renate. *Second Stage: The Alternative Theatre Movement in Canada.* Vancouver: Univ. of British Columbia Press, 1983.

Wagner, Anton, ed. *Contemporary Canadian Theatre: New World Visions.* Toronto: Simon & Pierre, 1985.

—————. "The Developing Mosaic: English-Canadian Drama to Mid-Century," in *Canada's Lost Plays, Volume Three.* Toronto: CTR Publications, 1980, pp. 4-39.

Wallace, Robert and Cynthia Zimmerman, eds. *The Work: Conversations with English-Canadian Playwrights.* Toronto: Coach House Press, 1982.

II. Individual Plays and Playwrights

Note: Wherever a book in this section has already appeared as an entry in Part I (Backgrounds, Surveys and General Studies), I have used the short form here. *Canadian Theatre Review* is indicated by *CTR*. An excellent selection of reviews of these twelve plays plus nineteen others can be found in L.W. Conolly, ed., *Modern Canadian Drama: Some Critical Perspectives*, in *Canadian Drama*, 11, no. 1 (1985), pp. 1-229.

MICHAEL COOK

A. BIOGRAPHY AND CRITICISM

Anthony, Geraldine, ed. *Stage Voices*, 207-32.

Bartlett, Donald R. "Notes Towards Putting Cook into Context." *Newfoundland Quarterly*, 78 (Fall 1982), 12-15.

Brissenden, Connie. "Michael Cook," in *Contemporary Dramatists*, 162-66.

Cook, Michael. "Introduction to *The Head, Guts and Sound Bone Dance*." *CTR*, 1 (Winter 1974), 74-76.

Fishman, Martin. "Michael Cook: A Playwright in His Own Right." *Canadian Drama*, 2 (Fall 1976), 181-87.

Lister, Rota. "Interview with Michael Cook." *Canadian Drama*, 2 (Fall 1976), 176-80.

Parker, Brian. "On the Edge: Michael Cook's Newfoundland Trilogy." *Canadian Literature*, 85 (Summer 1980), 22-41.

Perkyns, Richard. "*The Head, Guts and Sound Bone Dance*: An Introduction," in *Major Plays of the Canadian Theatre, 1934-1984*, pp. 444-48.

Wallace, Robert. "Michael Cook," in *Profiles in Canadian Literature*, Series 4, pp. 109-16.

————, and Cynthia Zimmerman, eds. *The Work*, 156-71.

B. JACOB'S WAKE: SELECTED REVIEWS

Ashley, Audrey M. "New Play a Ludicrous Cop-Out." *Ottawa Citizen*, 28 July 1975, p. 50.

Galloway, Myron. "*Jacob's Wake*: Newfie without a Hint of a Joke." *Montreal Star*, 14 July 1975, Sec. E, 1.

Portman, Jamie. "Bizarre Outport Saga 'Piece of Nonsense.'" *Vancouver Province*, 13 August 1975, p. 10.

DAVID FENNARIO

A. BIOGRAPHY AND CRITICISM

Collet, Paulette. "Fennario's *Balconville* and Tremblay's *En Pièces détachées*: A Universe of Backyards and Despair." *Canadian Drama*, 10 (Spring 1984), 35-43.

Conlogue, Ray. "Tough-Guy Playwright from the Point." *The Globe and Mail* (Toronto), 4 October 1980, Sec. E, 1.

Desson, Jim and Bruce K. Filson. "Where Is David Fennario Now?" *CTR*, 46 (Spring 1986), 36-41.

Fennario, David. *Without a Parachute*. Toronto: McClelland and Stewart, 1974.

Gilbert, S.R. "David Fennario," in *Contemporary Dramatists*, 241-43.

Goldie, Terry. "*On the Job* and *Nothing to Lose*." *Theatre History in Canada*, 2 (Spring 1981), 63-67.

Grigsby, Wayne. "The Bard from Balconville." *The Canadian Magazine*, 20 January 1979, pp. 16-18.

Horenblas, Richard. "David Fennario: Burning Houses Down." *Scene Changes*, 8 (March 1980), 26-29.

King, Dierdre. "The Drama of David Fennario." *Canadian Forum*, 60 (February 1981), 14-17.

Milliken, Paul. "Portrait of the Artist as a Working-Class Hero: An Interview with David Fennario." *Performing Arts in Canada*, 17 (Summer 1980), 22-25.

Peterson, Maureen. "Success Can't Spoil David Fennario." *Montreal Gazette*, 9 February 1980, p. 65.

Wallace, Robert and Cynthia Zimmerman, eds. *The Work*, 293-303.

B. BALCONVILLE: SELECTED REVIEWS

Abley, Mark. "The Shabby Intimacy of Daily Life." *Maclean's*, 94 (13 April 1981), 66.

Ashley, Audrey M. "Play Provides Biting Humour, Raw Language." *Ottawa Citizen*, 6 November 1979, p. 59.

Blazer, Fred. "Bilingual Drama is Universal." *The Globe and Mail* (Toronto), 10 February 1979, p. 37.

Burke, Tim. "Art in *Balconville* Mirrors Chunk of Life at Its Grittiest." *Montreal Gazette*, 16 February 1980, p. 93.

Conlogue, Ray. "Masterful Acting Abounds in Fennario's *Balconville*." *The Globe and Mail* (Toronto), 4 October 1979, p. 13.

Garebian, Keith. "*Balconville*." *Scene Changes*, 7 (March/April 1979), 33-34.

Knelman, Martin. "Bilingualism Among the Hopeless." *Saturday Night*, 94 (November 1979), 101-4.

Mallet, Gina. "Montreal Play Brings Slum to Life." *Toronto Star*, 4 October 1979, Sec. B, 1.

Peterson, Maureen. "Fennario's *Balconville* a Loveable Play." *Montreal Gazette*, 6 January 1979, p. 68.

Porter, Mackenzie. "Symbolic Promise of a Union." *Toronto Sun*, 5 October 1979, p. 88.

Wardle, Irving. "Nationalist Tension and Physical Congestion." *The Times* (London), 3 April 1981, p. 11.

DAVID FREEMAN

A. BIOGRAPHY AND CRITICISM

Anthony, Geraldine, ed. *Stage Voices*, 251-74.

Freeman, David. "The World of Can't." *Maclean's*, 77 (4 July 1964), 22, 44-45.

Gilbert, S.R. "David Freeman," in *Contemporary Dramatists*, 263-65.

Hendry, Tom. "David Freeman in the Theatre: A Major Surprise." *Saturday Night*, 87 (July 1972), 27-32.

Hofsess, John. "Will Success Spoil David Freeman?" *Maclean's*, 87 (February 1974), 35, 42.

McKeone, Carolyn A. "*Creeps* Revisited." *Scene Changes*, 8 (May 1980), 19-21.

Smith, Mary Elizabeth. "Freeman's *Creeps* and *Battering Ram*: Variations on a Theme." *Canadian Drama*, 4 (Spring 1978), 25-33.

Speirs, Rosemary. "Loser Turned Winner." *The Canadian Magazine*, 18 February 1978, pp. 4-9.

B. **CREEPS**: SELECTED REVIEWS

Barnes, Clive. "*Creeps*." *New York Times*, 5 December 1973, p. 52.

Clurman, Harold. "Theater." *The Nation*, 31 December 1973, p. 734.

Coe, Richard L. "Plight of Body, Flight of Mind: *Creeps*." *Washington Post*, 16 October 1973, Sec. B, 1, 11.

Cohen, Nathan. "A Ferociously Funny Play." *Toronto Star*, 6 February 1971.

Dafoe, Christopher. "Freeman's Play Bares Humanity of Spastics." *Vancouver Sun*, 23 March 1973, p. 33.

Fraser, John. "Six Years Later, *Creeps* Still Packs a Punch." *The Globe and Mail* (Toronto), 10 March 1977, p. 13.

Gartner, Zsuzsi. "*Creeps*: Power with a Twist." *The Globe & Mail* (Toronto), 30 August 1985, Sec. E, 6.

Kareda, Urjo. "New Theatre's First Production Beyond Praise." *Toronto Star*, 6 October 1971.

Kerr, Walter. "A Ring of Truth But After That?" *New York Times*, 16 December 1973, Sec. II, 5.

Oliver, Edith. "The Theater—Off Broadway." *The New Yorker*, 49 (17 December 1973), 99-100.

Sullivan, Dan. "An Insider Gives Us the *Creeps*." *Los Angeles Times*, 17 May 1982, Sec. VI, 1-2.

Watt, Douglas. "*Creeps* Packs a Terrific Wallop." *New York Daily News*, 5 December 1973.

Whittaker, Herbert. "*Creeps* Excellent Starter for Tarragon Theatre." *The Globe and Mail* (Toronto), 6 October 1971, p. 16.

DAVID FRENCH

A. BIOGRAPHY AND CRITICISM

Adams, John Coldwell. "From Coley's Point to Broadway." *Atlantic Advocate*, 70 (July 1980), 59-61.

Anthony, Geraldine, ed. *Stage Voices*, 234-50.

Carson, Neil. "Towards a Popular Theatre in English Canada." *Canadian Literature*, 85 (Summer 1980), 62-69.

Horenblas, Richard. "*One Crack Out*: Made in His Image." *Canadian Drama*, 2 (Spring 1976), 67-72.

Jewinski, Ed. "Jacob Mercer's Lust for Victimization." *Canadian Drama*, 2 (Spring 1976), 58-66.

Johnson, Chris. "Is That Us? Ray Lawler's *Summer of the Seventeenth Doll* and David French's *Leaving Home*." *Canadian Drama*, 6 (Spring 1980), 30-42.

MacCulloch, Clare. "Neither Out Far Nor in Deep." *Canadian Drama*, 2 (Spring 1976), 115-18.

Mullaly, Edward. "Canadian Drama: David French and the Great Awakening." *The Fiddlehead*, 100 (Winter 1974), 61-66.

Neary, Peter. "Of Many-Coloured Glass: Peter Neary Interviews David French." *Canadian Forum*, 53 (March 1974), 26-27.

Noonan, James. "The Comedy of David French and the Rocky Road to Broadway." *Thalia*, 3 (Fall/Winter 1980-81), 9-16.

Perkyns, Richard. "*Of the Fields, Lately*: An Introduction," in *Major Plays of the Canadian Theatre, 1934-1984*, pp. 479-83.

Thalenburg, Eileen and David McCaughna. "Shaping the Word: Guy Sprung and Bill Glassco." *CTR*, 26 (Spring 1980), 30-43.

Wallace, Robert and Cynthia Zimmerman, eds. *The Work*, 304-16.

Zimmerman, Cynthia. "David French," in *Profiles in Canadian Literature*, Series 4, pp. 117-23.

B. **JITTERS**: SELECTED REVIEWS

Barnes, Clive. "*Jitters* Opens a Can of Laughs." *New York Post*, 24 December 1979, pp. 20, 28.

Conlogue, Ray. "A Revived *Jitters* Triumphs." *The Globe & Mail* (Toronto), 17 January 1986, Sec. C, 11.

Edmonstone, Wayne. "*Jitters* Gives Actors the Chance to Do What They Like Doing Best." *Vancouver Sun*, 17 September 1979, Sec. C, 1.

Erdelyi, Joseph. "Playwright Conquers New Field." *Ottawa Citizen*, 20 February 1979, p. 53.

Gussow, Mel. "*Jitters* Finds Humor in Staging a Drama." *New York Times*, 6 November 1979, Sec. III, 9.

Johnson, Bryan. "A Few Laughs Get Past Opening-Night *Jitters*." *The Globe and Mail* (Toronto), 17 February 1979, p. 35.

Knelman, Martin. "Masochism as a Way of Life." *Saturday Night*, 94 (April 1979), 153-54.

McKendrick, Carol. "*Jitters* Entertaining." *Winnipeg Free Press*, 15 November 1980, p. 30.

Mallet, Gina. "Backstage *Jitters* Work Well on Centre Stage." *Toronto Star*, 17 February 1979, Sec. D, 3.

Peterson, Maureen. "*Jitters* Has the Makings of a Knock-Out Comedy." *Montreal Gazette*, 15 March 1980, p. 94.

Smith, Patricia Keeney. "A Play on a Play on a Play." *Maclean's*, 92 (5 March 1979), 54.

JOHN GRAY (with ERIC PETERSON)

A. BIOGRAPHY AND CRITICISM

Anderson, Ian. "Coming Home from Billy Bishop's War." *Maclean's*, 94 (16 March 1981), 17, 20.

Cruise, David. "John Gray, Writer." *Atlantic Insight*, 5 (August 1983), 22-27.

Galloway, Myron. "Life Is a One-Man Show [Eric Peterson]." *Montreal Star*, 24 February 1979, Sec. D, 8.

Godfrey, Stephen. "Author Churns Out the Hits with 'Controlled Dreaming.'" *The Globe & Mail* (Toronto), 7 September 1985, Sec. E, 3.

Knelman, Martin. "Roots." *Saturday Night*, 100 (December 1985), 69-71.

Steed, Judy. "John Gray's Progress." *Toronto Life*, 15 (May 1981), 66, 97-103.

————. "Mike and Eric and Chris and John: The Night Mike Nichols Met Billy Bishop." *The Canadian Magazine*, 26 May 1979, pp. 2-6.

Twigg, Alan. "John Gray: Filius," in *For Openers: Conversations with 24 Canadian Writers*. Vancouver: Harbour Publishing, 1981, pp. 97-106.

Usmiani, Renate. *Second Stage*, 67-71.

Wallace, Robert and Cynthia Zimmerman, eds. *The Work*, 44-59.

Wyman, Max. "The Billy Bishop Story Soars to Great Theatrical Heights." *Performing Arts in Canada*, 16 (Spring 1979), 18-21.

————. "From the Wild, Blue Yonder to the Great, White Way." *Vancouver Magazine*, 12 (July 1979), 65-71.

B. BILLY BISHOP GOES TO WAR: SELECTED REVIEWS

Ashwell, Keith. "Peterson Is a Stupendous Billy Bishop." *Edmonton Journal*, 24 January 1980, Sec. D, 9.

Barnes, Clive. "*Billy* Flies High at the Morosco." *New York Post*, 30 May 1980.

Beaufort, John. "Canada Visits Broadway with Biography and Song." *Christian Science Monitor*, 4 June 1980, p. 18.

Corbeil, Carole. "*Billy Bishop* Lands Safely." *The Globe and Mail* (Toronto), 13 January 1982, p. 17.

Galloway, Myron. "Canadian Musical Celebrates Flying Ace." *Montreal Star*, 16 February 1979, Sec. B, 4.

Gussow, Mel. "Capital Sees *Billy Bishop Goes to War*." *New York Times*, 13 March 1980, Sec. III, 20.

Hopkins, Thomas. "Can You Bake a Cherry Bomb, Billy Boy, Billy Boy?" *Maclean's*, 91 (4 December 1978), 70.

Johnson, Bryan. "*Billy Bishop Goes to War*: Flying Ace a Soaring Success." *The Globe and Mail* (Toronto), 14 February 1979, p. 13.

Kerr, Walter. "*Billy Bishop* Flies In." *New York Times*, 30 May 1980, Sec. III, 3.

Knelman, Martin. "Dancing in the Sky with Billy Bishop." *Saturday Night*, 94 (June 1979), 50-51.

Lardner, James. "Lighter Than Air." *Washington Post*, 6 March 1980, Sec. D, 1.

Mallet, Gina. "*Billy Bishop* Deserves Some Medals." *Toronto Star*, 14 February 1979, Sec. C, 3.

Porter, Mackenzie. "Gray's Believable Bishop Stirring Salute to Heroism." *Toronto Sun*, 15 February 1979, p. 92.

Sullivan, Dan. "Billy Bishop Goes to War and Likes It." *Los Angeles Times*, 17 October 1980, Sec. VI, 1.

Wardle, Irving. "*Billy Bishop Goes to War*." *The Times* (London), 21 August 1980, p. 9.

Wyman, Max. "Give *Billy Bishop* Show a Victory Roll." *Vancouver Sun*, 12 July 1979, Sec. B, 5.

JOHN HERBERT

A. BIOGRAPHY AND CRITICISM

Anthony, Geraldine, ed. *Stage Voices*, 165-206.

Carson, Neil. "Sexuality and Identity in *Fortune and Men's Eyes*." *Twentieth Century Literature*, 18 (July 1972), 207-18.

Fulford, Robert. "A Canadian Play Makes Its Way Around the World." *Saturday Night*, 90 (October 1975), 8, 12.

Herbert, John. "My Life and Hard Times in Cold, Bitter, Suspicious Toronto." *Saturday Night*, 86 (December 1971), 21-24.

Hofsess, John. "*Fortune and Men's Eyes*—A Report from the Set in a Quebec City Prison." *Maclean's*, 83 (December 1970), 81-83.

Lister, Rota. "Interview with John Herbert." *Canadian Drama*, 4 (Winter 1978), 173-76.

McLarty, James. "The World According to John Herbert." *Motion*, 1 (March-April 1973), 16-21.

Messenger, Ann P. "Damnation at Christmas: John Herbert's *Fortune and Men's Eyes*," in *Dramatists in Canada*, ed. W.H. New, 173-78.

Perkyns, Richard. "Fortune and Men's Eyes: An Introduction," in *Major Plays of the Canadian Theatre, 1934-1984*, pp. 276-81.

Teague, Francis. "Prisons and Imprisonment in Canadian Drama." *Journal of Canadian Fiction*, 19 (1977), 112-21.

Tyson, Brian F. "'This Man's Art and That Man's Scope': Language and the Critics in *Fortune and Men's Eyes*." *Canadian Drama*, 4 (Spring 1978), 34-39.

B. **FORTUNE AND MEN'S EYES**: SELECTED REVIEWS

Barnes, Clive. "Question Marks at Stage 73." *New York Times*, 23 October 1969, p. 55.

Bryden, Ronald. "Theatre." *The Observer* (London), 14 July 1968.

Cohen, Nathan. "When *Fortune and Men's Eyes* Opened." *Toronto Star*, 7 September 1967.

Fraser, John. "*Fortune and Men's Eyes* Stands the Test of Time." *The Globe and Mail* (Toronto), 20 November 1975, p. 18.

French, Philip. "Serving Time." *New Statesman*, 19 July 1968, pp. 88-89.

Oliver, Edith. "Theater." *The New Yorker*, 43 (4 March 1967), p. 134.

Pedwell, Susan. "Gripping Play Offers Slice of Life Behind Bars." *Calgary Herald*, 19 March 1980, Sec. B, 14.

Pritchett, Oliver. "The Power Politics of Homosexual Life." *The Guardian* (London), 21 July 1968.

Sullivan, Dan. "A Distressing *Fortune and Men's Eyes*." *New York Times*, 24 February 1967, p. 29.

Whittaker, Herbert. "Toronto's Jack Brundage Has a Winner." *The Globe and Mail* (Toronto), 4 March 1967, p. 18.

SHARON POLLOCK

A. BIOGRAPHY AND CRITICISM

Baldridge, Harold. "Calgary." *CTR*, 2 (Spring 1974), 118-20.

Bessai, Diane. "Introduction," in Sharon Pollock, *Blood Relations and Other Plays*. Edmonton: NeWest Press, 1981, pp. 7-9.

Dunn, Margo. "Sharon Pollock: In the Centre Ring." *Makara*, 1 (August-September 1976), 2-6.

Gilbert, S.R. "Sharon Pollock," in *Contemporary Dramatists*, 642-45.

Hofsess, John. "Families." *Homemaker's*, 15 (March 1980), 41-60.

———. "Sharon Pollock Off-Broadway: Success as a Subtle Form of Failure." *Books in Canada*, 12 (April 1983), 3-4.

Nunn, Robert C. "Sharon Pollock's Plays: A Review Article." *Theatre History in Canada*, 5 (Spring 1984), 72-83.

Page, Malcolm. "Sharon Pollock: Committed Playwright." *Canadian Drama*, 5 (Autumn 1979), 104-11.

Perkyns, Richard. "*Generations*: An Introduction," in *Major Plays of the Canadian Theatre, 1934-1984*, pp. 605-8.

Wallace, Robert and Cynthia Zimmerman, eds. *The Work*, 115-26.

Whittaker, Herbert. "Canadian West at Stratford." *The Globe and Mail* (Toronto), 22 July 1974, p. 14.

B. **WALSH**: SELECTED REVIEWS

Allen, Bob. "Stratford Discovers the West." *Vancouver Province*, 5 April 1974, p. 3.

Ashley, Audrey M. "Stratford Director, Cast Are Playwright's Delight." *Ottawa Citizen*, 25 July 1974, p. 50.

Bale, Doug. "Longshot Steals Show at Stratford Festival." *London Free Press*, 25 July 1974.

Freedman, Adele. "NAC Brings Little to Wild West Yarn." *The Globe and Mail* (Toronto), 12 May 1983, p. 25.

Messenger, Ann P. "More Utile than Dulce." *Canadian Literature*, 65 (Summer 1975), 90-95.

Portman, Jamie. "Calgary II." *CTR*, 2 (Spring 1974), 121-23.

———. "*Walsh* Signals Red-Letter Event for TC." *Calgary Herald*, 9 November 1973.

Whittaker, Herbert. "*Walsh* Beautiful, Tedious Too." *The Globe and Mail* (Toronto), 13 November 1973, p. 16

———. "*Walsh* Serves Up Sad History Straight." *The Globe and Mail* (Toronto), 25 July 1974, p. 13.

JAMES REANEY

A. BIOGRAPHY AND CRITICISM

Anthony, Geraldine, ed. *Stage Voices*, 139-64.

Dragland, Stan. "James Reaney's 'Pulsating Dance In and Out of Forms,'" in *The Human Elements*, ed. David Helwig. Ottawa: Oberon, 1978, pp. 112-33.

Huebert, Ronald. "James Reaney: Poet and Dramatist." *CTR*, 13 (Winter 1977), 125-28.

James Reaney Special Issue. *Essays on Canadian Writing*, 24-25 (1982-83); rpt. as *Approaches to the Work of James Reaney*, ed. Stan Dragland. Downsview: ECW Press, 1983.

Lee, Alvin. *James Reaney*. New York: Twayne, 1969.

———, and Eleanor R. Goldhar. "James Reaney," in *Profiles in Canadian Literature*, Series 4, pp. 17-28.

Miller, Mary Jane. "The Use of Stage Metaphor in *The Donnellys*." *Canadian Drama*, 8, no. 1 (1982), 34-41.

Noonan, James. "The Critics Criticized: An Analysis of Reviews of James Reaney's *The Donnellys* on National Tour." *Canadian Drama*, 3 (Fall 1977), 174-82.

————. "Foreword" and "Concluding Essay," in James Reaney, *The Donnellys*. Victoria: Press Porcépic, 1983, pp. 1-8; 275-88.

Parker, Gerald. "History, Story and Story-Style: James Reaney's *The Donnellys*." *Canadian Drama*, 4 (Spring 1978), 150-59.

————. "'The Key word . . . is "listen"': James Reaney's 'Sonic Environment.'" *Mosaic*, 14 (Fall 1981), 1-14.

Perkyns, Richard. "The Innocence of the Donnellys: James Reaney's Three-Ring Circus." *Canadian Drama*, 3 (Spring 1977), 162-73.

Reaney, James. *Fourteen Barrels from Sea to Sea*. Erin, Ont.: Press Porcépic, 1977.

————. "Ten Years at Play." *Canadian Literature*, 41 (Summer 1969), 53-61; rpt. in *Dramatists in Canada*, ed. W.H. New, 70-78.

————. "'Your Plays Are Like Movies—Cinemascope Ones.'" *Canadian Drama*, 5 (Spring 1979), 32-40.

Reaney, J. Stewart. *James Reaney*. Toronto: Gage, 1977.

Roberts, Eric. "*Sticks and Stones*: History, Play, and Myth." *Canadian Drama*, 4 (Fall 1978), 160-72.

Smith, Patricia Keeney. "James Reaney, Playmaker." *Canadian Forum*, 60 (October 1980), 9-12.

Woodman, Ross. *James Reaney*. Toronto: McClelland and Stewart, 1972.

B. **THE ST NICHOLAS HOTEL**: SELECTED REVIEWS

Carroll, Michael. "*The Donnellys*: A Canadian Phenomenon in Print and on the Stage." *The Canadian Review*, 3 (September 1976), 34-36.

Leggatt, Alexander. "Letters in Canada 1976: Theatre." *University of Toronto Quarterly*, 46 (Summer 1977), 383-85.

Salter, Denis. "*The Donnellys: Part II. The St. Nicholas Hotel, Wm. Donnelly, Prop.*" *Canadian Drama*, 5 (Spring 1979), 66-68.

Souchotte, Sandra. "Assessing *The Donnellys*." *CTR*, 7 (Summer 1975), 131-35.

Whittaker, Herbert. "More About Those Legendary Donnellys." *The Globe and Mail* (Toronto), 18 November 1974, p. 14.

In addition James Reaney has reprinted twenty reviews of *The Donnellys* in *Fourteen Barrels from Sea to Sea*, his account of the Trilogy's national tour in the fall of 1975. The reviews cover performances in London (Ont.), Winnipeg, Vancouver, Edmonton, Calgary, Ottawa, Halifax, Hamilton and Toronto. The following are the most informative:

Beaven, Scott. "The Donnellys Production Extraordinary." *The Albertan* (Calgary), 30 October 1975.

Dawson, Eric. "*The Donnellys: St. Nicholas Hotel*." *The Charlatan* (Ottawa), 14 November 1975.

Fraser, John. "NDWT's Weighty Donnelly Saga Makes a Sterling Return." *The Globe and Mail* (Toronto), 12 December 1975.

Galloway, Myron. "The Donnellys' Death." *Montreal Star*, 1 December 1975.

Kucherawy, Dennis. "*Donnellys*: 'Weep for One . . . Not for Four.'" *The Gazette* (London, Ont.), 10 October 1975.

ERIKA RITTER

A. BIOGRAPHY AND CRITICISM

Brown, Barry. "Interview: Erika Ritter." *Books in Canada*, 11 (April 1982), 26-28.

Conlogue, Ray. "Ritter Stood Up to Research to Keep Her *Pilot* on Course." *The Globe and Mail* (Toronto), 17 January 1980, p. 15.

Milliken, Paul. "Erika Ritter's Search for Integrity on the Stage." *Performing Arts in Canada*, 19 (Summer 1982), 33-37.

Wallace, Robert and Cynthia Zimmerman, eds. *The Work*, 277-91.

Zimmerman, Cynthia. "Erika Ritter," in *The Oxford Companion to Canadian Literature*, 707.

B. **AUTOMATIC PILOT**: SELECTED REVIEWS

Allen, Bob. "*Automatic Pilot* in High Gear." *Vancouver Province*, 17 May 1971, p. 12.

Ashwell, Keith. "Another Nasty Play Headed for New York." *Edmonton Journal*, 29 January 1981, Sec. D, 15.

Brennan, Brian. "Play Is Entertaining, but 'Very Toronto.'" *Calgary Herald*, 28 November 1980, Sec. C, 17.

Conlogue, Ray. "This *Pilot* Deserves Automatic Success." *The Globe and Mail* (Toronto), 18 January 1980, p. 15.

————. "Stand-Up Comic Toned Down." *The Globe and Mail* (Toronto), 11 September 1980, p. 19.

Czarnecki, Mark. "Bound for Glory of the Commercial Kind." *Maclean's*, 93 (14 July 1980), 54.

Dafoe, Christopher. "A Painfully Amusing Study of Emotions." *Vancouver Sun*, 12 November 1980, Sec. H, 1.

Edmonstone, Wayne. "*Pilot* Flawed but Flying." *Vancouver Sun*, 16 May 1981, Sec. B, 8.

Friedlander, Mira. "*Automatic Pilot*." *Scene Changes*, 8 (March 1980), 35-36.

Johnson, Audrey. "*Automatic Pilot*: It's More than a Comedy." *Victoria Times-Colonist*, 13 November 1980, p. 48.

Mallet, Gina. "This *Pilot*'s a Bit Off Course." *Toronto Star*, 18 January 1980, Sec. D, 1.

————. "*Automatic Pilot* Offers Better Flight." *Toronto Star*, 2 July 1980, Sec. D, 1.

GEORGE RYGA

A. BIOGRAPHY AND CRITICISM

Carson, Neil. "George Ryga and the Lost Country." *Canadian Literature*, 45 (Summer 1970), 33-40; rpt. in *Dramatists in Canada*, ed. W.H. New, 155-62.

Gerson, Mark. "The International Acceptance of Playwright George Ryga." *Performing Arts in Canada*, 19 (Fall 1982), 43-46.

Hay, Peter. "George Ryga: Beginnings of a Biography." *CTR*, 23 (Summer 1979), 36-44.

Innes, Christopher. *Politics and the Playwright: George Ryga*. Toronto: Simon & Pierre, 1985.

Moore, Mavor. *4 Canadian Playwrights*, 68-75.

————. "Introduction," in *Two Plays by George Ryga*. Winnipeg: Turnstone Press, 1982, pp. 1-7.

Parker, Brian. "The Ballad-Plays of George Ryga," in *The Ecstasy of Rita Joe and Other Plays*. Toronto: New Press, 1971, pp. vii-xx.

————. "Is There a Canadian Drama?" in *The Canadian Imagination*, ed. David Staines, 152-87.

Parker, Dorothy. "George Ryga," in *Contemporary Dramatists*, 682-86.

————. "George Ryga," in *Profiles in Canadian Literature*, Series 4, pp. 61-68.

Ryga, George. "Theatre in Canada: A Viewpoint on Its Development and Future." *CTR*, 1 (Winter 1974), 28-32.

Teague, Francis. "Prisons and Imprisonment in Canadian Drama." *Journal of Canadian Fiction*, 19 (1977), 112-21.

Watson, David and Christopher Innes. "Political Mythologies: An Interview with George Ryga." *Canadian Drama*, 8, no. 2 (1982), 160-72.

Worthington, Bonnie. "Ryga's Women." *Canadian Drama*, 5 (Fall 1979), 139-43.

B. THE ECSTASY OF RITA JOE: SELECTED REVIEWS

Donnelly, Tom. "Theater Journal: Two Views." *Washington Post*, 9 May 1973, Sec. F, 4.

Howard, Irene. "Vancouver Theatre Diary: Two Companies and Their Audience." *Canadian Forum*, 47 (February 1968), 252-54.

Kucherawy, Dennis. "Play Stirs New Controversy," *Vancouver Province*, 30 November 1981, Sec. B, 6.

Popkin, Henry. "*The Ecstasy of Rita Joe*: A Drama of American Indian Life." *Christian Science Monitor*, 11 June 1973, p. 12.

Portman, Jamie. "*Ecstasy of Rita Joe* Still Manages to Shock and Scourge." *Vancouver Province*, 12 April 1976, p. 10.

Richards, Jack. "World Premiere Lays Bare Tragedy of Canadian Society." *Vancouver Sun*, 24 November 1967, p. 6.

Shales, Tom. "*Ecstasy of Rita Joe*." *Washington Post*, 3 May 1973, Sec. B, 1, 8.

Skene, Reg. "*Ecstasy of Rita Joe* a Powerful Piece of Theatre." *Winnipeg Free Press*, 26 November 1981, p. 55.

Wardle, Irving. "A Pogrom in Canada." *The Times* (London), 23 September 1975, p. 12.

RICK SALUTIN and THEATRE PASSE MURAILLE

A. BIOGRAPHY AND CRITICISM

Arnott, Brian. "The Passe Muraille Alternative," in *The Human Elements*, ed. David Helwig. Ottawa: Oberon, 1978, pp. 97-111.

Copeman, Peter. "Rick Salutin and the Popular Dramatic Tradition: Towards a Dialectical Theatre in Canada." *Canadian Drama*, 10 (Spring 1984), 25-34.

————. "Rick Salutin: The Meaning of It All," *CTR*, 34 (Spring 1982), 190-97.

Miller, Mary Jane. "The Documentary Drama of Paul Thompson." *Saturday Night*, 89 (July 1974), 35-37.

————. "Two Versions of Rick Salutin's *Les Canadiens*." *Theatre History in Canada*, 1 (Spring 1980), 57-69.

Noonan, James. "Rick Salutin," in *The Oxford Companion to Canadian Literature*, 725-26.

Nunn, Robert C. "Performing Fact: Canadian Documentary Theatre," *Canadian Literature*, 103 (Winter 1984), 51-62.

Salutin, Rick. *1837: William Lyon Mackenzie and the Canadian Revolution*. Toronto: Lorimer, 1976.

Usmiani, Renate. *Second Stage*, 43-65.

Wallace, Bob. "Paul Thompson at Theatre Passe Muraille: Bits and Pieces." *Open Letter*, Second Series, 7 (Winter 1974), 49-71.

————, and Cynthia Zimmerman, eds. *The Work*, 237-63.

Wilson, Paul. "Blyth Spirit [Paul Thompson]." *Books in Canada*, 12 (April 1983), 10-13.

B. **1837: THE FARMERS' REVOLT**: SELECTED REVIEWS

Ashley, Audrey M. "Skimpy Sketches Illustrate Drama." *Ottawa Citizen*, 9 November 1976, p. 71.

O'Toole, Lawrence. "*1837*: Dull History Played as Fiercely Involving Anarchy." *The Globe and Mail* (Toronto), 13 September 1974, p. 13.

Pappert-Martinello, Margaret. "Revolutionary Parallels." *Essays on Canadian Writing*, 7/8 (Fall 1977), 196-99.

Skene, Reg. "*Farmers' Revolt* Slowed by Stretches of Theatrical Tedium." *Winnipeg Free Press*, 2 April 1981, p. 27.

Whittaker, Herbert. "*1837* Engrossing Handling of History." *The Globe and Mail* (Toronto), 19 January 1973, p. 15.

Wood, Susan. "Found History." *Canadian Literature*, 81 (Summer 1979), 111-12.

Wyman, Max. "An Indisputable Star in a Troupe Not Meant to Have any Stars." *Vancouver Sun*, 29 March 1976, p. 43.

GEORGE F. WALKER

A. BIOGRAPHY AND CRITICISM

Galloway, Myron. "George Walker—Resolving the World's Chaos." *Montreal Star*, 3 March 1979, Sec. D, 9.

Gass, Ken. "Introduction," in *Three Plays by George Walker*. Toronto: Coach House Press, 1978, pp. 9-15.

Hallgren, Chris. "George Walker: The Serious and the Comic." *Scene Changes*, 7 (March-April 1979), 23-25.

Johnson, Chris. "George F. Walker: B-Movies Beyond the Absurd." *Canadian Literature*, 85 (Summer 1980), 87-103.

Johnston, Denis W. "George F. Walker: Liberal Idealism and the 'Power Plays,'" *Canadian Drama*, 10, no. 2 (1984), 195-206.

Knelman, Martin. "The Enigma of George Walker." *Saturday Night*, 97 (February 1982), 59-60.

Lane, William. "Introduction," in George F. Walker, *The Power Plays*. Toronto: Coach House Press, 1984, pp. 9-14.

———. "Introduction," in *Zastrozzi: The Master of Discipline*. Toronto: Playwrights Co-op, 1979, pp. 3-6.

Milliken, Paul. "Walker's Living Theatre Ignites the Imagination." *Performing Arts in Canada*, 18 (Fall 1981), 43-46.

O'Hara, Jane. "George Walker: The Odd Man Out in Canadian Theatre." *Maclean's*, 95 (8 March 1982), 16, 19-20.

Usmiani, Renate. *Second Stage*, 35-38.

Wallace, Robert and Cynthia Zimmerman, eds. *The Work*, 212-25.

Wasserman, Jerry. "'Making Things Clear': The *film noir* Plays of George F. Walker." *Canadian Drama*, 8, no. 1 (1982), 99-101.

Wynne-Jones, Tim. "Acts of Darkness," *Books in Canada*, 14 (April 1985), 11-14.

B. **ZASTROZZI**: SELECTED REVIEWS

Galloway, Myron. "*Zastrozzi* Cast Superb." *Montreal Star*, 28 November 1978, Sec. A, 12.

Huebert, Ronald. "Letters in Canada 1978: Drama." *University of Toronto Quarterly*, 48 (Summer 1979), 362-70.

Johnson, Bryan. "*Zastrozzi* Wields a Satanic Rapier." *The Globe and Mail* (Toronto), 3 November 1977, p. 17.

Mallet, Gina. "Theatre Finds Strength with Style." *Toronto Star*, 3 November 1977, Sec. F, 1.

Messenger, Ann. "Canajun, Eh?" *Canadian Literature*, 86 (Fall 1980), 89-93.

Rich, Frank. "Serban Directs *Zastrozzi* at the Public." *New York Times*, 18 January 1982, Sec. C, 14.